THE TIMES
THE SUNDAY TIMES

Good University Guide

2021

John O'Leary

⌐ in 2020 by Times Books

An imprint of HarperCollins Publishers
Westerhill Road
Bishopbriggs
Glasgow G64 2QT
www.harpercollins.co.uk
times.books@harpercollins.co.uk

First published in 1993. Twenty-sixth edition 2020

© Times Newspapers Ltd 2020

The Times is a registered trademark of Times Newspapers Ltd

ISBN 978-0-00-836828-9

Catherine North was the lead consultant with Andrew Farquhar for UoE Consulting Limited,
which has compiled the main university league table and the individual subject tables for this *Guide*
on behalf of *The Times*, *The Sunday Times* and HarperCollins Publishers.

Please see chapters 1 and 13 for a full explanation of the sources of data used in the ranking tables.
The data providers do not necessarily agree with the data aggregations or manipulations appearing
in this book and are also not responsible for any inference or conclusions thereby derived.

Project editor: Alan Copps
Design and layout: Davidson Publishing Solutions

A catalogue record for this book is available from the British Library.

Printed and bound by CPI Group (UK) Ltd, Croydon, CR0 4YY.

MIX
Paper from
responsible sources
FSC™ C007454

This book is produced from independently certified
FSC™ paper to ensure responsible forest management.

For more information visit: www.harpercollins.co.uk/green

Contents

About the Author

John O'Leary is a freelance journalist and education consultant. He was the Editor of *The Times Higher Education Supplement* from 2002 to 2007 and was previously Education Editor of *The Times*, having joined the paper in 1990 as Higher Education Correspondent. He has been writing on higher education for more than 30 years and is a member of the executive board of the QS World University Rankings. He is a member of the Higher Education Commission and the author of *Higher Education in England*, published in 2009 by the Higher Education Funding Council for England. He has a degree in politics from the University of Sheffield.

Acknowledgements

We would like to thank the many individuals who have helped with this edition of *The Times and Sunday Times Good University Guide*, particularly Rosemary Bennett, Education Editor of *The Times*, Alastair McCall, Editor of *The Sunday Times Good University Guide*, and Catherine North, the lead consultant with Andrew Farquhar, for UoE Consulting Limited, which has compiled the main university league table and the individual subject tables for this *Guide* on behalf of *The Times*, *The Sunday Times* and HarperCollins Publishers.

To the members of *The Times and Sunday Times Good University Guide* Advisory Group for their time and expertise: Patrick Kennedy, Consultant, Collective Intelligence Limited; Christine Couper, Head of Planning and Statistics, University of Greenwich; James Galbraith, Senior Strategic Planner, University of Edinburgh; Alison Hartrey, Head of Planning, SOAS, London; Mark Langer-Crame, Senior Planning Officer, Cardiff University; Daniel Monnery, Head of Corporate Strategy, Northumbria University; Aaron Morrison, Principal Planning Officer, De Montfort University; Jackie Njoroge, Head of Strategic Planning, University of Salford; Komal Patel, Strategic Planning Officer, Imperial College, London; Dr Sarah Taylor, Head of Strategy Development, Aberystwyth University; David Totten, Head of Planning, Queen's University, Belfast; Jenny Walker, Planning Officer, Loughborough University; to Denise Jones, Emily Raven and Pip Day of HESA for their technical advice; to Jack Clover, Catherine Lally, Martin Ince and Sue O'Leary for their contributions to the book.

We also wish to thank all the university staff who assisted in providing information for this edition.

Timeline to a University Place

This book is designed to help you find a university place in September 2021. That may seem a long time away, but a decision that can change your life needs a lot of consideration. Add to that the fact that the application process is somewhat long-winded and there is less time than you might think – for example, if you want to study medicine starting in September 2021 you will have to have had some practical experience of helping to care for people, have taken an aptitude test during the summer and completed your application by 15 October 2020, almost a year before your studies will start. Planning well ahead of application and decision deadlines will always give you greater flexibility and choice. The less time you give yourself, the more limited will become your choices.

So where to start? The dates below indicate the key staging points along the way to a university place.

Key dates
February to July 2020
This is the time to develop your thoughts on the subject you would like to study and on where you would like to be at university. See overleaf for where to find advice in this book on choosing a subject and a university.

March 2020 onwards
Attend university open days. Open Days are a good way to gain a personal impression of what a university feels like, where it is located, and what studying in a particular department or faculty would be like. You will only have the time and resources to attend a small number of Open Days, so careful planning is necessary, not least because Open Days at different universities can often clash. The calendar for Open Days for 2020 (as announced by the beginning of the year) appears alongside each university's profile in Chapter 15.

July 2020
Registration starts for UCAS Apply, the online application system through which you will make your application. You will have a maximum of five choices when you come to complete your application form.

September 2020
UCAS will begin to accept completed applications.

15 October 2020
Deadline for applications to Oxford or Cambridge (you can only apply to one of them), and for applications to any university to study medicine, dentistry or veterinary science. Note that for some courses you will need to have completed a pre-application assessment test by this date.

15 January 2021
Deadline for applications for all other universities and subjects (excluding a few art and design courses with a deadline of 24 March 2021). It is advisable to get your application in ahead of this deadline; aim for the end of November 2020.

End of March 2021

Universities should have given you decisions on your applications by now if you submitted them by 15 January 2021.

April onwards

Apply for student loans to cover tuition fees and living costs.

Early May 2021

You will need to have responded to all university decisions. You have to select first choice, if your first offer is conditional, a second choice, and reject all other offers. Once you have accepted an offer, apply for university accommodation if you are going to require it.

3 August 2021

Scottish examination results. If your results meet the offer from your first choice (or, failing that, your second choice), your place at university will be confirmed. If not, you can enter Clearing for Scottish universities in order to find a place on another course.

12 August 2021

A-level results announced. If your results meet the offer from your first choice (or, failing that, your second choice), your place at university will be confirmed. If not, you can enter Clearing to find a place on another course offered by any university.

Mid to late September 2021

Arrive at university for Freshers' Week.

How This Book Can Help You

The process of making a successful application to university has many stages. Fundamental to the whole process are your decisions on which subject to pick and where to study it.

How do I choose a course?
As you will be taking a course that will last three or sometimes four years, you will need enthusiasm for, and some aptitude in, the subject. The options of studying full-time or part-time also need to be considered.

» The first half of chapter 2 provides advice on choosing a subject area and selecting relevant courses within that subject.

» Chapter 13 provides details for 67 different subject areas (as listed on page 36). For each subject there is specific advice and a league table that provides our assessment of the quality of universities offering courses.

How will my choice of subject affect my employment prospects?
As the course you choose will also influence your job prospects at its conclusion, your initial subject decision will have an impact on your life long after you complete your degree.

» The employment prospects and average starting salaries for the main subject groups are given in chapter 3.

» The subject tables in chapter 13 give the employment prospects for each university offering a course.

» Universities are now doing more to increase the employability of their graduates. Some examples are given in chapter 3.

How do I choose a university?
While choosing your subject comes first, the place where you study will also play a major role. You will need to decide upon what type of university you wish to go to: campus, city or smaller town? How well does the university perform? How far is the university from home? Is it large or small? Is it specialist or general? Do you want to study abroad?

» Central to our *Guide* is the main *Times and Sunday Times* league table in chapter 1. This ranks the universities by assessing their performance not just according to teaching quality and the student experience but also through seven other factors, including research quality, the spending on services and facilities, and graduate employment prospects.

» The second half of chapter 2 provides advice on the factors to consider when choosing a university.

» Chapter 15, the largest chapter in the book, contains two pages on each university, giving a general overview of the institution as well as data on student numbers, contact details, accommodation provision, and the fees for 2020–21. Note that fees and student support for 2021–22 will not be confirmed until August 2020, and you must check these before applying.

» For those considering Oxford or Cambridge, details of admission processes and of all the undergraduate colleges can be found in chapter 14.

» If you are considering studying abroad, chapter 11 provides guidance and practical information.

» Specific advice for international students coming to study in the UK is given in chapter 12.

How do I apply?

» Chapter 5 outlines the application procedure for university entry. It starts by advising you on how to complete the UCAS application, and then takes you through the process that we hope will lead to your university place for autumn 2021.

Can I afford it?

Note that most figures in chapters 4 and 7 refer to 2021 and there will be changes for 2021, which you will need to check.

» Chapter 4 describes how the system of tuition fees works and what you are likely to be charged, depending upon where in the UK you plan to study.
» Chapter 7 provides advice on the tuition fee loans and maintenance loans that are available, depending upon where you live in the UK, other forms of financial support (including university scholarships and bursaries), and how to plan your budget.
» Chapter 8 provides advice on where to live while you are at university. Sample accommodation charges for each university are given in chapter 15.

How do I find out more?

The Times and Sunday Times Good University Guide website at **https://www.thetimes.co.uk/gooduniversityguide** will keep you up to date with developments throughout the year and contains further information and online tables (subscription required).

You can also find much practical advice on the UCAS website (**www.ucas.com**), and on individual university websites. There is a wealth of official statistical information on the Discover Uni website (which has replaced Unistats) **www.discoveruni.gov.uk**.

Introduction

Although the number of 18-year-olds will rise for the first time for over a decade in 2021, the size of the main pool of applicants for higher education places will still be among the smallest in modern times. With a record number of places likely to be available, the level of competition should remain historically low. Almost 98% of applicants received at least one offer in 2019 – the highest proportion on record – and there is little reason to think it will fall far in the coming year.

There is no time to lose, however. The buyers' market that applicants find themselves in may not last long. The 18-year-old population is expected to be back to its 2010 peak by 2024, with thousands more prospective students each year. Although there are bound to be uncertainties surrounding the level of applications from European Union countries after the Brexit transition period, there is no sign of the demand from other international students weakening.

In virtually every area of higher education, opportunities should be plentiful in 2021. Offer rates rose in almost all subjects in 2019 – even highly selective courses like medicine and dentistry continue to take more students each year, and some of the promises made in last year's General Election would suggest still higher intakes. Growing numbers are entering university through Clearing, with 2019 setting yet another record as 14% of those taking up places found their course after Results Day.

There has even been progress in the hitherto intractable problem of low recruitment among disadvantaged groups. Although young people from poor backgrounds and some ethnic minorities remain severely under-represented in universities, their numbers rose significantly in 2019, when 17% of those from the most disadvantaged groups received a 'contextual' offer that was lower than the norm for their chosen course. Our social inclusion table tracks the record of individual universities.

Although the mix of subjects available at individual universities may change, as managers respond to student demand, universities will be as anxious as ever to recruit undergraduates in 2021. Fee levels had not been determined when this *Guide* went to press, but even if they were reduced, undergraduate fees would remain universities' main source of income. Almost 500,000 undergraduates were admitted in 2019, as numbers began to rise again, but some universities still struggled to fill their places.

The climate should be favourable, therefore, for those thinking of starting a degree in 2021. But is a degree still worth the price you will have to pay? Not if you listen to many of today's politicians and commentators. Graduates are left with unmanageable debts after sub-standard teaching on courses that lead nowhere, they say. Partly as a result of the negative publicity universities have received over the past two years, as many as three-quarters of people think higher education represents poor value for money.

In fact, Government statistics show graduates earning at least £90,000 more on average than non-graduates over a working lifetime, as well as being much less likely to be unemployed and more likely to remain healthy. But, as this *Guide* has demonstrated over a quarter of a century, there are wide variations between universities and courses. The Institute for Fiscal Studies has reported that the male graduates of 23 institutions earn less than non-graduates throughout their twenties and the same is true for female graduates at nine institutions. At the other end of the scale, the IFS found 36 institutions for men and ten for women where graduates were earning more than £60,000 after ten years – far more than those with lower qualifications.

The fine detail that is becoming available on employment rates and salary levels well into graduates' careers makes it more important than ever – and easier – to carry out thorough research before completing an application, or deciding not to do so. There are more options for 18-year-olds to go straight into work, perhaps through the halfway house of a degree apprenticeship, with the attractive combination of a qualification without fees, for those who are sure of their early career aspirations.

As yet, however, school and college leavers are as likely as before to opt for traditional higher education. The salary premium enjoyed by graduates appears to have declined over recent years with the sharp growth in the proportion of graduates in the working-age population, but it is still higher than in most other parts of the world.

New statistics will continue to come thick and fast, however, to test that proposition. The Government is planning to use graduate salary averages in the next round of its Teaching Excellence Framework, for example. With so many more graduates competing for jobs, a degree will never again be an automatic passport to a fast-track career. But it is a fair assumption that most of the better-paid jobs in the future will require post-school education, whether it is a traditional degree, a higher-level apprenticeship, or in-company training.

Even for those who cannot or do not wish to afford the costs associated with three or more years of full-time education when they leave school, university remains a possibility. As well as degree apprenticeships, the modular courses adopted by most universities enable students to work through even a traditional degree at their own pace, dropping out for a time if necessary, or switching to part-time attendance. Distance learning is another option, and advances in information technology now mean that some nominally full-time courses are delivered mainly online.

Being able to win a place is one thing, but you should also consider, as far as you can, whether you will be happy at your chosen university. The vast majority of students enjoy their undergraduate years, but there is growing concern about mental health among young people who are away from home for the first time, some of whom feel challenged academically and isolated socially. Of course, you hope you will not be one of them, but it is worth exploring what support the universities you are considering offer to those who are affected. Student Minds, with other national organisations, has drawn up a university mental health charter, for example, while a health start-up, Fika, has launched an app to help young people improve their emotional fitness. Does your prospective university subscribe to either of them, or have its own well-established system for safeguarding mental health?

Most graduates do not regret their decision to go to university. Students from all over the world flock to British universities, and they offer a valuable resource for those on their doorstep. No league table can determine which is the right university for any candidate, but this *Guide* should provide some of the information necessary to draw up a shortlist for further investigation and make the right choice in the end.

The methodology for the new edition remains stable. The *Guide* has always put a premium on consistency in the way that it uses the statistics published by universities and presents the results. The overriding aim is to inform potential students and their parents and advisors, not to make judgments on the performance of universities. As such, it differs from the Government's Teaching Excellence Framework (TEF), which uses some of the same statistics but makes allowance for the prior qualifications of students and uses an expert panel to place the results in context. Our tables use the raw data produced by universities to reflect the undergraduate experience, whatever advantages or disadvantages those institutions might face. We also rank all 131 universities, while the TEF uses only three bands, leaving almost half of the institutions in our table on the same middle tier.

The TEF represents the first official intervention in this area since the Quality Assurance Agency's assessments of teaching quality were abolished more than a decade ago. Scores in those reports correlated closely with research grades, and the first discussions on the framework in the Coalition Government envisaged one comparison taking account of both teaching and research. This remains our approach, to look at a broad range of factors (including the presence of excellent researchers on the academic staff) that will impact on undergraduates.

An era of change

Higher education has undergone numerous changes in the 26 years that this book has been published, and more are likely in England, with a new government poring over the recommendations of the Augar Review. In England, the Office for Students has taken on the responsibilities for regulating universities that were the province of the Higher Education Funding Council. Research is now overseen by a different body, making universities less able to juggle their finances between different budgets.

In the short term, fees of £9,250 are here to stay in England and Wales, following the announcement of a three-year freeze and the adoption of a new system in the Principality. In Scotland, too, the current regime of free higher education for Scottish residents and those from other EU countries is unlikely to change.

The pattern of applications and enrolments has already changed since the introduction of higher fees. Students are opting in larger numbers for subjects that they think will lead to well-paid jobs. While there has been a recovery in some arts and social science subjects, the trend towards the sciences and some vocational degrees is unmistakeable. Languages have suffered particularly, and so have courses associated with parts of the economy that were hardest hit in the recession. Building is one example, where numbers are only now beginning to recover even though the subject is in the top ten for employment prospects, with four out of five graduates going straight into a professional job.

The vast majority of students take a degree at least partly to improve their career prospects, so some second-guessing of the employment market is inevitable. But most graduate jobs are not subject-specific and the best brains in the country are hard-pressed to predict employment hotspots four or five years ahead, when today's applicants will be looking for jobs. Computer science is a good example of the pitfalls. Demand for the subject plummeted when the "dotcom bubble" burst and courses closed. Now much of the IT industry is booming again and there is a skills shortage. Applications for the subject have shot up, but no one can be certain of market conditions in such a fast-moving industry so far ahead.

Just as it may be unwise to second-guess employment prospects, the same goes for the competition for places in different subjects. Universities may close or reduce the intake to courses that have low numbers of applicants while some of the more selective institutions may make more places available, especially to candidates who achieve good grades at A-level. Bristol, Birmingham, Exeter and University College London have all taken hundreds more students than usual since the restrictions were relaxed for high-grade candidates. Now others plan to follow suit – as long as they can attract enough students.

Even before the increase to £9,250 fees in 2017, it seems that universities of all types saw the expansion of undergraduate provision as a sensible strategy. But even those that are expanding may do so only in areas where they are strong and extra students can be taught at reasonable cost. In the absence of clear announcements, applicants are still best advised to go for the courses and universities that meet their requirements, rather than trying to second-guess the system.

Using this *Guide*

The merger of *The Times and Sunday Times* university guides six years ago began a new chapter in the ranking of higher education institutions in the UK. The two guides had 35 editions between them and, in their new form, provide the most comprehensive and authoritative assessments of undergraduate education at UK universities.

There are no new names in the main table this year, even though ministers are keen for new institutions to shake up the higher education system. Even those with university titles – the first criterion for inclusion in our table – take time to build up the body of data required to make meaningful comparisons.

Some famous names in UK higher education have never been ranked because they do not fit the parameters of a system that is intended mainly to guide full-time undergraduates. The Open University, for example, operates entirely through distance learning, while the London and Manchester Business Schools have no undergraduates. Birkbeck University of London, which operates a broadly part-time course model, has dropped out of the table this year.

There are now 67 subject tables, and others will be added in due course because there is growing demand for information at this level. Successive surveys have found that international students are more influenced by subject rankings than those for whole institutions, and there is no reason to believe that domestic applicants think differently.

Since the separation of National Student Survey (NSS) scores, outlined below, there has been no change in the basic methodology behind the tables, however. The nine elements of the main table are the same, with the approach to scores in the 2014 Research Excellence Framework mirroring as closely as possible those for previous assessments. In order to reflect the likelihood of undergraduates coming into contact with outstanding researchers, the proportion of eligible academics entered for assessment is part of the calculation, as well as the average grades achieved.

This year's tables

This year's results again show considerable movement, perhaps reflecting the high level of competition for undergraduates. The division of NSS scores continues to have an effect, with the four sections of the survey categorised as 'Teaching Quality' given more weight than the remaining five. The survey itself was extended and toughened up in 2017, causing a general decline in scores which was only partially reversed in 2019.

For this edition of the *Guide* only, there are no new scores for graduate prospects, as HESA completes a new system for measuring destinations, carrying out surveys a year after graduation rather than six months. The figures used in the tables are the latest available, dating from the end of 2017, and replicate those in the 2020 *Guide*.

It seems that nothing can shake the dominance of Cambridge and Oxford at the head of the main table – and the majority of the subject tables. Cambridge has maintained a clear lead over its ancient rival, although the gap has narrowed slightly between Oxford and third-placed St Andrews, our University of the Year. Cambridge also tops 27 of the subject tables, compared with five at Oxford – and also at Loughborough and St Andrews. Throughout all the years of the *Guide*, Oxford and Cambridge have seldom been challenged, especially in terms of the undergraduate education they offer.

St Andrews remains easily Scotland's top university in the table and Queen's, Belfast the same in Northern Ireland, while in Wales, Swansea has held off Cardiff for the second year in a row. Other changes in the upper reaches of the table have seen the London School of Economics climb three places to sixth and Harper Adams shoot up 16 places and into the top 20 to occupy the highest-ever positon by a post-1992 university, making it our Modern University of the Year.

The biggest rise of all is over 30 places by West London, to 52nd place, more than making up for a big fall last year. Others celebrating impressive rises include Central Lancashire (up 30 places to 75th) and Hull, which almost recouped last year's losses with a rise of 26 places.

Those going in the other direction include Buckingham (down 49 places to 92nd) and Salford and Leeds Trinity, both of which have fallen 30 places this year.

More modern universities than ever feature above some older foundations. The first edition of *The Times Good University Guide* predicted the development of a new pecking order in an era of growing competition between universities, many of which had just acquired that title. It has taken longer than many expected, but at last one (Harper Adams) has reached the top 20 and four more (Nottingham Trent, Coventry, the University for the Creative Arts and the Arts University Bournemouth) feature in the top 50.

Making the right choices

Anyone hoping to embark on a degree in 2021 (or any other time) will be well advised to tread carefully and muster as much comparative information as possible before making their choices.

Guide Award Winners

University of the Year	**St Andrews**
Runner-up	**Harper Adams**
Shortlisted	**London School of Economics**
	Royal Holloway, London
	Staffordshire
Scottish University of the Year	**Strathclyde**
Welsh University of the Year	**Aberystwyth**
Modern University of the Year	**Harper Adams**
Sports University of the Year	**Stirling**
International University of the Year	**Lancaster**
University of the Year for	
Teaching Quality	**Sheffield Hallam**
Student Experience	**Dundee**
Graduate Employment	**Manchester**
Student Retention	**Norwich, University of the Arts**
Social Inclusion	**Bradford**

This *Guide* is intended as a starting point, a tool to help navigate the statistical minefield that will face applicants, as universities present their performance in the best possible light. There is advice on fees and financial questions, as well as all-important employment issues, along with the usual ranking of universities and 67 subject tables.

While some of the leading universities have expanded considerably in recent years, most will remain selective, particularly in popular subjects. Although nearly all applicants received at least one offer in 2019, that does not mean that they secured the university or course of their dreams. The demand for places is far from uniform, and even within the same university the level of competition will vary between subjects. The entry scores quoted in the subject tables in Chapter 13 offer a reliable guide to the relative levels of selectivity, but the figures are for entrants' actual qualifications. The standard offers made by departments will invariably be lower, and the grades those departments were prepared to accept were often lower still.

Making the right choice requires a mixture of realism and ambition. Most sixth-formers and college students have a fair idea of the grades they are capable of attaining, within a certain margin for error. Even with five choices of course to make, there is no point in applying for a degree where the standard offer is so far from your predicted grades that rejection is virtually certain. If your results do turn out to be much better than predicted, there will be an opportunity through the Adjustment system, or simply through Clearing, to trade up to an alternative university. Some 16,000 applicants took advantage of the new opportunity to 'self-release' from their chosen university in 2019, although only 11,000 of them eventually accepted another offer.

Since the relaxation of recruitment restrictions, universities that once took pride in their absence from Clearing have continued to recruit after A-level results day. As a result, the use of insurance choices – the inclusion of at least one university with lower entrance standards than your main targets – has been declining. It is still a dangerous strategy, but there is now more chance of picking up a place at a leading university if you aimed too high with all your first-round choices. Over 30,000 courses were available on the first day of Clearing last year and almost 10% of those placed subsequently went to 'high-tariff' universities. Some may even come to you if you sign up to allow universities to approach unplaced candidates on Results Day if their grades are similar to other entrants'.

The long view

School-leavers who enter higher education in 2021 were not born when our first league table was published and most will never have heard of polytechnics, even if they attend a university that once carried that title. But it was the award of university status to the 34 polytechnics, a quarter of a century ago, that was the inspiration for the first edition of *The Times Good University Guide*. The original poly, the Polytechnic of Central London, had become the University of Westminster, Bristol Polytechnic was now the University of the West of England and – most mysteriously of all – Leicester Polytechnic had morphed into De Montfort University. The new *Guide* charted the lineage of the new universities and offered the first-ever comparison of institutional performance in UK higher education.

The university establishment did not welcome the initiative. The vice-chancellors described the table as "wrong in principle, flawed in execution and constructed upon data which are not uniform, are ill-defined and in places demonstrably false." The league table has changed considerably since then, and its results are taken rather more seriously. While consistency has been a priority for the *Guide* throughout its 25 years, only six of the original 14 measures have survived. Some of the current components – notably the National Student Survey – did not exist in 1992, while others have been modified or dropped at the behest of the expert group of planning officers from different types of universities that meets annually to review the methodology and make recommendations for the future.

While ranking is hardly popular with academics, the relationship with universities has changed radically, and this *Guide* is quoted on numerous university websites. As Sir David Eastwood, now vice-chancellor of the University of Birmingham, said in launching an official report on university league tables that he commissioned as Chief Executive of the Higher Education Funding Council for England: "We deplore league tables one day and deploy them the next."

Most universities have had their ups and downs over the years, with the notable exceptions of Oxford and Cambridge. Both benefited from the introduction of student satisfaction ratings and from the extra credit given to the top research grades – the two measures that carry an extra weighting in our table. They also have famously high entry standards, much the largest proportions of first and upper-second class degrees and consistently good scores on every other measure. Several other famous names have been among the chasing pack throughout. Imperial College and University College London have seldom been out of the top five, with St Andrews joining them in recent years, while the London School of Economics, Durham and Warwick have all been fixtures in the top ten.

There have been spectacular rises, however. Coventry, for example, was only 12 places off the bottom in the 2006 *Guide* and is now well established in the top 50, having reached the highest position ever for a modern university four years ago. Harper Adams, which now enjoys that distinction, was not even a university until 2012.

Since this book was first published, the number of universities has increased by a third and the full-time student population has rocketed. Individual institutions are almost unrecognisable from their 1993 forms. Nottingham, for example, had fewer than 10,000 students then, compared with more than 30,000 now. Manchester Metropolitan, the largest of the former polys, has experienced similar growth. Yet there are universities now which would have been too small and too specialist to qualify for the title in 1992. The diversity of UK higher education is celebrated as one of its greatest strengths, and the modern universities are neither encouraged nor anxious to compete with the older foundations on some of the measures in our table.

The coming years, let alone the next 20, may see another transformation in the higher education landscape, with the private sector competing strongly with established universities in some fields and distance learning becoming more popular as there is greater investment in Massive Open Online Courses (MOOCs). A sharp rise in the number of 18-year-olds will increase the demand for higher education places over the next five years, but it remains to be seen whether the finances of universities and the regulatory restrictions they might face will enable them to satisfy that demand. There may, indeed, be university closures and mergers, although they have been predicted before and seldom come about. Universities are among the most enduring of the UK's institutions, and will take some shifting.

1 The University League Table

What Makes a Top University?

What distinguishes a top university and who is to say that one course is better than another? Critics of league tables insist that they are misleading because every university has different priorities, every course has a different way of approaching a subject, and students must choose the one that suits them best. So they must. Not everyone would find the top universities in our *Guide* to their taste, even if they were able to secure a place. But that does not mean there are not important differences in the quality of universities and the courses they offer.

Universities publish reams of statistics about themselves – more than ever now that governments insist on greater transparency. But even some of the official attempts to provide prospective students with better information have left many readers more confused, rather than less. Some would place the Teaching Excellence Framework in this category, with its use of benchmarks to allow for students' prior qualifications and an expert panel to override some results, yet still only placing universities and colleges in one of three bands.

The table in this chapter has been developed over 26 years to focus on the fundamentals of undergraduate education and make meaningful comparisons in an accessible way. The institutions will have their own ideas about what should go into comparisons of this type, but ours has stood the test of time because it uses the statistics that universities themselves employ to measure their own performance and combines them in a straightforward way that generations of students have found revealing.

Every element of the table has been chosen for the light it shines on the undergraduate experience and a student's future prospects. The selection of these measures and the way in which they are combined give a particular view of universities' overall strengths. Unlike some others, *The Times and Sunday Times Good University Guide* has placed a premium on consistency, confident that the measures are the best currently available for the task.

Some changes have been forced upon us. Universities stopped assessing teaching quality by subject, when this was the most heavily weighted measure in the table, for example. However, the subsequent development of the National Student Survey (NSS) has enabled the student experience to be reflected in the table. More than two thirds of final year undergraduates give their views on the quality of their courses, a remarkable response rate that makes the results impossible to dismiss.

Four years ago, we split the student satisfaction measure in two while keeping the overall contribution of the NSS to the table unchanged, and we have retained this approach. The "teaching quality" indicator reflects the average scores of the survey's sections on teaching, assessment and feedback, learning opportunities and academic support, while the "student experience" indicator is drawn from the average of the sections on organisation and management, learning resources, the student voice and the learning community, as well as the final question on overall satisfaction. Teaching quality is favoured over student experience and accounts for 67% of the overall student satisfaction score, with student experience making up the remaining 33%.

The basic information that applicants need in order to judge universities and their courses does not change, however. A university's entry standards, staffing levels, completion rates, degree classifications and graduate employment rates are all vital pieces of intelligence for anyone deciding where to study.

Research grades, while not directly involving undergraduates, bring with them considerable funds and enable a university to attract top academics.

Any of these measures can be discounted by an individual, but the package has struck a chord with readers. The ranking has built a reputation as the most authoritative arbiter of changing fortunes in higher education.

The measures used are kept under review by a group of university administrators and statisticians, which meets annually. The raw data that go into the table in this chapter and the 67 subject tables in chapter 13 are all in the public domain and are sent to universities for checking before any scores are calculated.

The various official bodies concerned with higher education do not publish league tables, and the Higher Education Statistics Agency (HESA), which supplies most of the figures used in our tables, does not endorse the way in which they are aggregated. But there are now numerous exercises, from the Teaching Excellence Framework to the annual "performance indicators" published by HESA on everything from completion rates to research output at each university, that invite comparisons.

Any scrutiny of league table positions is best carried out in conjunction with an examination of the relevant subject table – it is the course, after all, that will dominate your undergraduate years and influence your subsequent career.

How *The Times and Sunday Times* league table works

The table is presented in a format that displays the raw data, wherever possible. In building the table, scores for student satisfaction (combining the teaching quality, student experience scores) and research quality were weighted by 1.5; all other measures were weighted by 1.

For entry standards, student/staff ratio, good honours and graduate prospects, the score was adjusted for subject mix. For example, it is accepted that engineering, law and medicine graduates will tend to have better graduate prospects than their peers from English, psychology and sociology courses. Comparing results in the main subject groupings helps to iron out differences attributable simply to the range of degrees on offer. This subject-mix adjustment means that it is not possible to replicate the scores in the table from the published indicators because the calculation requires access to the entire dataset.

The indicators were combined using a common statistical technique known as z-scores, to ensure that no indicator has a disproportionate effect on the overall total for each university, and the totals were transformed to a scale with 1,000 for the top score. The z-score technique makes it impossible to compare universities' total scores from one year to the next, although their relative positions in the table are comparable. Individual scores are dependent on the top performer: a university might drop from 60% of the top score to 58% but still have improved, depending on the relative performance of other universities.

Only where data are not available from HESA are figures sourced directly from universities. Where this is not possible scores are generated according to a university's average performance on other indicators, apart from the measures for research quality, student/staff ratio and services and facilities spend, where no score is created.

The organisations providing the raw data for the tables are not involved in the process of aggregation, so are not responsible for any inferences or conclusions we have made. Every care has been taken to ensure the accuracy of the tables and accompanying information, but no responsibility can be taken for errors or omissions.

The *Times and The Sunday Times* league table uses nine important indicators of university activity, based on the most recent data available at the time of compilation:

» Teaching quality
» Student experience
» Research quality
» Entry standards
» Student/staff ratio

» Services and facilities spend
» Completion
» Good honours
» Graduate prospects

Teaching quality and student experience

The student satisfaction measure has been divided into two components which give final-year undergraduates' views of the quality of their courses. The National Student Survey (NSS) published in 2019 was the source of the data.

Where no data were available in the 2019 survey, the score from the 2018 survey was used. Where no data from the 2018 survey were available, the 2017 score was used.

» The National Student Survey covers eight aspects of a course, with an additional question gauging overall satisfaction. Students answer on a scale from 1 (bottom) to 5 (top) and the score in the table is the percentage of positive responses (4 and 5) in each section
» The teaching quality indicator reflects the average scores of the first four sections, which contain 14 questions
» The student experience indicator is drawn from the average scores of the remaining four sections, containing 12 questions, and the additional question on overall satisfaction.
» Teaching quality accounts for 67% of the overall score covering student satisfaction, with student experience making up the remaining 33%.
» The survey is based on the opinion of final-year undergraduates rather than directly assessing teaching quality. Most undergraduates have no experience of other universities, or different courses, to inform their judgements. Although all the questions relate to courses, rather than other aspects of the student experience, some types of university – notably medium-sized campus universities – tend to do better than others, while those in London in particular tend to do worse.

Research quality

This is a measure of the quality of the research undertaken in each university. The information was sourced from the 2014 Research Excellence Framework (REF), a peer-review exercise used to evaluate the quality of research in UK higher education institutions undertaken by the UK Higher Education funding bodies. Additionally, academic staffing data for 2013–14 from the Higher Education Statistics Agency have been used.

» A research quality profile was given to every university department that took part. This profile used the following categories: 4* world-leading; 3* internationally excellent; 2* internationally recognised; 1* nationally recognised; and unclassified. The Funding Bodies have directed more funds to the very best research by applying weightings, and for the 2015 Guide we used the weightings adopted by HEFCE (the funding council for England) for funding in 2013–14: 4* was weighted by a factor of 3 and 3* was weighted by a factor of 1. Outputs of 2* and 1* carried zero weight. This meant a maximum score of 3. In the interests of consistency, the above weightings continue to be applied this year.

» The scores in the table are presented as a percentage of the maximum score. To achieve the maximum score all staff would need to be at 4* world-leading level.

» Universities could choose which staff to include in the REF, so, to factor in the depth of the research quality, each quality profile score has been multiplied by the number of staff returned in the REF as a proportion of all eligible staff.

Entry standards

This is the average score, using the UCAS tariff (see page 32), of new students under the age of 21 who took A and AS-Levels, Scottish Highers and Advanced Highers and other equivalent qualifications (eg, International Baccalaureate). It measures what new students achieved rather than the entry requirements suggested by the universities. The data comes from HESA for 2017–18. The original sources of data for this measure are data returns made by the universities to HESA.

» Using the UCAS tariff, each student's examination results were converted to a numerical score. HESA then calculated an average for all students at the university. The results have then been adjusted to take account of the subject mix at the university.

» A score of 144 represents three As at A-level. Although all but five of the top 40 universities in the table have average entry standards of at least 144, it does not mean that everyone achieved such results – let alone that this was the standard offer. Courses will not demand more than three subjects at A-level and offers are pitched accordingly. You will need to reach the entry requirements set by the university, rather than these scores.

Graduate prospects

This measure is the percentage of the total number of graduates undertaking further study or in a professional job six months after graduation. The professional employment marker is derived from the latest Standard Occupational Classification (SOC2010) codes. The data came from the HESA Destination of Leavers from HE (DLHE) Record for 2017 graduates. The results have been adjusted for subject mix.

» HESA's survey of graduates six months after graduation is the only research to show what at least 80% of them do immediately after leaving university. The timing of HESA's survey has been altered to show the destinations of graduates a year after graduation, so no new figures were available this year.

Good honours

This measure is the percentage of graduates achieving a first or upper-second class degree. The results have been adjusted to take account of the subject mix at the university. The data comes from HESA for 2017–18. The original sources of data for this measure are data returns made by the universities themselves to HESA.

» Four-year first degrees, such as an MChem, are treated as equivalent to a first or upper-second.
» Scottish Ordinary degrees (awarded after three years of study) are excluded.
» Universities control degree classification, with some oversight from external examiners. There have been suggestions that, since universities have increased the numbers of good honours degrees they award, this measure may not be as objective as it should be. However, it remains the key measure of a student's success and employability.

Completion

This measure gives the percentage of students expected to complete their studies (or transfer to another institution) for each university. The data comes from the HESA performance indicators published in March 2019 and based on students entering in 2016–17, except Buckingham (2015–16).
» This measure is a projection, liable to statistical fluctuations.

Student/staff ratio

This is a measure of the average number of full-time equivalent students to each member of the academic staff, apart from those purely engaged in research. In this measure a low value is better than a high value. The data comes from HESA for 2017–18. The original sources of data for this measure are data returns made by the universities themselves to HESA.

» The figures, as calculated by HESA, allow for variation in employment patterns at different universities. A low value means that there are a small number of students for each academic member of staff, but this does not, of course, ensure good teaching quality or contact time with academics.
» Student/staff ratios vary by subject; for example, the ratio is usually low for medicine. In building the table, the score is adjusted for the subject mix taught by each university.
» Adjustments are also made for students who are on industrial placements, either for a full year or for part of a year.

Services and facilities spend

The expenditure per student on staff and student facilities, including library and computing facilities. The data comes from HESA for 2016–17 and 2017–18. The original data sources for this measure are data returns made by the universities to HESA.

» This is a measure calculated by taking the expenditure on student facilities (including sports, grants to student societies, careers services, health services, counselling, etc.) and library and computing facilities (books, journals, staff, central computers and computer networks, but not buildings) and dividing this by the number of full-time-equivalent students. Expenditure is averaged over two years to even out the figures (for example, a computer upgrade undertaken in a single year).

2019 rank	2018 rank		Teaching quality (%)	Student experience (%)	Research quality (%)	Entry standards (UCAS points)	Graduate prospects (%)	Good honours (%)	Completion rate (%)	Student-staff ratio	Services & facilities spend per student(£)	Total	Page
1	1	Cambridge	n/a	n/a	57.3	224	86.8	93.4	98.3	11.2	3,854	1000	364
2	2	Oxford	n/a	n/a	53.1	215	83.5	94.0	98.6	10.4	3,354	962	492
3	3	St Andrews	88.5	87.9	40.4	208	79.6	89.8	96.3	11.7	3,220	944	520
4	4	Imperial College London	75.1	77.9	56.2	206	90.4	89.2	96.5	11.4	3,767	845	432
5	5	Loughborough	83.4	85.8	36.3	162	86.9	83.8	92.1	13.4	3,286	834	468
6	9	London School of Economics	72.3	68.5	52.8	189	86.2	90.5	95.4	11.1	2,968	828	464
7	7	Durham	78.8	75.0	39.0	195	84.9	92.1	96.4	15	3,052	808	392
8	6	Lancaster	79.5	79.3	39.1	157	89.1	78.7	93.6	12.6	3,427	801	442
9	8	University College London	74.7	75.4	51.0	187	83.8	89.7	94.5	10.5	2,671	780	562
10	10	Warwick	79.6	79.2	44.6	180	83.2	84.3	95.1	13	2,537	778	564
11	13	Bath	79.4	81.8	37.3	182	87.5	88.3	96.6	15.6	2,541	777	332
12	12	Exeter	79.3	80.1	38.0	172	85.5	87.9	95.8	15.5	2,987	776	406
13	11	Leeds	79.8	80.4	36.8	166	81.2	86.9	92.4	13.4	3,043	744	444
14	14	Birmingham	78.4	77.9	37.1	165	85.8	86.6	94.9	13.9	3,036	737	340
=19	=19	Bristol	78.7	77.2	47.3	177	80.6	89.8	95.8	13.5	2,309	730	356
16	17	Glasgow	77.4	78.2	39.9	200	85.3	84.8	89.9	13.7	2,549	718	410
17	=33	Harper Adams	83.4	82.4	5.7	134	72.9	74.4	91.3	13.7	3,793	715	420
18	=19	Manchester	77.3	77.2	39.8	167	80.7	83.1	92.9	13.3	3,144	708	470
19	24	Royal Holloway, London	81.3	80.6	36.3	140	73.5	82.6	92.1	14.7	2,802	704	518
20	18	Southampton	79.1	78.6	44.9	160	82.1	84.9	89.3	13.5	2,454	700	538
21	16	Nottingham	78.0	78.0	37.8	161	86.0	84.1	93.8	14.5	2,663	693	486
22	22	York	82.6	81.0	38.3	158	82.0	80.5	92.8	14.6	1,810	692	582
23	15	East Anglia	79.1	79.0	35.8	147	77.1	87.2	90.7	13.6	2,842	691	394
24	27	Dundee	83.5	83.8	31.2	172	81.7	78.9	88.5	13.9	2,517	690	390
25	28	Edinburgh	73.3	72.6	43.8	190	77.5	89.5	92.1	11.9	2,169	686	400

2019 rank	2018 rank		Teaching quality (%)	Student experience (%)	Research quality (%)	Entry standards (UCAS points)	Graduate prospects (%)	Good honours (%)	Completion rate (%)	Student-staff ratio	Services & facilities spend per student (£)	Total	Page
26	25	Sheffield	80.6	82.1	37.6	157	84.4	81.5	92.8	15.2	2,290	684	526
27	26	Aberdeen	80.6	81.1	29.9	184	80.9	87.1	90.2	16.1	2,445	680	316
28	21	Newcastle	77.9	78.7	37.7	159	85.8	81.3	95.1	14.2	2,304	677	476
29	31	Liverpool	79.4	80.0	31.5	147	85.4	80.6	92.9	14.3	2,445	656	456
30	=35	King's College London	74.3	72.5	44.0	169	84.5	86.7	91.8	12.4	2,670	654	438
31	30	Swansea	81.2	81.5	33.7	135	85.6	78.0	90.8	15.4	2,372	653	554
32	23	Surrey	76.9	78.2	29.7	156	81.0	85.0	92.6	16.1	2,678	649	550
33	=35	Heriot-Watt	77.9	77.9	36.7	163	79.3	79.7	86.8	17.8	3,217	648	422
34	32	Cardiff	78.2	77.5	35.0	159	81.7	83.3	91.8	14.1	2,379	645	368
35	=38	Queen's, Belfast	77.5	77.4	39.7	152	82.4	84.0	91.8	15.9	2,416	636	506
36	=44	Strathclyde	78.3	78.9	37.7	200	79.6	83.4	88.5	19.5	1,867	634	544
37	29	Essex	79.5	80.3	37.2	111	74.3	74.5	85.4	15.9	3,521	630	404
=38	40	Reading	77.3	75.2	36.5	132	76.0	81.7	93.0	15.8	2,785	628	510
=38	41	Sussex	76.6	76.4	31.8	148	80.4	75.6	90.7	15.8	2,678	628	552
40	37	Nottingham Trent	83.0	81.7	6.5	135	81.7	74.4	87.6	14.5	2,434	625	488
41	=38	Leicester	77.7	78.0	31.8	133	75.4	78.4	92.3	14	2,749	619	452
42	=33	Creative Arts	83.8	78.0	3.4	143	72.7	75.1	80.1	12.9	2,666	614	382
43	=51	Arts Bournemouth	84.9	82.9	2.4	154	80.5	66.1	90.0	15.1	1,730	613	324
44	53	SOAS, London	75.5	71.2	27.9	156	70.9	81.7	81.4	11.3	2,608	606	532
45	=48	Aberystwyth	88.3	86.1	28.1	120	78.2	69.0	81.6	16.9	1,768	596	320
46	=48	Keele	82.5	82.5	22.1	127	82.1	74.2	88.7	14	2,087	586	434
47	=44	Stirling	79.5	75.6	30.5	163	78.7	76.3	86.7	16.4	1,865	583	542
48	56	Aston	78.3	77.3	25.8	133	79.1	84.4	92.0	17.4	1,983	578	328
49	=46	Queen Mary, London	73.5	74.3	37.9	144	78.7	83.2	89.9	13.1	2,352	574	504
50	=46	Coventry	82.3	81.5	3.8	126	80.9	76.1	83.9	14.6	2,411	572	380

2019 rank	2018 rank		Teaching quality (%)	Student experience (%)	Research quality (%)	Entry standards (UCAS points)	Graduate prospects (%)	Good honours (%)	Completion rate (%)	Student-staff ratio	Services & facilities spend per student(£)	Total	Page
51	42	Lincoln	79.5	79.3	10.3	128	81.4	75.1	88.1	14.7	2,123	570	454
52	83	West London	85.7	84.7	1.6	124	74.0	74.3	78.1	14.8	2,669	565	566
53	57	Staffordshire	83.3	79.8	16.5	120	80.8	72.3	78.4	15.4	2,484	564	540
54	55	Kent	76.8	76.6	35.2	135	78.3	79.1	89.0	18	1,827	558	436
55	59	Edge Hill	82.1	79.1	4.9	134	77.2	74.0	85.1	14.1	2,230	554	398
=56	54	Leeds Arts	83.1	79.0	n/a	158	57.1	79.9	88.8	11.9	1,287	552	446
=56	51=	Portsmouth	80.5	79.3	8.6	115	85.4	75.0	85.4	15.4	2,222	552	500
=58	60	Ulster	81.8	80.3	31.8	128	71.9	76.0	83.3	17.4	2,143	549	560
=58	58	West of England	83.8	83.1	8.8	126	76.3	75.4	84.3	15.3	2,007	549	568
60	50	Liverpool Hope	82.5	79.3	9.2	117	83.8	68.0	79.9	14.5	2,103	545	458
61	62	Huddersfield	81.2	78.3	9.4	131	80.0	74.6	84.2	17.5	2,417	540	428
=62	69	Manchester Metropolitan	80.7	78.9	7.5	133	70.7	73.2	83.5	15.5	2,719	535	472
=62	66	Norwich Arts	81.6	77.7	5.6	137	60.6	71.8	88.6	15	2,638	535	484
64	=63	Oxford Brookes	77.3	77.0	11.4	131	77.4	75.7	89.6	15.1	2,248	531	494
=65	61	Northumbria	79.7	78.3	9.0	145	75.4	77.3	84.0	16.3	2,224	524	482
=65	67	Sheffield Hallam	83.7	81.1	5.4	119	73.8	74.7	85.7	17.2	2,318	524	530
67	80	St George's, London	71.9	71.9	22.2	158	93.8	80.3	93.3	11.1	2,560	521	522
68	71	Goldsmiths, London	76.5	72.0	33.4	131	58.3	81.9	78.5	15.1	2,902	520	416
69	70	Roehampton	79.2	77.2	24.5	111	72.2	68.7	74.3	14.2	2,759	519	514
70	=63	Bangor	83.8	81.8	27.2	131	67.8	71.4	84.1	17	1,714	518	330
71	=94	Chichester	83.3	79.9	6.4	123	64.6	73.1	88.0	14.4	1,833	515	376
72	84	Falmouth	81.1	76.5	4.6	131	77.0	78.0	86.8	18.3	1,488	514	408
73	68	City, London	76.2	77.1	22.6	145	73.4	73.1	88.5	17.8	2,495	511	378
74	65	De Montfort	79.9	80.0	8.9	111	83.8	75.1	85.0	19.9	2,246	508	386
75	=105	Central Lancashire	81.3	78.7	5.6	133	76.9	71.8	79.6	14.2	2,241	506	372

2019 rank	2018 rank		Teaching quality (%)	Student experience (%)	Research quality (%)	Entry standards (UCAS points)	Graduate prospects (%)	Good honours (%)	Completion rate (%)	Student-staff ratio	Services & facilities spend per student(£)	Total	Page
76	72	Plymouth	82.4	79.9	15.9	132	73.6	70.9	83.6	16.2	2,020	504	496
77	=103	Hull	80.8	77.1	16.7	126	76.0	70.4	83.0	16.2	2,370	499	430
78	74	Liverpool John Moores	80.5	79.1	8.9	142	74.9	73.8	84.7	16.9	1,802	498	460
=79	=94	Arts London	76.3	70.1	8.0	137	72.2	71.3	86.2	14.8	2,397	495	326
=79	73	Chester	82.7	79.1	4.1	114	70.1	69.7	80.5	15.5	2,803	495	374
81	102	York St John	83.9	79.9	4.1	114	73.6	68.6	87.7	18	2,068	490	584
82	97	Queen Margaret, Edinburgh	80.7	76.5	6.6	151	72.9	79.0	81.9	18.6	1,775	488	502
83	96	Robert Gordon	83.0	80.4	4.0	157	81.1	69.9	86.8	20.4	1,449	487	512
84	100	Greenwich	79.9	78.4	4.9	137	70.3	77.0	82.0	17.4	2,329	484	418
85	77	St Mary's, Twickenham	82.2	79.0	4.0	119	72.6	75.3	81.0	16	1,741	483	524
86	107	London South Bank	80.4	77.9	9.0	114	87.7	69.5	77.5	15.6	2,156	480	466
87	=85	Teesside	83.1	79.5	3.6	120	81.3	68.0	79.8	18	2,464	477	556
88	90	Hertfordshire	78.8	78.3	5.6	115	80.6	64.9	83.7	16	2,700	476	424
=89	=115	Royal Agricultural	81.8	82.3	1.1	118	63.5	63.5	91.2	20.9	2,803	475	516
=89	=85	Solent	82.2	79.0	0.5	118	70.4	71.3	77.9	15.6	2,112	475	534
91	75	Derby	81.6	78.6	2.5	123	76.2	65.7	79.1	14.5	2,042	474	388
=92	43	Buckingham	80.6	80.5	n/a	121	81.5	69.7	84.0	15.8	1,926	472	360
=92	91	Worcester	85.1	82.8	4.3	120	75.0	67.1	81.8	17.2	1,629	472	578
94	78	Bournemouth	77.3	75.4	9.0	122	68.7	76.4	85.3	17	2,325	465	324
95	=81	Gloucestershire	81.0	78.0	3.8	123	72.9	71.3	80.9	18.7	2,055	461	414
=96	=87	Birmingham City	81.0	77.3	4.3	123	76.8	71.6	82.6	17.9	2,123	460	342
=96	101	Glasgow Caledonian	78.7	76.5	7.0	167	73.7	79.9	83.7	20.2	1,651	460	412
=98	=105	Abertay	84.5	81.3	5.1	142	73.4	65.8	77.4	19.6	1,919	459	318
=98	79	Winchester	80.5	78.5	5.8	113	63.7	76.4	86.3	16.4	1,683	459	574
100	76	Brunel	73.1	73.4	25.4	125	70.9	75.7	86.5	18	2,418	458	358

2019 rank	2018 rank		Teaching quality (%)	Student experience (%)	Research quality (%)	Entry standards (UCAS points)	Graduate prospects (%)	Good honours (%)	Completion rate (%)	Student-staff ratio	Services & facilities spend per student(£)	Total	Page
101	120	Edinburgh Napier	76.2	75.9	4.6	148	73.8	75.7	82.2	17.9	2,136	455	402
=102	113	Bishop Grosseteste	81.2	75.8	2.1	112	72.9	69.0	90.2	20.2	2,212	453	346
=102	109	Plymouth Marjon	86.7	82.7	0.0	125	63.7	77.1	78.4	22.2	1,996	453	498
=102	89	Wales Trinity St David	84.6	78.6	2.6	109	66.0	72.9	77.2	15.2	1,779	453	558
105	98	Bradford	74.3	74.3	9.2	132	82.8	80.2	83.0	17.2	2,076	448	352
106	=110	Kingston	79.3	78.3	5.1	124	64.5	72.5	84.1	16.6	2,559	444	440
107	=110	Middlesex	75.5	74.0	9.7	123	73.5	67.2	78.9	16.7	3,030	443	474
108	92	West of Scotland	81.4	78.0	4.3	139	80.7	71.3	80.9	22.4	2,205	442	570
109	93	Sunderland	79.9	77.2	5.8	115	67.1	64.7	80.4	15.8	2,657	441	548
110	=103	Bath Spa	76.5	72.2	7.9	118	66.9	78.8	86.2	18.7	2,100	438	334
111	81=	Salford	78.5	76.8	8.3	130	73.6	73.7	78.3	16.2	1,980	437	526
112	108	Cardiff Metropolitan	80.7	80.0	3.9	123	65.9	67.4	79.6	18.8	2,565	434	370
113	117	Buckinghamshire New	81.9	79.7	1.5	117	68.8	60.4	79.3	15.8	2,647	427	360
114	=110	South Wales	82.5	79.5	4.0	125	63.4	67.3	79.8	15.6	1,580	412	536
115	119	Newman	82.5	81.2	2.8	118	64.7	60.9	76.6	14.5	1,696	408	478
116	99	Northampton	78.8	73.9	3.2	105	68.2	68.0	80.6	16.8	2,728	407	480
117	=87	Leeds Trinity	77.1	74.8	2.0	109	68.1	79.3	82.4	19.9	1,940	403	450
118	118	Canterbury Christ Church	81.0	75.7	4.5	110	64.7	68.8	80.6	14.8	1,847	401	366
119	114	Westminster	75.2	75.1	9.8	127	70.4	70.5	81.7	19.3	1,857	395	572
120	122	Anglia Ruskin	82.4	79.0	5.4	113	68.3	74.0	78.2	18.5	1,464	388	322
121	125	Cumbria	78.9	73.8	1.2	126	73.6	67.4	82.7	16.8	1,611	383	384
122	123	Brighton	79.8	75.8	7.9	117	67.2	72.2	81.3	18.5	1,587	380	354
123	124	Leeds Beckett	80.4	79.3	4.1	112	63.2	70.3	76.4	19.3	1,954	377	448
124	127	Wolverhampton	81.3	78.8	5.9	112	68.9	66.2	72.9	18	1,913	374	576
125	126	Bolton	85.6	82.1	2.9	116	57.4	60.8	72.8	14.2	1,488	368	348

2019 rank	2018 rank		Teaching quality (%)	Student experience (%)	Research quality (%)	Entry standards (UCAS points)	Graduate prospects (%)	Good honours (%)	Completion rate (%)	Student-staff ratio	Services & facilities spend per student(£)	Total	Page
126	131	London Metropolitan	77.9	75.7	3.5	101	70.7	60.8	65.7	17.8	3,129	355	462
127	=115	East London	78.0	76.1	7.2	111	65.3	68.1	75.5	18.9	2,018	350	396
128	121	Bedfordshire	80.4	77.4	7.0	101	70.6	63.9	66.3	17	2,089	348	336
129	130	Suffolk	80.0	76.0	n/a	117	65.0	66.8	72.2	18.8	2,387	340	546
130	129	Wrexham Glyndŵr	79.2	74.3	2.3	113	63.5	70.4	74.8	21.2	1,673	313	580
131	132	Ravensbourne, London	72.1	66.1	n/a	113	68.7	63.9	89.7	31.6	1,460	250	508

Notes on the Table

University College Birmingham and Birkbeck, University of London, blocked the release of their performance data and do not appear in this year's table.

2 Choosing What and Where to Study

Choosing a degree is one of the biggest decisions any student will ever take – both in terms of the likely costs and the influence it may have on the direction of his or her life. That is not just a matter of future earning power, although the current political and media debates might suggest that it is. Many graduates end up living and working near their university; they often make their closest friends in their student days and may even meet their future partner there. And that is without considering the three or four years you will spend as an undergraduate, which should develop your intellect and shape you as a person.

Of course, with fees now exceeding £9,000, no one is suggesting that you should ignore career prospects – although it is dangerous to read too much into employment statistics that are collected only six months after graduation. Indeed, any assumptions about the link between particular courses and future salaries are no more than that; the world is changing too rapidly to pick winners several years ahead of joining the graduate labour market, although some subjects and universities have a record that inspires more confidence than others. This chapter will suggest some of the signs to take into account in selecting the course that is right for you, if indeed you are certain that your immediate future should be in higher education at all.

Most young people with the necessary qualifications decide that university is right for them – 60% of the working age population of London are now graduates. But applications and enrolments since the introduction of much higher fees are beginning to show clear patterns that favour certain subjects and universities – and may make life increasingly difficult for others. It is not surprising that growing numbers should decide to play it safe, as they see it, in choosing what and where to study. Although most graduate jobs continue to be open to students of any discipline, some arts subjects may now seem more of a gamble, and there may be pressure at home to go for a science or business subject if you have the right qualifications.

Your choices must be realistic, however. The course must not only be within your capabilities but will have to maintain your interest for at least three years – possibly much longer than that if it is then going to determine your field of employment. Ideally, higher education should broaden your options in later life, not narrow them. Most of today's graduates will work in several different fields during their careers. In any case, no one can be sure which skills will be required in four or more years' time, when today's applicants enter the graduate labour market.

Some subjects and universities will be more marketable than others, but which ones? Even some of the subjects producing highly employable graduates at the moment may see artificial intelligence decimate employment opportunities in the medium term. This *Guide* gives some pointers to developments in the graduate labour market – medicine is unlikely to go into decline, for example – but times do change. Computer science, for instance, went through years of falling numbers after the dotcom bubble burst, before recovering strongly in recent years. Applications for the group of subjects that includes architecture and building are only now returning to the totals reached before the 2008 recession.

Why applicants have reached some of the conclusions they have remains a mystery. Languages, for example, have been hardest hit in terms of applications and enrolments. Yet business leaders are constantly stressing the need for linguists. In this case, decisions made on entry to the sixth-form may be the biggest factor behind falling applications – the numbers taking languages at A-level have been dropping for a number of years, perhaps because they are seen as more difficult than other arts subjects. A similar problem seems to be affecting mathematics at the moment.

There will be many factors influencing your choice of university and course, ranging from the limitations imposed by your qualifications to favoured geographical locations. You may want to stay within reach of home – or to get as far away as possible. You may have heard good things about a particular course from friends, or a teacher. This *Guide* – and the tables it contains – offers a reality check to supplement such opinions, and the opportunity to narrow down your options.

What influences a choice?

Most important factors in choosing a university (median marks out of 10)

1	The course: curriculum, assessment type and structure	8.4
2	Reputation of the University	7.7
3	University's perceived ability to boost career	7.1
4	Accessibility by major transport	6.7
5	Facilities: gym, library, IT and labs	6.3
6	Distance from family home	6.1
7	Affordability of town/city	6.1
8	Availability of accommodation	5.9
9	Support services: enrichment, counselling and diversity	5.8
10	Culture: arts, food and attractions	5.7
11	Size of town or city	5.6
12	Nightlife	4.6
13	Sports available	3.9
14	Family or friends' links with university	3.9
15	Regional weather	3.6

Source: SPCE Labs 2018 (sample of 2,000 current and past UK students)

Is higher education for you?

Before you start, there is one important question to ask yourself: what do you want out of higher education? The answer will make it easier to choose where (and if) to be a student. With about three school-leavers in ten going on to university, it is easy to drift that way without much thought, opting for the subject in which you expect the best A-level grades, and looking for a university with a reasonable reputation and a good social life. Your career will look after itself – you hope.

With graduate debt soaring, however, and job prospects varying widely between subjects and universities, now is the time to look at your own motivation. Fewer young people than predicted have opted out of higher education since higher fees were introduced, but apprenticeships and big firms' training schemes are now offering attractive alternatives. Many of those who do choose higher education appear to be rethinking their choice of course to give themselves the best possible chance of a satisfying and lucrative career.

Love of a subject is an excellent reason for taking a degree, and one that allows you to focus almost exclusively on the search for a course that corresponds with your passions. If, however, higher education is a means to an end, you need to think about career ambitions and look carefully at employment rates for any courses you might consider. These are examined in more detail in chapter 3.

Many graduates look back on their student days as the best years of their lives, and there is nothing wrong with wanting to have a good time. Remember, though, that you will be paying for it later (literally) and there will be more studying than partying. If you have not enjoyed sixth-form or college courses, you may be better off in a job and possibly becoming one of the hundreds of thousands each year who return to education later in life.

Setting your priorities

Even in the world of £9,250 fees, there are good reasons to believe that the right degree will still be a good investment. Most research suggests that, on average, a degree would add more than £100,000 to lifetime earnings. Although the salary premium enjoyed by graduates has declined, a recent Labour Force Survey showed working-age graduates earning almost 50% more on average than non-graduates.

The majority of graduate jobs are not subject-specific; employers value the transferable skills that higher education confers. Rightly or wrongly, however, most employers are influenced by which university a graduate attended, so the choice of institution remains as important as ever. The Institute for Fiscal Studies found that the male graduates of 23 universities and the female graduates of nine were earning less than those without degrees after ten years.

Those who want to add value to their degree in the jobs market will find that growing numbers of universities are offering employment-related schemes that are considered in more detail in chapter 2. In many cases, this will involve work experience or extra activities organised by the careers service. A growing number of universities now run certificated employability programmes, while others, such as Liverpool John Moores, have built such skills into degree courses. Such programmes are also highlighted in chapter 2 and in the university profiles in chapter 15.

Narrowing down the field

Once you have decided that higher education is for you, the good news is that, as long as you start early enough, finding the right university can be relatively straightforward. Media attention focuses on the scramble for places on a relatively small proportion of courses where competition is intense, but there are plenty of places at good universities for candidates with the basic qualifications – it's just a matter of finding the one that suits you best. For older applicants, relevant work experience and demonstrable interest in a subject may be enough to win a place.

If anything, the problem is that of too much choice, although universities have reduced the number of degree combinations in anticipation of tougher financial conditions. Students prepared to move away from home will still have more than 100 universities and numerous specialist colleges to consider, most with hundreds – even thousands – of course combinations on offer. Institutions come in all shapes and sizes, so there is work to do at the outset narrowing down your options.

Most applicants start by choosing a subject, rather than a university, and this may reduce the field considerably – there are only eight institutions offering veterinary medicine for example, although the total will be more than 100 in subjects such as psychology, law and English. By the time you have factored in personal preferences about the type or location of your ideal university, the list of possibilities may already be reduced to manageable proportions.

After that, you can take a closer look at what the courses contain and what life is really like for students. Prospectuses and university websites will give you an accurate account of course combinations, and important facts like the accommodation available to new students, but it is their job to sell the university. To get a true picture, you need more – preferably a visit not just to the university, but to the department where you would be studying. If that is not possible, there are plenty of other sources of objective information, such as the National Student Survey which is available online, with a range of additional data about the main courses at each institution, at **www.officeforstudents.org.uk/advice-and-guidance/student-information-and-data**.

A few students' unions publish alternative prospectuses, giving a "warts and all" view of the university, and those that do not provide this service may be able to arrange a brief discussion with a current student, either by phone or email. Your school or college may put you in contact with someone who went to a university that you are considering. Guides and collections of statistics may give you valuable information about a course or a university, but there is no substitute for personal experience.

What to study?

Most people seeking a place in higher education start by choosing a subject and a course, rather than a university. If you take a degree, you are probably going to spend at least three years immersed in your subject. It has to be one you will enjoy and can master – not to mention one that you are qualified to study. Many economics degrees require maths A-level, for example, while most medical schools demand chemistry or biology. The UCAS website (**www.ucas.com**) contains course profiles, including entrance requirements, which is a good starting point, while universities' own sites contain more detailed information. In chapter 13, we describe 67 subject areas and provide league tables for each of them.

Your school subjects and the UCAS tariff

The official yardstick by which your results will be judged is the UCAS tariff, which gives a score for each grade of most UK qualifications considered relevant for university entrance, as well as for the International Baccalaureate (IB). The tariff changed two years ago. The new points system is shown on page 32, but most applicants are not affected – two-thirds of offers are made in grades, rather than tariff points. This allows universities to stipulate the grades that they require in specific subjects, if they wish, and to determine which vocational qualifications are relevant to different degrees. In certain universities, some departments, but not others, will use the tariff to set offers. Course profiles on the UCAS website and/or universities' own sites should show whether offers are framed in terms of grades or tariff points. It is important to find out which, especially if you are relying on points from qualifications other than A-level or Scottish Highers, more of which are included in the new tariff.

Entry qualifications listed in the *Guide* relate not to the offers made by universities, but to the actual grades achieved by successful candidates who are under 21 on entry. For ease of comparison, a tariff score is included even where universities make their offers in grades.

"Soft" subjects

There is a related issue for many of the most selective universities about the subjects studied in the sixth-form or at college. Not only have growing numbers of students been applying with

UCAS tariff scores for main qualifications:

A-levels		AS levels	
Grade	**Points**	**Grade**	**Points**
A*	56	A	20
A	48	B	16
B	40	C	12
C	32	D	10
D	24	E	6
E	16		

Scottish Advanced higher		Scottish higher	
Grade	**Points**	**Grade**	**Points**
A	56	A	33
B	48	B	27
C	40	C	21
D	32	D	15

International Baccalaureate			
Higher level		**Standard level**	
H7	56	S7	28
H6	48	S6	24
H5	32	S5	16
H4	24	S4	12
H3	12	S3	6

The Extended Essay and Theory of Knowledge course are awarded A 12, B 10, C 8, D 6, E 4

For other qualifications see: ucas.com/ucas/ucas-tariff-points

vocational (usually BTEC) qualifications, but the variety of A-level courses now available includes many subjects that top universities usually will not consider on a par with traditional academic subjects. For many years, a minority of universities have refused to accept General Studies as a full A-level for entrance purposes (although even some leading universities do). The growth of supposedly "soft" subjects, such as media studies and photography, has prompted a few universities to produce lists of subjects that will only be accepted alongside at least two traditional academic subjects.

The Russell Group of 24 leading universities published an extremely useful report, called Informed Choices, which it has now turned into a website, on the post-16 qualifications preferred by its members for a wide range of degrees. Although the original report named media studies, art and design, photography and business studies among the vocational subjects that would normally be given this label, it did not subscribe to the notion of a single list of "soft" subjects. The report suggested you choose at most a single vocational course and primarily select from a list of "facilitating subjects", which are required for many degrees and welcomed generally at Russell Group universities. The list comprised: maths and further maths, English, physics, biology, chemistry, geography, languages (classical and modern) and history. In addition, their guide indicates the "essential" and "useful" A-level subjects for 60 different subject areas studied at Russell Group universities.

For most courses at most universities, there are no such restrictions, as long as your main subjects or qualifications are relevant to the degree you hope to take. Nevertheless, when choosing A-levels it would be wise to bear the Russell Group lists in mind if you are likely to apply to one or more of the leading universities. At the very least, it is an indication of the subjects that admissions tutors may take less seriously than the rest. Although only the London School of Economics has published a list of "non-preferred" subjects (see below), others may adopt less-formal weightings.

Vocational qualifications
The Education Department downgraded many vocational qualifications in school league tables from 2014. This has added to the confusion surrounding the value placed on diplomas and other qualifications by universities. The engineering diploma has won near-universal approval from universities (for admission to engineering courses and possibly some science degrees), but some of the other diplomas are in fields that are not on the curriculum of the most selective universities. Regardless of the points awarded under the tariff, it is essential to contact universities direct to ensure that a diploma or another vocational qualification will be an acceptable qualification for your chosen degree.

Admission tests
The growing numbers of applicants with high grades at A-level have encouraged the introduction of separate admission tests for some of the most oversubscribed courses. There are national tests in medicine and law that are used by some of the leading universities, while Oxford and Cambridge have their own tests in a growing number of subjects. The details are listed on page 34. In all cases, the tests are used as an extra selection tool, not as a replacement for A-level or other general qualifications.

Making a choice
You're A-levels or Scottish Highers may have chosen themselves, but the range of subjects across the whole university system is vast. Even subjects that you have studied at school may be

---

"Traditional academic" and "non-preferred" subjects
The London School of Economics expects applicants to offer at least two of the traditional subjects listed below, while any of the non-preferred subjects listed should only be offered with two traditional subjects.

Traditional subjects

- Ancient history
- Biology
- Classical civilisation
- Chemistry
- Computing
- Economics
- Electronics
- English
- Further mathematics
- Geography
- Government and politics
- History
- Law
- Mathematics
- Modern or classical languages
- Music
- Philosophy
- Physics
- Psychology
- Religious studies
- Sociology

Non-preferred subjects

- Any Applied A-level
- Accounting
- Art and design
- Business studies
- Citizenship studies
- Communication and culture
- Creative writing
- Design and technology
- Drama/theatre studies
- Film studies
- Health and social care
- Home economics
- Information and communication technology
- Leisure studies
- Media studies
- Music technology
- Physical education/ Sports studies
- Travel and tourism

General studies, critical thinking, thinking skills, knowledge and enquiry and project work A-levels will only be considered as fourth A-level subjects and will not therefore be accepted as part of a conditional offer.

Admissions tests

Some of the most competitive courses now have additional entrance tests. The most significant tests are listed below. Note that registration for many of the tests is before 15 October and you will need to register for them as early as possible. All the tests have their own websites. Institutions requiring specific tests vary from year to year and you must check course website details carefully for test requirements. In addition over 50 universities also administer their own tests for certain courses. Details are given at: **www.ucas.com/undergraduate/applying-university/admissions-tests**

Law

Law National Admissions Test (LNAT): for entry to law courses at Bristol, Durham, Glasgow, King's College London, London School of Economics, Nottingham, Oxford, SOAS, University College, London. Register from August; tests held from September to June.

Mathematics

Mathematics Admissions Test (MAT): for entry to mathematics at Imperial College, London and mathematics and computer science at Oxford. Test held in early November.

Sixth Term Examination Papers (STEP): for entry to mathematics at Cambridge and Warwick (also occasionally requested by other universities). Register by end April; tests held in June. Test of Mathematics for University Admission: results accepted by Bath, Cardiff, Durham, Nottingham, Lancaster, London School of Economics, Sheffield, Southampton, Warwick. Register during September, test held at the end of October.

Medical subjects

BioMedical Admissions Test (BMAT): for entry to medicine at Brighton and Sussex Medical School, Cambridge (also for veterinary medicine), Imperial College London, Keele (international applicants only), Lancaster, Leeds (also for dentistry), Oxford and University College London. Register by 1 October; test held early November.

Graduate Medical School Admissions Test (GAMSAT): for graduate entry to medicine and dentistry at Cardiff, Exeter, Liverpool, Nottingham, Plymouth, St. George's, University of London, Swansea, Keele and St Andrews and Dundee in partnership with University of the Highlands & Islands (Scotgem). Register by early August; test held mid-September

Health Professions Admissions Test (HPAT-Ulster): for certain health profession courses at Ulster.Register by start January; test held late January.

UK Clinical Aptitude Test (UKCAT): for entry to medical and dental schools at Aberdeen, Anglia Ruskin, Aston, Birmingham, Bristol, Cardiff, Dundee, East Anglia, Edge Hill, Edinburgh, Exeter, Glasgow, Hull York Medical School, Keele, Kent and Medway, King's College London, Leicester, Liverpool, Manchester, Newcastle, Nottingham, Plymouth, Queen Mary, University of London, Queen's University Belfast, Sheffield, Southampton, St Andrews, St George's, University of London, Sunderland, Warwick. Register between May and mid-September; tests held between July and early October.

Cambridge University

Pre-interview or at-interview assessments take place for all subjects. Full details given on the Cambridge admissions website. See also STEP and BMAT above.

Oxford University

Pre-interview tests take place in many subjects that candidates are required to register for specifically by early October. Full details given on the Oxford admissions website. Tests held in early November, usually at candidate's educational institution. See also LNAT, MAT and BMAT above.

quite different at degree level – some academic economists prefer their undergraduates not to have taken A-level economics because they approach the subject so differently. Other students are disappointed because they appear to be going over old ground when they continue with a subject that they enjoyed at school. Universities now publish quite detailed syllabuses, and it is a matter of going through the fine print.

The greater difficulty comes in judging your suitability for the many subjects that are not on the school or college curriculum. Philosophy and psychology sound fascinating (and are), but you may have no idea what degrees in either subject entail – for example, the level of statistics that may be required. Forensic science may look exciting on television – more glamorous than plain chemistry – but it opens fewer doors, as the type of work portrayed in Silent Witness is very hard to find.

Academic or vocational?

There is frequent and often misleading debate about the differences between academic and vocational higher education. It is usually about the relative value of taking a degree, as opposed to a directly work-related qualification. But it also extends to higher education itself, with jibes about so-called "Mickey Mouse" degrees in areas that were not part of the higher education curriculum when most of the critics were students.

Such attitudes ignore the fact that medicine and law are both vocational subjects, as are architecture, engineering and education. They are not seen as any less academic than geography or sociology, but for some reason social work or nursing, let alone media studies and sports science, are often looked down upon. The test of a degree should be whether it is challenging and a good preparation for working life. Both general academic and vocational degrees can do this.

Nevertheless, it is clear that the prospect of much higher graduate debt is encouraging more students into job-related subjects. This is understandable and, if you are sure of your future career path, possibly also sensible. But much depends on what that career is – and whether you are ready to make such a long-term commitment. Some of the programmes that have attracted public ridicule, such as surf science or golf course management, may narrow graduates' options to a worrying extent, but often boast strong employment records.

Most popular subject areas by applications 2019		Most popular subjects by acceptances 2019	
1 Nursing	167,185	1 Nursing	30,390
2 Psychology	128,795	2 Psychology	24,395
3 Law	123,300	3 Law	22,895
4 Computer Science	97,680	4 Computer Science	18,660
5 Design studies	89,420	5 Design studies	18,225
6 Management studies	82,310	6 Management studies	16,280
7 Medicine	80,995	7 Business studies	16,240
8 Business studies	65,585	8 Sports and exercise science	14,805
9 Other subjects allied to medicine	64,445	9 Social Work	13,090
10 Sports and exercise science	64,015	10 Other subjects allied to medicine	13,055

Source: UCAS End of Cycle report 2019   Source: UCAS End of Cycle report 2019

Subject areas covered in this *Guide*

The list below gives each of the 67 subject areas that are covered in detail later in the book (in chapter 13). For each subject area in that chapter, there is specific advice, a summary of employment prospects and a league table of universities that offered courses in 2017–18, ranked on the basis of an overall score calculated from research quality, entry standards, teaching quality, student experience and graduate employment prospects.

Accounting and Finance
Aeronautical and Manufacturing
  Engineering
Agriculture and Forestry
American Studies
Anatomy and Physiology
Animal Science
Anthropology
Archaeology and Forensic Science
Architecture
Art and Design
Biological Sciences
Building
Business Studies
Celtic Studies
Chemical Engineering
Chemistry
Civil Engineering
Classics and Ancient History
Communication and Media Studies
Computer Science
Creative Writing
Criminology
Dentistry
Drama, Dance and Cinematics
East and South Asian Studies
Economics
Education
Electrical and Electronic Engineering
English
Food Science
French
General Engineering
Geography and Environmental Sciences

Geology
German
History
History of Art, Architecture and Design
Hospitality, Leisure, Recreation and Tourism
Iberian Languages
Italian
Land and Property Management
Law
Librarianship and Information Management
Linguistics
Materials Technology
Mathematics
Mechanical Engineering
Medicine
Middle Eastern and African Studies
Music
Nursing
Other Subjects Allied to Medicine
Pharmacology and Pharmacy
Philosophy
Physics and Astronomy
Physiotherapy
Politics
Psychology
Radiography
Russian
Social Policy
Social Work
Sociology
Sports Science
Theology and Religious Studies
Town and Country Planning and Landscape
Veterinary Medicine

As you would expect, many vocational courses are tailored to particular professions. If you choose one of these, make sure that the degree is recognised by the relevant professional body (such as the Engineering Council or one of the institutes) or you may not be able to use the skills that you acquire. Most universities are only too keen to make such recognition clear in their prospectus; if no such guarantee is published, contact the university department running the course and seek assurances. In education, for example, by no means all degrees qualify you to teach.

Even where a course has professional recognition, bear in mind that a further qualification may be required to practise. Both law and medicine, for example, demand additional training to become a fully qualified solicitor, barrister or doctor. Nor is either degree an automatic passport to a job: only about half of all law graduates go into the profession. Both law and medicine also offer a postgraduate route into the profession for those who have taken other subjects as a first degree. Law conversion courses, though not cheap, are increasingly popular, and there are a growing number of graduate-entry medical degrees.

One way to ensure that a degree is job-related is to take a "sandwich" course, which involves up to a year in business or industry. Students often end up working for the organisation which provided the placement, while others gain valuable insights into a field of employment – even if only to discount it. The drawback with such courses is that, like the year abroad that is part of most language degrees, the period away from university inevitably disrupts living arrangements and friendship groups. But most of those who take this route find that the career benefits make this a worthwhile sacrifice. Growing numbers of traditional degrees now offer shorter periods of work experience.

Employers' organisations calculate that more than half of all graduate jobs are open to applicants from any subject, and recruiters for the most competitive graduate training schemes often prefer traditional academic subjects to apparently relevant vocational degrees. Newspapers, for example, often prefer a history graduate to one with a media studies degree; computing firms are said to take a disproportionate number of classicists. A good degree classification and the right work experience are more important than the subject for most non-technical jobs. But it is hard to achieve a good result on a course that you do not enjoy, so scour prospectuses, and email or phone university departments to ensure that you know what you are letting yourself in for. Their reaction to your approach will also give you an idea of how responsive they are to their students.

Studying more than one subject

You may find that more than one subject appeals, in which case you could consider Joint Honours – degrees that combine two subjects – or even Combined Honours, which will cover several related subjects. Such courses obviously allow you to extend the scope of your studies, but they should be approached with caution. Even if the number of credits suggests a similar workload to Single Honours, covering more than one subject inevitably involves extra reading and often more essays or project work.

The numbers taking such degrees is falling, but there are advantages to them. Many students choose a "dual" to add a vocational element to make themselves more employable – business studies with languages or engineering, for example, or media studies with English. Others want to take their studies in a particular direction, perhaps by combining history with politics, or statistics with maths. Some simply want to add a completely unrelated interest to their main subject, such as environmental science and music, or archaeology and event management – both combinations that are available at UK universities.

At most universities, however, it is not necessary to take a degree in more than one subject in order to broaden your studies. The spread of modular programmes ensures that you can take courses in related subjects without changing the basic structure of your degree. You may not be able to take an event management module in a single-honours archaeology degree, but it should be possible to study some history or a language. The number and scope of the combinations offered at many of the larger universities is extraordinary. Indeed, it has been criticised by academics who believe that "mix-and-match" degrees can leave a graduate without a rounded view of a subject. But for those who seek breadth and variety, close scrutiny of university prospectuses is a vital part of the selection process.

What type of course?

Once you have a subject, you must decide on the level and type of course. Most readers of this *Guide* will be looking for full-time degree courses, but higher education is much broader than that. You may not be able to afford the time or the money needed for a full-time commitment of three or four years at this point in life.

Part-time courses

Tens of thousands of people each year opt for a part-time course – usually while holding down a job – to continue learning and to improve their career prospects. The numbers studying this way have dropped considerably, but loans are available for students whose courses occupy between a quarter and three-quarters of the time expected on a full-time course. Repayments are on the same conditions as those for full-time courses, except that you will begin repaying after three years of study even if the course has not been completed by then. The downside is that universities have increased their fees in the knowledge that part-time students will be able to take out student loans to cover fees, and employers are now less inclined to fund their employees on such courses. At Birkbeck, University of London, a compromise has been found with full-time courses taught in the evening. For courses classified as part-time, students pay fees in proportion to the number of credits they take.

Part-time study can be exhausting unless your employer gives you time off, but if you have the stamina for a course that will usually take twice as long as the full-time equivalent, this route should still make a degree more affordable. Part-time students tend to be highly committed to their subject, and many claim that the quality of the social life associated with their course makes up for the quantity of leisure time enjoyed by full-timers.

Distance learning

If you are confident that you can manage without regular face-to-face contact with teachers and fellow students, distance learning is an option. Courses are delivered mainly or entirely online or through correspondence, although some programmes offer a certain amount of local tuition. The process might sound daunting and impersonal, but students of the Open University (OU), all of whom are educated in this way, are frequently among the most satisfied in the country, according to the results of the annual National Student Survey. Attending lectures or oversized seminars at a conventional university can be less personal than regular contact with your tutor at a distance.

Of course, not all universities are as good at communicating with their distance-learning students as the OU, or offer such high-quality course materials, but this mode of study does give students ultimate flexibility to determine when and where they study. Distance learning is becoming increasingly popular for the delivery of professional courses, which are often needed to supplement degrees. The OU takes students of all ages, including school-leavers, not just mature students.

In addition, there is now the option of Massive Open Online Courses (MOOCs) provided by many of the leading UK and American universities, usually free of charge. As yet, most such courses are the equivalent of a module in a degree course, rather than the entire qualification. Some are assessed formally but none is likely to be seen by employers as the equal of a conventional degree, no matter how prestigious the university offering the course. That may change – some commentators see in MOOCs the beginning of the end of the traditional, residential university – but their main value for now is as a means of dipping a toe in the water of higher education. For those who are uncertain about committing to a degree, or who simply want to learn more about a subject without needing a high-status qualification, they are ideal.

A number of UK universities offer MOOCs through the Futurelearn platform, run by the Open University (**www.futurelearn.com**). But the beauty of MOOCs is that they can come from all over the world. Perhaps the best-known providers are Coursera (**www.coursera.org**), which originated at Stanford University, in California, and now involves a large number of American and international universities including Edinburgh, and edX (**www.edx.org**), which numbers Harvard among its members. MOOCs are also being used increasingly by sixth-formers to extend their subject knowledge and demonstrate their enthusiasm and capability to admissions tutors. They are certainly worth considering for inclusion in a personal statement and/or to spark discussion at an interview.

Foundation degrees

Even if you are set on a full-time course, you might not want to commit yourself for three or more years. Two-year vocational Foundation degrees have become a popular route into higher education in recent years. Many other students take longer-established two-year courses, such as Higher National Diplomas or other diplomas tailored to the needs of industry or parts of the health service. Those who do well on such courses usually have the option of converting their qualification into a full degree with further study, although many are satisfied without immediately staying on for the further two or more years that will be required to complete a BA or BSc.

Other short courses

A number of universities are experimenting with two-year degrees, encouraged by the Government, squeezing more work into an extended academic year. The so-called "third semester" makes use of the summer vacation for extra teaching, so that mature students, in particular, can reduce the length of their career break. Several universities are offering accelerated degrees as part of a pilot project initiated under the coalition government. But only at the University of Buckingham, the UK's longest-established private university, is this the dominant pattern for degree courses. Other private institutions – notably BPP University – are following suit.

A growing number of short courses, usually lasting a year, are designed for students who do not have the necessary qualifications to start a degree in their chosen subject. Foundation courses in art and design have been common for many years and are the chosen preparation for a degree at leading departments, even for many students whose A-levels would win them a degree place elsewhere. Access courses perform the same function in a wider range of subjects for students without A-levels, or for those whose grades are either too low or in the wrong subjects to gain admission to a particular course. Entry requirements are modest, but students have to reach the same standard as regular entrants to progress to a degree.

Higher and Degree Apprenticeships

Apprenticeships have been a serious alternative to university for more than a decade. But now students can have the best of both worlds at a growing number of universities, with higher or degree apprenticeships, which combine study at degree level with extended work experience with a named industrial or business partner. The programmes are already popular but are only available in a limited range of subjects, such as accountancy, healthcare sciences, management and some branches of engineering. A survey by the *Sunday Times* found only about 8,500 people taking degree apprenticeships in 2018, but universities were – and still are – planning to expand rapidly.

Such apprenticeships take up to five years to complete and leave the graduate with a Bachelor's or even a Master's degree. Employers including Deloitte, BMW and the BBC are offering higher-level apprenticeships, although naturally not all are with household names such as these. Students are paid employees of the sponsoring company, with a contract of employment and holiday entitlement, as well as salaries averaging £17,875 a year in 2019. Some are available through UCAS, but most require a direct application to the company. The best starting point to weigh up the options is the gov.uk website, which has a 'Find an Apprenticeship' section. Once you register, you can set up email and text alerts to inform you about new apprenticeship roles. You can also find a range of vacancies at **www.ratemyapprenticeship.co.uk**, which carries thousands of reviews.

Further details of the structure of courses and the areas in which apprenticeships are available can be found at **www.gov.uk/government/publications/higher-and-degree-apprenticeships**. In addition, *Which? University* and the National Apprenticeship Service have produced a more detailed publication, *The Complete Guide to Higher and Degree Apprenticeships*, which is available online and in print.

Yet more choice

No single guide can allow for personal preferences in choosing a course. You may want one of the many degrees that incorporate a year at a partner university abroad or, for the moment at least, to try a six-month exchange on the Continent through the European Union's Erasmus Programme. Either might prove a valuable experience and add to your employability. Or you might prefer a January or February start to the traditional autumn start – there are plenty of opportunities for this, mainly at post-1992 universities.

Universities with highest and lowest offer rates

Highest		Lowest	
1 Bucks New	97.9%	1 Oxford	22.2%
2 Aberystwyth	97.3%	2 Cambridge	29.4%
3 Portsmouth	96.0%	3 Leeds Arts	37.3%
4 Roehampton	95.4%	4 Arts, London	38.7%
5 Newman	94.5%	5 LSE	39.6%
6 Abertay	94.0%	6 Imperial College	46.2%
7 Cardiff Metropolitan	93.5%	7 St Andrews	49.2%
8 Royal Holloway, London	93.3%	8 Edinburgh	51.8%
9 Bangor	93.2%	9 Dundee	54.3%
10 Bishop Grosseteste	92.9%	10 Arts, Bournemouth	56.3%

UCAS: Applications 2018

In some subjects – particularly engineering and the sciences – the leading degrees may be Masters courses, taking four years rather than three (in England). In Scotland, most degree courses take four years and some at the older universities will confer a Masters qualification. Those who come with A-levels may apply to go straight into the second year. Relatively few students take this option, but it is easy to imagine more doing so in future at universities that charge students from other parts of the UK the full £9,250 for all years of the course.

Best paid graduates

(Median salary six months after graduating)

1	Imperial College London	£30,000
2	London School of Economics	£29,000
3	Oxford	£27,040
4	Cambridge	£27,000
5	St George's, London	£26,600
6	Warwick	£26,500
=7	Bath	£26,000
=7	King's College London	£26,000
=7	London South Bank	£26,000
=7	University College London	£26,000

HESA 2017 graduates

Where to study

Once you have decided what to study, there are still several factors that might influence your choice of university or college. Obviously, you need to have a reasonable chance of getting in, you may want reassurance about the university's reputation, and its location will probably also be important to you. On top of that, most applicants have views about the type of institution they are looking for – big or small, old or new, urban or rural, specialist or comprehensive. Campus universities tend to produce the highest levels of student satisfaction, but big city universities continue to attract sixth-formers in the largest numbers. You may surprise yourself by choosing somewhere that does not conform to your initial criteria but working through your preferences is another way of narrowing down your options.

Entry standards

Unless you are a mature student or have taken a gap year, your passport to your chosen university will probably be a conditional offer based on your predicted grades, previous exam performance, personal statement, and school or college reference. Many universities followed Birmingham's lead in making unconditional offers to candidates in selected subjects who have a strong academic record and are predicted high grades. But, with ministers making critical comments about the practice, it appears that far fewer unconditional offers will be made for courses beginning in 2020 and 2021.

Most popular universities by applications 2019

1	Manchester	65,060
2	Leeds	61,220
3	Edinburgh	60,905
4	Birmingham	52,480
5	Nottingham	52,415
6	University College London	50,090
7	Manchester Metropolitan	49,875
8	Bristol	49,245
9	King's College London	46,535
10	Nottingham Trent	40,595

Source: UCAS End of Cycle report 2018

Supply and demand dictate whether you will receive an offer, conditional or otherwise. Beyond the national picture, your chances will be affected both by the university and the subject you choose. A few universities (but not many) at the top of the league tables are heavily oversubscribed in every subject; others will have areas in which they excel but may make relatively modest demands for entry to other courses. Even in many of the leading universities, the number of applicants for each place in languages or engineering is still not high. Conversely, three As at A-level will not guarantee a place on one of the top English or law degrees, but there are enough universities running courses to ensure that three Cs will put you in with a chance somewhere.

University prospectuses and the UCAS website will give you the "standard offer" for each course, but in some cases, this is pitched deliberately low in order to leave admissions staff extra flexibility. The standard A-level offer for medicine, for example, may not demand A*s, but nearly all successful applicants will have one or more. In Scotland, universities have started to publish two sets of standard offers: their normal range and another with lower grades for applicants from disadvantaged backgrounds.

As already noted, the average entry scores in our tables give the actual points obtained by successful applicants – many of which are far above the offer made by the university, but which give an indication of the pecking order at entry. The subject tables (in chapter 13) are, naturally, a better guide than the main table (in chapter 1), where average entry scores are influenced by the range of subjects available at each university.

Location

The most obvious starting point is the country you study in. Most degrees in Scotland take four years, rather than the UK norm of three. It goes without saying that four years cost more than three, especially given the loss of the year's salary you might have been earning after graduation. A later chapter will go into the details of the system but suffice to say that students from Scotland pay no fees, while those from the rest of the UK do. Nevertheless, Edinburgh and St Andrews remain particularly popular with English students, despite charging them £9,250 a year for the full four years of a degree starting in 2020. The number of English students going to Scottish universities has increased almost every year since the fees went up, despite the fact that there would be no savings, perhaps because the institutions have tried harder to attract them. Fees – or the lack of them – are by no means the only influence on cross-border mobility: the number of Scots going to English universities rose sharply, in spite of the cost, probably because the number of places is capped in Scotland, but not any longer in England.

Close to home

Far from crossing national boundaries, however, growing numbers of students choose to study near home, whether or not they continue to live with their family. This is understandable for Scots, who will save themselves tens of thousands of pounds by studying at their own fees-free universities. But there is also a gradual increase in the numbers choosing to study close to home either to cut living costs or for personal reasons, such as family circumstances, a girlfriend or boyfriend, continuing employment or religion. Some simply want to stick with what they know.

The trend for full-time students who do go away to study, is to choose a university within about two hours' travelling time. The assumption is that this is far enough to discourage parents from making unannounced visits, but close enough to allow for occasional trips home to get the washing done, have a decent meal and see friends. The leading universities recruit from all over the world, but most still have a regional core.

University or college?

This *Guide* is primarily concerned with universities, the destination of choice for the vast majority of higher education students. But there are other options – and not just for those searching for lower fees. A number of specialist higher education colleges offer a similar, or sometimes superior, quality of course in their particular fields. The subject tables in chapter 13 chart the successes of various colleges in art, agriculture, music and teacher training in particular. Some colleges of higher education are not so different from the newer universities and may acquire that status themselves in future.

Further education colleges

The second group of colleges offering degrees are further education (FE) colleges. These are often large institutions with a wide range of courses, from A-levels to vocational subjects at different levels, up to degrees in some cases. Although their numbers of higher education students have been falling in recent years, the current fee structure presents them with an opportunity because they tend not to bear all the costs of a university campus. For that reason, too, they may not offer a broad student experience of the type that universities pride themselves on, but the best colleges respond well to the local labour market and offer small teaching groups and effective personal support.

FE colleges are a local resource and tend to attract mature students who cannot or do not want to travel to university. Many of their higher education students apply nowhere else. But, as competition for university places has increased, they also have become more of an option for school-leavers to continue their studies, as they always have been in Scotland.

Their predominantly local, mature student populations do FE colleges no favours in statistical comparisons with universities. But it should be noted that the proportion of college graduates unemployed six months after graduation tends to be higher than at universities, and average graduate salaries lower. However, 14 further education colleges secured 'gold' ratings in the first year of the Government's Teaching Excellence Framework (TEF) – although more than twice as many found themselves in the 'bronze' category.

Both further and higher education colleges are audited by the Quality Assurance Agency and appear in the National Student Survey, as well as the TEF. In all three, their results usually show wide variation. Some demonstrate higher levels of satisfaction among their students than most universities, for example, while others are at the bottom of the scale.

Private universities and colleges

The final group of colleges that present an alternative to university was insignificant in terms of size until recently, but may also prosper under the current fee regime, thanks to recent legislation. This is the private sector, seen mainly in business and law, but also in some other specialist fields.

By far the longest established – and the only one to meet the criteria for inclusion in our main table – is the University of Buckingham, which is profiled on page 360. The best-known "newcomer" currently is BPP University (see page 587), which became a full university in 2013 and offers degrees, as well as shorter courses, in both law and business subjects. Like Buckingham, BPP offers two-year degrees with short vacations to maximise teaching time – a model that other private providers are likely to follow. Fees will be £9,000 a year for UK students taking BPP's three-year degrees in 2020 and £13,500 a year for the accelerated version.

The New College of the Humanities, which graduated its first students in 2015, started out with fees of nearly £18,000 a year for all undergraduates, guaranteeing small-group teaching and some big-name visiting lecturers in economics, English, history, law and philosophy. The college is now matching the 'public sector' at £9,250 a year and has been bought by the Boston-based Northeastern University.

Two other private institutions have been awarded full university status. Regent's University, attractively positioned in London's Regent's Park, caters particularly for the international market with courses in business, arts and social science subjects priced at £17,500 a year for 2019–20. However, about half of the students at the not-for-profit university, which offers British and American degrees, are from the UK or other parts of Europe. The University of Law, as its name suggests, is more specialised. It has been operating as a college in London for more than 100 years and claims to be the world's leading professional law school. Law degrees, as well as professional courses, with fees for three-year degrees set at £9,250 in 2020–21 for UK and EU students and £11,100 for the two-year version. For non-EU students, the equivalent fees are £13,750 and £16,400 respectively. The university has opened its tenth campus, in Nottingham, to add to those in London, Birmingham, Bristol, Chester, Guildford, Manchester and Leeds, as well as at Exeter, Reading, and Liverpool universities.

There are also growing numbers of specialist colleges offering degrees, especially in the business sector. The ifs School of Finance, for example, also dates back more than 100 years and now has university college status (as ifs University College) for its courses in finance and banking.

Some others that rely on international students have been hit by tougher visa regulations, but the Government is keen to encourage the development of a private sector to compete with the established universities. Two newcomers will focus on engineering, for example. The Dyson Institute of Engineering and Technology, based at Malmesbury, in Wiltshire, welcomed its first 33 undergraduates in 2017. Funded entirely by Sir James Dyson, there are no fees, and students will work at the nearby Dyson headquarters for 47 weeks a year. The New Model in Technology and Engineering, in Hereford, has received more than £20m in Government funding and promises to "totally reimagine and redesign the higher education experience". It will take its first students in 2020.

Top 10 Universities for Quality of Teaching, feedback and support 2019 % satisfied with teaching quality		Top 10 Universities for Overall Student Experience 2018	
1 St Andrews	88.5%	1 St Andrews	87.9%
2 Aberystwyth	88.3%	2 Aberystwyth	86.1%
3 Plymouth Marjon	86.7%	3 Loughborough	85.8%
4 West London	85.7%	4 West London	84.7%
5 Bolton	85.6%	5 Dundee	83.8%
6 Worcester	85.1%	6 West of England	83.1%
7 Arts Bournemouth	84.9%	7 Arts Bournemouth	82.9%
8 Wales Trinity St David	84.6%	8 Worcester	82.8%
9 Abertay	84.5%	9 Plymouth Marjon	82.7%
10 York St John	83.9%	10 Keele	82.5%

Source: National Student Survey 2019

Source: National Student Survey 2019

So far, there are few multi-faculty private institutions, but the range of specialisms is certainly growing. There are two high-profile colleges specialising in football, for example, and, from this year, an Interdisciplinary School, based in London. Inevitably, they will take time to build up a track record, but there should be a market in the areas they offer. A listing of some of the more popular private institutions begins on page 587.

City universities

The most popular universities, in terms of total applications, are nearly all in big cities with other major centres of population within the two-hour travelling window. For those looking for the best nightclubs, top sporting events, high-quality shopping or a varied cultural life – in other words, most young people, and especially those who live in cities already – city universities are a magnet. The big universities also, by definition, offer the widest range of subjects, although that does not mean that they necessarily have the particular course that is right for you. Nor does it mean that you will actually use the array of nightlife and shopping that looks so alluring in the prospectus, either because you cannot afford to, because student life is focused on the university, or even because you are too busy working.

Campus universities

City universities are the right choice for many young people, but it is worth bearing in mind that the National Student Survey shows that the highest satisfaction levels tend to be at smaller universities, often those with their own self-contained campuses. It seems that students identify more closely with institutions where there is a close-knit community and the social life is based around the students' union rather than the local nightclubs. There may also be a better prospect of regular contact with tutors and lecturers, who may also live on or near the campus. Few UK universities are in genuinely rural locations, but some – particularly among the more recently promoted – are in relatively small towns. Several longer-established institutions in Scotland and Wales also share this type of setting, where the university dominates the town.

Importance of Open Days

The only way to be confident that this, or any other type of university, is for you is to visit. Schools often restrict the number of open days that sixth-formers can attend in term-time, but some universities offer a weekend alternative. The full calendar of events is available at **www.opendays.com** and on universities' own websites. Bear in mind, if you only attend one or two, that the event has to be badly mismanaged for a university not to seem an exciting place to someone who spends his or her days at school, or even college. Try to get a flavour of several institutions before you make your choice.

How many universities to pick?

When that time comes, of course, you will not be making one choice but five; four if you are applying for medicine, dentistry or veterinary science. (Full details of the application process are given in chapter 5.) Tens of thousands of students each year eventually go to a university that did not start out as their first choice, either because they did not get the right offer or because they changed their mind along the way. UCAS rules are such that applicants do not list universities in order of preference anyway – indeed, universities are not allowed to know where else you have applied. So do not pin all your hopes on one course; take just as much care choosing the other universities on your list.

The value of an "Insurance Choice"

Until recently, nearly all applicants included at least one "insurance" choice on that list – a university or college where entry grades were significantly lower than at their preferred institutions. This practice has been in decline, presumably because candidates expecting high grades think they can pick up a lower offer either in Clearing or through UCAS Extra, the service that allows applicants rejected by their original choices to apply to courses that still have vacancies after the first round of offers. However, it is easy to miscalculate and leave yourself without a place that you want. You may not like the look of the options in Clearing, leaving yourself with an unwelcome and potentially expensive year off at a time when jobs are thin on the ground.

The lifting of recruitment restrictions in 2015 has increased competition between universities and seen more of the leading institutions taking part in Clearing. For those with good grades, this makes it less of a risk to apply only to highly selective universities. However, if you are at all uncertain about your grades, including an insurance choice remains a sensible course of action. Even if you are sure that you will match the standard offers of your chosen universities, there is no guarantee that they will make you an offer. Particularly for degrees demanding three As or more at A-level, there may simply be too many highly qualified applicants to offer places to all of them. The main proviso for insurance choices, as with all others, is that you must be prepared to take up that place. If not, you might as well go for broke with courses with higher standard offers and take your chances in Clearing, or even retake exams if you drop grades. Thousands of applicants each year end up rejecting their only offer when they could have had a second, insurance, choice.

Reputation

The reputation of a university is something intangible, usually built up over a long period and sometimes outlasting reality. Before universities were subject to external assessment and the publication of copious statistics, reputation was rooted in the past. League tables are partly responsible for changing that, although employers are often still influenced by what they remember as the university pecking order when they were students.

The fragmentation of the British university system into groups of institutions is another factor: the Russell Group (**www.russellgroup.ac.uk**) represents 24 research-intensive universities, nearly all with medical schools; the million+ group (**www.millionplus.ac.uk**) contains many of the former polytechnics and newer universities; the University Alliance (**www.unialliance.ac.uk**) provides a home for 18 universities, both old and new, that did not fit into the other categories; while GuildHE (**www.guildhe.ac.uk**) represents specialist colleges and the newest universities. The Cathedrals Group (**www.cathedralsgroup.ac.uk**) is an affiliation of 16 church-based universities and colleges, some of which are also members of other groups.

Many of today's applicants will barely have heard of a polytechnic, let alone be able to identify which of today's universities had that heritage, but most will know which of two universities in the same city has the higher status. While that should matter far less than the quality of a course, it would be naïve to ignore institutional reputation entirely if that is going to carry weight with a future employer. Some big firms restrict their recruitment efforts to a small group of universities (see chapter 3), and, however short sighted that might be, it is something to bear in mind if a career in the City or a big law firm is your ambition.

Checklist

Choosing a subject and a place to study is a major decision. Make sure you can answer these questions:

Choosing a course

» What do I want out of higher education?
» Which subjects do I enjoy studying at school?
» Which subject or subjects do I want to study?
» Do I have the right qualifications?
» What are my career plans and does the subject and course fit these?
» Do I want to study full-time or part-time?
» Do I want to study at a university or a college?

Choosing a university

» What type of university do I wish to go to: campus, city or smaller town?
» How far is the university from home?
» Is it large or small?
» Is it specialist or general?
» Does it offer the right course?
» How much will it cost?
» Have I arranged to visit the university?

Facilities

A 2015 survey commissioned by university directors of estates found that the quality of campus facilities was an important factor in choosing a university for two thirds of applicants. Only the course and the university's location had a higher priority. Accommodation is the main selling point for those living away from home, but sports facilities, libraries and computing equipment also play an important part. Even campus nightclubs have become part of the facilities race that has followed the introduction of higher fees.

Many universities guarantee first-year students accommodation in halls of residence or university-owned flats. But it is as well to know what happens after that. Are there enough places for second- or third-year students who want them, and if not, what is the private market like? Rents for student houses vary quite widely across the country and there have been tensions with local residents in some cities. All universities offer specialist accommodation for disabled students – and are better at providing other facilities than most public institutions. Their websites give basic information on what is provided, as well as contact points for more detailed inquiries.

Special-interest clubs and recreational facilities, as well as political activity, tend to be based in the students' union – sometimes known as the guild of students. In some universities, the union is the focal point of social activity, while in others the attractions of the city seem to overshadow the union to the point where facilities are underused. Students' union websites are included with the information found in the university profiles (chapter 15).

Sources of information

With more than 130 universities to choose from, the Discover Uni and UCAS websites, as well as guides such as this one, are the obvious places to start your search for the right course. Discover Uni, the successor to Unistats, includes figures for average salaries at course level, as well as student satisfaction ratings and some information on contact hours, although this does not distinguish between lectures and seminars. The site does not make multiple comparisons easy to carry out, but it does contain a wealth of information for those who persevere. Once you have narrowed down the list of candidates, you will want to go through undergraduate prospectuses. Most are available online, where you can select the relevant sections rather than waiting for an account of every course to arrive in the post. Beware of generalised claims about the standing of the university, the quality of courses, friendly atmosphere and legendary social life. Stick, if you can, to the factual information.

While the material that the universities publish about their own qualities is less than objective, much of what you will find on the internet may be completely unreliable, for different reasons. A simple search on the name of a university will turn up spurious comparisons of everything from the standard of lecturing to the attractiveness of the students. These can be seriously misleading and are usually based on anecdotal evidence, at best. Make sure that any information you consider comes from a reputable source and, if it conflicts with your impression, try to cross-check it with this *Guide* and the institution's own material.

Useful websites

The best starting point is the UCAS website (**www.ucas.com**), there is extensive information on courses, universities and the whole process of applying to university. UCAS has an official presence on Facebook (**www.facebook.com/ucasonline**) and Twitter (**@UCAS_online**) and now also has a series of video guides (**www.ucas.tv**) on the process of applying, UCAS resources and comments from other students.

For statistical information which allows limited comparison between universities (and for full details of the National Student Survey), visit: **www.discoveruni.gov.uk**.

On appropriate A-level subject choice, visit: **www.russellgroup.ac.uk/for-students/school-and-college-in-the-uk/subject-choices-at-school-and-college/** or **www.informedchoices.ac.uk**.

Narrowing down course choices: **www.ukcoursefinder.com**.

For a full calendar of university and college open days: **www.opendays.com**.

Students with disabilities:
Disability Rights UK: **www.disabilityrightsuk.org/how-we-can-help**.

3 Assessing Graduate Job Prospects

Debate has raged over the past year – and, periodically, for much longer than that – over the extent to which universities and individual courses should be judged on how much their graduates earn, with ministers using this criterion alone to identify "underperforming degrees" and question their value. Universities have responded that there is more to higher education than future earning potential and commissioned a survey which found that only one student in three is motivated to take a degree by the prospect of a higher salary than they would expect otherwise, although half saw it as the first step in building a career.

Professor Julia Buckingham, President of Universities UK and Vice-Chancellor of Brunel University, asked: "What message does it send to our young people when they hear that the value of their university education and experience is judged solely on the money they earn when they graduate? Do we really want to send a message to our nursing and social care students or our trainee teachers that their degree holds less value simply because they earn less than other graduates?"

That, in essence, is why *The Times and Sunday Times Good University Guide* has never used salary figures in its league tables. There are other complications, such as the locations of universities in areas of high or low employment, high or low average wages. But it would be rash of any applicant, with fees at £9,250 a year, not to consider their employment prospects when choosing a degree. We do take account of graduate employment rates and distinguish between different types of employment. Indeed, we might give them a higher weighting if destinations were not surveyed a mere six months after graduation, when many graduates are doing internships, travelling or sampling the jobs market before determining a career path.

From later in 2020, a new system will be in place tracing graduate outcomes a year after graduation. One cohort of graduates has already answered the new survey, which includes questions on how meaningful or important they feel their activity to be and whether they are using the skills they gained from higher education. The results promise to be an improvement; the drawback is that the changeover means there are no new graduate employment figures to use in this edition of the *Guide*.

The tables in this chapter and the figures for graduate prospects in the institutional and subject league tables relate to those who graduated in 2017 and replicate those in the 2019 Guide. Comparisons of previous editions suggest that they remain a reasonable indication of institutional strengths and weaknesses, although the smaller numbers involved in some subject tables can make for bigger swings year on year.

If anything, the overall employment prospects for graduates have improved in the period since the 2017 survey was carried out. An annual survey by Pearson UK published at the end of 2019 found that graduate openings had continued to grow, with 85% of businesses either maintaining or increasing their graduate recruitment. It was the sixth year in a row that respondents had reported increases in graduate openings, despite frequent claims by commentators and some politicians that too many people are going to university.

It appears to be the case that the salary premium enjoyed by graduates has declined in recent years, as the number of students has grown, and the state of the economy has deteriorated. Research by the Higher Education Statistics Agency and economists at Warwick University found that graduates born in 1990 earned 11% more than non-graduates at the age of 26, compared to the 19% graduate premium at the same age enjoyed by graduates born in 1970.

However, the researchers do not assume that this indicates a long-term decline in the graduate premium, both because the premium tends to grow as a career progresses and because those born in 1990 (or the preceding years) would have been applying for jobs when the financial crash of 2008 had decimated opportunities. Future reports will demonstrate whether there is now a moderate or still a considerable difference in the salary expectations of graduates and other workers.

Even at the reduced rate, graduates are likely to earn about £90,000 more than others in the course of a working life. And if at any point, their annual earnings slip below £26,575, they will not be required to make repayments on any student loans (although they will still rack up interest).

In general, then, a degree is still a worthwhile investment financially, aside from the other benefits. But how can you be sure, four or five years before joining the employment market, whether this will remain the case and, if so, which course to choose? The answer, of course, is that you cannot be sure, and there are plenty in the media, Parliament and elsewhere who doubt the value of higher education. It will not pay off for everyone, which is why it is vital to find a course that will suit you and, at the very least, not close off options for the type of career you think you might want.

Median earnings by degree subject five years after graduation (2010 graduates)

Medicine and Dentistry	£47,300	Historical & Philosophical Studies	£25,400
Economics	£37,900	Law	£25,200
Veterinary Science	£34,900	Biological Sciences	£24,500
Mathematical Sciences	£33,100	Social Studies	£24,500
Engineering and Technology	£32,600	Combined Subjects	£24,200
Architecture, Building and Planning	£30,900	English Studies	£24,000
Nursing	£28,500	Education	£23,700
Computer Science	£27,800	Mass Communications & Documentation	£22,800
Languages	£27,400	Psychology	£22,600
Physical Sciences	£27,100	Agriculture & Related Subjects	£20,500
Business & Administrative Studies	£26,800	Creative Arts & Design	£20,200
Subjects Allied to Medicine	£26,400		

Source: Department for Education, Graduate Outcomes March 2018

Analysts are constantly claiming that many of the jobs available to the graduates of the future do not exist yet, while a growing proportion of the current options will disappear through automation and the impact of technology on current occupations. No doubt they are right, but employers will still need the analytical skills that come with a well-rounded degree, particularly if accompanied by so-called 'soft skills' honed through work-related experience outside the classroom or laboratory.

For now, the UK Labour Force Survey, run by the Office for National statistics, finds that while 71.6% of non-graduates were employed in 2018, the figure rose to 87.7% for graduates. Even this represents a narrowing of the gap between the two groups. Apprentices, whether at degree level or otherwise, tend to do better (including in salary terms) in their early twenties, but drop behind thereafter.

In addition, the 2018 Labour Force survey underlined the fact that a degree is an expectation in a growing number of occupations – 40% of graduates work in the public sector, health, or education, and a further 21% in banking and finance. Energy, water, fisheries, agriculture and forestry attract only 2% of all graduates, less than their share of the workforce as a whole.

Of course, what matters to readers of this book is how the market might look in a post-Brexit world, struggling to cope with the fourth industrial revolution, not the picture today. But for all the uncertainties, there would have to be seismic changes in the economy for graduates not to be in a much better position than those without a degree. That has been the case for several decades, and all projections suggest that a growing proportion of the jobs created in the coming years will require a degree.

This does not mean, however, that every degree will be a passport to a well-paid job, nor that it will be worth the debts that graduates are going to accrue in the current era of high fees. Recent salary figures for graduates five and ten years into their careers show startling differences between universities and subjects in the earning power of their graduates.

Graduate employment and underemployment

There are 14 million graduates in the UK, and in Inner London they make up 56% of the adult population. Even in the North East, Britain's least graduate region, 34% of those over 20 have a degree. As a result, today's graduates may take longer than their predecessors to find the right opening and may experiment with internships before committing themselves. Self-employment is also a growing option, rather than just a last resort.

This change in employment patterns explains why underemployment has become a hot topic in the public debate about higher education. It is an important subject but is also one with little precision. This *Guide* uses the definition from the Higher Education Statistics Agency (HESA) of a graduate job. But employers' ideas of which jobs require a degree, and of the jobs for which they prefer graduates, change over time. Nurses now require a degree, partly because the job has changed and requires skills that were not needed 20 years ago. The same is true of many occupations. In others it may be possible to do the job without a degree, but having one makes it much easier to get hired and to progress when you have been.

Nevertheless, a survey by consultants Accenture found that 60% of 2013 and 2014 graduates considered themselves underemployed or working in a job that did not require a degree. Eight out of ten said they had considered the availability of jobs in their intended field before selecting their degree course, but only 55% were working in their chosen field. Almost 60% said they would take a lower salary for a more fulfilling job.

What graduates are doing six months after graduation by subject studied

	Subject	Professional job %	Professional job and studying %	Studying %	Non-professional job and studying %	Non-professional job %	Unemployed %	Professional job and/or studying %
=1	Dentistry	96	2	1	0	0	1	**99.3**
=1	Medicine	95	1	3	0	0	1	**99.3**
3	Nursing	94	1	1	0	1	2	**96.9**
4	Veterinary medicine	94	0	2	0	1	3	**96.5**
5	Physiotherapy	94	2	1	0	2	2	**95.9**
6	Radiography	94	1	1	0	2	3	**95.5**
7	Pharmacology & pharmacy	72	10	10	1	4	3	**92.8**
8	Land and property management	79	3	5	0	5	9	**86.6**
9	Civil engineering	67	3	14	1	6	9	**84.8**
10	Building	75	4	5	0	7	9	**84.1**
11	Subjects allied to medicine	62	3	16	2	10	6	**83.4**
12	Town and country planning and landscape	58	6	16	2	11	8	**81.2**
13	Architecture	68	4	9	0	10	9	**81.1**
14	Electrical and electronic engineering	64	2	14	1	10	9	**80.2**
15	Mechanical engineering	62	2	15	1	10	10	**80.0**
16	Physics & astronomy	38	3	38	1	10	11	**79.8**
17	Chemical engineering	52	2	24	1	7	13	**79.4**
18	General engineering	59	2	18	0	9	12	**79.0**
19	Anatomy & physiology	42	4	31	2	14	8	**78.8**
20	Law	33	6	34	5	14	8	**78.2**
21	Economics	56	5	16	1	11	11	**77.8**
22	Materials technology	49	2	24	2	11	11	**77.7**
23	Chemistry	39	2	34	2	12	10	**77.5**
24	Computer science	64	2	11	1	11	12	**77.4**
25	Russian	50	0	23	4	13	10	**77.1**
26	Mathematics	45	4	26	1	13	11	**76.6**
27	Food science	54	3	16	3	16	8	**75.8**
28	Education	56	2	16	2	19	5	**75.5**
29	German	50	4	20	2	17	8	**75.4**
30	Social work	59	3	10	2	18	8	**74.5**
=31	Aeronautical and manufacturing engineering	57	2	15	1	14	12	**74.2**
=31	Geology	31	2	38	3	15	10	**74.2**
33	Theology & religious studies	32	3	33	5	18	8	**73.7**
34	Politics	41	3	26	4	17	10	**73.1**
=35	Accounting & finance	53	8	9	2	18	10	**72.3**
=35	French	48	3	19	2	18	10	**72.3**
37	Middle Eastern and African studies	43	3	24	2	14	14	**71.9**
38	Celtic studies	23	6	41	2	25	3	**71.5**
39	Biological sciences	30	2	35	3	18	10	**71.3**

Subject	Professional job %	Professional job and studying %	Studying %	Non-professional job and studying %	Non-professional job %	Unemployed %	Professional job and/or studying %
40 Sport science	39	5	23	4	23	6	**70.6**
41 Geography & environmental sciences	39	3	26	3	19	11	**70.3**
42 Business studies	55	3	10	2	20	10	**69.5**
43 Classics & ancient history	33	3	31	3	20	11	**69.4**
44 Librarianship & information management	55	4	9	1	19	12	**69.1**
45 Iberian languages	47	3	18	2	21	10	**69.0**
46 English	34	3	26	5	23	8	**68.7**
47 Music	41	5	19	3	25	7	**68.2**
48 History of art, architecture and design	37	2	26	3	23	9	**67.9**
49 Philosophy	35	3	26	4	19	13	**67.8**
50 History	31	3	29	4	22	10	**67.7**
51 Linguistics	39	3	22	3	26	7	**66.9**
52 Archaeology and forensic science	35	3	25	5	23	11	**66.5**
53 Italian	44	3	16	2	22	12	**66.3**
54 Art & design	54	1	8	2	25	10	**65.3**
55 Psychology	30	5	24	6	26	9	**65.0**
56 Anthropology	36	3	24	2	21	15	**64.7**
57 East and south Asian studies	45	1	16	2	21	15	**64.0**
58 Communication and media studies	49	2	10	2	27	10	**63.0**
=59 Social policy	35	4	21	3	26	11	**62.7**
=59 Drama, dance and cinematics	49	2	9	2	29	9	**62.7**
61 American studies	32	1	24	5	27	11	**62.2**
62 Criminology	34	3	20	5	31	8	**61.2**
63 Hospitality, leisure, recreation & tourism	48	1	7	2	31	10	**58.7**
=64 Agriculture and forestry	43	5	8	2	28	14	**57.8**
=64 Sociology	30	2	21	5	32	10	**57.8**
66 Creative writing	27	3	21	5	30	13	**56.8**
67 Animal science	25	2	18	4	44	6	**49.1**
AVERAGE	**52**	**3**	**17**	**2**	**17**	**8**	**74.3**

Note: Thhe table is ranked on the proportion of graduates in professional jobs and/or further study six months after leaving university. This total is shown in the final column in bold. **Source:** Higher Education Statistics Agency, 2016–17

The graduate labour market

Government reports take a longer-term view of the whole labour market. The first "experimental statistics" from its Longitudinal Education Outcomes (LEO) data were published at the end of 2016, showing average salaries and employment status three, five and ten years after graduation. Some of the measures were updated in the 2016–17 tax year and published in 2019. You may be encouraged by the long-term effects of higher education that they revealed. The original reports showed that 55% of graduates a year out of college had

What graduates earn six months after graduation by subject studied

Subject	Professional employment (£)	Non-professional employment (£)
=1 Dentistry	31,000	—
=1 Medicine	31,000	—
3 Veterinary Medicine	30,000	—
=4 Chemical Engineering	27,500	18,000
=4 General Engineering	27,500	16,380
=6 Economics	27,000	18,000
=6 Mechanical Engineering	27,000	17,500
8 Electrical and Electronic Engineering	26,500	16,497
=9 Aeronautical and Manufacturing Engineering	26,000	17,000
=9 Building	26,000	17,316
=9 Civil Engineering	26,000	15,808
=9 Physics & Astronomy	26,000	16,500
=9 Social Work	26,000	16,000
=14 Computer Science	25,000	16,500
=14 Land and Property Management	25,000	—
=14 Librarianship & Information Management	25,000	16,881
=14 Materials Technology	25,000	18,000
=14 Mathematics	25,000	17,472
19 Middle Eastern and African Studies	24,000	15,000
=20 Politics	23,000	17,000
=20 Town and Country Planning and Landscape	23,000	17,000
=22 Chemistry	22,500	16,653
=22 Education	22,500	15,933
24 Radiography	22,125	—
25 Physiotherapy	22,100	16,575
=26 Accounting & Finance	22,000	18,000
=26 Agriculture and Forestry	22,000	18,000
=26 Anatomy & Physiology	22,000	15,600
=26 Business Studies	22,000	17,971
=26 East and South Asian Studies	22,000	16,500
=26 Food Science	22,000	17,000
=26 French	22,000	17,500
=26 Iberian Languages	22,000	17,000
=26 Nursing	22,000	18,000
=26 Other Subjects Allied to Medicine	22,000	16,000
=26 Philosophy	22,000	17,000
37 Classics & Ancient History	21,600	16,000
38 Geography & Environmental Sciences	21,505	16,643
39 Theology & Religious Studies	21,500	15,912
=40 Biological Sciences	21,000	16,000
=40 Geology	21,000	16,575

Subject	Professional employment	Non-professional employment
=40 German	21,000	18,000
=40 History	21,000	16,497
=40 Italian	21,000	17,400
=40 Russian	21,000	16,000
46 History of Art, Architecture and Design	20,280	16,000
=47 American Studies	20,000	17,000
=47 Anthropology	20,000	17,063
=47 Architecture	20,000	16,640
=47 Hospitality, Leisure, Recreation & Tourism	20,000	17,000
=47 Linguistics	20,000	16,354
=47 Social Policy	20,000	16,224
=47 Sociology	20,000	16,400
=47 Criminology	20,000	17,000
55 Law	19,998	17,000
=56 English	19,500	16,224
=56 Psychology	19,500	16,500
58 Archaeology and Forensic Science	19,185	16,536
=59 Art & Design	19,000	15,808
=59 Celtic Studies	19,000	—
=59 Communication and Media Studies	19,000	16,185
=59 Pharmacology & Pharmacy	19,000	16,640
=59 Sport Science	19,000	16,000
=59 Animal Science	19,000	17,056
65 Drama, Dance and Cinematics	18,720	16,000
66 Music	18,500	16,380
67 Creative Writing	18,000	16,068
TOTAL	**22,128**	**16,640**

Note: The salaries table is ranked by the median salary of those in professional employment in each subject area.

Source: Higher Education Statistics Agency, Destination of Leavers from Higher Education, 2016–17

steady employment, but that a decade after graduation, the figure had hit 69%. In addition, the data show that graduates are on a steadily ascending salary ladder, with median earnings rising from £16,500 a year after graduation to £31,000 a decade after. The figures also show predictable differences between subjects in employment and salary rates, as well as illustrating the lasting impact of university choice. Among law graduates, for example, the top earners at Oxford and Cambridge averaged more than £75,000 (and the lowest some £35,000) after five years, compared with under £10,000 for low earners from the University of East London.

The material in this *Guide* – particularly in the subject tables – should help to create a more nuanced picture. A close examination of individual universities' employment rates in your subject – possibly supplemented by the salary figures on the Discover Uni website (**www.discoveruni.org.uk**) – will tell you whether national trends apply to your chosen course.

Inevitably, future graduate expectations are clouded by the uncertainty caused by Brexit. But even without this big unknown, there would be swings in employment trends before anyone starting a degree course in 2021 manages to graduate. For the boom years of graduate employment to return, there will have to be stronger recruitment by small- and medium-sized companies, as well as the big battalions. Increasingly, there will also be a greater proportion of self-employed graduates, universities report growing demand for the services they provide for students who want to set up their own company. If you think you may be one, it would be worth exploring the entrepreneurship offer of your chosen university because they vary considerably in scale and sophistication.

Subject choice and career opportunities

For those thinking of embarking on higher education in 2021, the signs are positive. But in any year, some universities and some subjects produce better returns than others. The tables on the pages that follow give a more detailed picture of the differences between subjects at a national level, while the rankings in chapters 1 and 13 include figures for each university and subject area. There are a few striking changes, but mainly among subjects with relatively small and fluctuating numbers of graduates.

In the employment table, subjects are ranked on "positive destinations", which include the jobs categorized by HESA as requiring a degree, and include those undertaking further study, whether or not combined with a job. Some similar tables do not make a distinction between different types of job. These tend to give the misleading impression that all universities and subjects offer uniformly rosy employment prospects.

The definition of a graduate job is a controversial one. The statistics include internships and temporary jobs, which may or may not lead to permanent employment. New universities in particular often claim that the whole concept of a graduate job immediately after graduation fails to reflect reality for their alumni, especially in subjects such as media studies or art. In any case, a degree is about enhancing your whole career, your way of working and your view of the world, not just your first job out of college.

That said, the tables in this chapter will help you assess whether your course is likely to pay off in career terms, at least to start with. They show both the amount you might expect to earn with a degree in a specific subject, and the odds of being in work. They reflect the experience six months after graduation of those who completed their degrees in 2017, so the picture may have improved by the time you leave university. But there is no reason to believe that the pattern of success rates for specific subjects and institutions will have changed radically.

The table of employment statistics does reveal some unexpected results. For example, only 68% of business studies graduates are working in graduate jobs or doing further study. Accounting and finance graduates are only two percentage points better off. The social workers and town and country planners fare a lot better. The figures also explode a few popular myths, such as the suggestion that young people avoid engineering because salaries are low. All six branches of engineering are in the top dozen subjects for graduate earnings, and five of them are in the top 20 for successful graduate destinations.

The employment table also shows that graduates in some subjects, especially sciences such as physics, chemistry and geology, are more likely to undertake further study than in others, such as those in art and design or hospitality. In Celtic studies, almost half of graduates continued to study, and the figure is above 30% for several branches of science. A range of professions now regard a Master's degree as a basic entry-level qualification.

Those going into subjects such as art and design appreciate that it too has its own career peculiarities. Periods of freelance or casual work may be an occupational hazard at the start of a career and may become an enduring choice. Less surprisingly, doctors and dentists are virtually guaranteed a job if they complete a degree, as are nurses. HESA found that only one graduate in 100 in medicine or dentistry was unemployed six months after graduating. The picture is pretty similar for vets and physiotherapists.

The second table, on pages 54–55, gives average earnings of those who graduated in 2017, recorded six months after leaving university. It contains interesting, and in some cases surprising, information about early career pay levels. Few would have placed social work in the top ten for graduate pay. However, nursing is now one of a large group of subjects sharing 26th place, having been in the top 20 a few years ago.

It is important, of course, to consider the differences between starting salaries and the long-term prospects of different jobs. After all, those years at university should teach you about the benefits of long-term strategic thinking. Over time, the accountants may well end up with bigger rewards, despite being only £91 a year better off than the nurses in our early-career snapshot.

In any case, it is important to realise that once you ignore the stellar incomes available to medics and other elite professionals, early graduate incomes vary less than you might think from subject to subject. Eleven subjects ranging from accountancy to food science and Iberian languages tie for 26th spot in our salary ranking. A further six tie for 40th. But the difference between these two groups is less than £1,000 a year, with the first set on £22,000 and the second on £21,100. That's why you should consider the lifetime earnings you might derive from these subjects, and your own interests and inclinations, at least as much as this snapshot.

There are reasons for longer-term optimism in HESA surveys on the occupations and views of graduates three and a half years into their careers. The last one, published in 2017, painted a more positive picture than surveys conducted six months after graduation. Of the UK graduates surveyed, 88% were in employment, 6% were studying full-time and 2.2% were unemployed. The majority of those who had been unemployed six months after graduation were in work by this stage, and 87.5% were fairly or very satisfied with their careers to date.

Enhancing your employability

Graduate employability has become the holy grail of degree education since the introduction of higher fees in most of the UK. Virtually every university has adopted some kind of initiative to enhance their graduates' prospects. Many have incorporated specially designed employability modules into degree courses; some are certificating extra-curricular activities to improve their graduates' CVs; and many more are stepping up their efforts to provide work experience to complement degrees.

Opinion is divided on the value of such schemes. Some of the biggest employers restrict their recruitment activities to a small number of universities, believing that these institutions attract the brightest minds and that trawling more widely is not cost-effective. In 2018–19, High Fliers reported that the universities most targeted were Manchester, Bristol, Birmingham, Warwick and University College London. Although some top law firms and others in the City of London have introduced institution-blind applications, big employers' links with their favourite recruiting grounds are likely to continue. Widening the pool of universities from which they set out to recruit is costly, and can seem unnecessary if employers are getting the people they think they need. They will expect outstanding candidates who went to other universities to come to them, either on graduation or later in their careers. But most graduates do not work in the City and most students do not go to universities at the top of the league tables.

University schemes

If a university offers extra help towards employment, it is worth considering whether its scheme is likely to work for you. Some are too new to have shown results in the labour market yet, but they may have been endorsed by big employers or introduced at an institution whose graduates already have a record of success in the jobs market. They might involve classes in CV writing, interview skills, personal finance, entrepreneurship and negotiation skills, among many other topics. There can be guest lectures and demonstrations, or mock interviews, by real employers, to assess students' strengths and weaknesses. In time, these extras may turn into mandatory parts of a degree, complete with course credit.

Hertfordshire, for example, has demonstrated a sustained focus on its students' job prospects. Employer groups are consulted on the curriculum and often supply guest lecturers on degree courses. Like some other universities, such as Derby, it offers career development support to graduates throughout their working life and has a good record for graduate employment. The University of Exeter is helping students to build their employability skills and certificating them. It believes that the Exeter Award will encourage employers to take more notice of graduate attainment beyond exam results.

The value of work experience

The majority of graduate jobs are open to applicants from any discipline. For these general positions, employers tend to be more impressed by a good degree from what they consider a prestigious university than by an apparently relevant qualification. Here numeracy, literacy and communications – the skills needed to function effectively in any organisation – are of vital importance. Specialist jobs, for example in engineering or design, are a different matter. Employers may be much more knowledgeable about the quality of individual courses, and less influenced by a university's overall position in league tables, when the job relies directly on knowledge and skills acquired as a student. That goes for medicine and architecture as well as computer games design or environmental management.

In virtually all fields of employment, however, work experience has become increasingly valuable. It is common for major and smaller employers to hire graduates who had already worked for them, whether in holiday jobs, internships or placements. Sandwich degrees, extended programmes that include up to a year at work, have always boosted employment prospects. Graduates – often engineers – frequently end up working where they undertook their placement. And while a sandwich year will make your course longer, it will not be subject to a full year's fees.

Many conventional degrees now include shorter work placements that should offer some advantages in the labour market. Not all are arranged by the university – most big graduate employers offer some provision of this nature, although access to it can be competitive.

A growing (but, as yet, relatively small) number are also offering degree apprenticeships, in partnership with a wide range of universities. Even Cambridge has some at postgraduate level and is developing more. They generally take longer than a traditional degree, but there are no fees and apprentices are paid a salary. Although there is no guarantee of employment at the end of the course, employment rates from sandwich degrees suggest that companies are likely to want to retain those in whom they have invested considerable time and money.

If you opt for a traditional degree without a work placement, you may want to consider arranging your own part-time or temporary employment. The majority of full-time students now take jobs during term time, as well as in vacations, to make ends meet. But such jobs can boost your CV as well as your bank balance. Even working in a bar or a shop shows some experience of dealing with the public and coping with the discipline of the workplace. Inevitably, the more prosperous cities are likely to offer more employment opportunities than rural areas or conurbations that were hard hit in the recession.

Consider part-time degrees

Another option, also favoured by ministers in successive governments, is part-time study. Although enrolments have fallen sharply both before and since the big 2012 increases in fees, there are now loans available for most part-time courses. Employers may be willing to share the cost of taking a degree or another relevant qualification, and the chance to earn a wage while studying has obvious attractions. Bear in mind that most part-time courses take twice as long to complete as the full-time equivalent. If your earning power is linked to the qualification, it will take that much longer for you to enjoy the benefits.

Plan early for your career

Whatever type of course you choose, it is sensible to start thinking about your future career early in your time at university. There has been a growing tendency in recent years for students to convince themselves that there would be plenty of time to apply for jobs after graduation, and that they were better off focusing entirely on their degree while at university. In the current employment market, all but the most obviously brilliant graduates need to offer more than just a degree, whether it be work experience, leadership qualities demonstrated through clubs and societies, or commitment to voluntary activities. Many students finish a degree without knowing what they want to do, but a blank CV will not impress a prospective employer.

Half of the leading employers in the High Fliers surveys mentioned above say that they are not interested in graduates without previous work experience and that any such applicants would have "little or no chance" of a place on their graduate programmes. Nearly half of all final year students in the survey had done course placements, internships, or vacation work with graduate employers whilst at university, completing an average of more than six months work experience. He may be overstating the case, but Martin Burchall, High Fliers' Managing Director, claimed that work placements and internships were now "just as important as getting a 2:1 or first-class degree".

Useful websites

Prospects, the UK's official graduate careers website: **www.prospects.ac.uk**
For career advice, internships and student and graduate jobs: **www.milkround.com**
For graduate employment (and other) statistics: **www.discoveruni.org.uk**
High Fliers research: **www.highfliers.co.uk**

4 Understanding Tuition Fees

Even last year's General Election has not cleared the uncertainty surrounding tuition fees for students from England, Wales and Northern Ireland. Scots will continue to enjoy free tuition, as long as they stay north of the border for their higher education.

But universities in England will have to wait for the Government's response to the Augar Review. The Conservative manifesto promised to consider carefully its "thoughtful" proposals for lower fees, but there was no suggestion during the campaign that this meant they would be implemented.

Augar's central proposal to reduce undergraduate fees for home students from £9,250 to £7,500 from 2021-22 would apply only in England. But the implications would be felt in Wales and Northern Ireland if universities there were charging up to £1,750 more than that for all but local students. At the time of writing, there was no indication whether fees would be reduced in any of the three countries, although they are likely to rise for students from other EU countries after the Brexit transition period. There has been a guarantee of no increase in 2020–21, but nothing beyond that.

This chapter is necessarily written on the premise of no change, which is at least likely in Scotland. The Scottish government has been adamant that it will not abandon its no-fees policy for Scots, the Welsh Assembly has only recently reformed its student finance system, and at the time of writing, Northern Ireland had no government of its own to consider potential change.

In England, for 2020/21 anyway, all English universities are planning on the assumption that fees for full-time honours degrees will remain at £9,250. Even the small discount previously applied by University College, Birmingham has now vanished. However, bursaries and fee waivers will bring down the actual cost for those from low-income families.

Those bursaries, scholarships and fee waivers mean that the actual amounts students pay in fees in England, let alone other parts of the UK, will vary much more widely than media reporting might suggest. But this only matters to those who qualify for an award, usually by virtue of family income or their academic performance; most students will pay the maximum. Some universities are charging an average fee after bursaries that is quite a lot lower than the headline £9,250. The Office for Students predicts that by 2022/23, assuming the current fee levels, the lowest actual charges at mainstream universities will be at the prestigious and endowment-rich London School of Economics and Imperial College, charging £8,144 and £8,291 respectively.

Some further education colleges – where nearly 200,000 students are studying on higher education courses – offer average fees of £6,000-8,000 if you are paying the full price. However, FE colleges may not all be in the business of affordable higher education. Bradford College is charging £8,750 for bachelor-level courses in 2019/20, only a whisker short of the full fee at the city's nearby university. The same goes for Newcastle College, one of the country's largest.

This *Guide* quotes the higher headline fees, but even these will vary according to whether you are studying full-time or part-time, and whether you are taking a Foundation degree or an Honours programme. Non-European medical students at Imperial College, London, will pay £44,000 a year in 2020 for their clinical years, a figure that will rise with inflation. Meanwhile, UK and EU students taking one Foundation course at nearby Kingston University will pay £5,300, although other Foundation years there will cost £7,800 for 2020 entry.

Here we focus on full-time Honours degrees for British and other EU undergraduates: these students make up the biggest group on any UK campus, and are the group for whom maximum fees shot up to £9,000 in 2012 and have since risen to £9,250.

One twist to bear in mind is that some universities guarantee that your fee will be fixed at the first-year level for the whole of your course. Reading is an example. Manchester, on the other hand, is among many that warn fees may go up for existing students as and when the government raises the maximum it can charge.

Fees and loans

Student numbers dropped in the first year of higher fees, in 2012, but prospective students now appear to have resigned themselves to the new regime. Numbers rose to record levels in 2019 after a decline caused mainly by the reduced size of the 18-year-old age group and the collapse in part-time education. The proportion of 18-year-olds going to university has continued to rise.

There is little sign that applicants are basing their choices on the marginal differences in fee levels and bursaries at different universities, and numbers from the poorest socio-economic groups are at record levels, although they remain severely under-represented compared with more affluent groups. Concern remains, however, over the impact on part-time courses and, in years to come, on the numbers prepared to continue to postgraduate study.

Most readers of *The Times and Sunday Times Good University Guide* will be choosing full-time undergraduate or Foundation degree courses. The fees for 2020 entry are listed alongside each university's profile in chapter 15. Details of English universities' bursaries and scholarships are on the website of the Office for Students (OfS) in the pages on access and participation plans.

Institutions in Scotland, Wales and Northern Ireland will continue to have lower charges for their own residents, but will charge varying amounts to students from other parts of the UK. Only those living in Scotland and studying at Scottish universities will escape all fees, although there will be reduced fees for those normally living in Wales and Northern Ireland.

The number of bursaries and scholarships offered to reduce the burden on new students has been falling since OFFA, the former Office for Fair Access, suggested that such initiatives do little to attract students from low-income households. As a result, the Government turned the grants paid to the poorest students into loans, although it is proposing to restore some maintenance grants, for example for nurses.

Variations among universities

The lowest full-time fee at an English university in 2020–21 will probably be the £4,100 a year cost of a Foundation degree in education and development of young people at York St John University. In Northern Ireland it is still possible to start a Foundation Degree for £2,600 a year. But even there, UK Honours degree students from outside the Province will pay £9,250 and local and other EU students, up to £4,275. The price for non-EU students is £14,060.

At most university-level institutions, every full-time degree will cost £9,250. Generally, the only exceptions will be during work placements or years abroad, when fees cannot exceed £1,850 (20% of the full-year fee) for work placements and £1,385 for a year abroad, and are often less.

Many universities will continue to devote a substantial proportion of the income they receive from higher fees to access initiatives, whether in the form of bursaries or outreach activities. As a result, the average fee paid by a student in 2019/20 after waivers and other support was £8,836.

In the case of the London School of Economics, more than half of its additional fee income above £6,000 is spent in this way and yields some bursaries of up to £4,000 a year for 2019–20. A more usual figure is in the 15-30% range.

The lowest spending on bursaries and fee waivers is at Newman University, where 10.1% of higher fee income went on access expenditure at the time of the last survey. However, this did not prevent Newman finishing in our top 15 for social inclusion. The highest levels of support are provided by colleges with a strong local educational mission. Bury College spends all its above-the-line cash on student support and Furness College, 97.7%

These measures appear to be having some success in attracting students from disadvantaged backgrounds, although young people from the most affluent neighbourhoods are still more than twice as likely to go to higher education as those from the most disadvantaged areas. A little over a fifth of young people from less affluent areas went to university in 2019/20, compared with nearly half of young people overall.

For 2020–21 at least, fees for students from other EU countries will be the same as for those from the UK, but charges will be higher, sometimes massively higher, for those from other countries.

Higher fees have had less effect on the demand for higher education than many universities dared hope in the run-up to the fees hike, but financial considerations will still be important to the decision-making process for many students. In the current economic circumstances, students will want to keep their debts to a minimum and are bound to take the cost of living into account. They will also want the best possible career prospects. and may choose their subject accordingly.

Alternative options

Some further education colleges will offer substantial savings on the cost of a degree, or of a Foundation degree, but they tend to have very local appeal, and generally offer a limited range of vocational subjects. Similarly, the private sector may be expected to compete more vigorously in future, following the success of two-year degrees at the University of Buckingham and BPP University in particular. Most will continue to undercut traditional universities, although Regent's University, one of the latest to be awarded that title, is charging £17,500 in the current year for all students, irrespective of their place of origin, although less for some foundation years. The New College of the Humanities, also in London, now charges the standard £9,250, having originally come in at twice the price charged by mainstream institutions. The non-EU fee is £14,000.

Impact on subject and university choice

Fee levels have had little impact on students' choices of university, but that is not the case for choices of subject. Predictions that old universities and/or vocational subjects would prosper at the expense of the rest have been shown to be too simplistic. Some, but not all, arts subjects have suffered, while in general science courses have prospered. For many young people, the options have not changed. If you want to be a doctor, a teacher or a social worker, there is no alternative to higher education. And, while there are now more options for studying post A-level, it remains to be seen whether they offer the same promotion prospects as a degree.

Even among full-time degrees, the pattern of applications and enrolments has varied considerably since the introduction of higher fees. In 2018, the big losers among disciplines included technology subjects and languages and literature, European and global. Winners included medicine and, perhaps unexpectedly, the social sciences. Notably less popular are melange degrees such as combinations of the arts, sciences and social sciences, or combined arts and sciences. Perhaps these choices seem too indecisive for the modern age. There was a small decline in applicant numbers, and less prestigious institutions felt the pinch the most. Medicine, dentistry and veterinary science have been growing in popularity and new medical schools are opening to meet the demand for more doctors.

In general terms, over the seven years since higher fees were introduced, science and business subjects have done better than the arts, as students have made their own assumptions about future career prospects. IT, engineering, physical sciences and law are ahead of 2010 application numbers and languages and linguistics are down.

Anyone hoping to start a course in 2021 would be unwise to jump to conclusions about levels of competition in different subjects. Universities vary the courses they offer, in response to the perceived demand from students, much more frequently than they used to. A drop in applications may mean less competition for places, or it may lead universities to close courses, possibly intensifying the race for entry. The only reliable forecast is that competition for places on the most popular courses will remain stiff, just as it has been since before students paid any fees.

There is considerable enthusiasm in the current UK government for the radical idea of delivering degrees in two years. At the moment, support for this concept comes mainly from private institutions. The University of Law, for example, already does degrees in this way. It charges £11,100 per year, a saving of £5,550 on a three-year course, which the same institution also offers at the standard £9,250, alongside less expensive online options. A two-year course also gets you into the workforce faster and reduces spending on living costs. However, this approach also cuts out much chance of holiday earnings and of sandwich courses or placements, where students can often get paid and gain work experience. It remains to be seen whether the idea will catch on with traditional universities and if so, whether it will be applicable to the full range of academic subjects.

Finally, there is the option of studying for a degree with no fees at all, by taking a degree apprenticeship sponsored by an employer. So far, the range of subjects in which these are available is relatively narrow – they have to go through a cumbersome accreditation procedure – but a growing number of universities are beginning to offer them. The numbers taking degree apprenticeships are still small, but big increases are planned and the idea has political support.

Naturally enough, many degree apprenticeships are in professional areas, such as childcare, policing and social work, but there are others in the sciences, business subjects, IT and some social sciences. Students spend the majority of their time at work with their sponsoring employer – and receiving a wage, rather than having to access loans – with varying periods at university. Some big names are involved, such as the Morrisons supermarket chain.

Degree apprenticeships – known as graduate apprenticeships in Scotland – are too new to be certain of the long-term prospects for those who take them. For those who last the course of up to five years, the immediate employment levels are guaranteed to be excellent, and many employers expect to pay those who complete the qualification more than traditional graduates because they will have been with them for longer and be more valuable in the short term. But it is impossible to say whether the qualification will have the same currency and be as portable as a traditional degree in mid-career.

Getting the best deal

There will still be a certain amount of variation in student support packages in 2021 and it will be possible to shop around, particularly if your family income is low. But remember that the best deal, even in purely financial terms, is one that leads to a rewarding career. By all means compare the full packages offered by individual universities, but consider too whether marginal differences of a few hundred pounds in headline fees, repaid over 30 years, matter as much as the quality of the course and the likely advantages it will confer in the employment market. Scottish students can save themselves £27,750 by opting to study north of the border. That is a very different matter to the much smaller saving that is available to students in England, particularly if the Scottish university is of comparable quality to the alternatives elsewhere. So it is all a matter of judgement.

Those who are eligible for means-tested bursaries may not be able to ignore the financial assistance they offer. No one has to pay tuition fees while they are a student, but you still have to find thousands of pounds in living costs to take a full-time degree. In some cases, bursaries may make the difference between being able to afford higher education and having to pass up a potentially life-changing opportunity. Some are worth up to £3,000 a year, although most are less generous than this, often because large numbers of students qualify for an award.

Some scholarships are even more valuable, and are awarded for sporting and musical prowess, as well as academic achievement. Most scholarships are not means-tested, but a few are open only to students who are both high performers academically and from low-income families.

Tuition fees by region for courses starting in 2020

Student's home region	Studying in England	Studying in Scotland	Studying in Wales	Studying in Northern Ireland
England	£9,250	Up to £9,250*	£9,000	£9,250
Scotland	£9,250	No fee	£9,000	£9,250
Wales**	£9,250	Up to £9,250	£9,000	£9,250
Northern Ireland	£9,250	Up to £9,250	£9,000	£4,275
EU	£9,250	No fee	£9,000	£4,275
Other international	Variable	Variable	Variable	Variable

*Note that Honours Degrees in Scotland take four years and some universities charge £9,250 for each year.

**Students who live in Wales will be entitled to tuition fee loans and means-tested maintenance grants.

NB: Correct at time of going to press.

Source: UCAS

How the £9,250 fee system works

What follows is a summary of the position for British students in late 2019. While there are substantial differences between the four countries of the UK, there is one important piece of common ground. Up-front payment of fees is not compulsory, and students can take out a fee loan from the Student Loans Company to cover them (see chapter 7). This is repayable in instalments after graduation when earnings reach £25,725 for English students, a threshold set by the Government.

Undergraduate fees are remaining unchanged at £9,250, and this is the most you can borrow to pay fees, with lower sums for private colleges (up to £6,165) and part-time study, where the cap is £6,935 at public institutions and £4,625 at private ones. There are different levels of fees and support for UK students who are not from England. For the moment at least, students from other EU countries will pay the same rate as home students in the UK nation in which they study. Those from outside the EU will usually pay quite a lot more. The latest information on individual universities' fees at the time of going to press is listed alongside their profiles in chapter 15.

With changes, large or small, becoming almost an annual occurrence, it is essential to consult the websites of the relevant Government agencies.

Potential EU applicants, in particular, should use the web sites below to keep up to date.

Fees in England

In England, the maximum tuition fee for full-time undergraduates from the UK or anywhere in the European Union will be £9,250 a year in 2020/21. As we have seen, most courses will demand fees of £9,250 or close to it.

In many public universities, the lowest fees will be for Foundation degrees and Higher National Diplomas. Although some universities have chosen to charge the full £9,250 a year for all courses, these two-year courses will remain a cost-effective stepping stone to a full degree, or a qualification in their own right, at many universities and further education colleges. Those universities that offer extended work placements or a year abroad as part of a degree course, will charge much less than the normal fee for this "year out". The maximum cost for a placement year is 20% of the tuition fee (£1,850), and for a full year abroad, 15%. If you spend only part of the year abroad, you will probably have to pay the whole £9,250.

Fees in Scotland

At Scottish universities and colleges, students from Scotland and those from other EU countries outside the UK pay no fees directly. The universities' vice-chancellors and principals have appealed for charges to be introduced at some level to save their institutions from falling behind their English rivals in financial terms, but Alex Salmond, when he was Scotland's First Minister, famously declared that the "rocks will melt with the sun" before this happens.

Students whose home is in Scotland and who are studying at a Scottish university apply to the Student Awards Agency for Scotland (SAAS) to have their fees paid for them. Note, too, that three-year degrees are rare in Scotland, so most students can expect to pay four years of living costs.

Students from England, Wales and Northern Ireland studying in Scotland will pay fees at something like the scale that applies in England and will have access to finance at similar levels to those available for study in England. It is worth noting, however, that some courses offer considerable savings. Robert Gordon University in Aberdeen, for example, has a fee of £6,000 per year for some four-year courses, including a BA in Accounting and Finance.

The majority of Scottish universities offer a "free" fourth year to bring their total fees into line with English universities, but Edinburgh and St Andrews are charging £9,250 in all four years of their degree courses.

Fees in Wales

In previous years, Welsh universities have applied a range of fees up to £9,000, but all have now opted for £9,000. Students who live in Wales will be able to apply for a Tuition Fee Loan as well as a Tuition Fee Grant, wherever they study. You can get a combined loan and grant for up to £9,000 if you study in Wales, or £9,250 for Scotland, England or Northern Ireland, but only a loan, of up to £6,165, for study in a private institution.

Fees in Northern Ireland

The two universities of Northern Ireland are charging local students £4,275 a year for 2020–21. Students can receive a fee loan to postpone paying this until their earnings are above £18,935, with an interest rate matching RPI or Bank of England base rate plus 1%, whichever is lower. For students from elsewhere in the UK, the fee is £9,250 for Queen's, Belfast and for the University of Ulster. It is £4,275 for EU students from outside the UK.

Useful websites

Particularly after the General Election, when changes in fee levels and interest rates for student loans were mooted but not confirmed, it is essential to consult the latest information provided by Government agencies. The following websites will outline any major developments:

England: **www.gov.uk/student-finance**
Wales: **www.studentfinancewales.co.uk**
Scotland: **www.saas.gov.uk**
Northern Ireland: **www.studentfinanceni.co.uk**
Office for Students: **www.officeforstudents.org.uk**

5 Making Your Application

The process of applying to university is deliberately straightforward. It all takes place online and there is plenty of help available. But too many people take their eye off the ball at this crucial stage. Surprising numbers of applicants each year spell their own name wrongly, or enter an inaccurate date of birth, or the wrong course code. And that is to say nothing of the damage that can be done in the personal statement and teachers' references.

While UCAS will decode misspelt names, other errors in grammar or spelling present admissions officers with an easy starting point in cutting applications down to a more manageable number. Of course, your grades will be the most important factor in winning a degree place, but what goes on the application form is more important than many students realise. The art of conveying knowledge of, and enthusiasm for, your chosen subject – preferably with supporting evidence from your school or college – can make all the difference.

In years to come, applications may be made after students have their results. There has been increasing criticism of the inaccuracy of predicted grades as the main guide to selection, and pressure to put the process back. For the moment, however, decisions have to be made months before final exams are taken, let alone marked. You will be able to make up to five choices, although you do not have to use all five if you do not want to. Some people make only a single application, perhaps because they do not want to leave home or they have very particular requirements – but you will give yourself the best chance of success if you go for the maximum.

At the time of writing, no major changes were planned for 2020 or 2021. There was a trial of names-blind applications at 16 universities to test whether this would counter unconscious bias among admissions officers, but the results were inconclusive. Perhaps the most important recent change allowed candidates to submit a new personal statement if their initial applications are unsuccessful and they use the UCAS Extra process. UCAS has also made it easier to switch courses if you already have a confirmed place. Previously, students looking to "trade up" had to phone the university where they had accepted an offer and ask to be released. Now they can go online and use the UCAS Track system to place themselves in Clearing.

Although fewer than 2% of accepted applicants changed course under the old system, the ease of using the new procedure and its impersonal nature may encourage more to try their luck elsewhere. Be sure to contact your preferred university and ensure that you have a place before taking the plunge.

The application process

Most applications for full-time higher education courses go through UCAS, although there is still a different process for the music conservatoires. The trend is towards the UCAS model even among specialist providers, however: the art and design courses that used to recruit using the separate "Route B" scheme have long since moved to the main system, for example.

Degree apprenticeships are exceptions to this rule. Most require an application to the employer, rather than the university. Many recruit through the **www.gov.uk/apply-apprenticeship** website, which also has links to vacancy information.

Some universities that have not filled all their places on conventional degrees, even during Clearing, will accept direct applications up to and sometimes after the start of the academic year, but UCAS is both the official route and the only way into the most popular courses.

All UCAS applications are made online. The Apply electronic system is accessed via the UCAS website and is straightforward to use. For those who do not have the internet at home and prefer not to use school or college computers, the UCAS website lists libraries all over the UK where you can make your application. Apply is available 24 hours a day, and, when the time comes, information on the progress of your application may arrive at any time.

Registering with Apply

The first step in the process is to register. If you are at a school or college, you will need to obtain a "buzzword" from your tutor or careers adviser – it is used when you log on to register. It links your application to the school or college so that the application can be sent electronically to your referee (usually one of your teachers) for your reference to be attached. If you are no longer at a school or college, you do not need a "buzzword", but you will need details of your referee. More information is given on the UCAS website.

To register, go to the UCAS website and click on "Apply". The system will guide you through the business of providing your personal details and generating a username and password, as well as reminding you of basic points, such as amending your details in case of a change of address. You can register separate term-time and holiday addresses – a useful option for boarders, who could find offers and, particularly, the confirmation of a place, going to their school when they are miles away at home. Remember to keep a note of your username and password in a safe place.

Throughout the process, you will be in sole control of communications with UCAS and your chosen universities. Only if you nominate a representative and give them your unique nine-digit application number (sent automatically by UCAS when your application is submitted), can a

---

The main screens to be completed in UCAS Apply

» Personal and contact details and some additional non-educational details for UK applicants.

» Student finance, a section for UK-resident applicants.

» Your course choices.

» Details of your education so far, including examination results and examinations still to be taken.

» Details of any jobs you have done.

» Your personal statement.

» A declaration that you confirm that the information is correct and that you will be bound by the UCAS rules.

» Pay for the application (applications for 2020 cost £25, or £20 to apply to just one course).

» A reference from one of your teachers.

parent or anyone else give or receive information on your behalf, perhaps because you are ill or out of the country.

Video guides on the application process are available on the UCAS website. Once you are registered, you can start to complete the Apply screens. The sections that follow cover the main screens.

Personal details

This information is taken from your initial registration, and you will be asked for additional information, for example, on ethnic origin and national identity, to monitor equal opportunities in the application process. UK students will also be asked to complete a student finance section designed to speed up any loan application you might make.

Choices

In most subjects, you will be able to apply to a maximum of five universities and/or colleges. The exceptions are medicine, dentistry and veterinary science, where the maximum is four, but you can use your fifth choice as a back-up to apply for a different subject.

The other important restriction concerns Oxford or Cambridge, because you can only apply to one or the other; you cannot apply to both universities in the same year, nor can you apply for more than one course there. For both universities you may need to take a written test (see page 34) and submit examples of your work, depending on the course selected. In addition, for Cambridge, many subjects will demand a pre-interview assessment once the university has received your application from UCAS, while the rest will set written tests to be taken at interview.

The deadline for Oxbridge applications – and for all medicine, dentistry and veterinary science courses – is 15 October. For all other applications the deadline is 15 January (or 24 March for some specified art and design courses). The other exceptions to this rule are the relatively small but growing number of courses that start in January or February. If you are considering one of these, contact the university concerned for application deadlines.

Most applicants use all five choices. But if you do choose fewer than five courses, you can still add another to your form up to 30 June, as long as you have not accepted or declined any offers. Nor do you have to choose five different universities if more than one course at the same institution attracts you – perhaps because the institution itself is the real draw and one course has lower entrance requirements than the other. Universities are not allowed to see where else you have applied, or whether you have chosen the same subject elsewhere. But they will be aware of multiple applications within their own institution. Remember that it is more difficult to write a convincing personal statement if it has to cover two subjects.

For each course you select, you will need to put the UCAS code on the form – and you should check carefully that you have the correct code and understand any special requirements that may be detailed on the UCAS description of the course. It does not matter what order you enter in your choices as all your choices are treated equally. You will also need to indicate whether you are applying for a deferred entry (for example, if you are taking a gap year – see page 78).

Education

In this section you will need to give details of the schools and colleges you have attended, and the qualifications you have obtained or are preparing for. The UCAS website gives plenty of advice on the ways in which you should enter this information, to ensure that all your relevant qualifications are included with their grades. While UCAS does not need to see qualification certificates, it can double-check results with the examination boards to ensure that no one is tempted to exaggerate their results.

In the Employment section that follows, add details of any paid jobs you have had (unpaid or voluntary work should be mentioned in your personal statement).

UCAS top ten personal statement tips

1   Express interest in the subject and show real passion.
2   Go for a strong opening line to grab the reader's attention.
3   Relate outside interests to the course.
4   Think beyond university.
5   Get the basics right.
6   Don't try to sound too clever.
7   Take time and make it your best work.
8   Don't leave it until the last minute – remember the 15 January deadline!
9   Get a second opinion.
10 Honesty is the best policy

Personal statement

As the competition for places on popular courses has become more intense, so the value attached to the personal statement has increased. Admissions officers look for a sign of potential beyond the high grades that growing numbers of applicants offer. Many academics responsible for admissions value success in extracurricular activities such as drama, sport or the Duke of Edinburgh's Award scheme. But your first priority should be to demonstrate an enthusiasm for and understanding of your subject beyond the confines of the exam syllabus.

This is not easy in a relatively short statement that can easily sound trite or pretentious. You should resist any temptation to exaggerate, let alone lie, particularly if there is any chance of an interview. A claim to have been inspired by a book that you have not read will backfire instantly under questioning and, even without an interview, academics are likely to see through grandiose statements that appear at odds with a teacher's reference.

Genuine experiences of after-hours clubs, lectures or visits, work experience or actual reading around the syllabus are much more likely to strike the right note. If you are applying for medicine, for example, any practical work experience or volunteering in medical or caring settings should be included. Take advice from teachers and, if there is still time before you make your application, look for some subject-related activities that will help round out your statement.

Admissions officers are also looking for evidence of character that will make you a productive member of their university and, eventually, a successful graduate. Taking responsibility in any area of school or college life suggests this – leading activities outside your place of learning even more so. Evidence of initiative and self-discipline is also valuable, since higher education involves much more independent study than sixth-formers are used to.

Your overall aim in writing your personal statement is to persuade the admissions officer to pick yours out from the piles of applications. That means trying to stand out among an often rather dull and uniform set of statements based around the curriculum and the more predictable sixth-form activities. Everyone is going to say they love reading, for example; narrow your interest down to an area of (real) interest. Don't be afraid to include the unusual, but bear in mind that an academic's sense of humour may not be the same as yours.

Give particular thought to why you want to study your chosen subject – especially if it is not one you have taken at school or college. You need to show that your interests and skills are well suited to the course and, if it is a vocational degree, that you know how you envisage using the qualification. Admissions officers want to feel that you will be committed to their subject for the full length of the course, which could be three, four or even five years, and capable of achieving good results. If your five choices cover more than one subject, be careful not to focus too much on one; try to make more general comments on your academic strengths and enthusiasms. And, since the same statement goes to all your chosen departments, avoid expressing any preference for an individual institution.

Your school or college should be the best source of advice, since they see personal statements every year, but there are others. The UCAS website has a useful checklist of themes that you may wish to address, while sites such as **www.studential.com** also provide tips. But do not fall into the trap of cutting and pasting from the model statements included on such sites – both UCAS and individual universities have software that will spot plagiarism immediately. In one year, no fewer than one in 20 applicants came to grief in this way. Plagiarists of this type are unlikely to be disqualified, but they destroy the credibility of their application.

Try not to cram in more than the limited space will allow – admissions officers will have many statements to go through, and judicious editing may be rewarded. As long as you write clearly – preferably in paragraphs and possibly with sub-headings – it will be up to you what to include. It is a *personal* statement. But consider the points listed below and make sure that you can answer all the questions raised. Once you have completed your statement show it to others you trust. It is really important to have others read your statement before submitting it – sometimes things that are clear to you may not be to fresh eyes.

The Apply system allows 4,000 characters (including spaces) or 47 lines for your statement. While there is no requirement to fill all the space, it should not look embarrassingly short. Indeed, your statement now has to be at least 1,000 characters long. UCAS recommends using a word-processing package to compile the statement before pasting it into the application system. This is because Apply will time-out after 35 minutes of inactivity, so there is a danger of losing valuable material. Working offline also has the advantage of leaving you with a copy and making it easier to show it to others.

References

Hand-in-hand with your personal statement goes the reference from your school, college or, in the case of mature students, someone who knows you well, but is not a friend or family member. Since 2014, even referees who are not your teachers have been encouraged to predict your grades, although they are allowed to opt out of this process. Whatever the source, the reference has to be independent – you are specifically forbidden to change any part of it if you send off your own application – but that does not mean you should not try to influence what it contains.

Key points to consider in writing your personal statement

» What attracts you to this subject (or subjects, in the case of dual or combined honours)?

» Have you undertaken relevant work experience or voluntary activities, either through school or elsewhere?

» Have you taken part in other extra-curricular activities that demonstrate character – perhaps as a prefect, on the sports field or in the arts?

» Have you been involved in other academic pursuits, such as Gifted and Talented programmes, widening participation schemes, or courses in other subjects?

» Which aspects of your current courses have you found particularly stimulating?

» Are you planning a gap year? If so, explain what you intend to do and how it will affect your studies. Some subjects – notably maths – actively discourage a break in studies.

» What other outside interests might you include that show that you are well-rounded?

Timetable for applications for university admission in 2021

At the time of writing UCAS had not confirmed the exact dates for the application schedule. Please check the UCAS website for the most recent information.

2020

January onwards	Find out about courses and universities. Check schedule of open days.
February onwards	Attend open days.
early July	Registration starts for UCAS Apply.
mid September	UCAS starts receiving applications.
15 October	Final day for applications to Oxford and Cambridge, and for most courses in medicine, dentistry and veterinary science.

2021

15 January	Final day for all other applications from UK and EU students.
16 January–end June	New applications continue to be accepted by UCAS, but only considered by universities if the relevant courses have vacancies.
late February	Start of applications through UCAS Extra.
24 March	Final day for applications to art and design courses that specify this date.
end March	Universities should have sent decisions on all applications received by 15 January.
early May	Final time by which applicants have to decide on their choices if all decisions received by end March (exact date for each applicant will be confirmed by UCAS). **If you do not reply to UCAS, they will decline your offers.** UCAS must have received all decisions from universities if you applied by 15 January.
early June	Final time by which applicants have to decide on their choices if all decisions received by early May.
start of July	Any new application received from this time held until Clearing starts. End of applications through UCAS Extra.
early July	International Baccalaureate results published.
3 August	SQA results published. Scottish Clearing starts. (to be confirmed)
12 August	A-level results published. Full Clearing and Adjustment starts. (to be confirmed)
end August	Adjustment closes. Last time for you to meet any offer conditions, after which university might not accept you.
late October	End of period for adding Clearing choices and last point at which a university can accept you through Clearing.

Most schools and colleges conduct informal interviews before compiling a reference, but it does no harm to draw up a list of the achievements that you would like to see included, and ensure your referee knows what subject you are applying for. Referees cannot know every detail of a candidate's interests and most welcome an aide-memoire.

The UCAS guidelines skirt around the candidate's right to see his or her reference, but it does exist. Schools' practices vary, but most now show the applicant the completed reference. Where this is not the case, the candidate can pay UCAS £10 for a copy, although at this stage it is obviously too late to influence the contents. Better, if you can, to see it before it goes off, in case there are factual inaccuracies that can be corrected.

Timing

The general deadline for applications through UCAS is 15 January, but even those received up to 30 June will be considered if the relevant courses still have vacancies. After that, you will be limited to Clearing, or an application for the following year. In theory – and usually in practice – all applications submitted by the January deadline are given equal consideration. But the best advice is to get your application in early: before Christmas, or earlier if possible. Applications are accepted from mid-September onwards, so the autumn half-term is a sensible target date for completing the process. Although no formal offers are made before the deadline, many admissions officers look through applications as they come in and may make a mental note of promising candidates. If your form arrives with the deadline looming, you may appear less organised than those who submitted in good time; and your application may be one of a large batch that receives a more cursory first reading than the early arrivals. Under UCAS rules, last-minute applicants should not be at a disadvantage, but why take the risk?

Next steps

Once your application has been processed by UCAS, you will receive an email confirming that your application has been sent to your university choices and summarising what will happen next. The email will also confirm your Personal ID, which you can use to access "Track", the online system that allows you to follow the progress of your application. Check all the details carefully: you have 14 days to contact UCAS to correct any errors. Universities can make direct contact with you through Track, including arranging interviews.

After that, it is just a matter of waiting for universities to make their decisions, which can take days, weeks or even months, depending on the university and the course. Some obviously see an advantage in being the first to make an offer – it is a memorable moment to be reassured that at least one of your chosen institutions wants you – and may send their response almost immediately. Others take much longer, perhaps because they have so many good applications to consider, or maybe because they are waiting to see which of their applicants withdraw when Oxford and Cambridge make their offers. Universities are asked to make all their decisions by the end of March, and most have done so long before that.

Interviews

Unless you are applying for a course in health or education that brings you into direct contact with the public, the chances are you will not have a selection interview. For prospective medics, vets, dentists or teachers, a face-to-face assessment of your suitability will be crucial to your chances of success. Likewise in the performing arts, the interview may be as important as your exam grades. Oxford and Cambridge still interview most applicants in all subjects, and a few of the top universities see a significant proportion. But the expansion of higher education has made it impractical to interview everyone, and many admissions experts are sceptical about interviews.

What has become more common, however, is the "sales" interview, where the university is really selling itself to the candidate. There may still be testing questions, but the admissions staff have already made their minds up and are actually trying to persuade you to accept an offer. Indeed, you will probably be given a clear indication at the end of the interview that an offer is on its way. The technique seems to work, perhaps because you have invested time and nervous energy in a sometimes lengthy trip, as well as acquiring a more detailed impression of both the department and the university.

The difficulty can come in spotting which type of interview is which. The "real" ones require lengthy preparation, revisiting your personal statement and reading beyond the exam syllabus. Impressions count for a lot, so dress smartly and make sure that you are on time. Have a question of your own ready, as well as being prepared to give answers.

While you would not want to appear ignorant at a "sales" interview, lengthy preparation might be a waste of valuable time during a period of revision. Naturally, you should err on the side of caution, but if your predicted grades are well above the standard offer and the subject is not one that normally requires an interview, it is likely that the invitation is a sales pitch. It is still worth going, unless you have changed your mind about the application.

Offers

When your chosen universities respond to your application, there will be one of three answers:

» Unconditional Offer (U): This used to be a possibility only if you applied after satisfying the entrance requirements – usually if you were applying as a mature student, while on a gap year, after resitting exams or, in Scotland, after completing Highers. However, a number of universities competing for bright students now make unconditional offers to those who are predicted high grades – just how high will depend on the university. If you are fortunate (and able) enough to receive one, do not assume that grades are no longer important because they may be taken into consideration when you apply for jobs as a graduate.
» Conditional Offer (C): The vast majority of students will still receive conditional offers, where each university offers a place subject to you achieving set grades or points on the UCAS tariff.
» Rejection (R): You do not have the right qualifications, or have lost out to stronger competition.

Unconditional offers have been the subject of considerable controversy over the past two years, following evidence from UCAS that applicants who received them were much more likely than others to miss their predicted grades. More than 20 universities making the highest proportions of unconditional offers were 'named and shamed' by the Education Secretary of the time, who argued that it was unethical to restrict such offers to those who made the university their first choice. Many of those on the list – and others – have now abandoned the practice, but unconditional offers are unlikely to disappear entirely in 2020 or 2021.

One danger, from the student's point of view, is that an unconditional offer might tempt a candidate to lower his or her sights and accept a place that would not have been their first choice otherwise. As long as this is not the case, however, there is no reason to spurn such an offer if it comes, as long as you do not take your foot off the pedal in the run-up to examinations.

If you have chosen wisely, you should have more than one offer to choose from, so you will be required to pick your favourite as your firm acceptance – known as UF if it was an unconditional offer and CF if it was conditional. Candidates with conditional offers can also accept a second offer, with lower grades, as an Insurance choice (CI). You must then decline any other offers that you have.

You do not have to make an Insurance choice – indeed, you may decline all your offers if you have changed your mind about your career path or regret your course decisions. But most people prefer the security of a back-up route into higher education if their grades fall short. Some 35,000 took up their Insurance Choice in 2018 – a decline on previous years but still 7% of all those finding places. You must be sure that your firm acceptance is definitely your first choice because you will be allocated a place automatically if you meet the university's conditions. It is no good at this stage deciding that you prefer your Insurance choice because UCAS rules will not allow a switch.

The only way round those rules, unless your results are better than your highest offer (see Adjustment, below), is through direct contact with the universities concerned. Your firm acceptance institution has to be prepared to release you so that your new choice can award you a place in Clearing. Neither is under any obligation to do so but, in practice, it is rare for a university to insist that a student joins against his or her wishes. Admissions staff will do all they can to persuade you that your original choice was the right one – as it may well have been, if your research was thorough – but it will almost certainly be your decision in the end.

UCAS Extra

If things do go wrong and you receive five rejections, that need not be the end of your higher education ambitions. From the end of February until the end of June, you have another chance through UCAS Extra, a listing of courses that still have vacancies after the initial round of offers. Extra is sometimes dismissed (wrongly) as a repository of second-rate courses. In fact, even in the boom years for applications, most Russell Group universities still have courses listed in a wide variety of subjects.

You will be notified if you are eligible for Extra and can then select courses marked as available on the UCAS website. In order to assist students who choose different subjects after a full set of rejections in their original application, you will be able to submit a new personal statement for Extra. Applications are made, one at a time, through UCAS Track. If you do not receive an offer, or you choose to decline one, you can continue applying for other courses until you are successful. About half of those applying through Extra normally find a place. Increases in the success rate from the initial round of applications prompted a fall of more than 20% in the numbers using Extra in 2018, but it remains a valuable route for those who need it. Why wait for the uncertainty of Clearing if there are places available on a course that you want?

Results Day

Rule Number One on results day is to be at home, or at least in easy communication – you cannot afford to be on some remote beach if there are complications. The day is bound to be stressful, unless you are absolutely confident that you achieved the required grades – more of a possibility in an era of modular courses with marks along the way. But for thousands of students, Track has removed the agony of opening the envelope or scanning a results noticeboard. On the morning of A-level results day, the system informs those who have already won a place on their chosen course. You will not learn your grades until later, but at least your immediate future is clear.

If you get the grades stipulated in your conditional offer, the process should work smoothly and you can begin celebrating. Track will let you know as soon as your place is confirmed and the paperwork will arrive in a day or two. You can phone the university to make quite sure, but it should not be necessary and you will be joining a long queue of people doing the same thing.

If the results are not what you hoped – and particularly if you just miss your grades – you need to be on the phone and taking advice from your school or college. In a year when results are better than expected, some universities will stick to the letter of their offers, perhaps refusing to accept your AAC grades when they had demanded ABB. Growing numbers will forgive a dropped grade to take a candidate who is regarded as promising, rather than go into Clearing to recruit an unknown quantity. Admissions staff may be persuadable – particularly if there are extenuating personal circumstances, or the dropped grade is in a subject that is not relevant to your chosen course. Try to get a teacher to support your case, and be persistent if there is any prospect of flexibility.

If your results are lower than predicted, one option is to ask for papers to be re-marked, as growing numbers do each year. The school may ask for a whole batch to be re-marked, and you should ensure that your chosen universities know this if it may make the difference to whether or not you satisfy your offer. If your grades improve as a result, the university will review its decision, but if by then it has filled all its places, you may have to wait until next year to start.

If you took Scottish Highers, you will have had your results for more than a week by the time the A-level grades are published. If you missed your grades, there is no need to wait for A-levels before you begin approaching universities. Admissions staff at English universities may not wish to commit themselves before they see results from south of the border, but Scottish universities will be filling places immediately and all should be prepared to give you an idea of your prospects.

Adjustment

If your grades are better than those demanded by your first-choice university, there is an opportunity to "trade up". The Adjustment Period runs from when you receive your results until 31 August, and you can only use it for five 24-hour periods during that period, so there is no time to waste. First, go into the Track system and click on "Register for Adjustment" and then contact your preferred institutions to find another place. If none is available, or you decide not to move, your initial offer will remain open. The number of students switching universities in this way has not increased as much as many observers expected, perhaps because Clearing has become much more flexible. Indeed, there was another big drop in 2019, but there were still 600 successful candidates. The process has become an established part of the system and, without the previous restrictions on the number of students they could recruit, many leading universities see it as a good source of talented undergraduates. UCAS does not publish a breakdown of which universities take part, but it is known that many students successfully go back to institutions that had rejected them at the initial application stage. Even if you are eligible for Adjustment, you may decide to stick with the offer you have, but it is worth at least exploring your options.

Clearing

If you do not have a place on Results Day, there will still be plenty of options through the UCAS Clearing scheme. More than 73,000 people – more than one successful applicant in seven – found a place through this route in 2019, despite another drop in the number of applicants. This included 23,000 who went straight to Clearing without submitting an initial application. With recruitment restrictions lifted, universities that used to regard their absence from Clearing as a point of pride are appearing in the vacancy lists. It is likely that this trend will continue in 2021, as more universities seek to expand, particularly in arts, social science and business subjects.

Although the most popular courses may still fill up quickly, many remain open up to and beyond the start of the academic year. And, at least at the start of the process, the range of courses with vacancies is much wider than in Extra. Most universities will list some courses, and most subjects will be available somewhere.

Clearing runs from A-level Results Day until the end of September, matching students without places to full-time courses with vacancies. As long as you are not holding any offers and you have not withdrawn your application, you are eligible automatically. You will be sent a Clearing number via Track to quote to universities.

There are now two ways of entering Clearing: the traditional method of ringing universities that still have vacancies, or by using the system introduced in 2017 which allows universities to approach candidates with suitable grades for one of their courses. You will be given the option of signing up for this service in an email from UCAS and issued with a code word to be used by universities contacting you on Results Day or subsequently. You will be approached by a maximum of five universities or colleges. UCAS advises students to approach universities themselves in any case, but the new system does add an extra string to their bow and may take some of the anxiety out of Clearing.

Assuming you are making your own approaches, the first step is to trawl through the lists on the UCAS website, and elsewhere, before ringing the university offering the course that appeals most, and where you have a realistic chance of a place – do not waste time on courses where the standard offer is far above your grades. Universities run Clearing hotlines and have become adept at dealing with a large number of calls in a short period, but you can still spend a long time on the phone when the most desirable places are beginning to disappear. If you can't get through, send an email setting out your grades and the course that interests you.

The best advice is to plan ahead and not to wait for Results Day to draw up a list of possible Clearing targets. Many universities publish lists of courses that are likely to be in Clearing on their websites from the start of August. Think again about some of the courses that you considered when making your original application, or others at your chosen universities that had lower entrance requirements. But beware of switching to another subject simply because you have the right grades – you still have to sustain your interest and be capable of succeeding over three or more years. Many of the students who drop out of degrees are those who chose the wrong course in a rush during Clearing.

In short, you should start your search straight away if you do find yourself in Clearing, and act decisively, but do not panic. You can make as many approaches as you like, until you are accepted on the course of your choice. Remember that if you changed your personal statement for applications in Extra, this will be the one that goes to any universities that you approach in Clearing, so it may be difficult to return to the subjects in your original application.

Most of the available vacancies will appear in Clearing lists, but some of the universities towards the top of the league tables may have a limited number of openings that they choose not to advertise – either for reasons of status or because they do not want the administrative burden of fielding large numbers of calls to fill a handful of places. If there is a course that you find particularly attractive – especially if you have good grades and are applying late – it may be worth making a speculative call. Sometimes candidates holding offers drop grades and you may be on the spot at the right moment.

What are the alternatives?

If your results are lower than expected and there is nothing you want in Clearing, there are several things you can do. The first is to resit one or more subjects. The modular nature of most courses means that you will have a clear idea of what you need to do to get better grades. You can go back to school or college, or try a "crammer". Although some colleges have a good success rate with re-takes, you have to be highly focused and realistic about the likely improvements. Some of the most competitive courses, such as medicine, may demand higher grades for a second application, so be sure you know the details before you commit yourself.

Other options are to get a job and study part-time, or to take a break from studying and return later in your career. You may have considered an apprenticeship before applying to university, but the number and variety are growing all the time, so it may be worth another look. The UCAS Progress service provides information on apprenticeship opportunities post-16 and a new search tool has been established for higher and degree apprenticeship vacancies.

The part-time route can be arduous – many young people find a job enough to handle without the extra burden of academic work. But others find it just the combination they need for a fulfilling life. It all depends on your job, your social life and your commitment to the subject you will study. It may be that a relatively short break is all that you need to rekindle your enthusiasm for studying. Many universities now have a majority of mature students, so you need not be out of place if this is your chosen route.

Taking a gap year

The other popular option is to take a gap year. In most years, about 7% of applicants defer their entry until the following year while they travel, or do voluntary or paid work. A whole industry has grown up around tailor-made activities, many of them in Asia, Africa or Latin America. Some have been criticised for doing more for the organisers than the underprivileged communities that they purport to assist, but there are programmes that are useful and character-building, as well as safe. Most of the overseas programmes are not cheap, but raising the money can be part of the experience.

Various organisations can help you find voluntary work. Some examples include vInspired (**www.vinspired.com**), Lattitude Global Volunteering (**www.lattitude.org.uk**) and Plan my Gap Year (**www.planmygapyear.co.uk**). Voluntary Service Overseas (**www.vsointernational.org**) works mainly with older volunteers but has an offshoot, run with five other volunteering organisations, International Citizen Service (**www.volunteerics.org**), that places 18–25-year-olds around the world.

The alternative is to stay closer to home and make your contribution through organisations like Volunteering Matters (**http://volunteeringmatters.org.uk**) or to take a job that will make higher education more affordable when the time comes. Work placements can be casual or structured, such as the Year in Industry Scheme (**www.etrust.org.uk**). Sponsorship is also available, mainly to those wishing to study science, engineering or business. Buyer beware: we cannot vouch for any of these and you need to be clear whether the aim is to make money or to plump up your CV. If it is the second, you may end up spending money, not saving it.

Many admissions staff are happy to facilitate gap years because they think it makes for more mature, rounded students than those who come straight from school. The longer-term benefits may also be an advantage in the graduate employment market. Both university admissions officers and employers look for evidence that candidates have more about them than academic ability. The experience you gain on a gap year can help you develop many of the attributes they are looking for, such as interpersonal, organisational and teamwork skills, leadership, creativity, experience of new cultures or work environments, and enterprise.

There are subjects – maths in particular – that discourage a break because it takes too long to pick up study skills where you left off. From the student's point of view, you should also bear in mind that a gap year postpones the moment at which you embark on a career. This may be important if your course is a long one, such as medicine or architecture.

If you are considering a gap year, it makes sense to apply for a deferred place, rather than waiting for your results before applying. The application form has a section for deferments. That allows you to sort out your immediate future before you start travelling or working, and leaves you the option of changing your mind if circumstances change.

Useful websites

The essential website for making an application is, of course, that of UCAS:
www.ucas.com/undergraduate/applying-to-university
For applications to music conservatoires: **www.ucas.com/conservatoires**
For advice on your personal statement:
www.ucas.com/ucas/16-18-choices/search-and-apply/writing-ucas-progress-personal-statement

Gap years

To help you consider options and start planning: **www.gapadvice.org**
For links to volunteering opportunities in the UK: **www.do-it.org**
For links to many gap year organisations: **www.yearoutgroup.org**
Also see above.

6 Where Students Come From

Admissions review

When we published our first social inclusion ranking in last year's edition of *The Times and Sunday Times Good University Guide*, it prompted much comment and interest from higher education institutions, the organisations charged with regulating them, and from commentators and readers alike. It touched a nerve, as the first multi-indicator assessment of the diversity of admissions to British universities.

The fairness of admissions to universities has been moving steadily up the political agenda. Since last year's publication of our first ranking, the appetite for change has grown considerably. The Office for Students announced it will investigate the university admissions process, while Universities UK, the sector's own lobby group, launched a Fair Admissions Review, inviting contributions from the universities themselves, schools, colleges, parents, students, recent graduates, employers and anyone else with a perspective on the debate. Both are due to report later this year.

The political parties have been quick to join the debate. All are agreed on the need for fairer admissions, even if there is disagreement on quite how to get there. Possibly, the most radical proposal on the table stems from a motion passed at last year's Labour Party conference, which called for a cap on admissions from independent schools to universities so that they admit in future "the same proportion of private school students as in the wider population (currently 7%)". Were that to be enacted, the admissions procedures of up to 47 universities would be affected, and even if a more representative figure of 14% of sixth-formers who are privately educated were used, 31 universities would be affected, 19 of them members of the Russell Group. Such a move would require primary legislation, however, as admissions are in the gift of individual universities.

There are wildly differing rates of admissions to universities across any number of indicators – social, ethnic, regional and educational:

Comprehensive school-educated: The proportions of students educated in comprehensive schools ranged from 100% at Newman University, in Birmingham to 38.4% at Imperial College London. Five of the top seven universities in the country – Cambridge, Oxford, Imperial College, the LSE and Durham – recruit fewer than half their students from the non-selective state schools in which around 80% of school leavers are educated;

First generation students: a widely-used measure to demonstrate a university's willingness to step out of their comfort zone and recruit students with no family history in higher education. This ranged from 74.8% at Newman (top again) and 70.7% at the University of Bedfordshire to 13.8% and 14.2% at Oxford and Cambridge respectively;

Ethnic minorities: the proportions of students drawn from ethnic minorities on British campuses ranges from 76.7% at Aston in the heart of multi-cultural Birmingham to 2.3% at Harper Adams, in the heart of rural Shropshire, barely 35 miles away;

Regional recruitment: at the University of Cambridge, just 62 undergraduates were admitted from northeast England and 49 from Scotland in 2018, compared to 686 from Greater London and 539 from southeast England.

The pace of change

The debate over what to do about these disparities in recruitment will rage for some years yet, while at the same time moves to eradicate them, or at the very least to close the gap, will continue to inch forward, prompting squeals of indignation and urges for a greater pace of change in equal measure.

State- versus independent-educated is at the heart of some of the most heated debates, even if it is too simplistic a device to be used in isolation as a measure of social inclusion/ exclusion. However, recent pronouncements from universities, from Oxford and Cambridge down, about their efforts to diversify in this regard among others, have led to mutterings about social engineering and middle-class dinner party debates about whether it is better to pull the children out of independent school for sixth form and send them to the local state school instead. (Answer: in most cases, don't, as being educated in an independent school still confers a significant advantage in applying to Oxbridge and most Russell Group universities). Illustrating the concerns within the independent sector, however, Barnaby Lenon, chairman of the Independent Schools Council, told *The Times* last year: "Independent schools report that their marginal candidates no longer tend to get in to Cambridge…" to which comprehensive school head teachers might retort that "None of ours ever did".

If the pace of change is too fast for some, for others it is quite the reverse. Baroness Valerie Amos was the first vice-chancellor of African-Caribbean descent when she was appointed to lead SOAS, University of London in 2015. She is more alive than most to the under-recruitment of ethnic minorities to universities and their subsequent underperformance (in most instances) when they get there. "Our universities are racially and culturally diverse, compared to many other sectors, but we are failing a generation of students if we don't act now to reduce the Bame attainment gap," she said last year on publication of a joint Universities UK/National Union of Students report on Black, Asian and Minority Ethnic Student Attainment at UK Universities: #closingthegap.

"It is important that universities act and are transparent in their approach so black, Asian and minority ethnic students are given the best chance of success. Inaction is not an option. Universities should be places where opportunity and aspiration come together."

The table

So why produce a social inclusion table? As well as providing a benchmark by which to measure change going forward, the key reason is that today's applicants want to know about the composition of the student body they will be joining. In the same way, today's students are interested in where their university ranks on green issues, through assessments such as that by People and Planet.

Our social inclusion tables show why so much attention is being focused on the fairness or otherwise of the present university admissions process. Broadly speaking, the universities at the top of our academic ranking – those with the highest entry standards, the best job prospects and most competition for places – find themselves at the bottom of our social inclusion ranking. They recruit the bulk of their students from a narrow cross-section of British society.

Some of the indicators used to rank universities are different to those used last year; they include "output" measures for the first time (those that cover what happens when students arrive at the university, such as looking at the black attainment gap) and not just input measures (relating to student recruitment of various under-represented groups).

We have also split the single table of last year into two rankings this year, Scotland standing alone on account of its different measure of social deprivation – the Scottish Index of Multiple Deprivation (SIMD) – which captures better the position in the 15 Scottish universities than the POLAR4 (Participation Of Local Areas) measure used for the rest of the UK, but is not directly comparable.

We have once again resisted the suggestion to include some or all the measures contained within the social inclusion tables as part of our wider academic ranking. There is good reason for this: a university with a poor record for social inclusion may still have an excellent record for teaching and research. It might be a very good university with an outstanding global and national reputation, but with a socially-narrow recruitment profile. By using the two multi-indicator, multi-institution tables that we publish together (alongside the relevant subject table) prospective students can identify the universities which are the best fit for them academically and where they might feel most at home socially or in tune politically. The importance of that last factor will vary from applicant to applicant.

Based on the most recent data available at the time of compilation, *The Times and The Sunday Times* social inclusion ranking for England and Wales uses eight equally-weighted indicators covering:

- » recruitment from non-selective state schools
- » recruitment from all ethnic minorities
- » a measurement of the black attainment gap
- » recruitment from deprived areas (using POLAR4)

- » a measurement of the deprived areas dropout gap
- » recruitment of first-generation students
- » recruitment of mature students (those 21 or older on admission)
- » recruitment of disabled students

For Scottish institutions, there is no measure of the deprived areas dropout gap and the deprived areas measure is based on SIMD, rather than POLAR4, as outlined above.

The two universities in Northern Ireland, Queen's Belfast and Ulster, are excluded from the ranking. Differences in their school system with a high proportion of selective grammar schools, and shortcomings in other datasets, make comparisons with the rest of the UK on social mix invalid.

Except for the admissions data for non-selective state schools, all the other indicators are in the public domain. The uniqueness of this social inclusion ranking is in combining the data to build an overall picture of the social mix at each institution and to measure university performance in the two key areas of black attainment and whether more students from the most deprived areas fail to complete their courses than those recruited from more advantaged districts.

The table is presented in a format that displays the raw data in all instances. No adjustment is made for university location, so a university with a strong, local recruitment pattern in an area of low ethnic minority population will not do well on the two measures covering the ethnicity of the intake. This was most notably the case with Glyndŵr, the most socially inclusive university in the UK according to our ranking, but which had just 5.7% of its 2018 entrants drawn from ethnic minorities.

However, by combining the eight indicators using a common statistical technique known as z-scoring, we have ensured no single indicator has a disproportionate effect on the overall total for each university. The totals for each university were transformed to a scale with 1,000 for the top score and the performance of all universities measured relative to that of the university ranked no 1.

Just as with our academic ranking, the organisations providing the raw data for the table are not involved in the process of aggregation and are not responsible for any conclusion or inferences we have made. Every care has been taken to ensure the accuracy of the table and accompanying analysis, but no responsibility can be taken for errors or omissions.

The indicators used and what can be learned from them are outlined in turn below.

Non-selective state school admissions

For many years, the Higher Education Statistics Agency has published as part of its annual Performance Indicators, the proportion of students admitted to universities from all state schools. Among the entrants included in this proportion are those attending the 164 state grammars in England and the voluntary grammars in Northern Ireland. However, state school admissions to all universities stripped of the academically-selective grammar school sector are not published elsewhere. Removing the grammar school sector from the equation reveals the proportion of students admitted to each university in 2017–18 from the largely non-selective state secondary schools attended by around 80% of university applicants.

At five universities, fewer than half the students admitted came from comprehensives and academies – Imperial College London (38.4%), Cambridge (40.9%), Oxford (41.3%), Durham (46.6%) and the London School of Economics (48.8%). Oxford is the only university in the country where privately-educated students are the biggest school grouping (41.8% independent/41.3% non-selective/16.9% grammar schools), while at Imperial, Cambridge, LSE and St George's more than one in five students are recruited from selective grammars.

The majority of universities (93 in all) admit more than 80% of their students from non-selective state schools, and just 20 take less than 70% of their intake from this demographic, 15 of these universities being members of the Russell Group of highly selective, research-led universities.

Ethnic minority admissions

Data gathered from the 2018 admissions cycle by UCAS shows the proportion of entrants to each university drawn from black, Asian, mixed and other ethnic minorities.

Eight London universities feature in the top ten – all with at least 62% of their students drawn from ethnic minorities – ranking behind Aston which recruited 76.7% of its students from ethnic minorities in 2018. Bradford (72.5%), our University of the Year for Social Inclusion, is the only other non-London university in the top ten. The most ethnically diverse London universities are City, University of London (74.3%), Brunel, London (72.2%), Middlesex and East London (both 68.2%), Queen Mary (68.1%), London Metropolitan (67.4%), Westminster (66.6%) and West London (62.3%). Queen Mary, London is by some distance the most ethnically diverse of the Russell Group.

The least ethnically diverse university is Harper Adams, in rural Shropshire, which specialises in predominantly land-based courses, where 2.3% of the intake was drawn from ethnic minorities in 2018. Harper Adams is followed by Bishop Grosseteste, in Lincoln (4.2%), Plymouth Marjon (4.4%), Wrexham Glyndŵr (5.7%) and York St John (5.8%).

Black attainment gap

A new measure for this edition, the data shows the percentage point difference between the proportion of black ethnic minority students and white students, who achieved first class or upper second class degrees in 2018. This is one of the key indicators in identifying underperformance by ethnic minorities while at university, with black ethnic minority students traditionally achieving the smallest proportion of top class degrees. Ironically, the very small numbers of black ethnic students involved in the calculations make this statistic highly volatile. So, while the University of Edinburgh actually shows a higher proportion of firsts and 2:1s among its black graduates (94.7%) compared to white graduates (90.8%), this data is derived from just 19 black graduates with degree classifications, 18 of whom got a first or 2:1.

The universities with the widest negative percentage point gap for black attainment (showing low attainment by black students) were Cardiff Metropolitan (-42.9%), Canterbury Christ Church (-42.2%), Gloucestershire (-36%), Wales, Trinity St David (-34.4%) and Sheffield Hallam (-32.6%).

Those where black students performed the best in relation to their white counterparts were Edinburgh (+4%, see caveat, above), Bradford (-3%), Durham (-3.7%), Liverpool (-4.5%) and Oxford (-5.7%) – four of the top five places taken by Russell Group institutions, so often lagging in other areas of the social inclusion ranking.

Deprived areas

This data is drawn again from the 2018 UCAS admissions cycle and looks at the home postcode of all university recruits, putting them into one of five pots, according to the level of participation in higher education. For England and Wales, this indicator records the proportion of students recruited from Quintile 1 (of POLAR4 data) – the 20% of areas that have the lowest participation rates in higher education. In Scotland, this indicator records the proportion of students recruited from postcodes which fall into the bottom 20%, those with the highest levels of deprivation measured by the Scottish Index of Multiple Deprivation (SIMD20).

Like all indicators, this one has limitations, chief among which is that London has relatively high participation rates in higher education, so very few London-based university entrants fall into Quintile 1, meaning that London universities score relatively poorly across the board on this measure, even if they have a socially diverse intake of students.

The universities of Sunderland (30.6%) and Teesside (29.2%) record the highest proportions of students recruited from Quintile 1. Both institutions recruit heavily within northeast England, which has the lowest participation rate in higher education in England. The Royal Agricultural University (0.5%) and King's College London and Imperial College London (both 3.8%) have the lowest rates of recruitment from Quintile 1.

Deprived areas dropout gap

This indicator is used in the England and Wales social inclusion ranking only. Drawing upon the same POLAR4 data as above, it measures student outcomes from each of the five social quintiles. The proportion of students dropping out who were recruited from Quintile 1 is compared to the proportion dropping out who were recruited from Quintiles 2, 3, 4 and 5. A negative score in this section of the ranking indicates a higher proportion of students is dropping out from Quintile 1 than those recruited from more advantaged areas. Already under-represented in the student population overall, this measure identifies those universities where those who do get in are more likely to fail to see their courses through.

The universities with the biggest negative percentage point gap – where a higher proportion of students from the most deprived areas fail to complete their courses than among the rest of the student population – are SOAS, London (-11%), Essex (-7.7%), Staffordshire (-6.2%), Suffolk (-6%) and Leeds Beckett (-5.2%). The universities performing most strongly here, where a smaller proportion of students from the most deprived areas drop out compared to the rest of the student population, are London Metropolitan (+6%), Goldsmiths, London (+5%), City, London (+4.6%), East London (+4.5%) and Brunel (+2.4%).

First generation students

A new measure for this edition, it records the proportion of students recruited from homes where neither parent attended university. This indicator is considered one of the most informative in assessing the overall inclusiveness of university recruitment strategies. Once again, performance varies considerably from those recruiting 60% or more first generation students – Newman (74.8%), Bedfordshire (70.7%), Bradford (67.3%), Bishop Grosseteste (66.6%) and Leeds Trinity (61.3%) – to those where fewer than 25% of students come from homes where parents did not go to university – Oxford (13.8%), Cambridge (14.2%), Bristol (21.9%), Imperial (22.6%), and Durham (23.5%).

Mature students

The proportion of entrants to university aged over 21 on admission is calculated from the overall number of entrants recorded by HESA in 2017–18. Mature students are returners to education and often win places with "life" qualifications, rather than A-levels. This immediately makes the group more diverse than the young entrants, who come mostly straight from school or via a gap year.

The age of the student population can have a major impact on the social scene on campus. Older students, particularly those with partners (and even children) are less likely to be found clubbing or propping up the bar late into the evening. Universities with a very small proportion of mature undergraduates – Bath (1.9%), Imperial College London (2.1%), Loughborough (2.2%), the LSE (2.8%) and Oxford (3.2%) – are likely to have a livelier campus social life than Wrexham Glyndŵr (72% mature admissions), Suffolk (65.3%), Bucks New (62.5%), Sunderland (59%) and London Metropolitan (58.3%) .

Disabled students

This indicator measures the proportion of all students in higher education in receipt of Disability Support Allowance (DSA). It is part of the bigger HESA dataset on widening participation, published in February 2019 and is based on data from the 2017–18 academic year.

As with the other indicators, there is a significant difference between the universities at the top – Wrexham Glyndŵr where HESA record 22.1% of students as being in receipt of DSA and Trinity St David (20.3%) – and those at the bottom – West of Scotland (2.1%) and Glasgow Caledonian (2.4%).

The overall picture

It is not possible to appear near the top of the social inclusion rankings if an institution is only achieving well on one or two of the measures of social inclusion that *The Times and The Sunday Times* have chosen. Success in the tables comes from broadly-based achievement in recruiting from areas of society least represented in higher education, and then seeing those students complete their degrees and achieve well. Equally, a university that appears near the bottom is not just falling short in one or two regards; it reflects a pattern of recruitment – or poor performance – affecting swathes of society.

A different set of metrics looking at the same subject matter might produce a very different looking table, which is why it is necessary to be clear about what is being measured here. Based on the measures we have chosen the top three in the academic rankings – Cambridge, Oxford and St Andrews – appear at the bottom (or third bottom in Oxford's case) of our social inclusion rankings. Wrexham Glyndŵr, next to bottom in the academic ranking, is top for social inclusion. Fifteen of the bottom 20 universities for social inclusion in England and Wales (and two of the bottom three in Scotland) are Russell Group universities.

Used in conjunction, our academic and social inclusion rankings provide an intriguing insight to likely academic and professional success, the quality of the student experience, and the mix of students likely to be found in the university lecture theatres and the after-hours clubs and bars. But whatever the student recruitment profile of the institution you are considering, don't rule it out on that basis. If applicants from non-traditional backgrounds don't apply to universities pledging to broaden their intake, then it will only make it easier for the status quo to prevail.

Social Inclusion Ranking for England and Wales

	Institution	State educated (non-grammar) (%)	Ethnic (%)	Black attainment gap (%)	Deprived areas (%)	Deprived areas dropout gap (%)	First generation students (%)	Disabled (%)	Mature (%)	Total
1	Wrexham Glyndŵr	99.2	5.7	-25.5	23.6		56.8	22.1	72.0	1,000
2	Bishop Grosseteste	95.3	4.2		24.2		66.6	13.4	40.7	900
3	Bradford	92.8	72.5	-3.0	13.6	-1.7	67.3	9.1	26.3	885
4	Sunderland	97.2	27.5	-26.4	30.6	2.2	59.2	5.1	59.0	865
5	East London	96.6	68.2	-19.0	9.4	4.5	54.7	6.4	47.7	855
6	London Metropolitan	95.7	67.4	-27.0	8.8	6.0	50.6	6.6	58.3	845
7	Wolverhampton	97.1	52.0	-26.3	20.7	0.9	59.8	7.7	45.4	830
8	Plymouth Marjon	93.8	4.4		20.9	0.0	59.2	15.1	31.1	830
9	London South Bank	94.9	59.0	-16.0	7.5	0.4	51.2	10.8	46.7	814
10	Teesside	98.1	13.4	-13.9	29.2	-4.3	56.9	10.3	42.4	811
11	Bedfordshire	97.3	60.5	-26.0	11.3	0.4	70.7	5.0	50.6	804
12	Bolton	97.9	37.0	-30.0	22.1	-2.0	57.9	11.9	47.0	799
13	Newman	99.4	46.0	-21.0	17.7	-4.0	74.8	8.3	34.6	793
14	Suffolk	98.5	9.3	-17.0	27.1	-6.0	59.6	7.7	65.3	788
15	Huddersfield	95.4	38.7	-21.1	16.5	1.5	56.4	8.5	21.3	752

16	West London	96.0	62.3	-22.0	7.1	-0.8	51.6	6.7	54.7	749
17	Central Lancashire	96.7	23.3	-16.5	19.2	-0.7	52.5	6.8	38.7	745
18	Leeds Trinity	97.2	22.2		20.1	0.0	61.3	7.0	17.6	737
19	Bucks New	93.5	52.7	-9.0	9.4	-4.0	48.8	3.0	62.5	725
20	De Montfort	95.2	50.1	-19.6	14.3	-1.1	51.7	11.1	13.4	723
21	Derby	96.6	25.6	-16.3	21.0	-3.4	51.7	9.7	27.2	723
22	Middlesex	96.5	68.2	-17.0	5.4		58.5	5.5	26.9	714
23	Anglia Ruskin	93.7	29.2	-18.0	16.0	0.2	55.0	5.0	34.3	713
24	Wales Trinity Saint David	97.7	7.2	-34.4	14.1		34.7	20.3	44.5	706
25	Kingston	93.6	61.9	-19.2	8.0	-2.9	56.8	7.3	31.0	697
26	Cumbria	95.7	11.6	-21.0	21.5	-2.0	53.8	7.8	33.6	697
27	Brunel	88.7	72.2	-15.0	4.0	2.4	50.2	6.6	9.8	696
28	Aston	84.8	76.7	-11.0	9.5	0.1	52.1	4.9	6.0	691
29	Goldsmiths, London	87.5	51.0	-23.0	5.0	5.0	44.3	8.4	20.7	688
30	Birmingham City	97.7	53.7	-18.5	12.5	-2.0	55.5	5.2	21.3	683
31	City	87.5	74.3	-21.0	4.2	4.6	51.2	3.7	14.2	683
32	Worcester	95.0	13.0	-21.5	15.9	-2.7	51.7	10.1	36.6	679
33	Staffordshire	98.6	18.4	-29.8	26.4	-6.2	57.2	9.5	33.5	671
34	Hull	91.0	11.9	-10.1	22.0	-4.6	49.2	5.6	33.1	663
35	St Mary's, Twickenham	92.5	34.1	-17.0	6.7	-2.0	51.6	10.8	20.2	657
36	South Wales	97.0	10.3	-19.5	21.1		43.9	7.4	25.5	656
37	Greenwich	91.3	55.2	-21.1	8.9	-2.4	55.8	5.0	31.0	654
38	Salford	95.6	33.8	-13.8	18.0	-4.2	46.3	5.7	26.0	653
39	Creative Arts	92.7	23.0	-25.0	12.4	0.5	50.5	10.8	15.3	652
40	Northampton	96.6	44.1	-19.8	12.7	-2.9	51.1	6.1	25.0	651
41	Edge Hill	96.7	6.5	-21.3	20.3	-2.0	55.8	6.8	21.4	648
42	Winchester	91.8	9.7	-24.3	13.4	0.0	49.5	12.2	14.6	639
43	Westminster	94.5	66.6	-22.0	5.6	-1.9	54.5	4.4	20.5	630
44	Keele	82.6	34.6	-14.3	16.7	-1.7	43.5	7.0	15.1	627
45	Chester	93.6	8.0	-28.7	19.1	-0.9	54.4	7.4	24.0	624
46	Coventry	91.2	56.4	-17.7	10.5	-1.7	47.2	3.8	19.5	622
47	Chichester	93.1	6.7		18.2	-3.1	49.7	8.9	18.9	615
48	Bangor	92.0	7.1	-19.9	14.4		41.2	9.8	27.5	615
49	Portsmouth	90.9	28.4	-25.8	13.0	0.1	48.4	8.7	12.0	613
50	Norwich Arts	94.3	11.4		17.0	-4.0	45.4	11.9	13.0	611
51	Queen Mary, London	79.3	68.1	-15.0	4.6	-1.6	46.0	7.5	9.2	607
52	Hertfordshire	94.0	58.5	-28.6	7.5	0.0	50.0	4.7	19.1	606
53	Manchester Metropolitan	94.3	31.4	-29.8	15.8	0.1	52.1	5.3	14.8	604
54	Liverpool Hope	87.7	10.1		20.0	-5.0	54.1	8.8	18.6	602
55	Plymouth	88.3	11.1	-15.2	14.8	-3.6	45.3	8.0	24.9	598
56	Sheffield Hallam	93.7	19.6	-32.6	20.0	-2.0	51.6	7.5	19.0	595
57	Canterbury Christ Church	91.7	26.2	-42.2	15.9	-0.7	58.3	6.2	33.7	594
58	Bath Spa	91.3	7.4		12.9	-1.9	43.3	11.3	13.3	588
59	Arts, London	91.3	29.1	-26.5	6.9	-3.7	39.9	15.6	18.1	586
60	Solent	96.3	16.2	-24.4	15.3	-2.5	50.3	6.1	18.5	580
61	Liverpool John Moores	89.9	12.1	-28.7	18.9	-2.4	55.3	6.9	15.8	577

Social Inclusion Ranking for England and Wales cont

Institution	State educated (non-grammar) (%)	Ethnic (%)	Black attainment gap (%)	Deprived areas (%)	Deprived areas dropout gap (%)	First generation students (%)	Disabled (%)	Mature (%)	Total
62 Leicester	80.4	52.0	-18.7	9.7	-0.2	39.3	5.3	12.5	574
63 Lincoln	93.0	10.3	-26.1	18.1	-2.1	52.3	6.7	10.6	569
64 Arts Bournemouth	92.6	12.8		10.0		39.5	11.4	13.8	568
65 Roehampton	94.3	57.3	-26.0	5.5	-3.6	52.7	5.0	20.1	568
66 Bournemouth	90.5	15.1	-24.6	10.5	-1.4	49.0	7.7	19.2	567
67 York St John	93.6	5.8		18.4	-3.5	47.8	7.6	10.9	563
68 Brighton	87.9	21.0	-24.3	11.2	-3.9	46.9	9.8	19.8	558
69 Liverpool	76.2	15.7	-4.5	10.0	-1.4	42.8	5.3	9.2	556
70 Kent	91.1	37.6	-27.4	10.3	-1.1	45.6	7.2	9.0	556
71 Royal Holloway, London	75.0	39.8	-15.0	5.3	1.3	39.2	6.1	6.5	548
72 Ravensbourne University London	93.5	39.9	-25.0	6.1		45.8	6.8	14.6	547
73 Falmouth	91.3	6.2		9.8	-1.1	34.6	11.1	13.5	544
74 West of England	90.6	17.1	-31.9	14.8	-2.0	43.4	7.7	21.2	537
75 St George's, London	65.2	61.8	-20.0	5.9		35.5	7.2	25.9	536
76 Nottingham Trent	88.9	23.6	-23.2	13.3	-2.6	45.7	6.2	9.3	532
77 Gloucestershire	92.5	10.9	-36.0	14.7	-3.4	47.7	9.8	22.3	531
78 Leeds Arts	96.6	11.7		10.5	-5.0	41.6	12.0	7.0	530
79 King's College London	63.5	54.4	-12.2	3.8	-0.9	36.2	5.5	14.7	522
80 Northumbria	89.7	10.1	-28.5	18.7	-4.8	52.0	6.1	17.0	522
81 East Anglia	79.3	22.3	-15.5	11.6	-3.7	39.6	7.6	12.5	521
82 Surrey	78.3	37.5	-16.2	7.3	-1.4	42.8	4.6	8.6	518
83 Aberystwyth	89.6	6.5	-28.4	12.0		40.0	10.8	13.2	513
84 Sussex	78.5	22.1	-24.8	8.2	0.0	42.0	7.7	11.0	513
85 Manchester	72.4	30.1	-11.6	8.8	-2.3	34.2	7.5	7.9	511
86 Cardiff Metropolitan	92.3	14.4	-42.9	17.7		48.3	6.5	25.5	504
87 Essex	88.7	44.3	-18.9	11.8	-7.7	47.8	4.2	14.1	503
88 Harper Adams	80.1	2.3		6.5	-4.0	38.7	16.3	5.3	494
89 Swansea	85.4	16.3	-17.1	9.9		37.6	4.6	15.2	488
90 Oxford Brookes	64.4	16.2	-20.4	6.1	-4.1	40.2	11.3	20.9	476
91 Lancaster	78.8	17.3	-25.8	10.2	0.6	38.0	5.7	4.2	468
92 Sheffield	74.6	19.1	-15.8	9.3	-3.4	33.1	7.5	10.8	467
93 SOAS, London	74.6	55.2	-15.0	3.9	-11.0	42.4	8.7	18.9	458
94 Southampton	71.5	22.9	-10.6	7.7	-4.6	35.8	6.0	10.9	458
95 Leeds Beckett	91.6	19.7	-30.4	17.3	-5.2	39.0	4.9	13.1	455
96 Loughborough	71.5	26.4	-25.0	7.1	-0.9	34.8	8.3	2.2	445
97 Warwick	57.7	38.2	-13.8	6.5	-1.3	31.9	5.1	5.9	441
98 Reading	73.8	29.5	-25.3	6.3	-2.7	36.8	6.2	7.9	421
99 Nottingham	66.0	26.4	-18.2	7.1	-1.9	31.9	5.3	7.3	420

100	Birmingham	66.1	28.9	-15.6	6.7	-2.2	28.3	5.3	6.3	416
101	Cardiff	75.0	17.4	-20.6	9.4		32.3	4.6	11.8	409
102	Royal Agricultural	59.6			0.5		34.4	12.9	17.1	408
103	York	71.2	13.1	-16.8	8.2	-3.1	31.4	5.2	8.5	405
104	London School of Economics	48.0	53.2	-10.0	6.7		29.2	3.7	2.8	399
105	Newcastle	65.2	13.2	-16.9	9.1	-3.2	34.7	4.3	6.1	389
106	Buckingham	73.8			6.9		33.2	4.2	20.0	373
107	Leeds	68.9	18.5	-28.9	8.3	-2.2	33.8	5.2	7.5	369
108	University College London	54.0	47.5	-13.7	4.0		26.9	3.4	5.0	360
109	Durham	46.5	12.2	-3.7	5.6	-3.0	23.5	5.5	4.0	359
110	Bristol	52.9	16.0	-8.4	4.6	-3.2	21.9	4.9	5.0	341
111	Exeter	51.6	10.2	-19.7	7.2	-3.1	27.8	7.2	6.2	337
112	Bath	54.5	17.2	-15.7	5.2		25.7	5.4	1.9	309
113	Oxford	41.3	18.1	-5.7	4.1		13.8	7.5	3.2	308
114	Imperial College London	38.2	50.0		3.8	-1.8	22.6	3.5	2.1	260
115	Cambridge	41.0	22.8	-14.8	4.7		14.2	4.1	4.5	232

Rankings based on unrounded data

Social Inclusion Ranking for Scotland

Institution	State educated (non-grammar) (%)	Ethnic (%)	Black attainment gap (%)	Deprived areas (%)	First generation students (%)	Disabled (%)	Mature (%)	Total
1 West of Scotland	98.8	9.6	-46.2	29.4	47.3	2.1	51.4	1,000
2 Queen Margaret, Edinburgh	95.4	8.4		9.9	41.4	9.7	39.4	983
3 Abertay	93.8	5.9		19.1	45.1	7.1	35.9	952
4 Glasgow Caledonian	96.2	11.1	-46.8	23.5	45.2	2.4	40.9	922
5 Highlands and Islands	98.8	5.0		8.3	44.4	5.3	53.1	874
6 Dundee	83.9	10.5	-6.5	15.8	37.3	4.8	29.0	848
7 Edinburgh Napier	90.8	10.0	-30.8	10.9	39.1	5.3	37.2	827
8 Heriot-Watt	80.5	14.5	-10.0	11.2	31.8	5.7	18.3	796
9 Robert Gordon	94.8	10.0	-16.9	6.5	33.7	5.5	32.6	775
10 Strathclyde	87.9	10.8	-35.9	16.6	36.3	2.9	33.1	755
11 Stirling	88.4	6.4	-51.9	15.9	37.7	6.4	24.9	695
12 aberdeen	81.8	10.2	-16.5	6.0	28.2	4.7	26.4	630
13 Edinburgh	58.6	11.6	4.0	8.1	22.4	5.4	12.5	548
14 Glasgow	78.3	9.1	-33.0	12.3	27.0	3.0	23.9	535
15 St Andrews	52.2	12.1		7.5	17.0	5.2	6.6	317

7 Financing Your Studies

The debate on student finance – in the General Election and in virtually any public forum – is all about tuition fees. But for those who have decided to aim for a degree, the most immediate concern is how to make ends meet for three or four years (if not more) at university. How much money will they need and where it will come from?

Students are notoriously bad at estimating how much they will spend in the course of a term, and at assessing how much they will earn after graduation, which is when the time may come to repay their loans. While 64% of students attempt to budget, according to research for the NatWest Student Living Index, that leaves 36% who don't. The same survey finds that 43% of students run out of money before the end of each semester.

To help you see your way past those scary totals, this chapter looks at the funding available to students in different parts of the UK, how to plan for a possibly precarious existence, and how to pay back what is required once you graduate. A note of caution: by September 2021, or at some point during your degree, everything may change. Fees may be reduced, but you can only plan on the basis of the current system. At the time of writing, that means fees of £9,250 in England (nothing in Scotland) with student loans for both fees and maintenance. In the past, these fees have increased in line with inflation, although at the moment they are being held.

What will not change is the need to find enough money to live on at university and the likelihood that for most, some debt will be involved. Under the current system, those debts are likely to be considerable. But assuming they come mainly from student loans, they should be manageable and may well not be repaid in full. You will not repay anything until you are earning £25,725 a year, and then only 9% of anything you make above that amount, however much you earn.

When you do get a student loan, your first surprise is that the interest clock starts ticking on it from the day the first payment hits your bank account, usually the first day of your first term. It keeps ticking until the April after you finish the course, which is when you might or might not start repaying. If you are a part-time student, and earning over £25,725, you'll have to start repaying four years after you started getting the loan, even if you are still studying, perhaps for a higher degree.

During your course, the interest rate on your loan will be RPI plus 3%. RPI, the Retail Price Index, is a standard measure of UK inflation and at the time of writing, RPI plus 3% adds up to a total of 5.4%. That would mean interest of £500 a year on a single year's tuition fee of £9,250. The interest you are racking up will, paradoxically, go down to RPI alone if you leave college and get a job paying less than £25,725 a year. Then it goes onto a sliding scale of RPI plus up to 3% until you reach a salary of £46,305 after which it remains at RPI plus 3%, however much you earn. Note that as with much else in this chapter, these threshold numbers are likely to change over time, usually upwards. Note, too, that the rate of RPI plus 3% will be applied to your debt automatically if you don't keep in touch with the Student Loans Company and inform them of your circumstances.

One constant, however, is that after 30 years in England (the figure varies elsewhere in the UK), the debt is written off. Because the repayments seem modest for anyone with a qualifying income, and because of the 30-year rule, student debt is a lot more forgiving than a mortgage or a credit card, where the bills keep on coming even if you are out of work. The Student Loans Company is, after all, probably the only lender in Britain who will hand you tens of thousands of pounds without a credit check.

The last significant change in this system, in 2016/2017, was the abolition of grants for students from low-income families in England, and their replacement by loans. As with the introduction of fees, there is no immediate impact on students. Repayments still begin only after graduation, and when the borrower's salary reaches £25,725. But the prospect of yet more debt does appear to be deterring some applicants from this already under-represented section of society. That did not happen when fees went up in 2012, but no one can be sure what will happen over time.

There are different arrangements in other parts of the UK, which are addressed later in this chapter. But wherever you study, there are two quite different timescales to consider. In the short term, you need enough money to live on and maybe have some fun, while the long-term calculation is whether your degree is value for money. Much commentary on the subject conflates the two, focusing on the total debt that the average student will have at graduation. That is likely to be an intimidating figure, and one that should not be ignored by those contemplating a degree, but it has little to do with whether you can afford three or more years as an undergraduate.

Affordability

The introduction of £9,000 fees, now fixed at a maximum of £9,250 for three or four-year courses, added enormously to graduates' debts. But tuition fee loans are paid straight to the university, so the student's calculation is more about bridging the gap between a maintenance loan and the real cost of living. In England, a maintenance loan was worth up to £8,944 (or £11,672 in London) in 2019/20. The maximum figure was reduced to £7,529 for those living with parents. With hall fees topping £5,000 a year at some universities, that might seem an attractive option. For a year when you were studying abroad for at least one term, the maximum award was £10,242. If you are over 60 when the course starts, you can apply for a loan of up to £3,783.

There will be a financial gap for most students. But don't panic. Students have always had a challenge to make ends meet, typically through a combination of parental help, part-time employment and institutional bursaries.

Analysis by the National Union of Students suggests that it is not possible to get by on student loans alone. Savings, earnings, and help from family and friends have to be added to the pot. The Natwest survey mentioned above put the average monthly contribution per student from the Bank of Mum and Dad at £222. Information provided here will help you understand how big your pot needs to be, and what you can expect to be added and taken away from it. But it takes careful budgeting to avoid adding credit card debt to the income-contingent variety offered by the Government and repaid (or not) over 30 years.

Value for money

Contrary to some alarmist media coverage of graduate employment prospects, most surveys suggest that on average, a degree is still a worthwhile investment in terms of future salary expectations, even after adding in the amounts you might otherwise have earned while you were a student.

Only when you are sure you can cope with the costs of student life should you move on to the longer-term question of whether your chosen degree will make it worth repaying £40,000 or more in student loans. Even in purely financial terms, there are too many uncertainties to be sure of the answer. You may never earn the £25,000-plus per year which triggers repayments, although few students go to university with that expectation. In practice, very few will be in that position, and they will mostly be there because of positive life decisions that they have taken. At the other extreme, your degree may help you land such a well-paid job that university was cheap at the price. Most graduates will be somewhere in the middle, and in any case, the system is too new for any to have experienced the impact of loan repayments of 9% of salary above the threshold for more than a few years.

In 2019 the Department for Education published figures showing, in a somewhat broad-brush way, that graduate salaries have continued to rise. They put average earnings for new graduates at over £19,000 a year, with those three years after graduating on over £30,000. This implies, incidentally, that the bulk of graduates are repaying their student finance at this stage in their working lives. The 2018 figures showed that someone with a bachelor-level degree earns about £10,000 a year more than a non-graduate, with an extra £5,000 a year mark-up for a higher degree, and that this premium had held steady for a decade. However, the *Financial Times* pointed out that over that decade, the median non-graduate income had risen from about £19,000 to about £23,000 while the graduate premium had stayed unchanged, in effect falling as a percentage of total income.

The Government's decision to raise the threshold for starting repayments from £21,000 to an initial £25,000 is expected to mean that, on average, graduates pay back £15,700 less over a full career. The biggest advantage will be for those on relatively low incomes, who will appreciate the more gradual repayments and who become even more likely never to finish paying.

This Guide should help to fill in some of the detail on employment rates for different courses at different universities, while salary data by course is available on the Discover Uni website (**www.discoveruni.gov.uk**). But, no one can be certain of salary prospects over an entire career, which is increasingly likely to span several forms of employment. Many satisfying jobs are open only to graduates, while in others the majority of entrants have degrees. There is also growing debate about the effects on employment of machine learning and artificial intelligence. This debate is beyond the scope of this chapter, but there is evidence that traditionally graduate jobs are far from immune to this form of disruptive innovation.

Planning your finances

Like maximum fees, national student support schemes are the responsibility of the devolved UK administrations. There are separate sections for Northern Ireland, Wales and Scotland that follow the advice given for English students below.

At the time of writing, the government had decided to keep the basic rate of fees at £9,250 per year for England, partly as a political response to its unpopularity with young people. This standstill is bad news for university finance managers, who might have expected an inflation-linked increase, but excellent for you. Despite this stasis, it is essential to consult the information

Scottish maintenance bursaries and loans 2019-20

Young student (under 25 at start of course)				Independent student (25+)			
Income	Loan	Bursary	Total	Income	Loan	Bursary	Total
Up to £20,999	£5,750	£2,000	£7,750	Up to £20,999	£6,750	£1,000	£7,750
£21,000-£23,999	£5,750	£1,125	£6,875	£21,000-£23,999	£6,750	–	£6,750
£24,000-£33,999	£5,750	£500	£6,250	£24,000-£33,999	£6,250	–	£6,250
Over £34,000	£4,750	–	£4,750	Over £34,000	£4,750	–	£4,750

Nursing and Midwifery students are eligible for bursaries of £8,100 for the first three years and £6,075 for the fourth year of a course. There is a separate dental bursary scheme.

Source: Students Awards Agency Scotland

provided by Government agencies. It is worth checking the following websites for the latest information:

» England: **www.gov.uk/student-finance**
» Wales: **www.studentfinancewales.co.uk**
» Scotland: **www.saas.gov.uk**
» Northern Ireland: **www.studentfinanceni.co.uk**

Student loans for English students

More than 80% of students take out a student loan, and it is not difficult to see why. The National Union of Students estimates that undergraduates spend £12,000 a year outside London and £13,500 in the capital. These are the figures for living costs alone, not fees or other course costs, the main element is £4,834 on rent. While some other estimates are marginally lower, most students find it impossible to cover all their living costs without a loan or significant family

Maintenance Loan entitlement, England 2019-20

Household income	Living at home	Living away from home but not in London	Living away from home and studying in London
£25,000	£7,529	£8,944	£11,672
£30,000	£6,895	£8,303	£11,020
£35,000	£6,260	£7,661	£10,367
£40,000	£5,626	£7,019	£9,714
£42,875	£5,261	£6,650	£9,339
£45,000	£4,991	£6,377	£9,062
£50,000	£4,357	£5,735	£8,049
£55,000	£3,722	£5,093	£7,756
£58,215 and over	£3,314	–	–
£60,000	–	£4,452	£7,103
£62,212 and over	–	£4,168	–
£65,000	–	–	£6,451
£69,888 and over	–	–	£5,812

Source: Student Finance England

support. NUS research suggests that money worries are among students' biggest concerns and are one of the main reasons why they might drop out of a course or consider doing so. Incidentally, anyone who drops out of university still has to repay the loan they ran up while there. The only ways out of paying are to wait 30 years, become permanently unable to work, or die. Unpaid student debt does not become a charge against an estate.

Most experts such as Martin Lewis of moneysavingexpert.com, who writes regularly on student finance, agree that student loans are a good deal compared with other forms of borrowing. In particular, he counsels against using family savings to pay fees upfront, especially since the Government's own estimates suggest that most graduates will not repay the whole amount that they borrow.

Tuition fees loan
You can borrow up to the full amount needed to cover your tuition fees wherever you study in the UK, and this loan is not dependent upon your household income.

Tuition fees loans for part-time students
The most that universities or colleges can charge for part-time courses is 75% of the full-time fee, a maximum of £4,625 per year at private institutions and £6,935 per year at public ones. New part-time students are able to apply for a tuition fee loan that is not dependent on household income or on age, a factor that led to some courses having a surprising number of pensioner students. Eligibility depends on the "intensity" of the course being at least 25% of a

---

Funding timetable
It is vital that you sort out your funding arrangements before you start university. Each funding agency has its own arrangements, and it is very important that you find out the exact details from them. The dates below give general indications of key dates.

March/April
» Online and paper application forms become available from funding agencies.
» You must contact the appropriate funding agency to make an application. This will be the funding agency for the region of the UK that you live in, even if you are planning to study elsewhere in the UK.
» Complete application form as soon as possible. At this stage select the university offer that will be your first choice.
» Check details of bursaries and scholarships available from your selected universities.

May/June
» Funding agencies will give you details of the financial support they can offer.
» Last date for making an application to ensure funding is ready for you at the start of term (exact date varies significantly between agencies).

August
» Tell your funding agency if the university or course you have been accepted for is different from that originally given them.

September
» Take letter confirming funding to your university for registration.
» After registration, the first part of funds will be released to you.

full-time course. If a course takes six years to complete and the full-time equivalent takes three, the intensity will be 50%. In practice, most courses achieve more than 25% intensity.

Maintenance loan

Maintenance loans are means-tested. The amount you can borrow depends on several factors, including your family income, where you intend to study, and whether you expect to be living in the family home.

Although you are legally an adult once you turn 18, your student finance options depend heavily on your family income, frequently termed "household income", which in practice usually means your parents' earnings. If your parents are separated, divorced or widowed, only the income of the parent with whom you normally live will be assessed. However, if that parent has married again, entered into a civil partnership, or has a partner of the opposite sex, then both their incomes will be taken into account. If you are over 25, married, or in some other way visibly independent of your parents, their income ceases to be a factor. If you have not been in contact with them for a year or more, you can apply to be regarded as "estranged." This last is a complex field touching on issues such as forced marriage. It requires genuine evidence, not just a statement from you that you have fallen out with your parents.

The maximum loan for those living at home is £7,529, but only if the combined household income is £25,000 or less. The size of the loan is then reduced on a sliding scale to £4,991 for household incomes over £45,000. For students living away from home outside London, the maximum loan is £8,944, and for those living away from home in London, £11,672, but again these are rates for a household income of £25,000 or less. For students outside London, the loan is reduced on a sliding scale to £6,377 for those whose parents earn £45,000 and above, while for students in London the loan reduces to £9,062 for incomes of £45,000 and above. You can get up to £9,963 for a year studying abroad as part of a UK course. Final-year students receive less than those in earlier years, on the theory that they don't have a summer vacation to survive.

These complex figures mean that 65% of the maintenance loan is available to you regardless of your family circumstances, while the remaining 35% is means-tested. Note, too, that there is extra cash available for future teachers, social workers and healthcare workers, including doctors and dentists.

Scams

One new hazard for students seeking loans has emerged in recent years in the form of an email scam that appears to offer tax refunds in an attempt to steal personal data and money. The scammers are using fake university addresses or aping the branding of the GOV.UK website or credit card companies, and the emails guide students through links to websites where they are instructed to enter personal and bank details.

HMRC has said this is the first such attack it has seen directly targeting university students in high volumes. It said it would never inform anyone about tax refunds by email, text or voicemail and that any such communication should be regarded as a scam. If you get such a message, don't click on it. Instead, forward it to HMRC's phishing email address that can be found on its website.

Repaying loans

As we have seen, full-time students begin accumulating interest from day one of their course and will start repaying in the April after graduation if they earn over £25,725. They will then pay 9% of their income above this figure. Repayments will stop during any period in which annual income falls below the threshold. Repayments are normally taken automatically through income tax and National Insurance. If the loan has not been paid off after 30 years, no further repayments will be required. During the repayment period, the amount of interest will vary according to how much you earn. If you earn less than £25,725, interest will be at the rate of inflation as measured by the Retail Price Index; between £25,000 and £46,305 you will be charged inflation plus up to 3%; and if you earn more than this, interest will be at inflation plus the full 3%.

The Student Loans Company website (**www.studentloanrepayment.co.uk**) has information to guide prospective students through these arrangements and gives examples of levels of repayment.

Student loans and grants for Northern Ireland students

Maintenance loans for 2019/20 vary from a maximum of £3,750 for students living at home, £4,840 for those studying away from home, up to £5,770 for those living overseas and £6,780 for those studying in London. Only 25% of the loan is means-tested. There are also extra sums for people taking courses longer than 30 weeks a year, worth up to £108 a week if you are in London. Maintenance grants range from £3,475 for students with household incomes of £19,203 or below, to zero if the figure is £41,540 or above. Your maximum loan is reduced by the size of any grant you receive. Loan repayments of 9% of salary start once your income reaches £18,935 for 2019/20, less than in England, and interest is calculated on the retail price index or 1% above base rate, whichever is lower, again less than for England. The loan will be cancelled after 25 years, also quicker than in England.

As in England, there are also special funds for people with disabilities and other special needs, and for those with children or adult dependants. Students studying in the Republic of Ireland can also borrow up to €3,000 a year to pay their Irish student fees and may be able to get a bursary to study there. Tuition fee loans are available for the full amount of tuition fees, regardless of where you study in the UK.

Fees for local students at the province's two universities are a lot lower than for England, Scotland or Wales, at £4,275 for 2019/20. These rates also apply to anyone from the rest of the EU, including the Republic of Ireland, except for the English, Welsh and Scots, who pay £9,250.

Student loans and grants for Welsh students

For 2019/20 the maximum maintenance award is £7,840 for students living at home, £9,225 for those living away from home and outside London, and £11,530 for those living in London. The cunning part is that these sums are mainly an outright grant to those from less prosperous households. So, if total household income is £18,370 or less, £8,100 of the £9,225 is a grant and only £1,125 a loan, but if income is over £59,200, then £8,225 is repayable and only £1,000 is a grant. The same logic applies to other levels of support, while part-time students can get a loan or grant up to the precise figure of £4,987.50.

Tuition fee loans are available to cover the first £9,000 of tuition fees in Wales, or £9,250 for Welsh students in Scotland, England or Northern Ireland (£6,165 for a private provider). If you are studying part-time in Wales (or at the Open University) you can apply for a loan of up to £2,625. Elsewhere in the UK you can apply for up to £6,935 or, if your course is offered by a private provider, £4,625.

Repayment of loans starts once a graduate's income reaches £25,725. Interest repayments and the length of loan are as for England (see above). In addition, students in Wales are also able to apply for Welsh Government support for parents of young children, for adult learners, for those with adult dependants and for those with disabilities. This support can cover carer costs as well as equipment and general expenditure.

Student loans and grants for Scottish students

Scottish students pay no tuition fees at their own universities and can apply for up to £9,250 per year as a loan for fees elsewhere in the UK. You must reapply for this loan each year.

The Scottish Government has a commitment to a minimum income, currently £7,750 per year, for students from poorer backgrounds. So, in 2019/20, students from a family with an income below £20,999 could get a £2,000 Young Students' Bursary (YSB) as well as a loan of £5,750. The bursary component does not have to be repaid, but the loan does. It tapers off to zero for family incomes of £34,000, at which point the maximum loan also falls from £5,750 to £4,750. The loan does not vary in size depending on whether you live at home or where you are studying in the UK. Higher loans but more limited bursaries are available for "independent" students – those who are married, mature (25 or over) or without family support.

Note that you must be under 60 on the first day of your course. Repayment of the loan starts when your income reaches £18,935 and is set at 9% of your income above that threshold. The Scottish government, whose Student Awards Agency Scotland runs this system, plans to raise the repayment threshold to £25,000 in April 2021, to match the figure for England. Interest is linked to the Retail Price Index. Repayments will continue until the loan is paid off, with any outstanding amount being cancelled after 35 years, five years later than for the English.

As elsewhere in the UK, there are special funds for people with disabilities and other special needs, and for those with children or adult dependants. No tuition fee loans are required by Scottish students studying in Scotland, but such loans are available for Scottish students studying elsewhere in the UK.

Living in one country, studying in another

As each of the countries of the UK develops its own distinctive system of student finance, the effects on students leaving home in one UK nation to go and study in another have become knottier. UK students who cross borders to study pay the tuition fees of their chosen university and are eligible for a fee loan, and maybe a partial grant, to cover them. They are also entitled to apply for the scholarships or bursaries on offer from that institution. Any maintenance loan or grant will still come from the awarding body of their home country. If you are in this position, you must check with the authorities in your home country about the funding you are eligible for. You should also contact your own government about support on offer if you are in the Channel Islands or the Isle of Man.

While the UK remains in the European Union, EU students from outside the UK must be charged the same tuition fees as those paid by nationals of the country where they are studying, rather than the higher – often much higher – fees paid by students from outside the EU. They can also apply for a fee loan and may be considered for some of the scholarships and bursaries offered by individual institutions. Only students who have been living and studying in the UK for at least three years can apply for a maintenance loan or grant. Those who haven't, will need to apply for assistance from the authorities in their own country. Tuition fee rules for non-UK European Union students are the same in Scotland as for Scottish students – that is, they do not have to pay tuition fees. There are also no fees to pay for exchange students coming to the UK, including those on the Socrates Programme.

Applying for support

English students should apply for grants and loans through Student Finance England, Welsh students through Student Finance Wales, Scottish students through the Student Awards Agency for Scotland, and those in Northern Ireland through Student Finance NI or their Education and Library Board. You should make your application as soon as you have received an offer of a place at university. Maintenance loans are usually paid in three instalments a year into your bank or building society account. The third is the biggest as it is meant to last through the summer break. European Union students from outside the UK will usually be sent an application form for tuition fee loans by the university that has offered them a place.

Don't expect things to happen automatically. For instance, you will have to tell the finance system to pay your fees to the college. You'll never see this money yourself, only the repayments you end up making.

University scholarships and bursaries

As well as taking out student loans for both tuition and living costs, you can shop around for university bursaries, scholarships and other sponsorship packages, and seek out supplementary support to which you may be entitled. There may be reductions for a range of other groups, including local students, which vary widely from university to university and which are usually detailed on university websites. The details of the financial support offered by all universities in England are listed in the access agreements published on the website of the Office for Students, **www.officeforstudents.org.uk**. There is money for people with disabilities or family responsibilities; or for those taking subjects such as social work or medicine, with wide public benefit, as well as a range of charities with their own criteria.

Nevertheless, UK students are said to be missing out on over £150 million in scholarships, according to research by The Scholarship Hub, a free online database of over 3,000 scholarships and bursaries. Leading organisations offering scholarships, grants or bursaries to UK students said they often struggle to get enough suitable applicants.

A bewildering variety of awards are on offer at UK universities. Most bursaries are dependent on your financial circumstances, while scholarships are available through open competition. In general, bursaries that provide students with the money to make ends meet at university have (rightly) proved more popular than fee waivers giving relief from repayments that may stretch over 30 years. Some universities offer eligible students the choice of accommodation discounts, fee waivers or cash. Most also have hardship funds for those who find themselves in financial difficulties. Many charities for specific industries or professions have a remit to support education, and many have bursaries for anyone studying a related subject. It might be worth seeking out some options online. The Directory of Grant-Making Trusts at **https://www.dsc.org.uk/wp-content/uploads/2019/08/Look-inside-DGMT-2020-21.pdf** lists a wealth of bodies that make one-off or regular awards to all kinds of causes, often including deserving students. You may have to visit a library to see it for free.

Do take note of the application procedures for scholarships and bursaries. They vary from institution to institution, and even from course to course within individual institutions. There may be a deadline you have to meet to apply for an award. In some cases, the university will work out for you whether you are entitled to an award by referring to your funding agency's financial assessment. If your personal circumstances change part-way through a course, your entitlement to a scholarship or bursary may be reviewed.

If you feel you still need more help or advice on scholarships or bursaries, you can usually find it on a university's website or in its prospectus. Most institutions also maintain a helpline. Some questions you will need answered include; whether the bursary or scholarship is automatic or conditional and, if the latter, when you will find out whether your application has been successful. For some awards, you won't know whether you have qualified until you get your exam results. Another obvious question is how the scholarship or bursary on offer compares with awards made by another university you might consider applying to. Watch out for institutions that list entitlements that others don't mention, but which you would get anyway.

Students with disabilities

Extra financial help is available to disabled students, whether studying full-time or part-time, through Disabled Students' Allowances, which are paid in addition to the standard student finance package. They are available for help with education-related conditions such as dyslexia, and for other physical and mental disabilities. They do not depend on income and do not have to be repaid. The cash is available for extra travel costs, equipment and to pay helpers. For 2019/20 the maximum for students in England for a non-medical helper is £22,603 a year, or £16,951 a year for a part-time student. In addition, there is a maximum equipment allowance of £5,684 for the duration of the course and £1,899 (£1,424 part-time) for general expenses a year, although the government warns that most students get less than these amounts. There is also needs-based funding for travel costs. For postgraduates, the maximum award is a flat payment of £10,993 for full-time students and less for those studying part-time.

The National Health Service has its own Disabled Students Allowance system, worth a look if you are in the health field. On that theme, the NHS Business Services Authority has a Student Services Arm which runs the NHS Learning Support Grants and the NHS Education Support Grant, again worth investigating if you are planning to study health or social work.

Further sources of income

If you are feeling daunted by the potential costs of study, take comfort from this section, which outlines just some of the ways you can raise additional funds.

Taking a gap year

Gap years (see page 78) have become increasingly popular both for travelling and to earn some money to help pay for higher education. Many students will simply want to travel, but others will be more focused on boosting the bank balance in preparation for life as a student. Work opportunities can be structured or casual. An example of the structured variety in the science and engineering field is EDT (**www.etrust.org.uk**).

Further support

There are various types of support available for students in particular circumstances, other than the main loans, grants and bursaries.

» Undergraduates in financial difficulties can apply for help to their university's student hardship fund. These are allocated to provide support for anything from day-to-day study and living costs to unexpected or exceptional expenses. Many universities have committed to increasing the size of their hardship funds. The university decides which students need help and how much money to award them. These funds are often targeted at older or disadvantaged students, and at finalists who are in danger of dropping out. The sums range up to a few thousand pounds, are not repayable and do not count against other income.

» Students with children can apply for a Childcare Grant, worth up to £169.35 a week if you have one child and up to £290.27 if you have two or more children under 15, or under 17 with special educational needs, calculated on the basis of 85% of your childcare costs; and a Parents' Learning Allowance, for help with course-related costs, of between £50 and £1,716 a year.

» Any students with a partner, or another adult family member who is financially dependent on them, can apply for an Adult Dependants' Grant of up to £3,007 a year for 2019/20.

Part-time work

The need to hold down a part-time job during term time is now a fact of life for almost half of students. Students from a working-class background are more likely to need to earn while they learn.

If you need to earn during term time, it is important to ensure that you do not work so many hours that it affects your studies. A survey by the NUS found that 59% of students who worked felt it had an impact on their studies, with 38% missing lectures and over a fifth failing to submit coursework because of their part-time jobs. You may find that new universities are better geared up to cope with working students than more traditional institutions.

Student employment agencies, which can now be found on many university campuses, can help you get the balance right. These introduce employers with work to students seeking work, sometimes offering jobs within the university itself. But they also abide by codes of practice that regulate both minimum wages and the maximum number of hours worked in term time, typically 15 hours a week. Some firms, such as the big supermarkets, offer continuing part-time employment to their school part-time employees when they go to university. Some students make use of their expertise in areas like web design to earn some extra money, but most take on casual work in shops, restaurants, bars and call centres.

Most students, including those who don't work during term time, get a job during vacations. A Government survey found that 86% of students in their second year of study or above worked during their summer vacation. Most of this kind of work is casual, but some is formalised in a scheme like STEP (**www.step.org.uk**) or may be part of a sponsorship programme. Many vacation jobs are mundane, but it is possible to find more interesting work. Some students broaden their experience by working abroad, others work as film extras, take on tutoring, or do a variety of jobs at big events such as festivals. It is also a good idea to try to use the summer holidays to get some work experience in a field that has some relevance to your career aspirations. Even if you don't get paid, this can significantly enhance your chances of finding employment after graduation. Many new graduates end up being hired by businesses where they have previously worked.

What you will need to spend money on
Living costs

Certain costs are unavoidable. You have to have a roof over your head, eat enough, clothe yourself, and probably do a certain amount of travelling. But the cost of even these essential items can be cut significantly through a mixture of shopping around and careful budgeting. If you set aside a certain amount of money a week for food, you will find it goes much further if you keep takeaways and ready-meals to a minimum and stick to a shopping list when you go to a supermarket. And you might even end up healthier. Some catering outlets at your university or in the students' union may well offer good value meals, but probably the most economical way to eat is to cook and share meals with fellow students with whom you may be living in a shared house. Make sure you make full use of student travel cards and other offers and facilities available locally to help you cut the cost of travel. In certain locations, a bicycle is a worthwhile investment (as is buying a lock for it).

If you can keep your essential costs down, you will have more for what you would probably prefer to spend your money on – going out and personal items. Most students spend a proportion of their budget on socialising, and this is certainly an important part of the university experience. You can have fun and keep your leisure costs down by making the most of your student union's facilities and events.

It is easy to let "other costs" get out of hand to the extent that they start to eat into your budget for day-to-day living. Mobile phone bills are a case in point: the latest edition of an annual survey of student life by NatWest put average spending at £13.10 per month, but extras like downloading games or music, or sending pictures, can add significantly to your bill. Most of all, try to avoid getting tied up with an expensive and inflexible contract.

The same survey shows that students spend £84 a month on groceries and household items, £28 on alcohol, but just £12 on books and other course-related material. An earlier survey by Sodexo suggested that half of all students have altered their eating and socialising habits for lack of money.

Studying costs

A NUS survey estimated that the average student spent about £1,000 a year on costs associated with course work and studying, mainly books and equipment. The amount you spend will be determined largely by the nature of your course. Additional financial support may be available for certain expenditure, but this is unlikely to cover you fully for spending on books, stationery, equipment, fieldwork or elective courses. A long reading list could prove very expensive if you tried to buy all the required books brand new. Find out as soon as possible which books are available either in your university library or local libraries. Another approach is to buy books second-hand from students who no longer need them. Your students' union or your university may run second-hand book sales, or offer a service helping students to buy and sell books.

Overdrafts and credit cards

Other costs it is best to avoid include the more expensive forms of debt. Many banks offer free overdraft facilities for students, but if you go over the limit without prior arrangement, you can end up paying way over the odds for your borrowing. Credit cards can be useful if managed properly. The best way to manage a credit card is to set up a direct debit to pay off your balance in full every month, which means you will avoid paying any interest. One of the worst ways is to pay only the minimum charge each month, which can cost you a small fortune over a long period. If you are the kind of person who spends impulsively and doesn't keep track of your spending, you are probably better off without a credit card. Have a debit card instead. That way, you can't spend money you don't have.

Insurance

One kind of additional spending that can save you money is getting insurance cover for your possessions. Most students arrive at university with laptops and other goodies such as games consoles, sports equipment, musical instruments, mobile phones and bikes that are tempting to thieves. It is estimated that around a third of students fall victim to crime at some point during university. If you shop around, you should be able to get a reasonable amount of cover for these items without it costing you an arm and a leg. It may also be possible to add this cover cheaply to your parents' domestic contents policy (probably at their expense).

Planning your budget

One in four freshers spend their first student loan instalment within a month, according to Endsleigh Insurance. But university websites, the National Union of Students (**https://www.nus.org.uk/en/advice/money-and-funding/money-management-tips**) and many others offer guidance on preparing a budget, usually with the basic headings provided for you to complete. First, list all your likely income (bursaries, loans, part-time work, savings, parental support) and then see how this compares with what you will spend. Try to be realistic, and not too optimistic, about both sides of the equation. With care, you will end up either only slightly in the red, or preferably far enough in the black for you to be able to afford things you would really like. Remember that there are often bargains available in student shops at well below high street prices.

Above all, keep track of your finances so that your university experience isn't ruined by money worries, or by finding that you can't go to the ball because the cash machine has eaten your card. Spreadsheets make doing this simpler, and it is one skill you can learn at college that you are going to need for the rest of your life.

If all else fails, your campus almost certainly has a student money adviser who is a member of NASMA, the National Association of Student Money Advisers. You can find them via **www.nasma.org.uk**. NASMA reports that some students, especially those with children, are struggling financially. One problem is that more than two-thirds of young people aged 18–24 say they received no financial education at school. This chimes with the experience of NASMA, which finds that many students have low levels of basic financial awareness and planning ability. In addition, advisers have noticed that students are increasingly likely to spend money they cannot afford on TV and online gambling, so try to avoid this temptation.

Useful websites

For the basics of fees, loans, grants and other allowances:
www.gov.uk/student-finance
www.gov.uk/browse/education/student-finance

UCAS provides helpful advice:
www.ucas.com/ucas/undergraduate/undergraduate-finance-and-support

For England, visit Student Finance England: **www.sfengland.slc.co.uk**
Office for Students: **www.officeforstudents.org.uk**
For Wales, visit Student Finance Wales: **www.studentfinancewales.co.uk**
For Scotland, visit the Student Awards Agency for Scotland: **www.saas.gov.uk**
For Northern Ireland, visit Student Finance Northern Ireland: **www.studentfinanceni.co.uk**

All UK student loans are administered by the Student Loans Company: **www.slc.co.uk**

For guidance on the tax position of students, visit HM Revenue and Customs:
www.gov.uk/student-jobs-paying-tax

For finding out about availability of scholarships: **www.thescholarshiphub.org.uk**

8 Finding Somewhere to Live

Students spend an average of £147 a week on rent, according to the 2018 NUS/Unipol Student Accommodation Costs Survey, while the maximum £8,944 maintenance loan (for 2019/20) provides only £172 per week for someone outside London and living away from home. So it is no exaggeration to say that choosing where to live is the most important decision a student has to make, after the choice of course. Getting it right will have an impact on your entire university experience. It will determine how much money you have left for other activities, but more importantly, will influence your work and your whole state of mind. Particularly in your first year – and especially if it is your first time away from home – you are likely to be happier and more successful academically in accommodation of reasonable quality, preferably in a setting that helps you meet other students.

Fortunately, there is more choice than ever, with a range of private providers supplementing what universities and individual landlords provide. Many universities guarantee to provide accommodation for first-year undergraduates, and even those which cannot do this will offer help in finding somewhere of reasonable quality.

All has not been plain sailing in the current academic year, however, with some private providers failing to complete developments by the start of term and an incident in Bolton raising safety concerns as fire ripped through a relatively new private hall of residence with cladding. Some students accepted by Bristol University in Clearing were housed in Newport, 30 miles away in South Wales, because there were no hall places left. At the neighbouring University of the West of England, students complained that "pods" erected in a car park as temporary accommodation were too small and isolated to live in. Chris Skidmore, the Universities Minister, called a special meeting of universities and accommodation providers to thrash out concerns.

Whatever you choose has to be affordable. But if your budget will stand it, you may well start off in a hall of residence or university flat. Three-quarters of applicants hope to live in halls, but only 60% actually do so, according to a 2016 report by Unite Students. The company's most recent UK survey showed halls gaining in popularity among second and third-year undergraduates, with the proportion opting for shared houses in their second year falling to little more than half.

With tastes apparently changing and the numbers going to university remaining high, student housing has become the biggest growth area in the property market, with rising rents and billions of pounds committed to student residences each year.

Despite considerable investment in housing by universities themselves, property consultants JLL estimate that more than a third of residential places for students are now in private hands. Particularly in the big student cities, but increasingly in other university towns as well, student accommodation now comes in all shapes, sizes and prices. Most of the developments are in big complexes, but there are also niche providers such as Student Cribs, which convert properties to a rather higher spec than the traditional landlord and rents them to students. It now operates in 24 cities.

Of the big providers, Unite Students has 50,000 beds in 22 towns and cities, some provided in partnership with universities and others in developments that serve more than one institution. UPP manages over 35,000 residential places in complexes it has built for universities, usually on campus, and where rents are negotiated with the university, often in consultation with the students' union. The National Student Accommodation Survey found that 10% of students were living in private halls in 2019, up from 8% two years ago. By contrast, 27% live in university accommodation, 54% have a private landlord, 6% live with their parents, and a lucky 1% own their home.

There is now an award for the best private halls of residence – won in 2019 by Host, which has accommodation in 19 UK cities. A survey for the 2019 Student Housing Awards found that traditional campus universities such as Queen's University Belfast and Lancaster tend to have well-liked halls, although some newer institutions such as Derby and Edge Hill also do well.

For most students, it will not matter whether the owner of their accommodation is the university, a private landlord or larger organisation if the quality and the price are right. But successive reports by the National Union of Students have told a story of increasingly unaffordable rents, often poor facilities and rushed decisions by inexperienced students. While those who can afford it – or think they can – are living in luxury, NUS has found others coping with mice, slugs, mould, cold, or all of these, not to mention other, even less agreeable, surprises. So it is worth putting some effort into basic decisions on this subject.

Term-time accommodation of full-time and sandwich students 2017–18

University provided accommodation	356,325	19.5%
Private sector halls	150,725	8.3%
Parental home	355,365	19.4%
Own residence	317,300	17.4%
Other rented accommodation	531,715	29.1%
Other	67,810	3.7%
Not in attendance/unknown	65,310	3.6%
Source HESA 2018 (adapted)		

Living at home

Although student loan repayments start only after graduation, many undergraduates are understandably cautious about the debts they run up. So the option of avoiding big accommodation charges is a tempting one for those who are attracted by a local university. The pattern of recent applications shows that the trend towards studying at home is accelerating, albeit only gradually, and there is no reason to think that this will change in the near future. This may be a permanent shift, given the rising costs of student housing and the willingness of many young people, student or not, to live with their parents well into their twenties.

The proportion of students living at home was already rising before undergraduate fees went up. Including mature students, many of whom live in their own home rather than their parents', the proportion is now close to 20%. Among younger students, women are more likely than men to stay at home, and Asian women are particularly likely to take this option. Home study is also four times more common at post-1992 universities than older institutions, again reflecting the larger numbers of mature students with family responsibilities at the newer universities and a generally younger and more affluent student population at the older ones. Research has shown that mature students, who are in a majority at some newer universities, spend less time on campus than others and are less involved in campus sports and activities. In London, University College has published advice for students on coping with long commuting. The National Student Accommodation Survey puts students' average journey time to lectures at 20 minutes, but 30 minutes in London. Students living with family often make far longer journeys to college than this, and there is evidence that "commuter students" do less well academically.

For those considering studying from home, there are important considerations to get right, of which the relationship with your parents and the availability of quiet space are the most obvious. You will still be entitled to a maintenance loan, although for 2019/20 it is a maximum of £7,529 in England, rather than £8,944 if you were living away from home outside London, or £11,672 in London. There is no higher rate for anyone living at home in London, which seems unreasonable given the

Top Ten Problems for Student Tenants

1	Noisy housemates	45%
2	Damp	35%
3	Housemates stealing food	33%
4	Lack of water/heating	32%
5	Disruptive building work	20%
=6	Rodents and pests	16%
=6	Inappropriate landlord visits	16%
=8	Dangerous living conditions	5%
=8	Break-in or burglary	5%
10	Bedbugs	3%

Source: National Student Accommodation Survey 2019

Based on 2,196 responses **www.savethestudent.org**

high cost of transport and other essentials there. There may be advantages in terms of academic work if the alternative involves shopping, cooking and cleaning as well as the other distractions of a student flat. The downside is that you may miss out on a lot of the student experience, especially the social scene and the opportunity to make new friends.

A 2018 report by the Higher Education Policy Institute found that students who live at home are less likely than others to say they are learning a lot at university, and a survey by the Student Engagement Partnership suggests that they find life unexpectedly "tiring, expensive and stressful". Issues affecting their quality of life include travel, security and the lack of their own space. But remember that you can always move on later if you think you are missing out. Many initially home-based students do so in their second year.

Living away from home

Most of those who can afford it, still see moving away to study as integral to the rite of passage that student life represents. Some have little option, for instance if the course they want is not available locally in spite of the expansion of higher education. Others are happy to travel to secure their ideal place and widen their experience. If you insist on a degree from a household-name global university, the odds are that you'll have to travel to get there.

For the lucky majority, the search for accommodation will be over quickly because the university can offer a place in one of its halls of residence or self-catering flats. The choice may come down to the type of accommodation and whether or not to do your own cooking. But for others, there will be an anxious search for a room in a strange city. Most universities will help with this if they cannot offer accommodation of their own.

Going to university will oblige those who take the away route to think for the first time about the practicalities of living independently. This can make the decision about where to live – in terms of location and the type of accommodation – doubly difficult. It may even influence your choice of university, since there are big differences across the sector and the country in the cost and standard of accommodation, and in its availability.

How much will it cost?

Rents vary so much across the UK that national averages are almost meaningless. The 2019 NatWest Student Living Index found a range from £326 a month in Belfast and £374 in Dundee to £700 in London and £570 in Brighton, the next-dearest. At all but three of the 35 student cities in the survey – Belfast, Dundee and Cardiff – rents averaged more than £400 a month.

However accurate such figures may be, they conceal a wide range of actual rents, particularly in London. This was always the case, but has become even more obvious with the rapid growth of a luxury market at the same time as many students are willing to accept sub-standard accommodation to keep costs down.

A series of recent reports suggest that the need for good Wi-Fi has overtaken reasonable rents as students' top priority in choosing accommodation. A survey by mystudenthalls.com found that a big, bright room, good Wi-Fi, friendly people, a clean kitchen and a good gym are the top things students say they value in a place to live. Their parents worry more about security, the bar and the social life, perhaps hoping their kids will have the wild college life that they misremember.

But obviously you have to be able to afford the rent in the first place. The 2018 edition of the NUS/Unipol Accommodation Cost survey found that in 2018/19, average rents were equal to 73% of the maximum financial support per student, up from 58% in 2011/12. And as the report says, even this support is means-tested against household income, so many students get less.

Another issue raised in this survey is the need for cash up front for deposits, and/or a guarantee, probably from your parents, that the rent will be paid.

Most universities with a range of accommodation find that their most expensive rooms fill up first, and that students appear to have higher expectations than they used to. More than half of all the rooms in the NUS survey had en-suite facilities.

It is important to remember that both your living costs and your potential earnings should be factored into your calculations when deciding where to live. While living costs in London are by far the highest, potential part-time earnings are, too. Taking account of both income and outgoings, the 2019 NatWest index made Cardiff the most affordable student city, followed by Bristol and Leicester. London was the dearest on this measure, ahead of Edinburgh and Aberystwyth. Students were found to earn the most in Bristol, followed by Manchester – £1,386 and £1,374 per term-time month respectively. Bottom of the league are Aberystwyth at £859 and Dundee on £886.

The choices you have

The NUS puts accommodation into 16 categories, ranging from luxurious university halls to a bedsit in a shared house. The choices include:

» University hall of residence, with individual study bedrooms and a full catering service. Many will have en-suite accommodation.
» University halls, flats or houses where you have to provide your own food.
» Private, purpose-built student accommodation.
» Rented houses or flats, shared with fellow students.
» Living at home.
» Living as a lodger in a private house.

This chapter will help you decide where you would like to live and whether you can afford it.

Making your choice

Finance is not the only factor you should consider when deciding where to live. It is worth investing time to find the right place, and to avoid the false economy of choosing somewhere cheap, but where you may end up feeling depressed and isolated. Most students who drop out of university do so in the first few months, when homesickness and loneliness can be felt most acutely.

Being warm and well fed is likely to have a positive effect on your studies. Perhaps for these reasons, most undergraduates in their first year plump for living in university halls, which offer a convenient, safe and reliable standard of accommodation, along with a supportive community environment. The sheer number of students – especially first years – in halls makes this form of accommodation an easy way of meeting people from a wide range of courses and making friends.

If meals are included, this extra adds further peace of mind both for students and their parents. The last NUS survey, which covered students in 2018–19, found that the difference in cost between full board and self-catering was just £37 a week on average, not unreasonable for two hot meals a day. But only 4% of places are now catered, compared with 58% in the standard format of en-suite rooms and a shared kitchen. So, some basic cooking skills might help build your popularity and self-confidence when you first reach university.

Wherever you choose to live, there are some general points you will need to consider, such as how safe the neighbourhood seems to be, and how long it might take you to travel to and from classes, especially during rush hour. A survey of travel time between term-time accommodation and the university found that most students in London can expect a commute of at least 30 minutes and often over an hour, while students living in Wales are usually much less than 30 minutes away from their university.

In chapter 15, we provide details of what accommodation each university offers, covering the number of places, the costs, and their policy towards first-year students.

What universities offer

You might think that opting to live in university accommodation is the most straightforward choice, especially since first-year students are given priority in the allocation of places in halls of residence, and it is possible to arrange university accommodation in advance and at a distance. Searching for private housing can often be a matter of having to be in the right place at the right time, and many potential students start the hunt in the November before they go to college. However, you may still need to select from a range of options, because most universities will have a variety of accommodation on offer. You will need to consider which best suits your pocket and your preferred lifestyle.

New student accommodation

At the top end of the market, private firms usually lead the way, at least in the bigger student cities. Companies such as UPP, Unite Students and Liberty Living offer some of the most luxurious student accommodation the UK has seen, either in partnership with universities or in their own right. Rooms in these complexes are nearly always en-suite and with internet access and may include other facilities such as your own phone line and satellite TV. Shared kitchens are top-quality and fitted out with the latest equipment.

This kind of accommodation naturally comes at a higher price, but offers the advantages of flexibility both in living arrangements and through a range of payment options. An earlier NUS survey found little difference between the rents charged by higher education institutions for their own accommodation and those for rooms managed by private companies under contract. But private providers operating outside institutional links charged over £20 a week more. A survey carried out independently for the "Purpose-Built Student Accommodation" industry, ie the private sector providers, found that those using this option had better academic outcomes and better physical health.

Halls of residence

Many new or recently refurbished university-owned halls offer a standard of accommodation that is not far short of the privately-built residences. This is partly because rooms in these halls can be offered to conference delegates during vacations. Even though these halls are also at the pricier end of the spectrum, you will probably find that they are in great demand, and you may have to get your name down quickly to secure one of the fancier rooms. That said, you can often get a guarantee of accommodation if you give a firm acceptance of an offered place by a certain date in the summer.

If you have gained your place through Clearing, this option may not exist, although rooms in private halls might still be on offer at this stage. This year's experiences underline the importance of ensuring, as far as possible, that any new developments are on time and have the seal of approval (even in the absence of a formal arrangement) of the university. Cladding is a particular concern and not one that is easily assuaged. The cladding in last November's Bolton fire, for example, appears to have met building regulations and not to be the type used on Grenfell Tower.

While a few halls are single-sex, most are mixed, and often house over 500 students. In student villages, the numbers are now counted in thousands. They are therefore great places for making friends and becoming part of the social scene. Most of the university applicants surveyed for the 2017 Reality Check report by the Higher Education Policy Institute, in association with Unite, regarded the course and their accommodation as the two key places to meet new friends. Many also agreed that the ability to make friends was more important than the specification of the accommodation. Two-thirds put a priority on the availability of social events where they lived, particularly in their first term.

One possible downside is that big student housing developments can also be noisy places where it can be difficult at times to get down to some work. In another Unite survey, 44% of those responding identified noise as the biggest challenge in student accommodation, including some expensive private provision. For those who had experienced it, peace and quiet was a higher priority than access to public transport or good nightlife. The more successful students learn, before too many essay deadlines and exams start to loom, to get the balance right between all-night partying and escaping to the library for some undisturbed study time. Remember that many libraries, especially new ones, are now open 24 hours a day.

University self-catering accommodation

An alternative to halls offered by most universities, are smaller, self-catering properties fitted out with a shared kitchen and other living areas. Students looking for a more independent and flexible lifestyle often prefer this option, which is now the norm at many universities. The Reality Check report found that 83% of female university applicants, and 79% of the men, felt confident of their cooking abilities. The women were also more likely to say they could clean the house and cope with laundry. As well as having to feed yourself, you may also have heating and lighting bills to pay. University properties are often on campus or nearby, so travel costs should not be a problem.

Catering in university accommodation

Many universities have responded to a general increase in demand from students for a more independent lifestyle by providing more flexible catering facilities. A range of eateries, from fast food outlets to more traditional refectories, can usually be found on campus or in student villages. Students in university accommodation may be offered pay-as-you-eat deals as an alternative to full-board packages.

What after the first year?

After your first year of living in university residences you may well wish, and will probably be expected, to move out to other accommodation. The main exceptions are the collegiate universities, particularly Oxford and Cambridge but also others, which may allow you to stay on in college for another year or two, and particularly for your final year. Students from outside the EU are also often guaranteed accommodation. At a growing number of universities, where there is a sufficiently large stock of residential accommodation, it is not uncommon for students to move back into halls for their final year.

Practical details

Whether or not you have decided to start out in university accommodation, you will probably be expected to sign an agreement to cover your rent. Contract lengths vary. They can be for around 40 weeks, which includes the Christmas and Easter holiday periods, or for just the length of the three university terms. These term-time contracts are common when a university uses its rooms for conferences during vacations, and you will be required to leave your room empty during these weeks. Check whether the university has secure storage space for you to leave your belongings. Otherwise you will have to make arrangements to take all your belongings home or store them privately between terms. International students may be offered special arrangements by which they can stay in halls during the short vacation periods. Organisations like **www.hostuk.org** can arrange for international students to stay in a UK family home at holiday times such as Christmas.

Parental purchases

One option for affluent families is to buy a house or flat and take in student lodgers. This might not be the safe financial bet it once appeared, but it is still tempting for many parents. Agents Knight Frank have had a student division since 2007, mostly working with new developers to sell specially adapted homes. Those who are considering this route tend to do so from their first year of study to maximise the return on their investment.

Being a lodger or staying in a hostel

A small number of students live as a lodger in a family home, an option most frequently taken up by international students. The usual arrangement is for a study bedroom and some meals to be provided, while other facilities such as the washing machine are shared. Students with particular religious affiliations or from a particular country may wish to consider living in a hostel run by a charity catering for a specific group. Most of these are in London. There are also specialist commercial providers such as Mansion Student India, which runs housing for Indian students in the UK.

Renting from the private sector

Around a third of students live in privately rented flats or houses. Every university city or town is awash with such accommodation, available via agencies or direct from landlords. Indeed, this type of accommodation has grown to the point where so-called "student ghettoes," in which local residents feel outnumbered, have become a hot political issue in some cities. Into this traditional market for rented flats and houses have come the new private-sector complexes and residences, adding to the options. Some are on university campuses, but others are in city centres and usually open to students of more than one university. Examples can be seen online; some sites are listed at the end of this chapter.

While there are always exceptions, a much more professional attitude and approach to managing rented accommodation has emerged among smaller providers, thanks to a combination of greater regulation and increasing competition. Nevertheless, it is wise to take certain precautions when seeking out private residences.

How to start looking for rented property

Start this process as soon as you have accepted a place. Contact your university's accommodation service and ask for its list of approved rented properties. Some have a Student Accommodation Accreditation Scheme, run in collaboration with the local council. To get onto an approved list under such schemes, landlords must show they are adhering to basic standards of safety and security, such as having an up-to-date gas and electric safety certificate. University accommodation officers should also be able to advise you on any hidden charges. For instance, you may be asked to pay a booking or reservation fee to secure a place in a particular property, and there are sometimes fees for references or for drawing up a tenancy agreement. The practice of charging a "joining fee", however, has been outlawed.

It is wise to speak to older students with first-hand experience of renting in the area. Certain companies may be notorious among second and third years and you can try to avoid them. In addition to websites and accommodation services designed for students, you can also use sites such as Gumtree that cater for the population at large.

Making a choice

Once you have made an initial choice of the area you would like to live in and the size of property you are looking for, the next stage is to look at possible places. If you plan to share, it is important that you all have a look at the property. If you will be living by yourself, take a friend with you when you go to view a property, since he or she can help you assess what you see objectively, and avoid any irrational or rushed on-the-spot decisions. Don't let yourself be pushed into signing on the dotted line there and then. Take time to visit and consider a number of options, as well as checking out the local facilities, transport and the general environment at various times of the day and different days of the week.

If you are living in private rented accommodation, it is likely that at least some of your neighbours will not be students. Local people often welcome students, but resentment can build up, particularly in areas of towns and cities that are dominated by student housing. It is important to respect your neighbours' rights, and not to behave in an anti-social manner.

Preparing for sharing

The people you are planning to share a house with may have some habits that you find at least mildly irritating. How well you cope with some of the downsides of sharing will be partly down to the kind of person you are and where you are on the spectrum between laid back and highly strung. But it will help a lot if you are co-habiting with people whose outlook on day-to-day living is not too far out of line with your own. According to Unite Students, 31% of female students find sharing more difficult than they had expected, compared with 22% of men.

Some students sign for their second-year houses as early as November. While it is good to be ahead of the rush, you may not yet have met your best friends at this stage. If you have not selected your own group of friends, universities and landlords can help by taking personal preferences and lifestyle into account when grouping tenants together.

Potential issues to consider when deciding whether to move into a shared house include whether any of the housemates smoke, or own a loud musical instrument. It will also be important to sort out broadband arrangements that will work for everyone in the house, and that you will be able to access the university system. It is a good idea to agree a rota for everyone to share in the household cleaning chores from the start. Otherwise, it is almost certain that you will live in a state of unhygienic squalor, or that one or two individuals will be left to clear up everyone else's mess.

The practical details about renting

It is a good idea to ask whether your house is covered by an accreditation scheme or code of standards. Such codes provide a clear outline of what constitutes good practice as well as the responsibilities of both landlords and tenants. Adhering to schemes like the National Code of Standards for Larger Student Developments compiled by Accreditation Network UK (**www.anuk.org.uk**) may well become a requirement for larger properties, including those managed by universities, now that the Housing Act is in force. Student accommodation provider Liberty Living has published the National Code at **https://www.libertyliving.co.uk/media/7125/national-code-of-standards.pdf**

At the very least, make sure that if you are renting from a private landlord, you have his or her telephone number and home address. Some can be remarkably difficult to contact when repairs are needed or when deposits are due to be returned.

Multiple occupation

If you are renting a private house it may be subject to the 2004 Housing Act in England and Wales (similar legislation applies in Scotland and Northern Ireland). Licenses are compulsory for all private Houses in Multiple Occupation (HMOs) with three or more storeys and that house five or more unrelated residents. The provisions of the Act also allow local authorities to designate whole areas in which HMOs of all sizes must be licensed. The regulations may be applied in sections of university towns and cities where most students live. This means that a house must be licensed, well-managed and must meet various health and safety standards, and its owner subject to various financial regulations. There is more on this at gov.uk under Private Renting.

Tenancy agreements

Whatever kind of accommodation you go for, you must be sure to have all the paperwork in order and be clear about what you are signing up to before you move in. If you are taking up residence in a shared house, flat or bedsit, the first document you will have to grapple with is a tenancy agreement or lease offering you an 'assured shorthold tenancy'. Since this is a binding legal document, you should be prepared to go through every clause with a fine-tooth comb. Remember that it is much more difficult to make changes or overcome problems arising from unfair agreements once you are a tenant than before you become one.

You would be well advised to seek help in the likely event of your not fully understanding some

---

Security in Student Housing

» Before you rent check that front and back doors have five-lever mortise locks as well as standard catch locks and use them when you go out

» Invest in a light-timer, so the house looks occupied even when you're out and don't advertise your departure on social media

» If you put your desk in a window, make sure you move your laptop, phone and any other valuable equipment away when you're not using them

» Get insurance for your valuables and take them home if you're leaving the house for any length of time. You may be able to add your valuables to your parents' home insurance

» Ask the landlord or letting agency to make sure previous tenants have returned any keys and discuss any security concerns with them

» Registering your valuables (see www.immobilise.com) makes it more likely you'll be re-united if things do get stolen and invest in a good bike lock

Source: www.savethestudent.org and NUS (adapted)

of the clauses. Your university accommodation office or students' union is a good place to start. They should know all the ins and outs, and have model tenancy agreements to refer to. A Citizens Advice Bureau or Law Advice Centre should also be able to offer you free advice. In particular, watch out for clauses that may make you jointly responsible for the actions of others with whom you are sharing. If you name a parent as a guarantor to cover any costs not paid by you, they may also be liable for charges levied on all tenants for damage that was not your fault. A rent review clause could allow your landlord to increase the rent at will, whereas without such a clause, they are restricted to one rent rise a year. Make sure you keep a copy of all documents, and get a receipt (and keep it somewhere safe) for anything you have had to pay for that is the landlord's responsibility.

Contracts with private landlords tend to be longer than for university accommodation. They will frequently commit you to paying rent for 52 weeks of the year. Leaving aside the cost, there are probably more advantages than disadvantages to this kind of arrangement. It means you don't have to move out during vacations, which you will have to in most university halls. You can store your belongings in your room when you go away (but don't leave anything really valuable behind if you can help it). You may be able to negotiate a rent discount for periods when you are not staying in the property. The other advantage, particularly important for cash-strapped students, is that you have a base from which to find work and hold down a job during the vacations. Term dates are also not as dictatorial as they might be in halls. If you rent your own house, then you can come back when you wish.

Deposits

On top of the agreed rent, you will need to provide a deposit or bond to cover any breakages or damage. This will probably set you back the equivalent of another month's rent. The deposit should be returned, less any deductions, at the end of the contract. However, be warned that disputes over the return of deposits are common, with the question of what constitutes reasonable wear and tear often the subject of disagreements between landlord and tenant. To protect students from unscrupulous landlords who withheld deposits without good reason, the 2004 Housing Act introduced a National Tenancy Deposit Scheme under which deposits are held by an independent body. This is designed to ensure that deposits are fairly returned, and that any disputes are resolved swiftly and cheaply. There are details at **citizensadvice.org.uk**. You may also be asked to find guarantors for your rent payments – in practice, usually your parents.

Inventories and other paperwork

You should get an inventory and schedule of condition of everything in the property. This is another document that you should check carefully and make sure that everything listed is as described. Write on the document anything that is different. The NUS suggests taking photographs of rooms and equipment when you first move in (setting the correct date on your camera), to provide you with additional proof should any dispute arise when your contract ends and you want to get your deposit back. If you are not offered an inventory, then make one of your own. You should have someone else witness and sign this, send it to your landlord, and keep your own copy. Keeping in contact with your landlord throughout the year and developing a good relationship with him or her will also do you no harm, and may be to your advantage in the long run.

You should ask your landlord for a recent gas safety certificate issued by a qualified CORGI engineer, a fire safety certificate covering the furnishings, and a record of current gas and electricity meter readings. Take your own readings of meters when you move in to make sure these match up with what you have been given, or make your own records if the landlord doesn't supply them. This also applies to water meters if you are expected to pay water rates (although this isn't usually the case). The NUS issues its own advice on how to keep down energy bills, at **http://studentswitchoff.org/save-energy-rented-accommodation**. The NUS says that the average student in private rented accommodation spends £500 a year on energy, so you can save money and get a glow of green virtue by cutting back.

Finally, students are not liable for Council Tax. If you are sharing a house only with other full-time students, then you will not have to pay it. However, you may be liable to pay a proportion of the Council Tax bill if you are sharing with anyone who is not a full-time student. You may need to get a Council Tax exemption certificate from your university as evidence that you do not need to pay Council Tax.

Safety and security

Once you have arrived and settled in, remember to take care of your own safety and the security of your possessions. You are particularly vulnerable as a fresher, when you are still getting used to your new-found independence. This may help explain why so many students are burgled or robbed in the first six weeks of the academic year. Take care with valuable portable items such as mobile phones, tablet computers and laptops, all of which are tempting for criminals. Ensure you don't have them obviously on display when you are out and about and that you have insurance cover. If your mobile phone is stolen, call your network or 08701 123123 to immobilise it. Students' unions, universities and the police will provide plenty of practical guidance when you arrive. Following their advice will reduce the chance of you becoming a victim of crime, and help you to enjoy living in the new surroundings of your chosen university town.

Useful websites

For advice on a range of housing issues, visit: **www.nus.org.uk/en/advice/housing-advice**

The Shelter website has separate sections covering different housing regulations in England, Wales, Scotland and Northern Ireland: **www.shelter.org.uk**

As examples of providers of private hall accommodation, visit:
www.upp-ltd.com
http://www.unitestudents.com/
www.libertyliving.co.uk
http://thestudenthousingcompany.com
www.student-cribs.com

A number of sites will help you find accommodation and/or potential housemates, including:
www.accommodationforstudents.com
www.uniplaces.com
www.sturents.com,
 www.studentpad.co.uk
www.studentcrowd.com
www.let4students.com
http://student.spareroom.co.uk
http://uk.easyroommate.com

Accreditation Network UK is at: **www.anuk.org.uk**
www.hostuk.org helps international students meet British people and families in their homes

9 Enjoying University Sport

The quality of the sports facilities will not be the clinching factor in most applicants' choice of university – and nor should it be – but nearly a third say it played some part in their decision-making. Universities are well aware of this and have upgraded their provision accordingly. Some of the best and most extensive sports facilities in the UK are now to be found on campuses. Such has been the scale of investment in recent years that nationally, they are said to be worth an astonishing £20 billion.

Birmingham has a new £55m sports centre, including the only 50m pool in the region, to add to its already impressive facilities. Nottingham opened a £40m sports complex in 2016, while Solent recently opened a £28m sports development. Such facilities attract elite performers and are often used for high-level teaching, but they are also available for day-to-day use by undergraduates.

There may never be a better opportunity to pursue your favourite sport, take up a new one, or simply to keep fit than during your undergraduate years. Practically every university now has excellent sports facilities and even the most demanding course timetable will leave room to take advantage of them. More than half of all students exercise regularly, according to research published in 2018, and another 40% do so for at least half an hour a week.

Especially at the big universities – but also at many of the smaller ones – sporting provision is now both diverse and high quality. Half of all universities were chosen as training bases for Great Britain squads in the run-up to the 2012 Olympic Games and 30 hosted other nations' teams. Comparing such facilities is not easy, but most universities display them prominently on their websites and offer taster sessions on open days. There are brief descriptions of the bigger developments in the university profiles in Chapter 15.

At the elite level, university sport has never been stronger. At the Rio Olympics in 2016, over half Team GB's medals were won by university students or alumni, and many more are hoping to be selected for the Tokyo Games. Five of the gold medal-winning ladies hockey team in Rio (and the coach) were Loughborough graduates, for example. Indeed, Loughborough would have been 17th in the overall medal table, and it was not the only successful university – St Mary's, Twickenham, would have been 25th. Such successes are the result of considerable investment in sports scholarships and training programmes, as well as campus facilities.

Naturally, most students will never aspire to such heights, but may still welcome the chance to use top-grade facilities. Research for British Universities and Colleges Sport (BUCS) suggests that at least 1.7 million students take part in regular physical activity, from gym sessions to competitive individual or team sports. There are good reasons, beyond fitness, for doing so, according to BUCS reports. Those who were physically active expect higher grades and are more confident of securing a graduate job than less active students. In 2013, graduates who had played and/or volunteered in sport were found to be earning at least £4,000 more than those who had not, and were 25% less likely to have been unemployed. Nine out of ten employers thought that participation in university sport helped to develop valuable skills in potential employees.

Sporting opportunities

Some specialist facilities may be reserved at times for elite performers, but all universities are conscious of the need for wider access. Surveys show that two-thirds of sessions at university sports facilities are taken by students, roughly a quarter by the local community and the rest by staff. Many institutions still encourage departments not to schedule lectures and seminars on Wednesday afternoons, to give students free time for sport. There are student-run clubs for all the major sports and – particularly at the larger universities – a host of minor ones. In addition, there are high-quality gyms, with staff on hand to devise personalised training regimes and to run popular activities such as Zumba and Pilates. The cost varies widely between universities, and membership fees can represent a large amount to lay out at the start of the year, but most provide good value if you are going to be a regular user.

Sport for all

For most universities, it is in the area of "sport for all" that most attention has been focused. Beginners are welcomed and coaching provided in a range of sports, from Ultimate Frisbee to tai-chi, that would be difficult to match outside the higher education system. Check on university websites to see whether your usual sport is available, but do not be surprised if you come across a new favourite when you have the opportunity to try out something different as a student. Many universities have programmes designed to encourage students to take up a new sport, with expert coaching provided.

All universities are conscious of the need to provide for a spread of ability – and disability. Sports scholarships for elite performers are now commonplace, but there will be plenty of opportunities, too, for beginners. University teams demand a hefty commitment in terms of training and practice sessions – often several times a week – and in many sports standards are high. University teams often compete in local and national leagues.

For those who are looking for competition at a lower level, or whose interests are primarily social, there are thriving internal, or intramural, leagues. These provide opportunities for groups from halls of residence or faculties, or even a group of friends, to form a team and participate on a regular basis. A BUCS survey found 41,000 participants in the intramural programmes of 41 institutions. The largest programme was at the University of Brighton, where more than 6,000 students were playing sports ranging from football, rugby and badminton to softball, orienteering and fencing. Nor is university sport a male preserve – student teams were among the pioneers in mixed sport and are still strong in areas such as women's cricket, football and rugby.

Some universities have cut back sports budgets, but representative sport continues to grow. There are home nations competitions at international level in some sports and in London over 30 institutions take part in the London Universities Sport League. This now involves almost 450 teams – male, female and mixed – competing at a variety of levels in 15 different sports, not all of which are in the main national competitions.

First-year sport

Halls of residence and university-owned flats will often have their own sports teams. At some universities, these are part of the intramural network of leagues, while others have separate arrangements for first years. In such cases, a Sports Captain, elected the year previously as part of the Junior Common Room, takes responsibility for organising trials and picking the teams, as well as arranging fixtures for the year. Hall sport is a great way of meeting like-minded people from your accommodation and over the course of the years, friendly rivalries often develop with other halls or flats. Generally there will be teams for football (five-a-side and 11-a-side), hockey, netball, cricket, tennis, squash, badminton and even golf. If your lodgings are smaller then don't worry, they are often twinned with similar flats to enable as many first-year students as possible to get involved in freshers' sport.

Other opportunities

You may even end up wanting to coach, umpire or referee – and this is another area in which higher education has much to offer. Many university clubs and sports unions provide subsidised courses for students to gain qualifications that may be of use to the individual in later life, as well as benefiting university teams in the short term. Or you might want to try your hand at some sports administration, with an eye to your career. In most universities there is a sports (or athletic) union, with autonomy from the main students' union, which organises matches and looks after the wider interests of those who play. There are plenty of opportunities for those seeking an apprenticeship in the art of running a club, or larger organisation. Solent University, for example, deploys students on volunteer coaching placements in local schools and community groups, working with Southampton FC's Saints Foundation. The placements increase a university's community engagement as well as enhancing student employability.

Universities that excel

A few universities are known particularly for sport. Men's teams from Exeter and Loughborough have played national Premier League hockey, for example, while Bath and Loughborough have teams in the Netball Super League. The University of London women's volleyball team has won the English Volleyball Championships, and "Team Bath" have tasted success in the FA Cup. Several of this elite group had a head start as former physical education colleges. Loughborough, our Sports University of the Year, is undoubtedly the best-known of them, but Leeds Beckett and Brunel are others with a similar pedigree. Other universities with different traditions, such as Bath and East Anglia, also have a variety of outstanding facilities, while the likes of Stirling and Cardiff Metropolitan have the same in a narrower range of sports.

As in so much else, Oxford and Cambridge are in a category of their own. The Boat Race and the Varsity Match (in rugby union) are the only UK university sporting events with a big popular following – although there are varsity matches in many university cities that have become big occasions for students – and there is a good standard of competition in other sports. But you should not assume that success in school sport will be a passport to an Oxbridge place, for the days of special consideration for sporty undergraduates are long gone.

Representative sport

Competitive standards have been rising in university sport, as have the numbers taking part in it. More than 6,000 students competed in eight sports at the 2019 BUCS Nationals in Sheffield. BUCS is the national organisation for higher education sport in the UK, providing a comprehensive, multi-sport competition structure and managing the development of services and facilities for participative, grass-roots sport and healthy campuses, through to high-performance elite athletes. Its mission is to raise the profile of student sport and drive the university sport agenda by influencing government and key stakeholders in the sector.

BUCS (**www.bucs.org.uk**) runs competitions in 47 sports, and ranks participating institutions based on the points earned in the competitive programme. Over 4,700 teams compete in BUCS leagues, making the organisation the largest provider of league sport across Europe. More than a third of those teams are female and many others mixed. There is also international competition in a number of sports, and the World Student Games have become one of the biggest occasions in the international sporting calendar.

British Universities and Colleges Sports (BUCS) league table positions

University	2018–19	2017–18	2016–17	University	2017–18	2016–17	2015–16
Loughborough	1	1	1	Southampton	31	30	32
Nottingham	2	2	4	Strathclyde	32	33	26
Durham	3	3	2	King's College London	33	25	37
Edinburgh	4	6	3	Essex	34	35	34
Exeter	5	4	5	Manchester Met (MMU)	35	34	36
Bath	6	5	6	Brunel	36	43	38
Birmingham	7	8	7	Oxford Brookes	37	38	35
Bristol	8	7	9	East Anglia	38	40	43
Newcastle	9	9	10	Leicester	39	37	39
Northumbria	10	14	8	West of England (UWE)	40	36	28
Stirling	11	11	12	Aberdeen	41	41	50
Oxford	12	15	13	York	42	42	46
Nottingham Trent	13	12	15	East London	43	52	42
Cardiff	14	10	11	Lancaster	44	44	49
Leeds Beckett	15	13	14	Hertfordshire	45	45	45
Cardiff Metropolitan	16	20	21	St Mary's, Twickenham	46	54	47
Sheffield	17	19	19	Plymouth	47	51	51
Swansea	18	17	33	Reading	48	39	44
Leeds	19	24	16	Derby	49	59	57
Cambridge	20	31	18	Kent	50	48	48
Liverpool	21	27	30	Portsmouth	51	47	55
Manchester	22	16	17	Coventry	52	63	52
Bournemouth	23	28	31	Brighton	53	55	61
Warwick	24	26	23	Hartpury University	54	65	=68
Imperial College	25	22	24	Chichester	55	=57	56
St Andrews	26	18	25	Queen Mary, London	56	46	=64
Glasgow	27	21	22	Worcester	57	64	60
University College London	28	23	27	Dundee	58	49	54
Sheffield Hallam	29	32	20	LSE	59	53	53
Surrey	30	29	29	Heriot-Watt	60	62	=64

University	2017–18	2016–17	2015–16	University	2017–18	2016–17	2015–16
Sussex	61	50	41	Sunderland	96	90	99
South Wales	62	60	5	Queen Margaret Edinburgh	97	98	110
De Montfort	63	66	75	Salford	98	93	=101
Royal Holloway	64	=57	62	Northampton	99	100	83
Gloucestershire	65	56	40	Harper Adams	100	94	98
Liverpool John Moores	66	61	66	Queen's, Belfast	101	=127	106
Bangor	67	67	63	Roehampton	102	96	91
Central Lancashire	68	72	67	Bedfordshire	103	110	=95
Solent	69	74	58	UCFB (Football Business)	104	107	116
Robert Gordon	70	70	74	Birmingham City	105	102	109
Aberystwyth	71	69	=68	Highlands and Islands	106	109	112
Lincoln	72	71	73	Teesside	107	=105	103
Hull	73	73	76	Huddersfield	108	101	=101
Anglia Ruskin	74	79	70	Westminster	109	103	114
Chester (Chester)	75	68	72	Buckinghamshire New	110	104	97
City, London	76	77	86	Ulster	111	113	120
Edinburgh Napier	77	80	79	FXU (Falmouth & Exeter Union)	112	121	104
Canterbury Christ Church	78	75	78	Universities at Medway	113	=105	=122
Keele	79	76	77	Bolton	114	114	=136
Plymouth, Marjon	80	78	82	Royal Agricultural University	115	113	115
Wolverhampton	81	97	93	Newman	116	124	118
Middlesex	82	84	81	Leeds Trinity	117	108	107
University of London	83	111	71	Cranfield University	118	115	117
West of Scotland	84	87	=95	Greenwich	119	119	113
Edge Hill	85	81	80	Bath Spa	120	120	119
York St John	86	89	94	Doncaster Coll & Uni centre	121	=127	135
Winchester	87	83	100	St George's, London	122	112	108
Abertay	88	82	85	Royal Veterinary College	123	=117	126
London South Bank	89	92	92	Scotland's Rural College	124	133	–
Staffordshire	90	88	90	Chester (Warrington)	125	=125	130
Bradford	91	95	87	London Metropolitan	126	116	124
Kingston	92	85	84	SOAS	127	=127	132
Aston	93	91	89	Wrexham Glyndŵr	128	=125	=138
Liverpool Hope	94	99	105	Brooksby Melton College	=129	=136	
Glasgow Caledonian	95	86	88	AECC University College	=129	=140	

Compiled from results in league, cup and individual competitions across a range of sports.
Loughborough scored 6,158 to top the table. Cambridge in 20th place scored 1,671.
A further 23 institutions scored less than 20 points on BUCS scale.

University sports facilities

Even the smallest university should provide reasonable indoor and outdoor sports facilities – a sports hall, modern gym equipment and outdoor pitches (usually including an all-weather surface and floodlights). Many will also have a swimming pool and extras such as climbing walls, but some smaller universities make arrangements for students to use local sports centres and clubs when it is not feasible to provide for minority sports. The same goes for the really expensive sports, like golf, which is usually the subject of an arrangement with one or more local clubs that give students a discount. Specialist facilities, like boat houses and climbing huts, obviously depend on location, but the most landlocked university is likely to have a sailing club that organises regular activities away from campus, and a skiing club that runs at least annual trips to the mountains.

Developments at many universities have come in partnership with local authorities or national sporting bodies, which usually give local people some access to the facilities. University campuses are also ideal locations for national coaching centres, and many have been established in recent years. Although elite coaching generally takes place in closed sessions, students may occasionally find themselves rubbing shoulders with star players.

University campuses now boast a significant proportion of the UK's 50-metre pools, for example, the latest of which, at Birmingham and Surrey universities, have some of the most advanced facilities in the country. Innovative schemes include Leeds Beckett's development of the Headingley cricket and rugby league grounds, providing teaching space for students during the week and improved facilities for players and spectators on match days.

Beyond scrutinising the website and prospectus for the extent of university facilities, there are two important questions to ask: how much do they cost and where are they? Neither is easy to track down on the average university website.

How much?

University prospectuses tend to major on the quality of the sports facilities without being as forthcoming about the prices. Students who are used to free (if inferior) facilities at school often get a nasty surprise when they find that they are expected to pay to join the Athletic Union and then pay again to use the gym or play football. Because most university sport is subsidised, the charges are reasonable compared to commercial facilities, but the best deal may require a considerable outlay at the start. Some campus gyms and swimming pools now charge more than £300 a year, for example, which is still considerably cheaper than paying per visit if you intend to use the facilities regularly (and provides an incentive to carry on doing so). Some universities are offering sports facility membership as part of the £9,250 fee, but most offer a variety of peak and off-peak membership packages – some for the entire length of your course.

Outdoor sports are usually charged by the hour, although clubs will also charge a membership fee. You may be required to pay up to £90 for membership of the Athletic Union, although most universities also offer pay-as-you-play options. Fees for intramural sport are seldom substantial; teams will usually pay a fee for the season, while courts for racket sports tend to be marginally cheaper per session than in other clubs.

How far away?

The other common complaint by students is that the playing fields are too far from the campus – understandable in the case of city-centre universities, but still aggravating if you have to arrange your own transport. This is where campus universities have a clear advantage. For the rest, there has to be some trade-off between the quality of outdoor facilities and the distance you have to travel to use them. But universities are beginning to realise that long journeys depress usage of important (and expensive) facilities, and some have tried to find suitable land closer to lectures and halls of residence. Indoor sports centres should all be within easy reach.

Sport as a degree subject

Sports science and other courses associated with sport had seen consistent increases in applications until the imposition of higher fees, and their popularity has now returned. Nearly 15,000 students started courses in 2018, making it one of the eight most popular degree choices. A separate ranking for the subject is on page 274. If you are hoping to be rewarded with an academic qualification for three years on the sports field, you will be disappointed because there is serious science involved.

However, sport is a growing employment field and one that demands qualifications like any other. It is even spawning whole new higher education institutions. The University College of Football Business (UCFB) is already offering undergraduate degrees at Wembley Stadium, its original home at Burnley's Turf Moor ground, and at the Etihad Stadium, in Manchester. And now Gary Neville, the former Manchester United captain and television pundit, has opened University Academy '92, in Manchester, in partnership with Lancaster University, offering sport, business and media degrees.

Many degrees in the sports area focus on management, with careers in the leisure industry in mind – golf course management, for example, has proved popular with students despite being a target of those who see anything beyond the traditional academic portfolio as "dumbing down". The question is not whether the courses are up to standard, but whether a less specialised one will offer more career flexibility if a decline in popularity for the particular sport limits future opportunities.

Sports scholarships

The number and range of sports scholarships have expanded just as rapidly as courses in the subject, but the two are usually not connected. Sports scholarships are for elite performers, regardless of what they are studying – indeed, they exist at universities with barely any degrees in the area. Imported from the USA, scholarships now exist in an array of sports. At Birmingham University, for example, there are specialist golf awards (as there are at a number of other universities) and a scholarship for triathletes, as well as others open to any sport.

The value of scholarships varies considerably – sometimes according to individual prowess. The Royal and Ancient scholarships for golfers, for example, range from £500 for promising handicap golfers to £10,000 for full internationals, and are available at 17 universities. All of them demand that you meet the normal entrance requirements for your course and maintain the necessary academic standards, as well as progressing in your sport. In practice, most departments will be flexible about attendance and deadlines, as long as you make your requests well in advance.

Many sports scholarships offer benefits in kind, in the form of coaching, equipment or access to facilities. The Government-funded Talented Athlete Scholarship Scheme (TASS), which is restricted to students at English universities who have achieved national recognition at under-18 level and are eligible to represent England in one of 32 different sports, is one such example. No fewer than 165 current or former TASS athletes took part in the Rio Olympics and Paralympics, winning 78 medals, 35 of them gold. The scholarships are worth £3,500 a year and can be put towards expenses such as competition and training costs, equipment or mentoring. In 2018–19, more than 600 student athletes were supported across a wide range of sports.

The Scottish equivalent, Winning Students Scotland, awards scholarships worth up to £6,000 a year for training, competition fees and other expenses such as student accommodation. Further details of the two schemes are available at **www.tass.gov.uk** and **www.winningstudents-scotland.ac.uk**.

Leading performers in many sports still look first to US universities – often unfamiliar ones – for sports scholarships. In some sports, such as American football or basketball, this is the main route into professional sport, while in others it may provide bigger awards – and in some cases better coaching – than are available in the UK. Half of the UK's six-strong tennis team at the 2017 World Student Games were from US universities, including Clemson University, in South Carolina, and the University of North Florida – neither of them household names on this side of the Atlantic. For the most promising athletes, US scholarships can cover the full cost of university; for others they may be worth only a few thousand dollars, but may make the difference in gaining admission. Further details are available at **www.fulbright.org.uk/study-in-the-usa/undergraduate-study/funding/sports-scholarships**.

Part-time work

University sports centres are an excellent source of term-time (and out-of-term) employment. You may also be trained in first aid, fire safety, customer care and risk assessment – all useful skills for future employment. The experience will help you secure employment in commercial or local authority facilities – and even for jobs such as stewarding at football grounds and music venues. Most universities also have a sabbatical post in the Athletic Union or similar body, a paid position with responsibility for organising university sport and representing the sporting community within the university.

10 How Parents Can Help

Parents have become much more active in recent years both during the admissions process for higher education and when their children are at university. For a time, this was dismissed as 'helicopter parenting' by a generation who could not accept their children becoming adults, but growing concerns about mental health in young people and a succession of tragic incidents in universities have changed attitudes markedly. There is still a fine line between support and meddling, but it is a balance that every parent wants to get right – and naturally the same applies to step-parents and guardians.

Most students are adults, capable of making their own decisions, but they may still welcome help and advice, especially if it is their first foray beyond the family home. Two-thirds of students would be happy for their university to share concerns with parents or a trusted adult if there were "extreme" problems, according to a recent survey, and a further 15% thought universities should be able to contact parents in "any circumstances" where there were mental health worries. Of course, every family is different and individual relationships will determine how much help is required. But many parents take an active role in selecting courses, may have their say subsequently on the quality of the student experience – and contribute large sums towards their children's time at university.

The introduction of £9,000 fees was meant to make the student responsible for his or her higher education – including paying for it – but parents' involvement has, if anything, increased under the current system. That is because most parents are paying towards students' living costs, not their tuition. Maintenance loans may be larger than they were, but very few students will get by on them alone. For undergraduates outside London, they range from £8,944 for students with a family income below £25,000 to £4,168 with a family income above £65,000 for 2019–20. Those parents who can, are often anxious to spare their children yet more debt on top of the cost of tuition. Surprising numbers of students from affluent families are not taking out loans at all and are relying instead on support from parents or sometimes grandparents. Up to half the students at some leading universities are doing without Government maintenance loans, although throughout England, well over 80% are taking them up.

Nearly half of all parents in the UK think university is now poor value for money, according to a survey by HSBC. But a larger proportion also believe that higher education is essential to their children's career prospects and are willing to help them through it. Nine out of ten expect to make a financial contribution to their children's time at university – and to spend up to eight years paying off the debts they incur in the process.

Operating the "bank of mum and dad" may be the most indispensable role played by parents, but there are plenty of others, from chauffeur on open days to cookery coach in anticipation of their first experience of living away from home. The scale of parental involvement naturally depends on individual relationships, but the right advice and encouragement before, during and after the selection process can be invaluable. Many parents have been to university themselves and will be more adept than a teenager at reading between the lines of a self-congratulatory prospectus or website. But it is important to remember who is going to be the student and not to allow your own (inevitably dated) preconceptions to muddy the waters. Those who are not graduates are just as capable of doing the necessary research to offer a second opinion on universities and courses.

Laying the ground

The first thing any parent can do to smooth the path to university is to be encouraging about the value of higher education. Ideally, this should have started long before the application process, but it is especially important at this point. Now that student debt and variable graduate employment prospects have become frequent media topics, it is only natural for sixth-formers and others to have second thoughts about higher education.

The lure of a regular wage packet will be tempting, should one be available, and there are plenty of young people who are not suited to full-time higher education. More big companies are choosing to employ promising 18-year-olds, rather than rely entirely on graduate recruitment, and there has been a rapid development of higher-level apprenticeships. Even after the years of enormous university expansion, most people still do not go to university. Nevertheless, those who are capable of going generally do not regret the decision. Many people look back on their student days as the best period of their life, as well as the one that shaped their personality and their career. Given the right choice of course, time as a student should still pay off for the individual in terms of lifetime earnings, as well as personal development. A little reassurance at this stage may make all the difference.

Making the choice

Any parent wants to help a son or daughter through the difficult business of choosing where and what to study. How big a role you play will depend on a number of factors, not the least of which is the extent to which your advice is wanted. If the quality of advice available at school or college is good, parental involvement may be marginal. But often that is not the case, and you may have to call on other resources, including your own research. Avoid second-hand opinions gleaned through the media or dinner party gossip. You may think that some subjects are a sure-fire route to lucrative employment, while others are shunned by employers, but are you right? And do you really know the strengths and weaknesses of more than 100 universities? Above all, do not try to rewind your own career decisions through your children. The fact that you enjoyed – or hated – a subject or a university does not mean that they will. You may have always regretted missing out on the chance to go to Oxbridge or to become a brain surgeon, but they have their own lives to lead. Many students who switch courses or drop out complain that they were pressured into their original choice by their parents. The tables in chapters 1 and 3 offer a reality check, but even they cannot take account of the differences within institutions. The subject tables in chapter 13 show that the best graduate employment rates are often not at the obvious universities.

Parents are encouraged by many schools and colleges to play an active role in the process of choosing a course. At the most basic (but vital) level, this means keeping an eye on deadlines, but it is also about acting as a sounding board and trying to guide your child towards the right university and course. Check that choices are being made for sensible reasons, not on the basis of questionable gossip or trivial criteria. But beyond that, you should stay in the background unless there is a very good reason to play a more substantive role. Make a point of looking for important aspects of university life that the applicant might miss. Security, for example, usually does not feature near the top of a teenager's list of priorities; likewise, other practical issues, such as the proximity of student accommodation to lectures, the library and the students' union.

Many universities now publish guides specifically for parents and put on programmes for them at Open Days. The latter may be a way of separating prospective applicants from their more demanding "minders", but the programmes themselves can be interesting and informative. Do not worry that you will be an embarrassment by attending Open Days – many thousands of parents do so, and you may add a critical edge to the proceedings. Like prospectuses, Open Days are part of the sales process, and it is easy for a sixth-former to be carried away by the excitement surrounding a lively university campus. You are much more likely to spot the defects – even if they are ignored in the final decision. The Open Days in 2020 that had been announced at the time of going to press are included alongside each university's profile, in Chapter 15. The website **www.opendays.com** also provides a calendar of these events. As Open Days at popular institutions are often on the same day, providing assistance in planning visits is important. Where there is a clash, universities and individual departments are always happy for prospective applicants to visit on another occasion. Ring ahead or email the department to see if an academic will be available to answer questions.

Most of today's sixth-formers and college students seem happy to have their parents' help and advice – even if they do not take it in the end. Research by the Knowledge Partnership consultancy found that more than half of the parents of first-year undergraduates felt they had exerted some influence on their children's choices of university and course, although only about 7% characterised this as "a lot".

UCAS also publishes its own guide for parents, offering useful tips and outlining the deadlines that applicants will have to meet. The school should be on top of the timing and offering the necessary advice, but there is no harm in providing a little back-up, especially on parts of the process that take time and thought, such as writing the personal statement. There is little a parent can do as the offers and/or rejections come rolling in, other than to be supportive. If the worst happens and there is a full set of rejections, you may have to start the advice process all over again for a new round of applications through UCAS Extra. If so, a cool head is even more necessary, but the same principles apply.

Results Day

Then, before you know it, results day is upon you. Make sure you are at home, rather than in some isolated holiday retreat. Your son or daughter needs to have access to instant advice at school or college, and to be able to contact universities straight away if Clearing or Adjustment is required. And your moral support will be much more effective face-to-face, rather than down a telephone line. Whatever happens, try not to transmit the anxiety that you will inevitably be feeling to your son or daughter, especially if the results are not what was wanted. It is easy to make rash decisions about re-sitting exams or rejecting an insurance offer in the heat of the moment. Try to slow the process down and encourage clear and realistic thinking. Make sure you know in advance what might be required, such as where to access Clearing lists, and if Clearing or Adjustment is being used, you will need to be on hand to offer advice and help with visits to possible universities. For most applicants, Clearing or Adjustment is all but over in a week, so the agony should be short-lived.

Before they go

Little more than a month after the tension of results day, everything should be ready for the start of term. Unless your son or daughter chooses to stay at home to study – as one in five now does, either in their own or their parents' home – there will be forms to fill in to secure university accommodation, as well as student loans to sort out and registration to complete. You can perform useful services, like supplying recipe books if the first year is to be spent in self-catering accommodation, but now is the time for independence to become reality. Make sure that important details like insurance are not forgotten, but otherwise stand clear.

Then it is just a matter of agreeing a budget, assuming you are in a position to make a financial contribution. How large that contribution is will depend on family circumstances and your attitude to independent living. Some parents want to ensure that their children leave university debt-free; others could never afford to do that. The important thing is that students and parents know where they stand.

Student finance and parental involvement

After a mortgage, a university degree can be the most significant debt families have to repay, according to HSBC. The debt usually combines student loans for tuition fees and maintenance and is repayable only when a graduate is paid £25,000 a year and can never amount to more than 9% of his or her salary above that threshold. The immediate priority, however, is budgeting for the cost of living, which the National Student Money Survey puts at £806 a month on average, ranging from £650 a month in Wales to £900 in London.

Hundreds of thousands of undergraduates – particularly mature students – pay their own way through university. Many undergraduates of all ages supplement their income with term-time and vacation jobs. But every survey shows that families play an important (and growing) role where students move straight from school to higher education. Nearly three-quarters of all students receive some money from their parents, and roughly half say the family contribution is crucial to their ability to afford a university education.

Costs are likely to be higher if the choice is an overseas university, although most American institutions have generous scholarships and employment opportunities. Even so, HSBC found that most parents were prepared to pay more for the experience, although they would prefer that their children stayed closer to home.

A frank discussion on what the family can afford is essential before the student leaves home. It is all too easy for a young person who has never had to budget for themselves to get into financial difficulties in the social whirl that is the first term of a degree course. In the worst cases, this can lead to excessive term-time employment to keep up with spiralling debts and pressures that contribute towards a student dropping out.

After they've left

Any new student is going to be nervous if he or she is leaving home for the first time and having to settle into a strange environment. But in most cases, it is not going to last long because everyone is in the same boat and freshers' weeks hardly leave time for homesickness. Students will not want to let their apprehension show. The people who are most likely to be emotional are the parents – especially if they are left with an empty nest for the first time. It can take a while to get used to an orderly, quiet house after all those years of mayhem.

Resist any temptation to decorate a student's bedroom and turn it into an office – it is more common than you might think, and psychologists say it can do lasting damage to family relationships. Keep in touch by phone, text or email, but try not to pry. You're not going to be told everything anyway – which is probably just as well. They will be back soon enough and, just as you were getting used to having the place to yourself, a weekend visit or the Christmas vacation will remind you how life used to be. If things are not going smoothly at university, this may be the time for reassurance – more students drop out at Christmas of their first year than any other time.

Keeping in contact

Growing numbers of parents now want to play their part in ensuring that their children get value for money at university, but there is a fine line between constructive involvement and unwelcome interference. Universities report that anxious mothers and fathers are more inclined than ever to question what their children are getting for their now substantial fees. There have been stories of parents challenging not just the amount and quality of tuition, but even the marking of essays and exams. The phenomenon, first reported in the USA, has given rise to the phrase "helicopter parents" – so called because they hover over their children's education when they should be letting go. No one wants to think of themselves in that category, but it is not surprising – or reprehensible – that parents are taking more of an interest.

One of the reasons that some overstep the mark is that they are shocked that the amount of teaching and size of seminar groups are not what they recall from their own "free" higher education. The new fees were meant to herald improvements in the student experience, including more contact hours, but these have been marginal in most universities. It may be that fewer and larger seminars are here to stay in the arts and social sciences, where almost all state support for teaching was withdrawn, and more learning opportunities will be provided online.

An associated reason for greater parental involvement is that family relationships have changed. Many teenage applicants are glad to accept a lift to an open day to get a second opinion on a university and their prospective course. They are also more likely than previous generations of students to come home at the weekend – or to live there in the first place – and to air any grievances. It is up to each family to decide when parental intervention is justified – and would be welcomed. Universities are in a difficult position when such intervention takes place; traditionally, they have only been prepared to deal with students, not parents. But recent tragic cases have encouraged greater flexibility.

The majority of students will go through their time at university without major mishaps, but parents are often the first to spot signs of unhappiness. They should not be afraid to discuss it and, if necessary, take things further with the university. Most students' unions, as well as universities themselves, have professional counselling services that are a good starting point.

Useful websites

Many universities have sections on their websites for parents of prospective students.
UCAS has a Parents section and a guide on its website:
www.ucas.com/ucas/undergraduate/getting-started/ucas-undergraduate-parents-and-guardians
To find out more about open days, visit: **www.opendays.com**

11 Going Abroad to University

Just as British students were beginning to get a taste for foreign study, Brexit has come along to complicate the issues. For the moment (as far as the 2020–21 academic year), the saga should have no impact, even for those contemplating a spell at a Continental university. But it has introduced a note of uncertainty which may put a dent in the growing numbers choosing to widen their horizons.

Students from the UK were late to the party that has attracted millions of their counterparts in other countries to go abroad for part or all of a degree. Poor linguistic skills, the cost, and the availability of good universities at home have all kept the numbers down. UK universities are second only to those in the US in all the international rankings and, at present at least, there are plenty of places available.

There is evidence, however, that going abroad, even for part of a degree, may be good for future career prospects. Surveys can exaggerate the impact because the minority who choose to go abroad – and can afford to do so – may be more outgoing and have other advantages in any case. Nevertheless, one report found that UK students who study abroad are 9% more likely to gain a 1st or 2:1 degree and 24% less likely to be unemployed after they graduate.

Ever since £9,000 fees were introduced, there has been speculation that more students would apply to universities on the Continent, where the equivalent charges are low or even non-existent. Schools say that many more sixth-formers have been considering it and the numbers going abroad as part of a UK degree have grown by 50% in recent years, topping 30,000. But France still has three times as many studying abroad and Germany more than four times as many, according to UNESCO. Nepal, with half the UK's population, has roughly the same number of students overseas.

The Government and universities themselves have been encouraging students to take advantage of overseas opportunities but, even before Brexit takes place, the predicted surge in applications to European universities has not really materialised. There has been an increase in the numbers going to universities in the USA, where the fees gap has narrowed, at least with state universities, but it is still very much a minority pursuit. There were over 11,000 UK students at US universities last year, but many were postgraduates and/or the children of Britons working on that side of the Atlantic.

Research by the British Council has shown that one student in three is interested in some form of overseas study. And there is now a wide range of opportunities for them to consider. Some universities have international summer schools and many degrees include the opportunity of a semester or a year abroad, either studying or with an employer.

Some of the obstacles that have held British students back are now being removed. The maximum fee for a year abroad while studying at a UK university is £1,385, for example, and many universities are charging less than that. But there is still one important disincentive to taking a full degree overseas: although support from the Student Loans Company continues for a year abroad during a UK degree course, it is not available for degrees from non-UK institutions.

Universities in some countries – notably the Netherlands and the USA – now mount frequent recruitment campaigns in the UK. Numbers of British students have been rising sharply at Dutch universities, where fees in 2020/21 will be little more than €2,100 for most courses, but they still account for only about 1,000 of the 2.5-million student population. How Brexit will affect fees for UK students in the Netherlands and other EU countries in the long term is not yet clear. The normal fees for international students are between €800 a year for arts degrees and €32,000 for medicine.

Leading independent schools report serious interest in American universities and attendance at the Fulbright Commission's recruitment fairs continues to rise, but the numbers enrolling remain modest, despite attractive incentives in the form of scholarships, bursaries and campus employment opportunities.

Nevertheless, it would be surprising if high fees at home and an increasingly international graduate labour market did not encourage continuing growth in overseas study. Most students who go abroad are motivated by a desire to study at a "world-class" institution, according to a study commissioned by the Government. Often the trigger is failure to win a place at a leading UK university and being unwilling to settle for second best. Other motivations include a desire for adventure and a belief that overseas study might lead to an international career. The question is how to judge a university that may be thousands of miles from home against more familiar names in the UK. This chapter will make some suggestions, including the use of the growing number of global rankings that are available online.

It is possible to have your academic cake and eat it by going on an international exchange or work placement organised by a UK university, or even to attend a British university in another country. Nottingham University has campuses in China and Malaysia; Middlesex can offer Dubai or Mauritius, where students registered in the UK can take part or all of their degree. Other universities, such as Liverpool, also have joint ventures with overseas institutions which offer an international experience (in China, in Liverpool's case) and degrees from both universities.

In most cases, however, an overseas study experience means a foreign university – through a partnership with a UK institution. Until recently, this was usually for a postgraduate degree – and there are still strong arguments for spending your undergraduate years in the UK before going abroad for more advanced study. Older students taking more specialised programmes may get more out of an extended period overseas than those who go at 18 and, since first degrees in the UK are shorter than elsewhere, it may also be the more cost-effective option.

If cost is the main consideration, however, even the generally longer courses at Continental universities can work out cheaper than a degree in the UK. The main obstacle, apart from British students' traditional reluctance to take degrees anywhere else, concerns the language barrier. Although there are now thousands of postgraduate courses taught in English at

Continental universities, first-degree programmes are still much thinner on the ground. A few universities, like Maastricht and others in the Netherlands, are offering a wide range of subjects in English. But most European universities teach undergraduates in the host language – and, up to now, that has always deterred UK students.

The obvious alternative lies in American, Australian and Canadian universities, all of which are keen to attract more international students. Here, cost and distance are the main obstacles. Four-year courses add considerably to the cost of affordable-looking fees, while the state of the pound has been another serious disadvantage. Add in the natural reluctance of most 18-year-olds to commit to life on the other side of the world (or even just the Atlantic), and the prospect of a dramatic increase in student emigration is considerably reduced.

Where do students go to?

There is remarkably little official monitoring of how many students leave the UK, let alone where they go. But it seems that for all the economic advantages of studying in Continental Europe, the USA remains by far the most popular student destination. Most surveys put Canada, France and Germany, Ireland and Australia as the biggest attractions outside the USA.

A few British students find their way to unexpected locations, like South Korea or Slovakia, but usually for family reasons or to study the language. The figures suggest that British students are more attracted to countries that are familiar or close at hand, and where they can speak English. Many are doubtless planning to stay in their adopted country after they graduate, although visa regulations may make this difficult.

Studying in Europe

More than 10,000 UK students now attend Continental European universities and colleges, according to UNESCO. But international statistics pick up those whose parents emigrated or are working abroad, as well as those who actually leave the UK to take a degree. A minority are undergraduates, if only because the availability of courses taught in English is so much greater at postgraduate level.

The increased interest in Continental universities arises both from the generally low fees they charge and from the growth in the number of courses offered in English. Some countries charge no fees at all, even to international students, and public universities in the European Union are obliged to charge other member countries' students the same as local residents, as well as allowing them to get a job while studying.

At present, undergraduates can study at a French university for €170 a year but, not surprisingly, nearly all first degrees are taught in French. Little more than 100 programmes taught in English and listed on the Campus France website (**www. campusfrance.org/en**) are at the Licence (Bachelors equivalent) level – and many of them have some teaching in French. Germany is much the same, despite attracting large numbers of international students. The DAAD website (**www.daad.de/en**) lists 235 undergraduate programmes taught wholly or mainly in English, but many are at private universities like Jacobs University in Bremen, which charges €20,000 a year. There are cheaper alternatives in the public sector, where tuition fees have been abolished, but they remain relatively scarce.

Any potential saving has to be considered with care. In spite of the Bologna process – an intergovernmental agreement which means that degrees across Europe are becoming more similar in content and duration – most Continental courses are longer than their UK equivalents, adding to the cost and to your lost earnings from attending university. And, of course, you will have higher travel costs. It is harder to generalise about the cost of living. It can be lower than the UK in southern Europe, but frighteningly high in Scandinavia.

Obviously, the cost of an international experience and the commitment involved is much reduced if you opt for an exchange scheme or other scheme arranged by a UK university, many of which have partners all over the world. There are opportunities for everything from a summer school of less than a month to a full year abroad, and a number of universities now have targets to increase the numbers taking advantage of such schemes.

The most common offering has been the EU's Erasmus scheme, which funds exchanges of between three months and a year, the work counting towards your degree. More than 2 million students throughout Europe have used the scheme, and there are 2,000 universities to choose from in 30 countries. It is uncertain whether UK students will have access to the scheme after Brexit but, for the moment at least, applications are made through universities' international offices, and must be approved by the UK university as well as by the Erasmus administrators. Erasmus students do not pay any extra fees and they are eligible for grants to cover the extra expense of travelling and living in another country.

Studying in America

American universities remain the first choice of British students going abroad to take a degree, just as the UK is the first choice for Americans. Regardless of any special relationship, this is not surprising since international rankings consistently show US and UK universities to be the best in the world (as well as teaching in English). Around half of the British students taking courses in the USA are undergraduates.

Already by far the most popular student destination, the attractions of an American degree have multiplied since fees trebled in England. The Fulbright Commission, which promotes American higher education, has seen a 30% increase in the number of Britons taking US university entrance exams. Even before the latest rise in UK fees, the top American universities had seen demand rise sharply, and this is spreading to universities further down the rankings.

The sheer depth of the US university system means that if you are thinking of studying abroad, the USA is almost bound to be on the list of possibilities. Tuition fees at Ivy League institutions are notoriously high – Harvard's are $47,730 in 2019–20 and the university put the full cost of attendance at $73,500 a year – but generous student aid programmes ensure

Top Ten destinations for UK undergraduates studying abroad

			Best Student Cities in the World	
1	United States	10,316	1 London	United Kingdom
2	Netherlands	2,723	2 Tokyo	Japan
3	Germany	2,255	3 Melbourne	Australia
4	Australia	2,235	4 Munich	Germany
5	France	2,139	5 Berlin	Germany
6	Canada	1,668	6 Montreal	Canada
7	Ireland	1,427	7 Paris	France
8	Spain	995	8 Zurich	Switzerland
9	Denmark	947	9 Sydney	Australia
10	Bulgaria	890	10 Seoul	South Korea

Source: 2018 Unesco figures

QS ranking 2019

that most pay far less than the "sticker price". Outside the Ivy League, the fee gap for UK students was narrowing, but fees at many state universities have shot up in the last few years as politicians have tried to balance the books. Texas A&M University, for example, ranked in the top 200 in the world, puts undergraduates' total costs at $54,000. Fees are $26,851 at the State University of New York, although the university puts the average cost for those living on campus at $34,348. Only at much lower-ranked state universities do the costs compare with those in the UK. At South Dakota State University, for example, fees and living costs are estimated to be less than $12,000 a year for undergraduates.

The individual systems of state universities and private universities mean that there is a great variation in the financial support given to international students. Fulbright advises students considering a US degree to assess and negotiate a funding package at the same time as pursuing their application. Otherwise, they may end up with a place they cannot afford, losing valuable time in the quest for a more suitable one.

Which countries are best?

Anyone going abroad to study will be in search of a memorable and valuable all-round experience, not just a good course. Most international students are motivated by location – both the country and the city in which a university is based – as well as by the reputation of the institution. QS publishes an annual ranking of student cities, based on quality of life indicators as well as the number of places at world-ranked universities. London topped the ranking in 2019, with Tokyo second, Melbourne third and Munich fourth.

Many Asian countries are looking to recruit more foreign students, both as part of a broader internationalisation agenda and to compensate for falling numbers of potential students at home. Japan is a case in point. The high cost of living may put off many potential students, as may the unfamiliarity of its language, but more support is being offered to attract foreign students and more courses are being taught in English. However, as with any non-English speaking country, the language of instruction is only part of the story. You will need to know enough of the local language to manage the shops and the transport system, and, of course, to make friends and get the most out of being there.

Another option of growing interest is China, although Western students are often put off by the dormitory accommodation that is the norm at most universities. The country has already grown massively in importance. Its university system is growing in quality, with the leading institutions climbing the world rankings and improving their facilities. Familiarity with China is unlikely to be a career disadvantage for anyone in the 21st century. Until the recent disturbances, many saw Hong Kong, which has several world-ranked universities and a familiar feel for Britons, as the perfect alternative to mainland Chinese universities.

Will my degree be recognised?

Even in the era of globalisation, you need to bear in mind that not all degrees are equal. At one extreme is the MBA, which has an international system for accrediting courses, and a global admissions standard. But with many professional courses, study abroad is a potential hazard. To work as a doctor, engineer or lawyer in the UK, you need a qualification which the relevant professional body will recognise. It is understandable that to practise law in England, you need to have studied the English legal system. For other subjects, the issues are more to do with the quality and content of courses outside UK control.

There are ways of researching this issue in advance. One is to contact NARIC, the National Recognition Centre for the UK (**www.naric.org.uk**). NARIC exists to examine the compatibility and acceptability of qualifications from around the world. The other approach is to ask the UK professional body in question – maybe an engineering institution, the relevant law society or the general teaching, medical or dental councils – about the qualification you propose to study for.

Which are the best universities?

Going abroad to study is a big and expensive decision, and you want to get it right. Whether your ultimate aim is to become an internationally mobile high-flyer, or simply to broaden your experience, you will want to know that the university you are going to is taken seriously around the world.

At the moment, there are three main systems for ranking universities internationally. One is run by QS (Quacquarelli Symonds), an educational research company based in London (**www.topuniversities.com**). Another is by Shanghai Ranking Consultancy, a company set up by Shanghai Jiao Tong University, in China, and is called the Academic Ranking of World Universities (ARWU) (**www.shanghairanking.com**). The third is produced by *Times Higher Education* (**www.timeshighereducation.com/world-university-rankings**), a weekly magazine with no connection to *The Times*, which published the QS version until 2010.

There are several more international ranking systems that an online search might throw up, but most are either specialist – like the Webometrics ranking of universities' web activity – or limited in their readership and influence. Some are still developing: the European Commission's U-Multirank (www.umultirank.org), for example, remains limited in the subjects it covers, but may become a more widely-used source of information in time.

The QS system uses a number of measures including academic opinion, employer opinion, international orientation, research impact and staff/student ratio to create its listing, while the ARWU uses measures such as Nobel Prizes and highly-cited papers, which are more related to excellence in scientific research. *Times Higher Education* added a number of measures to the QS model, including research income and a controversial global survey of teaching quality.

Naturally, the different methodologies produce some contrasting results – the three main rankings each have a different university at the top, for example. The table on these pages is a composite of the three main rankings, which places Stanford at the top and includes three UK universities in the top ten. In practice, however, if you go to a university that features strongly in any of the tables, you will be at a place that is well-regarded around the world. After all, even the 200th university on any of these rankings is an elite institution in a world with more than 5,000 universities.

The main international rankings focus mainly on research and tend to favour universities which are good at science and medicine. Places that specialise in the humanities and the social sciences, such as the London School of Economics, can appear in deceptively modest positions. In addition, the rankings look at universities in the round, and contain only limited information on specific subjects. QS published the first 26 global subject rankings in 2011 and has since increased this to 42. One advantage of the QS ranking system is that 10% of a university's possible score comes from a global survey of recruiters, so this column of the table provides some idea of where the major employers like to hire. Note that the author of this *Guide* has a role in developing the QS rankings.

Top Universities in the World

Rank	(Last year)	Institution	Country
2020	**(2019)**		
1	**(1)**	Stanford University	USA
2	**(2)**	Massachusetts Institute of Technology (MIT)	USA
3	**(3)**	Harvard University	USA
4	**(5)**	University of Oxford	UK
5	**(4)**	University of Cambridge	UK
6	**(6)**	California Institute of Technology (Caltech)	USA
7	**(7)**	Princeton University	USA
8	**(8)**	University of Chicago	USA
9	**(9)**	Yale University	USA
=10	**(10)**	ETH Zurich (Swiss Federal Institute of Technology)	Switzerland
=10	**(=12)**	UCL (University College London)	UK
=12	**(=12)**	Imperial College London	UK
=12	**(11)**	Columbia University	USA
14	**(=15)**	University of Pennsylvania	USA
=15	**(14)**	Cornell University	USA
=15	**(=15)**	University of California, Berkeley (UCB)	USA
17	**(17)**	Johns Hopkins University	USA
18	**(19)**	University of Michigan	USA
19	**(18)**	University of California, Los Angeles (UCLA)	USA
20	**(21)**	University of Toronto	Canada
21	**(20)**	Duke University	USA
22	**(22)**	University of Edinburgh	UK
=23	**(=23)**	Tsinghua University	China
=23	**(=23)**	Northwestern University	USA
25	**(26)**	The University of Tokyo	Japan
26	**(25)**	University of California, San Diego (UCSD)	USA
27	**(27)**	New York University (NYU)	USA
28	**(=30)**	Peking University	China
29	**(32)**	National University of Singapore (NUS)	Singapore
30	**(28)**	University of Washington	USA
31	**(29)**	University of Melbourne	Australia
32	**(=30)**	University of Manchester	UK
=33	**(34)**	King's College London (KCL)	UK
=33	**(35)**	University of British Columbia	Canada
35	**(36)**	Kyoto University	Japan
36	**(45)**	Nanyang Technological University (NTU)	Singapore
=37	**(37)**	Ecole Polytechnique Fédérale de Lausanne (EPFL)	Switzerland
=37	**(33)**	University of Wisconsin-Madison	USA
39	**(=40)**	Ludwig-Maximilians-Universität München	Germany
40	**(39)**	University of Texas at Austin	USA
=41	**(38)**	Australian National University (ANU)	Australia

Rank	(Last year)	Institution	Country
=41	(42)	Technische Universität München	Germany
43	(44)	Ruprecht-Karls-Universität Heidelberg	Germany
=44	(48)	University of Hong Kong (HKU)	Hong Kong
=44	(=46)	University of Illinois at Urbana-Champaign	USA
=46	(=40)	McGill University	Canada
=46	(52)	The University of Queensland (UQ)	Australia
48	(=46)	Carnegie Mellon University	USA
49	(49)	London School of Economics and Political Science (LSE)	UK
50	(53)	Washington University in St. Louis	USA
51	(=50)	University of North Carolina, Chapel Hill	USA
=52	(54)	The Hong Kong University of Science and Technology (HKUST)	Hong Kong
=52	(57)	Karolinska Institute, Stockholm	Sweden
54	(=50)	The University of Sydney	Australia
55	(=63)	Brown University	USA
=56	—	Université PSL (Paris Sciences & Lettres)	France
=56	(=63)	University of Copenhagen	Denmark
58	(60)	University of Bristol	UK
59	(56)	Sorbonne University	France
60	(59)	Seoul National University (SNU)	South Korea
61	(61)	The Chinese University of Hong Kong (CUHK)	Hong Kong
=62	(=73)	Monash University	Australia
=62	(58)	University of California, Santa Barbara (UCSB)	USA
64	—	The University of New South Wales (UNSW)	Australia
65	(66)	Katholieke Universiteit Leuven	Belgium
=66	(65)	Delft University of Technology	Netherlands
=66	(70)	University of Southern California	USA
68	(62)	University of Minnesota	USA
69	(69)	University of California, San Francisco	USA
=70	(=77)	Zhejiang University	China
=70	(71)	Utrecht University	Netherlands
=72	(67	University of Amsterdam	Netherlands
=72	(68)	University of Zurich	Switzerland
74	(=77)	Boston University	USA
75	(72)	Rockefeller University	USA
=76	(=73)	University of Maryland, College Park	USA
=76	(=85)	Erasmus University, Rotterdam	Netherlands
=78	(84)	University of Groningen	Netherlands
=78	(83)	Université de Paris-Sud	France
=80	(76)	The University of Warwick	UK
=80	(79)	University of Colorado at Boulder	USA
82	—	Fudan University	China
=83	(=80)	KAIST – Korea Advanced Institute of Science and Technology	South Korea
=83	(=96)	Shanghai Jiao Tong University	China
85	(91)	University of California, Davis (UCD)	USA

86	(=80)	Leiden University	Netherlands
=87	(93)	City University of Hong Kong	Hong Kong
=87	—	Ecole Polytechnique	France
=89	(=94)	Tokyo Institute of Technology	Japan
=89	(92)	University of Helsinki	Finland
=89	(=96)	University of Geneva	Switzerland
=92	(=73)	Purdue University	USA
=92	—	University of Oslo	Norway
=92	(=94)	Wageningen University	Netherlands
95	—	Aarhus University	Denmark
96	(=99)	McMaster University	Canada
97	(=87)	Uppsala University	Sweden
98	(98)	University of Glasgow	UK
99	(=85)	Pennsylvania State University	USA
100	—	University of Science and Technology	China

Averaged from positions in the QS World University Ranking (QS), the Academic Ranking of World Universities (ARWU) and *Times Higher Education* (THE) for 2019

Other options for overseas studies

For the growing numbers who want to study abroad without committing themselves to a complete degree, a number of options are available. A language degree will typically involve a year abroad, and a look at the UCAS website will show many options for studying another subject alongside your language of choice. UK universities offer degrees in information technology, science, business and even journalism with a major language such as Chinese.

Many degrees offer a year abroad, either studying or in a work placement, even to those who are not taking a language. At Aston University, for example, 70% of students do a year's work placement and a growing number do so abroad. China and Chile have been among recent destinations. Other universities offer the opportunity to take shorter credit-bearing courses with partner institutions overseas. American universities are again the most popular choice. The best approach is to decide what you want to study and then see if there is a UK university that offers it as a joint degree or with a placement abroad. Make sure that all the universities involved are well-regarded, for example by looking at their rankings on one or other of the websites of global rankings.

Useful websites

Prospects: studying abroad: **www.prospects.ac.uk/postgraduate-study/study-abroad**
Association of Commonwealth Universities: **www.acu.ac.uk**
Campus France: **www.campusfrance.org/en**
College Board (USA): **www.collegeboard.org**
DAAD (for Germany): **www.daad.de/en**
Study in Holland: **www.studyinholland.co.uk**
Education Ireland: **www.educationinireland.com/en**
Erasmus Programme (EU): **www.erasmusplus.org.uk**
Finaid (USA): **www.finaid.org**
Fulbright Commission: **www.fulbright.org.uk**
Study in Australia: **www.studyinaustralia.gov.au**
Study in Canada: **www.studyincanada.com**

12 Coming to the UK to Study

International students have continued to come to the UK in large numbers, despite the uncertainties created by Brexit. Those from other parts of the European Union have been guaranteed that fee levels and access to loans will remain unchanged for courses beginning in 2020, but no decisions had been announced for 2021 onwards when the *Guide* went to press. At some stage, it seems inevitable that EU students will be charged (much higher) international fees, so demand for places may grow in the short term as those who are able to, bring their plans forward.

Students from outside the EU are, of course, unaffected by Brexit, although some appear to have been put off by what they perceive as a less welcoming attitude in the UK since the 2016 referendum. This has been counterbalanced by the advantages they have seen from the fall in the value of the pound, which has made a UK higher education cheaper in real terms than it has been for many years.

Universities are understandably anxious about the long-term consequences of tougher visa controls and leaving the EU, but the Government has stressed that it remains keen to attract the "brightest and the best" to universities both as students and academics. Universities in the UK have been a magnet for international students for many years – only the huge higher education system in the USA attracts more. Global surveys have shown that UK universities are seen as offering high quality in a relatively safe environment, with the added advantage of allowing students to learn and immerse themselves in English. Even after the fall in the value of the £, the UK remains an expensive destination by international standards, but shorter than average courses both at undergraduate and Master's level redress the balance to some extent. The UK's 9% share of the world's young people who choose to study outside their own country is important to its universities and welcomed by British students.

More than four million people now travel abroad to study, and universities in many parts of the world compete aggressively to attract them. The students concerned may see other countries' universities as better than their own, or they may want to master another language and/or experience another culture, but most also see international study as a boost to their career prospects. Surveys in a number of countries have shown that employers – particularly those engaged in global markets – favour applicants with an international education.

While international students have continued to favour UK universities, the numbers of undergraduates coming from individual countries have varied considerably over recent years and the UK's overall 'market share' has declined. The source of most stability has been China, which sends four times as many students as any other country – more than 106,000 at all levels in 2018. Elsewhere, there has been more fluctuation, often due to economic or political factors. Most significant has been the decline in students coming from the Indian sub-continent, where tougher visa policies have hit hardest. But even here there has been a significant recovery recently, and India itself is now second only to China for the numbers coming to the UK, at around 20,000.

Universities in the UK continue to be extremely proactive in the recruitment of international students, participating in international fairs and sometimes opening their own offices in target countries. The fees such students pay is the obvious motivation, but universities also value the cultural richness that a diverse international intake contributes to student life.

Why study in the UK?
Aside from the strong reputation of UK degree courses and the opportunity to be taught and surrounded by English, research shows that most graduates are handsomely rewarded when

The top countries for sending undergraduates to the UK

EU countries (top 20)		%	Non-EU countries (top 20)		%
France	8,713	9.7	China	41,594	27.9
Italy	7,649	8.5	Hong Kong	13,181	8.8
Cyprus (European Union)	7,262	8.1	Malaysia	11,909	8.0
Romania	7,230	8.0	United States	6,504	4.4
Spain	6,183	6.9	India	6,303	4.2
Germany	6,032	6.7	Singapore	5,409	3.6
Poland	5,968	6.6	Nigeria	4,463	3.0
Bulgaria	5,271	5.9	Korea (South)	3,206	2.1
Greece	5,007	5.6	Canada	3,170	2.1
Ireland	4,802	5.3	Norway	3,110	2.1
Lithuania	3,660	4.1	United Arab Emirates	3,013	2.0
Portugal	3,276	3.6	Kuwait	2,825	1.9
Belgium	2,036	2.3	Saudi Arabia	2,594	1.7
Sweden	1,981	2.2	Russia	2,528	1.7
Czech Republic	1,855	2.1	Pakistan	2,385	1.6
Hungary	1,721	1.9	Switzerland	2,333	1.6
Netherlands	1,637	1.8	Qatar	2,175	1.5
Finland	1,607	1.8	Thailand	1,926	1.3
Slovakia	1,328	1.5	Oman	1,542	1.0
Latvia	1,094	1.2	Vietnam	1,537	1.0
Total (all non-UK EU)	**89,871**		**Total (all non-EU)**	**149,222**	

Note: First degree non-UK students

they return home. A Government-commissioned report showed that UK graduates earn much higher salaries than those who studied in their own country. The starting salaries of UK graduates in China and India were more than twice as high as those for graduates educated at home, while even those returning to the USA enjoyed a salary premium of more than 10%.

Some premium is to be expected – you are likely to be bright and highly motivated if you are prepared to uproot yourself to take a degree. And, unless they have government scholarships, most students have to be from a relatively wealthy background to afford the fees and other expenses of international study. A higher salary will probably be a necessity to compensate for the cost of the course. But the scale of increase demonstrated in the report suggests that a UK degree remains a good investment. Three years after graduation, 95% of the international graduates surveyed were in work or further study. More than 90% had been satisfied with their learning experience and almost as many would recommend their university to others.

A popular choice

Nearly all UK universities are cosmopolitan places that welcome international students in large numbers. Almost one student in five is from outside the UK – 6% from the EU and 14% from the rest of the world. The most recent surveys by i-graduate, the student polling organisation, put the country close behind the USA among the world's most attractive study destinations. More full-time postgraduates – the fastest-growing group – come from outside the UK than within it. In many UK universities you can expect to have fellow students from over 100 countries.

More than 90% of international students declare themselves satisfied with their experience of UK universities in i-graduate surveys, although they are less enthusiastic in the Government's National Student Survey and more likely than UK students to make official complaints. Nevertheless, satisfaction increased by eight percentage points in four years, according to i-graduate, reflecting greater efforts to keep ahead of the global competition. International students are particularly complimentary about students' unions, multiculturalism, teaching standards and places of worship. Their main concerns tend to be financial, partly because of a lack of employment opportunities. However, promised new arrangements for graduates to remain in the UK to work for two years after they complete a degree course should meet some of those concerns. The system is due to come in during 2021 and to benefit those who begin courses in 2020.

A growing number of students are taking UK degrees through a local institution, distance learning or a full branch campus of a UK university. Indeed, there are now more international students taking UK first degrees in their own country than there are in Britain. The numbers grew by 70% in a decade and are likely to rise further if UK Government policies obstruct universities' efforts to increase the number of students coming to Britain. Most branch campuses are in Asia or the Middle East, but some universities are now planning campuses in other parts of the EU. Coventry has already set up in Poland.

Where to study in the UK

The vast majority of the UK's universities and other higher education institutions are in England. Of the 132 universities profiled in this *Guide*, 107 are in England, 15 in Scotland, eight in Wales and two in Northern Ireland. Fee limits in higher education for UK and EU students are determined separately in each administrative area, which in some cases has brought benefits for EU students. All undergraduates from other EU countries are currently charged the same fees as those from the part of the UK where their chosen university is located, which is why EU students currently pay no tuition fees in Scotland, for example.

Within the UK, the cost of living varies by geographical area. Although London is the most expensive, accommodation costs can also be high in many other major cities. You should certainly find out as much as you can about what living in Britain will be like. Further advice and information is available through the British Council at its offices worldwide, at more than 60 university exhibitions that it holds around the world every year, or at its Education UK website (**https://study-uk.britishcouncil.org**). Another useful website for international students is provided by the UK Council for International Student Affairs (UKCISA) at **www.ukcisa.org.uk**.

Universities in all parts of the UK have a reputation for high quality teaching and research, as evidenced in global rankings such as those shown on page 133. They maintain this standing by investing heavily in the best academic staff, buildings and equipment, and by taking part in rigorous quality assurance monitoring. The new Office for Students is the chief regulatory body for higher education in England, overseeing organisations such as the Quality Assurance Agency for Higher Education (QAA), which remains the arbiter of standards. Professional bodies also play an important role in relevant subjects.

Although many people from outside the UK associate British universities with Oxford and Cambridge, in reality most higher education institutions are nothing like this. Some universities do still maintain ancient traditions, but most are modern institutions that place at least as much emphasis on teaching as on research and offer many vocational programmes, often with close links to business, industry and the professions. The table below shows the universities that are

The universities most favoured by EU and non-EU students

Institution (top 20)	EU students	Institution (top 20)	Non-EU students
Coventry University	2,809	The University of Manchester	5,743
University College London	2,721	University College London	5,351
King's College London	2,611	Coventry University	5,098
The University of Aberdeen	2,541	The University of Liverpool	4,965
The University of Glasgow	2,182	University of the Arts, London	4,556
The University of Edinburgh	2,014	The University of Edinburgh	4,087
The University of Manchester	1,975	King's College London	3,376
University of the Arts, London	1,890	Imperial College of Science, Technology and Medicine	3,081
The University of Warwick	1,788	The University of Sheffield	3,032
The University of Westminster	1,668	University of Nottingham	2,953
The University of Essex	1,505	The University of Warwick	2,729
Imperial College of Science, Technology and Medicine	1,453	The University of Birmingham	2,697
Middlesex University	1,409	The University of Leeds	2,460
The University of Bath	1,351	The University of St Andrews	2,408
The University of Surrey	1,322	The University of Sussex	2,255
The University of Southampton	1,306	The University of Exeter	2,228
Queen Mary University of London	1,251	City, University of London	2,162
The University of Kent	1,194	Newcastle University	2,144
The University of Greenwich	1,134	The University of Bristol	2,092
The University of Exeter	1,130	University of Durham	2,046

Note: First degree non-UK students

most popular with international students at undergraduate level. Although some of those at the top of the lists are among the most famous names in higher education, others achieved university status only in the last 30 years.

What subjects to study?

One of the reasons for such diversity is that strongly vocational courses are favoured by international students. Many of these in professional areas such as architecture, dentistry or medicine take one or two years longer to complete than most other degree courses. Traditional first degrees are mostly awarded at Bachelor level (BA, BEng, BSc, etc.) and last three to four years. There are also some "enhanced" first degrees (MEng, MChem, etc.) that take four years to complete. The relatively new Foundation degree programmes are almost all vocational and take two years to complete as a full-time course, with an option to study for a further year to gain a full degree. The table below shows the most popular subjects studied by international students. Remember, though, that you need to consider the details of any university course that you wish to study and to look at the ranking of that university in our main league table in chapter 1 and in the subject tables in chapter 13.

The most popular subjects for international students

Subject Group	EU students	Non-EU students	Total students	% of all international students
(12) Business Studies	13,204	25,703	38,907	16.3
(01) Accounting & Finance	2,388	15,026	17,414	7.3
(39) Law	4,084	10,171	14,255	6.0
(19) Computer Science	6,528	5,325	11,853	5.0
(09) Art & Design	4,290	7,295	11,585	4.8
(23) Economics	2,982	7,411	10,393	4.3
(44) Mechanical Engineering	2,116	6,282	8,398	3.5
(10) Biological Sciences	4,147	3,647	7,794	3.3
(53) Politics	3,815	3,858	7,673	3.2
(54) Psychology	4,106	3,185	7,291	3.0
(25) Electrical and Electronic Engineering	1,347	5,271	6,618	2.8
(18) Communication and Media Studies	3,124	3,206	6,331	2.6
(43) Mathematics	1,710	4,521	6,232	2.6
(21) Drama, Dance and Cinematics	3,330	2,231	5,560	2.3
(45) Medicine	1,250	3,736	4,987	2.1
(08) Architecture	1,640	3,072	4,712	2.0
(35) Hospitality, Leisure, Recreation & Tourism	2,469	1,915	4,384	1.8
(16) Civil Engineering	807	3,572	4,379	1.8
(49) Other Subjects Allied to Medicine	1,506	1,952	3,459	1.4
(14) Chemical Engineering	614	2,790	3,404	1.4
Total	**89,871**	**149,222**	**239,093**	

English language proficiency

The universities maintain high standards partly by setting demanding entry requirements, including proficiency in English. For international students, this usually includes a score of at least 5.5 in the International English Language Testing System (IELTS), which assesses English language ability through listening, speaking, reading and writing tests. Under visa regulations introduced in 2011, universities are able to vouch for a student's ability in English. This proficiency will need to be equivalent to an "upper intermediate" level (level B2) of the CEFR (Common European Framework of Reference for Languages) for studying at an undergraduate level (roughly equivalent to an overall score of 5.5 in IELTS).

There are many private and publicly funded colleges throughout the UK that run courses designed to bring the English language skills of prospective higher education students up to the required standard. However, not all of these are Government approved. Some private organisations such as INTO (**www.intostudy.com**) have joined with universities to create centres running programmes preparing international students for degree-level study. The British Council also runs English language courses at its centres around the world.

Tougher student visa regulations were introduced in 2012 and have since been refined. Although under the current system, universities' international students should not be denied entry to the UK, as long as they are proficient in English and are found to have followed other immigration rules, some lower-level preparatory courses taken by international students have been affected. It is, therefore, doubly important to consult the official UK government list of approved institutions (web address given at the end of this chapter) before lodging an application.

How to apply

You should read the information below in conjunction with that provided in chapter 5, which deals with the application process in some detail.

Some international students apply directly to a UK university for a place on a course, and others make their applications via an agent in their home country. But most applying for a full-time, first degree course do so through the Universities and Colleges Admissions Service (UCAS). If you take this route, you will need to fill in an online UCAS application form at home, at school or perhaps at your nearest British Council office. There is plenty of advice on the UCAS website about the process of finding a course and the details of the application system.

Whichever way you apply, the deadlines for getting your application in are the same. Under the regulations at the time this *Guide* went to press, for those applying from within an EU country, application forms for most courses starting in 2021 must be received at UCAS by 15 January 2021. Note that applications for Oxford and Cambridge and for all courses in medicine, dentistry and veterinary science have to be received at UCAS by 15 October 2020, while some art and design courses have a later deadline of 24 March 2021.

If you are applying from a non-EU country to study in 2021, you can submit your application to UCAS at any time between 1 September 2020 and 30 June 2021. Most people will apply well before the 30 June deadline to make sure that places are still available and to allow plenty of time for immigration regulations, and to make arrangements for travel and accommodation.

Entry and employment regulations

Visa regulations have been the subject of continuing controversy in the UK and many new rules and regulations have been introduced, often hotly contested by universities. Recent governments have been criticised for increasing visa fees, doubling the cost of visa extensions, and ending the right to appeal against refusal of a visa.

The current points system for entry – known as Tier 4 – came into effect in 2009. Under this scheme, prospective students can check whether they are eligible for entry against published criteria, and so assess their points score. Universities are also required to provide a Confirmation of Acceptance for Studies (CAS) to their international student entrants, who must have secured an unconditional offer, and the institution must appear as a "Tier 4 Sponsor" on the Home Office's Register of Sponsors. Prospective students have to demonstrate that, as well as the necessary qualifications, they have English language proficiency and enough money for the first year of their specified course. This includes the full fees for the first year and, currently, living costs of £1,265 a month, up to a maximum of nine months, if studying in London (£1,015 a month in the rest of the UK). Under the current visa requirements, details of financial support are checked in more detail than before.

All students wishing to enter the UK to study are required to obtain entry clearance before arrival. The only exceptions are British nationals living overseas, British overseas territories citizens, British Protected persons, British subjects, and non-visa national short-term students who may enter under a new Student Visitor route. Visa fees are £348 for a Tier 4 visa, plus an annual healthcare surcharge. As part of the application process, biometric data will be requested and this will be used to issue you with a Biometric Residence Permit (BRP) once you have arrived in the UK. You will need a BRP to open a bank account, rent accommodation or establish your eligibility for benefits and services or to work part-time, for example. The details of the regulations are continually reviewed by the Home Office. You can find more about all the latest rules and regulations for entry and visa requirements at **www.gov.uk/tier-4-general-visa**.

Until now, the rules and regulations governing permission to work have varied according to your country of origin and the level of course you undertake. Those from a European Economic Area (EEA) country (the EU plus Iceland, Liechtenstein and Norway) or Switzerland, have not needed permission to work in the UK, although you have needed to be ready to show an employer your passport or identity card to prove you are a national of an EEA country. However, the regulations that will apply after the UK leaves the EU are unknown at the time of writing and you will need to check for the latest information before making an application.

Students from outside the EEA who are here as Tier 4 students are allowed to work part-time for up to 20 hours a week during term time and full-time during vacations. These arrangements apply to students on degree courses; stricter limits were introduced in 2010 for lower-level courses. If you wish to stay on after you have graduated, you can apply for permission under Tier 2 of the points-based immigration system, but you will need a sponsor and the work must be considered "graduate level", commanding a salary of at least £23,000. The new work visa would offer an "unsponsored route" where universities would not need to maintain responsibility for their graduates while they try to access the jobs market.

Bringing your family

Since 2010, international students on courses of six months or less have been forbidden to bring a partner or children into the UK, and the latest reforms extend this prohibition to all undergraduates except those who are government sponsored. Postgraduates studying for 12 months or longer will still be able to bring dependants to the UK, and most universities can help to arrange facilities and accommodation for families as well as for single students. The family members you are allowed to bring with you are your husband or wife, civil partner (a same-sex relationship that has been formally registered in the UK or your home country) or long-term partner and dependent children. You can find out more about getting entry clearance for your family at **www.ukcisa.org.uk**.

Support from British universities

Support for international students is more comprehensive than in many countries, and begins long before you arrive in the UK. Many universities have advisers in other countries. Some will arrange to put you in touch with current students or graduates who can give you a first-hand account of what life is like at a particular university. Pre-departure receptions for students and their families, as well as meet-and-greet arrangements for newly-arrived students, are common. You can also expect an orientation and induction programme in your first week, and many universities now have "buddying" systems where current students are assigned to new arrivals to help them find their way around, adjust to their new surroundings and make new friends. Each university also has a students' union that organises social, cultural and sporting events and clubs, including many specifically for international students. Both the university and the students' union are likely to have full-time staff whose job it is to look after the welfare of students from overseas.

International students also benefit from free medical and subsidised dental and optical care and treatment under the UK National Health Service (non-EU students will have had to pay a healthcare surcharge when paying for their visa to benefit from this), plus access to a professional counselling service and a university careers service.

At university, you will naturally encounter people from a wide range of cultures and walks of life. Getting involved in student societies, sport, voluntary work, and any of the wide range of social activities on offer will help you gain first-hand experience of British culture, and, if you need it, will help improve your command of the English language.

Useful websites

The British Council, with its dedicated Study UK site designed for those wishing to find out more about studying in the UK:
https://study-uk.britishcouncil.org/

The UK Council for International Student Affairs (UKCISA) provides a wide range of information on all aspects of studying in the UK:
www.ukcisa.org.uk

UCAS, for full details of undergraduate courses available and an explanation of the application process:
www.ucas.com/undergraduate/applying-university/ucas-undergraduate-international-and-eu-students

For the latest information on entry and visa requirements:
www.gov.uk/tier-4-general-visa

Register of sponsors for Tier 4 educational establishments:
www.gov.uk/government/publications/register-of-licensed-sponsors-students

For a general guide to Britain, available in many languages:
www.visitbritain.com

13 Subject by Subject Guide

The 67 subject tables in this chapter drill down into the experience students are likely to have on their chosen course and the career prospects they might expect when they graduate. Knowing where a university stands in the pecking order of higher education is a vital piece of information for any applicant, but the quality of the course is what matters most – particularly in the short term. Recent surveys suggest that the majority of applicants agree and take more notice of the subject tables than the institutional rankings which tend to attract the headlines.

As the 2014 Research Excellence Framework confirmed, the most modest institution may have a centre of specialist excellence, and even famous universities have mediocre departments. This chapter offers some pointers to the leading universities in a wide range of subjects. Since universities mount frequent reviews of the courses they offer, it is possible that not all institutions listed in a particular subject area will be running courses in 2021.

Many subjects, such as dentistry or sociology, have their own table, but others are grouped together in broader categories, such as "other subjects allied to medicine". Scores are not published where the number of students is too small for the outcome to be statistically reliable.

The subject tables include scores from the National Student Survey (NSS). These distil the views of final-year undergraduates on various aspects of their course, with the results presented in two columns. The teaching quality indicator reflects the average scores in the sections of the survey focusing on teaching, assessment and feedback, learning opportunities and academic support. The student experience indicator is drawn from the average of the organisation and management, learning resources, student voice and learning community sections, as well as the survey's final question, on overall satisfaction.

The three other measures used are research quality, students' entry qualifications and graduate employment prospects. The Education table uses a fifth indicator: Ofsted grades, a measure of the quality of teaching based on the outcomes of Ofsted inspections of teacher training courses. None of the measures is weighted. A full explanation of the measures is given on the next page.

Cambridge is again the most successful university. It tops 27 of the 67 tables, while Loughborough, Oxford and St Andrews all lead in five subjects, and Glasgow in four. Birmingham, Edinburgh, Leeds, Strathclyde and Warwick are all top in two subjects. Eleven other universities are top in one subject.

Research quality

This is a measure of the quality of the research undertaken in the subject area. The information was sourced from the 2014 Research Excellence Framework (REF), a peer-review exercise used to evaluate the quality of research in UK higher education institutions, undertaken by the UK Higher Education Funding Bodies. The approach mirrors that in the main table, with the REF results weighted and then multiplied by the percentage of eligible staff entered for assessment.

For each subject, a research quality profile was given to those university departments that took part, showing how much of their research was in various quality categories. These categories were: 4* world-leading; 3* internationally excellent; 2* internationally recognised; 1* nationally recognised; and unclassified. The funding bodies decided to direct more funds to the very best research by applying weightings. The English, Scottish and Welsh funding councils have slightly different weightings. Those used by HEFCE (the funding council for England) are employed in the tables: 4* is weighted by a factor of 3 and 3* is weighted by a factor of 1. Outputs of 2* and 1* carry zero weight. This results in a maximum score of 3. In the interest of consistency, the above weightings continue to be applied this year.

The scores in the table are presented as a percentage of the maximum score. To achieve the maximum score, all staff would need to be at 4* world-leading level. Universities could choose which staff to include in the REF, so, to factor in the depth of the research quality, each quality profile score has been multiplied by the number of staff returned in the REF as a proportion of all eligible staff.

Entry standards

This is the average new UCAS tariff score for new students under the age of 21, based on A and AS-Levels and Scottish Highers and Advanced Highers and other equivalent qualifications (including the International Baccalaureate), taken from HESA data for 2017–18. Each student's examination grades were converted to a numerical score using the UCAS tariff. The points used in the tariff appear on page 32.

Teaching quality and student experience

The student satisfaction measure is divided into two components. These measures are taken from the National Student Survey (NSS) results published in 2018 and 2019. The latest year's figures are used when only one is available, but an average of the two years' results is used in all other cases. Students at some universities boycotted the 2019 NSS, leaving individual departments below the 50% threshold for publication. Where 2019 NSS data were not available, the latest available scores for Teaching Quality and Student Experience were adjusted by the percentage point change in each subject between that year and 2019. This applies mainly to Oxford and Cambridge, which last met the threshold as entire universities in 2016. The adjusted scores were used for z-scoring only, and do not appear in the final table.

The NSS covers eight aspects of a course, with an additional question gauging overall satisfaction. Students answer on a scale from 1 (bottom) to 5 (top) and the score in the table is calculated from the percentage of positive responses (4 and 5) in each section. The teaching quality indicator reflects the average scores for the first four sections of the survey. The student experience indicator is drawn from the average scores of the remaining sections and the additional question on overall satisfaction. Teaching quality is favoured over student experience and accounts for 67% of the overall student satisfaction score, with student experience making up the remaining 33%.

Graduate prospects

This is the percentage of graduates undertaking further study or in a professional job (positive destinations), in the annual survey by HESA six months after graduation. Because of the relatively small numbers in some departments, two years of data (2016 and 2017 graduates) are aggregated to make the scores more reliable. No new graduate employment figures have been published by HESA since the last edition of the *Guide* because it is changing the timing of its surveys to measure destinations a year after graduation.

A low score on this measure does not necessarily indicate unemployment – some graduates may have taken jobs that are not categorised as professional work. The averages for each subject are given at the foot of each subject table in this chapter and in two tables in chapter 3 (see pages 52–55).

Note that in the tables that follow, when a figure is followed by *, it refers solely to data from 2015–16 because no data for 2016–17 are available.

The subjects listed below are covered in the tables in this chapter:

Accounting and Finance
Aeronautical and
    Manufacturing Engineering
Agriculture and Forestry
American Studies
Anatomy and Physiology
Animal Science
Anthropology and Forensic
    Science
Archaeology
Architecture
Art and Design
Biological Sciences
Building
Business Studies
Celtic Studies
Chemical Engineering
Chemistry
Civil Engineering
Classics and Ancient
    History
Communication and Media
    Studies
Computer Science
Creative Writing
Criminology
Dentistry
Drama, Dance and
    Cinematics

East and South Asian Studies
Economics
Education
Electrical and Electronic
    Engineering
English
Food Science
French
General Engineering
Geography and
    Environmental Sciences
Geology
German
History
History of Art, Architecture
    and Design
Hospitality, Leisure,
    Recreation and Tourism
Iberian Languages
Italian
Land and Property
    Management
Law
Librarianship and
    Information Management
Linguistics
Materials Technology
Mathematics
Mechanical Engineering

Medicine
Middle Eastern and
    African Studies
Music
Nursing
Other Subjects Allied to
    Medicine (see page 248
    for subjects included in
    this category)
Pharmacology and Pharmacy
Philosophy
Physics and Astronomy
Physiotherapy
Politics
Psychology
Radiography
Russian and East European
    Languages
Social Policy
Social Work
Sociology
Sports Science
Theology and Religious
    Studies
Town and Country Planning
    and Landscape
Veterinary Medicine

Accounting and Finance

A decline in the numbers applying to study accounting in 2018 did not stop record numbers starting degrees in these two popular subjects for the fourth year in a row. Finance, the smaller of the two areas, saw applications continue to increase, but there was a 4% drop for accountancy. The numbers enrolling for finance degrees passed 2,500 for the first time, while in accounting the total was again well over 7,000.

Leeds retains the leadership of the table, with the London School of Economics leaping into second place from outside last year's top ten. Although still not in the top 50 in either of our measures of student satisfaction, much-improved scores have propelled the LSE, which already had the top research grades, up the table. Leeds has good scores across the board, without topping any single measure.

There are high rates of student satisfaction throughout the table. The best are at the University of Central Lancashire, which is only just in the top 50 overall. Leading employment scores are also well scattered. At Loughborough, 96.5% of graduates went straight into a professional job or further study, and at Queen's Belfast 94%, but at six universities the proportion was 50% or less.

Employment rates in the two areas come a surprisingly long way down the table of subjects – only 35th of 67 subject areas. Those who do find graduate jobs have starting salaries around the average for all subjects, at £22,000 in 2017.

Glasgow and Strathclyde have much the highest entry grades, benefiting from the conversion rate for Scottish qualifications in the UCAS tariff. Some of the leading universities demand maths A-level and all welcome it, but there is considerable variation in entry standards, from over 200 points at Glasgow and Strathclyde to less than 100 at 11 universities. More than 150 universities and colleges expect to offer accounting or finance, either alone or in combination, in 2020.

Accounting and Finance	Teaching quality %	Student experience %	Research quality %	Entry standards (UCAS points)	Graduate prospects %	Overall score
1 Leeds	89.9	92.4	39.3	177	87.0	100.0
2 London School of Economics	77.5	77.3	52.3	188	93.6	98.9
3 Warwick	83.1	85.0	40.4	188	88.9	98.6
4 Glasgow	82.4	87.1	22.1	220	88.7	98.2
5 Strathclyde	74.6	76.3	44.3	214	89.5	97.9
6 Bath	82.6	84.3	41.8	173	87.5	97.3
7 York	86.1	87.7	24.0	172*	—	95.8
=8 Lancaster	80.7	83.4	42.6	149	88.9	95.4
=8 Queen's, Belfast	81.3	82.4	32.7	159	94.0	95.4
10 Loughborough	76.0	85.4	32.6	157	96.5	94.7
11 Exeter	81.5	84.2	24.4	162	90.6	94.0
12 Liverpool	87.5	88.3	20.1	157	82.1	93.6
13 Aberdeen	78.2	79.0	24.9	181	88.0	93.5
14 Birmingham	81.0	80.8	29.1	145	91.8	93.2
15 Ulster	83.6	82.6	40.4	125	83.9	93.1
16 Nottingham	75.6	80.6	32.6	155	90.3	92.8
=17 Sussex	81.4	85.7	23.7	142	90.6	92.6
=17 Swansea	85.6	87.0	22.0	129	90.4	92.6

Accounting and Finance cont

		Teaching quality %	Student experience %	Research quality %	Entry standards (UCAS points)	Graduate prospects %	Overall score
19	Reading	82.2	82.6	29.3	136	87.9	92.4
20	Sheffield	80.3	84.1	26.8	146	86.6	92.3
21	Manchester	78.0	84.3	33.3	169	73.2	92.2
22	Stirling	79.5	82.1	25.2	171	77.6	91.9
23	Heriot-Watt	81.3	83.6	18.8	161	83.6	91.8
24	Durham	75.9	80.4	23.1	157	90.8	91.6
25	Newcastle	77.6	78.4	20.7	154	93.1	91.5
26	East Anglia	81.1	82.4	28.1	143	81.1	91.3
=27	City	80.5	84.3	28.7	163	68.2	90.8
=27	Robert Gordon	86.2	85.7	2.6	184	74.6	90.8
=29	Kent	77.9	78.1	24.8	139	90.2	90.7
=29	Southampton	80.7	82.6	24.0	148	79.6	90.7
31	Cardiff	76.6	77.0	32.0	160	73.6	90.1
32	Queen Mary, London	71.9	75.4	31.3	157	81.9	89.8
33	Nottingham Trent	87.7	87.6	4.6	128	86.3	89.7
34	Liverpool John Moores	91.0	88.0	—	129	84.0	89.5
=35	Aberystwyth	91.9	90.2	14.5	107	74.8	89.2
=35	Bristol	73.0	75.7	32.1	168	70.8	89.2
=35	Dundee	79.0	79.6	12.1	165	79.1	89.2
38	Edinburgh	68.7	73.9	25.8	185	74.8	88.8
39	Lincoln	86.5	87.3	4.8	113	83.6	87.9
40	Keele	84.8	86.9	10.2	116	79.0	87.7
=41	Edinburgh Napier	83.3	85.6	2.3	147	75.2	87.6
=41	Portsmouth	83.1	82.7	9.5	109	88.0	87.6
43	De Montfort	81.8	84.4	10.7	99	90.3	87.3
44	Aston	78.3	78.2	19.7	138	73.4	87.1
=45	Derby	86.6	83.7	0.9	107	86.2	86.8
=45	Northumbria	81.9	82.6	4.0	136	78.4	86.8
47	Westminster	81.8	83.8	2.4	140	74.5	86.3
=48	Buckingham	89.3	94.0	—	106	71.7	86.2
=48	Central Lancashire	93.8	94.3	4.4	130	50.0	86.2
=48	West of Scotland	83.2	82.0	2.9	146	70.4	86.2
=48	Worcester	90.0	91.1	0.9	109	70.8	86.2
52	Hull	80.0	80.4	10.2	124	78.4	86.1
=53	Bangor	89.8	92.6	23.4	94	53.7	86.0
=53	Chester	91.4	88.5	0.5	95	75.9	86.0
=53	South Wales	88.8	89.4	0.2	120	68.9	86.0
56	Royal Holloway, London	74.0	78.7	27.0	134	—	85.9
57	Greenwich	86.3	87.4	3.3	130	65.4	85.8
=58	Glasgow Caledonian	77.7	77.4	1.8	173	68.3	85.7
=58	London South Bank	86.4	87.2	2.1	107	75.7	85.7
60	Essex	78.8	83.5	25.1	104	68.7	85.6

=61	Coventry	84.2	85.6	1.6	117	75.0	85.5
=61	Surrey	72.4	75.9	15.8	158	69.3	85.5
=63	Huddersfield	81.1	79.6	4.1	127	77.3	85.3
=63	Plymouth	84.9	86.9	13.1	124	58.2	85.3
65	Bradford	77.8	82.1	11.8	129	70.7	85.2
66	Oxford Brookes	83.8	82.7	5.1	122	69.7	85.0
67	Leicester	68.9	72.7	24.3	126	77.5	84.7
68	Gloucestershire	84.9	77.9	—	102	82.2	84.4
69	Hertfordshire	83.0	85.2	0.9	111	72.1	84.1
70	Solent	83.4	87.1	—	112	69.4	83.9
71	Brunel	74.3	79.7	23.0	112	65.0	83.6
=72	Abertay	85.6	85.0	—	136	55.2	83.5
=72	Teesside	84.1	79.3	2.0	102	75.0	83.5
=72	West of England	79.2	82.6	5.5	113	71.1	83.5
75	West London	89.6	89.2	—	107	56.7	83.3
=76	Liverpool Hope	83.1	80.2	—	105	74.3	83.2
=76	Manchester Metropolitan	82.1	80.0	4.7	126	62.1	83.2
=78	Bolton	93.0	92.3	—	83	56.3	82.7
=78	Edge Hill	74.9	75.6	—	128	77.1	82.7
80	Middlesex	72.6	78.1	10.5	122	67.7	82.2
81	Birmingham City	82.5	82.3	1.3	108	63.8	82.0
82	Staffordshire	91.0	87.7	2.6	103	46.7	81.9
83	Winchester	89.8	88.0	—	98	52.4	81.7
84	Leeds Beckett	82.6	83.2	0.8	99	63.9	81.5
85	Wolverhampton	85.5	85.1	2.4	93	57.1	81.1
=86	Bucks New	82.7	87.8	1.8	118	47.0	80.8
=86	Northampton	82.2	79.2	1.0	92	66.8	80.8
=86	Roehampton	74.3	79.5	4.5	105	69.0	80.8
=89	Salford	75.1	78.3	5.9	124	58.2	80.7
=89	Cardiff Metropolitan	80.8	82.3	—	107	60.0	80.7
91	Chichester	81.6	81.3	—	109*	57.4	80.5
92	East London	81.6	78.7	0.8	105	59.7	80.4
93	Sheffield Hallam	78.3	79.8	0.6	114	59.4	80.3
=94	Bournemouth	73.7	75.2	8.8	116	57.5	79.6
=94	Leeds Trinity	88.8	83.8	—	85*	50.0	79.6
96	Brighton	73.8	69.8	6.5	107	59.9	78.3
=97	Kingston	74.1	78.2	9.2	116	43.9	78.0
=97	London Metropolitan	78.1	78.8	0.6	76	63.6	78.0
99	Anglia Ruskin	77.0	76.3	3.4	89	48.4	76.3
100	Canterbury Christ Church	68.3	71.6	—	103	60.5	76.0
=101	Bedfordshire	68.4	73.6	3.1	105	54.1	75.9
=101	Sunderland	66.4	66.0	0.4	104	66.7	75.9

Employed in professional job	53%	Employed in non-professional job and Studying		2%
Employed in professional job and studying	8%	Employed in non-professional job		18%
Studying	9%	Unemployed		10%
Average starting professional salary	£22,000	Average starting non-professional salary		£18,000

Aeronautical and Manufacturing Engineering

Unlike other branches of engineering, the aeronautical variety is growing in popularity with six successive increases in the number of applications, including 8% growth in the last two years. The number of places has not kept pace with the most recent increases in demand, making higher entry requirements inevitable.

Cambridge retains its accustomed lead in the table, with Imperial College London back as its nearest challenger after a rise in student satisfaction. Cambridge has the best scores in the table for research and entry standards, while the University of the West of Scotland (UWS), in a share of 15th place, again has a clear lead in both of our measures of student satisfaction. Coventry, two places higher, is the only other university to register 90% satisfaction with the quality of teaching.

Most of the courses in this ranking focus on aeronautical or manufacturing engineering, but the category includes some with a mechanical title. In addition, manufacturing degrees often go under the rubric of production engineering, which has seen broadly stable levels of demand with around 3,000 applications a year.

Although they do not feature in our tables, degree apprenticeships at leading firms like Rolls-Royce provide an attractive alternative to a conventional degree in this area. The subjects share ninth place out of the 67 subject groups for starting salaries following traditional degrees, but they are not in the top 30 for the proportion of graduates going straight into professional jobs or further study. Almost 60% of the 2017 graduates went straight into high-level work, and at tenth-placed Newcastle over 95% either went into such jobs or continued studying.

Many universities demand maths and physics at A-Level, and give extra credit for further maths, computing and/or design technology. Entry grades are high at the leading universities, with Cambridge averaging almost 240 points per entrant and four others over 200. Coventry, UWS and the University of the West of England remain the only post-1992 universities in the top 20.

Aeronautical and Manufacturing Engineering	Teaching quality %	Student experience %	Research quality %	Entry standards (UCAS points)	Graduate prospects %	Overall score
1 Cambridge	83.7*	85.5*	67.0	239	93.6	100.0
2 Imperial College London	73.3	77.3	59.6	221	86.2	92.8
3 Bristol	84.1	88.4	52.3	204	78.0	92.2
4 Bath	81.0	86.1	37.4	198	85.9	90.7
5 Leeds	83.8	83.7	40.9	173	83.5	89.3
6 Glasgow	70.7	73.4	47.2	209	82.8	88.5
=7 Southampton	74.7	75.9	52.3	181	78.7	87.4
=7 Swansea	78.5	81.6	45.5	149	86.2	87.4
9 Loughborough	76.8	81.1	41.8	168	84.1	87.3
10 Newcastle	71.0	72.7	30.2	—	95.2	86.5
11 Nottingham	77.7	71.4	40.8	168	80.5	85.5
12 Strathclyde	70.9	75.1	37.2	208	73.2	85.0
13 Coventry	91.0	89.2	10.3	137	80.9	84.1
14 Manchester	73.7	73.0	35.1	170	77.4	83.5
=15 Surrey	75.2	75.0	30.8	163	75.0	82.3

=15	West of Scotland	93.3	93.9	9.0	152	65.6	82.3
=17	Liverpool	73.3	77.8	32.1	143	80.1	82.2
=17	Sheffield	66.6	71.9	36.0	156	82.8	82.2
19	Ulster	88.0	85.6	—	131	80.6	81.2
20	West of England	80.4	80.8	10.6	133	81.3	80.8
21	Plymouth	76.9	79.1	15.7	126	83.7	80.6
22	Queen Mary, London	67.6	74.8	46.7	133	71.4	79.8
23	Queen's, Belfast	66.5	65.4	36.7	148	77.4	79.7
24	Portsmouth	76.2	77.4	9.1	111	88.9	79.5
25	Sussex	69.7	74.2	—	142	87.5	78.4
26	Brunel	63.8	65.6	23.7	144	82.1	78.3
27	Hertfordshire	71.7	73.2	16.5	111	83.6	77.9
28	Staffordshire	78.2	71.4	5.7	116	79.3	76.9
29	Aston	78.2	79.1	20.6	126	61.5	76.2
30	City	76.6	84.2	23.1	133	55.6	75.8
31	South Wales	82.8	78.9	—	122	65.0	75.0
32	Sheffield Hallam	70.5	63.9	17.8	122	71.4	74.6
33	Bucks New	75.8	67.3	—	111	74.1	73.6
34	Salford	66.1	71.3	4.4	129	68.8	72.5
35	Wolverhampton	71.2	72.4	4.4	101	—	71.6
36	Teesside	67.5	62.2	5.8	121	—	71.1
37	Central Lancashire	60.2	61.0	7.1	137	—	70.3
38	Kingston	70.6	68.2	2.9	116	57.9	69.4
39	Brighton	67.6	74.3	7.4	121	52.0	68.9

Employed in professional job	57%	Employed in non-professional job and Studying		1%
Employed in professional job and studying	2%	Employed in non-professional job		14%
Studying	15%	Unemployed		12%
Average starting professional salary	£26,000	Average starting non-professional salary		£17,000

Agriculture and Forestry

The numbers starting degrees in agriculture fell below 2,000 for the first time in five years in 2018, while enrolments for forestry or arboriculture dropped below 100. The two subjects are in the bottom four for graduate prospects, with a 14% unemployment rate that is among the highest in the sector. Those who do find professional jobs – nearly half of the 2017 cohort – command salaries that are around average for all subjects, at £22,000.

Nottingham leads the table for the third year in a row, but it cannot match the student satisfaction rates at neighbouring Nottingham Trent, which is restricted to fourth place overall, largely because of a low research score. Neither university teaches agriculture in Nottingham – NTU has a specialist campus in Brackenhurst, while Nottingham students are taught on the university's biosciences campus at Sutton Bonnington.

Queen's Belfast, which recorded much the best score in the Research Excellence Framework, is back in second place after recording the year's biggest rise to follow last year's biggest fall. Third-placed Reading is the UK's sole representative in the QS world rankings for agriculture – indeed, the only one in the top 50. Newcastle and Kent were the only universities to see 80% of their 2017 graduates go straight into highly-skilled employment or continue their studies.

There are two specialist institutions in the table: the Royal Agricultural University and Harper Adams, which is the leading modern university in the main table in *The Times and Sunday Times Good University Guide*, but only eighth for agriculture and forestry. Unusually, 35 points cover the average entry grades at all 12 universities in the specialist ranking.

Agriculture and Forestry	Teaching quality %	Student experience %	Research quality %	Entry standards (UCAS points)	Graduate prospects %	Overall score
1 Nottingham	89.7	91.2	36.4	151	68.8	100.0
2 Queen's, Belfast	69.2	68.1	56.3	146	78.9	97.5
3 Reading	80.0	79.3	50.7	134	75.9	96.4
4 Nottingham Trent	95.5	94.0	4.1	147	69.8	96.3
5 Newcastle	77.4	79.4	28.4	138	80.8	94.8
6 Aberystwyth	87.3	87.7	38.2	134	63.7	94.5
7 Bangor	85.6	81.8	29.7	125	77.1	92.9
8 Harper Adams	82.7	81.7	5.7	136	74.5	91.4
9 Kent	65.9	62.8	–	140	80.5	88.2
10 Royal Agricultural	82.0	82.8	2.1	122	54.1	83.7
11 Greenwich	–	–	19.5	132	43.1	83.5
12 Cumbria	93.2	86.8	–	116	48.6	83.4

Employed in professional job	43%	Employed in non-professional job and Studying	2%
Employed in professional job and studying	5%	Employed in non-professional job	28%
Studying	8%	Unemployed	14%
Average starting professional salary	£22,000	Average starting non-professional salary	£18,000

American Studies

The top five are unchanged in the new American Studies table, with Birmingham still in the lead. It has the best graduate prospects and high scores across the board. Second-placed Manchester achieved the best grades in the Research Excellence Framework, while Sussex, in third place, has the highest entry scores. Two points cover the top three on this measure.

Applications for degrees in American Studies have fallen since their heyday before £9,000 fees were introduced. Another decline in 2018 left only 260 students beginning degrees. Yet 57 institutions plan to offer the subject in 2019.

The subject has become a fixture in the bottom ten of our employment table. Those who find graduate-level work have average starting salaries of £20,000, but only a third of graduates in 2017 were in this happy position. Three out of ten graduates went on to take another course.

American Studies is unusual for having higher scores in the sections of the National Student Survey (NSS) focusing on teaching quality than those dealing with the broader student experience. Ninth-placed Hull and Winchester, in 13th, both top 90% in each of our satisfaction measures.

Degrees classified by UCAS as American studies include a variety of courses such as international relations and black studies. Most concentrate on the culture and politics of the USA and Canada. A growing number of courses offer the opportunity of a year at an American or Canadian university as part of a four-year degree. The leading universities are likely to expect English or history at A-level or the equivalent.

American Studies	Teaching quality %	Student experience %	Research quality %	Entry standards (UCAS points)	Graduate prospects %	Overall score
1 Birmingham	88.0	83.9	48.8	151	81.2	100.0
2 Manchester	88.2	82.5	49.1	152	65.2	97.6
3 Sussex	78.5	75.2	45.6	153	78.8	95.6
4 Kent	79.7	74.8	47.3	111	79.4	91.7
5 Nottingham	75.2	71.4	39.9	140	73.7	90.9
6 Leicester	84.3	84.4	34.3	127	63.2	90.5
7 Portsmouth	89.6	81.2	32.2	104	70.0	89.7
8 East Anglia	79.1	71.8	33.1	147	60.4	89.5
9 Hull	93.1	92.6	26.1	112	50.4	88.4
10 Swansea	84.4	82.1	18.5	122	70.2	87.6
11 Goldsmiths, London	80.6	76.3	34.9	128	54.2	87.5
12 Essex	78.8	79.0	46.9	96	58.2	86.7
13 Winchester	93.0	92.7	—	107	76.2	86.6
14 Manchester Metropolitan	79.7	81.9	29.0	120*	—	86.3
15 Keele	81.9	73.9	29.8	115*	57.9	85.7
16 Liverpool	80.1	77.1	33.4	—	39.3	81.9
17 Derby	88.6	76.1	13.5	—	30.7	79.3
18 York St John	84.1	84.5	—	100	51.7	78.6
19 Canterbury Christ Church	76.1	58.8	16.3	96	41.3	75.0

Employed in professional job	32%	Employed in non-professional job and Studying		5%
Employed in professional job and studying	1%	Employed in non-professional job		27%
Studying	24%	Unemployed		11%
Average starting professional salary	£20,000	Average starting non-professional salary		£17,000

Anatomy and Physiology

There were almost seven applications to the place for degrees in anatomy and physiology in 2018, despite universities expanding their intakes for the sixth year in a row. There was a small increase in applications, and the numbers starting degrees topped 4,850. None of the 45 universities in the table averaged less than 100 points on the UCAS tariff, but only three averaged more than 200 points.

The table covers a broad range of courses, including the biomedical science degrees that have been growing in popularity over recent years. Very few actually have the title of anatomy or physiology, but they include degrees in cell biology, neurosciences and pathology. Entry requirements often include at least two science subjects – usually biology and chemistry – although some post-1992 universities will accept just one science.

St Andrews has overtaken Cambridge to lead this year's table. St Andrews has a rare 100% score for graduate prospects, while Cambridge has the highest entry standards. Brighton and Salford, both outside the top ten, have much the best of a generally positive set of student satisfaction scores.

There are big changes in the table outside the top six. Cardiff has fallen 13 places to 17th, having entered the ranking last year in fourth place. The most dramatic rises are by East London and Ulster, both of which have gone up 12 places to stand on the verge of the top 30.

Anatomy and physiology are in the top 20 for graduate prospects and close to that group for starting salaries. As well as St Andrews, Newcastle, Brighton, Huddersfield, Glasgow Caledonian, St George's London, Cardiff Metropolitan and Queen Margaret all saw over 90% of leavers go straight into graduate-level employment or continue their studies. The table is 50% larger than it was a decade ago, with one more university – Birmingham – joining since last year.

Anatomy and Physiology	Teaching quality %	Student experience %	Research quality %	Entry standards (UCAS points)	Graduate prospects %	Overall score
1 St Andrews	90.6	91.5	37.6	204	100.0	100.0
2 Cambridge	–	–	52.5	240	84.0	98.7
3 Newcastle	91.8	86.7	47.8	179	91.8	97.0
4 Dundee	86.0	89.1	55.4	188	79.8	94.7
5 Oxford	–	–	50.9	222	76.3	92.5
6 Glasgow	81.8	83.9	33.4	199	84.7	92.4
7 Glasgow Caledonian	92.1	91.8	8.1	165	97.5	92.2
8 University College London	77.5	77.8	55.4	193	78.7	92.0
9 Loughborough	88.2*	92.3*	52.1	150*	79.2	91.7
10 Bristol	82.9	82.7	49.7	176	75.0	90.3
11 Huddersfield	90.2	86.5	7.8	139	99.7	89.6
12 Brighton	96.7	95.8	4.8	128	95.3	89.3
13 Leeds	79.3	80.7	40.9	165	82.1	89.1
=14 Aberdeen	86.8	88.5	34.7	184	70.3	89.0
=14 Salford	96.7	95.4	12.7	126	90.5	89.0
16 Liverpool	86.7	86.9	31.7	147	83.3	88.7
17 Cardiff	83.1	85.3	33.3	152	–	88.6
18 Manchester	83.2	80.7	38.3	166	76.4	88.2
19 Sussex	68.9	71.9	46.8	160	84.9	87.3
20 King's College London	75.8	77.0	38.0	163	78.4	86.5
21 Birmingham	76.8	74.1	31.5	163	–	86.2
22 Swansea	72.3	76.2	44.7	155	–	86.1
23 Queen's, Belfast	72.4	72.1	33.3	157	85.0	85.9
24 Edinburgh	65.1	63.8	52.8	188	68.7	84.7
25 St George's, London	74.3	73.8	20.0	128	94.4	84.6
=26 Nottingham	77.2	77.1	26.5	156	77.5	84.3
=26 Cardiff Metropolitan	79.6	76.4	–	146	93.8	84.3
28 Leicester	81.6	80.7	36.5	135	73.0	84.1

29 Central Lancashire	85.5	86.2	8.3	—	74.4	83.0
30 Manchester Metropolitan	81.4	80.7	12.0	135	82.2	82.9
31 East London	89.8	88.0	—	127	79.7	82.3
32 Coventry	85.0	85.8	4.5	119	82.2	81.7
33 Ulster	82.1	80.4		134	83.1	81.4
34 Queen Mary, London	62.8	69.3	26.1	139	85.7	81.3
35 Portsmouth	72.9	69.6	8.1	131*	89.5	81.1
36 Plymouth	79.2	77.2	—	139	79.9	80.1
37 Oxford Brookes	83.4	82.8	21.3	134	63.6	79.9
38 Westminster	84.7	81.1	21.2	113	68.6	79.5
39 Queen Margaret, Edinburgh	62.1	58.3	—	137	97.4	79.2
40 Keele	78.5	82.5	16.5	130	68.4	79.1
41 Anglia Ruskin	71.5	67.2	2.2	126	88.2	79.0
42 Reading	72.5	72.1	26.6	128	67.4	77.9
43 Greenwich	72.1	83.2	2.2	123*	—	76.9
44 Bangor	73.4	71.8	—	118	77.8	76.1
45 Derby	70.5	70.3	1.6	105	68.8	72.1

Employed in professional job	42%	Employed in non-professional job and Studying		2%
Employed in professional job and studying	4%	Employed in non-professional job		14%
Studying	31%	Unemployed		8%
Average starting professional salary	£22,000	Average starting non-professional salary		£15,600

Animal Science

The Animal Science table was first published only five years ago and was a reflection of growing interest in the group of subjects under this heading. Extracted from the agriculture category, degree courses range from animal behaviour to equine science and veterinary nursing. Almost 2,700 students started courses in 2018, about 10% of them finding a place through Clearing. Most degrees will require biology and probably chemistry.

Glasgow remains well clear at the top of the table, with by far the highest entry standards among the 17 universities in the ranking and the top score in the National Student Survey for the overall student experience. Reading, which registered the best results in the Research Excellence Framework (REF), has moved up to second. Only 11 of the 17 universities in the table entered the REF in this category. Canterbury Christ Church, one of the REF absentees and only four places off the bottom of the table, is the only university to reach 90% for satisfaction with teaching quality.

Only 6% of those graduating from animal science degrees in 2017 were unemployed at the end of the year, placing it among the ten best subjects on this measure. However, animal science remains rooted to the bottom of our employment table because it had by far the largest proportion of graduates – almost half – beginning their careers in lower-level jobs. Some universities' employment scores are worryingly low – below 5% in Edinburgh Napier's case and under 30% at four more. Yet all the graduates of Middlesex's degree in veterinary nursing found professional employment or continued studying in 2016 and 2017.

Animal Science

		Teaching quality %	Student experience %	Research quality %	Entry standards (UCAS points)	Graduate prospects %	Overall score
1	Glasgow	87.7	92.7	42.3	195	66.7	100.0
2	Reading	81.8	78.4	50.7	144	56.3	89.9
3	Liverpool	74.9	81.3	32.9	150	82.9	89.0
4	Nottingham	72.7	78.9	36.4	153	75.4	88.5
5	Aberystwyth	87.3	87.7	38.2	130	65.7	88.1
6	Middlesex	83.8	68.8	—	147	100.0	84.5
7	Nottingham Trent	86.8	84.1	4.1	149	71.1	83.7
8	Bristol	77.7	63.4	33.2	143	28.6	79.6
9	Lincoln	81.6	78.2	—	139	66.7	79.0
10	Harper Adams	82.7	81.7	5.7	139	45.2	77.7
11	Plymouth	88.9	85.6	—	146	23.2	76.2
12	Royal Veterinary College	73.7	71.8	—	139	56.1	75.0
13	Chester	81.2	75.8	7.9	123	31.8	72.9
14	Canterbury Christ Church	90.2	86.4	—	88	40.0	69.9
15	Edinburgh Napier	62.8	54.2	—	167	4.8	68.2
16	Anglia Ruskin	52.0	36.7	24.6	135	25.0	67.6
17	Greenwich	—	—	19.5	109	24.3	67.5

Employed in professional job	25%	Employed in non-professional job and Studying	4%
Employed in professional job and studying	2%	Employed in non-professional job	44%
Studying	18%	Unemployed	6%
Average starting professional salary	£19,000	Average starting non-professional salary	£17,056

Anthropology

Applications to study anthropology topped 10,000 for the first time in 2018, an increase of almost 10% continuing one the most unexpected success stories following the introduction of £9,000 fees. Anthropologists feared that higher fees would endanger courses, but applications and enrolments have more than doubled since then. Although the numbers starting degrees remain below 2,000, there are now 26 universities in the table, all of which expect to offer the subject in 2020.

Some attribute the subject's rise in popularity to television series, but there has been no firm explanation. Much of the growth has come in joint Honours degrees, pairing the subject with everything from accountancy to linguistics or law. There are no subject-specific requirements for most degree courses, although some universities favour candidates who have taken sociology, biology or another science in the sixth-form.

Cambridge remains at the head of the table, with Oxford in second place. However, neither was in the top six in the Research Excellence Framework, where Birmingham, in eighth place, achieved the best grades. For the third year in a row, students at East London, only six places off the bottom of the table, were the most satisfied with the quality of teaching, while St Andrews, in 12th place, had the highest scores for the broader student experience.

Anthropology has tended to be the preserve of old universities, but there are seven post-1992 institutions in the latest table. Portsmouth is the only one to feature in the top ten, and had by far the best graduate prospects in the table. Employment prospects will be the main concern of those considering a degree in anthropology. It is only just outside the bottom ten for the proportion of graduates going straight into "professional" jobs or further study, and it ties with East and South Asian Studies for the unwanted distinction of the highest unemployment rate. The picture is a little better in the earnings table, but anthropology is still in the bottom 20, with average starting salaries in professional jobs of £20,000 in 2017.

Anthropology	Teaching quality %	Student experience %	Research quality %	Entry standards (UCAS points)	Graduate prospects %	Overall score
1 Cambridge	—	—	40.4	213	84.8	100.0
2 Oxford	—	—	38.8	202	79.1	98.8
3 University College London	80.4	78.7	49.3	173	74.4	98.1
4 Exeter	82.5	82.2	41.0	171	77.4	97.8
5 London School of Economics	84.4	80.7	41.3	178	69.9	97.5
6 Edinburgh	84.5	81.5	42.2	181	59.9	96.3
7 Portsmouth	88.3	85.8	32.2	102	91.7	95.7
8 Birmingham	74.5	70.4	50.9	156	81.0	95.6
9 Sussex	83.0	78.6	34.4	151	79.7	95.2
10 Manchester	82.4	79.5	36.7	160	73.1	95.1
11 Durham	79.5	75.2	29.1	176	79.4	94.5
12 St Andrews	89.2	86.5	25.0	183	54.8	94.2
13 Queen's, Belfast	88.8	79.5	49.0	151*	42.4	93.5
14 Kent	85.8	84.5	20.5	134	76.7	92.3
15 Aberdeen	84.3	82.2	31.8	160	55.3	92.0
16 SOAS, London	70.4	70.2	31.1	163	75.6	90.1
17 Brunel	83.7	75.6	29.3	118	63.9	89.0
18 Roehampton	87.4	84.6	27.7	107	51.7	88.1
19 Goldsmiths, London	80.5	72.8	34.5	126	53.7	87.6
20 Leeds	79.4	75.3	—	149	80.8	87.1
21 East London	90.5	67.2	13.7	—	53.7	87.0
22 Liverpool John Moores	75.7	73.5	15.1	157	65.1	86.8
23 Bournemouth	80.7	77.2	19.9	106	62.4	85.4
24 Bristol	76.0	73.3	11.2	153	62.1	85.2
25 Oxford Brookes	72.7	69.5	17.3	118	49.3	80.4
26 Wales Trinity St David	74.6	64.4	17.3	96	48.3	78.5

Employed in professional job	36%	Employed in non-professional job and Studying	2%
Employed in professional job and studying	3%	Employed in non-professional job	21%
Studying	24%	Unemployed	15%
Average starting professional salary	£20,000	Average starting non-professional salary	£17,063

Archaeology and Forensic Science

There are no specific subject requirements for a degree in archaeology, although geography, history and science subjects are all considered relevant. Entry standards are relatively low – only 11 of the 58 universities in the table average more than 150 points. More than 10% of those starting courses in 2018 came through Clearing.

Only 450 students started archaeology degrees in 2018, although there were over 2,300 takers for programmes classified by UCAS as forensic and archaeological science. More than 50 universities and colleges plan to offer degrees in the area in 2020. Applications fell in 2018, but the subjects have regained the levels of demand seen before £9,000 fees arrived.

For most students, money is not the attraction – archaeology is in the bottom ten in our earnings table. But graduates' immediate prospects have been improving – the subjects are just outside the top 50 in the employment table, with two-thirds of leavers going into graduate-level jobs or continuing their studies.

The top three in the table are unchanged since last year. Cambridge leads and has the highest entry standards, but Dundee – holder of the best research grades – is only a fraction of a point behind, with Oxford third.

Further down the table, however, there has been plenty of movement. Lincoln has gone up 13 places to become the only modern university in the top 20 and Anglia Ruskin is up 18 places to the verge of the top 30. Birmingham City, having shot up 40 places last year, has dropped 13 in the latest edition.

As is often the case, the most satisfied students are not at the leading universities. The best scores in the sections of the National Student Survey relating to teaching quality were at Worcester, in 27th place, while in the remaining sections tenth-placed Queen's Belfast is the lead. The top graduate prospects were at eighth-placed Liverpool.

Archaeology	Teaching quality %	Student experience %	Research quality %	Entry standards (UCAS points)	Graduate prospects %	Overall score
1 Cambridge	—	—	47.2	213	84.8	100.0
2 Dundee	84.7	82.5	55.4	186	82.2	99.7
3 Oxford	—	—	42.9	197	81.6	97.8
4 University College London	89.2	85.0	51.4	168	73.6	96.8
5 Durham	84.8	77.4	41.2	172	73.6	93.7
6 York	91.1	87.0	35.1	143	78.1	93.5
7 Glasgow	88.5	85.4	16.4	187	75.0	93.2
8 Liverpool	83.7	79.4	33.5	143	85.7	92.3
9 Exeter	81.2	82.0	33.6	159	77.0	91.6
10 Queen's, Belfast	89.2	89.4	36.9	126	72.1	90.7
11 Swansea	86.3	83.9	39.4	121	78.1	90.6
12 Birmingham	80.3	77.2	40.3	146*	72.6	89.8
13 Kent	87.1	83.9	33.1	132	72.2	89.6
14 Leicester	81.9	78.2	37.2	125	79.3	89.3
15 Newcastle	81.4	80.5	25.8	142	78.5	88.9
16 Southampton	78.0	70.0	43.5	147	70.8	88.7
17 Reading	87.0	81.7	44.7	125	62.3	88.4

18	Sheffield	77.7	76.2	31.6	139	73.7	87.2
19	Lincoln	88.4	88.5	—	136	80.3	87.1
20	Aberdeen	82.3	79.8	29.4	—	66.7	86.6
21	Huddersfield	86.2	79.9	—	136	82.6	86.1
=22	Bradford	75.9	66.0	23.6	138	80.3	85.7
=22	Manchester	—	—	24.7	145	64.4	85.7
=24	Nottingham	79.5	78.8	23.7	136	68.4	85.2
=24	Nottingham Trent	88.5	81.8	4.1	135	72.2	85.2
26	Bangor	84.3	76.7	24.3	126*	—	85.1
27	Worcester	92.6	86.2	8.1	106	74.1	85.0
28	Derby	91.6	87.3	3.6	130	67.2	84.9
=29	Birmingham City	84.5	79.1	—	129	80.9	84.7
=29	Teesside	84.1	83.5	—	128	79.5	84.7
31	Hull	81.0	78.0	31.7	114	66.0	84.3
32	Anglia Ruskin	88.4	85.8	24.6	115	56.6	83.7
=33	De Montfort	90.0	85.5	—	115	72.5	83.5
=33	Edinburgh	77.2	68.4	20.9	186	48.1	83.5
=33	Warwick	78.0	71.6	—	166	70.4	83.5
36	Glasgow Caledonian	79.7	67.4	4.7	167	65.3	83.3
37	Cardiff	76.5	67.6	31.1	131	63.8	83.1
38	West of England	82.9	87.1	—	123	72.7	82.8
39	Robert Gordon	73.0	76.6	8.8	150	68.2	82.3
40	Staffordshire	83.8	86.2	—	127	64.9	81.6
=41	London South Bank	85.9	83.9	—	120	65.7	81.3
=41	West London	81.7	85.5	—	125	67.3	81.3
43	Coventry	78.8	80.3	—	123	71.7	80.9
=44	Central Lancashire	76.0	73.7	9.8	130	63.9	80.1
=44	Wales Trinity St David	81.4	71.6	17.3	104	65.0	80.1
=44	West of Scotland	77.5	81.6	—	118	71.0	80.1
=47	Chester	89.5	80.1	15.4	102	52.7	79.8
=47	Greenwich	86.2	85.5	—	133	52.0	79.8
49	Bournemouth	75.8	75.4	19.9	122	56.0	79.4
50	Winchester	73.8	72.2	7.5	100	76.2	78.9
51	Liverpool John Moores	72.9	69.2	—	150	62.0	78.7
52	South Wales	77.1	75.0	—	127	56.1	76.9
53	Keele	58.5	55.5	—	134	78.3	75.9
54	Abertay	62*	67.7*	—	159	57.1	75.8
=55	Canterbury Christ Church	84.0	77.1	16.3	101	41.2	75.7
=55	Wolverhampton	83.7	74.7	—	114	49.2	75.7
57	Manchester Metropolitan	70.6	65.7	—	136	44.7	72.7
58	Cumbria	77.9*	67.3*	1.5	100*	46.7	71.9

Employed in professional job	35%	Employed in non-professional job and Studying	5%
Employed in professional job and studying	3%	Employed in non-professional job	23%
Studying	25%	Unemployed	11%
Average starting professional salary	£19,185	Average starting non-professional salary	£16,536

Architecture

It is extremely rare for every student to be satisfied with the quality of teaching throughout a degree, but Solent managed the maximum score in architecture and was less than 1 percentage point off repeating the feat in the sections of the National Student Survey dealing with the broader student experience. The university, which is restricted to a share of 18th place overall, partly because it did not enter the Research Excellence Framework in architecture, has a record of high scores in the subject, topping 90% on both satisfaction measures last year.

Bath remains top of the table, with Cambridge close behind, but there is a big change immediately behind them with Loughborough entering the table in third place. Other substantial moves see Manchester School of Architecture – a joint enterprise between Manchester and Manchester Metropolitan universities – jump ten places into the top ten, while the University of the Arts London is up 12 places to enter the top 20.

Architecture is not in the top 40 subjects for starting salaries in professional jobs, but graduates know that this soon changes. After five years at work, female architects earn 11% more than the average graduate and men 6% more. The workload on degree courses is above average – 16 hours a week, compared to 14 for all subjects – but initial employment prospects are good. Architecture is in the top 12 of the 67 subject groups for the proportion of graduates finding high-level work or continuing to study. Seven out of ten graduates went straight into a professional role in 2017 and the subject was close to the top ten for overall graduate prospects.

More than a dozen universities saw at least nine out of ten leavers go straight into graduate-level work or continue studying. They were led by Falmouth, which managed 100% employment for the second year in a row. Nowhere did the proportion fall below 60%.

Qualification usually takes seven years, in which the first degree is but a step on the way. That is a considerable financial commitment, especially when course materials can add another £1,000 to the burden. There are no particular subjects required for entry to most degrees in architecture, although some universities prefer candidates with art A-level or equivalent, and most welcome maths.

Architecture	Teaching quality %	Student experience %	Research quality %	Entry standards (UCAS points)	Graduate prospects %	Overall score
1 Bath	87.1	86.1	52.9	205	96.6	100.0
2 Cambridge	—	—	49.0	221	90.9	97.7
3 Loughborough	87.7	87.7	58.3	165	—	96.4
4 Sheffield	86.1	87.3	36.6	179	96.4	95.3
5 University College London	77.7	74.6	54.1	199	91.0	95.2
6 Cardiff	84.2	80.4	40.7	186	94.5	94.9
7 Strathclyde	88.1	78.9	23.0	198	93.5	93.5
8 Newcastle	82.3	82.8	43.7	175	89.9	93.1
9 Queen's, Belfast	89.8	86.4	35.2	153	91.1	92.2
10 Manchester School of Architecture	85.1	85.0	12.6	170	94.7	90.0
11 Liverpool	79.1	81.0	43.5	151	86.5	89.4
12 Edinburgh	74.9	74.1	35.1	181	87.5	89.3
13 Dundee	83.4	83.7	8.7	178	87.3	87.5
14 Oxford Brookes	84.9	83.5	17.6	157	85.6	87.1

15	West of England	88.9	89.0	10.6	149	86.0	86.8
16	Arts London	82.7	77.1	—	181	90.6	86.5
17	Kent	74.1	75.0	33.3	154	85.6	86.3
=18	Nottingham	75.9	74.2	14.8	167	90.1	85.9
=18	Solent	100.0	99.2	—	97	92.6	85.9
=18	Ulster	81.7	77.2	28.6	128	88.2	85.9
21	Northumbria	89.6	90.7	5.9	153	82.3	85.7
22	Plymouth	87.1	85.3	13.2	130	88.3	85.5
23	Coventry	88.6	88.7	10.3	128	86.3	85.0
=24	Reading	72.9	78.0	40.0	136	—	84.1
=24	Robert Gordon	82.6	79.7	8.3	163	81.2	84.1
26	Arts Bournemouth	93.4	86.0	2.4	134	82.2	83.9
=27	Derby	85.5	83.7	6.7	130	86.6	83.6
=27	Greenwich	89.0	81.2	2.0	147	82.5	83.6
=27	Westminster	84.9	81.6	10.7	141	82.3	83.6
30	Nottingham Trent	82.0	84.2	3.4	131	88.1	82.9
31	Creative Arts	83.2	82.8	3.4	137	84.6	82.6
32	Liverpool John Moores	83.8	82.8	4.9	152	78.8	82.5
=33	De Montfort	65.7	67.2	35.9	109	89.0	81.5
=33	Portsmouth	80.4	81.0	—	116	91.7	81.5
=35	London South Bank	78.9	75.8	19.6	103	82.6	80.3
=35	Cardiff Metropolitan	91.8	91.7	—	92	82.1	80.3
=37	Birmingham City	81.9	79.6	9.6	126	75.3	79.5
=37	Sheffield Hallam	88.1	87.3	13.4	112	69.5	79.5
39	Falmouth	68.6	67.8	—	104	100.0	79.1
40	Brighton	84.9	77.4	13.1	114	69.8	78.1
41	Norwich Arts	90.2	78.9		106	73.7	77.6
42	Huddersfield	72.8	77.3	—	137	76.5	77.2
=43	London Metropolitan	84.6	75.1	7.2	99	75.3	77.1
=43	Middlesex	88.0	80.8	13.3	122	60.0	77.1
=43	Salford	69.9	66.8	19.6	120	75.6	77.1
46	East London	89.8	84.7	8.1	113	63.0	77.0
47	Kingston	77.7	74.9	10.1	127	69.2	76.8
48	Leeds Beckett	75.7	70.7	5.6	123	74.1	76.3
49	Edinburgh Napier	67.7	73.6	5.7	133	74.3	75.8
50	Anglia Ruskin	79.6	68.5	5.2	89	78.6	75.2
=51	Central Lancashire	66.7	61.7	3.0	129	77.8	74.6
=51	Lincoln	56.2	54.6	3.2	124	89.6	74.6
53	Wolverhampton	85.4	81.0	5.6	97	60.9	73.6
54	Northampton	71.4	59.9	—	102	78.6	73.0
55	Glasgow Caledonian	70.5	68.4	9.1	—	69.2	72.2
56	Ravensbourne, London	62.0	57.1	—	99	66.7	67.4

Employed in professional job	68%	Employed in non-professional job and Studying	0%
Employed in professional job and studying	4%	Employed in non-professional job	10%
Studying	9%	Unemployed	9%
Average starting professional salary	£20,000	Average starting non-professional salary	£16,640

Art and Design

The two universities which tied for the lead in art and design in last year's *Guide* have been well and truly separated in the new edition. Oxford remains in first place, thanks partly to its customary high entry standards, but Newcastle has dropped to sixth after a fall of more than ten percentage points in our two measures of student satisfaction. Loughborough and Lancaster are now Oxford's nearest challengers, both less than a point behind.

Art and design are among the big recruiters in higher education, with over 120,000 students applying for places in 2018. The numbers enrolling in the larger area of design have fallen for the last three years, but there were still more than 18,000 starters in 2018. Demand for fine art also fell, with 4,435 embarking on degrees.

The subjects always feature in the lower reaches of the tables for employment and earnings, but artists and designers accept that they may have a period of lowly paid self-employment early in their career while they find a way to pursue their vocation. Only Lancaster, Portsmouth, Bournemouth Arts and Staffordshire, in 39th place, saw more than 80% of 2017 graduates find professional jobs or postgraduate courses. However, specialist arts universities and arts faculties of generalist institutions have increased their focus on employability in recent years. Only three of the 85 universities in the latest table dropped below 50% positive destinations, compared with 17 three years previously, although two of this year's top five are below 60% on this measure.

Although outside the top 50 overall, Canterbury Christ Church has the best scores in the sections of the National Student Survey devoted to teaching quality, while fourth-placed Essex is the leader in the rest of the survey.

Most courses in art and design are at post-1992 institutions, but older foundations monopolise the top ten. Higher entry standards are partly responsible, although most artists would argue that entry grades are of less significance than in other subjects. Selection in art and design rests primarily on the quality of candidates' portfolios and many undergraduates enter through a one-year Art Foundation course. Trinity St David is the highest-placed modern university, in 11th place.

Art and Design	Teaching quality %	Student experience %	Research quality %	Entry standards (UCAS points)	Graduate prospects %	Overall score
1 Oxford	—	—	39.7	238	70.0	100.0
2 Loughborough	84.2	81.4	35.3	184	76.0	99.7
3 Lancaster	76.8	77.7	48.0	165	81.4	99.5
4 Essex	94.2	91.0	46.9	—	56.5	97.3
5 University College London	84.8	80.2	44.7	193	55.9	96.9
6 Newcastle	71.5	69.7	37.3	206	70.8	96.6
7 Glasgow	68.5	68.2	37.2	211	—	95.8
8 Aberystwyth	93.4	87.5	21.6	133	76.0	95.2
9 Leeds	74.4	71.4	33.6	172	74.8	94.7
10 Goldsmiths, London	84.5	82.9	25.9	188	59.8	94.4
11 Wales Trinity St David	88.7	82.1	39.2	118	70.4	93.8
12 Portsmouth	92.0	87.4	—	124	88.3	93.5
13 Ulster	75.7	67.8	57.2	138	66.5	93.2

14	Manchester Metropolitan	84.7	78.8	9.7	174	71.6	92.9
15	Arts Bournemouth	84.2	80.9	2.4	160	80.4	92.7
16	Dundee	82.9	81.7	39.9	160	56.0	92.6
17	Southampton	79.1	74.0	35.4	168	60.9	92.2
18	Nottingham Trent	82.8	80.9	4.7	156	79.1	92.1
19	Edinburgh	77.7	67.8	27.9	182	64.0	92.0
20	Brunel	74.9	70.7	32.8	139	76.8	91.8
=21	Robert Gordon	89.0	81.6	11.5	158	66.2	91.5
=21	Westminster	82.8	73.6	22.5	154	68.9	91.5
=23	Bangor	91.2	83.8	—	139	75.0	90.8
=23	Coventry	82.9	80.9	18.1	132	73.9	90.8
=23	Kingston	85.2	77.7	10.1	182	60.7	90.8
26	Kent	64.2	60.4	44.3	137	78.8	90.6
=27	Chichester	93.8	84.5	—	138	70.0	90.0
=27	De Montfort	86.1	85.0	10.2	123	75.2	90.0
29	West of England	89.0	83.1	15.0	150	60.3	89.9
30	Northumbria	83.9	81.0	13.3	158	63.4	89.8
31	Liverpool John Moores	83.2	77.5	7.2	170	62.5	89.1
32	Falmouth	79.5	75.3	3.0	149	76.5	89.0
33	Sheffield Hallam	89.7	85.4	15.5	128	62.1	88.8
34	Bournemouth	81.1	76.9	15.0	118	76.1	88.6
=35	Central Lancashire	87.4	81.6	3.9	143	66.1	88.4
=35	Heriot-Watt	66.7	62.7	31.1	165	66.1	88.4
37	London South Bank	82.1	76.8	12.8	108	78.5	88.1
38	Lincoln	78.2	76.2	7.1	143	72.8	88.0
39	Staffordshire	79.6	74.6	2.3	116	85.1	87.9
40	Teesside	84.1	80.6	2.9	126	74.3	87.8
41	Salford	90.6	85.9	8.0	140	57.4	87.6
42	Creative Arts	83.4	76.2	3.4	150	65.8	87.4
43	Huddersfield	80.8	75.9	4.8	135	71.8	87.1
44	Plymouth	85.1	82.7	14.7	148	53.8	87.0
45	Reading	64.4	61.7	38.9	144	64.8	86.8
46	Bath Spa	73.3	66.5	9.6	160	66.1	86.1
47	Abertay	87.3	77.2	—	142	61.9	85.9
=48	Brighton	82.5	76.8	13.1	151	53.6	85.8
=48	Norwich Arts	83.0	79.0	5.6	143	60.5	85.8
=48	Leeds Arts	81.0	75.9	—	165	59.5	85.8
51	Hertfordshire	81.6	76.2	5.8	111	73.9	85.7
52	Arts London	77.0	71.1	8.0	148	64.9	85.6
53	Canterbury Christ Church	96.6	88.3	7.3	—	43.4	85.3
=54	Birmingham City	84.1	79.7	9.6	129	58.9	85.1
=54	Edinburgh Napier	75.5	74.2	—	168	61.2	85.1
56	Greenwich	82.9	78.4	3.5	133	62.9	85.0
57	Glasgow Caledonian	84.5	79.5	1.8	188	42.0	84.9
58	Worcester	80.4	79.3	11.1	130	59.7	84.8
59	South Wales	85.1	81.5	3.3	130	59.5	84.6

Art and Design cont

		Teaching quality %	Student experience %	Research quality %	Entry standards (UCAS points)	Graduate prospects %	Overall score
60	Derby	76.5	72.4	5.1	125	70.7	84.5
=61	London Metropolitan	84.9	79.8	4.7	124	60.7	84.4
=61	Cardiff Metropolitan	86.2	82.4	7.9	127	55.4	84.4
63	Wolverhampton	87.7	83.3	8.9	103	60.3	84.1
64	Anglia Ruskin	82.7	79.2	8.5	137	54.3	84.0
65	Chester	83.3	80.2	6.2	110	64.2	83.9
66	Cumbria	83.3	77.1	6.1	139	54.3	83.7
=67	Bucks New	78.1	72.0	6.1	122	66.1	83.5
=67	Middlesex	76.6	73.0	13.3	132	58.8	83.5
69	Ravensbourne, London	76.7	72.0	—	121	70.1	83.0
70	West London	85.5	83.8	4.5	122	53.3	82.8
71	Gloucestershire	82.6	75.5	—	128	59.2	82.5
72	Solent	84.9	82.7	1.6	113	57.2	82.2
73	Oxford Brookes	72.8	68.5	10.4	161	50.4	82.1
74	Sunderland	79.5	70.9	9.8	123	56.8	81.9
75	Winchester	79.9	79.0	—	98	67.9	81.7
76	Hull	75.7	57.0	11.2	125	61.5	81.2
77	Northampton	85.0	73.6	2.9	117	54.2	81.0
78	Glyndŵr	80.5	76.9	7.8	112	52.1	80.1
79	Leeds Beckett	83.9	76.7	1.2	119	50.8	80.0
80	Bolton	82.9	76.9	—	116	52.2	79.7
81	York St John	85.8	79.2	—	122	45.9	79.6
82	Suffolk	79.5	72.1	—	116	54.5	79.0
83	East London	65.9	64.0	9.8	114	59.7	77.9
84	Bedfordshire	74.9	72.5	—	100	59.8	77.8
85	Liverpool Hope	49.2	39.5	—	135	78.6	76.6

Employed in professional job	54%	Employed in non-professional job and Studying	2%
Employed in professional job and studying	1%	Employed in non-professional job	25%
Studying	8%	Unemployed	10%
Average starting professional salary	£19,000	Average starting non-professional salary	£15,808

Biological Sciences

The numbers starting degrees in the biological sciences have fallen marginally for the last two years, but only after record enrolments in the five years before that. Botany, zoology and microbiology actually enjoyed small increases in 2018, but general biology degrees and those in molecular biology, biochemistry and biophysics declined. Nevertheless, almost 95,000 applications showed that these are clearly the most popular sciences. With 143 universities and colleges planning programmes for undergraduates, there will be more options than ever in 2020.

Cambridge remains top for the 15th year in a row, and Oxford is back up to second after losing that position last year for the first time in the same period. The average grades for entrants to Cambridge's Natural Sciences degree are among the highest in any subject, while fourth-placed Imperial College has the best score for graduate prospects. Ulster, just outside the top 30 after choosing not to enter the Research Excellence Framework in these subjects, has the most satisfied students, topping both of our measures derived from the National Student Survey.

Satisfaction rates are generally good – only three of the 100 universities dropped below 70% on teaching quality. Graduates are less enthusiastic, however: three years after graduation almost 40% of biologists wish they had chosen a different subject – one of the biggest proportions in the arts or sciences. Employment rates and graduate salaries have been improving, but are still in the bottom half of all subjects. Four out of ten graduates stay on for a postgraduate qualification, either full or part-time.

Microbiology provides the stiffest competition at entry, with six applications to the place, but the leading universities' requirements can be tough across all the subjects in this category. Many will demand two sciences at A-level, or the equivalent – usually biology and chemistry – for any of the biological sciences..

Biological Sciences	Teaching quality %	Student experience %	Research quality %	Entry standards (UCAS points)	Graduate prospects %	Overall score
1 Cambridge	—	—	52.5	240	83.9	100.0
2 Oxford	—	—	50.9	217	83.9	96.8
3 Dundee	83.0	83.9	55.4	180	85.2	95.8
4 Imperial College London	73.7	75.4	61.6	198	88.4	95.6
5 St Andrews	88.3	86.3	37.6	207	73.4	93.8
6 York	87.1	87.8	41.9	174	77.4	93.0
7 Strathclyde	78.3	79.8	52.2	197	76.6	92.9
8 Sheffield	82.1	85.8	57.4	160	77.8	92.8
9 University College London	77.6	77.9	55.4	189	77.6	92.6
=10 Exeter	86.8	86.0	39.7	172	77.8	92.4
=10 Lancaster	83.3	83.6	46.5	159	82.3	92.4
12 Warwick	82.4	86.1	37.1	157	86.9	92.3
13 King's College London	83.6	84.6	38.0	172	79.0	91.6
14 Bristol	81.9	83.0	46.8	167	76.1	91.1
15 Edinburgh	73.6	75.0	62.9	192	70.1	90.8
16 Durham	77.9	74.0	32.9	199	80.7	90.7
17 Bath	78.0	83.8	31.5	177	82.6	90.6
18 Sussex	76.3	78.6	46.8	153	80.3	89.5
19 Manchester	78.8	77.2	38.3	167	78.8	89.4
=20 Birmingham	76.2	75.2	38.1	168	81.6	89.2
=20 Glasgow	76.8	82.1	33.4	195	72.4	89.2
22 Southampton	82.3	85.8	34.2	151	76.5	88.8
=23 Nottingham Trent	83.5	85.2	24.1	128	87.2	88.7
=23 Swansea	86.1	86.5	38.6	130	75.9	88.7
25 Aberystwyth	89.5	87.6	38.2	116	75.6	88.5
26 Liverpool	79.0	83.0	33.9	150	77.6	88.0

Biological Sciences cont

	Teaching quality %	Student experience %	Research quality %	Entry standards (UCAS points)	Graduate prospects %	Overall score
27 Kent	75.1	77.2	39.1	135	85.1	87.9
28 Leeds	76.9	76.9	40.9	160	74.9	87.7
=29 Aberdeen	80.6	82.9	34.7	167	66.8	86.9
=29 Leicester	82.2	83.4	36.5	137	72.8	86.9
31 Ulster	92.0	95.5	—	124	81.1	86.7
=32 Aston	77.7	74.8	39.1	120	82.0	86.4
=32 Glasgow Caledonian	79.8	81.6	8.1	176	78.0	86.4
=32 Royal Holloway, London	84.0	85.4	25.7	135	74.4	86.4
35 East Anglia	77.9	79.5	38.8	134	75.1	86.2
36 Heriot-Watt	76.2	70.6	26.3	164	77.7	85.9
37 Queen's, Belfast	72.2	74.4	47.3	147	72.7	85.8
=38 Portsmouth	83.7	76.9	24.3	104	84.5	85.5
=38 Surrey	78.5	79.1	37.5	149	68.4	85.5
40 Keele	82.1	83.1	16.5	133	78.2	85.3
41 Central Lancashire	87.2	87.7	8.3	131	75.8	85.1
42 Nottingham	74.4	75.1	26.5	151	77.2	85.0
=43 Newcastle	76.6	79.8	28.4	148	72.7	84.9
=43 Teesside	86.1	85.3	—	122	84.3	84.9
45 Hull	81.1	78.5	31.7	120	74.3	84.7
46 Stirling	74.9	77.3	49.0	169	56.9	84.6
47 Reading	86.6	83.6	26.6	128	66.1	84.3
48 Robert Gordon	78.6	79.2	4.9	158	77.0	84.0
=49 Cardiff	71.5	71.9	33.3	158	71.2	83.9
=49 Edge Hill	91.7	93.9	6.2	123	67.7	83.9
51 Huddersfield	83.3	81.3	7.8	130	77.3	83.8
52 Essex	85.1	82.8	17.8	100	77.9	83.7
53 Lincoln	85.6	86.4	—	127	77.5	83.6
=54 Abertay	90.7	90.9	4.3	121	67.2	82.9
=54 Northumbria	74.5	74.5	14.0	136	79.9	82.9
=54 Plymouth	88.0	85.2	17.4	142	59.5	82.9
57 West of Scotland	90.0	82.3	29.0	157	47.8	82.8
=58 Queen Mary, London	71.6	74.6	26.1	137	74.3	82.5
=58 Oxford Brookes	75.1	78.9	21.3	122	75.5	82.5
60 Sheffield Hallam	84.4	81.9	10.4	114	72.9	82.2
=61 Greenwich	77.9	85.7	7.4	142	70.1	82.0
=61 Sunderland	82.7	84.7	7.5	104	76.8	82.0
=61 Westminster	74.7	78.3	21.2	122	74.3	82.0
64 Queen Margaret, Edinburgh	80.1	75.7	—	154	72.7	81.9
65 Manchester Metropolitan	83.4	84.4	12.0	128	66.5	81.8
66 Roehampton	80.3	79.8	20.6	108	71.7	81.7
67 Liverpool John Moores	83.2	82.0	15.1	148	58.0	81.3
68 Brunel	74.9	74.9	18.2	124	72.9	81.0

69	Staffordshire	81.0	80.9	—	114	75.7	80.7
70	Worcester	88.4	86.3	10.9	111	60.2	80.3
71	Derby	80.5	77.9	1.6	130	70.4	80.2
72	Bolton	87.4	83.9	—	108*	68.0	80.0
=73	Bangor	80.3	81.2	31.5	136	50.1	79.9
=73	Bedfordshire	77.3	81.2	25.1	93	68.3	79.9
=73	Leeds Beckett	79.8	80.3	3.5	114	72.1	79.9
76	Bradford	72.3	75.0	9.5	118	75.6	79.6
77	Salford	83.0	81.0	12.7	125	59.3	79.5
=78	Edinburgh Napier	81.1	81.3	8.9	151	55.2	79.4
=78	Hertfordshire	77.3	75.0	10.9	101	74.7	79.4
80	St George's, London	57.8	62.0	20.0	151	78.4	79.3
81	Chester	74.1	75.2	12.0	110	72.7	79.1
82	London South Bank	77.3	78.7	35.0	100*	58.7	79.0
=83	South Wales	83.5	79.0	—	129	63.4	78.9
=83	Royal Veterinary College	73.9	80.5	—	133	70.0	78.9
=85	Gloucestershire	72.1	69.3	14.5	115	72.3	78.6
=85	Cardiff Metropolitan	78.2	82.2	—	107	71.6	78.6
=85	West of England	76.3	77.0	8.2	113	69.2	78.6
=88	Bath Spa	80.1	77.3	—	103	72.8	78.5
=88	East London	80.3	84.2	—	94	71.7	78.5
90	Brighton	88.1	83.2	4.8	104	59.7	78.4
91	London Metropolitan	72.1	75.3	—	112	76.6	78.1
92	Middlesex	74.7	66.8	10.0	111	72.2	77.9
93	Wolverhampton	75.6	77.1	—	111	70.0	77.4
94	Northampton	91.2	86.6	—	85	59.0	77.3
95	Coventry	69.5	72.3	4.5	88	79.9	76.9
96	Kingston	78.8	80.6	2.6	106	62.6	76.6
97	Anglia Ruskin	83.6	83.1	2.2	112	49.5	75.1
98	Canterbury Christ Church	73.2	66.7	11.9	91	63.3	74.2
99	Liverpool Hope	47.7	46.6	—	99	93.6	72.8
100	Bournemouth	73.5	69.5	4.7	116	51.4	72.4

Employed in professional job	30%	Employed in non-professional job and Studying		3%
Employed in professional job and studying	2%	Employed in non-professional job		18%
Studying	35%	Unemployed		10%
Average starting professional salary	£21,000	Average starting non-professional salary		£16,000

Building

Building is in the top ten subjects both for employment prospects and starting salaries in professional jobs – and yet there are still less than four applications per place. Applications and enrolments both fell in 2018 after something of a recovery over the previous five years, but the demand for places is down by more than a third since the recession of 2008, when the decline set in.

Almost 80% of those completing building degrees in 2017 went straight into graduate-level employment, and only five of the 35 universities in our table dropped below this mark. The proportion topped 90% at 15 universities.

The table is dominated by post-1992 universities, although older foundations fill the top five places.

Loughborough remains clear of the rest, with University College London still in second place, but every other university has shifted position this year. Loughborough achieved the best grades in the Research Excellence Framework, while students on UCL's Project Management for Construction degree have the highest entry grades. In general, entry requirements are lower than for most subjects – even the leading institutions average less than 160 points and four dropped below 100 in 2018.

The relatively low numbers of students on many building courses make for fluctuations in the scores, especially where satisfaction levels are concerned. Heriot Watt, the leader on the broad student experience, was not in the top 20 on this measure last year. Students at Coventry are the most satisfied with the quality of teaching.

Courses in this category include surveying and building services engineering, as well as construction. There is now the added complication for students from degree apprenticeships in construction, which do not appear in this table but are a potentially attractive alternative for those planning a career in the sector.

Building	Teaching quality %	Student experience %	Research quality %	Entry standards (UCAS points)	Graduate prospects %	Overall score
1 Loughborough	86.4	89.0	58.3	155	96.4	100.0
2 University College London	77.5	80.8	54.1	158	92.9	96.7
3 Heriot-Watt	85.2	93.4	38.1	157	92.9	96.1
4 Ulster	88.5	88.0	28.6	135	94.1	91.9
5 Reading	75.1	73.8	40.0	135	96.6	91.5
6 Oxford Brookes	86.9	86.8	17.6	123	93.6	87.9
7 Nottingham	76.1	76.6	14.8	144	–	87.1
8 West of England	88.3	90.2	10.6	121	92.9	86.7
=9 Coventry	89.1	90.6	10.3	129	87.5	86.1
=9 Robert Gordon	83.3	79.3	8.3	132	92.5	86.1
11 London South Bank	78.2	77.9	19.6	113	95.5	85.4
=12 Liverpool John Moores	80.6	79.7	4.9	143	87.0	85.0
=12 Nottingham Trent	82.3	79.7	3.4	122	96.3	85.0
14 Edinburgh Napier	84.3	85.3	5.7	138	83.7	84.2
15 Sheffield Hallam	76.9	76.8	13.4	116	93.8	84.0
=16 Aston	82.6	87.0	20.6	139	75.0	83.8
=16 Northumbria	73.3	73.2	5.9	137	90.4	83.8
18 Portsmouth	84.3	85.3	–	110	95.1	83.1
19 Salford	72.1	71.5	19.6	127	84.1	82.3
20 Plymouth	83.4	87.3	13.2	118	81.1	81.8
21 Anglia Ruskin	83.1	83.9	5.2	113	85.4	81.0
22 South Wales	68.7	70.7	–	122	92.3	80.4

23	Glasgow Caledonian	68.1	65.6	9.1	141	80.0	80.1
24	Westminster	69.5	66.9	10.7	121	86.0	79.9
25	Bolton	87.6*	81.3*	2.5	—	77.8	79.5
26	Wolverhampton	81.3	82.1	5.6	97	86.5	78.6
27	Greenwich	67.7	56.6	2.0	132	83.3	78.1
28	Leeds Beckett	68.9	69.3	5.6	103	90.0	77.9
29	Derby	85.5	83.7	5.6	97	81.3	77.7
30	Central Lancashire	71.4	70.4	3.0	120	80.0	77.0
31	Brighton	58.1	56.9	—	111	88.9	75.3
32	East London	84.2	80.2	8.1	96	70.6	74.0
33	Birmingham City	53.4	49.8	2.7	109	79.2	70.8
34	Kingston	43.4	51.7	—	114	80.0	70.1
35	Wales Trinity St David	65.5	62.8	—	99	72.4	69.5

Employed in professional job	75%	Employed in non-professional job and Studying	0%
Employed in professional job and studying	4%	Employed in non-professional job	7%
Studying	5%	Unemployed	9%
Average starting professional salary	£26,000	Average starting non-professional salary	£17,316

Business Studies

St Andrews has taken over the lead in business studies from Oxford for the first time since its one appearance on top of the table, three years ago. Although it still has the highest entry standards, in the absence of new satisfaction scores due to the continuing boycott of the National Student Survey, a drop of 16 points in average entry grades was Oxford's undoing. St Andrews is not top on any single measure but it is among the leaders on all of them.

The Business Studies table is the biggest in our *Guide*, with 120 universities. The various branches of business and management are the largest recruiters of undergraduates in the UK, with more than 50,000 students starting courses last autumn from over 250,000 applications. Although, for the third year in a row, fewer students embarked on degrees in management, there was a healthy increase of more than 11% for business studies. The two subjects also remain the biggest area in Clearing, with more than 4,000 students finding places through the service in 2018.

Some of the most famous business schools are absent from this ranking because they do not offer undergraduate courses. One exception is the Manchester Business School, which provides Manchester's undergraduate courses, as well as MBAs and executive education. The London School of Economics, which shares tenth place with York, was the top scorer in the Research Excellence Framework.

Student satisfaction levels have dipped since the introduction two years ago of more focused questions in the National Student Survey. West London, in 50th place overall, partly because it did not enter the Research Excellence Framework in this area, is the only university to reach 90% on either of our satisfaction measures. However, there is just one score below 65% for perceptions of teaching quality and only one for the broader student experience.

Three years after graduation, almost 39% of respondents say they would have chosen a different subject. Disappointments in the graduate employment market may be partly responsible. Although nearly six out of ten graduates went straight into a professional job in 2017, the subjects are outside the top 40 overall. Salary levels for those who do find professional employment are much better – business studies is among a large group of subjects sharing 26th place.

Business Studies	Teaching quality %	Student experience %	Research quality %	Entry standards (UCAS points)	Graduate prospects %	Overall score
1 St Andrews	84.7	86.3	43.8	211	85.5	100.0
2 Bath	81.1	84.3	41.8	189	83.2	96.6
=3 Loughborough	82.5	88.7	32.6	159	92.5	95.9
=3 Oxford	—	—	32.0	216	85.1	95.9
5 Warwick	77.0	81.5	40.4	189	86.2	95.5
6 Leeds	80.5	84.3	39.3	168	85.9	95.1
7 Strathclyde	77.6	79.7	44.3	207	71.7	94.5
8 Lancaster	78.6	80.3	42.6	152	89.3	94.1
9 University College London	73.8	76.1	43.9	180	87.3	94.0
=10 London School of Economics	71.0	73.3	52.3	172	85.4	93.2
=10 York	86.1	87.7	24.0	144	85.7	93.2
12 Exeter	74.1	80.9	24.4	169	94.0	92.5
13 King's College London	68.6	77.4	38.2	189	82.8	91.9
14 Southampton	79.3	83.9	24.0	156	85.6	91.8
=15 City	77.1	81.4	28.7	176	77.3	91.3
=15 Sheffield	77.1	81.7	26.8	150	87.7	91.3
17 Glasgow	71.1	74.5	22.1	195	86.7	91.0
18 Stirling	82.3	81.0	25.2	160	76.5	90.9
19 East Anglia	81.3	80.7	28.1	145	80.7	90.8
20 Bristol	77.1	77.5	32.1	164	77.3	90.5
21 Durham	73.5	72.0	23.1	172	88.5	90.2
22 Manchester	75.0	78.4	33.3	160	77.4	90.0
23 Nottingham	70.0	77.4	32.6	153	84.8	89.4
24 Aberdeen	71.4	75.3	24.9	182	78.6	89.2
25 Ulster	84.6	84.5	40.4	125	61.8	89.0
=26 Cardiff	73.3	75.9	32.0	161	76.0	88.8
=26 Sussex	73.7	78.8	23.7	146	85.1	88.8
28 Kent	75.2	77.4	24.8	139	84.9	88.7
29 Reading	74.6	74.2	29.3	136	84.6	88.5
30 Swansea	78.5	82.0	22.0	135	79.2	88.4
=31 Birmingham	67.1	70.2	29.1	163	87.2	88.3
=31 Heriot-Watt	79.0	79.0	18.8	154	74.9	88.3
33 Liverpool	75.1	78.0	20.1	149	81.8	88.2
34 Royal Holloway, London	77.1	77.6	27.0	140	75.4	87.8
=35 Aston	77.5	77.9	19.7	143	78.0	87.6
=35 Newcastle	68.8	72.4	20.7	158	87.2	87.6
=37 Bangor	81.4	84.2	23.4	129	69.0	87.3
=37 Nottingham Trent	79.9	80.4	4.6	132	87.0	87.3
=37 Queen's, Belfast	72.3	75.3	32.7	145	75.1	87.3

=37	Robert Gordon	80.4	81.0	2.6	171	72.5	87.3
41	Edinburgh	66.4	72.0	25.8	185	73.8	86.9
42	Falmouth	84.4	78.7	—	109	89.8	86.6
43	Glasgow Caledonian	83.4	83.1	1.8	183	56.6	86.2
44	Oxford Brookes	78.9	81.3	5.1	136	78.7	86.1
45	Surrey	69.3	74.9	15.8	160	79.7	86.0
=46	Aberystwyth	80.9	79.8	14.5	113	75.4	85.5
=46	Coventry	80.6	80.8	1.6	124	80.7	85.5
=46	West of England	81.0	83.6	5.5	117	77.8	85.5
49	SOAS, London	68.0	68.7	25.0	159	75.7	85.4
50	West London	90.0	90.6	—	106	66.7	85.2
51	Portsmouth	75.8	77.1	9.5	115	85.1	85.1
52	Lincoln	77.5	77.9	4.8	121	82.5	84.9
53	Suffolk	86.2	87.9	—	113	68.0	84.6
54	Essex	74.5	77.7	25.1	113	72.3	84.5
=55	Dundee	72.5	78.1	12.1	156	68.7	84.4
=55	Queen Mary, London	67.5	73.1	23.5	151	72.5	84.4
57	Harper Adams	73.9	81.3	—	133	81.3	84.3
=58	De Montfort	74.5	76.8	10.7	107	84.1	84.1
=58	South Wales	86.2	84.0	0.2	129	62.3	84.1
=60	Bournemouth	78.8	77.7	8.8	122	71.3	83.8
=60	Edinburgh Napier	74.9	78.6	2.3	150	71.0	83.8
=60	Hull	76.6	72.3	10.2	127	75.9	83.8
=60	Teesside	82.6	81.5	2.0	106	74.8	83.8
64	Central Lancashire	78.7	81.7	4.4	128	69.4	83.7
65	Abertay	81.0	85.6	—	113	71.7	83.6
66	Keele	77.7	78.3	10.2	124	69.3	83.5
67	Brunel	72.8	76.0	23.0	132	64.4	83.4
=68	Huddersfield	75.2	74.5	4.1	131	76.6	83.3
=68	Staffordshire	81.5	79.7	2.6	121	68.9	83.3
=70	Buckingham	78.0	80.2	—	115	76.8	83.2
=70	Plymouth	76.5	77.8	13.1	115	70.9	83.2
=70	Solent	82.1	80.8	—	113	71.2	83.2
=73	Queen Margaret, Edinburgh	76.9	78.5	—	135	72.0	83.1
=73	Sheffield Hallam	81.7	80.2	0.6	110	72.6	83.1
=75	Edge Hill	81.2	80.6	—	125	67.3	83.0
=75	Liverpool John Moores	77.5	77.4	—	136	70.8	83.0
77	Gloucestershire	79.8	77.7	—	118	73.4	82.9
=78	Chichester	86.3	83.2	—	110	63.3	82.8
=78	Derby	78.2	73.7	0.9	123	75.7	82.8
80	Bath Spa	78.7	79.3	—	107	75.5	82.5
81	Manchester Metropolitan	75.8	74.9	4.7	129	70.8	82.4
82	Northumbria	71.1	73.6	4.0	141	71.4	81.9
=83	Bucks New	84.6	82.1	1.8	118	56.4	81.8
=83	Worcester	81.4	74.1	0.9	121	66.3	81.8
85	Leicester	64.5	69.4	24.3	130	71.3	81.7

Business Studies cont	Teaching quality %	Student experience %	Research quality %	Entry standards (UCAS points)	Graduate prospects %	Overall score
86 West of Scotland	77.3	78.3	2.9	139	59.6	81.6
=87 Bradford	72.3	73.9	11.8	125	67.3	81.4
=87 Hertfordshire	76.3	79.2	0.9	113	70.0	81.4
89 Anglia Ruskin	83.8	81.2	3.4	98	61.2	81.3
90 Birmingham City	79.7	79.6	1.3	115	63.5	81.2
91 Chester	78.5	77.0	0.5	109	69.0	81.1
=92 Kingston	78.8	80.0	9.2	116	54.1	80.5
=92 Leeds Beckett	78.6	79.7	0.8	104	65.3	80.5
94 London South Bank	70.6	73.3	2.1	106	78.4	80.4
95 Liverpool Hope	76.5	75.1	—	105	70.8	80.3
96 Brighton	75.5	74.6	6.5	115	63.5	80.2
97 Westminster	69.2	75.1	2.4	135	66.3	80.0
=98 Bolton	78.4	77.0	—	122	58.3	79.9
=98 Royal Agricultural	70.0	79.5	—	107	73.5	79.9
100 St Mary's, Twickenham	77.2	73.3	—	100	68.9	79.6
101 Wales Trinity St David	82.7	78.9	—	91	59.1	79.3
102 Leeds Trinity	80.3	80.6	—	86	62.2	79.2
103 Arts London	71.0	66.8	—	128	69.4	79.1
104 Middlesex	72.6	73.7	10.5	118	57.1	79.0
105 Greenwich	72.8	74.5	3.3	129	57.4	78.9
106 Sunderland	77.8	75.1	0.4	102	59.9	78.5
107 Cardiff Metropolitan	73.3	71.3	—	112	64.8	78.4
108 Roehampton	73.8	73.0	4.5	104	62.1	78.3
109 Salford	67.1	72.9	5.9	120	64.0	78.2
110 York St John	76.7	74.6	0.8	105	57.9	78.1
111 Winchester	72.8	69.4	—	116	61.9	77.8
112 Wolverhampton	77.3	77.1	2.4	107	51.6	77.7
113 London Metropolitan	74.6	74.5	0.6	88	64.6	77.5
114 Bedfordshire	74.0	70.4	3.1	96	60.7	77.1
115 Canterbury Christ Church	72.8	72.9	—	103	53.3	75.7
=116 East London	70.1	73.1	0.8	103	55.7	75.6
=116 Newman	76.0	86.8	—	87	44.2	75.6
118 Northampton	70.7	68.7	1.0	95	56.7	74.8
119 Cumbria	66.0	67.2	5.6	99	47.8	72.7
120 Glyndŵr	67.5	59.5	—	97	51.0	71.8

Employed in professional job	55%	Employed in non-professional job and Studying	2%
Employed in professional job and studying	3%	Employed in non-professional job	20%
Studying	10%	Unemployed	10%
Average starting professional salary	£22,000	Average starting non-professional salary	£17,971

Celtic Studies

There was a rise of more than 20% in the number of students taking up places on full-time degrees in Celtic Studies in 2018 – but there were still only 115 of them. Applications did at least top 500 for the first time in three years, but only ten universities plan to offer the subjects in 2020 and just eight of them appear in our latest table.

The ranking is split between four universities from Wales, which naturally major in Welsh, and the remaining four, which focus on Gaelic or Irish studies. Ironically, it is the only one from England that tops the table, Cambridge occupying that position for the eighth year in a row. It registered the best performance in the 2014 Research Excellent Framework, although Glasgow, which has shot up five places to second, now has higher entry grades, thanks partly to the generous conversion rate for Scottish secondary qualifications in the UCAS tariff.

Students who do opt for Celtic studies are overwhelmingly satisfied with the experience – no university scores less than 80% in the sections of the National Student Survey (NSS) concerned with the broad student experience and only one – Bangor – misses that mark for the quality of teaching. Aberystwyth, third in the table overall, is the leader on both measures.

Cardiff, which has now dropped to fourth, had the best graduate prospects in a year when Celtic Studies registered the lowest unemployment of any group of subjects outside medicine, dentistry and nursing, contributing to a move of seven places up the employment table to 38th out of the 67 areas. Almost half of the 2017 graduates went on to take another course. Starting salaries for those in professional jobs were a different matter, however. Celtic studies remained in the bottom ten.

Celtic Studies	Teaching quality %	Student experience %	Research quality %	Entry standards (UCAS points)	Graduate prospects %	Overall score
1 Cambridge	—	—	54.0	189	81.8	100.0
2 Glasgow	89.6	85.2	41.1	209	75.0	99.3
3 Aberystwyth	92.4	89.9	23.7	145	79.6	95.4
4 Cardiff	88.6	81.8	32.5	153	84.3	95.2
5 Bangor	78.1	80.5	39.6	157	69.8	92.2
6 Queen's, Belfast	83.1	82.6	53.6	149	39.3	92.0
7 Swansea	84.4	82.1	19.4	166	68.6	91.7
8 Ulster	90.8	84.5	35.7	115	51.7	91.1

Employed in professional job	23%	Employed in non-professional job and Studying	2%
Employed in professional job and studying	6%	Employed in non-professional job	25%
Studying	41%	Unemployed	3%
Average starting professional salary	£19,000	Average starting non-professional salary	n/a

Chemical Engineering

Chemical engineering is in the top four subjects for starting salaries in professional jobs and the top 20 for graduate prospects. Yet applications have dropped almost a quarter in two years and the numbers starting degrees in the subject have fallen by 12% over the same period.

The demand for places is still higher than it was when £9,000 fees were introduced, however, and there are almost six applications to the place.

Entry standards for the full range chemical, process and energy engineering are higher than in other branches of engineering, but only four universities averaged more than 200 points in 2018. They include the top two – Cambridge, which has regained the leadership after a gap of a year, and Imperial College London. The others are Bath and Strathclyde, in fourth and fifth respectively. Degree courses normally demand chemistry and maths A-levels, or their equivalent, and often physics as well. Most courses offer industrial placements in the final year and lead to Chartered Engineer status.

The top two are separated by less than a single point and both feature in QS's top ten universities in the world for chemical engineering – Cambridge in the top three. The most satisfied students are at Wolverhampton, where the approval rate for teaching quality is among the highest in any subject. The university is the biggest climber in this year's table, moving up 15 places to 14th. Portsmouth, two places below it, has the best graduate prospects, an impressive 94% of 2017 leavers going straight into graduate-level employment or continuing to study.

Four out of five chemical engineers come with A-levels or equivalent qualifications, and more than half of the 29 universities in the table average more than 150 points at entry. This helps produce engineering's largest proportion of Firsts and 2:1s. Undergraduates are taught for about 20 hours a week in classrooms or laboratories, one of the highest figures for any subject.

Chemical Engineering	Teaching quality %	Student experience %	Research quality %	Entry standards (UCAS points)	Graduate prospects %	Overall score
1 Cambridge	83.7*	85.5*	62.0	237	86.2	100.0
2 Imperial College London	82.3	86.3	59.6	217	89.7	99.2
3 Nottingham	83.7	87.1	40.8	171	90.7	94.0
4 Bath	81.0	86.1	37.4	201	80.2	91.7
=5 Birmingham	73.0	73.4	47.0	181	88.5	91.4
=5 Strathclyde	69.9	75.1	37.2	214	87.0	91.4
7 Swansea	78.5	81.6	45.5	139	90.0	90.8
8 Lancaster	71.6	71.8	41.6	134	96.2	89.4
=9 Heriot-Watt	79.4	83.2	47.8	156	77.9	89.0
=9 Sheffield	75.7	83.4	36.8	153	86.2	89.0
11 Loughborough	75.5	80.4	41.8	163	81.4	88.6
12 University College London	65.2	70.0	44.6	183	84.5	88.2
13 Manchester	64.8	69.8	48.4	178	82.2	87.6
14 Wolverhampton	97.9	94.9	4.4	104*	—	86.4
15 Queen's, Belfast	69.6	72.6	36.7	152	81.0	85.0
16 Portsmouth	75.1	78.2	9.1	125	94.4	84.8
17 Leeds	56.3	66.5	30.7	176	87.1	84.4
18 Edinburgh	63.2	66.2	50.3	191	69.3	84.3
19 London South Bank	84.7	87.7	19.6	98	83.8	84.2
20 Newcastle	64.9	67.8	30.2	152	83.7	83.5
21 Teesside	83.3	82.7	5.8	110	86.3	82.9

22 Aberdeen	76.2	78.5	28.4	159	69.6	82.8
23 Chester	90.0	83.6	7.1	102	—	82.5
24 Bradford	80.4	84.3	7.7	119	81.0	81.9
25 Aston	78.2	79.1	20.6	121	76.7	81.6
26 Hull	67.1	70.2	16.5	108	86.7	80.1
27 West of Scotland	75.1	81.2	9.0	133	75.0	79.9
28 Surrey	71.9	75.8	30.8	142	65.3	79.6
29 Huddersfield	91.4	89.0	10.2	97*	60.6	77.3

Employed in professional job	52%	Employed in non-professional job and Studying	1%
Employed in professional job and studying	2%	Employed in non-professional job	7%
Studying	24%	Unemployed	13%
Average starting professional salary	£27,500	Average starting non-professional salary	£18,000

Chemistry

Chemistry has one of the highest workloads of any degree subject, in terms of teaching time. Undergraduates spend up to 25 hours a week in classrooms or laboratories, according to UCAS. But most students seem to enjoy the experience. Satisfaction rates are high throughout the table, with some of the best scores coming at universities outside the top 20. South Wales, in 35th place, partly because it did not enter the Research Excellence Framework in chemistry, has the best rate for teaching quality, while Nottingham Trent, in 10th, does best in the sections of the National Student Survey concerned with the broader student experience.

However, a third year of decline in both applications and enrolments in 2018 confirmed that chemistry's extended period of rising popularity among prospective students had come to an end. Entry standards at the leading universities remain high nevertheless –seven universities average more than 200 points, including four of the top five. Some courses require maths as well as chemistry, and most successful candidates for the leading universities take more than one science at A-level.

Cambridge and Oxford (in that order) remain clear at the top of the table, although neither has student satisfaction scores because responses to the National Student Survey did not reach the 50% threshold for publication. Cambridge has the highest entry standards and the best research grades – 97%of the work submitted for the Research Excellence Framework was considered world-leading or internationally excellent. Both Cambridge and Oxford are among the top six universities in the world for chemistry, according to QS.

Chemistry is just outside the top 20 for graduate prospects and salaries in graduate-level employment. Only two universities – Nottingham Trent and King's – saw positive destinations for more than 90% of 2017 graduates. Equally, only one university dropped (fractionally) below 60% on this measure. A total of 115 universities and colleges plan to offer the subject in 2020.

Chemistry

	Teaching quality %	Student experience %	Research quality %	Entry standards (UCAS points)	Graduate prospects %	Overall score
1 Cambridge	—	—	70.3	240	84.0	100.0
2 Oxford	—	—	63.1	229	89.8	98.8
3 St Andrews	85.9	89.9	50.3	208	83.0	96.2
4 York	88.4	86.4	44.6	187	86.1	95.5
5 Durham	83.7	80.5	49.1	208	85.6	95.4
6 Warwick	85.0	87.2	50.8	168	84.4	94.0
7 Strathclyde	88.0	85.5	40.1	195	79.8	93.1
8 Lancaster	86.8	87.2	37.5	162	85.7	92.9
9 Liverpool	78.9	77.9	55.6	151	88.1	92.6
=10 Nottingham	81.0	79.9	48.5	159	86.9	92.4
=10 Nottingham Trent	92.2	90.9	24.1	118	92.3	92.4
=12 Bristol	83.5	83.6	56.6	177	77.6	92.3
=12 University College London	75.9	77.1	56.0	182	83.9	92.3
14 Birmingham	86.9	86.1	37.3	163	82.8	91.9
15 Bath	81.9	82.4	43.0	176	82.1	91.6
16 Heriot-Watt	84.6	85.5	34.2	170	83.2	91.5
17 Glasgow	72.9	72.2	41.1	208	82.6	90.5
18 Keele	89.3	87.7	41.1	115	81.4	89.9
19 Leicester	87.1	86.3	32.8	129	83.6	89.8
20 Surrey	85.3	79.4	30.8	152	82.7	89.4
21 Edinburgh	74.8	70.6	48.4	200	76.9	89.3
22 Plymouth	93.5	90.7	25.3	117	79.5	88.7
23 West of Scotland	89.0	81.4	29.0	152	77.8	88.6
24 Imperial College London	63.8	64.6	54.6	195	81.8	88.5
=25 Cardiff	78.6	82.3	30.9	140	84.7	88.4
=25 Sheffield	78.2	84.5	38.9	155	78.4	88.4
27 Loughborough	81.4	86.4	23.9	145	82.4	88.1
28 Manchester	77.2	80.0	46.0	164	75.0	87.9
=29 Leeds	75.9	80.6	35.9	154	80.1	87.6
=29 Queen's, Belfast	76.1	77.0	34.7	159	80.8	87.6
31 East Anglia	78.2	79.6	39.2	150	78.1	87.5
32 Southampton	78.8	75.1	50.7	154	74.2	87.4
33 Bangor	81.9	82.8	19.1	119	84.6	86.5
34 Huddersfield	86.5	82.4	11.0	117	84.7	86.4
35 South Wales	94.6	88.0	—	119	81.3	86.3
=36 Greenwich	92.9	88.7	7.4	124	78.0	86.1
=36 Manchester Metropolitan	88.2	85.1	16.3	129	77.9	86.1
38 Newcastle	78.4	82.6	28.5	148	76.6	86.0
=39 Aberdeen	77.3	80.8	31.6	203	67.0	85.9
=39 Aston	85.1	85.4	20.6	120	78.9	85.9
41 Sussex	82.8	82.4	25.8	149	74.3	85.8
42 Queen Mary, London	78.8	80.1	37.0	130	74.2	85.0

43 Hull	82.5	82.0	24.2	116	77.3	84.7
44 Reading	77.2	75.9	27.3	115	81.5	84.6
45 Bradford	77.8	78.3	9.5	108	86.8	84.2
46 Sheffield Hallam	81.8	81.4	17.8	103	79.8	83.8
47 Liverpool John Moores	76.0	74.7	6.0	133	83.3	83.3
48 Central Lancashire	74.2	74.2	11.7	120	83.9	83.0
=49 Kent	78.1	73.6	27.5	122	74.7	82.8
=49 London Metropolitan	81.1	80.4	—	110	82.6	82.8
51 King's College London	64.8	66.1	—	152	90.0	82.6
52 Northumbria	87.1	85.0	14.0	147	59.7	80.8
53 Brighton	71.3	72.2	4.8	107	82.2	80.2
54 Kingston	81.7	81.1	2.6	96	62.9	76.2

Employed in professional job	39%	Employed in non-professional job and Studying	2%
Employed in professional job and studying	2%	Employed in non-professional job	12%
Studying	34%	Unemployed	10%
Average starting professional salary	£22,500	Average starting non-professional salary	£16,653

Civil Engineering

Cambridge has retained the lead in civil engineering that it won last year, registering the highest entry standards and the best research grades. But second-placed Glasgow, which benefits from a rare 100% employment score, has closed the gap slightly. Cambridge is ranked by QS as the fourth best university in the world for the subject, with Imperial College London – fourth in our table – only two places behind.

Both applications and enrolments were down in 2018, but 89 universities and colleges are planning undergraduate programmes in 2020. Graduate prospects are in the top ten for all subjects, with 70% of leavers going straight into professional jobs and earning average salaries of £26,000, which are also in the top ten of the 67 subject groups. The plentiful employment opportunities are reflected in the table, where 25 of the 55 universities saw at least nine out of ten graduates go straight into professional jobs or on to postgraduate study.

By contrast, only two universities reached 90% in either of our student satisfaction measures. West London had the best scores, with exactly the same proportion – 93.9% – satisfied with the quality of teaching and the broader student experience.

Some of the top degrees in civil engineering are four-year courses leading to an MEng; others are sandwich courses incorporating a period at work. The leading departments will expect physics and maths A-levels, or their equivalent. Fewer than half of all civil engineering undergraduates are admitted with A-levels, however, reflecting the popularity of BTEC. Almost half of the universities in the table are post-1992 institutions, but only Northumbria, in 15th position after a rise of 12 places, reaches the top 20.

Civil Engineering

		Teaching quality %	Student experience %	Research quality %	Entry standards (UCAS points)	Graduate prospects %	Overall score
1	Cambridge	83.7*	85.5*	67.0	239	93.5	100.0
2	Glasgow	82.2	85.7	47.2	200	100.0	96.3
3	Bath	81.0	86.1	52.9	185	97.5	95.1
4	Imperial College London	81.1	86.6	61.5	195	87.5	94.4
5	Southampton	83.4	87.4	52.3	179	93.5	94.3
6	Bristol	84.0	87.5	52.3	175	91.9	93.8
7	Aberdeen	87.9	89.5	28.4	159	95.7	91.9
8	Sheffield	77.2	82.6	43.1	165	97.2	91.3
9	Nottingham	86.3	84.6	40.8	161	87.8	90.6
10	Swansea	78.5	81.6	45.5	140	96.4	89.9
11	Heriot-Watt	80.3	82.7	47.8	163	84.7	89.4
12	Exeter	74.7	77.3	36.4	164	96.8	89.3
=13	Leeds	82.1	85.8	32.0	166	87.1	89.0
=13	Loughborough	81.6	85.6	26.9	147	95.3	89.0
15	Northumbria	88.1	89.2	30.7	143	86.7	88.8
=16	Liverpool	77.8	82.5	32.1	144	97.3	88.7
=16	Strathclyde	72.6	75.1	35.7	190	90.3	88.7
18	Birmingham	84.1	79.7	21.9	160	92.7	88.6
19	Cardiff	73.7	77.1	35.0	164	93.4	88.1
20	Ulster	88.0	85.6	28.6	120	92.6	88.0
21	Manchester	77.6	76.4	36.4	166	88.5	87.9
22	University College London	74.0	75.5	23.1	183	93.2	87.8
23	Edinburgh	66.9	75.1	50.3	181	85.7	87.5
24	Newcastle	76.9	77.5	40.9	142	88.9	86.9
25	Dundee	75.0	80.2	46.2	144	84.9	86.5
26	Queen's, Belfast	76.8	71.8	31.3	142	94.3	86.4
27	Surrey	76.5	80.1	30.8	142	89.7	86.0
28	Nottingham Trent	84.8	85.0	3.4	129	95.3	85.7
29	Central Lancashire	84.9	86.4	7.1	136	—	85.6
30	Edinburgh Napier	80.2	82.0	7.7	148	91.2	85.1
31	Abertay	91.2	90.1	16.3	104	85.7	85.0
32	London South Bank	88.9	88.9	19.6	118	82.2	84.9
33	Bradford	79.1	79.8	17.8	123	91.9	84.3
34	West London	93.9	93.9	—	119	81.0	83.9
35	Teesside	78.5	79.3	5.8	130	92.6	83.4
36	Plymouth	76.9	79.1	15.7	123	90.0	83.1
37	Coventry	77.7	79.7	10.3	120	90.8	82.6
38	Greenwich	73.4	69.3	5.5	142	92.9	82.0
39	Salford	76.6	78.6	19.6	123	84.1	81.9
40	Portsmouth	76.9	76.6	9.1	120	89.6	81.7
=41	Glasgow Caledonian	78.6	77.1	9.1	160	76.3	81.6
=41	West of Scotland	73.2	70.0	9.0	145	88.5	81.6

43	West of England	75.3	69.9	10.6	127	89.5	81.3
44	Anglia Ruskin	85.4	81.9	5.2	111	82.4	81.2
45	Wolverhampton	79.4	78.6	—	104	92.3	81.0
46	Brunel	61.9	71.5	23.7	146	85.5	80.5
=47	Derby	78.7	79.1	6.7	94	85.3	79.2
=47	Leeds Beckett	77.9	76.3	5.6	100	85.7	79.2
49	Liverpool John Moores	72.0	69.3	—	146	83.3	79.1
50	City	67.4	71.8	23.1	120	80.6	78.6
51	East London	79.7	81.1	2.3	115	72.1	77.4
52	South Wales	81.5	83.6	—	89	76.0	76.9
53	Kingston	75.9	80.0	2.9	103	66.1	74.2
54	Brighton	73.8	72.9	5.1	115	64.2	73.6
55	Bolton	60.1	63.9	—	127	59.1	68.7

Employed in professional job	67%	Employed in non-professional job and Studying	1%
Employed in professional job and studying	3%	Employed in non-professional job	6%
Studying	14%	Unemployed	9%
Average starting professional salary	£26,000	Average starting non-professional salary	£15,808

Classics and Ancient History

Six years of rising numbers of students starting classics degrees came to a halt in 2018, when both applications and enrolments were down by more than 8%. The demand for places is still running well ahead of the first year of £9,000 fees, however. The teaching of Latin and Greek has declined seriously in state schools, but most universities offering classics teach the subject from scratch, as well as to more practised students.

Cambridge has topped the table for 14 years in a row, and Oxford has now regained its accustomed second place after overtaking Durham. Cambridge has much the highest scores in the table for research, while Oxford has the highest average entry grades. In the table as a whole, Warwick enjoys the biggest rise, up nine places and into the top ten, while Birmingham experiences the biggest fall, down ten places to 17th.

Roehampton's students are the most satisfied with the quality of teaching and the broader student experience, although the university remains only one place off the bottom of the table because it was the only one of the 23 universities not to enter the Research Excellence Framework. Several universities teach the subjects as part of a modular degree scheme, but not as a degree in its own right, while most providers now broaden their offering with degrees in classical studies or classical civilisation that range beyond Latin or Greek.

Starting salaries for classicists in graduate-level employment are a little below half way in the table, at 37th, while the proportion going into such jobs or on to further study are lower, at 43rd of the 67 subject groups. More than a third of graduates opt for postgraduate courses, but the unemployment rate of 11% was above average in 2017. Glasgow, in 11th place, just pipped third-placed St Andrews to the best graduate prospects.

Classics and Ancient History	Teaching quality %	Student experience %	Research quality %	Entry standards (UCAS points)	Graduate prospects %	Overall score
1 Cambridge	—	—	65.0	208	76.7	100.0
2 Oxford	—	—	58.3	211	79.3	98.0
3 St Andrews	92.0	85.9	43.2	188	83.9	97.7
4 Durham	82.7	81.0	54.3	198	79.8	96.3
5 Exeter	85.9	82.0	45.0	173	80.5	94.3
6 University College London	84.9	81.6	42.7	178	72.4	92.2
7 Nottingham	88.6	79.0	52.0	144	70.4	91.6
8 Warwick	86.4	78.9	45.0	161	64.2	89.8
=9 Kent	87.1	83.2	33.1	121	78.7	89.0
=9 Liverpool	89.9	84.5	28.9	137	72.7	89.0
11 Glasgow	78.6	70.8	32.7	152	84.2	88.7
12 King's College London	80.4	71.9	43.6	159	70.9	88.6
13 Bristol	74.6	68.7	42.2	181	71.3	88.2
14 Reading	85.3	77.0	45.2	123	68.7	87.7
15 Leeds	85.4	83.6	29.1	151	67.4	87.6
16 Newcastle	77.6	73.8	44.7	146	69.1	87.0
17 Birmingham	75.2	71.3	40.3	156	71.7	86.7
18 Royal Holloway, London	85.6	77.3	20.4	141	73.2	86.2
19 Manchester	80.6	75.5	31.0	152	65.0	85.4
20 Swansea	86.3	83.9	25.0	122	67.4	85.3
21 Edinburgh	80.2	72.0	34.9	170	55.4	84.6
22 Roehampton	94.1	86.6	—	112	67.1	82.9
23 Wales Trinity St David	81.4	71.6	15.7	—	45.7	75.6

Employed in professional job	33%	Employed in non-professional job and Studying		3%
Employed in professional job and studying	3%	Employed in non-professional job		20%
Studying	31%	Unemployed		11%
Average starting professional salary	£21,600	Average starting non-professional salary		£16,000

Communication and Media Studies

Loughborough remains the leader in Communication and Media Studies for the third year in a row, but there are bigger moves further down the table than in almost any other subject. Goldsmiths has dropped no less than 57 places, for example, after a disastrous year for student satisfaction. By contrast, London South Bank has jumped 34 places and into the top 50 with one of the best scores for student perceptions of teaching quality.

Both media studies and journalism saw falling applications in 2018, although media studies managed a small increase in the numbers actually embarking on courses. Neither area has suffered the collapse in demand that sceptics in the media itself predicted when £9,000 fees were introduced, despite the fact that graduate employment rates remain poor. The subjects were in the bottom ten nationally both for graduate prospects and starting salaries in professional jobs in 2017. Fewer than half of those completing degrees at 12 of the 95 universities in the table went straight into such jobs or onto postgraduate courses.

The division of jobs into professional and non-graduate fields of employment hits communication and media studies harder than most other subjects. Academics in the field argue that it is normal for students completing media courses to take "entry level" work that is not classified as a graduate job.

Swansea, just outside the top ten overall, has by far the best score for graduate prospects, with a 92% success rate that is over seven percentage points ahead of its nearest rival. Marjon, in Plymouth, is a similar distance ahead for student satisfaction with the quality of teaching, but only just makes the top 40 overall after choosing not to enter the Research Excellence Framework. It is also the leader in the sections of the National Student Survey dealing with the broader student experience, but by a much smaller margin. Strathclyde has the highest entry standards, but no university averages 200 points.

The subjects used to be the preserve of post-1992 universities, but older institutions have been moving in and now monopolise the top 20. Glasgow Caledonian is the leading modern university, in 22nd place.

Communication and Media Studies	Teaching quality %	Student experience %	Research quality %	Entry standards (UCAS points)	Graduate prospects %	Overall score
1 Loughborough	84.2	86.1	62.3	154	78.9	100.0
2 Leeds	83.0	83.1	54.5	165	79.9	99.6
3 Exeter	84.9	80.2	46.2	171	71.4	97.5
4 Lancaster	80.7	81.2	51.4	148	82.1	97.0
5 Sheffield	82.6	82.6	37.9	156	84.5	96.9
=6 Cardiff	80.9	78.0	55.4	151	75.3	96.1
=6 Newcastle	81.4	79.2	37.8	164	79.5	96.1
8 Warwick	85.8	75.3	61.7	162	55.4	95.1
9 York	89.1	80.3	26.0	153	—	94.7
10 Southampton	88.4	78.2	42.7	147	67.1	94.0
11 Strathclyde	81.2	75.6	39.4	193	53.3	93.8
12 Stirling	85.3	81.1	36.0	170	58.9	93.4
13 Swansea	78.0	76.4	18.5	138	92.0	91.7
14 City	73.4	73.6	30.9	158	77.8	91.4
15 Leicester	75.0	75.5	46.1	129	78.3	91.1
16 Queen's, Belfast	87.8	84.5	38.3	152	50.0	91.0
17 Surrey	78.9	80.8	30.2	141	72.0	90.4
18 East Anglia	77.7	75.9	43.8	142	64.5	90.2
19 Sussex	71.7	70.2	43.6	145	72.3	90.0
20 King's College London	73.7	66.6	55.8	156	55.9	89.8
21 Royal Holloway, London	81.4	79.0	38.1	142	56.6	88.9
22 Glasgow Caledonian	80.9	76.6	15.2	172	57.9	88.8
23 Liverpool	79.7	79.0	27.5	136	68.2	88.7
24 Nottingham Trent	85.2	82.8	10.0	133	72.8	88.4
25 Keele	81.7	78.7	25.0	119	74.3	88.2
26 Northumbria	82.4	78.1	22.2	135	66.5	88.0

Communication and Media Studies cont

		Teaching quality %	Student experience %	Research quality %	Entry standards (UCAS points)	Graduate prospects %	Overall score
27	Robert Gordon	88.8	82.1	7.5	152	57.3	87.8
28	Oxford Brookes	76.2	74.5	25.3	142	67.0	87.4
=29	Edinburgh Napier	76.7	76.7	9.5	166	59.5	86.6
=29	Salford	74.8	73.1	36.9	132	62.6	86.6
=31	Brunel	83.6	77.4	23.0	116	67.5	86.4
=31	De Montfort	78.2	75.4	31.2	105	75.4	86.4
=31	Queen Margaret, Edinburgh	76.4	72.1	14.0	157	62.9	86.4
34	Kent	82.0	79.3	—	120	81.8	86.2
35	Hull	86.5	84.7	11.2	129	59.4	85.9
36	Central Lancashire	87.4	84.7	7.9	119	64.6	85.7
37	Liverpool John Moores	79.7	77.9	6.2	138	67.2	85.4
38	Liverpool Hope	79.6	80.4	—	110	84.8	85.3
39	Coventry	80.3	77.1	18.1	115	70.3	85.2
=40	Aberystwyth	86.3	84.1	9.2	110	66.8	85.0
=40	Manchester Metropolitan	77.1	75.5	29.0	122	61.9	85.0
=40	Plymouth Marjon	95.8	87.9	—	113	58.5	85.0
=40	West of England	79.2	77.5	18.6	118	67.8	85.0
44	Portsmouth	81.2	79.6	12.8	104	75.5	84.8
=45	Lincoln	75.9	72.7	4.0	135	72.3	84.3
=45	Solent	85.1	80.8	0.8	116	69.8	84.3
=45	Sunderland	82.4	79.5	13.0	117	64.4	84.3
48	London South Bank	87.3	78.7	12.8	101	66.9	84.2
49	St Mary's, Twickenham	82.2	77.4	9.1	127	62.1	84.1
50	Queen Mary, London	75.0	68.0	35.1	135	52.2	84.0
51	Teesside	82.4	83.1	2.9	106	73.6	83.8
52	Westminster	68.4	66.4	28.3	125	69.0	83.5
=53	Bournemouth	76.9	77.1	15.1	125	60.1	83.0
=53	Creative Arts	84.5	81.1	3.4	114	62.8	83.0
=53	Staffordshire	75.6	70.3	6.7	107	81.3	83.0
56	Sheffield Hallam	83.4	80.3	14.4	114	56.6	82.9
57	Edge Hill	83.3	77.7	10.2	131	50.9	82.7
58	Wolverhampton	80.6	75.6	33.2	95	57.8	82.6
59	Bangor	84.0	81.5	24.7	126	38.9	82.5
60	Derby	76.4	74.9	13.5	115	64.2	82.2
=61	Ulster	78.3	73.6	34.0	124	41.8	82.0
=61	Worcester	85.2	84.1	8.2	105	57.2	82.0
63	Glyndŵr	85.3	76.4	7.8	109	58.7	81.8
64	Gloucestershire	79.2	73.8	9.3	119	60.2	81.7
65	Greenwich	74.4	67.1	3.5	138	61.8	81.4
=66	Birmingham City	79.4	76.6	6.0	112	62.2	81.2
=66	Huddersfield	77.4	70.1	—	118	69.2	81.2
=66	Roehampton	68.3	68.2	26.4	104	69.5	81.2

69	Falmouth	76.4	70.2	—	120	68.8	81.1
=70	Canterbury Christ Church	81.8	75.7	7.3	101	64.2	81.0
=70	West of Scotland	73.3	66.9	11.3	137	56.0	81.0
72	Ravensbourne, London	72.3	64.8	—	111	78.8	80.5
73	Leeds Beckett	84.1	84.2	11.0	106	47.5	80.2
74	Winchester	79.2	76.4	15.8	105	54.0	80.1
75	West London	77.6	70.7	4.5	111	61.9	79.7
76	Bath Spa	71.8	66.4	13.9	114	62.2	79.6
77	Chester	79.0	71.0	4.3	96	66.8	79.4
78	Kingston	78.1	77.2	15.7	107	49.5	79.2
79	Goldsmiths, London	40.2	39.7	60.0	141	62.7	78.8
80	Suffolk	81.3	66.3	—	131	45.5	78.3
=81	Arts London	72.4	65.5	—	115	64.3	78.1
=81	Bedfordshire	84.0	78.0	8.2	89	52.0	78.1
=81	East London	74.7	73.5	13.9	106	51.7	78.1
84	Middlesex	72.7	70.7	11.0	117	51.3	77.9
85	Leeds Trinity	73.0	68.1	3.9	102	62.9	77.3
86	York St John	83.8	78.6	4.4	108	40.3	77.2
87	Brighton	75.4	66.1	16.2	111	44.0	76.6
88	Anglia Ruskin	76.2	71.8	26.4	94	40.4	76.4
=89	London Metropolitan	70.7	61.9	5.9	90	66.1	75.8
=89	Northampton	79.2	72.4	—	89	55.4	75.8
91	Cumbria	70.3	63.2	—	110	57.9	75.5
92	Chichester	76.9	68.8	—	115	40.7	74.7
93	South Wales	72.2	67.4	—	120	43.3	74.5
94	Bucks New	69.7	56.9	—	117	46.1	72.9
95	Bradford	71.3	64.6	—	123	27.8	71.1

Employed in professional job	49%	Employed in non-professional job and Studying	2%
Employed in professional job and studying	2%	Employed in non-professional job	27%
Studying	10%	Unemployed	10%
Average starting professional salary	£19,000	Average starting non-professional salary	£16,185

Computer Science

Both applications and enrolments for computer science degrees rose in 2018, and seem to have done so again in the latest admissions cycle. But the different specialisms vary in popularity, with degrees in artificial intelligence building quickly from a low base – still only 180 places in 2018 – and combinations within computer science also doing well. Overall, the demand for degree places is running at record levels and a growing number of universities are also offering degree apprenticeships in the more popular areas of computer science.

Some of the leading universities demand maths at A-level, or the equivalent, while others want computing or computer science. Entry standards vary more widely than in most subjects, with average scores on the UCAS tariff ranging from more than 200 points at the top four universities in the table to less than 100 points at four others. Top-placed Cambridge has the highest average grades, while Imperial College, its nearest challenger, produced the best scores in the Research Excellence Framework. QS ranks Cambridge among the top five universities in the world for computer science, with Oxford – fourth in our table – only one place behind.

The undergraduates most satisfied with their teaching are at Chester, which is only just in the top 60 overall. Those at West London, just outside the top 40, gave the best rating to the broader student experience. Satisfaction rates are generally high in computer science, with only bottom-placed Canterbury Christ Church averaging less than 60% in either of our measures drawn from the National Student Survey.

Overall, the subjects offer good prospects for graduates – they are close to the top 20 of the 67 subject groups, with two-thirds of leavers going straight into professional employment. The £25,000 average salary in such jobs puts computer science into a tie for 14th place. But the table shows the advantage of winning a place at one of the leading universities. Fifteen of the top 20 universities registered positive destinations for at least 90% of graduates in 2017, whereas only two of the bottom ten reached 70%. Liverpool Hope, in 36th place, had the best record of all, with 98% of graduates going straight into professional employment or continuing their studies.

Computer Science	Teaching quality %	Student experience %	Research quality %	Entry standards (UCAS points)	Graduate prospects %	Overall score
1 Cambridge	—	—	57.1	230	96.5	100.0
2 Imperial College London	74.8	80.9	64.1	221	92.5	97.5
3 St Andrews	88.1	87.1	33.4	220	90.8	97.1
4 Oxford	—	—	60.6	203	90.9	95.9
5 Bath	81.9	84.5	33.3	171	97.0	92.7
6 Exeter	79.6	81.2	40.7	166	97.1	92.4
7 Manchester	77.4	80.4	50.7	183	87.6	92.3
8 Swansea	83.6	82.7	47.5	148	92.7	92.0
9 Durham	73.1	77.2	38.8	194	94.7	91.9
10 Nottingham	80.2	82.5	45.4	168	88.0	91.5
=11 Birmingham	75.6	78.8	46.4	166	93.5	91.1
=11 Sheffield	77.8	80.8	51.1	158	90.1	91.1
=13 Aberystwyth	89.4	86.3	38.4	122	95.2	91.0
=13 Glasgow	68.9	71.9	50.3	195	91.0	91.0
15 Edinburgh	66.4	71.5	54.3	197	88.6	90.6
16 Southampton	72.0	76.2	48.2	172	90.9	90.2
17 Loughborough	85.2	88.8	18.7	155	93.1	90.1
18 University College London	62.3	67.4	62.7	192	89.4	90.0
=19 Newcastle	76.2	80.7	49.7	158	86.9	89.9
=19 Warwick	63.6	64.7	54.8	190	94.6	89.9
21 Leeds	72.7	73.5	41.6	167	94.7	89.6
=22 Royal Holloway, London	79.5	78.7	35.1	147	94.9	89.4
=22 York	74.5	75.9	46.9	153	92.3	89.4
=24 Bristol	66.0	66.9	49.2	188	88.7	88.6
=24 Lancaster	71.8	69.6	44.8	156	95.5	88.6
=24 King's College London	70.2	74.7	47.6	163	89.9	88.6
=24 Strathclyde	78.9	83.5	21.1	186	82.4	88.6

28 Liverpool	75.8	78.5	40.5	151	87.3	87.9
29 Aberdeen	70.0	77.5	37.4	194	77.3	87.4
30 Dundee	77.9	84.3	29.4	157	80.7	86.9
31 Cardiff	76.1	78.1	25.0	151	90.7	86.8
=32 Heriot-Watt	74.1	75.6	39.5	152	81.8	86.0
=32 Surrey	73.5	77.1	25.3	151	90.3	86.0
34 East Anglia	74.4	79.0	35.9	134	87.8	85.9
35 Leicester	77.8	79.0	30.2	133	87.0	85.7
36 Liverpool Hope	83.6	82.4	8.8	111	98.3	85.4
37 Kent	65.0	68.2	37.8	147	92.3	84.7
38 Brunel	78.4	77.0	25.2	135	84.3	84.6
39 Sussex	70.3	70.6	21.6	155	90.6	84.5
40 Staffordshire	87.0	83.7	0.4	126	88.4	84.4
41 West London	87.9	89.7	1.2	124	83.3	84.2
42 Queen's, Belfast	67.8	70.8	29.5	147	88.4	83.8
43 West of England	80.7	82.4	5.9	132	85.3	83.4
44 London South Bank	74.6	67.0	19.6	129	91.8	82.9
45 Essex	70.6	72.4	34.3	121	86.0	82.6
46 Aston	76.7	71.8	21.7	137	80.1	82.5
47 Abertay	78.1	74.3	3.4	162	78.0	82.3
48 Plymouth	73.1	68.5	21.8	137	84.2	82.1
49 Huddersfield	76.3	74.5	7.4	135	86.1	82.0
=50 Coventry	77.2	76.3	3.3	137	83.8	81.7
=50 Queen Mary, London	62.9	67.0	37.4	144	82.3	81.7
=50 Wales Trinity St David	90.1	83.8	1.0	108	78.6	81.7
53 Portsmouth	77.4	76.6	7.2	118	87.8	81.5
=54 Bangor	79.5	75.0	17.6	117	80.3	81.4
=54 Falmouth	80.1	79.8	—	124	84.6	81.4
=56 Salford	77.7	75.8	15.3	133	76.6	81.3
=56 Sheffield Hallam	82.2	80.7	14.4	117	75.7	81.3
58 Robert Gordon	79.4	75.8	4.3	140	78.0	81.2
59 Chester	94.8	85.8	1.3	103	70.9	81.1
60 Teesside	82.5	79.2	3.4	126	77.9	81.0
61 De Montfort	76.4	74.4	13.4	111	86.3	80.9
62 Hull	70.9	69.2	22.2	130	82.4	80.8
63 Edge Hill	82.5	79.8	0.3	139	72.8	80.7
64 Lincoln	69.8	75.7	13.6	135	81.5	80.5
65 Nottingham Trent	72.9	71.2	5.2	137	83.8	80.3
66 Derby	74.1	73.3	5.0	128	84.1	80.1
67 Worcester	87.0	80.0	—	117	73.0	80.0
=68 Manchester Metropolitan	79.0	75.1	5.6	133	74.2	79.9
=68 South Wales	82.6	82.1	3.6	129	69.6	79.9
=70 Arts London	89.8	83.6	—	99	73.7	79.8
=70 East London	85.6	86.0	2.3	106	73.0	79.8
=70 Keele	77.8	81.4	10.8	118	74.4	79.8
73 Bath Spa	82.0	72.8	13.9	106	—	79.5

Computer Science cont

		Teaching quality %	Student experience %	Research quality %	Entry standards (UCAS points)	Graduate prospects %	Overall score
74	Cardiff Metropolitan	74.9	79.8	—	119	82.4	79.4
=75	Bournemouth	76.8	74.4	8.5	127	75.0	79.3
=75	Oxford Brookes	66.0	66.8	13.0	131	86.5	79.3
=75	Glyndŵr	84.8	79.2	3.9	129	65.3	79.3
=78	Edinburgh Napier	74.7	71.7	5.2	135	76.4	79.1
=78	Reading	68.0	64.1	16.3	138	80.5	79.1
=80	Birmingham City	80.0	77.5	4.9	126	69.5	78.7
=80	City	72.9	66.7	21.8	149	64.3	78.7
82	Kingston	83.6	82.7	5.3	113	66.7	78.6
83	Ulster	72.0	69.6	16.6	130	72.1	78.3
=84	Greenwich	74.7	75.0	7.3	147	64.8	78.2
=84	Stirling	65.0	62.6	14.0	122	88.0	78.2
86	Liverpool John Moores	71.6	70.6	3.2	142	73.8	78.0
=87	Bolton	89.6	83.3	—	103	62.6	77.7
=87	Chichester	75.9	70.3	—	123	77.3	77.7
=87	Goldsmiths, London	70.9	72.8	29.2	134	59.6	77.7
90	Hertfordshire	69.3	72.1	7.8	120	79.3	77.6
91	West of Scotland	80.0	74.2	3.2	132	63.2	77.3
92	Northumbria	71.6	68.9	4.0	150	66.0	76.9
=93	Central Lancashire	71.8	69.1	—	137	71.1	76.5
=93	Westminster	71.2	70.6	2.9	124	73.9	76.5
95	Bradford	73.6	66.3	—	136	70.7	76.4
96	Leeds Beckett	78.3	75.8	0.2	109	69.4	76.2
97	Glasgow Caledonian	67.0	67.6	4.0	149	68.3	76.1
98	Gloucestershire	75.2	74.3	—	119	68.8	76.0
99	York St John	72.8	70.9	—	112	75.0	75.8
=100	Middlesex	75.9	78.3	14.2	126	53.6	75.7
=100	Solent	72.2	64.5	—	122	75.0	75.7
102	Wolverhampton	68.5	67.6	—	108	80.5	75.2
103	Anglia Ruskin	75.5	71.9	—	108	69.3	75.0
104	London Metropolitan	74.9	73.6	0.7	107	67.2	74.7
105	Sunderland	70.8	70.0	1.8	110	71.2	74.5
106	Northampton	78.8	71.0	—	102	64.8	74.2
107	Bucks New	82.6	81.1	—	99	54.9	74.0
108	Suffolk	69.2	66.3	—	115	63.6	72.3
109	Bedfordshire	70.9	68.7	9.1	97	61.4	72.2
110	Brighton	70.4	62.4	6.4	107	62.8	72.1
111	Canterbury Christ Church	57.8	58.5	—	96	49.5	64.4

Employed in professional job	64%	Employed in non-professional job and Studying	1%
Employed in professional job and studying	2%	Employed in non-professional job	11%
Studying	11%	Unemployed	12%
Average starting professional salary	£25,000	Average starting non-professional salary	£16,500

Creative Writing

Two more universities have joined our Creative Writing table this year, to add to the three newcomers in the last edition, despite the fact that the subject is bottom of the salaries table and only one place off it for the proportion of graduates going straight into professional jobs or continuing their studies. Indeed, 110 universities and colleges plan to offer the subject in 2020, including as part of joint honours degrees with subjects as diverse as law, dance and business, but more normally with English.

Both applications and enrolments were broadly steady in 2018, when approaching 900 students started undergraduate programmes. With fewer than four applications to the place, entry standards are generally low – only seven of the 53 universities averaged more than 150 points on the UCAS tariff. Top-placed Lancaster was not one of them, although it did average 150 points, as well as having by far the best graduate prospects – a 95% success rate that was a full ten percentage points ahead of its nearest challenger, London South Bank. The rate dropped below 40% at five universities in 2017 and below 20% at one.

Outside the bottom three universities, student satisfaction rates are generally high. They are highest at the University of the West of England, in 16th place overall, which topped 97% in both of our measures drawn from the National Student Survey. Bolton, ten places lower, runs it close, and eight universities reached at least 90% satisfaction with the quality of teaching.

Birmingham, which has gone up two places to second, has the highest entry standards, while Queen Mary, in fifth place, recorded the best performance in the 2014 Research Excellence Framework. The small numbers on many courses make for volatility in the table. Essex, for example, has shot up 28 places to 13th, and York St John is up 20 places to 24th. Most applicants recognise that professional employment will be uncertain and some are not even aiming for a full-time job on graduation.

Creative Writing	Teaching quality %	Student experience %	Research quality %	Entry standards (UCAS points)	Graduate prospects %	Overall score
1 Lancaster	84.9	83.8	47.0	150	95.5	100.0
2 Birmingham	83.7	79.8	37.0	174	81.0	97.9
3 Warwick	79.4	74.0	59.8	171	66.7	97.6
4 Royal Holloway, London	84.3	77.5	49.9	151	75.7	95.7
=5 Queen Mary, London	80.6	76.2	64.0	140	—	93.8
=5 Newcastle	71.6	68.5	54.3	164	—	93.8
7 Bangor	87.7	81.1	46.3	129	70.5	91.4
8 Queen's, Belfast	74.3	66.7	53.1	151	64.3	90.9
9 Nottingham	67.4	64.7	56.6	151	61.7	89.5
=10 Brunel	90.1	88.3	30.9	130	64.3	88.3
=10 Surrey	72.0	64.9	39.1	150	69.0	88.3
12 East Anglia	77.9	74.2	36.2	154	59.4	88.1
13 Essex	82.2	84.8	37.7	126	—	86.8
14 Aberystwyth	88.0	85.7	31.2	117	65.6	85.9
15 Manchester Metropolitan	84.4	77.9	29.0	122	68.4	85.4
16 West of England	97.5	97.2	35.4	116	46.3	85.3

		Teaching quality %	Student experience %	Research quality %	Entry standards (UCAS points)	Graduate prospects %	Overall score
17	Plymouth	90.5	82.0	30.5	117	60.5	84.8
18	London South Bank	91.5	84.9	12.8	97	84.6	83.8
19	Coventry	80.8	74.4	18.1	115	77.4	83.0
20	De Montfort	79.2	70.6	24.1	111	73.8	82.2
21	Liverpool John Moores	83.3	79.1	17.9	138	52.6	82.0
22	Liverpool Hope	89.1	86.4	26.9	104*	–	81.9
23	Birmingham City	79.0	74.5	30.9	104*	69.2	81.8
24	York St John	92.2	85.5	9.7	109	64.3	80.9
25	Hull	83.5	75.9	22.7	118	57.6	80.8
26	Bolton	95.5	92.7	14.4	96	60.0	80.2
=27	Portsmouth	75.8	65.9	17.1	103	80.4	79.9
=27	Westminster	83.8	71.6	28.9	99	62.3	79.9
29	Greenwich	82.6	81.3	14.4	125	53.5	79.6
=30	Bath Spa	70.8	66.1	23.5	120	64.5	79.4
=30	Chester	83.8	76.5	10.7	113	65.6	79.4
32	Edge Hill	79.9	76.1	12.1	129	54.9	79.1
33	Roehampton	84.8	77.5	20.8	111	54.0	78.8
34	Derby	81.3	72.5	13.5	104	69.8	78.7
=35	Central Lancashire	79.8	65.5	9.9	129	56.6	78.0
=35	Falmouth	85.1	81.1	–	119	61.8	78.0
=35	Winchester	86.5	83.7	–	126	54.2	78.0
38	Worcester	81.7	78.8	8.2	114	56.8	76.9
39	St Mary's, Twickenham	85.7	71.6	14.6	96	61.8	76.7
40	Kingston	73.0	68.1	15.7	124	52.2	76.2
41	Salford	69.9	65.8	7.8	127	57.3	75.3
42	Chichester	77.9	73.2	16.3	105	53.3	75.2
43	Gloucestershire	81.2	66.9	9.3	112	54.2	75.1
44	Bedfordshire	96.2	82.0	45.8	82*	17.6	74.3
45	Solent	94.9	87.4	–	108	40.0	74.1
46	Bournemouth	72.9	65.5	15.1	138	33.3	73.8
47	Anglia Ruskin	83.3	75.3	16.3	103	40.0	73.2
48	Sheffield Hallam	81.4	71.6	14.6	109	35.1	72.0
49	Middlesex	63.7	57.9	11.0	–	56.5	70.4
50	Canterbury Christ Church	74.7	67.1	8.0	89	42.1	67.4
51	South Wales	58.1	48.5	12.8	109*	43.2	66.6
52	Northampton	35.6	35.3	15.3	109	34.6	59.4
53	East London	55.6	34.9	–	94*	32.2	57.5

Employed in professional job	27%	Employed in non-professional job and Studying	5%
Employed in professional job and studying	3%	Employed in non-professional job	30%
Studying	21%	Unemployed	13%
Average starting professional salary	£18,000	Average starting non-professional salary	£16,068

Criminology

Loughborough has joined the Criminology table in first place, the second time in three years that a new entrant has gone straight to the top. The previous example was Lancaster, which has now dropped to second. Loughborough's degree is too new to have had graduates in 2017 but it has the best satisfaction rate for the broad student experience and good scores on the other measures. Sheffield drops to third, despite having graduate prospects that are at least 20 percentage points ahead of all but one of the other 66 universities.

The table is now in its fourth year and is still growing. Keele and Liverpool have also joined this year, and no fewer than 155 universities and colleges plan to offer undergraduate programmes in the subject in 2020. Their numbers are being swelled by new degrees in professional policing, part of a drive for more graduates in the force which also involved degree apprenticeships, but criminology was already growing sufficiently to justify a table of its own.

Sociology or psychology is welcomed by some departments, but there are no specific entry requirements for criminology degrees, apart possibly from GCSE maths, since the course is likely to involve the use of statistics. Edinburgh Napier, in 18th place has the highest entry standards, just ahead of Stirling in 11th, although no university averages more than 170 points. For the second year in a row, students at Glyndŵr are by far the most satisfied with the quality of teaching, while Kent has the best research score.

Criminology remains in the bottom six subjects for the proportion of graduates going straight into professional employment or further study, but those who find professional jobs are paid an average of £20,000, placing the subject in the top 50 on this measure. Many criminology graduates eventually find employment in the police force, prison service, the Home Office, charities or law practices. Although the unemployment rate is a respectable 8%, more than a third of graduates start out in lower-level jobs.

Criminology	Teaching quality %	Student experience %	Research quality %	Entry standards (UCAS points)	Graduate prospects %	Overall score
1 Loughborough	84.4	88.1	40.6	155	—	100.0
2 Lancaster	77.1	79.6	51.4	156	74.5	97.9
3 Sheffield	76.4	74.1	26.8	153	95.5	96.9
4 Durham	80.4	76.1	28.7	161	71.8	95.4
5 Nottingham	80.0	78.8	43.5	144	68.2	95.2
6 Manchester	79.2	76.7	27.2	158	70.3	94.4
=7 Birmingham	77.2	73.1	40.1	155	—	94.1
=7 Kent	76.4	77.9	59.0	123	69.4	94.1
=7 Swansea	85.2	83.8	20.4	134	74.4	94.1
10 Leeds	77.1	71.8	40.1	156	65.3	93.8
11 Stirling	79.1	74.5	33.8	167	55.6	93.4
12 York	76.2	75.2	47.5	148	57.1	92.7
=13 Essex	78.4	78.6	44.3	113	73.3	92.3
=13 Sussex	81.1	77.6	27.9	141	64.7	92.3
15 Southampton	74.7	74.2	52.8	144	55.0	92.2
16 Aberystwyth	87.5	83.4	14.3	123	69.3	91.8

Criminology cont	Teaching quality %	Student experience %	Research quality %	Entry standards (UCAS points)	Graduate prospects %	Overall score
17 Keele	79.5	82.0	34.0	127	—	91.5
18 Edinburgh Napier	86.0	81.7	—	168	52.9	91.4
19 Portsmouth	83.3	78.9	12.1	120	78.8	91.1
=20 Leicester	80.8	81.4	26.3	132	61.7	91.0
=20 Queen's, Belfast	82.1	76.3	39.3	139	48.8	91.0
22 Nottingham Trent	82.4	82.8	5.1	126	74.9	90.4
23 Glyndŵr	94.9	86.8	—	100	66.7	89.4
24 Liverpool John Moores	81.1	77.5	5.8	137	66.4	89.2
25 Bradford	79.3	74.1	10.6	131	71.4	89.1
26 Northumbria	77.6	77.0	12.7	144	59.8	88.8
=27 Hull	77.9	74.7	14.3	123	73.0	88.7
=27 Surrey	81.0	77.8	—	164	50.6	88.7
29 Cardiff	71.9	72.0	30.8	151	51.3	88.3
30 Salford	79.8	77.3	27.7	122	55.0	88.2
31 Sheffield Hallam	87.4	82.9	14.4	113	54.1	88.1
=32 Central Lancashire	77.9	77.1	11.8	133	61.8	87.9
=32 Greenwich	86.7	83.8	2.1	128	53.3	87.9
34 Lincoln	78.3	79.6	5.8	121	69.9	87.6
35 Plymouth	81.9	77.3	16.0	124	55.5	87.5
=36 Edge Hill	82.4	79.2	12.1	134	49.5	87.4
=36 London South Bank	77.2	77.7	20.1	110	67.9	87.4
38 Westminster	86.5	83.7	—	115	60.3	87.3
39 Abertay	84.8	78.4	5.0	144	43.4	87.1
=40 Gloucestershire	78.6	80.1	—	116	72.4	86.9
=40 West London	81.4	74.6	—	113	74.2	86.9
=42 Coventry	82.1	77.4	—	120	66.1	86.8
=42 Derby	83.2	79.5	2.4	123	58.9	86.8
44 Teesside	80.2	76.0	15.0	107	65.5	86.6
=45 West of England	82.5	81.3	10.9	121	51.5	86.5
=45 South Wales	85.3	82.9	15.4	129	37.5	86.5
47 Liverpool Hope	77.3	73.0	8.6	108	73.7	86.1
48 Manchester Metropolitan	78.7	76.7	6.9	126	56.1	85.7
49 Liverpool	71.8	66.6	24.5	136	—	85.5
50 Birmingham City	77.4	72.9	3.8	122	63.8	85.3
51 Huddersfield	75.3	69.7	9.5	118	67.5	85.2
52 London Metropolitan	72.6	74.7	8.8	118	59.7	83.8
53 Winchester	78.0	82.4	4.4	113	51.9	83.7
=54 Kingston	79.7	76.0	—	114	54.3	83.3
=54 Royal Holloway, London	74.1	74.8	—	134	50.7	83.3
=54 Solent	72.3	66.8	—	118	70.7	83.3
57 Suffolk	85.0	79.3	—	106	45.1	82.7
58 Brighton	74.5	68.3	12.4	107	58.2	82.6

59	De Montfort	66.6	68.6	11.2	101	74.4	82.4
60	Roehampton	72.9	71.9	—	108	66.0	82.3
61	Leeds Beckett	83.9	79.4	6.4	102	40.3	82.1
62	Middlesex	68.6	64.4	14.9	117	57.9	81.8
63	Anglia Ruskin	80.7	75.5	5.4	103	43.2	81.2
=64	Chester	77.8	75.5	0.3	103	41.3	79.5
=64	City	67.2	62.1	20.8	143	26.7	79.5
66	Canterbury Christ Church	79.1	72.8	3.2	89	38.9	77.9
67	Northampton	70.8	66.7	—	98	51.9	77.6

Employed in professional job	34%	Employed in non-professional job and Studying	5%
Employed in professional job and studying	3%	Employed in non-professional job	31%
Studying	20%	Unemployed	8%
Average starting professional salary	£20,000	Average starting non-professional salary	£17,000

Dentistry

Scores in dentistry are so close that positions change frequently throughout the ranking, but Glasgow is building a healthy lead after three years at the top. It has the highest entry grades and the best scores in the sections of the National Student Survey that focus on teaching quality. It was not one of the four universities where every graduate went straight into professional employment or further study in 2017, but it was less than a percentage point off that achievement. Second-placed Dundee, Queen's Belfast, Birmingham and Central Lancashire were the 100% universities, but they did not benefit in the table because dentistry is one of the subjects where employment scores do not form part of the calculations so as not to exaggerate the impact of tiny numbers delaying their entry into the profession. None of the 15 universities in the table score less than 96.6% for graduate prospects.

Dentists are the best-paid graduates to emerge from higher education and the most likely to find a professional job. Only medics matched the £31,000 average salaries paid to the 96% of those who found such work after graduating in 2017. There is no figure for less skilled work because virtually everyone who completes a degree goes on to become a dentist.

Applications were up by over 6% in 2018 but still 30% lower than they were at the start of the decade, when the Government was increasing the number of places to cope with a national shortage of dentists. There are more than eight applications to the place and entry standards are high – nowhere averages less than 170 points on the UCAS tariff. Most schools demand chemistry and biology, and some also require maths or physics at A-level.

Dentistry degrees last five years, although several universities offer a six-year option for those without the necessary scientific qualifications. There is less flexibility than in most other subjects, as there are more mandatory modules, to ensure graduates have the required skills to enter practice. UCAS estimates that weekly teaching time rises to between 24 and 27 hours as the course progresses, but satisfaction rates are among the highest in any subject.

Dentistry

		Teaching quality %	Student experience %	Research quality %	Entry standards (UCAS points)	Graduate prospects %	Overall score
1	Glasgow	95.1	89.9	29.3	228*	99.2	100.0
2	Dundee	87.7	88.8	22.1	225	100.0	95.3
3	Queen's, Belfast	89.1	86.6	50.7	191	100.0	95.2
4	Newcastle	93.0	91.4	43.6	189	98.5	94.6
5	Queen Mary, London	84.6	86.0	48.3	182	97.5	91.2
6	Cardiff	78.1	78.0	36.8	194	99.3	88.0
7	Manchester	64.1	65.0	57.1	189	98.5	87.1
8	Bristol	78.6	71.2	47.1	179	99.0	86.6
9	Leeds	80.9	82.9	31.7	181	99.1	84.9
10	Liverpool	85.9	81.6	31.7	173	99.2	84.4
11	Birmingham	89.2	80.7	19.2	183	100.0	83.8
12	Central Lancashire	93.0	89.7	8.3	—	100.0	82.7
13	Sheffield	83.7	83.1	28.5	171	97.5	82.5
14	Plymouth	92.0	89.1	9.5	173	96.6	80.6
15	King's College London	61.2	53.2	40.9	187	99.1	79.8

Employed in professional job	96%	Employed in non-professional job and Studying	0%
Employed in professional job and studying	2%	Employed in non-professional job	0%
Studying	1%	Unemployed	1%
Average starting professional salary	£31,000	Average starting non-professional salary	n/a

Drama, Dance and Cinematics

Drama, dance and cinematics is one of the few areas where final-year undergraduates are more satisfied with the quality of teaching than other elements of their course, like the quality of resources and the organisation of the timetable. Four out of five students gave positive ratings to the teaching in the latest round of the National Student Survey, compared with little more than three-quarters for the broader student experience. Both are high rates, but the difference is significant.

There are big changes in the table, with second-placed Sussex and Westminster in 39th the only universities in the top 40 to occupy the same position as last year. Glasgow has gone up three places to head the table, while last year's leader, Essex, is down to fifth. Other moves are even more dramatic – Edinburgh Napier is up ten places to tenth, Loughborough up 17 places to enter the top 20 and West London's rise is 47 places.

All three subjects that contribute to this ranking saw the numbers starting courses fall in 2018, and only cinematics (which is paired with photography in the UCAS statistics) attracted a similar number of applications to the previous year. However, the table still contains more than 100 universities.

The subjects' popularity has never been reflected in high entry grades – quality of performance is a more important criterion on most courses. No university averages 200 points at entry and two average less than 100. Glasgow has the highest score, at 198 points. Ten universities top 90% for satisfaction with teaching quality, with Essex recording the highest rate of all. Lancaster is the leader for the broader student experience.

The Royal Conservatoire of Scotland has by far the best of a generally poor set of employment figures, with 91% of leavers going straight in to professional jobs or further study. Overall, drama, dance and cinematics are in the bottom ten for graduate prospects, despite an unemployment rate of 9% that is no higher than in most subjects, and they are three from the bottom of the salaries table. As in other performing arts, freelancing and periods of temporary employment are common for new graduates – more than 30% started out in low-level jobs in 2017.

Drama, Dance and Cinematics	Teaching quality %	Student experience %	Research quality %	Entry standards (UCAS points)	Graduate prospects %	Overall score
1 Glasgow	77.7	75.4	53.9	198	68.5	100.0
2 Sussex	93.6	90.7	45.6	153	76.7	99.9
3 Lancaster	94.0	91.9	48.0	167	64.6	99.5
4 Warwick	83.8	78.5	61.7	159	73.1	98.6
5 Essex	94.4	90.9	37.7	135	85.4	98.5
6 Queen Margaret, Edinburgh	89.9	81.2	14.0	187	74.4	97.6
7 Manchester	—	—	58.6	172	56.5	97.3
8 Exeter	82.7	85.2	46.3	157	75.3	97.2
9 Central School of Speech and Drama	—	—	47.7	143	76.3	96.6
10 Edinburgh Napier	81.7	81.8	37.9	167	66.7	94.7
11 Birmingham	71.2	72.1	36.9	174	75.9	94.1
12 Bristol	77.6	73.5	48.7	178	56.2	93.7
13 Royal Conservatoire of Scotland	82.7	79.7	11.3	146	91.1	93.5
14 Surrey	81.6	79.7	27.2	165	66.9	92.8
15 Loughborough	88.4	87.5	32.4	149	62.5	92.7
16 Leeds	81.5	83.4	28.0	161	66.3	92.6
17 Queen Mary, London	80.6	76.2	68.4	138	56.8	92.3
18 Sheffield	69.3	78.4	60.0	149*	63.9	91.8
19 Arts Bournemouth	85.0	84.5	2.4	152	79.2	91.5
20 Royal Holloway, London	77.9	76.4	50.6	146	61.1	91.1
=21 Aberystwyth	94.0	87.7	30.3	120	67.0	91.0
=21 East Anglia	80.3	81.0	43.8	164	49.5	91.0
23 York	76.2	74.9	26.0	169	64.4	90.9
24 Kent	79.9	74.0	44.3	132	69.3	90.4
25 Oxford Brookes	88.1	83.6	27.8	129*	68.3	90.3
26 Manchester Metropolitan	86.7	86.1	7.5	146	68.4	89.5
27 Coventry	86.5	84.3	18.1	127	72.0	89.1
28 Huddersfield	84.8	83.8	28.0	131	64.7	89.0
29 De Montfort	83.9	83.7	14.5	123	78.8	88.9
30 Queen's, Belfast	79.3	76.5	38.3	147	55.7	88.6
31 Aberdeen	78.2	68.4	29.3	153*	—	88.4
32 Edinburgh	65.7	52.5	48.0	182	52.0	88.3
33 East London	87.1	84.6	11.2	132	64.5	87.4
34 Reading	76.3	76.5	34.8	139	57.5	86.8
35 Nottingham Trent	73.2	68.8	10.0	158	68.7	86.7

Drama, Dance and Cinematics cont

		Teaching quality %	Student experience %	Research quality %	Entry standards (UCAS points)	Graduate prospects %	Overall score
36	Robert Gordon	91.0	81.5	11.5	—	52.9	86.6
37	Falmouth	80.0	74.5	6.2	137	73.4	86.5
38	West London	91.2	88.5	2.3	146	50.9	86.2
=39	Creative Arts	80.9	76.5	3.4	139	69.3	86.0
=39	Westminster	76.4	74.4	—	142	75.6	86.0
=41	Hertfordshire	78.8	76.3	5.3	130	74.9	85.7
=41	Staffordshire	87.4	81.7	—	118	73.9	85.7
43	Derby	86.3	78.8	5.1	119	69.0	85.0
44	Hull	87.4	84.9	11.2	129	54.8	84.8
45	Roehampton	76.0	73.2	46.6	116	55.5	84.6
46	Portsmouth	78.9	77.0	—	122	76.6	84.4
47	Liverpool Hope	73.9	71.2	3.0	129	77.3	84.2
=48	Birmingham City	80.1	73.5	11.6	130	63.2	84.1
=48	Nottingham	67.3	63.5	45.8	138	54.5	84.1
50	Middlesex	78.5	73.5	16.1	130	61.6	84.0
51	Goldsmiths, London	75.5	65.6	28.3	132	57.6	83.7
=52	Bath Spa	78.7	74.7	10.7	132	59.9	83.3
=52	Central Lancashire	78.3	74.1	3.9	138	61.6	83.3
54	Brunel	76.7	72.4	32.6	130	49.5	83.2
=55	Arts London	79.9	72.2	—	139	61.7	83.1
=55	Ulster	89.5	85.2	40.0	126	27.2	83.1
57	Lincoln	79.7	75.7	6.5	126	63.2	83.0
58	Norwich Arts	76.6	72.3	—	127	70.8	82.8
=59	London South Bank	79.6	72.9	—	122	70.1	82.7
=59	West of England	83.9	79.2	—	133	56.4	82.7
=61	Gloucestershire	81.8	77.1	—	131	59.5	82.5
=61	Newman	92.5	81.5	9.6	122	45.8	82.5
=61	Teesside	85.4	83.6	2.9	130	51.9	82.5
=61	West of Scotland	83.9	75.5	—	142	51.8	82.5
=65	Liverpool John Moores	77.3	76.6	—	140	57.4	82.2
=65	Northumbria	81.1	74.7	13.3	142	44.7	82.2
=67	Plymouth	78.4	74.5	20.2	132	48.2	82.0
=67	Wolverhampton	92.1	90.1	—	113	51.5	82.0
69	Bournemouth	69.8	71.9	15.1	143	54.6	81.9
70	London Metropolitan	86.7	81.8	—	107	62.2	81.5
71	Sheffield Hallam	88.3	84.5	14.4	117	42.4	81.2
72	Wales Trinity St David	81.3	70.0	—	122	61.8	81.0
73	Chichester	77.5	72.7	9.7	133	50.8	80.8
=74	Chester	82.1	79.1	4.3	120	53.9	80.7
=74	Kingston	80.7	74.7	15.7	128	45.3	80.7
=76	Worcester	80.8	82.1	3.5	124	51.4	80.6
=76	Leeds Arts	85.4	83.4	—	133	43.2	80.6

78 Sunderland	79.6	76.8	4.2	120	57.0	80.5
=79 Salford	80.7	75.6	7.2	134	45.4	80.4
=79 York St John	86.0	77.2	10.5	120	45.2	80.4
81 Solent	78.0	71.9	—	119	62.3	80.2
82 Edge Hill	71.8	65.4	3.8	136	56.6	79.6
83 Cardiff Metropolitan	94.0	89.6	—	107	42.1	79.5
84 Plymouth Marjon	82.4	70.9	—	122	52.6	79.3
85 South Wales	76.1	71.7	6.4	131	48.1	79.1
86 Northampton	86.8	78.3	—	114	48.0	78.9
87 Bedfordshire	75.7	80.0	5.6	99	61.7	78.4
=88 Brighton	70.8	64.1	13.1	127	50.7	78.0
=88 Winchester	78.7	75.6	11.2	117	43.9	78.0
90 Bolton	75.8	73.8	—	121	50.2	77.5
91 Greenwich	58.8	55.0	3.5	147	58.2	77.3
92 Canterbury Christ Church	81.7	76.4	15.2	102	43.7	77.2
=93 Bucks New	80.5	76.0	—	123	40.8	76.9
=93 Ravensbourne, London	66.5	60.1	—	112	69.7	76.9
95 St Mary's, Twickenham	70.0	60.6	9.1	124	51.8	76.7
96 Anglia Ruskin	67.7	66.9	16.9	126	43.5	76.5
97 Glyndŵr	93.2	77.4	—	88*	45.9	76.3
98 Suffolk	81.6	72.2	—	115	42.1	76.0
99 Bishop Grosseteste	75.0	62.3	—	118	49.5	75.5
100 Leeds Beckett	66.9	60.0	1.7	121	50.0	74.2
101 Cumbria	52.6	48.6	—	126	41.9	68.4

Employed in professional job	49%	Employed in non-professional job and Studying	2%
Employed in professional job and studying	2%	Employed in non-professional job	29%
Studying	9%	Unemployed	9%
Average starting professional salary	£18,720	Average starting non-professional salary	£16,000

East and South Asian Studies

Only 500 students started degrees in the various languages covered by East and South Asian Studies in 2018, but two more universities have joined the table – Newcastle in third place and Liverpool in eighth. Indeed, 35 universities are offering degrees in Chinese alone in 2020, despite the fact that applications have dropped by almost 40% since 2016 and the number of new entrants for single honours degrees has fallen below 100. Japanese, where applications rose by 2% in 2018, is the main draw, although only 215 students started degrees in that year.

Most undergraduates learn their chosen language from scratch, although universities expect to see evidence of potential in other modern language qualifications. East and South Asian studies are often included in broader modern languages or area studies degrees, but the School of Oriental and African Studies, in London, offers a range of languages, including Burmese, Indonesian, Thai, Tibetan and Vietnamese. South Asian Studies is available at only four universities.

Degrees in these subjects are afforded extra protection by the Government because of their small size and their economic and cultural importance. Cambridge retains the leadership of the table, registering the highest entry grades and the best graduate prospects. The most satisfied students are at Nottingham Trent, the only post-1992 university in the top ten.

The small numbers of graduates make for exaggerated swings in the employment and salaries tables. East Asian Studies ties with anthropology for the unwanted distinction of the highest unemployment rate – 15% – and is just outside the bottom ten for graduate prospects generally. But the subjects do much better in the comparisons of graduate earnings, sharing 26th place, with average starting salaries of £22,000 in professional jobs.

East and South Asian Studies	Teaching quality %	Student experience %	Research quality %	Entry standards (UCAS points)	Graduate prospects %	Overall score
1 Cambridge	—	—	45.0	220	88.9	100.0
2 Oxford	—	—	36.2	210	84.6	95.7
3 Newcastle	87.8	82.7	36.3	156	—	94.9
4 Manchester	76.0	74.0	48.9	157	67.2	91.7
5 Edinburgh	77.4	73.4	30.1	185	66.2	89.8
6 Nottingham	77.4	66.9	27.3	148	82.4	88.8
7 Nottingham Trent	92.5	90.6	10.0	125	76.2	88.7
8 Liverpool	80.1	77.1	33.4	138	—	88.3
9 Leeds	74.9	75.4	30.6	162	68.6	88.2
10 SOAS, London	80.9	70.2	26.3	163	59.5	86.5
11 Hull	85.2	81.8	22.7	117	—	86.4
12 Durham	67.2	66.6	34.6	173	—	85.8
13 Sheffield	74.3	72.6	16.7	156	61.6	82.9
14 Oxford Brookes	76.5	77.1	—	136	59.0	78.4
15 Central Lancashire	79.7	76.7	—	121	54.5	77.1

Employed in professional job	45%	Employed in non-professional job and Studying	2%
Employed in professional job and studying	1%	Employed in non-professional job	21%
Studying	16%	Unemployed	15%
Average starting professional salary	£22,000	Average starting non-professional salary	£16,500

Economics

Warwick has never been out of the top five for economics in almost 20 years that the table has been published, but this is the first time that it has reached the top. Higher satisfaction rates have done the trick, although it is also in the top seven on the other measures in the table. St Andrews could hardly be closer in second place, and both Cambridge and Oxford are within a point, despite each dropping two places.

Economics is famously competitive. Six universities, of which Warwick is not one, average more than 200 points at entry. The numbers starting degrees in the subject have risen by almost a quarter since higher fees were introduced and applications continue to rise, setting new records in each of the last five years. Consistently good prospects for graduates are an obvious attraction. The subject is in the top four for starting salaries in professional jobs, reflecting the value that employers place on a subject that they see combining the skills of the sciences and the arts. It is just outside the top 20 for the proportion of leavers going straight into graduate-level work or continuing their studies.

Many of those considering a degree in economics underestimate the mathematical skills required. Most of the leading universities demand maths at A-level or its equivalent as part of offers that are consistently high. The range of entry scores has been widening, however, as more universities have joined the table: nine have averages of less than 100 points in the latest table.

Economists from the leading universities invariably command some of the highest salaries on graduation. While the average salary for 2017 graduates in "professional" jobs was £27,000 by the end of the year, Cambridge economists averaged £37,000 at this point and £49,000 three years later. The London School of Economics took the laurels in the Research Excellence Framework, while East London in 65th place scores the highest for teaching quality and Cardiff Met, which shared 40th place, is the best for wider student experience.

Economics	Teaching quality %	Student experience %	Research quality %	Entry standards (UCAS points)	Graduate prospects %	Overall score
1 Warwick	81.2	81.6	49.6	197	92.8	100.0
2 St Andrews	87.4	87.6	23.6	215	92.5	99.7
3 Cambridge	—	—	45.0	233	94.1	99.6
4 Oxford	—	—	58.0	218	84.3	99.0
5 London School of Economics	68.8	66.3	70.7	203	89.8	97.7
6 Strathclyde	81.9	84.7	44.3	203	79.4	97.2
7 University College London	67.6	70.7	70.2	196	85.8	96.6
8 Leeds	78.3	80.6	39.3	174	88.1	95.3
9 Bath	70.6	77.5	41.8	187	90.8	94.8
10 Loughborough	81.8	85.1	32.6	157	87.3	94.6
=11 Bristol	75.6	77.5	43.6	178	83.6	94.1
=11 Glasgow	75.6	81.4	26.4	188	89.3	94.1
13 Nottingham	72.7	78.6	31.7	185	87.6	93.2
14 Exeter	72.5	76.4	26.9	181	91.9	92.9
15 Lancaster	72.9	78.1	42.6	150	87.4	92.5
16 Durham	71.6	71.6	23.1	201	90.1	92.3
17 East Anglia	85.2	86.8	25.7	136	79.9	91.7
18 Stirling	84.5	80.8	25.2	148	80.4	91.5
19 Heriot-Watt	82.8	82.9	18.8	141	85.7	91.3
20 Aberdeen	74.1	78.2	16.0	188	85.1	90.9
21 Liverpool	79.9	81.4	20.1	146	85.1	90.7
22 Aston	78.6	79.2	19.7	128	91.8	90.5
23 York	74.9	77.6	22.6	152	86.7	90.1
=24 Birmingham	74.1	75.5	26.6	158	84.3	90.0
=24 Queen Mary, London	75.4	81.0	31.3	151	78.6	90.0
26 Royal Holloway, London	76.8	78.2	31.3	122	85.9	89.9
=27 Edinburgh	69.2	75.1	30.2	191	77.3	89.7
=27 Huddersfield	87.7	89.2	4.1	120	—	89.7

Economics cont

	Teaching quality %	Student experience %	Research quality %	Entry standards (UCAS points)	Graduate prospects %	Overall score
=27 Surrey	72.8	77.3	33.0	153	80.5	89.7
=30 Southampton	74.5	77.6	23.4	145	85.8	89.5
=30 Swansea	79.2	82.0	22.0	129	83.6	89.5
=32 Essex	80.5	83.3	43.6	100	75.0	89.4
=32 Nottingham Trent	85.1	84.4	4.6	123	87.6	89.4
34 Sheffield	75.4	77.6	16.6	155	85.7	89.3
35 Manchester	71.0	74.9	26.8	168	79.7	88.8
=36 Kent	78.2	82.6	14.6	134	82.8	88.5
=36 Sussex	76.3	75.8	25.1	143	80.0	88.5
=38 Dundee	75.3	73.8	12.1	174	80.7	88.2
=38 Newcastle	67.1	71.4	20.7	155	90.7	88.2
=40 Cardiff Metropolitan	88.0	91.4	—	105	81.0	87.8
=40 West of England	86.3	86.5	5.5	116	79.2	87.8
42 Queen's, Belfast	73.6	73.5	32.7	142	74.8	87.4
43 Hertfordshire	91.7	91.1	0.9	98	75.9	87.2
44 SOAS, London	73.2	69.1	22.9	149	81.0	87.1
45 Bangor	82.5	87.9	23.4	97	70.6	86.5
46 London South Bank	83.9	79.3	—	104	86.7	86.4
47 Cardiff	68.3	69.7	32.0	154	74.8	86.3
48 Goldsmiths, London	86.6	82.9	16.8	113	67.7	86.2
=49 Salford	87.1	86.6	5.9	109	72.4	86.1
=49 Ulster	73.9	74.4	39.2	121	69.9	86.1
51 Coventry	78.8	82.5	1.6	113	84.3	85.8
52 Hull	77.2	80.2	10.2	114	79.7	85.4
53 Buckingham	76.8	77.9	—	116	86.0	85.1
54 De Montfort	78.2	79.5	10.7	94	82.2	85.0
55 Reading	69.9	72.1	29.3	129	73.5	84.8
=56 King's College London	70.3	70.5	—	181	78.3	84.7
=56 Plymouth	79.9	77.3	13.1	113	73.7	84.7
=56 Portsmouth	78.0	79.2	9.5	105	79.1	84.7
59 Leicester	72.0	74.0	21.4	127	73.4	84.3
60 Central Lancashire	87.6	85.7	4.4	102	66.7	84.2
61 London Metropolitan	88.0	90.4	—	104	65.4	84.1
62 Oxford Brookes	75.8	79.2	5.1	119	76.4	83.7
63 Greenwich	84.3	81.4	3.3	124	65.2	83.6
64 Keele	80.5	75.9	10.2	110	69.6	83.1
65 East London	91.9	90.9	0.8	87	59.6	82.9
66 Manchester Metropolitan	78.1	71.0	4.7	118	75.0	82.8
67 Aberystwyth	78.8	82.4	14.5	88	66.7	82.2
68 Birmingham City	79.3	78.0	1.3	110	70.0	81.9
69 City	71.9	77.2	15.1	135	59.7	81.2
70 Brighton	76.5	75.2	6.5	94	—	80.9

71 Sheffield Hallam		74.5	76.6	—	103	72.4	80.5
72 Bradford		65.0	68.2	12.7	117	71.9	79.7
73 Leeds Beckett		76.3	78.3	0.8	104	63.0	79.3
74 Anglia Ruskin		82.8	80.5	3.4	77	60.0	79.1
=75 Kingston		79.9	80.0	9.2	89	51.2	77.9
=75 Middlesex		70.7	72.3	10.5	100	61.5	77.9
77 Brunel		65.9	68.8	9.9	108	65.7	77.6
78 Northampton		77.8	74.4	—	94	50.8	75.6

Employed in professional job	56%	Employed in non-professional job and Studying		1%
Employed in professional job and studying	5%	Employed in non-professional job		11%
Studying	16%	Unemployed		11%
Average starting professional salary	£27,000	Average starting non-professional salary		£18,000

Education

The numbers starting teacher training degrees rose in 2018, but a decline in the larger group in the education category – those on courses classified as Academic Studies in Education – more than cancelled them out. Taken as a whole, education starts were down again in the latest admissions cycle, as some of the traditional graduate destinations, such as outdoor education, early years and local authority posts, dried up through lack of funding.

Almost five women for every man started teacher training degrees in 2018, which helps to explain the shortage of male teachers in primary schools. BEd courses remain the most common route into primary teaching, while secondary school teachers are more likely to take the Postgraduate Certificate in Education, or train through the Teach First or Schools Direct programmes, which are not included in these statistics.

The University of the West of Scotland pips Cambridge to the leadership of the education table – not something that happens often – dislodging Glasgow, which has slipped to third. UWS is one of nine universities with satisfaction rates of more than 90% for the quality of teaching and it has the best graduate prospects, with a success rate of 99%. All eight Scottish institutions in the table appear in the top 20. They benefit from the UCAS tariff points for Scottish secondary qualifications – but also have the top seven scores for graduate prospects. Employment scores at different universities are influenced by the variations in demand for new staff between primary and secondary schools, as well as between different parts of the UK.

Entry standards are not high – only Cambridge averages 200 points on the UCAS tariff – but only London Metropolitan has an average below 100. There are more than six applications to every place for teacher training, but the ratio for other education courses in the education category is much lower.

Neither University College London's Institute of Education, which is ranked top in the world in this field by QS, or Oxford, which achieved the top grades in the 2014 Research Excellence Framework, offer the BEd. UCL appears in the table because of the Institute's BA course in education, but Oxford is absent. Cambridge is one of those that do not offer Qualified Teacher Status but combines the academic study of education with other subjects. The table includes Ofsted inspection data for universities in England. Ten institutions – seven of them in the top 20 overall – tie for the best scores.

Morale is often said to be low in the teaching profession, but the official survey of graduates three years into their careers shows that those who studied education are among the least likely to wish they had taken a different subject. Competitive salaries in the early years of teaching may be one reason – education is just outside the top 20 of our 67 subject groups. The subject is also in the top 30 for the proportion going straight into professional jobs or continuing to study.

Education	Teaching quality	Student experience	Research quality	OFSTED Rating	Entry standards (UCAS points)	Graduate prospects	Overall score
1 West of Scotland	90.4	87.9	7.5	—	189	99.1	100.0
2 Cambridge	—	—	36.6	4.0	202	82.4	99.5
3 Glasgow	81.9	77.6	32.5	—	186	97.8	98.9
4 Strathclyde	84.8	78.9	19.8	—	196	89.0	97.6
5 Birmingham	85.9	87.4	40.9	4.0	151	83.8	97.0
=6 Edinburgh	77.2	77.4	23.1	—	189	98.8	96.8
=6 Stirling	81.1	72.6	29.2	—	182	96.0	96.8
8 Warwick	94.1	91.1	43.6	3.7	168	61.5	96.5
9 Dundee	84.6	83.4	11.7	—	180	94.9	95.8
10 Durham	76.3	66.8	38.9	4.0	161	89.4	94.3
11 Coventry	92.0	92.1	18.1	—	131	87.5	93.6
12 Aberdeen	74.8	71.7	7.6	—	186	94.9	92.1
13 Reading	88.8	88.5	25.8	3.0	139	88.0	92.0
14 Southampton	76.6	78.8	41.1	3.0	155	86.0	91.4
15 University College London	77.1	79.7	40.2	4.0	161	58.1	91.1
16 York	79.5	80.3	43.3	3.0	139	80.6	90.3
17 Brunel	92.1	87.1	20.4	4.0	119	65.9	90.2
18 Bangor	83.0	77.1	39.6	—	137	74.8	89.9
19 Manchester	68.3	68.5	46.0	4.0	137*	77.0	89.8
=20 St Mary's, Twickenham	83.8	83.2	1.8	4.0	126	88.6	89.7
=20 Royal Conservatoire of Scotland	73.5	66.2	—	—	179	97.4	89.7
=22 Brighton	84.4	80.6	1.6	4.0	124	88.4	89.2
=22 West London	92.7	93.3	7.6	—	113	—	89.2
24 Gloucestershire	87.0	87.8	—	3.7	135	81.2	89.1
25 West of England	93.9	91.6	5.3	3.0	132	80.1	88.9
=26 Liverpool John Moores	90.1	87.4	3.0	3.5	143	72.1	88.7
=26 Newcastle	85.0	77.4	33.1	3.1	132	—	88.7
28 East Anglia	79.4	80.0	27.2	3.0	149	77.9	88.5
29 Winchester	85.7	84.2	2.2	4.0	126	77.4	88.4
30 Huddersfield	88.0	84.5	5.9	3.1	136	81.9	87.9
31 Keele	79.4	78.2	25.0	3.5	130	74.2	87.6
=32 Liverpool Hope	88.0	85.8	7.3	3.0	123	86.1	87.5
=32 Sheffield	86.0	86.7	32.9	3.0	152	51.3	87.5
=34 Derby	86.8	82.3	1.1	3.4	131	80.1	87.1
=34 Nottingham Trent	84.0	82.8	2.6	3.3	146	76.3	87.1

36	Roehampton	81.5	80.2	20.2	3.0	124	84.0	86.9
37	Plymouth	88.1	86.9	9.4	3.0	129	74.3	86.5
38	De Montfort	83.1	82.8	11.2	—	120	80.7	86.2
39	Chichester	88.4	88.2	—	3.0	118	84.3	86.1
40	Sheffield Hallam	85.4	79.2	2.0	3.7	126	72.1	86.0
41	Birmingham City	85.0	80.5	1.8	3.0	129	84.8	85.9
42	Staffordshire	89.9	84.8	7.6	3.0	128	70.0	85.7
43	Sunderland	79.8	77.0	3.8	3.0	127	91.1	85.4
44	Hull	86.9	82.1	5.0	3.0	141	68.1	85.3
45	Cumbria	85.7	80.0	0.4	3.0	123	83.6	85.1
=46	Chester	79.8	75.7	1.4	3.7	126	76.2	85.0
=46	York St John	81.0	78.1	1.5	3.3	127	81.6	85.0
48	St Mark and St John	83.4	80.3	—	3.3	136	70.8	84.7
=49	Bedfordshire	88.4	82.6	3.1	3.1	110	76.9	84.5
=49	Edge Hill	79.9	77.3	1.4	3.0	131	85.2	84.5
=49	Northumbria	72.5	69.1	—	3.0	151	90.7	84.5
52	Worcester	86.6	85.6	2.5	3.0	125	71.5	84.4
=53	Aberystwyth	88.4	85.8	—	—	127	65.6	84.3
=53	Greenwich	86.2	81.9	0.8	3.3	140	60.4	84.3
55	Manchester Metropolitan	79.7	77.9	5.8	3.0	132	76.3	83.9
56	Middlesex	76.8	76.1	14.9	3.0	127	76.0	83.8
57	Hertfordshire	85.5	82.3	—	3.0	116	76.6	83.5
=58	Anglia Ruskin	92.8	88.7	0.8	3.0	122	56.5	83.3
=58	Leeds Trinity	81.9	78.9	—	3.0	122	78.7	83.3
=60	Canterbury Christ Church	85.0	80.3	2.8	3.0	114	74.2	83.0
=60	Cardiff	73.6	68.7	35.3	—	149	56.5	83.0
62	Teesside	83.8	75.8	15.0	—	111	70.2	82.9
63	Newman	80.9	80.2	2.2	3.0	126	70.0	82.5
=64	Central Lancashire	83.5	76.2	—	—	127	68.7	82.3
=64	Leeds	68.0	69.6	31.6	3.0	145	59.0	82.3
=64	London South Bank	78.7	77.2	—	3.0	103	88.2	82.3
=64	Ulster	86.7	84.7	27.5	—	113	48.6	82.3
68	Bolton	87.3	86.7	3.1	—	129	52.9	82.1
=69	Bath Spa	74.4	71.1	3.2	4.0	105	70.2	82.0
=69	Kingston	92.3	84.6	—	3.0	107	60.1	82.0
=69	Suffolk	84.8	72.9	—	—	140	60.7	82.0
=69	Wolverhampton	78.1	77.2	1.9	3.0	122	75.2	82.0
73	Northampton	81.7	77.4	1.8	3.0	120	70.3	81.8
=74	London Metropolitan	86.1	84.4	3.3	3.1	92	70.5	81.7
=74	Bishop Grosseteste	81.5	76.0	1.4	3.0	116	73.3	81.7
76	Oxford Brookes	74.3	71.3	3.3	3.0	133	73.6	81.4
=77	Portsmouth	79.4	77.7	—	3.3	108	68.0	80.7
=77	South Wales	81.5	77.1	—	—	132	60.9	80.7
79	Wales Trinity St David	86.2	81.7	—	—	113	56.4	79.7
80	East London	77.4	73.9	2.8	3.0	117	63.1	79.3
81	Leeds Beckett	78.2	72.4	2.3	3.0	115	62.7	79.0

Education cont

		Teaching quality	Student experience	Research quality	OFSTED Rating	Entry standards (UCAS points)	Graduate prospects	Overall score
82	Goldsmiths, London	73.8	68.2	17.4	3.0	108	61.5	78.9
83	Cardiff Metropolitan	76.1	72.6	–	–	112	52.0	74.6
84	Glyndŵr	68.7	62.3	–	–	120	52.3	71.9

Employed in professional job	56%	Employed in non-professional job and Studying	2%
Employed in professional job and studying	2%	Employed in non-professional job	19%
Studying	16%	Unemployed	5%
Average starting professional salary	£22,500	Average starting non-professional salary	£15,933

Electrical and Electronic Engineering

The heyday of electrical and electronic engineering appears to be past, for the moment at least, as many of the subjects' natural applicants have been diverted into computer science and the more specialist gaming courses that have grown in popularity. The demand for places declined again in 2018 and, with five applications to the place, selection is less competitive than in most other branches of engineering. Career prospects should not be the problem – electrical and electronic engineering are 14th in the overall table for graduate employment and postgraduate study and in the top eight for salaries in graduate-level jobs.

Cambridge has extended its lead slightly over second-placed Imperial College, with the best research grades and by far the highest entry standards. The QS rankings rate Cambridge in the top five universities in the world, with Imperial only two places lower. The scores are close together throughout the table, making for some big moves. Queen's Belfast has entered the top ten after a rise of nine places, while Ulster is up 15 places to 23rd. Hertfordshire has gone 20 places in the opposite direction, finishing in the bottom four.

Derby, in a share of 30th place, and Solent, just inside the top 50, tie for the highest score in the sections of the National Student Survey directly concerned with the quality of teaching, while Anglia Ruskin has the best rating for the broader student experience, despite being in the bottom ten overall.

Most of the top courses demand maths and physics at A-level, or the equivalent. Graduate prospects are excellent at the leading universities: 17 of the 66 universities in the table saw at least 90% of their 2017 graduates find professional work or continue their studies. However, the rate was below 70% at nine of the bottom 26 universities.

Electrical and Electronic Engineering		Teaching quality %	Student experience %	Research quality %	Entry standards (UCAS points)	Graduate prospects %	Overall score
1	Cambridge	83.7*	85.5*	67.0	239	93.5	100.0
2	Imperial College London	80.2	82.4	65.0	208	92.8	96.0
3	Southampton	81.8	84.4	53.3	186	90.7	92.9
4	Leeds	80.5	84.1	41.8	190	95.1	92.3

5 Strathclyde	81.4	83.3	41.7	212	86.6	92.2
6 University College London	74.4	77.0	59.0	192	84.1	90.2
7 Nottingham	83.9	85.5	40.8	157	91.6	89.7
8 Glasgow	64.2	73.2	47.2	215	91.8	89.6
9 Queen's, Belfast	77.9	72.9	47.3	147	96.1	88.2
10 Bath	80.8	83.8	28.6	170	90.8	88.1
11 Edinburgh	68.3	73.3	50.3	195	85.3	87.8
12 Manchester	80.8	79.9	37.0	166	85.9	87.4
=13 Loughborough	83.3	83.9	23.8	158	91.6	87.2
=13 Swansea	76.3	84.1	45.5	143	90.9	87.2
15 Surrey	83.2	86.3	36.3	156	82.3	86.9
16 Bristol	69.2	73.9	52.3	173	85.6	86.7
17 Sheffield	75.9	79.3	42.6	149	87.7	86.0
18 Exeter	72.9	72.8	36.4	155	94.2	85.9
19 Newcastle	71.1	82.0	39.4	152	89.5	85.5
20 Lancaster	75.4	67.3	41.6	157	87.5	85.2
=21 Bangor	81.9	89.9	31.9	136	82.7	84.9
=21 Birmingham	71.3	74.3	32.1	161	91.0	84.9
=23 Essex	76.0	83.2	34.3	127	91.3	84.5
=23 Heriot-Watt	72.8	69.0	47.8	158	82.7	84.5
=23 Ulster	81.6	81.4	22.8	136	90.2	84.5
26 East London	78.5	79.6	2.3	—	92.9	83.8
27 York	84.8	81.0	21.4	140	83.4	83.7
28 Northumbria	78.3	80.7	30.7	138	81.0	82.8
29 Aston	85.1	79.7	25.8	133	77.4	82.3
=30 Derby	92.6	91.4	6.7	122	79.5	82.2
=30 Queen Mary, London	70.2	72.7	41.9	140	83.0	82.2
=32 Cardiff	72.4	74.8	30.2	147	83.3	82.1
=32 London South Bank	87.0	85.9	19.6	137	74.1	82.1
34 Central Lancashire	81.1	77.5	11.7	130	88.9	81.7
35 Huddersfield	82.9	82.0	10.2	143	79.3	81.2
=36 Liverpool	70.6	79.0	30.4	137	82.2	81.0
=36 Liverpool John Moores	74.2	70.2	8.7	154	89.2	81.0
38 Bedfordshire	81.0	83.2	9.1	—	76.9	80.6
39 Sussex	67.3	72.3	24.0	132*	90.9	80.4
40 Aberdeen	74.6	80.9	28.4	167	65.0	80.3
41 Sheffield Hallam	79.5	75.3	17.8	128	82.2	80.2
42 Brunel	76.1	76.0	26.4	131	77.6	79.9
=43 Chester	87.1	85.8	7.1	103	—	79.4
=43 Portsmouth	76.0	73.8	7.2	114	93.2	79.4
45 Coventry	77.8	77.4	10.3	133	80.8	79.2
46 South Wales	80.2	79.9	—	131*	83.3	79.0
47 Kent	66.0	70.5	27.3	130	85.0	78.9
48 Plymouth	73.5	72.8	13.3	123	85.5	78.5
49 Solent	92.6	85.2	—	94	78.4	78.2
50 Glasgow Caledonian	79.4	74.7	4.7	154	71.3	78.0

Electrical and Electronic Engineering cont	Teaching quality %	Student experience %	Research quality %	Entry standards (UCAS points)	Graduate prospects %	Overall score
=51 Birmingham City	84.3	82.5	—	143	67.5	77.5
=51 Robert Gordon	72.6	73.6	8.8	151	75.0	77.5
=53 Hull	68.6	65.3	16.5	124	86.7	77.4
=53 West of England	76.3	78.0	10.6	127	76.3	77.4
55 Salford	83.7	78.4	4.4	132	68.6	77.0
56 Teesside	78.4	73.9	5.8	118	75.8	76.1
57 Manchester Metropolitan	71.0	71.8	16.3	139	68.9	75.7
58 Anglia Ruskin	88.5	94.0	9.1	—	50.0	75.6
59 Staffordshire	66.6	76.4	5.7	111	81.8	74.5
60 Westminster	80.1	75.9	2.9	117	66.7	74.1
61 De Montfort	68.9	64.3	12.5	112	78.6	74.0
62 Brighton	69.2	73.7	7.4	115	71.4	73.0
63 Hertfordshire	65.4	66.5	16.5	122	67.3	72.3
64 City	69.8	69.6	23.1	131	54.3	72.2
65 Reading	69.8	50.8	16.3	—	70.6	70.9
66 Greenwich	64.6	60.4	7.5	129	65.8	70.5

Employed in professional job	64%	Employed in non-professional job and Studying	1%
Employed in professional job and studying	2%	Employed in non-professional job	10%
Studying	14%	Unemployed	9%
Average starting professional salary	£26,500	Average starting non-professional salary	£16,497

English

The lead changes frequently in the English table, which is one of the largest in our *Guide*, with more than 100 universities. Durham is back on top after sharing first place with St Andrews two years ago and dropping to second in the last edition. It has higher entry standards and research grades than Oxford and Cambridge, which are in fourth and fifth place respectively. York and St Andrews share second place, but Bolton, just outside the top 30, has the most satisfied students.

English is among the biggest recruiters of undergraduates, despite the fact that the subject is usually in the lower reaches of the tables for graduate prospects and for starting salaries in professional jobs. But the attractions of a degree in English appear to be on the wane – applications have dropped in seven of the last eight years, falling by almost 10% in 2018. Entry standards are high at the leading institutions, although only three universities (led by Durham) average more than 200 points.

English produces consistently good levels of student satisfaction, with many of the top performers in the bottom half of the table overall. Only the bottom two failed to reach 70% in the sections of the National Student Survey directly concerned with the quality of teaching. Queen Mary, University of London, in 34th place overall, produced the best results in the Research Excellence Framework.

More than a third of English graduates go on to a postgraduate course, and unemployment has been no higher than average for all subjects for three years in succession, but approaching three in ten graduates start out in lower-level jobs. Employment rates have improved recently, and the subject has climbed out of the bottom 20. Seven universities saw fewer than half of their 2017 graduates go straight into professional work or further study, but there were 13 in this position in the last edition of the *Guide*.

English

	Teaching quality %	Student experience %	Research quality %	Entry standards (UCAS points)	Graduate prospects %	Overall score
1 Durham	83.1	73.9	57.9	206	82.0	100.0
=2 St Andrews	87.0	84.1	60.4	198	73.0	99.9
=2 York	87.7	83.5	61.5	164	83.3	99.9
4 Oxford	—	—	50.7	202	76.6	98.6
5 Cambridge	—	—	50.0	203	82.6	97.7
6 University College London	84.3	73.5	61.7	195	70.1	97.3
7 Exeter	84.2	80.3	46.2	171	82.1	96.9
8 Loughborough	93.1	90.0	32.4	149	81.4	96.6
9 Lancaster	84.7	80.6	47.0	160	81.0	96.1
10 Newcastle	82.6	83.3	54.3	159	76.9	95.8
=11 Birmingham	84.4	82.9	37.0	166	81.3	95.4
=11 Glasgow	79.8	76.5	52.0	187	73.5	95.4
13 Nottingham	78.4	75.4	56.6	162	78.9	94.8
14 Aberdeen	88.8	81.9	46.3	167	66.5	94.6
15 Warwick	77.8	73.1	59.8	174	73.3	94.5
16 Manchester	79.9	75.8	49.1	165	76.3	93.9
17 Sheffield	81.4	80.3	42.2	156	79.2	93.8
18 Sussex	81.4	78.1	45.6	153	75.6	93.0
19 Liverpool Hope	87.9	86.7	26.9	116	86.5	92.8
=20 Aberystwyth	91.2	89.3	31.2	121	75.9	92.6
=20 Royal Holloway, London	84.6	79.8	49.9	141	70.7	92.6
=22 King's College London	78.4	70.7	47.6	171	72.4	92.3
=22 Southampton	85.2	81.5	38.4	154	70.1	92.3
24 Edinburgh Napier	94.1	88.0	37.9	178	47.4	92.1
25 Kent	82.3	78.3	47.3	132	76.1	92.0
26 Leeds	81.2	78.0	38.6	161	72.6	91.9
27 Stirling	85.3	80.0	29.8	162	69.7	91.5
28 Dundee	86.7	83.7	32.8	166	61.8	91.3
29 Swansea	82.1	81.4	43.6	125	74.6	91.0
30 Bristol	73.6	65.5	30.0	179	81.4	90.6
31 Bolton	96.1	97.5	14.4	91	76.7	90.4
32 Strathclyde	83.8	75.7	39.4	183	54.7	90.3
33 Edinburgh	74.7	71.8	43.6	182	65.5	90.2
34 Queen Mary, London	78.0	72.0	64.0	132	65.1	90.1
=35 Liverpool	79.6	74.6	47.8	141	68.8	90.0
=35 West of England	91.6	90.1	35.4	111	63.9	90.0
=37 Cardiff	83.2	75.8	35.1	153	67.1	89.9

English cont

		Teaching quality %	Student experience %	Research quality %	Entry standards (UCAS points)	Graduate prospects %	Overall score
=37	Coventry	90.6	85.9	18.1	114	76.8	89.9
39	Leicester	80.2	73.5	45.4	127	70.9	89.2
40	Bangor	85.8	85.8	46.3	118	60.1	89.1
41	Plymouth	87.2	80.2	30.5	125	67.1	88.8
=42	De Montfort	85.1	83.6	24.1	104	78.3	88.7
=42	Surrey	77.2	68.8	39.1	144	72.7	88.7
44	Essex	81.9	80.0	37.7	110	72.1	88.4
45	Nottingham Trent	84.8	77.3	30.0	118	71.8	88.3
46	Huddersfield	84.4	78.5	29.9	128	67.0	88.0
47	Oxford Brookes	82.3	79.2	27.8	123	71.2	87.8
48	Edge Hill	85.4	83.2	12.1	126	73.9	87.7
49	Queen's, Belfast	75.4	71.2	53.1	148	58.6	87.6
50	Staffordshire	88.3	82.2	—	95	87.0	87.3
=51	East Anglia	77.6	74.9	36.2	151	61.3	87.1
=51	Keele	82.4	79.0	29.8	123	66.8	87.1
=53	Hull	88.7	83.5	22.7	119	62.0	86.9
=53	Teesside	86.4	78.1	15.6	102	77.9	86.9
55	Roehampton	88.6	82.8	20.8	107	66.9	86.8
56	London South Bank	91.5	84.9	12.8	97	70.0	86.6
57	Northumbria	84.1	77.2	27.2	138	59.6	86.5
58	Aston	84.6	83.3	23.4	123	62.6	86.4
=59	Portsmouth	83.8	81.6	17.1	101	75.6	86.3
=59	Solent	93.9	78.6	—	124	67.5	86.3
61	Lincoln	82.9	80.2	16.2	124	69.5	86.2
62	Greenwich	90.4	88.8	14.4	122	57.6	86.1
63	Liverpool John Moores	84.3	80.0	17.9	127	65.1	86.0
64	St Mary's, Twickenham	92.3	87.5	14.6	106	60.1	85.8
65	Manchester Metropolitan	81.7	77.6	29.0	120	62.5	85.5
66	Chester	92.4	87.2	10.7	113	57.2	85.3
67	Bishop Grosseteste	93.4	78.5	6.7	105	64.5	85.0
68	Bedfordshire	76.6	68.9	45.8	96	67.9	84.8
69	Reading	75.6	68.4	36.3	128	63.3	84.6
70	Sheffield Hallam	89.3	85.1	14.6	109	57.4	84.5
=71	Buckingham	81.9	80.2	—	125	72.2	84.4
=71	Hertfordshire	83.3	77.5	7.8	109	72.6	84.4
73	Bournemouth	88.1	83.3	15.1	109	58.8	84.3
74	Central Lancashire	83.8	85.6	9.9	120	62.1	84.2
75	Worcester	85.5	79.5	8.2	114	65.5	84.1
76	Newman	81.1	73.1	9.6	119	70.2	83.8
77	Birmingham City	80.3	75.8	30.9	108	59.0	83.5
78	Northampton	86.8	76.3	15.3	101	62.3	83.4
=79	Leeds Beckett	85.3	83.4	11.0	100	63.3	83.3

=79 Salford	81.8	76.7	7.8	115	67.9	83.3
=81 Brunel	76.3	75.0	30.9	111	61.1	83.0
=81 York St John	86.1	82.3	9.7	107	60.0	83.0
83 Westminster	82.9	76.2	28.9	98	57.1	82.8
84 Winchester	87.1	86.0	—	110	59.3	82.5
=85 Bath Spa	79.4	69.3	23.5	117	59.2	82.3
=85 East London	86.6	74.8	13.7	—	54.8	82.3
=85 Wolverhampton	81.6	81.8	7.6	95	67.9	82.3
88 Ulster	79.8	77.1	35.1	117	47.2	82.2
=89 Kingston	83.1	81.3	15.7	105	56.8	82.1
=89 Suffolk	97.8	94.5	—	108	41.2	82.1
91 Leeds Trinity	81.9	85.1	6.2	99	64.0	82.0
92 Derby	80.8	72.9	13.5	116	59.7	81.7
93 Sunderland	72.5	67.9	15.3	97	75.6	81.2
94 Falmouth	81.4	68.4	—	102	71.1	81.0
95 South Wales	75.4	72.9	12.8	121	60.7	80.7
96 Anglia Ruskin	82.2	78.7	16.3	102	53.4	80.6
97 Gloucestershire	78.9	68.1	9.3	111	60.6	79.9
98 Goldsmiths, London	74.9	66.8	34.9	120	45.1	79.5
99 Brighton	83.6	72.5	16.2	112	43.7	79.0
100 Canterbury Christ Church	83.8	71.4	8.0	101	50.9	78.5
101 Cumbria	87.3	78.9	—	103*‍	42.0	77.5
102 Cardiff Metropolitan	81.7	69.9	—	98	54.9	77.4
103 Plymouth Marjon	81.7	76.5	—	96*	48.5	76.5
104 Chichester	68.5	62.0	16.3	104	58.0	76.3
105 Middlesex	65.8	59.5	11.0	101	51.1	72.9

Employed in professional job	34%	Employed in non-professional job and Studying	5%
Employed in professional job and studying	3%	Employed in non-professional job	23%
Studying	26%	Unemployed	8%
Average starting professional salary	£19,500	Average starting non-professional salary	£16,224

Food Science

Glasgow has come straight in at the top of the Food Science table, which contains more than 40 universities for the first time after two years of increased enrolments nationally. This came to an end in 2018, however, when the numbers starting courses fell by more than 18%. With only 600 students enrolling, such statistics can be misleading, but the percentage drop in applications was even larger.

Food science is well inside the top 30 subject groups for both salaries and employment. Degrees range from professional cookery to food manufacturing, nutrition, dietetics and food security. There are even specialist baking science degrees at London South Bank.

Most of the universities offering food science are post-1992 institutions, but only three – Robert Gordon, Glasgow Caledonian and Plymouth – feature in the top ten. Others are making progress, however. The Royal Agricultural University has moved up 17 places to 14th in the new table, Kingston is up 19 and into the top 20 and Northumbria is only just outside it after a rise of 14 places.

Entry standards are modest – Glasgow has the highest, averaging over 200 points, but only ten other universities reach 150. Glasgow's course is too new to compile a score for graduate prospects, but the next five universities all saw more than 90% of leavers go into graduate-level employment or continue studying. None of them had the highest score on this measure; that distinction went to Hertfordshire, in 16th place overall, where the success rate was 97% in 2017.

Queen's Belfast registered the top score in the Research Excellence Framework, while Kingston, in 18th place, had the best scores in all parts of the National Student Survey. Student satisfaction is generally high in food science, with eight universities topping 90% for teaching quality and four for the broader student experience.

Food Science	Teaching quality %	Student experience %	Research quality %	Entry standards (UCAS points)	Graduate prospects %	Overall score
1 Glasgow	77.2	78.5	42.3	203	—	100.0
2 Surrey	90.4	90.2	37.5	151	95.3	97.7
3 Leeds	82.0	88.8	36.8	165	92.8	96.8
4 Robert Gordon	92.8	89.3	4.9	171	96.9	95.8
5 Glasgow Caledonian	90.9	86.1	8.1	171	94.7	95.0
6 Queen's, Belfast	69.1	74.8	56.3	157	91.8	94.4
7 Nottingham	81.6	83.7	36.4	157	85.1	93.5
8 Ulster	90.6	80.9	42.5	136	74.2	91.4
9 Plymouth	90.4	89.7	17.4	156	73.1	90.5
10 Reading	74.4	78.5	50.7	129	84.1	90.3
11 Newcastle	81.5	82.8	28.4	142	80.3	89.5
=12 Central Lancashire	91.5	91.4	8.3	137*	80.9	88.9
=12 Coventry	83.1	83.0	—	148	93.5	88.9
14 Royal Agricultural	80.6	81.7	2.1	—	91.7	88.3
15 Abertay	87.2	85.8	—	156	80.0	88.2
16 Hertfordshire	84.1	82.3	14.8	113	97.0	88.0
17 King's College London	66.2	63.6	46.8	150	78.0	87.5
18 Kingston	95.9	94.0	2.6	—	65.2	86.8
19 Worcester	84.6	79.7	—	127*	92.9	86.3
20 Liverpool John Moores	85.4	87.7	6.0	157	61.7	85.1
21 Northumbria	86.5	84.6	14.0	140*	64.8	85.0
22 Manchester Metropolitan	84.4	84.7	12.0	140	67.4	84.8
23 Cardiff Metropolitan	87.8	85.8	—	123	78.9	84.2
24 Leeds Beckett	82.5	88.1	—	115	86.1	84.0
25 Harper Adams	82.7	81.7	5.7	111	86.9	83.9
26 London Metropolitan	84.2	84.9	—	111*	82.8	82.8
27 Chester	74.6	71.8	12.0	112	88.9	82.7
28 Bournemouth	90.9	91.0	4.7	121	63.3	82.6
=29 Huddersfield	77.3	76.9	—	129	81.0	82.2
=29 Roehampton	73.5	81.0	20.6	121	72.0	82.2

31	Sheffield Hallam	83.8	83.0	3.7	117	73.1	81.8
32	Greenwich	66.0	72.2	19.5	130	71.4	80.4
33	Oxford Brookes	78.1	79.2	3.0	147	57.7	80.3
34	Queen Margaret, Edinburgh	72.2	66.4	—	157	58.7	78.6
35	Bath Spa	80.5	82.3	—	104	68.3	77.9
36	Westminster	80.6	81.0	—	123*	57.3	77.7
37	Edge Hill	69.9	76.5	—	133	64.3	77.5
38	St Mary's, Twickenham	75.1	70.8	—	109	74.1	77.3
39	London South Bank	78.7	78.5	—	102*	60.0	75.2
40	Liverpool Hope	69.8	62.6	—	97	61.9	71.3
41	Leeds Trinity	56.8	55.5	—	112	59.6	69.2

Employed in professional job	54%	Employed in non-professional job and Studying		3%
Employed in professional job and studying	3%	Employed in non-professional job		16%
Studying	16%	Unemployed		8%
Average starting professional salary	£22,000	Average starting non-professional salary		£17,000

French

Fewer than 300 students started degrees in French in 2018, less than half the total in the early years of the decade. The number of applications is now below 2,000 for the first time, having fallen for ten years running. Another 2,300 students opted for broader language courses, many of which included French, but these, too, were down in 2018. Not surprisingly, some universities are cutting back their language courses. Although 68 of them are offering full-time undergraduate courses in or including French starting in 2020, that is two less than a year ago.

French remains the most popular language at degree level, but there were only 40 fewer applications for Spanish in 2018, whereas the gap was more than 1,000 four years earlier. Entry standards remain relatively high, however. In spite of the falling numbers, there were six applications to the place in 2018 and many of the candidates came from high-achieving independent schools. Five universities average at least 200 points on the UCAS tariff and only one dropped below an average of 110 points. Many universities will teach the language from scratch, especially as part of joint degrees.

Cambridge remains well clear at the head of the table, but nearly every other university has changed position. Cambridge's three nearest challengers last year have all dropped at least five places in the latest edition, Lancaster crashing out of the top ten from second place, despite boasting much the best graduate prospects. Surrey has moved up five places to take second, just ahead of Oxford, with the top rates in both of our measures of student satisfaction.

Satisfaction rates are among the highest in any subject, with over 85% of final-year undergraduates giving positive ratings to the quality of teaching and 82% feeling the same about the broader student experience. Nationally, French is in the top 30 for starting salaries in graduate-level jobs, but just in the bottom half for employment prospects.

French

		Teaching quality %	Student experience %	Research quality %	Entry standards (UCAS points)	Graduate prospects %	Overall score
1	Cambridge	—	—	54.0	209	80.6	100.0
2	Surrey	97.2	95.2	39.1	160	76.2	96.0
3	Oxford	—	—	41.3	203	77.0	95.4
=4	St Andrews	91.4	92.6	26.4	211	72.0	94.8
=4	Strathclyde	84.3	85.5	42.0	205	71.9	94.8
6	Sheffield	90.4	84.1	41.2	145	84.8	94.3
7	Queen's, Belfast	83.8	82.1	53.6	155	78.3	94.2
8	Warwick	83.2	77.3	45.2	166	84.3	94.0
9	Exeter	85.8	83.8	35.1	169	84.5	93.7
10	Durham	81.0	73.2	34.6	197	86.3	93.6
11	York	89.3	82.7	37.3	162	78.9	93.1
=12	King's College London	85.0	83.9	42.1	165	77.0	93.0
=12	Southampton	83.0	80.4	42.7	163	81.3	93.0
14	Lancaster	72.7	70.1	47.0	155	97.1	92.9
15	Manchester	81.2	76.7	48.9	161	78.2	92.6
16	Newcastle	85.7	85.4	36.3	158	80.7	92.5
17	Reading	90.3	83.8	41.7	129	81.0	92.4
18	Royal Holloway, London	89.4	85.9	48.3	147	68.1	92.3
19	Stirling	90.5	86.9	29.8	160	78.2	92.2
20	Nottingham	84.9	81.5	39.4	148	81.5	92.0
21	Bristol	84.4	79.3	36.0	166	78.9	91.6
=22	Bangor	90.7	87.8	39.6	123	76.3	91.2
=22	Leeds	86.8	86.8	30.6	165	74.8	91.2
24	Birmingham	77.7	71.1	33.7	177	82.5	90.3
25	Glasgow	78.5	77.5	26.3	215	68.8	89.8
26	Cardiff	87.7	87.2	32.5	148	70.6	89.7
27	Aberystwyth	93.9	90.5	16.6	122	83.1	89.3
28	Kent	78.2	80.6	41.9	118	84.1	89.2
=29	Liverpool	74.8	76.1	33.4	143	86.3	88.5
=29	University College London	74.1	66.2	43.7	171	73.6	88.5
31	Heriot-Watt	79.6	79.3	26.3	174	73.2	88.2
32	Portsmouth	85.6	85.2	32.2	—	66.7	88.0
=33	Hull	96.6	90.2	22.7	115*	69.8	87.8
=33	Swansea	87.2	84.4	22.8	116	83.4	87.8
35	Bath	75.8	75.5	27.4	159	80.3	87.5
36	Aberdeen	77.0	79.2	29.3	172	70.0	87.3
37	Edinburgh	71.1	74.0	30.3	189	71.7	87.2
38	Queen Mary, London	91.4	83.1	35.1	128	58.0	86.6
39	Leicester	92.8	90.2	16.9	121	68.5	86.0
40	Chester	89.9	89.3	17.3	105	75.2	85.5
41	Manchester Metropolitan	92.5	83.1	29.0	118	45.5	82.5
42	Ulster	89.4	83.3	22.4	—	50.0	82.1

43 Aston	83.1	73.7	23.4	135	56.2	81.6
44 Nottingham Trent	86.2	80.5	7.6	115	70.0	81.5
45 Oxford Brookes	83.7	84.0	—	128*	68.0	80.5
46 Coventry	90.2	85.4	—	114*	58.1	79.1
47 Edinburgh Napier	81.5	82.0	—	144	57.9	78.9
48 Westminster	85.9	80.9	2.0	121	57.1	78.3

Employed in professional job	48%	Employed in non-professional job and Studying	2%
Employed in professional job and studying	3%	Employed in non-professional job	18%
Studying	19%	Unemployed	10%
Average starting professional salary	£22,000	Average starting non-professional salary	£17,500

General Engineering

Bristol is back on top of the General Engineering table after a year's absence. It has been swapping places with Cambridge, the long-time leader in this subject, for the last three editions of the *Guide*. Bristol registered the best graduate prospects and has outstanding scores in both of our measures of student satisfaction, with 99% of final-year undergraduates giving a positive rating to the quality of teaching. Cambridge has the highest entry standards and was just behind fourth-placed Oxford in the 2014 Research Excellence Framework.

The numbers starting general engineering courses fell slightly in 2018, but it was not for the want of candidates. Applications were up for the seventh year in succession, setting another record at a time when most branches of engineering were down. The table is still growing, with three universities joining it last year and another three – Dundee, Nottingham Trent and Surrey – listed for the first time in the new edition.

General engineering courses attract students who are looking for maximum career flexibility. It may also help that general engineering has become a fixture in the top five of the graduate earnings table, with median salaries of £27,500 in professional jobs. The subject has been dropping in the overall employment table, however. Having been in the top ten only four years ago, it is now only just inside the top 20.

Nevertheless, half of the top ten universities saw at least 90% of their 2017 graduates go straight into professional jobs or continue their studies. Most of the leading universities will require both maths and physics at A-level, with further maths, design technology and/or computing welcome additions. Entry standards vary widely between the leading universities, six of which average more than 200 points on the UCAS tariff, and those near the bottom, three of which average less than 100 points.

General Engineering	Teaching quality %	Student experience %	Research quality %	Entry standards (UCAS points)	Graduate prospects %	Overall score
1 Bristol	99.0	96.1	52.3	206	97.4	100.0
2 Cambridge	83.7*	85.5*	67.0	239	93.5	98.6
3 Glasgow	82.2	85.7	47.2	213	93.1	94.0
4 Oxford	—	—	68.7	234	88.3	93.7

	Teaching quality %	Student experience %	Research quality %	Entry standards (UCAS points)	Graduate prospects %	Overall score
5 Imperial College London	83.9	84.7	60.1	204	84.6	93.3
6 Nottingham	84.9	86.0	40.8	—	90.0	91.5
7 Heriot-Watt	79.9	82.9	47.8	183	—	90.3
8 Sheffield	76.5	82.9	51.4	167	91.4	89.8
9 Warwick	77.2	79.3	47.2	174	89.2	88.9
10 Durham	71.5	73.6	39.4	217	88.7	88.6
11 King's College London	76.2	76.2	56.6	170	—	87.9
12 Aberdeen	77.2	79.5	28.4	193	—	87.2
13 Dundee	75.0	80.2	34.1	189	—	87.0
14 Swansea	78.5	81.6	45.5	140	86.4	86.5
15 Liverpool John Moores	87.8	80.1	14.2	156	88.5	85.7
16 Exeter	67.4	66.8	36.4	167	96.7	85.5
17 Nottingham Trent	84.8	85.0	20.1	144	—	85.0
18 Lincoln	76.8	78.2	12.4	—	90.9	84.3
19 West of England	94.0	90.6	10.6	119	81.9	83.8
20 Ulster	88.0	85.6	22.8	125	79.5	83.4
21 Surrey	73.9	77.6	30.8	159	—	83.1
22 London South Bank	80.5	78.1	19.6	130	87.5	82.8
23 Queen Mary, London	82.3	67.3	46.7	133	69.2	81.2
24 Cardiff	73.7	77.1	30.2	139	77.4	80.8
25 Aston	78.2	79.1	20.6	122	81.3	80.6
=26 Leicester	73.7	74.2	34.4	125	79.1	80.5
=26 Liverpool	77.8	82.5	32.1	156	65.5	80.5
28 Bournemouth	84.1	76.3	8.5	126	81.7	80.3
29 Central Lancashire	67.4	67.4	7.1	152*	92.3	79.8
30 Bradford	79.8	82.1	7.7	128	79.6	79.5
31 Greenwich	73.5	70.9	5.5	—	84.6	78.9
32 Derby	78.7	79.1	6.7	109*	—	77.1
33 Coventry	77.7	79.7	10.3	94*	76.7	76.4
34 West of Scotland	75.8	74.0	9.0	—	69.2	74.8
35 Hull	67.1	70.2	16.5	123	—	74.6
36 City	69.7	73.8	23.1	112	67.0	74.4
37 Wolverhampton	77.4	72.1	—	71	80.6	73.8
38 Middlesex	76.4	78.4	—	121	62.4	72.7
39 Glasgow Caledonian	59.7	62.2	4.7	146	69.9	71.4
40 Edinburgh Napier	67.9	73.6	—	126	63.1	70.9
41 Northampton	63.0	57.6	—	91	77.8	69.6

Employed in professional job	59%	Employed in non-professional job and Studying	0%
Employed in professional job and studying	2%	Employed in non-professional job	9%
Studying	18%	Unemployed	12%
Average starting professional salary	£27,500	Average starting non-professional salary	£16,380

Geography & Environmental Sciences

Young people's ever-increasing interest in climate change has not translated into a boom for degrees in geography and environmental sciences. Physical and human geography, as well as the courses classified by UCAS as the science of aquatic and terrestrial environments, all saw falling applications and enrolments in 2018. Indeed, applications for physical geography were down by almost a quarter.

The demand for places had been growing, albeit gradually, despite middling early career prospects for graduates. Geography and environmental sciences are outside the top 40 in the employment table, with 30% of graduates starting out in lower-level jobs or unemployed. They fare a little better in the comparison of earnings, although the average starting salary of £21,505 in professional jobs is still below the mean for all subjects.

St Andrews has swapped places with Durham to take the lead in geography and environmental sciences, with Cambridge remaining in second place. St Andrews has the highest satisfaction rates in the sections of the National Student Survey dealing with the broad student experience, as well as good scores on our other measures. Staffordshire in 38th has the best rates for the quality of teaching, just ahead of Salford, which is up 19 places to a share of 40th position.

Physical geography courses may give preference to candidates with a science or maths A-level in addition to geography, while for environmental science, most of the leading universities will ask for two from biology, chemistry, maths, physics and geography at A-level or the equivalent. Both entry scores and graduate prospects vary widely in this table, and are influenced by which branch of geography is offered, as well as by the university. Three of the top four universities, led by fourth-placed Oxford, average more than 200 points, while four others have averages of less than 100 points.

Geography and Environmental Sciences	Teaching quality %	Student experience %	Research quality %	Entry standards (UCAS points)	Graduate prospects %	Overall score
1 St Andrews	93.6	92.5	44.2	203	77.2	100.0
2 Cambridge	—	—	57.3	207	83.3	99.1
3 Durham	84.6	79.7	55.0	193	85.0	98.6
4 Oxford	—	—	41.1	210	80.4	98.2
5 Bristol	78.3	80.4	61.3	180	84.8	97.0
6 Lancaster	81.4	81.6	46.5	157	87.3	94.8
7 London School of Economics	77.7	72.6	46.9	179	87.7	94.6
8 Exeter	80.7	82.0	43.7	167	82.6	94.1
=9 Birmingham	80.3	81.4	42.0	157	85.8	93.6
=9 Glasgow	80.3	79.3	42.4	182	78.3	93.6
=11 Loughborough	88.9	92.1	24.3	149	83.3	93.5
=11 Newcastle	82.3	83.8	43.1	159	80.5	93.5
13 University College London	81.7	77.3	52.3	171	73.3	93.2
14 Manchester	85.3	84.9	36.6	161	77.9	93.1
15 Nottingham	81.1	84.8	39.6	154	81.2	92.6
16 Royal Holloway, London	86.8	88.8	45.8	137	72.4	92.3
=17 Aberystwyth	87.2	88.0	38.6	115	83.8	92.2

Geography and Environmental Sciences cont

		Teaching quality %	Student experience %	Research quality %	Entry standards (UCAS points)	Graduate prospects %	Overall score
=17	Southampton	84.8	83.6	45.8	153	71.8	92.2
19	Leeds	76.8	78.5	42.3	162	82.9	92.1
20	Dundee	81.5	87.4	28.3	168	74.8	91.2
21	Swansea	82.6	86.0	39.4	129	80.2	91.1
=22	Aberdeen	78.9	79.2	38.2	186	68.3	90.8
=22	Sheffield	84.2	86.2	31.1	150	75.0	90.8
24	Stirling	82.5	82.2	30.3	164	73.8	90.6
25	Edinburgh	79.4	77.6	38.2	175	69.3	90.2
26	East Anglia	81.2	80.8	47.4	147	66.6	89.6
27	York	83.0	80.5	23.9	150	77.2	89.5
28	Liverpool	83.9	87.2	26.3	140	74.8	89.4
29	Hull	87.6	86.2	31.7	117	70.4	88.4
30	Cardiff	76.2	79.1	36.8	148	73.3	88.3
31	Sussex	75.0	76.2	35.8	147	76.6	88.1
32	Leicester	80.5	80.3	29.7	127	77.0	87.8
=33	Liverpool Hope	83.2	80.9	1.6	108	94.6	87.3
=33	King's College London	77.4	78.0	40.0	154	64.0	87.3
35	Coventry	91.0	92.1	2.0	124	73.8	87.2
36	Greenwich	82.9	77.7	7.4	—	79.2	87.0
37	Portsmouth	85.4	86.0	14.9	113	76.3	86.6
38	Staffordshire	96.3	92.3	—	97	74.4	86.5
39	Queen Mary, London	73.4	72.9	45.1	129	69.7	85.8
=40	Bangor	80.8	84.1	31.5	123	65.4	85.7
=40	Salford	94.8	85.4	16.7	109	61.5	85.7
=42	Queen's, Belfast	76.9	77.1	36.9	138	63.7	85.5
=42	Reading	75.9	76.3	35.0	127	70.4	85.5
=42	Ulster	89.3	90.9	17.2	112	62.7	85.5
45	Keele	89.2	87.3	16.4	118	63.1	85.4
46	Plymouth	82.3	82.3	25.8	121	65.4	85.0
47	Northumbria	85.5	87.0	15.4	131	61.2	84.9
48	Derby	83.0	86.2	3.6	112	78.3	84.8
49	West of England	90.5	90.5	6.4	113	63.8	84.6
50	Manchester Metropolitan	81.8	83.0	14.9	113	69.6	83.9
51	Liverpool John Moores	86.3	85.4	—	125	65.5	83.3
=52	Gloucestershire	85.3	86.5	14.5	114	60.4	83.2
=52	Nottingham Trent	80.8	78.1	4.1	113	76.8	83.2
54	Chester	83.0	80.9	6.4	106	67.5	81.8
55	Hertfordshire	79.9	77.8	—	105	75.5	81.5
56	Worcester	87.1	82.9	8.1	106	57.8	81.3
57	Sheffield Hallam	81.0	84.0	13.4	106	60.7	81.2
58	Kingston	76.8	76.6	6.9	106	72.7	81.0
59	South Wales	91.9	89.1	—	111	49.8	80.8

60 Central Lancashire	82.5	77.9	9.8	118*	56.5	80.4
61 Bournemouth	81.7	79.8	19.9	103	54.3	80.2
62 Oxford Brookes	75.6	75.6	17.3	121	58.8	80.0
63 Brighton	89.1	85.0	5.1	102	51.0	79.9
64 Cumbria	78.2	77.3	1.5	119	63.2	79.6
65 Winchester	80.1	77.9	7.5	97	—	79.2
66 Canterbury Christ Church	88.4	86.0	—	110	48.1	79.1
67 Leeds Beckett	77.9	79.6	5.6	103	61.8	78.9
68 Northampton	82.3	76.3	7.7	86	57.7	77.8
69 Edge Hill	71.1	73.4	6.2	111	62.0	77.1
70 St Mary's, Twickenham	71.7	49.5	—	96*	56.0	71.5
71 Bath Spa	61.7	63.1	—	107	53.3	70.6

Employed in professional job	39%	Employed in non-professional job and Studying	3%
Employed in professional job and studying	3%	Employed in non-professional job	19%
Studying	26%	Unemployed	11%
Average starting professional salary	£21,505	Average starting non-professional salary	£16,643

Geology

Both applications and enrolments in geology dropped by more than 10% in 2018, continuing a downward trajectory of recent years. The demand for places is down by almost a third since 2015, although 41 universities are offering courses starting in 2020.

The top three are unchanged in geology, with Imperial College still the leader and the holder of the best results in the 2014 Research Excellence Framework. Imperial, which often struggles in the National Student Survey, also has the highest level of satisfaction with the quality of teaching and shares top place for the broader student experience with Derby, which is in the bottom ten overall. Imperial is not one of the three universities where average entry standards top 200 points, however. Second-placed Cambridge's average of 240 points is among the highest in any subject.

Some of the leading universities expect candidates to have two scientific or mathematical subjects at A-level, or the equivalent. Undergraduates spend an average of 16 hours a week attending lectures and seminars, while fieldwork varies from the local areas around the campus, to placements both in the UK and overseas.

Only Celtic Studies has a higher proportion of graduates continuing their studies than geology. More than 40% took this route in 2017, helping the subject to finish in the top half of the table for graduate prospects. Durham, which is fourth overall, had the best score on this measure and was the only university to see 90% of graduates going straight into professional employment or continuing their studies.

Newcastle, which jumped 15 places into the top ten last year, has made the reverse journey in the latest edition, dropping 14 places and out of the top 20 after a big drop in satisfaction with teaching quality. Portsmouth is the only post-1992 university in the top 20.

Geology

		Teaching quality %	Student experience %	Research quality %	Entry standards (UCAS points)	Graduate prospects %	Overall score
1	Imperial College London	91.1	91.3	59.6	193	87.6	100.0
2	Cambridge	—	—	58.0	240	84.0	99.3
3	Oxford	—	—	52.1	209	82.2	96.5
4	Durham	84.4	81.7	42.2	176	91.2	94.8
5	Bristol	90.1	88.6	55.8	158	73.4	94.3
6	St Andrews	81.5	82.4	44.2	216	75.0	93.1
7	Southampton	81.5	84.4	58.3	149	79.1	92.6
8	Exeter	89.2	84.7	45.7	144	77.9	92.5
9	Royal Holloway, London	84.2	85.3	43.4	132	81.5	91.1
10	East Anglia	82.1	87.1	47.4	142	77.5	91.0
11	Leeds	82.1	84.2	41.9	157	78.0	90.8
=12	Glasgow	79.6	81.4	38.5	190	73.3	90.2
=12	Manchester	82.2	81.3	44.5	162	73.7	90.2
14	Aberdeen	80.1	83.1	38.2	160	78.7	90.0
15	Aberystwyth	89.9	87.6	34.9	103	79.3	89.9
16	Birmingham	76.6	78.2	38.6	150	81.9	88.7
17	Bangor	81.9	82.8	31.5	137	79.2	88.5
18	University College London	73.9	82.8	47.9	166	67.9	87.8
19	Leicester	82.1	83.4	37.2	131	71.6	87.6
20	Portsmouth	84.9	79.1	19.8	109	85.9	87.4
21	Edinburgh	74.8	74.5	38.2	194	68.3	87.3
22	Newcastle	76.9	89.5	35.4	136	—	87.2
23	Liverpool	81.1	85.8	30.3	136	72.0	87.1
24	Derby	88.5	91.3	3.6	107	81.7	86.8
25	Cardiff	78.6	82.3	21.3	133	75.0	85.4
26	Keele	84.1	85.5	12.2	105	78.6	85.3
27	Hull	82.8	77.8	31.7	109	66.7	84.3
28	Plymouth	78.7	78.8	25.3	118	62.4	82.2
29	Brighton	85.6	83.9	5.1	98	55.1	79.6
30	Kingston	75.0	71.4	6.9	105	68.8	78.6
31	Edge Hill	77.1	71.9	—	104*	67.7	78.1
32	South Wales	70.5	73.4	—	94*	43.0	71.2

Employed in professional job	31%	Employed in non-professional job and Studying	3%
Employed in professional job and studying	2%	Employed in non-professional job	15%
Studying	38%	Unemployed	10%
Average starting professional salary	£21,000	Average starting non-professional salary	£16,575

German

Cambridge is back on top of the table for German, a position it had held for 12 years before being displaced by Lancaster last year. Cambridge had the best results in the Research

Excellence Framework and has the highest entry standards. St Andrews, which has the best graduate prospects, is up six places to second, while Glasgow has made even more progress, jumping 12 places and into the top five.

Degree courses in German were struggling to attract students before other languages joined the decline. After another drop of 16% in 2018, the number of applications was less than half the total at the start of the decade. Only 100 students started degrees in German, although others learn the language as part of broader modern languages programmes. German has suffered more than other languages from the decline in the numbers taking courses in the sixth-form, but there has been a worldwide decline in the language that has been worrying the German government, as well as academic linguists.

Most universities in the table offer German from scratch as well as catering for those who took the subject at A-level. Employment prospects are better than in other modern languages, although the small numbers mean that the differences can be slight from year to year. German is in the top 30 for the proportion of graduates going into professional jobs or onto postgraduate courses, but 11 places lower in the salary table.

The highest rate of student satisfaction with teaching quality is at Aberystwyth, which is in a share of 17th place, but did not have enough entrants in 2018 to compile a score for that measure. King's College London, in fourth place, does best in the other sections of the National Student Survey. There are only three post-1992 universities in the ranking, with Chester the only one to feature in the top 30.

German	Teaching quality %	Student experience %	Research quality %	Entry standards (UCAS points)	Graduate prospects %	Overall score
1 Cambridge	—	—	54.0	209	80.6	100.0
2 St Andrews	84.8	88.8	26.4	206	89.7	96.4
3 Lancaster	81.6	82.5	47.0	—	85.7	95.7
4 King's College London	91.8	91.2	42.1	153	79.6	95.1
5 Glasgow	86.7	84.5	26.3	199	—	94.8
6 Oxford	—	—	41.3	195	79.3	94.7
7 Durham	81.0	73.2	34.6	197	86.3	94.1
8 Exeter	85.8	83.8	35.1	169	84.5	94.0
9 Nottingham	85.5	78.9	39.4	152	86.4	93.6
10 Sheffield	85.5	78.2	41.2	149	85.6	93.5
=11 Southampton	87.2	87.5	42.7	159	76.0	93.4
=11 Warwick	84.0	84.3	45.2	174	74.1	93.4
13 Birmingham	84.7	78.8	33.7	—	85.6	93.2
14 Cardiff	87.7	87.2	32.5	154	83.9	93.1
15 Newcastle	87.4	84.1	36.3	163	78.2	92.6
16 York	89.6	83.9	37.3	145*	—	92.3
=17 Aberystwyth	93.9	90.5	16.6	—	78.3	91.7
=17 Manchester	75.7	75.6	48.9	153	80.4	91.7
=19 Leeds	87.5	87.0	30.6	156	79.1	91.5
=19 Reading	86.1	77.1	41.7	117	86.1	91.5
21 Bristol	87.1	83.6	36.0	172	68.7	90.6

German cont		teaching quality %	Student experience %	Research quality %	Entry standards (UCAS points)	Graduate prospects %	Overall score
=22	Kent	79.4	84.7	41.9	120	77.4	89.0
=22	Queen Mary, London	88.4	81.5	35.1	122	76.7	89.0
24	Swansea	87.2	84.4	22.8	119*	86.2	88.8
25	Bath	75.8	75.5	27.4	159	83.3	88.4
=26	Bangor	90.7	87.8	39.6	120*	65.9	88.3
=26	Heriot-Watt	79.6	79.3	26.3	174	74.6	88.3
28	Chester	89.9	89.3	17.3	—	70.9	87.6
=29	Aston	83.6	81.7	23.4	136*	80.3	87.5
=29	Royal Holloway, London	77.8	74.2	48.3	—	70.2	87.5
31	Portsmouth	86.7	85.7	32.2	100	76.4	86.9
32	University College London	71.4	67.6	43.7	181	59.5	85.5
33	Liverpool	72.0	75.6	33.4	127	—	82.7
34	Nottingham Trent	89.1	84.6	7.6	115	69.6	81.6
35	Edinburgh	62.2	62.7	30.3	189	59.4	80.8
36	East Anglia	74.6	74.3	—	139	76.3	79.2
37	Hull	75.3	73.9	22.7	118*	58.2	78.0

Employed in professional job	50%	Employed in non-professional job and Studying		2%
Employed in professional job and studying	4%	Employed in non-professional job		17%
Studying	20%	Unemployed		8%
Average starting professional salary	£21,000	Average starting non-professional salary		£18,000

History

Both applications and enrolments for history degrees fell for the third year in a row in 2018. History remains among the 20 most popular subjects in higher education, but the numbers starting courses fell below 10,000 for the first time since £9,000 fees were introduced in 2012. Poor early career prospects may be responsible.

The subject is in the bottom 20 for employment, with more than a quarter of graduates starting out in low-level jobs. It is 40th in the earnings table, although surveys have suggested that historians often rise to the top later in their careers.

The top five for history are unchanged since last year, with Cambridge in a clear lead over Oxford. The best results in the Research Excellence Framework and the highest entry standards have given Cambridge top place for the fifth time in succession. The leading scores for our other measures are all to be found outside the top 20. Liverpool Hope, in 33rd, for example, has by far the best graduate prospects.

Once again, eight of the top ten universities for student satisfaction with teaching quality are post-1992 institutions; yet the top 20 in our table, even including the NSS results, are all older foundations. Suffolk, which is 83rd overall, narrowly failed to repeat last year's 100% rate for satisfaction with teaching quality but still has the best score on this measure as well as very high satisfaction with the wider student experience, in which it was just pipped by Leeds Beckett in

68th place. Unfortunately, Suffolk has to live with its score for graduate prospects in 2017 – an unusually low success rate of 27% – because no new graduate employment rates have been calculated in the last year while a new system is introduced.

Employment scores are disappointing at many universities in the table. Eleven of the 94 institutions saw less than half of those graduating in 2017 go into professional jobs or start postgraduate courses by the end of the year.

History	Teaching quality %	Student experience %	Research quality %	Entry standards (UCAS points)	Graduate prospects %	Overall score
1 Cambridge	—	—	56.3	211	80.9	100.0
2 Oxford	—	—	56.1	207	81.9	97.2
3 Durham	85.4	77.9	41.4	204	86.2	96.9
4 St Andrews	90.9	86.3	46.7	196	71.7	96.4
5 Sheffield	83.1	82.2	53.7	155	78.5	93.5
6 University College London	78.2	73.8	51.9	182	77.9	93.1
=7 Warwick	83.1	76.0	51.7	168	74.8	92.7
=7 York	83.3	76.9	43.3	172	79.6	92.7
9 Exeter	79.6	77.4	45.6	174	80.1	92.5
10 Leeds	83.7	80.2	43.6	170	74.0	91.8
=11 Birmingham	79.5	78.8	48.8	163	76.6	91.6
=11 Manchester	—	—	39.8	163	71.2	91.6
13 Lancaster	81.8	76.9	37.0	160	83.4	91.0
14 Nottingham	82.3	81.5	36.9	156	81.3	90.8
=15 Southampton	82.8	76.5	50.6	152	71.9	90.7
=15 Sussex	83.9	76.9	41.3	148	79.9	90.7
17 London School of Economics	72.5	65.5	46.8	182	79.5	90.2
18 Glasgow	78.9	73.3	47.7	178	67.2	90.0
19 Kent	84.1	76.6	41.3	138	79.0	89.7
=20 Aberdeen	83.0	80.3	36.1	183	64.7	89.5
=20 Royal Holloway, London	88.5	80.9	40.6	135	72.3	89.5
22 Loughborough	88.5	83.1	22.5	145	82.2	89.3
23 Lincoln	91.4	86.2	25.9	126	79.7	88.8
24 Strathclyde	81.6	78.0	42.0	190	56.0	88.7
=25 Dundee	84.7	82.5	30.4	168	64.9	88.0
=25 East Anglia	81.7	77.2	47.4	139	68.0	88.0
=27 Edinburgh	75.0	69.0	46.9	183	61.5	87.7
=27 King's College London	74.0	69.6	45.3	163	71.7	87.7
=27 Teesside	94.2	83.6	27.9	104	78.9	87.7
30 Queen Mary, London	83.5	78.4	43.7	136	67.3	87.6
31 Bristol	74.5	68.6	40.6	173	70.9	87.5
32 Northumbria	93.0	88.3	30.7	135	61.8	87.4
=33 Liverpool	84.1	80.7	38.9	138	67.2	87.2
=33 Liverpool Hope	89.5	86.2	15.7	114	87.3	87.2
35 Swansea	86.3	83.9	25.0	127	76.8	86.7

History cont

		Teaching quality %	Student experience %	Research quality %	Entry standards (UCAS points)	Graduate prospects %	Overall score
36	Queen's, Belfast	83.7	79.7	46.3	146	55.5	86.6
37	Newcastle	75.0	73.6	29.0	162	75.5	86.1
38	Aberystwyth	89.2	84.7	19.5	125	75.2	86.0
39	Portsmouth	87.2	87.0	32.2	101	73.4	85.8
=40	Hertfordshire	79.0	72.8	46.7	105	72.9	85.1
=40	Stirling	84.4	75.5	28.5	167	56.9	85.1
42	Huddersfield	87.2	85.6	22.3	120	71.8	85.0
=43	De Montfort	84.8	83.5	23.4	105	78.2	84.5
=43	Leicester	81.5	78.9	34.3	127	66.2	84.5
45	Coventry	93.8	85.7	5.6	115	77.2	84.4
46	Liverpool John Moores	88.0	81.8	15.9	136	68.3	84.2
47	Keele	76.2	72.0	32.8	125	76.1	84.1
48	Cardiff	76.5	67.6	31.4	153	68.0	84.0
49	Roehampton	89.7	83.4	21.4	102	71.1	83.6
50	Essex	84.2	83.9	34.8	101	64.0	83.3
51	Oxford Brookes	81.2	78.6	35.0	120	61.5	83.0
52	Reading	81.8	73.0	35.4	127	58.2	82.5
53	Hull	78.5	75.3	26.1	119	70.3	82.1
=54	Bangor	84.3	76.7	24.3	125	61.3	82.0
=54	Brunel	80.4	70.4	32.4	108	68.4	82.0
=54	Salford	95.4	90.1	—	110	68.3	82.0
57	SOAS, London	75.2	65.8	20.8	147	71.7	81.9
58	Newman	86.9	84.3	12.0	112	68.8	81.7
59	Northampton	88.8	88.3	21.5	98	59.6	81.3
60	Edge Hill	89.3	81.9	23.6	113	54.1	81.2
61	Ulster	90.8	85.1	24.0	117	48.2	81.1
62	Plymouth	88.4	82.4	22.6	117	53.1	80.9
=63	Nottingham Trent	83.0	77.3	17.5	117	66.1	80.8
=63	Sheffield Hallam	88.4	82.0	38.3	108	42.3	80.8
=65	Manchester Metropolitan	83.7	80.9	18.0	117	61.8	80.6
=65	Bishop Grosseteste	92.0	85.2	7.0	85	71.7	80.6
67	Worcester	87.5	79.7	19.5	116	56.4	80.5
=68	Leeds Beckett	93.1	91.7	11.0	96	56.3	80.0
=68	West of England	88.4	81.8	28.9	107	46.9	80.0
70	Derby	91.6	87.3	13.5	99	55.7	79.7
71	Central Lancashire	84.3	80.5	12.0	116	60.7	79.3
72	Goldsmiths, London	80.5	69.6	34.5	114	50.6	79.1
73	Staffordshire	89.7	87.8	—	89*	67.6	78.5
74	Greenwich	82.5	77.1	8.6	125	59.8	78.4
=75	Chester	89.5	80.1	9.1	113	52.3	78.1
=75	Winchester	83.8	78.0	19.1	108	53.4	78.1
77	Bath Spa	81.4	77.9	8.3	106	65.6	77.9

78 Westminster	80.1	75.5	11.8	102	64.1	77.3
79 St Mary's, Twickenham	88.0	81.0	11.0	96	54.3	77.2
80 Canterbury Christ Church	88.2	83.1	16.3	92	48.9	77.0
81 Gloucestershire	85.8	81.2	11.2	103	52.7	76.9
82 Chichester	82.1	67.1	15.8	100	60.6	76.7
83 Suffolk	98.9	90.3	—	119	27.3	75.1
84 Wolverhampton	82.3	73.1	18.8	97	44.4	74.4
=85 Wales Trinity St David	81.4	71.6	17.3	100	45.4	74.2
=85 York St John	85.1	77.5	—	107	50.4	74.2
87 Anglia Ruskin	81.0	69.6	15.3	102	45.7	73.8
88 Bradford	63.8*	58.9*	12.7	—	72.0	73.0
89 Brighton	82.3	71.5	13.1	97	41.9	72.7
90 Kingston	83.7	79.6	—	101*	42.1	71.9
91 Sunderland	71.3	61.7	7.7	102	53.9	70.9
92 South Wales	74.7	58.3	15.8	111	37.6	70.2
93 Leeds Trinity	69.9	54.3	10.3	85	55.7	69.3
94 East London	49.8	45.1	13.9	—	72.2	66.0

Employed in professional job	31%	Employed in non-professional job and Studying	4%
Employed in professional job and studying	3%	Employed in non-professional job	22%
Studying	29%	Unemployed	10%
Average starting professional salary	£21,000	Average starting non-professional salary	£16,497

History of Art, Architecture and Design

The numbers taking history of art degrees have held up better than in most of the humanities, and more than 60 institutions are offering the subject in 2020, several as part of a broader liberal arts programme. Employment levels have improved in recent years, lifting the subjects into the top 50 of the 67 subject groups. Cambridge and Aberystwyth were the only universities where 80% of the 2017 graduates went straight into professional jobs or postgraduate study, but only bottom-placed Brighton slipped below 50% on this measure. The relatively small numbers taking degrees in the history of art, architecture or design can make for considerable volatility in the statistics, but it was also in the top 50 in the most recent salaries table.

Aberystwyth, which joined our table in second place last year, has closed the gap slightly on Cambridge, the longstanding leader in the subject. St Andrews, in third place, has the most satisfied students and is the only university to register 90% approval for the quality of teaching. Oxford, one place lower, has the highest entry grades in a generally high-scoring subject. Although only Oxford and Cambridge average more than 200 points on the UCAS tariff, just three of the 29 universities have an average below 120 points and none is below 100.

The Courtauld Institute, an independent college of the University of London based in Somerset House, and previously the only specialist institution to top any of our league tables, had the best results in the Research Excellence Framework, when 95% of its submission was rated as world-leading or internationally excellent. It is now sixth in the table, after a rise of two places since last year.

History of Art, Architecture and Design

		Teaching quality %	Student experience %	Research quality %	Entry standards (UCAS points)	Graduate prospects %	Overall score
1	Cambridge	—	—	49.0	217	84.4	100.0
2	Aberystwyth	89.2	84.7	21.6	—	93.6	98.9
3	St Andrews	90.9	86.2	42.1	199	75.4	98.3
4	Oxford	—	—	39.7	221	77.8	95.5
5	York	85.0	79.1	53.2	151	77.9	94.5
6	Courtauld	80.4	70.2	66.0	182	67.2	93.9
7	Warwick	82.9	75.9	53.0	167	71.4	93.4
8	Manchester	—	—	54.0	166	67.4	92.9
9	Birmingham	79.6	78.8	43.7	159	79.4	92.3
10	University College London	78.1	73.6	44.7	189	68.8	91.6
11	Leeds	83.6	80.4	30.0	159	71.1	90.6
12	Aberdeen	83.1	80.4	36.1	—	65.5	90.2
13	Leicester	81.6	78.5	42.0	135	73.0	90.1
14	Exeter	79.8	78.0	35.1	169	67.7	89.9
15	East Anglia	81.7	77.2	36.9	155	68.4	89.8
16	Sussex	83.9	76.9	25.2	138	79.2	89.7
17	Nottingham	82.1	81.4	30.9	151	68.8	89.5
=18	Essex	83.7	83.3	46.9	114*	—	89.1
=18	Kent	83.7	76.8	44.3	129	65.1	89.1
20	Plymouth	88.4	82.4	14.7	152	63.3	88.5
21	Glasgow	79.5	74.1	37.2	170	59.3	88.2
22	Oxford Brookes	81.2	78.6	35.0	118	72.5	87.9
23	Manchester Metropolitan	83.7	80.9	9.7	150	—	87.3
=24	Edinburgh	75.4	69.2	27.9	172	68.0	86.9
=24	SOAS, London	75.2	65.8	40.9	150	69.2	86.9
26	Bristol	74.6	68.7	28.3	163	59.0	84.6
27	Goldsmiths, London	80.5	69.6	25.9	147	54.3	84.3
28	Liverpool John Moores	88.0	81.8	7.2	126	50.0	83.4
29	Brighton	83.4	74.0	13.1	106	40.0	78.9

Employed in professional job	37%	Employed in non-professional job and Studying	3%
Employed in professional job and studying	2%	Employed in non-professional job	23%
Studying	26%	Unemployed	9%
Average starting professional salary	£20,280	Average starting non-professional salary	£16,000

Hospitality, Leisure, Recreation & Tourism

The top two in hospitality, leisure and tourism remain the same, with Birmingham enjoying its fifth year at the top. But there is considerable movement further down the table. Even within the new top 20, Arts Bournemouth is up more than 20 places, while Gloucestershire, Manchester Metropolitan and London South Bank have all risen at least ten places. Among those dropping out of the leading group, Staffordshire and Edinburgh have fallen 19 and 21 places respectively.

Only eight of the 59 institutions in the latest table are pre-1992 universities, but they include six of the top ten. Entry standards are modest – only six universities average more than 150 points on the UCAS tariff. They are led by second-placed Strathclyde with 214 points. Birmingham benefits from by far the best results in the Research Excellence Framework, when 90% of its submission was considered world-leading or internationally excellent. Students at tenth-placed Sunderland are again the most satisfied with their course, producing an unusually high rate both for the quality of teaching and the broader student experience.

More than 100 universities and colleges are offering courses in one or more of the hospitality, leisure, recreation and tourism subjects in 2020. The grouping covers a variety of courses directed towards management in the leisure and tourism industries. Taken together with sports studies, it remains close to the top 20 for applications, although the numbers have dropped for four years in a row and are down by a quarter since the beginning of the decade.

Because so many graduates begin their careers in low-level jobs, the subjects are never far from the foot of the employment table. They are fifth from bottom in the most recent edition. The subjects do better in the earnings table, but are still in the bottom 20. Portsmouth, just outside the top 20, has the best graduate prospects, one of only three universities to see eight out of ten graduates go straight into professional employment or onto a postgraduate course. The proportion was below one in three at three universities.

Hospitality, Leisure, Recreation and Tourism	Teaching quality %	Student experience %	Research quality %	Entry standards (UCAS points)	Graduate prospects %	Overall score
1 Birmingham	76.3	77.7	63.7	176	73.9	100.0
2 Strathclyde	75.5	77.0	44.3	214*	54.5	96.0
3 Ulster	94.0	94.2	31.0	120	63.0	90.4
4 Liverpool John Moores	77.5	77.7	45.3	144	54.1	88.5
=5 Manchester	83.8	82.1	—	155	77.6	88.2
=5 Surrey	72.7	80.6	33.6	160	57.8	88.2
7 Lincoln	80.1	81.3	11.4	132	78.7	87.1
8 Glasgow Caledonian	90.4	87.6	15.2	154	44.6	85.6
9 Central Lancashire	94.5	92.9	5.1	125	61.0	85.4
10 Sunderland	98.7	97.9	2.4	99	69.3	85.2
11 Coventry	85.6	84.4	1.6	133	70.6	85.1
12 Gloucestershire	81.1	78.3	6.0	119	80.5	84.9
13 Arts Bournemouth	82.9	83.1	—	117	81.6	84.7
=14 De Montfort	87.6	79.2	—	124	74.1	84.4
=14 Manchester Metropolitan	85.8	85.9	4.7	135	63.0	84.4
=16 Edge Hill	81.1	80.3	7.7	141	—	84.3
=16 Leeds Beckett	85.9	86.5	12.6	117	64.9	84.3
18 London South Bank	77.2	80.2	35.0	99	62.0	83.4
19 Oxford Brookes	79.1	81.9	5.1	140	63.5	83.3
20 Huddersfield	79.9	77.1	—	137	70.6	83.2
21 Winchester	86.8	82.8	—	105	77.5	83.1
=22 Greenwich	81.6	78.9	3.3	146	59.6	82.9

	Teaching quality %	Student experience %	Research quality %	Entry standards (UCAS points)	Graduate prospects %	Overall score
=22 Portsmouth	76.9	78.0	8.1	101	83.2	82.9
24 Falmouth	93.2	88.1	—	113	63.0	82.8
=25 Bournemouth	80.3	77.5	9.0	121	67.9	82.6
=25 Staffordshire	86.3	88.2	19.1	105	56.8	82.6
=27 Chichester	87.8	85.8	—	117	65.5	82.4
=27 Queen Margaret, Edinburgh	81.3	82.5	—	129	67.1	82.4
29 Wolverhampton	92.1	89.9	5.6	119	53.2	82.2
=30 Bolton	85.5	85.8	—	126	61.0	81.8
=30 Edinburgh	49.4	46.9	26.1	176	65.6	81.8
=30 Robert Gordon	82.4	79.4	2.6	141	56.6	81.8
=30 Solent	80.4	81.7	0.6	122	69.1	81.8
34 Sheffield Hallam	82.5	79.8	8.5	113	64.5	81.5
35 Plymouth	84.0	79.8	13.1	120	52.9	80.9
36 Canterbury Christ Church	82.3	81.8	19.0	106	53.4	80.4
37 Chester	86.1	80.9	6.6	116	54.4	80.1
38 Hertfordshire	77.7	78.8	0.9	117	65.6	79.7
=39 Aberystwyth	75.2	78.8	14.5	123	53.3	79.6
=39 Salford	75.0	73.7	5.9	123	63.2	79.6
=39 Westminster	67.5	71.5	10.7	141	58.1	79.6
=42 Derby	79.0	77.6	0.9	134	55.2	79.4
=42 Edinburgh Napier	78.7	75.8	2.3	140	51.8	79.4
44 Brighton	80.7	80.9	10.9	115	51.8	79.1
45 West of Scotland	75.7	73.4	9.1	120	57.7	78.8
46 Liverpool Hope	76.9	77.5	10.9	110	57.7	78.7
47 West London	81.6	82.6	—	120	53.5	78.4
=48 East London	84.2	85.0	0.8	103	57.9	78.3
=48 Cardiff Metropolitan	75.6	76.0	7.7	119	56.5	78.3
50 South Wales	80.0	73.7	10.8	112	52.4	77.9
51 St Mary's, Twickenham	86.8	75.0	4.8	131	32.3	76.1
52 Wales Trinity St David	80.3	79.0	—	105	48.8	74.8
53 Bucks New	79.0	76.0	0.9	109	47.3	74.6
54 Northampton	75.5	66.7	—	112	53.0	74.3
55 Middlesex	71.0	70.2	10.5	135	32.7	73.8
56 London Metropolitan	69.3	66.5	—	98	51.9	71.0
57 Bedfordshire	69.7	68.8	6.7	72	47.0	68.6
58 Anglia Ruskin	66.1	71.9	3.4	106	30.0	67.5
59 Cumbria	64.1	60.8	3.2	—	45.7	67.4

Employed in professional job	48%	Employed in non-professional job and Studying	2%
Employed in professional job and studying	1%	Employed in non-professional job	31%
Studying	7%	Unemployed	10%
Average starting professional salary	£20,000	Average starting non-professional salary	£17,000

Iberian Languages

Spanish was only 15 behind French for the number of students starting degrees in 2018, but that will have been little consolation to university departments that shared in further declines nationally in both applications and enrolments. Only 270 students embarked on degrees in Spanish alone, although others among the 2,300 students entering broader modern language degrees will include Spanish in their programme of study. The table also includes Portuguese, but not one student has started a single honours degree in the language since 2012. Nevertheless, Portuguese will still be available –as part of a modern languages degree or other joint honours – at 22 universities in 2020. It can be combined with Czech, Russian, philosophy or theatre (among other subjects) at Bristol.

Cambridge has a clear lead at the top of the table, with Aberystwyth moving up 13 places to become its nearest challenger. Cambridge has the highest entry grades and produced the top results in the Research Excellence Framework. Although down 11 places from second overall after a collapse in student satisfaction, Lancaster has by far the best graduate prospects, with over 96% of graduates going straight into professional employment or further study. Only Aberystwyth comes within ten percentage points. The Welsh university is also the runner-up for student satisfaction, where third-placed Surrey is the new leader.

Iberian Languages are tied with French and nine other subjects for 26th place on graduate salaries in professional jobs. They are in the bottom half for overall graduate prospects, although most universities offering the languages have a reasonable employment record. Only three fell below 60% for the proportion of graduates going straight into professional jobs or further study in 2017. Just six of the 47 institutions in this year's table are post-1992 universities, none of them reaching the top 30. Coventry comes closest.

Iberian Languages	Teaching quality %	Student experience %	Research quality %	Entry standards (UCAS points)	Graduate prospects %	Overall score
1 Cambridge	—	—	54.0	209	80.6	100.0
2 Aberystwyth	93.9	90.5	16.6	—	88.7	96.3
3 Surrey	94.8	93.6	39.1	140	—	94.6
4 Durham	81.0	73.2	34.6	197	86.3	94.2
5 Glasgow	83.9	81.8	26.3	198	85.6	94.1
6 Exeter	85.8	83.8	35.1	169	84.5	94.0
7 St Andrews	86.5	85.5	26.4	198	79.8	93.7
8 Oxford	—	—	41.3	208	72.7	93.6
9 Newcastle	86.1	86.8	36.3	156	82.5	93.1
=10 Southampton	85.2	85.3	42.7	158	77.6	93.0
=10 Strathclyde	82.5	79.7	42.0	191	73.1	93.0
12 Queen's, Belfast	84.2	82.8	53.6	145	74.2	92.8
13 Lancaster	69.6	62.4	47.0	154	96.7	92.2
14 King's College London	83.9	83.1	42.1	161	76.0	92.1
15 Manchester	82.9	79.2	48.9	155	70.7	91.1
16 Leeds	82.5	86.2	30.6	160	79.7	90.8
17 Birmingham	88.3	83.6	33.7	168*	70.2	90.7
=18 Reading	90.3	87.5	41.7	120	—	90.4

Iberian Languages cont	Teaching quality %	Student experience %	Research quality %	Entry standards (UCAS points)	Graduate prospects %	Overall score
=18 Stirling	85.2	80.4	29.8	168	76.0	90.4
=20 Nottingham	80.1	74.9	39.4	153	78.4	89.9
=20 York	83.9	81.8	37.3	147	75.0	89.9
22 Sheffield	83.7	77.3	41.2	153	72.1	89.8
23 Warwick	75.7	77.4	45.2	165	–	89.4
24 Royal Holloway, London	82.5	79.8	48.3	144	66.7	89.2
25 Heriot-Watt	79.6	79.3	26.3	174	77.0	89.0
26 Bristol	74.3	72.6	36.0	160	81.2	88.9
27 Cardiff	87.7	87.2	32.5	142	68.6	88.4
28 Liverpool	83.3	87.1	33.4	134	74.2	88.3
29 Bath	75.8	75.5	27.4	164	79.2	87.8
30 University College London	69.8	61.6	43.7	184	71.3	87.6
31 Coventry	91.8	85.4	18.1	125	77.8	87.4
32 Aberdeen	75.9	77.5	29.3	176*	71.0	87.2
33 Kent	76.7	73.8	41.9	123	77.0	86.9
34 Bangor	90.7	87.8	39.6	106	63.4	86.6
35 East Anglia	74.6	74.3	33.1	139	75.0	85.5
36 Portsmouth	85.0	86.0	32.2	100	72.5	85.4
37 Edinburgh	69.1	65.7	30.3	182	71.1	85.2
38 Manchester Metropolitan	90.2	85.7	29.0	110	65.1	85.0
=39 Queen Mary, London	78.3	72.2	35.1	130	70.4	84.8
=39 Swansea	87.2	84.4	22.8	128	66.8	84.8
41 Hull	83.7	76.7	22.7	108*	71.0	82.6
42 Chester	89.9	89.3	17.3	118	59.3	82.3
43 Leicester	86.5	77.4	16.9	127	63.6	81.8
44 Aston	76.4	70.6	23.4	134	67.4	81.5
45 Ulster	89.4	83.3	22.4	–	49.6	80.6
46 Westminster	86.5	81.7	2.0	129	63.6	79.6
47 Nottingham Trent	86.3	82.4	7.6	115	53.7	77.3

Employed in professional job	47%	Employed in non-professional job and Studying	2%
Employed in professional job and studying	3%	Employed in non-professional job	21%
Studying	18%	Unemployed	10%
Average starting professional salary	£22,000	Average starting non-professional salary	£17,000

Italian

Only 25 students started degrees in Italian in 2018 – five fewer than in the previous year, but five more than in 2016. Such are the tiny numbers that modern languages departments are having to juggle, although an unknown number of students will be taking Italian as part of a broader package of languages, or as one or more modules in another degree. A total of 36 universities are offering Italian at degree level in 2020, but only seven have a single honours programme.

Most students have no previous knowledge of Italian, although they are likely to have taken another language at A-level. Entry standards remain surprisingly high, given the small numbers of applicants. Although top-placed Cambridge is the only university with an average of more than 200 points, most average over 150 and none drops below 100.

Cambridge, which also did best in the Research Excellence Framework, is well clear at the top of the table, but Kent has overtaken Oxford to become the nearest challenger, after a rise of five places. The small numbers of students make for a volatile table – this year, both UCL and Reading have broken into the top ten after rises of at least five places. Reading has much the highest scores in both of the measures derived from the National Student Survey (NSS), while Birmingham was well clear of the field on graduate prospects, with 95% of those completing courses in 2017 going straight into professional jobs or continuing to study.

Italian is outside the top 50 in the latest employment table, although it does better in the comparison of graduate salaries. Scores have generally been good in the NSS. As in other subjects, Oxford and Cambridge did not secure enough responses from students to compile scores, but every other university satisfied at least three quarters of final-year undergraduates on the quality of teaching.

Italian	Teaching quality %	Student experience %	Research quality %	Entry standards (UCAS points)	Graduate prospects %	Overall score
1 Cambridge	—	—	54.0	209	80.6	100.0
2 Kent	82.0	84.8	41.9	—	87.0	94.4
3 Oxford	—	—	41.3	196	76.6	93.5
4 Durham	81.0	73.2	34.6	197	86.3	93.0
5 Exeter	85.8	83.8	35.1	169	84.5	92.9
6 University College London	83.5	64.0	43.7	185	81.6	92.8
7 Manchester	81.2	76.7	48.9	149	84.1	92.4
8 Bristol	89.7	84.8	36.0	163	75.5	92.1
9 Reading	97.8	94.3	41.7	137	58.1	91.1
10 Warwick	82.4	79.0	45.2	159	72.1	90.7
11 Birmingham	76.0	73.4	33.7	161	95.1	90.4
12 Edinburgh	83.8	85.1	30.3	175	75.4	90.3
13 Bangor	90.7	87.8	39.6	—	56.4	89.3
14 Cardiff	87.7	87.2	32.5	156	66.0	88.8
15 Leeds	86.7	90.9	30.6	156	64.8	88.3
16 Glasgow	80.0	77.3	26.3	172	—	87.1
17 Bath	75.8	75.5	27.4	156	83.7	86.8
18 Portsmouth	85.8	86.1	32.2	100	76.1	85.8
19 Royal Holloway, London	75.8	76.5	48.3	—	56.1	83.6
20 Nottingham Trent	88.6	84.7	7.6	115	60.7	79.5

Employed in professional job	44%	Employed in non-professional job and Studying	2%
Employed in professional job and studying	3%	Employed in non-professional job	22%
Studying	16%	Unemployed	12%
Average starting professional salary	£21,000	Average starting non-professional salary	£17,400

Land and Property Management

Graduate salaries and employment levels in land and property management are among the best of any group outside the health professions. More than 80% of graduates go straight into professional employment, helping the subjects to a top-ten position for graduate prospects. Starting salaries of £25,000 in those jobs place land and property management 14th on that criterion. There were too few graduates in lower-level jobs at the end of 2017 to compile a national average.

The subject table reflects those high employment rates: six of the nine universities score over 90% for graduate prospects, with 94% of graduates at fourth-placed Reading finding high-level work or continuing to study. No university dropped below 70% on this measure. The table is still less than half the size it was in 2006, however, with no representation from Scotland or Wales. Nevertheless, 20 universities and colleges are offering courses in this area in 2020. They include degrees in woodland ecology and conservation, and surveying, as well as the real estate degrees that are the largest recruiters.

Cambridge has a predictably big lead, with the best research score and entry grades that are 66 points ahead of the next highest. Birmingham City, only three places from the bottom of the table, has the most satisfied students on both of our measures taken from the National Student Survey.

The subjects have acquired a reputation for recruiting disproportionate numbers from independent schools, but property firms now fund a "Pathways to Property" scheme to try to widen participation. Year 12 students in state schools and colleges are invited to a summer school at Reading's Henley Business School and an online course for prospective students to explore the real estate sector is in its first year.

Land and Property Management	Teaching quality %	Student experience %	Research quality %	Entry standards (UCAS points)	Graduate prospects %	Overall score
1 Cambridge	—	—	49.0	204	89.7	100.0
2 Ulster	81.0	80.8	28.6	129	90.0	94.2
3 Oxford Brookes	80.2	80.6	17.6	135*	92.4	93.8
4 Reading	69.8	69.9	40.0	138	94.4	92.6
5 Sheffield Hallam	81.0	80.1	13.4	115	92.1	92.2
6 Nottingham Trent	80.3	81.0	3.4	118	93.3	91.7
7 Birmingham City	81.4	81.6	2.7	119	90.9	91.5
8 Westminster	69.8	75.7	10.7	126	84.2	87.6
9 Greenwich	75.9	77.1	2.0	126	70.0	85.3

Employed in professional job	79%	Employed in non-professional job and Studying	0%
Employed in professional job and studying	3%	Employed in non-professional job	5%
Studying	5%	Unemployed	9%
Average starting professional salary	£25,000	Average starting non-professional salary	n/a

Law

Already one of the most popular choices for higher education, law has attracted record applications and converted them into record enrolments for four years in a row. The numbers starting degrees passed 26,000 in 2019. Entry standards reflect this: only in medical subjects and economics do so many universities make such testing demands. Seven of the 101 universities in the table average more than 200 points and a third average more than 150 points. However, so many universities now offer law that there are still five where the average was below 100 points in 2018.

Cambridge remains well ahead of its rivals at the head of the table without topping any of the five measures. The same goes for UCL and Oxford, which are second and third this year. Fourth-placed Glasgow again has the highest entry standards, benefiting from the UCAS conversion rate for Scottish secondary qualifications, while Lancaster, just outside the top 20, has the best score for graduate prospects. The students who are most satisfied with the quality of teaching are at Abertay, which has shot up 20 places to 13th, while West London, although not in the top 40 overall, has the best rating for the broader student experience.

Law is in the top 20 in the employment table but it is only 55th out of the 67 subjects for early career earnings, which average (just) less than £20,000 in professional jobs. Only about half of all graduates go on to practise law, and training contracts for those who do keep the median pay in graduate-level jobs relatively low. Those in lower-level employment are only £3,000 worse off, although the later rewards in professional jobs can be considerable. Recent surveys suggest that the average law graduate almost doubles his or her salary within ten years.

Aspiring solicitors in England go on to take the Legal Practice Course, while those aiming to be barristers take the Bar Vocational Course, so it is no surprise that 45% of all law graduates are engaged in postgraduate study six months after completing a degree. Note that in Scotland, most law courses are based on the distinctive Scottish legal system, which also has different professional qualifications.

Law	Teaching quality %	Student experience %	Research quality %	Entry standards (UCAS points)	Graduate prospects %	Overall score
1 Cambridge	—	—	58.7	219	89.8	100.0
2 University College London	76.3	76.7	57.7	211	89.2	96.5
3 Oxford	—	—	51.8	215	83.9	95.4
4 Glasgow	79.0	80.2	33.8	233	84.5	94.5
5 London School of Economics	72.6	63.9	64.5	196	85.8	93.3
6 King's College London	76.3	73.8	39.2	204	87.0	92.6
7 Aberdeen	81.5	83.0	20.9	190	90.2	92.3
8 Leeds	83.2	86.4	40.1	167	79.2	91.5
9 Dundee	81.1	84.5	16.3	184	89.4	91.2
=10 Durham	75.9	68.6	32.8	205	86.0	90.9
=10 Strathclyde	74.9	73.8	29.4	198	88.5	90.9
12 Edinburgh	69.2	70.4	40.8	210	85.4	90.8
=13 Abertay	94.1	87.2	1.2	156	88.0	90.3
=13 Nottingham	71.4	73.2	45.2	176	86.3	90.3
15 Bristol	73.3	68.5	50.5	186	79.3	89.8
16 Sheffield	78.8	80.0	31.9	159	85.8	89.7

Law cont

		Teaching quality %	Student experience %	Research quality %	Entry standards (UCAS points)	Graduate prospects %	Overall score
17	Kent	76.3	78.1	43.9	146	84.6	89.5
18	York	78.5	81.7	30.3	166	81.7	89.1
19	Warwick	72.8	74.6	41.9	179	80.1	89.0
20	Southampton	84.2	77.7	18.2	161	84.8	88.7
21	Exeter	75.3	75.9	21.4	173	86.9	88.2
=22	Lancaster	69.2	68.0	38.9	145	93.5	88.1
=22	Stirling	80.4	81.4	19.4	174	80.1	88.1
24	Queen's, Belfast	71.4	67.4	40.3	156	87.6	88.0
25	Birmingham	74.8	73.2	33.6	163	83.2	87.8
26	East Anglia	78.2	78.6	26.5	158	80.7	87.4
27	Newcastle	76.4	77.9	25.4	169	80.0	87.2
28	Reading	77.1	79.4	31.2	135	82.8	86.9
=29	Cardiff	77.2	77.0	27.2	160	78.8	86.7
=29	Glasgow Caledonian	75.5	74.4	1.8	197	86.0	86.7
=29	Heriot-Watt	74.9	79.0	18.8	181	79.2	86.7
=32	Sussex	76.3	74.8	23.3	153	84.2	86.6
=32	Swansea	81.3	81.2	20.4	131	83.8	86.6
34	Keele	77.0	77.8	30.5	119	85.2	86.2
35	Manchester	68.8	66.5	27.2	175	85.2	86.1
=36	Aberystwyth	82.0	82.7	14.3	119	84.8	85.6
=36	Liverpool	76.6	74.7	19.6	148	83.0	85.6
=36	London South Bank	81.1	78.5	20.1	105	87.9	85.6
39	Leicester	77.4	78.0	26.4	141	77.4	85.2
40	Queen Mary, London	72.1	70.4	23.7	162	79.7	84.7
=41	Lincoln	83.5	83.6	5.0	118	84.2	84.5
=41	Nottingham Trent	85.2	81.3	2.3	128	82.7	84.5
=41	Sunderland	91.3	88.2	0.7	101	81.2	84.5
=41	West London	88.8	91.3	—	108	80.8	84.5
45	Bangor	85.1	82.2	12.0	121	78.0	84.4
46	Gloucestershire	85.9	76.6	—	119	86.4	84.2
=47	SOAS, London	70.9	73.3	26.7	157	75.7	83.8
=47	Ulster	81.0	78.2	48.5	130	58.9	83.8
49	Robert Gordon	77.1	72.9	3.9	166	79.3	83.5
50	Hull	77.3	73.5	12.6	128	82.0	83.1
51	Aston	80.6	76.1	19.7	136	71.3	83.0
=52	Buckingham	75.1	74.8	—	116	92.8	82.9
=52	Portsmouth	67.1	70.0	32.2	118	84.3	82.9
=52	Sheffield Hallam	86.0	85.5	14.4	112	70.6	82.9
55	Plymouth	79.4	75.9	16.0	127	76.3	82.8
56	South Wales	87.9	86.7	—	117	73.8	82.6
57	Essex	73.6	74.4	31.6	111	76.6	82.5
58	Northumbria	81.8	81.0	2.5	136	74.9	82.3

59	St Mary's, Twickenham	84.8	84.1	—	114	76.8	82.1
=60	Edge Hill	83.2	79.8	12.1	121	70.1	81.7
=60	Teesside	81.2	77.3	15.0	111	74.0	81.7
62	Solent	88.2	89.8	—	104	71.4	81.6
63	De Montfort	78.2	79.6	5.2	102	81.9	81.3
64	Derby	78.8	76.4	2.4	117	80.0	81.2
65	Westminster	78.0	78.9	7.5	118	76.4	81.1
=66	Bolton	87.4	83.5	—	92	75.0	80.8
=66	Middlesex	72.0	70.5	21.4	110	79.1	80.8
68	London Metropolitan	81.1	79.2	0.3	97	81.2	80.7
69	Chester	75.7	74.4	—	107	85.3	80.6
=70	Bournemouth	70.8	72.8	8.8	119	82.4	80.5
=70	Greenwich	80.9	76.4	2.1	133	71.5	80.5
=72	Edinburgh Napier	80.0	70.7	—	173	64.9	80.3
=72	Liverpool John Moores	72.3	68.1	2.7	134	82.2	80.3
=74	Bradford	71.6	70.2	11.8	132	76.5	80.2
=74	West of England	79.4	78.9	3.5	115	74.1	80.2
=76	Brighton	84.1	81.4	6.5	102	69.5	80.0
=76	Brunel	69.9	69.3	20.3	122	75.6	80.0
=76	Manchester Metropolitan	72.3	72.2	14.9	122	75.0	80.0
79	Cumbria	91.0	81.7	—	108	64.0	79.7
80	Coventry	73.8	72.3	5.6	114	78.1	79.3
81	Central Lancashire	77.6	78.4	5.3	125	68.5	79.2
82	Oxford Brookes	75.5	75.8	5.1	119	70.1	78.4
83	Staffordshire	74.9	71.9	—	112	77.1	78.3
84	Salford	77.3	76.1	5.9	108	69.9	78.2
85	Surrey	64.9	62.1	8.5	147	76.2	78.1
86	Huddersfield	69.0	70.4	—	123	78.8	77.9
=87	Bedfordshire	83.7	82.9	3.6	79	66.2	77.3
=87	Birmingham City	74.0	78.3	2.8	110	69.7	77.3
=87	East London	72.3	70.2	8.6	102	73.8	77.3
=90	Hertfordshire	71.2	73.0	—	108	76.0	77.1
=90	Liverpool Hope	66.3	62.5	—	112	84.4	77.1
92	West of Scotland	83.7	83.2	—	127	54.1	77.0
93	Wolverhampton	78.7	79.2	2.7	97	65.2	76.6
94	Bucks New	75.9	81.5	—	123	60.3	76.2
95	Northampton	71.1	69.1	—	88	74.0	74.9
96	City	64.9	64.4	9.1	143	62.1	74.7
97	Anglia Ruskin	74.6	72.0	5.2	101	57.3	73.4
98	Canterbury Christ Church	81.2	74.9	3.2	115	45.2	72.9
99	Leeds Beckett	66.2	66.6	—	104	66.1	72.5
100	Kingston	64.8	63.3	—	104	64.5	71.4
101	Winchester	62.0	57.5	—	108	62.1	69.8

Employed in professional job	33%	Employed in non-professional job and Studying	5%
Employed in professional job and studying	6%	Employed in non-professional job	14%
Studying	34%	Unemployed	8%
Average starting professional salary	£19,998	Average starting non-professional salary	£17,000

Librarianship and Information Management

The table for Librarianship and Information Management has changed more than any other in this year's *Guide*, transforming from three to 22 universities. Sadly, this does not reflect a sudden boom in demand for librarians, but a change in the courses that qualify for the table. Universities offering degrees in information systems were asked if they would like to appear in this table rather than the one for computer science. Some chose not to make the switch, but others agreed that this category offered a better reflection of the content of their programmes.

Traditional librarianship has practically disappeared at undergraduate level and is now normally studied as a Master's degree; indeed, some postgraduate training is required to enter the profession after completing a first degree. The dwindling number of courses in this category mainly focused on broader information services, so a table that includes degrees classified by UCAS under information systems should be more valuable to prospective students.

Loughborough remains top of the new table, with the highest of a modest set of entry grades – 160 points on the UCAS tariff – and the best rating for the overall student experience. The other survivors from last year's table are Northumbria, in seventh place, and Manchester Metropolitan, only three places off the bottom. Cardiff, which recorded the best performance in the 2014 Research Excellence Framework, is second, and Aberystwyth, where students conferred the best ratings for teaching quality, third.

There are real contrasts in graduate prospects among universities in the new table, partly reflecting the different types of courses on offer. While Cardiff saw 92% of its graduates go straight into professional jobs or further study, the proportion was little more than half that figure at East London. Nine of the 22 universities had a success rate of less than 75%.

Librarianship and Information Management	Teaching quality %	Student experience %	Research quality %	Entry standards (UCAS points)	Graduate prospects %	Overall score
1 Loughborough	85.6	89.2	45.1	160	89.0	100.0
2 Cardiff	76.1	78.1	55.4	—	92.3	96.0
3 Aberystwyth	86.0	83.4	9.2	—	85.4	92.2
4 Brunel	78.4	77.0	23.0	146	80.4	90.5
5 Derby	79.5	77.2	13.5	139	78.9	88.3
6 De Montfort	76.4	74.4	31.2	113	82.9	87.6
7 Northumbria	71.6	68.9	21.0	147	73.0	86.4
8 Edinburgh Napier	74.7	71.7	9.5	141	79.4	86.1
9 Robert Gordon	79.4	75.8	7.5	—	76.9	86.0
10 Leeds Beckett	78.3	75.8	11.0	124	78.7	85.8
11 Sheffield Hallam	82.2	80.7	14.4	111	73.2	85.4
12 Birmingham City	80.0	77.5	6.0	123	—	85.2
13 Portsmouth	77.4	76.6	12.8	113	81.2	85.1
14 Gloucestershire	75.2	74.3	—	127	75.8	83.1
15 East London	85.6	86.0	13.9	112	46.8	82.7
16 Westminster	71.2	70.6	28.3	125	58.7	82.6
17 Anglia Ruskin	75.5	71.9	26.4	—	58.1	81.9
18 Wolverhampton	68.5	67.6	33.2	—	66.7	81.6

19 Hertfordshire	69.3	72.1	—	114	86.0	81.5
20 Manchester Metropolitan	79.0	75.4	4.7	129	51.2	80.9
21 Glasgow Caledonian	67.0	67.6	15.2	—	72.8	79.9
22 London Metropolitan	74.9	73.6	5.9	87	67.3	77.8

Employed in professional job	55%	Employed in non-professional job and Studying	1%
Employed in professional job and studying	4%	Employed in non-professional job	19%
Studying	9%	Unemployed	12%
Average starting professional salary	£25,000	Average starting non-professional salary	£16,881

Linguistics

Almost 70 universities are offering degrees in linguistics in 2020 even though only 535 students started courses in the subject in 2018. The category includes some degrees in English language and large numbers that pair linguistics with other subjects. In its pure form, linguistics examines how language works, and can lead to work in speech therapy or the growing field of teaching English as a foreign language.

Despite falls in the demand for places over the past two years, the subject has fared much better than might have been expected since the introduction of £9,000 fees, with both applications and enrolments higher than they were at that time. Almost three-quarters of the students are female. There are five applications for each place and entry standards are comparatively high, with 11 of the top 15 universities averaging more than 150 points on the UCAS tariff. Cambridge has the highest average, but has dropped to fourth place in the latest table.

Oxford retains the lead, despite having lower scores than Cambridge in the three measures in which they have published figures. As in other subjects, neither university reached the required 50% response rate in the National Student Survey, but Cambridge had the lowest satisfaction rates in the entire table on the last occasion that a score could be produced. Warwick and Lancaster, which, Cambridge apart, has the top score for graduate prospects, are now Oxford's nearest challengers.

Students at SOAS – not usually the easiest to impress in the National Student Survey – are the most satisfied with the quality of teaching, while those at Leeds gave the highest rating to the broader student experience.

Linguistics is outside the top 50 in the employment table, but does a little better in the comparison of earnings, sharing 47th place with eight others. Almost one graduate in three starts off in lower-level employment, and only Cambridge and Essex saw eight out of ten of those completing a linguistics degree go straight into professional work or onto a postgraduate course in 2017.

Linguistics	Teaching quality %	Student experience %	Research quality %	Entry standards (UCAS points)	Graduate prospects %	Overall score
1 Oxford	—	—	41.3	203	77.4	100.0
=2 Lancaster	84.2	84.1	47.0	154	78.3	98.0
=2 Warwick	84.1	83.6	45.2	165	—	98.0
4 Cambridge	—	—	54.0	216	87.9	97.6
5 Manchester	75.6	80.2	48.9	151	79.8	95.7

Linguistics cont	Teaching quality %	Student experience %	Research quality %	Entry standards (UCAS points)	Graduate prospects %	Overall score
6 University College London	78.6	81.8	43.7	185	66.3	95.6
7 Newcastle	88.5	79.6	36.3	153	69.1	94.8
8 Sheffield	76.1	79.7	42.2	155	76.0	94.2
9 Leeds	86.3	87.5	30.6	157	65.8	93.9
10 SOAS, London	93.6	84.2	26.0	160*	60.9	93.8
11 Aberdeen	77.6	77.2	46.3	143*	72.7	93.3
12 Kent	81.1	78.1	41.9	122	78.5	93.1
13 Edinburgh	69.5	70.3	57.7	193	56.6	92.7
14 York	80.3	79.4	37.3	146	68.9	92.2
15 Huddersfield	87.2	86.1	29.9	123	69.2	92.0
16 Glasgow	79.8	76.5	26.3	—	75.0	91.3
17 Central Lancashire	83.6	83.9	15.2	133	77.8	91.1
18 King's College London	72.2	73.9	42.1	154	69.0	90.9
19 Bangor	85.8	85.8	39.6	124	55.6	90.3
20 Manchester Metropolitan	85.3	79.1	29.0	111	71.7	90.0
21 Essex	70.2	72.6	36.0	125	80.4	89.5
=22 Queen Mary, London	72.2	68.9	50.3	120	69.6	89.0
=22 Nottingham Trent	89.3	80.4	10.0	126	69.6	89.0
24 Cardiff	83.2	75.8	35.1	—	59.3	88.8
25 Roehampton	81.7	76.4	21.8	101*	77.4	88.0
26 West of England	83.2	83.8	9.5	117	65.1	86.2
27 Reading	73.6	72.2	25.8	138	—	85.7
=28 Hertfordshire	81.3	81.8	—	110	69.2	84.3
=28 York St John	85.3	81.9	9.7	102	60.0	84.3
30 Wolverhampton	75.4	72.9	12.8	113*	69.6	84.0
31 Salford	86.7	85.1	4.8	110*	53.3	83.4
32 Brighton	85.0	75.7	16.2	114	47.7	82.7
=33 Ulster	79.8	77.1	22.4	112	33.7	79.5
=33 Westminster	80.8	75.1	2.0	104	51.9	79.5

Employed in professional job	39%	Employed in non-professional job and Studying	3%
Employed in professional job and studying	3%	Employed in non-professional job	26%
Studying	22%	Unemployed	7%
Average starting professional salary	£20,000	Average starting non-professional salary	£16,354

Materials Technology

Courses in this table cover four distinct areas: materials science, mining engineering, textiles technology and printing, and marine technology. The various subjects are highly specialised and attract relatively small numbers – fewer than 700 started courses in all of these areas combined in 2018, when there were falls in both applications and enrolments. There are now only 15 universities in the table, but 45 are offering courses in this area in 2020. The leading universities demand chemistry and sometimes also physics, maths or design technology at A-level or its equivalent.

Cambridge remains well ahead of the rest at the top of the table, with much the highest scores for entry standards and research: only 3% of the university's submission to the Research Excellence Framework was considered less than world-leading or internationally excellent. However, Loughborough, one place behind Oxford in third position, has the best graduate prospects. Like Sheffield and Swansea, it saw at least 95% of graduates go straight into professional jobs or further study. Loughborough also has the top score in our teaching quality measure derived from the National Student Survey, while Manchester does best in the sections focusing on the wider student experience. QS ranks Cambridge among the top four universities in the world for materials science, with Oxford three places lower and Imperial College London – fifth in our table – also in the top ten.

Materials technology does well in the national salaries table, holding down 14th place, with an average that reached £25,000 in 2017, and it is only eight places lower for graduate prospects after improvements in recent years. More than half of all graduates went straight into professional jobs, while nearly three in ten continued their studies, either full or part-time. Entry standards are relatively high, with only two universities averaging less than 120 points on the UCAS tariff.

Materials Technology	Teaching quality %	Student experience %	Research quality %	Entry standards (UCAS points)	Graduate prospects %	Overall score
1 Cambridge	—	—	78.3	240	84.0	100.0
2 Oxford	—	—	70.8	232	93.4	97.4
3 Loughborough	91.2	87.4	41.8	149	95.9	92.9
4 Sheffield	77.5	79.3	41.0	165	95.7	90.4
5 Imperial College London	65.7	69.2	62.3	196	82.8	90.0
6 Manchester	87.5	87.7	36.4	171	74.6	88.1
7 Exeter	81.6	83.3	36.4	147	87.8	87.5
8 Birmingham	73.5	73.5	49.3	163	83.7	87.4
9 Swansea	75.8	79.1	45.5	115	95.0	86.5
10 Sheffield Hallam	84.5	84.5	17.8	121	76.1	80.2
11 Queen Mary, London	60.8	73.7	40.0	134	76.4	79.1
12 Birmingham City	74.4	71.0	—	130	77.3	74.8
13 De Montfort	84.4	79.4	12.5	91	65.8	73.8
14 Bucks New	54.1	52.9	—	138*	55.0	64.1
15 Huddersfield	56.8	48.9	10.2	126	46.9	63.0

Employed in professional job	49%	Employed in non-professional job and Studying	2%
Employed in professional job and studying	2%	Employed in non-professional job	11%
Studying	24%	Unemployed	11%
Average starting professional salary	£25,000	Average starting non-professional salary	£18,000

Mathematics

The number of students starting maths degrees dropped unexpectedly by almost 1,000 – practically 11% – in 2019, wiping out the increases that university departments had enjoyed since the introduction of £9,000 fees. Harder maths A-levels, taken for the first time in 2017, have been blamed, with the numbers taking the qualification falling by almost 5,000 in 2019. The decline flies in the face of Government exhortations to take maths, which is often cited as one of the subjects most likely to lead to a lucrative career. Its popularity led four more universities to join the table in the last edition.

Including statistics and joint honours degrees, the number of applications, is still close to 50,000 a year.

Entry standards are high: the top three in this year's table all average more than 220 points and seven average at least 200. The scores are boosted by the fact that most successful candidates for the leading universities have taken two A-levels in the subject, as well as two or three others. But the table also covers a wide spread of entry scores: 20 universities average less than 120 points, five of which fall below 100.

Cambridge remains fractions of a point ahead of Oxford at the top of the table, without leading on any individual measure. QS places Cambridge and Oxford fifth and sixth respectively in its world ranking for maths. Oxford produced the best results in the Research Excellence Framework, but the best scores on the other measures are surprisingly widely spread through the table. Chichester, which is 58th out of the 73 universities, has the best graduate prospects, for example, almost six percentage points ahead of any other university. Students at DeMontfort, in 33rd position, are the most satisfied with the quality of teaching, while London Metropolitan, just inside the top 50 overall, does best in the remaining sections of the National Student Survey.

Maths is one of five subjects sharing 14th place for average salaries in professional jobs six months after graduation. However, it is still outside the top 20 in the table based on the proportion of graduates going straight into such jobs or embarking on another course. Three in ten continue their studies after graduation, while just under half find high-level employment.

Mathematics	Teaching quality %	Student experience %	Research quality %	Entry standards (UCAS points)	Graduate prospects %	Overall score
1 Cambridge	—	—	60.7	232	88.9	100.0
2 Oxford	—	—	67.5	222	90.6	99.2
3 St Andrews	85.2	86.5	44.2	235	88.5	98.3
4 Warwick	77.7	76.6	55.8	207	83.6	94.2
=5 Durham	78.9	77.6	44.0	215	86.4	94.1
=5 Imperial College London	75.2	78.5	59.7	198	84.5	94.1
7 University College London	79.2	77.7	42.0	191	90.2	93.5
8 Lancaster	82.4	81.0	45.8	165	88.2	93.3
9 Birmingham	86.5	85.3	34.1	176	83.9	92.8
10 Strathclyde	83.2	82.3	34.6	197	82.5	92.5
11 Heriot-Watt	82.3	80.9	42.3	180	83.0	92.4
12 Loughborough	87.2	88.3	31.0	162	84.0	92.2
13 Bristol	78.5	75.9	57.3	192	76.0	91.9
14 Edinburgh	73.9	77.1	43.7	203	84.0	91.7

=15	Manchester	79.2	79.5	44.3	183	79.1	91.0
=15	Nottingham	79.2	78.5	44.8	175	81.1	91.0
=17	Bath	76.2	75.1	35.7	191	85.0	90.5
=17	Glasgow	78.2	80.4	41.4	203	74.5	90.5
19	Southampton	80.6	79.7	41.9	165	80.4	90.4
20	Aberdeen	84.2	88.7	32.0	175	74.4	90.1
=21	Dundee	81.1	80.7	48.2	167	73.8	90.0
=21	Exeter	77.7	78.9	37.9	174	82.2	90.0
23	Sheffield	81.4	82.5	34.0	149	82.2	89.4
24	Kent	81.6	79.2	28.2	136	89.1	89.2
=25	Aberystwyth	93.4	90.7	19.4	125	78.2	88.9
=25	Queen's, Belfast	76.7	77.5	25.0	164	88.8	88.9
=27	Leeds	73.7	75.4	42.0	169	80.8	88.6
=27	London School of Economics	73.9	68.2	28.7	195	85.7	88.6
29	York	84.6	82.9	27.0	159	76.6	88.4
30	Essex	82.8	79.6	34.3	108	85.3	88.0
31	South Wales	93.1	90.8	10.1	127	79.0	87.9
32	Newcastle	81.4	82.9	32.0	161	73.0	87.6
33	De Montfort	94.0	91.9	—	88	90.0	87.5
34	Cardiff	79.0	80.7	31.6	168	74.1	87.4
=35	King's College London	75.4	76.0	37.1	168	76.2	87.2
=35	Salford	86.0	87.8	4.4	128	87.5	87.2
37	Sussex	72.9	72.9	28.5	147	89.0	87.1
38	Reading	82.7	77.6	35.3	132	76.5	87.0
39	Nottingham Trent	86.6	87.6	18.4	124	77.7	86.7
=40	Central Lancashire	90.0	88.6	19.8	117	71.4	85.9
=40	Liverpool John Moores	87.5	86.5	3.2	131	80.7	85.9
=40	Surrey	76.4	75.5	31.5	161	74.4	85.9
43	Stirling	82.8	80.3	14.0	156	76.6	85.8
44	Liverpool	79.7	80.3	29.8	145	72.9	85.7
=45	Keele	85.1	84.4	19.5	120	74.8	85.2
=45	Swansea	76.9	75.6	20.7	131	84.0	85.2
47	Sheffield Hallam	86.2	87.6	17.8	112	74.4	85.1
48	Portsmouth	84.3	80.2	11.2	108	84.2	85.0
49	London Metropolitan	92.4	93.2	13.5	75*	73.7	84.4
=50	East Anglia	71.8	76.2	33.7	149	72.3	84.0
=50	Hull	77.4	69.6	24.2	128	79.9	84.0
52	West of England	91.7	89.9	10.6	114	65.8	83.7
53	Liverpool Hope	75.4	79.4	8.8	112	88.0	83.6
54	Chester	83.7	83.0	7.1	110	78.8	83.5
55	Coventry	76.6	74.6	9.4	117	86.7	83.4
56	Derby	88.4	87.7	5.0	100	74.5	83.3
57	Greenwich	88.5	86.6	5.1	112	71.9	83.2
58	Chichester	72.5*	77.5*	—	104	96.3	83.1
=59	Middlesex	81.6	82.9	14.2	107	—	82.8
=59	Northumbria	77.6	76.5	16.7	133	74.3	82.8

Mathematics cont

		Teaching quality %	Student experience %	Research quality %	Entry standards (UCAS points)	Graduate prospects %	Overall score
61	Royal Holloway, London	74.3	71.1	35.5	134	68.4	82.5
62	City	82.7	82.6	30.2	130	57.7	82.3
63	Brunel	77.3	76.4	25.8	116	71.2	82.2
64	Leicester	68.3	73.0	25.0	129	77.7	81.8
65	Queen Mary, London	70.1	69.0	30.3	141	69.7	81.2
66	Wolverhampton	83.0	82.7	—	93	77.6	81.1
67	Hertfordshire	74.0	73.8	20.2	98	76.8	80.8
68	Oxford Brookes	85.0	69.7	13.9	135	62.3	80.5
69	Aston	70.3	71.5	21.7	124	72.9	80.3
70	Manchester Metropolitan	87.8	83.6	5.6	115	59.8	80.0
71	Plymouth	84.5	80.3	9.3	132	55.8	79.3
72	Brighton	82.4	77.7	6.4	111	63.1	78.7
73	Kingston	81.0	83.1	—	84	58.0	75.6

Employed in professional job	45%	Employed in non-professional job and Studying	1%
Employed in professional job and studying	4%	Employed in non-professional job	13%
Studying	26%	Unemployed	11%
Average starting professional salary	£25,000	Average starting non-professional salary	£17,472

Mechanical Engineering

Mechanical engineering is by far the biggest branch of engineering, attracting twice as many applicants as any of the other subjects, even after a 5% decline in 2018. Indeed, it is only just outside the top ten for all degree choices. The introduction of higher fees only increased the subject's popularity, as students looked for a sure route to well-paid employment. The numbers starting degrees in 2018 remained stable, having grown by more than 50% in a decade. It is not hard to see why. Mechanical engineering is among the top 15 subjects for early career prospects and in the top six for starting salaries in graduate-level employment. Almost two-thirds of graduates go straight into such jobs.

Cambridge is out on its own at the head of the mechanical engineering table this year, having shared top spot with Imperial College in the last edition of the *Guide*. Cambridge is ranked in the top three in the world for the subject by QS, with Imperial also in the top ten. Cambridge has the highest entry standards, the top research score and the best graduate prospects. But London South Bank, which has jumped 16 places and into the top 20, has easily the highest rates of student satisfaction and is the only university to score more than 90% in either of our measures drawn from the National Student Survey. Satisfaction with the quality of teaching is relatively low nationally, compared with other subjects, however.

More than 130 universities and colleges are offering mechanical engineering in 2020. Most of the leading universities demand maths – preferably with a strong component of mechanics – and another science subject (usually physics) at A-level or its equivalent. With more than six applications to the place, entry standards are high at the leading universities, three of which averaged more than 200 points in 2018. Only one institution, compared with three last year, averaged less than 100 points.

Mechanical Engineering	Teaching quality %	Student experience %	Research quality %	Entry standards (UCAS points)	Graduate prospects %	Overall score
1 Cambridge	80.1*	86.1*	67.0	239	93.5	100.0
2 Imperial College London	82.0	85.3	59.6	220	91.1	97.4
3 Bristol	74.8	79.8	52.3	194	89.3	92.1
4 Southampton	80.1	80.2	52.3	174	89.6	91.9
5 Leeds	81.9	83.1	40.9	194	86.1	91.7
6 Strathclyde	76.9	82.2	37.2	223	83.5	91.5
7 Heriot-Watt	83.2	82.5	47.8	170	86.3	91.2
8 Loughborough	83.3	85.9	41.8	169	87.8	91.1
9 Bath	77.8	80.0	37.4	198	89.0	90.9
10 Sheffield	80.3	85.3	36.0	174	89.9	90.4
11 Nottingham	78.5	81.7	40.8	168	86.5	89.1
=12 Glasgow	69.0	75.3	47.2	196	85.5	88.9
=12 Swansea	78.6	81.4	45.5	146	90.1	88.9
14 Lancaster	76.5	78.9	41.6	159	87.9	88.2
15 Birmingham	75.8	74.5	37.7	161	90.5	87.7
16 University College London	64.6	70.0	44.6	192	88.0	87.4
17 London South Bank	94.2	93.3	19.6	122	83.7	87.0
18 Edinburgh	61.8	70.3	50.3	193	84.4	86.8
19 Surrey	75.4	77.0	30.8	148	86.6	85.2
=20 Greenwich	83.3	83.1	29.5	129	82.5	85.1
=20 Liverpool	74.3	79.0	32.1	144	86.5	85.1
22 Cardiff	69.1	73.4	30.2	166	87.9	85.0
23 Exeter	65.8	68.7	36.4	167	88.3	84.7
24 Dundee	75.3	79.6	34.1	160	77.1	84.5
=25 Coventry	79.5	81.9	10.3	135	91.5	84.2
=25 Queen's, Belfast	70.6	73.0	36.7	146	85.8	84.2
27 Teesside	87.5	84.6	5.8	123	87.1	83.6
28 Newcastle	67.6	73.0	30.2	148	87.7	83.3
29 Bradford	82.7	84.6	7.7	128	86.4	83.1
30 Ulster	75.5	76.5	22.8	133	86.0	82.9
31 Plymouth	78.9	78.3	15.7	139	83.6	82.7
32 Aberdeen	75.8	78.4	28.4	164	71.3	82.6
33 Manchester	67.2	74.6	35.1	165	75.5	82.4
34 West of Scotland	83.1	84.1	9.0	135	79.2	82.1
35 Harper Adams	84.5	84.5	—	133	82.8	81.9
36 Aston	77.9	74.6	20.6	135	80.0	81.6
37 Sunderland	83.7	83.5	8.8	120	80.8	81.4
38 Central Lancashire	74.4	74.7	7.1	151	84.4	81.3
39 Huddersfield	71.3	71.2	10.2	130	92.2	81.0

Mechanical Engineering cont

		Teaching quality %	Student experience %	Research quality %	Entry standards (UCAS points)	Graduate prospects %	Overall score
40	West of England	78.9	78.9	10.6	130	80.7	80.8
=41	Queen Mary, London	60.4	67.7	46.7	143	75.7	80.3
=41	Portsmouth	78.6	79.1	9.1	107	86.4	80.3
=43	Northumbria	67.7	73.0	30.7	143	75.5	80.2
=43	Sussex	70.5	74.9	24.0	135	78.3	80.2
45	Oxford Brookes	72.9	71.7	13.9	138	82.3	80.1
46	Chester	80.6	86.8	7.1	108	—	80.0
47	Wales Trinity St David	88.5	84.4	1.0	117	75.0	79.9
48	Liverpool John Moores	75.6	77.0	4.7	139	80.3	79.7
49	Lincoln	78.1	79.5	—	123	84.0	79.6
50	De Montfort	74.6	80.1	12.5	107	82.9	79.2
51	Salford	76.9	83.0	4.4	137	73.0	78.8
52	Robert Gordon	69.4	72.0	8.8	157	75.8	78.6
53	Derby	73.2	73.2	6.7	120	84.1	78.5
54	Sheffield Hallam	72.4	74.4	17.8	116	76.9	78.0
55	Hertfordshire	67.4	71.5	16.5	115	79.3	77.0
=56	Hull	65.4	65.1	16.5	122	81.3	76.8
=56	Manchester Metropolitan	68.7	72.7	16.3	124	73.8	76.8
=58	Solent	84.9	80.8	—	115	66.7	76.5
=58	South Wales	72.8	75.2	—	85	88.9	76.5
60	Brighton	80.0	78.2	7.4	115	63.1	75.3
61	Staffordshire	74.1	74.4	5.7	111	70.3	74.9
=62	Brunel	55.2	60.9	23.7	132	75.3	74.5
=62	Glasgow Caledonian	75.7	72.8	4.7	158	54.5	74.5
64	Bolton	81.9	79.3	—	106	58.8	73.3
65	Birmingham City	71.2	72.2	—	107	70.1	73.0
66	Anglia Ruskin	63.7	62.1	9.1	109	73.0	72.2
67	Kingston	69.0	73.8	2.9	119	57.3	70.9
68	City	66.2	67.9	23.1	120	48.3	70.3

Employed in professional job	62%	Employed in non-professional job and Studying	1%
Employed in professional job and studying	2%	Employed in non-professional job	10%
Studying	15%	Unemployed	10%
Average starting professional salary	£27,000	Average starting non-professional salary	£17,500

Medicine

Applications for medicine shot up almost 10% in 2018 as 500 more places became available, and they rose even more as new medical schools opened for the current academic year at Edge Hill, Lincoln and Sunderland. With another 250 places coming on stream in 2020 as another school opens in Kent and those at Edge Hill and Sunderland expand their intakes, the trend is likely to continue. There were still almost nine applications to the place in 2018 and the highest entry standards of any subject. Eleven of the 34 schools in our table average 200 points or more at entry and only one less than 180. In spite of this – and the fact that you can only apply to four medical schools – medicine is in the top seven subjects for the volume of applications.

The subject carries unique prestige and shares top place in the employment table. Graduate prospects for individual schools are not used in the ranking (although they are still shown for guidance) to avoid small differences distorting positions in a subject where virtually all graduates become junior doctors or researchers. Thirteen schools reported full employment in 2017, and none dropped below 97%. The average starting salary of £31,000 for junior doctors was matched only by dentists.

There are significant changes in the top five, which now contains three Scottish universities, but not at the very top. Oxford has held that position for the last nine years with strong scores across the board. Edinburgh is now its nearest challenger, after jumping 13 places thanks to big increases in student satisfaction. An even bigger change in the opposite direction has taken Swansea down 23 places from third last year.

Dundee, in fourth place, has the highest entry standards, while Brighton and Sussex Medical School, in 18th, has the most satisfied students. It is the only school to reach 90% in the sections of the National Student Survey focused on the quality of teaching. There was little to choose between the top scorers in the Research Excellence Framework, but Lancaster produced the best results.

Nearly all schools demand chemistry and most biology. Physics or maths is required by some, either as an alternative or addition to biology. Universities will want to see evidence of commitment to the subject through work experience or voluntary work. Almost all schools interview candidates, and several use one of the two specialist aptitude tests (see chapter 2). Undergraduates have to be prepared to work long hours, particularly towards the end of the course, which will usually be five years long. Many students are now opting for the postgraduate route into the medical profession instead, although this is even longer.

Medicine	Teaching quality %	Student experience %	Research quality %	Entry standards (UCAS points)	Graduate prospects %	Overall score
1 Oxford	89.5*	88.1*	48.9	221	97.0	100.0
2 Edinburgh	78.8	79.7	49.8	231	98.7	97.5
3 Cambridge	76.4	72.1	52.0	232	98.8	96.6
4 Dundee	87.7	88.8	25.1	239	100.0	95.7
5 Glasgow	79.3	81.7	42.3	230	99.8	95.5
6 Keele	89.1	88.3	50.0	188	99.6	94.1
7 Imperial College London	77.6	83.1	54.6	201	99.3	93.4
8 Queen Mary, London	86.1	86.8	40.2	199	99.3	92.0
9 Aberdeen	85.8	86.4	20.2	232	99.4	91.9
10 Newcastle	85.8	81.5	44.8	193	99.8	91.4
=11 Bristol	82.0	77.6	47.5	196	100.0	91.0
=11 Exeter	79.4	78.9	41.6	209	99.6	91.0
13 Leeds	89.6	88.4	32.1	192	100.0	89.6
14 University College London	70.0	74.6	53.3	201	99.5	89.4

Medicine cont

	Teaching quality %	Student experience %	Research quality %	Entry standards (UCAS points)	Graduate prospects %	Overall score
15 Queen's, Belfast	86.8	87.5	34.6	192	99.7	89.2
=16 Lancaster	81.3	75.7	55.2	176	100.0	89.1
=16 St Andrews	89.4	92.2	19.8	207	98.2	89.1
18 Brighton and Sussex Medical School	92.7	92.5	34.3	174	100.0	88.3
19 Sheffield	87.0	85.7	36.5	183	100.0	88.0
20 Cardiff	78.1	78.0	34.5	203	100.0	87.2
21 Birmingham	82.8	84.5	31.5	191	99.8	86.4
22 East Anglia	82.0	85.6	31.8	188	99.4	85.9
23 King's College London	73.8	70.6	48.3	185	99.3	85.6
24 Plymouth	87.2	87.8	23.1	189	100.0	85.3
25 Leicester	83.2	83.0	33.3	180	99.4	84.7
26 Swansea	72.9	63.7	44.7	—	100.0	84.5
27 Nottingham	72.8	71.0	36.8	189	100.0	82.5
28 St George's, London	79.1	77.8	22.4	189	99.8	81.1
29 Hull-York Medical School	73.6	69.0	36.2	181	100.0	80.8
30 Southampton	69.1	69.8	35.6	186	100.0	80.2
31 Manchester	69.5	64.8	34.6	184	99.7	79.0
32 Liverpool	69.7	68.9	31.7	183	99.8	78.5
33 Warwick	70.2	67.6	26.2	—	100.0	75.4
34 Central Lancashire	72.8	67.0	8.3	177	—	71.0

Employed in professional job	95%	Employed in non-professional job and Studying	0%
Employed in professional job and studying	1%	Employed in non-professional job	0%
Studying	3%	Unemployed	1%
Average starting professional salary	£31,000	Average starting non-professional salary	n/a

Middle Eastern and African Studies

Middle Eastern and African Studies shared in an increase in the numbers starting degrees in non-European languages in 2019, but this remains one of the smallest categories in the *Guide*. Only 115 students started courses in Middle Eastern and African Studies combined in 2018 although larger numbers will have included modules from this group in a broader area studies degree. The subjects enjoy some official protection because they are classed as "vulnerable" and of national importance. There were only 45 applications for African Studies in 2018, a third of the totals in the years before the introduction of £9,000 fees.

St Andrews holds onto top place after sharing it with Cambridge last year. Students at St Andrews are the most satisfied with the quality of teaching, while Cambridge has the highest entry standards. Scores are close throughout much of the table, with the leaders on individual measures spread about. Westminster, in last place overall, does best in the sections of the National Student Survey dealing with the broad student experience, while Birmingham, only two places higher, produced the best performance in the 2014 Research Excellence Framework.

The small numbers can make for big swings in the national statistics. A £2,160 rise in the average starting salary in professional jobs took Middle Eastern and African Studies into the top 20 in the earnings table, but the subjects are in the bottom half for graduate prospects, with an unemployment rate that reached 14% at the end of 2017, one of the highest figures for any subject. Oxford graduates had the best immediate prospects. Applicants for courses in Arabic or African languages are not expected to have previous knowledge of the language, although they would normally be expected to demonstrate an aptitude for learning other languages.

Middle Eastern and African studies	Teaching quality %	Student experience %	Research quality %	Entry standards (UCAS points)	Graduate prospects %	Overall score
1 St Andrews	84.4	81.8	46.7	197	—	100.0
2 Cambridge	—	—	45.0	220	88.9	99.4
3 Durham	81.8	73.1	34.6	194	88.5	95.5
4 Edinburgh	78.2	73.5	30.1	176	89.2	92.3
5 Oxford	—	—	36.2	198	89.6	91.1
6 Manchester	77.3	63.0	48.9	147	75.0	89.6
7 Leeds	83.2	86.2	30.6	155	69.2	88.1
8 SOAS, London	82.0	75.2	26.3	151	76.0	87.1
9 Birmingham	73.5	67.8	50.9	137*	57.1	84.5
10 Exeter	59.7	59.1	36.0	167	76.7	84.3
11 Westminster	81.4	86.6	11.3	106*	66.7	78.3

Employed in professional job	43%	Employed in non-professional job and Studying	2%
Employed in professional job and studying	3%	Employed in non-professional job	14%
Studying	24%	Unemployed	14%
Average starting professional salary	£24,000	Average starting non-professional salary	£15,000

Music

It's all change in the music table, with only two of the top 60 universities occupying the same position as last year. Manchester has taken over the lead from Durham, although – like Oxford and Cambridge – its student satisfaction rates date from 2016 because students have boycotted the National Student Survey since then. Neither of the top two leads on any individual measure.

Both applications and enrolments rose in 2018 after a big decline in the previous year. The numbers starting courses are running at almost twice the level of a decade ago. The expansion of provision has meant that there are now fewer than four applications per place. Entry grades are relatively low at most universities –22 of the 79 universities in this year's table average less than 120 UCAS points – although music grades and the quality of auditions carry more weight in selecting students. Nine out of ten degree applicants come with A-levels, and most university departments expect music to be among them, although they may accept a distinction or merit in Grade 8 music exams.

The character of courses varies considerably, from the practical and vocational programmes in conservatoires to the more theoretical degrees in some of the older universities, and everything from creative sound design and new media to sonic arts elsewhere. No fewer than 171 universities, colleges and other providers are offering undergraduate courses in 2020.

Cambridge has the highest entry grades, but London South Bank, in 34th place, has the best scores in the sections of the National Student Survey dealing with the quality of teaching, and Lincoln, seven places higher, does best in the other sections. The Royal Academy of Music has the top employment score, with an impressive 93.4% of graduates going straight into professional work or postgraduate study in 2018. The four leading specialist institutions are all in the top six on this measure.

Music invariably finishes ahead of the other performing arts in the employment table, although it is still only just outside the bottom 20 overall. The 7% unemployment rate is one of the best in the table, but 28% of leavers were in non-graduate occupations six months after graduation. Music has slipped back into second to last place in the earnings table, however.

Music

		Teaching quality %	Student experience %	Research quality %	Entry standards (UCAS points)	Graduate prospects %	Overall score
1	Manchester	—	—	56.3	208	80.7	100.0
2	Durham	83.6	74.3	64.9	200	90.8	98.8
3	Southampton	86.3	78.1	70.7	175	85.5	97.2
4	Oxford	—	—	66.3	197	73.4	95.4
5	Birmingham	79.6	79.7	50.7	194	86.3	94.9
6	Bristol	92.5	87.9	48.0	190	70.6	94.7
7	Cardiff	92.9	92.0	47.0	164	74.1	93.4
8	Royal Holloway, London	83.9	79.7	55.0	190	72.8	93.3
9	Leeds	79.9	75.4	44.2	192	82.6	92.7
10	Cambridge	—	—	48.0	214	89.0	92.4
11	Sheffield	83.8	80.9	60.0	157	72.3	91.0
12	Glasgow	72.7	70.2	46.0	206	77.6	90.9
=13	Aberdeen	83.8	79.5	32.0	183	72.7	89.3
=13	Nottingham	79.3	73.4	55.4	162	73.5	89.3
15	York	81.3	82.0	37.1	174	74.3	89.2
16	Surrey	87.5	84.4	27.2	169	74.9	89.1
17	Goldsmiths, London	82.6	77.1	51.1	148	67.7	87.3
18	Edinburgh	64.1	66.1	48.0	206	69.5	87.1
19	Bangor	89.4	88.3	24.7	146	71.7	86.8
20	King's College London	74.9	69.5	43.5	169	72.9	86.6
21	Edinburgh Napier	86.1	84.6	—	176	75.4	85.7
22	Huddersfield	86.7	81.9	28.0	134	73.6	85.4
23	Royal Northern College of Music	80.6	80.3	12.3	138	88.9	85.1
24	Royal Academy of Music	74.8	74.8	23.9	128	93.4	84.8
25	Newcastle	70.7	66.5	40.8	155	75.9	84.3
26	De Montfort	86.7	85.6	14.5	118	80.0	83.6
27	Lincoln	90.8	92.3	6.5	123	—	83.5
=28	Brunel	84.9	71.2	32.6	136*	67.7	83.4
=28	Sussex	78.5	71.2	30.2	140	75.0	83.4

30 Ulster	87.2	83.6	40.0	144	50.3	83.3
31 Birmingham City	87.5	79.3	11.6	128	76.4	82.9
=32 Coventry	83.9	80.9	18.1	121	77.8	82.8
=32 Kent	73.7	70.6	44.3	129*	72.7	82.8
34 London South Bank	96.4	89.9	12.8	88	76.9	82.7
35 Oxford Brookes	77.3	78.3	30.2	130	72.9	82.6
36 Royal College of Music	74.2	74.8	10.9	125	92.6	82.4
37 Liverpool	83.3	78.6	31.4	150	53.4	81.9
38 Chester	82.1	79.1	4.3	129	81.4	81.8
=39 Hull	87.3	86.2	11.2	131	64.9	81.3
=39 Royal Conservatoire of Scotland	66.6	66.7	11.3	153	87.1	81.3
41 SOAS, London	76.4	61.8	60.0	122	58.3	81.2
=42 Manchester Metropolitan	92.8	85.4	7.5	123*	64.2	81.1
=42 Staffordshire	81.3	74.7	—	124	86.4	81.1
=44 Greenwich	81.4	68.6	—	155	75.0	81.0
=44 Plymouth	84.7	85.6	20.2	124	63.0	81.0
46 Queen's, Belfast	68.2	70.6	38.3	158	60.6	80.8
=47 Bath Spa	83.9	80.4	10.7	125	71.0	80.7
=47 Salford	87.9	84.1	7.2	142	59.7	80.7
=49 West London	81.6	80.9	2.3	141	70.6	80.3
=49 Winchester	84.6	82.5	11.2	132	64.3	80.3
51 Keele	72.1	73.2	41.7	126	62.6	79.9
52 City	76.0	67.5	34.0	138	60.0	79.7
53 Liverpool Hope	71.8	62.2	15.5	117	86.7	79.2
54 Falmouth	80.0	74.5	6.2	109	79.2	78.7
55 Middlesex	84.5	79.3	16.1	112	60.1	78.0
56 Anglia Ruskin	86.8	83.0	16.9	117	51.6	77.6
57 Hertfordshire	77.9	73.8	5.3	119	70.9	77.2
58 Brighton	91.9	86.7	13.1	110	46.0	76.9
59 Arts London	80.8	77.9	—	102*	73.7	76.6
60 West of Scotland	68.2	60.9	11.3	152	64.8	76.3
61 Wolverhampton	90.2	84.6	—	112	53.8	76.2
62 Derby	86.3	78.8	6.7	122	50.7	75.9
63 Bournemouth	75.6	71.5	15.0	—	58.8	75.5
64 Solent	86.8	83.1	—	118	51.6	75.3
65 South Wales	76.4	74.6	6.4	116	63.0	75.2
66 York St John	78.2	68.3	10.5	116	60.3	74.9
67 Gloucestershire	80.7	81.1	—	114	57.9	74.7
68 East London	85.0	81.3	11.2	113	45.8	74.6
=69 Edge Hill	71.8	65.4	3.8	139	—	74.5
=69 Leeds Beckett	87.2	80.7	1.7	115	48.4	74.5
=69 Sunderland	74.3	62.5	4.2	128*	64.0	74.5
72 Chichester	76.4	73.7	9.7	130	50.1	74.1
73 Central Lancashire	70.0	54.2	3.9	117	69.3	72.7
74 Kingston	77.9	72.9	—	114	52.4	72.0
75 Plymouth Marjon	82.4	70.9	—	115	46.7	71.7

Music cont

	Teaching quality %	Student experience %	Research quality %	Entry standards (UCAS points)	Graduate prospects %	Overall score
76 Westminster	61.7	58.5	22.5	119	56.3	71.3
77 Canterbury Christ Church	71.5	53.6	15.2	112	47.1	69.4
78 Northampton	73.4	69.9	—	97	51.7	68.9
79 Cumbria	52.6	48.6	—	137	39.1	63.0

Employed in professional job	41%	Employed in non-professional job and Studying	3%
Employed in professional job and studying	5%	Employed in non-professional job	25%
Studying	19%	Unemployed	7%
Average starting professional salary	£18,500	Average starting non-professional salary	£16,380

Nursing

Applications for nursing degrees have dropped by 30% in the two years after bursaries were replaced by loans in England. The total in 2018 was 25,000 lower than at any time in the previous six years. But, since nursing is by far the most popular subject in the UCAS system, there were plenty of applicants to go round, and the numbers starting courses dropped by only a few hundred and appear to have recovered in 2019. The latest enrolment is close to the record set in 2016 and the chances of winning a place were the highest in recent years.

Entry requirements were already comparatively low, considering the demand for places. Almost two-thirds of nursing students arrive without A-levels, many of them upgrading other health-related qualifications. Although only six universities averaged less than 120 points on the UCAS tariff in 2018, just four others topped 160 points. The highest aggregate was Glasgow's 201 points and Edinburgh's 189. The two Scottish rivals have swapped places at the top of the table again this year, with Edinburgh taking over the leadership.

Another Scottish university – Queen Margaret Edinburgh, in 7th position – has the most satisfied students, topping 97% in both of our measures drawn from the National Student Survey. There are high rates of satisfaction throughout the table, especially for teaching quality. The same applied to graduate prospects. Ten universities, including Suffolk, only five places off the bottom, saw all their 2018 graduates go straight into professional jobs or further study. Only four of the 72 universities in the table scored less than 95% on this measure. Nursing is in the top three subjects for graduate destinations, but only 26th for salaries in professional jobs.

Southampton, in ninth place, produced much the best results in the Research Excellence Framework, when 94% of its work was rated as world-leading or internationally excellent. Most of the universities offering nursing are post-1992 universities, with Huddersfield the highest-placed, but older foundations fill the top 13 places in the table. There are big changes in the latest ranking. Cardiff is up 21 places to enter the top ten and Central Lancashire has jumped 35 places and into the top 30, for example, while Essex is down 43 places and now only one off the bottom.

Nursing

	Teaching quality %	Student experience %	Research quality %	Entry standards (UCAS points)	Graduate prospects %	Overall score
1 Edinburgh	95.1	89.1	53.4	189	100.0	100.0
2 Glasgow	90.9	91.2	42.3	201	96.2	98.2
3 Manchester	86.2	80.4	57.1	147	97.7	93.2
=4 Birmingham	87.3	86.2	37.0	150	99.3	92.6
=4 Surrey	83.2	83.3	37.5	160	98.3	92.6
6 Liverpool	89.0	88.3	35.3	143	100.0	92.4
7 Queen Margaret, Edinburgh	98.1	97.1	1.5	159	98.2	92.0
8 Cardiff	80.2	73.6	36.8	163	99.0	91.9
9 Southampton	68.9	67.7	65.7	151	99.2	91.6
10 Ulster	88.4	89.0	27.7	138	99.7	90.9
=11 Keele	89.4	87.9	20.9	139	100.0	90.6
=11 York	82.1	79.5	40.2	150	96.3	90.6
13 Leeds	77.9	72.8	31.7	153	99.8	90.3
14 Huddersfield	88.2	83.2	13.2	148	99.3	90.0
15 Manchester Metropolitan	89.2	87.3	12.0	143	99.6	89.9
16 West of Scotland	88.8	84.3	29.0	134	97.8	89.7
=17 Bangor	78.1	70.1	34.7	147	99.3	89.6
=17 South Wales	90.8	86.5	2.2	150	99.1	89.6
19 Portsmouth	86.3	83.6	24.3	133	100.0	89.5
=20 Coventry	89.9	86.8	4.5	144	99.4	89.3
=20 Queen's, Belfast	80.6	78.4	34.7	136	98.8	89.3
=22 Northumbria	83.3	76.7	14.0	149	99.6	89.0
=22 Swansea	82.9	83.2	14.5	148	98.3	89.0
24 Hull	85.9	78.4	16.7	146	97.8	88.9
25 Nottingham	74.4	64.6	31.4	152	99.2	88.8
26 East Anglia	73.3	72.2	24.9	154	99.0	88.6
=27 City	86.4	83.1	20.5	138	96.7	88.4
=27 King's College London	71.1	64.7	34.6	153	98.1	88.4
=29 Central Lancashire	81.5	76.4	8.3	156	97.7	88.2
=29 Dundee	90.2	87.4	22.1	118	98.8	88.2
31 Greenwich	84.2	83.1	2.2	150	98.5	88.1
32 Plymouth	80.5	74.9	9.5	152	98.3	87.9
33 Derby	87.4	81.3	7.3	132	100.0	87.7
34 Liverpool John Moores	83.3	80.8	6.0	148	97.4	87.6
=35 Bedfordshire	84.7	79.2	25.1	121	99.0	87.5
=35 Stirling	76.2	68.2	34.1	133	99.0	87.5
37 Worcester	88.1	85.3	2.6	132	98.6	87.1
=38 Chester	82.4	76.5	12.0	133	99.5	87.0
=38 Middlesex	84.0	80.9	10.0	131	99.1	87.0
=38 Staffordshire	88.4	83.9	—	132	99.4	87.0
41 Anglia Ruskin	86.7	83.8	3.1	133	98.6	86.9
=42 Glasgow Caledonian	79.0	73.9	8.1	143	98.9	86.8

Nursing cont

		Teaching quality %	Student experience %	Research quality %	Entry standards (UCAS points)	Graduate prospects %	Overall score
=42	Lincoln	72.2	75.6	22.6	134	100.0	86.8
44	West of England	82.2	80.3	8.2	136	98.1	86.7
=45	Birmingham City	82.0	75.1	1.5	144	98.4	86.6
=45	Leeds Beckett	92.6	89.8	3.5	112	100.0	86.6
47	Kingston/St George's, London	77.5	79.9	2.6	140	100.0	86.5
48	Wolverhampton	84.0	79.0	11.0	145	93.8	86.4
49	London South Bank	79.2	75.5	13.7	128	99.9	86.3
=50	Canterbury Christ Church	81.9	74.7	2.2	136	99.3	86.1
=50	Northampton	82.4	77.9	1.6	135	98.8	86.1
=52	De Montfort	84.8	81.6	13.0	128	95.9	86.0
=52	Teesside	85.3	80.6	2.4	133	97.6	86.0
54	Cumbria	81.8	75.5	0.7	138	98.6	85.9
55	Sheffield Hallam	80.2	76.8	3.7	136	98.5	85.8
56	Edge Hill	82.6	79.6	2.0	145	94.7	85.7
57	West London	87.0	84.9	2.5	130	95.2	85.4
58	Robert Gordon	81.1	73.5	4.9	122	99.4	84.8
=59	Abertay	69.3	65.6	—	146	100.0	84.6
=59	Brighton	79.3	74.8	4.8	125	98.7	84.6
61	Salford	71.9	68.5	3.8	141	98.6	84.5
62	Hertfordshire	81.1	78.1	4.0	116	99.1	84.3
63	Bradford	64.2	64.3	9.5	148	98.1	84.2
64	Sunderland	83.2	77.1	7.5	141	90.0	84.0
=65	Bournemouth	76.0	70.2	4.7	126	98.7	83.8
=65	Oxford Brookes	67.1	65.1	3.0	143	98.8	83.8
67	Brunel	69.8	73.6	18.2	—	96.3	83.7
68	Suffolk	77.4	73.1	—	111	100.0	82.7
69	Edinburgh Napier	72.7	70.8	5.3	122	96.2	82.1
70	Bucks New	79.3	79.4	1.0	115	91.3	80.7
71	Essex	67.2	57.4	—	117	99.4	80.5
72	Bolton	89.0	84.3	—	138	66.5	75.5

Employed in professional job	94%	Employed in non-professional job and Studying	0%
Employed in professional job and studying	1%	Employed in non-professional job	1%
Studying	1%	Unemployed	2%
Average starting professional salary	£22,000	Average starting non-professional salary	£18,000

Other Subjects Allied to Medicine

Strathclyde tops the table for the large group of subjects 'allied to medicine' for the fourth year in a row. They include the likes of audiology, complementary therapies, counselling, health services management, health sciences, nutrition, occupational therapy, optometry, ophthalmology, orthoptics, osteopathy, podiatry and speech therapy. Physiotherapy and radiography now have rankings of their own. Performance in the table is naturally influenced by which specialisms are offered. Strathclyde, which has degrees in prosthetics and orthotics, and speech and language pathology, has good scores across the board, without leading on any individual measure.

The withdrawal of NHS bursaries has hit applications in virtually all the subjects in this group. As in nursing, however, universities have upped the offer rate to the point where there were increases in enrolments of about 3% in 2018. A place just outside the top ten for graduate prospects will have helped, with two-thirds of graduates going straight into professional jobs in 2017 and only 6% unemployed. As a group, the subjects are level with nursing for median salaries in professional jobs, inside the top 30 in the earnings table.

Most of the institutions in the table are post-1992 universities, but only Kingston features in the top ten. It has shot up 30 places to third, with the top rating for the quality of teaching in the National Student Survey. Robert Gordon, which is only a fraction behind on this measure, does best in the rest of the survey and is up six places to 14th overall. Cambridge, not surprisingly, has much the highest entry grades, but did not enter the Research Excellence Framework in the relevant category and is only tenth in the table as a result. Fourth-placed Southampton was the star performer in the REF.

The scores for graduate prospects vary considerably, with Kingston, Leeds, Sunderland, Swansea and Wolverhampton – the latter only just in the top 60 overall – all reaching 100%. At two others, however, the success rate was below 60%.

Subjects Allied to Medicine

	Teaching quality %	Student experience %	Research quality %	Entry standards (UCAS points)	Graduate prospects %	Overall score
1 Strathclyde	86.9	86.9	52.2	183	92.9	100.0
2 University College London	87.4	87.0	48.4	176	93.5	99.1
3 Kingston	95.9	94.0	2.6	—	100.0	97.5
4 Southampton	77.1	77.2	65.7	159	97.8	97.4
5 Lancaster	87.3	87.5	55.2	160	87.5	97.1
6 Dundee	78.9	82.2	31.3	194	95.5	96.8
=7 Cambridge	—	—	—	240	84.0	96.4
=7 Manchester	78.8	77.9	57.1	162	95.0	96.4
9 Cardiff	85.5	84.3	36.8	160	97.5	96.2
10 Leeds	82.6	86.6	31.7	154	100.0	95.1
11 Newcastle	83.3	83.4	47.8	164	84.9	94.7
12 Swansea	81.2	78.6	44.7	136	100.0	93.9
13 Sunderland	92.0	75.0	7.5	—	100.0	93.7
14 Robert Gordon	95.8	96.0	4.9	161	87.5	93.5
15 Aston	80.7	81.6	39.1	140	98.7	93.4
16 Exeter	79.4	77.7	41.1	167	87.8	93.3
17 King's College London	83.1	80.6	34.6	157	—	93.1
18 City	88.8	88.6	20.5	144	94.2	93.0
=19 East Anglia	80.9	81.7	24.9	158	96.2	92.9
=19 Glasgow Caledonian	88.0	86.5	8.1	177	88.4	92.9
=21 Oxford Brookes	91.9	90.8	3.0	146	97.4	92.5

		Teaching quality %	Student experience %	Research quality %	Entry standards (UCAS points)	Graduate prospects %	Overall score
=21	Reading	83.5	74.6	42.3	157	85.7	92.5
23	Birmingham	83.4	82.6	31.5	151	87.9	91.9
=24	Plymouth	88.2	83.8	9.5	149	96.1	91.8
=24	Sheffield	79.2	81.8	38.3	152	87.5	91.8
26	Liverpool	80.9	81.8	35.3	134	94.9	91.6
27	Warwick	81.5	85.2	25.3	158	82.9	90.6
=28	Hull	85.8	78.4	16.7	—	88.9	89.8
=28	London South Bank	88.2	82.1	13.7	136	91.1	89.8
=30	Bedfordshire	84.7	79.2	25.1	120	96.2	89.7
=30	Huddersfield	90.2	86.2	13.2	129	90.2	89.7
32	London Metropolitan	84.2	84.9	5.2	—	90.0	89.3
33	Birmingham City	85.3	83.4	1.5	141	95.5	89.2
34	Surrey	70.6	76.2	37.5	157	83.5	88.9
=35	Portsmouth	91.5	86.9	24.3	128	78.3	88.8
=35	Queen Margaret, Edinburgh	85.4	78.4	6.7	163	83.1	88.8
37	Cumbria	85.9	83.0	0.7	138	94.0	88.6
=38	Northampton	88.9	81.9	1.6	136	90.6	88.2
=38	South Wales	83.1	80.4	2.2	141	94.0	88.2
40	Sheffield Hallam	89.6	86.2	3.7	135	82.8	87.3
41	West of England	82.7	83.6	8.2	137	85.4	87.0
=42	Lincoln	83.4	84.4	22.6	129	78.8	86.8
=42	Ulster	78.9	80.1	27.7	137	79.2	86.8
44	Teesside	87.6	83.1	2.4	128	87.5	86.7
45	Northumbria	72.0	75.4	14.0	148	90.0	86.6
=46	Bradford	77.0	76.2	9.5	139	89.6	86.2
=46	Greenwich	79.2	81.9	2.2	148	84.7	86.2
48	West of Scotland	75.4	72.3	29.0	127	85.7	85.9
49	De Montfort	83.9	84.5	13.0	112	87.1	85.8
50	Queen Mary, London	69.6	75.6	48.3	128	—	85.5
51	York St John	83.4	80.7	1.9	134	84.1	85.4
52	Anglia Ruskin	86.5	87.2	3.1	112	86.6	85.3
53	Manchester Metropolitan	84.8	78.1	12.0	135	76.9	85.1
54	Salford	84.5	85.0	3.8	138	76.0	84.9
55	Cardiff Metropolitan	87.9	86.3	3.6	124	77.8	84.7
=56	Coventry	81.6	81.7	4.5	127	83.4	84.6
=56	Derby	79.3	76.3	7.3	135	83.6	84.6
58	Canterbury Christ Church	77.0	66.9	2.2	136	90.4	84.0
59	Wolverhampton	60.6	59.6	11.0	145	100.0	83.9
60	Hertfordshire	80.1	79.6	4.0	121	85.4	83.8
61	Worcester	84.6	79.7	2.6	125	78.3	83.5
62	Bournemouth	75.0	70.2	4.7	130	88.1	83.2
=63	Bucks New	79.3	79.4	1.0	128	—	83.1

Subjects Allied to Medicine cont

=63 Central Lancashire	77.8	72.2	8.3	138	77.8	83.1
=63 Nottingham	80.2	72.9	31.4	142	60.0	83.1
66 Brunel	60.5	67.0	18.2	128	94.4	82.8
67 Staffordshire	95.2	87.5	—	94	75.0	82.5
68 Liverpool John Moores	70.1	71.6	6.0	145	80.5	82.3
69 St Mary's, Twickenham	75.1	70.8	4.8	123	86.0	82.2
70 Brighton	80.7	81.2	4.8	117	75.5	81.7
71 Glyndŵr	70.2	70.2	3.6	133	83.8	81.4
72 Bangor	78.8	70.6	34.7	112	64.6	81.1
73 Middlesex	71.2	72.2	10.0	123	79.7	80.8
74 Leeds Beckett	76.7	80.0	3.5	116	76.7	80.7
75 Plymouth Marjon	85.6	82.2	—	110	69.2	80.1
76 Newman	80.3	85.9	—	128	58.9	79.0
77 Essex	76.7	80.8	—	104	73.6	78.5
78 Westminster	74.6	70.2	21.2	116*	57.1	77.2
79 Chester	69.9	68.9	12.0	108	70.7	77.0
80 East London	72.9	74.2	7.6	108	62.3	75.8

Employed in professional job	62%	Employed in non-professional job and Studying	2%
Employed in professional job and studying	3%	Employed in non-professional job	10%
Studying	16%	Unemployed	6%
Average starting professional salary	£22,000	Average starting non-professional salary	£16,000

Pharmacology and Pharmacy

Pharmacology and pharmacy are quite different courses, leading to different careers.
Departments in England are evenly split between those specialising in the two disciplines,
with only four covering both. While the MPharm degree, which is the only direct route to
professional registration as a pharmacist, takes four years, pharmacology is available either as
a three-year BSc or as an extended course. The MPharm is now offered at 29 institutions, while
another nine are running a BSc in the subject or as part of a broader degree. Most degrees in
either area require chemistry and another science or maths at A-level or the equivalent.

Applications for the group as a whole, which includes toxicology degrees, were down for
the seventh year in a row in 2018, dropping over 25% in that time. However, as in other health
subjects, changes in the offer rate have ensured that the numbers starting courses have not
fluctuated to the same extent. The numbers starting courses in 2018 were higher than when
the decline in applications set in, but there were little more than five applications per place,
compared with seven in 2011. Entry standards have fallen accordingly, with nine universities in
the latest table averaging less than 120 points, two of them less than 90.

Cambridge remains top of the table, the university's normal high entry standards making
the difference. Only Strathclyde, in 10th place, comes within 45 points of Cambridge's average.
Dundee and UCL have both shot up 15 places into the top five, but neither can prevent Queens
Belfast, the star of the 2014 Research Excellence Framework taking second place. Anglia
Ruskin, just in the top 40 overall, has the best scores for teaching quality in the National Student
Survey, while Keele has the highest for wider student satisfaction.

The employment table does not suggest subjects that should be struggling to attract applicants – pharmacology and pharmacy remain seventh out of 67 subject groups, with 82% of graduates going straight into professional jobs and only 3% unemployed. At four universities – Ulster, Lincoln, Kent and Reading – the rate was 100%. The earnings table is a different matter, however: partly because of the training structure for pharmacists, the subjects are seldom in the top 40. In the latest edition, they remain in the bottom ten.

Pharmacology and Pharmacy	Teaching quality %	Student experience %	Research quality %	Entry standards (UCAS points)	Graduate prospects %	Overall score
1 Cambridge	—	—	52.5	240	84.0	100.0
2 Queen's, Belfast	86.1	87.6	60.0	160	97.6	98.8
=3 Bristol	91.6	88.8	47.0	163	90.2	97.7
=3 Dundee	86.0	89.1	55.4	173	88.9	97.7
5 University College London	84.4	85.3	51.3	175	93.6	97.4
6 Nottingham	84.0	84.8	51.2	161	98.7	97.3
7 Bath	82.9	85.4	56.2	157	96.5	97.0
8 Manchester	82.7	85.2	57.1	157	95.1	96.7
9 Cardiff	83.1	85.3	36.8	178	97.7	96.5
10 Strathclyde	68.8	77.9	52.2	226	94.6	96.3
11 Ulster	85.4	84.4	42.5	149	100.0	96.2
12 Aberdeen	90.7	88.7	34.7	180	81.0	95.5
13 Kent	—	—	42.3	137	100.0	94.9
14 East Anglia	81.5	85.3	38.1	144	99.2	94.4
15 Keele	88.4	90.9	20.9	143	95.4	94.2
=16 Glasgow	76.5	79.2	33.4	194	92.9	93.9
=16 Robert Gordon	83.2	82.8	4.9	188	99.4	93.9
18 Leeds	79.6	84.6	40.9	167	88.5	93.6
19 Aston	81.7	83.5	39.1	131	98.0	93.3
20 Queen Mary, London	84.1	88.1	40.2	126	—	93.0
21 Birmingham	83.0	80.7	19.2	155	99.4	92.9
22 Reading	83.9	78.1	34.2	125	100.0	92.5
23 King's College London	76.8	78.6	46.8	149	92.1	92.3
24 Newcastle	83.8	78.4	47.8	160	75.0	91.4
25 Portsmouth	86.3	85.4	24.3	108	95.6	91.2
26 Liverpool John Moores	81.0	84.6	6.0	145	99.6	91.0
27 Glasgow Caledonian	89.8	90.2	8.1	174	72.2	90.7
28 Nottingham Trent	86.4	85.0	24.1	115	—	90.4
29 Central Lancashire	77.1	80.1	8.3	146	98.7	89.6
30 Wolverhampton	81.6	78.3	11.0	139	94.1	89.4
31 Kingston	89.2	89.8	2.6	120	83.5	88.7
32 Liverpool	74.5	81.7	31.7	151	80.3	88.6
=33 De Montfort	79.1	78.6	13.0	115	97.9	88.3
=33 Lincoln	75.9	76.6	22.6	110	100.0	88.3
35 Hull	85.8	78.4	16.7	—	81.1	88.1

36	Bradford		77.0	77.4	9.5	127	97.2	87.9
37	Huddersfield		75.2	70.6	13.2	134	99.2	87.7
38	Hertfordshire		78.8	80.3	10.9	119	92.2	87.4
39	Coventry		81.2	82.6	4.5	120	88.5	87.0
40	Anglia Ruskin		91.9	82.5	3.1	83	—	86.6
41	Brighton		74.0	74.3	4.8	123	99.2	86.4
=42	Queen Margaret, Edinburgh		89.8	81.2	1.5	127	75.0	86.3
=42	Sunderland		75.3	74.9	7.5	123	95.2	86.3
44	Greenwich		72.1	83.2	2.7	130	92.6	86.2
45	Westminster		84.7	81.1	21.2	113	73.1	85.9
46	Sussex		68.9	71.9	8.0	154	—	83.6
=47	East London		83.1	88.1	7.6	89	59.8	81.1
=47	London Metropolitan		78.0	81.1	5.2	118	62.9	81.1

Employed in professional job	72%	Employed in non-professional job and Studying	1%
Employed in professional job and studying	10%	Employed in non-professional job	4%
Studying	10%	Unemployed	3%
Average starting professional salary	£19,000	Average starting non-professional salary	£16,640

Philosophy

Philosophy's long run of increased popularity with prospective students, dating back five years, came to an end in 2018 when both applications and enrolments fell. Both figures remained higher than in the years before £9,000 fees were introduced, but the numbers starting courses dropped by over 8%. Winchester has dropped out of the table, although almost 80 universities and colleges are offering the subject in 2020.

Oxford remains on top for philosophy, with the highest entry standards and the best grades in the Research Excellence Framework. Bangor, just inside the top 30, again has the highest levels of student satisfaction, topping 97% in the sections of the National Student Survey directly concerned with teaching quality. The best graduate prospects in 2017 were at the London School of Economics, which was the only institution to see 90% of philosophers go straight into professional jobs or postgraduate courses. The proportion was below 50% at four of the 50 universities in the table.

The subject is in the bottom 20 nationally for the proportion of graduates going straight into professional jobs or continuing to study. A third take the postgraduate route, but the 13% unemployment rate is among the highest among the 67 subject groups. Those in professional employment are paid relatively well, however. Although no longer in the top 20, median salaries of £22,000 are firmly in the top half of the table.

Relatively few philosophy undergraduates studied the subject at A-level – some departments actively discourage it. Degrees can require more mathematical skills than many candidates expect, especially when there is an emphasis on logic in the syllabus. There is wide variation in entry standards, with Oxford, Cambridge and St Andrews averaging more than 200 points, but three universities dropping below 100 and another eight averaging less than 110 points.

Philosophy

		Teaching quality %	Student experience %	Research quality %	Entry standards (UCAS points)	Graduate prospects %	Overall score
1	Oxford	—	—	61.3	219	84.4	100.0
2	Cambridge	—	—	51.6	210	83.3	99.1
3	St Andrews	85.5	86.6	52.7	201	68.5	97.8
=4	Birmingham	83.0	72.6	52.8	160	85.7	95.9
=4	University College London	76.2	73.2	55.6	189	81.4	95.9
6	Exeter	78.0	76.4	41.0	179	84.4	94.3
7	Newcastle	78.3	71.3	54.3	155	84.8	94.2
8	London School of Economics	70.6	69.4	48.6	178	90.5	93.8
9	Warwick	80.7	76.9	47.7	175	73.2	93.6
10	Sheffield	81.2	81.2	48.3	154	72.8	92.9
=11	Durham	79.4	72.4	30.1	191	80.6	92.7
=11	Lancaster	78.0	75.4	53.0	150	78.2	92.7
13	Southampton	86.8	83.8	31.7	144	75.1	91.7
14	Royal Holloway, London	82.2	82.7	30.5	138	84.7	91.6
15	Aberdeen	85.7	82.6	39.1	156*	62.4	90.9
16	King's College London	78.1	73.0	53.9	173	57.6	90.4
=17	Edinburgh	74.3	70.3	49.7	168	68.9	90.2
=17	York	81.4	76.2	30.7	148	78.5	90.2
19	Bristol	75.3	69.3	40.9	177	71.1	90.1
20	Sussex	76.8	74.0	34.2	146	82.9	90.0
=21	Leeds	78.8	76.5	39.5	159	66.3	89.4
=21	Liverpool	83.2	77.4	28.4	134	78.2	89.4
23	Nottingham	83.0	77.1	28.2	145	73.0	89.0
24	Manchester	75.6	71.7	31.9	165	74.3	88.7
25	Liverpool Hope	94.2	91.8	—	109	77.3	87.6
26	Hertfordshire	81.6	76.0	32.9	110	76.4	87.4
27	Kent	80.4	75.7	31.0	122	72.7	86.9
28	Bangor	97.5	96.2	—	128	59.2	86.8
29	Keele	86.5	83.1	23.7	117	65.0	86.4
30	Queen's, Belfast	77.5	77.0	40.3	149	53.1	86.0
31	Essex	78.9	76.4	44.0	101	65.3	85.7
32	Central Lancashire	96.6	90.4	8.3	101*	60.9	85.6
33	Bath Spa	88.5	80.0	—	112	80.0	85.4
34	Dundee	81.4	81.1	27.7	166	41.5	84.5
35	Stirling	76.7	70.6	22.7	147	64.7	84.3
36	Brighton	90.9	85.0	13.1	103	59.7	84.0
37	East Anglia	79.1	75.0	28.6	133	56.8	83.8
38	Oxford Brookes	91.1	86.4	8.4	107	58.9	83.7
39	Cardiff	69.3	65.3	36.3	143	64.5	83.6
=40	Glasgow	71.0	69.0	18.9	167	62.2	83.0
=40	Reading	80.0	76.2	28.6	118	55.8	83.0
42	Anglia Ruskin	89.5	79.9	—	84	72.7	82.2

=43	Manchester Metropolitan	82.8	77.4	12.5	121	58.1	82.0
=43	Nottingham Trent	89.0	78.1	10.0	116	53.1	82.0
45	Roehampton	83.3	76.3	—	92	77.6	81.7
46	St Mary's, Twickenham	84.3	80.5	7.0	94	64.0	81.1
47	Gloucestershire	82.4	81.4	6.9	107	58.3	80.5
48	West of England	86.7	87.9	18.6	107	36.9	80.1
49	Hull	83.4	78.9	10.5	112	48.8	79.6
50	Leeds Trinity	74.3	62.2	—	104	48.0	72.9

Employed in professional job	35%	Employed in non-professional job and Studying		4%
Employed in professional job and studying	3%	Employed in non-professional job		19%
Studying	26%	Unemployed		13%
Average starting professional salary	£22,000	Average starting non-professional salary		£17,000

Physics and Astronomy

Physics and astronomy attract some of the highest entry grades of any subject, with nine of the 46 institutions in our latest table averaging at least 200 points and another ten at least 170. Only two universities drop below 110 points, the equivalent of BBC at A-Level. Most demand physics and maths at A-level for both physics and astronomy, as well as good grades overall. There are almost six applications to the place.

The top four in the table are unchanged, with St Andrews heading Cambridge for the second year in succession. Cambridge, which is in the top four universities in the world for physics, according to QS, produced the best grades in the Research Excellence Framework. Cambridge also has the highest entry standards, its 2018 entrants averaging 240 points. But St Andrews' traditional strength in the National Student Survey (NSS) helps to keep it on top; it is one of four universities with rates of more than 90% in both of our satisfaction measures. The other three are all in the bottom 15 of the table, with the West of Scotland recording highest scores of all.

The subjects enjoyed eight successive increases in the numbers starting physics degrees, spanning the introduction of £9,000 fees, and applications have resumed their upward trend. Enrolments were steady in 2018, when exactly the same number (280) started degrees in astronomy or astrophysics, and remained similar in the last admissions cycle. The "Brian Cox effect" has been credited with the recent popularity of both physics and astronomy, in recognition of the engaging Manchester University professor's many television appearances.

More than 40% of those completing degrees in physics or astronomy stay on for a postgraduate course, helping the subjects to a place in the top 20 for graduate prospects. They are higher still in the earnings table, average salaries of £26,000 six months after graduation taking physics and astronomy into the top ten. Three universities saw 90% of graduates go straight into professional jobs or continue studying in 2017. Eighth-placed Birmingham again had the top rate, and only at Dundee did the proportion of positive destinations drop below 60%.

Physics and Astronomy	Teaching quality %	Student experience %	Research quality %	Entry standards (UCAS points)	Graduate prospects %	Overall score
1 St Andrews	91.2	93.7	51.0	225	90.8	100.0
2 Cambridge	—	—	55.7	240	84.0	97.7
3 Oxford	—	—	52.1	226	90.4	95.9
4 Durham	79.8	76.8	46.2	221	89.2	94.3
5 Warwick	85.7	84.4	46.1	189	84.9	93.3
=6 Lancaster	86.4	83.6	37.6	176	88.8	91.9
=6 Leeds	89.5	85.8	41.8	161	85.5	91.9
8 Birmingham	79.8	79.5	33.8	200	91.9	91.7
9 Nottingham	83.1	82.1	48.3	171	84.0	91.6
10 Manchester	79.9	80.7	44.9	204	81.6	91.5
11 Bath	81.9	82.4	40.0	183	84.8	90.8
12 Heriot-Watt	88.4	89.8	44.1	179	72.7	90.3
13 Exeter	79.9	81.8	42.4	194	80.4	90.2
14 Bristol	78.1	78.0	43.7	179	84.7	89.9
15 Glasgow	73.9	75.8	42.0	207	83.1	89.8
16 York	87.6	82.4	35.8	166	83.3	89.7
17 Southampton	79.1	78.6	44.1	167	84.3	89.5
18 Surrey	80.9	83.5	39.6	163	84.5	89.3
19 Royal Holloway, London	87.6	86.8	31.5	158	84.4	89.2
20 Imperial College London	61.8	61.5	49.6	217	87.6	89.0
21 University College London	70.3	71.4	45.1	183	87.1	88.8
=22 Edinburgh	72.8	71.9	48.7	204	76.9	88.7
=22 Leicester	88.6	85.9	40.8	140	79.6	88.7
24 Queen's, Belfast	84.5	84.0	44.4	156	73.7	87.8
25 Aberdeen	79.8	82.3	32.0	174	82.9	87.7
26 Strathclyde	79.7	81.8	45.3	193	67.5	87.4
27 Swansea	84.5	82.8	33.0	140	81.7	86.6
28 Sheffield	82.2	85.0	36.8	155	75.9	86.5
29 Cardiff	78.6	82.3	34.9	161	79.4	86.4
30 Liverpool	81.6	80.2	31.5	148	82.2	86.1
31 Loughborough	84.0	87.2	19.0	153	83.7	85.6
32 West of Scotland	95.5	98.4	19.1	129	72.7	84.9
33 King's College London	72.5	74.5	35.8	158	80.2	84.5
34 Hertfordshire	87.7	87.8	20.2	115	83.3	84.2
35 Sussex	81.1	81.5	24.7	146	79.5	84.0
36 Keele	86.0	84.2	31.8	108	76.8	83.7
=37 Northumbria	94.0	95.1	30.7	129	61.1	83.5
=37 Nottingham Trent	90.9	91.3	20.1	116	76.1	83.5
39 Aberystwyth	89.9	87.6	12.4	108	80.0	82.0
40 Kent	78.2	76.8	30.7	126	75.5	81.8
41 Queen Mary, London	70.7	72.7	27.6	126	80.1	80.4
=42 Dundee	86.1	84.6	34.1	165	46.4	79.8

=42 Portsmouth	79.1	75.7	21.8	110	77.4	79.8
44 Salford	82.6	84.7	4.4	113	72.6	77.0
45 Hull	71.1	66.4	24.2	120	68.9	76.0
46 Central Lancashire	71.0	70.9	19.8	128	64.3	74.9

Employed in professional job	38%	Employed in non-professional job and Studying	1%
Employed in professional job and studying	3%	Employed in non-professional job	10%
Studying	38%	Unemployed	11%
Average starting professional salary	£26,000	Average starting non-professional salary	£16,500

Physiotherapy

More than 95% of physiotherapy graduates go straight into professional jobs – enough to take the subject into the top five in our employment table and close to the top 20 for graduate salaries. Applications are well above the level before £9,000 fees arrived and over 60 universities and colleges are offering undergraduate courses in physiotherapy, or a related subject such as osteopathy or chiropractic, starting in 2020. Most of the leading courses demand biology A-level or equivalent, but some may also want another science or maths. The Chartered Society of Physiotherapy accredits all degrees in the subject in the UK.

The top four in the table are unchanged, although Robert Gordon has closed the gap a little on Southampton, in first place. Southampton had the best results in the Research Excellence Framework and is one of 11 universities with maximum scores for graduate prospects. The others are spread around the table and include Cumbria, in last place overall. Robert Gordon, the leader two years ago, has the highest entry standards and is close to maximum points for student satisfaction with teaching quality. Brighton, which has broken into the top 30 in the new edition, does best in the remaining sections of the National Student Survey and tops 95% in both of our satisfaction measures.

The ranking is in its seventh year, the subject having appeared previously as part of the table for "other subjects allied to medicine". The table is still growing, with Wolverhampton and London South Bank joining this year. Two-thirds of the universities in the table are post-1992 institutions, but only two feature in the top ten. Entry standards have been rising and vary less than in most subjects. Two Scottish universities average more than 200 points, but all but four of the remainder are within 50 points of each other on the UCAS tariff. Nowhere does the average drop below 120 points.

Physiotherapy	Teaching quality %	Student experience %	Research quality %	Entry standards (UCAS points)	Graduate prospects %	Overall score
1 Southampton	87.1	84.4	65.7	177	100.0	100.0
2 Robert Gordon	99.1	94.5	4.9	215	100.0	99.1
=3 Cardiff	83.1	85.3	36.8	168	98.7	95.7
=3 East Anglia	89.0	90.6	24.9	183	97.0	95.7
5 Birmingham	76.8	74.1	63.7	178	94.6	95.2
6 Salford	96.7	95.4	3.8	160	100.0	94.9

Physiotherapy cont	Teaching quality %	Student experience %	Research quality %	Entry standards (UCAS points)	Graduate prospects %	Overall score
=7 Liverpool	86.7	86.9	35.3	152	98.4	94.8
=7 Nottingham	77.2	77.1	40.6	169	98.3	94.8
9 Glasgow Caledonian	92.1	91.8	8.1	208	93.3	94.4
10 Ulster	85.4	84.4	27.7	155	98.8	94.2
11 Bradford	93.4	92.8	9.5	165	97.7	94.1
12 Worcester	92.8	89.9	2.6	149	100.0	93.3
13 Oxford Brookes	83.4	82.8	3.0	160	100.0	92.7
14 Leeds Beckett	92.1	93.0	3.5	136	100.0	92.6
15 Huddersfield	90.2	86.5	13.2	139	98.6	92.3
16 Coventry	85.0	85.8	4.5	151	99.3	92.2
17 Central Lancashire	85.5	86.2	8.3	137	100.0	92.0
18 Wolverhampton	81.9	77.3	11.0	164	—	91.9
=19 Brunel	78.7	79.8	18.2	144	99.0	91.7
=19 West of England	85.0	85.0	8.2	144	98.8	91.7
21 Sheffield Hallam	89.7	89.3	3.7	145	97.9	91.6
=22 Keele	78.5	82.5	20.9	137	98.9	91.5
=22 Manchester Metropolitan	81.4	80.7	12.0	160	97.0	91.5
=24 London South Bank	80.0	76.2	13.7	159	—	91.2
=24 Teesside	89.4	89.0	2.4	125	100.0	91.2
26 Bournemouth	79.6	74.4	4.7	148	100.0	91.1
27 Kingston/St George's, London	74.3	73.8	2.6	158	100.0	91.0
28 Northumbria	93.6	92.5	14.0	157	91.9	90.8
29 Hertfordshire	92.1	92.0	4.0	133	96.9	90.7
30 Brighton	96.7	95.8	4.8	131	95.1	90.4
31 York St John	88.6	86.4	1.9	154	94.6	90.0
32 Plymouth	79.2	77.2	9.5	149	96.7	89.9
33 Queen Margaret, Edinburgh	62.1	58.3	1.5	193*	96.8	89.5
34 King's College London	75.8	77.0	34.6	161	90.2	89.1
35 East London	89.8	88.0	7.6	124	91.2	86.8
36 Cumbria	59.8	50.5	0.7	129	100.0	86.0

Employed in professional job	72%		Employed in non-professional job and Studying	1%
Employed in professional job and studying	10%		Employed in non-professional job	4%
Studying	10%		Unemployed	3%
Average starting professional salary	£22,100		Average starting non-professional salary	£16,575

Politics

Fifteen more universities have joined the politics table over the past decade, as demand for the subject has soared. Buckingham and London South Bank are the latest recruits. Applications grew by 50% in five years and were stable in 2018, when the numbers starting courses were within 50 of the record enrolment set in the previous year. Even after considerable expansion of provision, there are still almost six applications to every place. Graduate salaries may be one slightly surprising reason. Politics is among the top 20 subjects for starting salaries in professional jobs, which averaged £23,000 in 2017. The subject is mid-way in the employment table.

The top four in the table remain the same with Warwick leading for the second year running without posting the best score on any individual indicator. Second-placed Oxford has the highest entry standards, while Essex, in fifth place, was well ahead of the field in the Research Excellence Framework, with 87% of its work considered world-leading or internationally excellent. Most of the leading scores from the National Student Survey are to be found much further down the table. Students at Canterbury Christ Church, in 73rd place, were the most satisfied with the quality of teaching, while Northampton, only one place higher overall, has the top rating for the broader student experience. There are some dramatic moves in the latest table – notably Huddersfield's 32-place rise into the top 40 and Surrey's 30-place fall into the bottom ten.

Both entry standards and graduate prospects show considerable variation among the 84 universities in the table. Three universities average more than 200 points at entry, while at another 11, the average is less than 100. The London School of Economics, in seventh place overall, was the only university to see 90% of leavers go straight into professional employment or postgraduate study in 2017, but another 17 topped 80%, while four were below 50%.

Politics	Teaching quality %	Student experience %	Research quality %	Entry standards (UCAS points)	Graduate prospects %	Overall score
1 Warwick	86.5	84.1	52.7	182	84.4	100.0
2 Oxford	—	—	61.1	216	83.4	98.6
3 St Andrews	88.9	84.0	38.4	205	72.3	97.5
4 Cambridge	—	—	38.2	213	84.8	96.6
5 Essex	84.9	84.5	69.6	111	79.5	96.4
6 Sheffield	82.6	78.0	48.3	160	85.3	96.2
7 London School of Economics	70.5	65.3	54.6	185	90.8	95.3
8 Lancaster	78.2	75.8	53.0	150	81.7	94.2
9 University College London	67.2	67.5	57.0	186	85.0	94.1
10 Loughborough	84.8	84.1	22.5	147	86.6	92.9
=11 Bristol	83.8	77.6	30.4	176	75.5	92.7
=11 Exeter	77.3	78.0	29.8	171	85.5	92.7
13 York	79.3	77.1	36.9	151	83.1	92.4
14 Bath	75.4	76.4	27.4	167	89.6	92.3
=15 Aberystwyth	86.9	83.9	40.2	115	76.5	91.9
=15 Strathclyde	77.2	76.6	41.6	193	65.8	91.9
17 Leeds	80.5	78.4	25.1	162	80.4	91.2
18 Durham	74.6	65.4	27.0	191	83.4	91.0
=19 Newcastle	81.3	77.0	22.0	154	81.2	90.4
=19 Stirling	80.8	72.3	33.8	182	66.8	90.4
21 Edinburgh	68.1	64.2	44.5	185	76.9	90.2
22 Nottingham	75.1	73.6	30.8	157	81.4	90.0
23 Manchester	76.8	73.6	28.4	163	78.6	89.9

Politics cont

		Teaching quality %	Student experience %	Research quality %	Entry standards (UCAS points)	Graduate prospects %	Overall score
24	King's College London	75.9	72.0	29.0	182	73.2	89.8
=25	Royal Holloway, London	81.1	77.9	30.5	134	78.0	89.7
=25	Sussex	75.2	73.8	33.6	145	81.8	89.7
27	Glasgow	74.7	72.3	30.5	191	69.6	89.6
28	Birmingham	74.2	71.5	31.1	153	82.6	89.5
29	Aberdeen	80.4	80.3	18.4	185	67.0	89.2
=30	Dundee	80.6	80.2	10.8	163	79.1	89.1
=30	East Anglia	80.8	79.8	35.5	135	69.9	89.1
32	Swansea	85.1	81.4	18.5	124	76.1	88.2
33	Southampton	72.7	71.8	37.0	145	75.8	88.1
34	Portsmouth	80.0	75.8	32.2	102	81.1	87.9
=35	Cardiff	78.2	72.5	30.4	147	71.3	87.8
=35	SOAS, London	78.7	77.0	30.5	166	61.7	87.8
37	Kent	79.0	73.1	27.8	134	73.5	87.3
38	Aston	75.4	72.7	38.6	117	73.4	86.8
=39	Greenwich	85.6	86.0	8.6	124	71.7	86.5
=39	Huddersfield	86.7	78.2	9.5	126	73.7	86.5
41	Keele	78.0	77.5	24.0	115	76.1	86.2
42	Queen's, Belfast	76.0	72.6	35.0	144	63.1	86.1
43	City	81.8	79.4	24.6	136	61.7	86.0
=44	Buckingham	88.4	83.6	—	117	75.6	85.8
=44	Reading	71.1	66.7	37.0	128	75.4	85.8
46	Coventry	89.0	84.2	5.6	106	72.5	85.6
47	Queen Mary, London	71.8	69.2	28.1	141	73.9	85.5
48	Plymouth	83.1	76.1	25.8	115	63.6	85.0
49	Lincoln	82.7	77.8	7.7	113	76.8	84.9
50	Nottingham Trent	82.9	80.7	5.1	119	73.9	84.7
51	Hull	81.5	72.6	10.8	120	74.8	84.5
52	Oxford Brookes	78.4	75.8	17.8	120	70.1	84.2
53	Salford	85.5	75.3	4.8	115	72.0	83.9
54	Westminster	80.9	80.1	14.3	110	68.2	83.8
55	Northumbria	81.3	76.9	12.7	134	62.5	83.6
56	Leeds Beckett	89.0	86.8	—	94	68.4	83.4
57	West of England	81.7	81.2	13.8	118	61.8	83.3
=58	Liverpool	75.8	72.9	12.0	136	69.3	83.2
=58	Manchester Metropolitan	87.2	82.2	18.0	120	50.3	83.2
=60	Brunel	70.1	65.7	32.4	114	71.2	82.9
=60	De Montfort	78.7	78.0	10.7	100	74.2	82.9
62	Bradford	73.2	71.1	12.7	114	77.9	82.7
63	Leicester	69.2	67.5	20.0	121	76.7	82.6
64	Liverpool Hope	78.3	75.9	7.0	97	76.6	82.3
65	Central Lancashire	85.1	77.2	12.0	122	52.2	81.6

66 Ulster	83.3	75.4	20.9	112	51.5	81.5
67 East London	84.5	73.4	13.7	95	60.1	81.0
68 London South Bank	81.7	72.7	—	92	75.0	80.9
69 Sheffield Hallam	81.5	69.7	14.4	102	57.8	79.9
70 Kingston	83.6	77.7	—	101	59.0	79.4
71 London Metropolitan	77.5	74.5	1.2	102	65.5	79.0
72 Northampton	88.8	90.6	—	64	54.6	78.9
73 Canterbury Christ Church	93.9	85.3	3.2	96	37.2	78.6
74 Derby	67.5	72.8	13.5	119	59.8	78.2
=75 West of Scotland	75.1	66.2	—	137	58.1	78.1
=75 Wolverhampton	81.4	70.4	—	89	64.0	78.1
=77 Chichester	73.1	73.4	15.8	91*	—	78.0
=77 Goldsmiths, London	74.0	68.6	16.8	108	54.8	78.0
=77 Surrey	61.7	57.9	12.5	147	66.8	78.0
80 Middlesex	74.3	66.5	14.9	87	—	76.7
81 Bournemouth	66.8	62.2	15.1	113	—	75.7
82 Chester	77.5	74.9	—	104	47.9	75.4
83 Winchester	80.7	75.9	—	93	45.8	75.1
84 Brighton	73.5	67.1	13.1	96	41.7	73.6

Employed in professional job	40%	Employed in non-professional job and Studying	3%
Employed in professional job and studying	3%	Employed in non-professional job	19%
Studying	24%	Unemployed	11%
Average starting professional salary	£22,000	Average starting non-professional salary	£16,500

Psychology

Only nursing attracts more applications than psychology, and the subject table is among the biggest in the *Guide*, with 116 universities. There is no sign of decline in the subject's popularity: applications were up by nearly 5% in 2018 and the numbers starting courses continued to rise at an even faster rate, the sixth successive increase leaving them 50% higher than in 2008. Psychology's successes are nothing to do with its performances in the graduate employment market; it is just outside the bottom ten for the proportion of graduates with "positive destinations", and for average starting salaries in professional-level jobs. Although unemployment is no higher than the average for most subjects, nearly a third of graduates begin their careers in low-level jobs.

Most undergraduate programmes are accredited by the British Psychological Society, which ensures that key topics are covered, but the clinical and biological content of courses still varies considerably. Some universities require maths and/or biology A-levels among three high-grade passes, but others are much less demanding. The contrast is obvious in the ranking, with 23 universities averaging at least 160 points at entry but another 20 falling below 110 points. Oxford has the highest entry grades in the table, and remains top with Cambridge moving up to second. Exeter, which has dropped five places to 12th, has the best graduate prospects and is one of only five universities where more than 80% of 2017 graduates found professional employment or continued studying.

Seventh-placed Loughborough achieved the highest scores in the Research Excellence Framework. Bolton, sharing 45th place despite a string of awards for its psychology degrees, has the highest levels of satisfaction with the quality of teaching. St Andrews, in third position, has the best scores in the sections of the National Student Survey devoted to other aspects of the student experience and is the only university to reach 90% on this measure.

Psychology	Teaching quality %	Student experience %	Research quality %	Entry standards (UCAS points)	Graduate prospects %	Overall score
1 Oxford	—	—	58.6	217	78.4	100.0
2 Cambridge	—	—	57.5	211	78.3	96.7
3 St Andrews	89.1	90.4	45.4	206	71.2	95.6
4 Bath	76.5	81.9	56.2	194	82.1	94.4
5 King's College London	83.9	83.7	54.1	180	—	94.0
6 University College London	75.1	78.0	57.0	191	76.6	92.4
7 Loughborough	81.0	84.4	62.3	161	71.4	91.7
=8 Cardiff	83.5	84.1	55.7	170	68.6	91.6
=8 York	84.3	84.9	46.7	159	76.1	91.6
10 Lancaster	83.2	83.6	38.5	159	81.5	91.3
11 Bristol	71.4	77.1	49.4	179	83.1	91.0
12 Exeter	75.3	77.3	43.3	173	83.6	90.8
13 Newcastle	77.2	80.7	50.0	162	75.3	89.8
14 Aberdeen	84.0	83.5	38.7	169	65.8	88.8
15 Sheffield	80.7	82.7	38.8	149	76.2	88.7
=16 Glasgow	66.2	74.9	52.9	183	75.4	88.6
=16 Southampton	80.5	83.9	47.8	157	67.0	88.6
18 Sussex	77.0	74.8	42.3	153	79.5	88.4
19 Royal Holloway, London	82.7	86.0	37.8	155	68.6	88.3
20 Birmingham	67.3	71.3	55.8	165	78.7	88.1
21 Bangor	88.1	88.5	32.0	130	72.0	87.9
22 Swansea	75.0	74.7	44.7	136	83.1	87.7
23 Kent	73.9	81.2	38.8	147	79.3	87.5
24 Stirling	78.9	82.1	40.1	157	68.8	87.4
=25 Strathclyde	83.5	81.4	23.5	191	60.3	87.1
=25 Warwick	74.7	78.3	43.1	162	70.4	87.1
27 Durham	71.6	70.7	37.1	183	73.4	86.9
28 Nottingham	73.9	78.8	36.4	164	72.9	86.8
29 Surrey	78.6	79.6	22.0	150	76.4	86.0
=30 Manchester	76.5	78.7	44.9	157	63.5	85.9
=30 Nottingham Trent	81.8	83.0	19.3	134	78.0	85.9
32 Portsmouth	81.7	83.1	21.0	122	79.9	85.6
33 Leeds	76.2	81.2	33.0	159	66.5	85.5
34 Edinburgh	62.4	65.7	52.8	192	66.8	85.4
35 Essex	78.7	83.9	41.0	111	73.3	85.1
=36 Liverpool	77.3	77.3	34.6	143	69.0	84.8

=36 West London	90.6	87.8	7.6	115	74.0	84.8
38 East Anglia	75.1	79.3	33.2	150	66.4	84.3
39 Aston	76.3	78.5	39.1	128	69.3	84.2
40 Staffordshire	86.2	83.9	8.2	117	74.2	83.5
41 Northumbria	82.1	82.9	18.7	138	64.8	83.4
42 Aberystwyth	90.5	89.4	—	124	66.3	83.0
=43 Central Lancashire	79.6	79.8	12.2	130	72.4	82.7
=43 De Montfort	82.5	83.0	11.2	109	75.9	82.7
=45 Bolton	91.0	87.9	3.6	118	64.5	82.6
=45 Edinburgh Napier	84.9	87.8	5.3	162	54.7	82.6
47 Derby	88.7	83.6	8.4	122	64.3	82.4
48 Liverpool John Moores	83.4	80.5	7.8	137	66.5	82.3
49 Leicester	77.3	81.8	29.6	133	60.9	82.2
=50 Liverpool Hope	83.3	79.5	5.5	110	75.9	81.9
=50 Plymouth	80.4	83.4	33.8	131	53.6	81.9
=52 Coventry	76.3	76.0	7.8	126	77.5	81.8
=52 Hull	78.6	73.9	26.8	122	67.4	81.8
=54 Lincoln	78.8	80.9	7.9	130	70.0	81.6
=54 Queen's, Belfast	70.6	78.6	40.2	146	56.3	81.6
56 Dundee	73.0	76.4	22.7	162	56.7	81.0
57 Abertay	85.8	81.4	15.1	111	62.0	80.9
=58 Buckingham	84.8	83.4	—	112	69.7	80.8
=58 Keele	79.8	79.7	17.7	125	62.3	80.8
60 Reading	70.2	68.3	42.3	135	61.2	80.7
61 Cumbria	86.5	80.2	—	114	67.3	80.5
62 Ulster	79.6	81.3	23.2	124	56.9	80.4
=63 Glasgow Caledonian	73.0	70.8	8.1	186	55.1	80.1
=63 Huddersfield	76.7	72.6	9.5	122	72.0	80.1
=65 Bradford	81.0	82.6	9.5	122	60.5	79.8
=65 Chester	89.0	85.0	7.9	115	54.3	79.8
=67 Edge Hill	77.2	73.5	18.8	130	61.0	79.7
=67 Roehampton	77.1	75.9	26.4	107	63.9	79.7
69 Teesside	70.5	72.3	15.0	112	76.2	79.5
70 Manchester Metropolitan	78.4	78.9	12.0	126	60.6	79.4
=71 Gloucestershire	74.4	76.4	—	118	73.8	79.0
=71 Hertfordshire	75.9	80.0	6.0	107	70.8	79.0
=73 Heriot-Watt	67.1	60.7	26.9	162	59.3	78.9
=73 Queen Margaret, Edinburgh	72.2	70.5	8.6	145	64.9	78.9
=75 Sheffield Hallam	83.2	82.1	3.7	117	58.5	78.8
=75 Worcester	81.3	82.7	7.1	119	57.7	78.8
=77 Birmingham City	86.4	82.7	—	112	58.7	78.7
=77 Oxford Brookes	73.4	73.9	18.1	132	60.2	78.7
=77 West of Scotland	76.7	73.5	9.4	151	54.5	78.7
80 Queen Mary, London	64.9	72.2	26.1	137	63.3	78.6
=81 Bedfordshire	80.8	78.6	25.1	93	58.6	78.5
=81 London South Bank	71.5	69.4	8.6	105	78.3	78.5

Psychology cont

	Teaching quality %	Student experience %	Research quality %	Entry standards (UCAS points)	Graduate prospects %	Overall score
=83 East London	74.1	75.5	8.3	109	70.4	78.4
=83 Sunderland	84.6	77.0	7.5	114	57.0	78.4
85 Goldsmiths, London	69.7	68.9	40.4	130	52.8	78.3
86 West of England	83.1	83.8	8.2	117	52.5	78.2
87 Chichester	85.3	85.7	10.3	101	52.9	78.0
=88 Bournemouth	81.1	81.5	13.0	113	53.4	77.9
=88 City	68.0	72.3	24.1	140	56.9	77.9
=88 Westminster	73.1	73.8	9.3	115	67.4	77.9
91 York St John	83.8	80.9	11.0	111	52.2	77.8
92 Greenwich	78.1	79.4	6.7	127	53.5	77.3
93 Wolverhampton	73.8	74.8	—	109	69.4	77.0
=94 Leeds Trinity	81.6	81.0	—	109	57.3	76.9
=94 St Mary's, Twickenham	87.2	84.6	4.8	101	49.3	76.9
=96 London Metropolitan	78.3	72.7	—	107	65.1	76.7
=96 Solent	78.5	78.3	—	111	60.5	76.7
=96 South Wales	80.7	77.3	0.9	123	53.7	76.7
99 Brunel	66.3	68.6	26.6	122	59.0	76.5
100 Middlesex	71.3	72.2	7.6	113	64.2	76.2
101 Suffolk	83.4	76.2	—	96	59.0	76.1
102 Salford	74.4	74.6	3.8	125	56.7	76.0
103 Cardiff Metropolitan	76.2	75.6	—	108	61.9	75.9
104 Bucks New	81.2	84.5	—	126	44.4	75.8
105 Wales Trinity St David	84.6	81.1	—	104	49.6	75.6
106 Bath Spa	73.7	69.3	—	109	63.7	75.1
107 Winchester	76.9	79.6	6.5	107	51.0	75.0
108 Leeds Beckett	78.7	79.7	6.5	110	48.1	74.9
=109 Kingston	77.7	72.4	6.5	107	51.0	74.3
=109 Newman	77.4	77.2	0.8	109	51.3	74.3
111 Canterbury Christ Church	75.4	76.7	2.2	111	49.8	73.8
112 Anglia Ruskin	77.9	74.2	12.6	105	43.9	73.6
113 Glyndŵr	69.9	68.5	3.6	—	59.0	73.3
114 Brighton	73.7	69.5	12.4	115	42.5	72.5
115 Bishop Grosseteste	62.5	58.1	—	111	62.3	71.0
116 Northampton	71.1	71.4	0.4	100	47.3	70.6

Employed in professional job	30%	Employed in non-professional job and Studying	6%
Employed in professional job and studying	5%	Employed in non-professional job	26%
Studying	24%	Unemployed	9%
Average starting professional salary	£19,500	Average starting non-professional salary	£16,500

Radiography

Leeds has taken over the leadership of the Radiography table, ending Bangor's four-year reign. Both universities were among seven where every graduate found professional employment or continued studying in 2017, but declines in student satisfaction and entry standards have seen Bangor drop to fifth this year. Robert Gordon, which shares second place with Exeter, has the highest entry standards and much the best rates in both of our measures of student satisfaction, but is handicapped by a research score that is in the bottom ten of the 25 universities.

The table is in its seventh year, radiography having been listed previously among "other subjects allied to medicine" in the *Guide*. Diagnostic courses usually involve two years of studying anatomy, physiology and physics followed by further training in sociology, management and ethics, and the practice and science of imaging. The therapeutic branch covers much of the same scientific content in the first year, but follows this with training in oncology, psycho-social studies and other modules. Degrees require at least one science subject, usually biology, among three A-levels or the equivalent. Entry grades are not high, but they have been rising: only one university averaged less than 120 points in the latest survey.

Radiography was among the top six subjects for graduate prospects in 2017. An impressive 95% of graduates went straight into professional jobs and just 3% were unemployed six months after completing a degree. The other universities with 100% scores for graduate prospects are Robert Gordon, Bradford, Cumbria, Salford and Derby. City and Ulster were the only universities where fewer than nine out of ten graduates went straight into professional jobs or further study – and both of them scored at least 86%, enough to register the top graduate prospects in some subjects. The subject has slipped slightly in the earnings table, but it is still 24th for salaries in those professional jobs.

Radiography	Teaching quality %	Student experience %	Research quality %	Entry standards (UCAS points)	Graduate prospects %	Overall score
1 Leeds	88.8	84.9	31.7	174	100.0	100.0
=2 Exeter	83.8	85.9	42.4	161	99.0	99.0
=2 Robert Gordon	96.1	93.5	4.9	181	100.0	99.0
4 Cardiff	85.5	84.3	36.8	155	97.7	97.3
5 Bangor	78.8	70.6	34.7	155	100.0	96.3
6 Liverpool	84.7	84.8	35.3	130	97.2	94.8
7 Glasgow Caledonian	82.9	77.8	8.1	180	95.5	94.3
8 Teesside	85.9	79.2	2.4	168	97.3	93.9
9 Cumbria	85.9	83.0	0.7	151	100.0	93.8
=10 Salford	84.6	79.5	3.8	140	100.0	92.7
=10 West of England	91.5	91.4	8.2	130	96.8	92.7
12 Keele	85.9	87.0	20.9	125	—	92.6
13 Queen Margaret, Edinburgh	77.4	67.8	1.5	161	97.2	91.1
14 Sheffield Hallam	83.7	82.4	3.7	148	94.5	90.9
15 Hertfordshire	85.7	85.1	4.0	132	95.9	90.7
16 Birmingham City	79.5	73.3	1.5	136	98.2	90.1
17 Bradford	62.5	63.8	9.5	147	100.0	89.8
18 Suffolk	83.1	81.7	—	131	96.2	89.7

Radiography cont

	Teaching quality %	Student experience %	Research quality %	Entry standards (UCAS points)	Graduate prospects %	Overall score
19 Derby	79.3	76.3	—	120	100.0	89.6
20 London South Bank	74.1	70.7	13.7	120	98.4	89.3
=21 Canterbury Christ Church	79.2	68.4	2.2	127	98.0	89.0
=21 Portsmouth	70.3	67.9	24.3	126	95.3	89.0
23 Ulster	78.9	80.1	27.7	142	86.4	88.7
24 City	85.9	87.1	20.5	121	87.0	87.8
25 Kingston/St George's, London	65.1	61.5	2.6	118	94.7	84.2

Employed in professional job	94%	Employed in non-professional job and Studying	0%
Employed in professional job and studying	1%	Employed in non-professional job	2%
Studying	1%	Unemployed	3%
Average starting professional salary	£22,125	Average starting non-professional salary	n/a

Russian and Eastern European Languages

Both applications and enrolments for degrees in Russian and East European languages fell again in 2018, when only 35 students embarked on single honours programmes – less than half the total a decade ago. Many others are learning Russian as part of a broader modern languages programme, but these have also been in decline, enrolments dropping by another 10% in the current academic year. Only 24 universities are advertising programmes in Russian in 2020, even as part of a broader modern languages degree.

Cambridge is top for the sixth year in a row, recording the highest entry standards and the best research score. It is well clear of Oxford in second place. Glasgow has much the best graduate prospects – nine percentage points ahead of any other university – but has dropped out of the top ten this year after a collapse in student satisfaction. St Andrews is top in both of the measures derived from the National Student Satisfaction. Portsmouth, the only post-1992 university in the table, is its nearest challenger on these measures.

Most undergraduates learn Russian or another Eastern European language from scratch. Despite the small numbers, entry standards remain high throughout the table: the top two average more than 200 points on the UCAS tariff and only Portsmouth has an average of less than 130 points.

As in other subjects, the small numbers inevitably make for exaggerated swings in the statistics. Russian dropped ten places and then went up 13 in successive years to its current position of 25th. Half of all graduates went straight into professional employment in 2017 and a further 27% continued studying. Another big swing saw average starting salaries in professional jobs drop by £3,000, taking the subjects 20 places down the earnings table from their previous position in the top 20.

Russian and Eastern European Languages	Teaching quality %	Student experience %	Research quality %	Entry standards (UCAS points)	Graduate prospects %	Overall score
1 Cambridge	—	—	54.0	209	80.6	100.0
2 Oxford	—	—	41.3	207	85.7	94.9
3 Durham	81.1	73.2	34.6	197	86.3	92.5
4 Exeter	85.8	83.8	35.1	169	84.6	92.2
5 St Andrews	90.2	87.9	26.4	186*	76.7	91.0
6 Manchester	80.5	77.8	48.9	162	68.2	90.5
7 Bristol	82.1	80.7	36.0	175	72.7	89.5
8 University College London	72.8	70.1	43.7	179	72.6	88.8
9 Birmingham	76.0	73.4	33.7	161	87.9	88.7
10 Nottingham	78.8	71.6	39.4	139	85.7	88.5
11 Sheffield	84.2	81.8	41.2	146	58.6	86.4
12 Glasgow	68.3	67.2	26.3	163	96.9	86.3
13 Leeds	70.1	69.7	30.6	160	87.1	86.0
14 Portsmouth	85.8	86.1	32.2	100	76.1	84.6
15 Bath	75.8	75.5	27.4	—	73.9	84.2
16 Edinburgh	67.4	66.3	30.3	184	55.7	80.6

Employed in professional job	50%	Employed in non-professional job and Studying		4%
Employed in professional job and studying	0%	Employed in non-professional job		13%
Studying	23%	Unemployed		10%
Average starting professional salary	£21,000	Average starting non-professional salary		£16,000

Social Policy

The London School of Economics has lost its accustomed place at the top of the Social Policy table, dropping to third after a surprise decline in entry standards and a low score for satisfaction with the student experience. Strathclyde, which shared top place with the LSE two years ago, is the new leader, although it has no employment score because its programme was too new to have graduates in 2017. Fifth-placed Bath is the leader on that measure, the only university to see 90% of graduates go straight into professional employment or continue studying.

Students at Bolton, just outside the top 20, are the most satisfied with the quality of teaching, while Loughborough, in fourth, received the top rating for the broader student experience. In research, the LSE was 15 percentage points ahead of its nearest challenger, Kent.

The demand for places on social policy degrees fluctuated in the aftermath of £9,000 fees, but both applications and enrolments grew for the fourth year in a row in 2018. There were fewer than four applications for every place, however. Nevertheless, there are still 44 universities in the latest table, and 77 universities and colleges plan to offer the subject in 2020. Entry standards are generally modest: only three universities average more than 180 points on the UCAS tariff, while another 11 dropped below 120 points.

Nationally, the subject is in the bottom ten for employment, with almost three graduates in ten starting out in low-level jobs. This is reflected in the table, where at six universities, less than half of the graduates found professional work or continued studying, and only five universities reached 80%. The picture is only a little more positive in the comparison of starting salaries in graduate-level jobs, where social policy shares 47th place with eight other subjects.

Social Policy	Teaching quality %	Student experience %	Research quality %	Entry standards (UCAS points)	Graduate prospects %	Overall score
1 Strathclyde	88.1	80.4	31.9	185	—	100.0
2 Glasgow	90.4	83.9	41.8	189	61.2	97.5
3 London School of Economics	71.4	62.6	74.9	163	87.4	97.4
4 Loughborough	87.1	85.6	40.6	154	75.6	95.6
5 Bath	77.5	79.5	43.4	150	90.4	95.4
6 Leeds	80.5	79.0	47.6	158	72.7	94.2
7 Kent	85.7	81.6	59.0	127	72.2	93.7
8 Nottingham	81.3	78.5	43.5	149	77.5	93.6
9 Bristol	71.5	68.8	47.9	154	80.8	91.9
10 Bangor	87.3	82.1	39.6	130	72.1	91.7
=11 Birmingham	73.8	67.9	40.1	151	82.7	91.3
=11 Edinburgh	68.9	65.1	53.4	191	57.5	91.3
=13 Swansea	85.2	83.8	22.7	131	78.8	90.4
=13 York	77.3	76.3	47.5	124	78.4	90.4
15 Southampton	78.5	72.8	52.8	137*	—	89.9
16 Queen's, Belfast	81.5	—	26.2	144*	69.0	88.8
17 Sheffield	77.3	72.8	26.8	144*	73.1	88.2
=18 Salford	84.7	77.9	27.7	132	66.1	87.9
=18 Stirling	71.1	72.0	33.8	165	62.5	87.9
20 Coventry	82.1	84.4	5.6	—	70.6	87.6
21 Bolton	92.4	83.1	1.0	—	60.0	87.4
22 Liverpool Hope	81.7	77.2	8.6	124	83.3	87.0
23 Aston	71.3	67.1	38.6	122	75.8	85.8
24 Edge Hill	82.4	79.2	5.7	135	—	85.4
25 Keele	79.5	82.0	25.0	130*	58.5	85.1
26 Cardiff	71.9	72.0	30.8	130	65.6	84.3
27 Central Lancashire	77.8	75.6	11.8	122	65.9	82.6
28 De Montfort	71.2	73.1	11.2	124	74.1	82.4
29 Wolverhampton	90.1	85.2	—	117	54.6	82.2
30 West of Scotland	80.8	74.8	9.4	—	57.1	82.1
31 Ulster	80.5	78.4	39.2	115	33.9	80.4
=32 Chester	77.8	75.5	0.3	117	60.0	79.2
=32 Lincoln	74.3	72.5	5.8	117*	62.5	79.2
34 Middlesex	70.5	69.3	14.9	122	55.9	78.5
35 Plymouth	81.4	76.7	16.0	—	37.3	77.7
36 Canterbury Christ Church	79.1	72.8	3.2	—	48.3	77.6
37 London Metropolitan	71.2	66.6	8.8	98	63.7	76.4
38 Brighton	79.5	73.5	12.4	106	37.5	75.4
39 Bedfordshire	71.3	68.8	16.3	108	45.0	75.1

		Teaching quality %	Student experience %	Research quality %	Entry standards (UCAS points)	Graduate prospects %	Overall score
40	Wales Trinity St David	74.6	64.4	—	110	53.5	75.0
41	Birmingham City	59.6	63.7	3.8	122*	62.2	74.9
42	Northampton	76.5	74.1	—	100	47.9	74.4
43	Goldsmiths, London	70.9	67.9	13.5	99*	—	74.2
44	Anglia Ruskin	60.3	43.1	5.4	109	58.8	70.8

Employed in professional job	35%	Employed in non-professional job and Studying	3%
Employed in professional job and studying	4%	Employed in non-professional job	26%
Studying	21%	Unemployed	11%
Average starting professional salary	£20,000	Average starting non-professional salary	£16,224

Social Work

Stirling has overtaken Edinburgh at the top of the Social Work table, having moved up 15 places in three years. It is one of six Scottish universities in the top 20 and has a rare 100% employment score, as well as the top rating for satisfaction with teaching quality, but did not have enough students taking social work in 2018 for average entry grades to be published. Students at Oxford Brookes in 27th place are the most satisfied with the broad student experience. Kent produced the best results in the Research Excellence Framework, but remains outside the top 20 overall. Eighteen of the 78 universities in the table did not enter the assessments.

The Frontline programme, modelled on Teach First, is trying to attract graduates of other subjects to train as social workers but, for the moment, social work degrees remain the main. route into the profession. Enrolments remain relatively healthy, although applications have dropped from 80,000 to less than 50,000 during the current decade. The number of applications per place has dropped from more than seven in 2010 to under four over the same period. No universities average less than 100 points at entry, but only Edinburgh and Leeds have averages of more than 160 points.

Remarkably, social work does better in the comparison of earnings in professional jobs than in the table based on overall graduate prospects. A median salary of £26,000 in graduate-level employment places it in the top ten of the 67 groups, whereas it is only just in the top 30 for the proportion of graduates going straight into such jobs or continuing to study. Unemployment is relatively low, at 8%, but one graduate in five started out in low-level employment in 2017. A total of 22 universities saw positive destinations for at least 90% of their 2017 graduates, but the rate was under 60% at six others.

Social Work	Teaching quality %	Student experience %	Research quality %	Entry standards (UCAS points)	Graduate prospects %	Overall score
1 Stirling	95.4	80.4	33.8	—	100.0	100.0
2 Edinburgh	84.6	77.9	53.4	176	78.3	98.8
3 Lancaster	85.5	79.8	51.4	152	93.2	98.0
4 Birmingham	84.6	81.2	40.1	155	87.7	95.9
5 Nottingham	75.5	67.7	43.5	158	94.3	94.7
6 York	75.8	59.3	47.5	148	95.8	93.2
7 Hull	88.9	83.1	14.3	149	90.6	93.0
=8 Leeds	73.7	75.6	47.6	167	72.8	92.9

Social Work cont

		Teaching quality %	Student experience %	Research quality %	Entry standards (UCAS points)	Graduate prospects %	Overall score
=8	Queen's, Belfast	77.9	81.4	39.3	136	96.2	92.9
10	West of England	89.4	86.2	10.9	141	96.5	92.8
11	Glasgow Caledonian	82.9	84.6	8.1	157	89.7	91.9
=12	Bath	85.4	74.5	43.4	148	72.0	91.8
=12	Bolton	92.4	83.1	1.0	—	89.5	91.8
=12	Plymouth	92.7	83.7	16.0	136	88.8	91.8
=15	Robert Gordon	82.8	79.7	18.0	144	93.6	91.6
=15	Strathclyde	77.9	81.5	31.9	156	78.4	91.6
17	Ulster	84.4	83.5	39.2	127	87.3	91.5
18	Dundee	83.5	78.0	31.1	142	84.2	91.4
19	East Anglia	72.4	61.7	45.8	143	92.9	91.2
20	East London	94.0	87.4	10.6	125	90.8	90.5
21	Kent	70.1	68.5	59.0	134	85.8	90.4
22	London South Bank	85.6	74.8	20.1	136	90.4	90.2
23	Swansea	75.4	72.8	22.7	148	90.7	90.0
24	Solent	88.3	89.0	—	140	90.0	89.9
25	West of Scotland	80.1	77.7	9.4	145*	90.9	89.3
26	Salford	82.6	78.6	27.7	137	80.4	89.2
27	Oxford Brookes	92.7	96.3	—	127	85.2	88.8
28	Bournemouth	86.3	81.4	4.7	131	91.1	88.3
29	Sussex	75.8	69.0	27.9	141	84.0	88.2
30	Portsmouth	85.7	78.7	12.1	130	87.9	88.1
=31	De Montfort	85.0	83.8	11.2	119	93.1	87.7
=31	Lincoln	81.4	77.4	5.8	133*	94.2	87.7
33	Bucks New	88.4	83.6	—	140	78.1	87.2
34	Bedfordshire	82.2	72.5	16.3	129	87.1	87.1
35	Liverpool Hope	86.1	78.0	8.6	130	84.0	87.0
=36	Central Lancashire	82.1	78.1	11.8	142	76.3	86.9
=36	Huddersfield	84.3	79.9	9.5	139	76.9	86.9
38	Liverpool John Moores	91.2	89.4	5.8	141	63.4	86.6
39	Anglia Ruskin	80.7	68.6	5.4	132	93.3	86.5
40	Nottingham Trent	83.7	81.3	5.1	138	77.4	86.3
41	Manchester Metropolitan	86.1	84.1	6.9	144	64.6	85.8
42	Teesside	73.3	71.8	15.0	132	89.4	85.7
43	Sheffield Hallam	88.1	87.3	—	120	84.2	85.5
=44	Brighton	84.0	75.5	12.4	111	92.1	85.4
=44	Edge Hill	85.8	77.7	5.7	135	74.1	85.4
=44	West London	81.1	78.1	—	140	80.0	85.4
=47	Bradford	80.1	81.4	10.6	143	67.6	85.2
=47	Brunel	72.8	71.1	28.5	—	81.8	85.2
=47	Northumbria	78.6	73.7	12.7	152	64.5	85.2
=50	Derby	85.8	81.9	5.6	122	80.9	85.1

=50	Staffordshire	70.1	67.9	—	142	95.0	85.1
52	Coventry	87.8	83.1	5.6	126	73.0	84.8
=53	Birmingham City	78.9	78.9	3.8	134	80.4	84.7
=53	Middlesex	73.3	70.3	14.9	135	82.9	84.7
=55	Greenwich	78.2	63.9	2.2	172	56.2	84.2
=55	Keele	64.4	45.7	25.0	135	95.8	84.2
57	Suffolk	83.0	80.8	—	122	81.7	83.7
58	Hertfordshire	63.5	59.2	4.0	139	91.7	82.2
=59	Goldsmiths, London	80.5	67.3	13.5	106	83.9	81.7
=59	London Metropolitan	72.7	69.5	8.8	118	86.3	81.7
=59	Worcester	89.2	86.6	—	119	63.5	81.7
=59	Kingston/St George's, London	75.4	69.4	—	131	78.5	81.7
63	Cardiff Metropolitan	77.0	74.5	—	130	73.6	81.5
64	South Wales	87.7	79.6	15.4	112	59.7	81.2
65	Winchester	75.3	74.4	—	126	77.0	81.1
66	Bangor	81.0	77.0	—	146	52.4	81.0
67	Gloucestershire	76.3	69.1	—	118	80.5	80.3
68	Wolverhampton	77.5	73.6	—	125	71.1	80.2
69	Essex	83.1	74.0	—	109*	75.7	79.9
70	Chester	79.2	76.8	0.3	124	65.5	79.8
=71	Chichester	87.2	79.4	—	109	64.0	79.3
=71	Leeds Beckett	88.4	83.2	6.4	108	57.0	79.3
73	Canterbury Christ Church	74.5	69.9	2.2	121	72.4	79.2
74	Cumbria	81.6	82.3	—	125	56.0	79.1
75	Northampton	74.9	72.3	—	116	72.1	78.4
76	Newman	80.9	79.9	2.2	120	54.9	78.1
77	Sunderland	75.9	76.2	1.9	119	57.8	77.0

Employed in professional job	59%	Employed in non-professional job and Studying	2%
Employed in professional job and studying	3%	Employed in non-professional job	18%
Studying	10%	Unemployed	8%
Average starting professional salary	£26,000	Average starting non-professional salary	£16,000

Sociology

Sociology is one of the more unexpected success stories of higher education in the era of £9,000 fees. Applications have risen by 75% since fees went up in most of the UK, following another 4,000 increase in 2018. The record numbers starting degrees in the subject are approaching 9,000, compared with little more than 5,000 in 2012. The Sociology table now contains 94 institutions, and 136 universities and colleges are advertising degrees or Foundation degrees in 2020.

Immediate job prospects cannot be responsible for the boom: sociology is in the bottom three for the proportion of graduates finding professional work or continuing their studies. Less than a third of sociologists found such work, while considerably more started out in low-level jobs. The median salary of £20,000 among those who did find graduate-level work was only just in the top 50 of the 67 subject groups.

Cambridge remains top of the table, with by far the highest entry standards and as one of six universities where more than 80% of sociologists went straight into professional jobs or began postgraduate courses. Lincoln, in 46th place, had the top score on this measure, despite falling 27 places overall after a drop in student satisfaction. The proportion of graduates enjoying 'positive destinations' was under 40% at five others.

The students most satisfied with the quality of teaching were at Plymouth, which has jumped 27 places to 28th place this year, while fourth-placed Loughborough did best in the sections of the National Student Survey focusing on the broader student experience. The best performance in the Research Excellence Framework was at Kent, in 16th position. As in the 2008 assessments, the sociology panel was no respecter of reputations: neither Cambridge nor the London School of Economics is among the top eight universities on this measure, despite being in the top six in the world, according to QS.

Degree courses starting in 2020 will include subjects such as urban studies, women's studies and some communication studies, as well as sociology itself, and a large number of institutions teach the subject as part of a combined studies or modular programme. Entry standards are moderate: eight of the 94 universities in the table average less than 100 points on the UCAS tariff and another 33 less than 120 points.

Sociology	Teaching quality %	Student experience %	Research quality %	Entry standards (UCAS points)	Graduate prospects %	Overall score
1 Cambridge	—	—	39.2	213	84.8	100.0
2 Bristol	88.5	83.7	46.7	161	78.4	98.9
3 Lancaster	77.1	79.6	51.4	170	82.8	97.6
4 Loughborough	89.8	94.6	40.6	154	69.2	97.5
5 Exeter	78.7	79.5	41.0	167	78.9	95.6
6 Bath	77.5	79.5	43.4	154	83.9	95.4
7 King's College London	83.1	80.6	42.2	157	—	94.8
8 London School of Economics	72.8	71.4	45.2	164	80.7	93.7
9 Glasgow	75.2	72.2	41.8	182	70.3	93.6
10 Durham	82.7	78.5	28.7	170	66.3	92.8
11 Edinburgh	71.7	67.0	48.8	187	65.6	92.6
12 Warwick	80.6	79.2	31.7	148	75.3	92.5
13 Manchester	77.8	75.5	50.4	152	64.3	92.3
14 Nottingham	80.0	78.8	43.5	149	64.9	92.1
15 Leeds	77.1	71.8	47.6	151	67.5	91.7
=16 Birmingham	79.0	74.9	31.1	151	74.1	91.4
=16 Kent	73.7	75.9	59.0	120	73.7	91.4
=16 York	76.2	75.2	45.1	138	73.5	91.4
19 Aberdeen	81.6	80.4	31.0	186	45.8	90.8
20 Stirling	79.8	76.6	33.8	164	57.8	90.5
=21 Bangor	87.3	82.1	39.6	123	57.1	90.3
=21 Sussex	80.0	77.0	29.7	143	70.2	90.3
23 Newcastle	79.5	77.3	30.3	147	66.9	90.2
24 Surrey	81.0	77.8	30.2	148	63.4	90.0

25	Sheffield	75.4	72.0	26.8	141	78.0	89.3
26	Essex	78.4	78.6	44.3	109	67.9	88.9
27	Southampton	74.9	75.2	52.8	135	55.6	88.8
28	Plymouth	91.8	88.7	16.0	117	55.0	88.1
29	Portsmouth	82.2	77.5	32.2	102	70.8	88.0
30	Keele	79.5	82.0	25.0	121	66.5	87.6
=31	Edinburgh Napier	86.0	81.7	5.3	148	55.7	86.9
=31	Oxford Brookes	81.9	79.2	17.8	124	65.2	86.9
33	Glasgow Caledonian	83.0	79.9	12.7	180	39.1	86.8
=34	Bradford	79.3	74.1	10.6	134	72.2	86.7
=34	Central Lancashire	86.1	84.5	11.8	105	67.7	86.7
36	Robert Gordon	82.5	86.7	4.9	153	53.5	86.6
=37	Coventry	82.1	77.4	5.6	106	82.0	86.4
=37	Leicester	80.8	81.4	18.4	122	63.0	86.4
39	Abertay	84.8	78.4	5.0	147	56.3	86.2
40	Queen Margaret, Edinburgh	86.4	83.8	—	127	63.3	86.1
41	Cardiff	71.9	72.0	30.8	145	58.3	85.8
42	Aston	74.9	68.2	38.6	117	63.0	85.7
43	Northumbria	77.6	77.0	12.7	135	64.9	85.6
=44	Nottingham Trent	83.0	84.5	5.1	118	64.2	85.4
=44	Teesside	80.2	76.0	15.0	115	68.5	85.4
46	Lincoln	75.5	73.8	—	120	85.7	85.3
47	Liverpool	71.8	66.6	24.5	134	69.3	85.2
=48	Bedfordshire	86.3	83.7	16.3	92	61.8	85.0
=48	Newman	89.5	86.6	2.2	96	63.6	85.0
50	Gloucestershire	78.6	80.1	14.5	116	64.1	84.8
51	Anglia Ruskin	88.1	78.4	26.4	107	44.6	84.6
52	Salford	79.8	77.3	27.7	124	48.2	84.5
53	West of England	82.5	81.3	10.9	120	55.8	84.3
54	Ulster	80.5	78.4	39.2	114	40.6	84.2
=55	Liverpool Hope	77.3	73.0	8.6	112	73.9	84.1
=55	West of Scotland	80.8	74.8	9.4	139	53.4	84.1
57	Westminster	86.5	83.7	—	113	57.7	83.9
58	Leeds Beckett	88.9	84.8	6.4	103	51.8	83.7
59	Manchester Metropolitan	78.7	76.7	14.9	123	55.9	83.6
60	Brunel	78.9	77.4	26.0	109	52.2	83.4
61	Queen's, Belfast	71.4	71.3	26.2	134	55.1	83.3
62	Staffordshire	77.4	74.9	—	123	68.8	83.2
=63	Derby	83.2	79.5	13.5	112	50.0	83.0
=63	Wolverhampton	86.0	83.1	—	101	59.4	83.0
=65	Edge Hill	82.4	79.2	5.7	125	50.7	82.8
=65	Greenwich	86.7	83.8	—	123	46.3	82.8
=67	Huddersfield	72.9	66.1	9.5	121	72.2	82.7
=67	Hull	78.0	73.9	14.3	116	57.9	82.7
=67	Liverpool John Moores	81.5	77.8	5.8	121	54.1	82.7
=70	Roehampton	70.0	69.3	24.9	99	71.4	82.4

		Teaching quality %	Student experience %	Research quality %	Entry standards (UCAS points)	Graduate prospects %	Overall score
=70	Sheffield Hallam	87.4	82.9	14.4	106	40.3	82.4
72	London South Bank	77.2	77.7	20.1	102	50.0	81.2
73	Goldsmiths, London	70.8	67.2	33.4	115	48.2	80.9
74	East London	81.3	72.9	13.7	105	48.3	80.8
75	Suffolk	85.0	79.3	—	123	38.9	80.5
76	South Wales	77.5	73.4	—	118	55.9	80.3
=77	Chester	77.8	75.5	6.4	108	50.3	79.7
=77	Royal Holloway, London	74.1	74.8	—	132	50.0	79.7
=79	Bucks New	83.1	82.6	—	96	47.7	79.6
=79	London Metropolitan	72.6	74.7	—	88	73.0	79.6
81	Sunderland	80.6	74.9	1.9	109	48.7	79.5
82	Birmingham City	75.9	71.7	3.8	107	56.5	79.3
83	Winchester	78.0	82.4	4.4	112	42.5	79.2
84	Bath Spa	81.6	74.0	13.9	106	37.4	79.1
85	De Montfort	66.6	68.6	11.2	—	65.0	79.0
86	St Mary's, Twickenham	76.8	69.0	—	95	62.2	78.7
87	City	67.2	62.1	20.8	143	39.8	78.4
88	Brighton	75.6	68.7	12.4	110	44.5	78.3
=89	Canterbury Christ Church	79.1	72.8	—	106	44.8	77.6
=89	Middlesex	69.6	63.3	14.9	112	50.5	77.6
91	Kingston	79.7	76.0	—	99	44.3	77.5
92	Worcester	80.9	78.6	—	104	32.4	76.5
93	Bournemouth	66.3	67.7	4.7	113	53.3	76.3
94	Northampton	72.7	65.4	—	91	55.6	75.6

Employed in professional job	30%	Employed in non-professional job and Studying	5%
Employed in professional job and studying	2%	Employed in non-professional job	32%
Studying	21%	Unemployed	10%
Average starting professional salary	£26,000	Average starting non-professional salary	£16,400

Sports Science

Loughborough, the most famous name in university sport, is back on top of the Sports Science table for the first time in seven years, unseating Exeter after a rise of three places. All the universities at the top of the table have excellent sports facilities and successful teams, but it is their performance in sports degree courses and research that counts in this context. Appropriately, competition is fierce here, too, with two percentage points covering the top five institutions.

Loughborough has good scores across the board, without leading on any one measure. Glasgow has the highest entry grades, while the best graduate prospects are at Essex. Birmingham had much the best grades in the Research Excellence Framework, but it is Kingston, just outside the top 40, that tops both of our measures of student satisfaction.

The UCAS category of sport and exercise science covers more than 40 specialisms, from sports therapy to equestrian sport studies and marine sport technology. Many courses contain more science and less physical activity than some candidates expect. Essex, for example, requires maths or one of the sciences at A-level. Many universities now offer sports scholarships for elite performers, but most are not tied to a particular course and, officially at least, do not mean that the normal entry requirements are waived.

Sports science has been one of the big growth areas of UK higher education over the past decade, with a 50% increase in undergraduate entrants. It is now among the top ten subjects for applications, and 156 universities and colleges are offering courses starting in 2020. Both applications and enrolments for sport and exercise science degrees dipped for the second year in a row in 2018, however. Sports science has one of the lowest unemployment rates, at 6%, and is in the top 40 graduate prospects, but it is in the bottom five for starting salaries in professional jobs.

Sports Science	Teaching quality %	Student experience %	Research quality %	Entry standards (UCAS points)	Graduate prospects %	Overall score
1 Loughborough	83.5	89.4	52.1	168	83.3	100.0
2 Exeter	83.6	88.2	50.8	163	84.8	99.5
3 Bath	84.5	85.5	54.0	164	82.5	99.4
4 Birmingham	83.7	84.2	63.7	155	81.7	99.3
5 Edinburgh	81.3	88.0	26.1	196	81.3	98.2
=6 Durham	90.5	86.2	28.7	167	82.2	97.8
=6 Glasgow	72.4	73.8	42.3	202	83.6	97.8
8 Nottingham	87.2	90.1	31.4	165	—	97.1
9 Surrey	87.8	80.9	33.6	166	—	96.4
10 Leeds	81.7	88.8	50.5	150	72.1	94.6
11 Aberdeen	85.9	85.8	34.7	190	60.0	94.1
12 East Anglia	88.7	88.0	27.2	159	71.3	93.9
13 Liverpool John Moores	79.0	81.5	45.3	158	72.8	93.6
14 Swansea	77.5	82.5	38.8	148	78.6	92.9
15 Nottingham Trent	90.7	91.4	7.3	149	78.1	92.7
16 Essex	81.5	85.6	25.8	127	86.5	92.4
17 Robert Gordon	84.4	84.1	4.9	172	75.9	91.9
18 Stirling	78.7	76.0	33.6	156	73.4	91.3
19 Portsmouth	85.9	85.2	8.1	134	83.3	90.9
20 Aberystwyth	89.3	87.7	23.5	121	74.0	90.4
21 Bradford	82.5	83.2	9.5	156*	75.0	90.2
22 Edge Hill	92.3	89.7	7.7	151	65.5	90.0
23 Liverpool Hope	89.3	89.2	10.9	121	78.0	89.9
24 Lincoln	83.0	84.7	11.4	140	75.9	89.4
25 Bucks New	92.4	91.8	0.9	124	74.1	88.9
=26 Bangor	79.3	81.4	30.6	139	67.6	88.6
=26 Northumbria	86.1	87.0	4.4	153	67.8	88.6
28 Abertay	86.1	80.6	8.9	145	70.8	88.5
=29 Staffordshire	81.6	78.8	19.1	127	76.6	88.3

Sports Science cont

		Teaching quality %	Student experience %	Research quality %	Entry standards (UCAS points)	Graduate prospects %	Overall score
=29	Ulster	81.4	80.6	31.0	137	65.9	88.3
=31	Brunel	75.2	73.5	46.4	135	66.7	88.2
=31	Chester	88.2	88.7	6.6	120	75.4	88.2
=33	Chichester	87.6	86.8	15.2	130	67.1	87.9
=33	Gloucestershire	82.3	83.7	6.0	140	73.7	87.9
=35	Coventry	81.9	82.7	4.5	135	77.2	87.8
=35	Manchester Metropolitan	85.8	85.4	12.0	132	69.7	87.8
=35	Roehampton	79.5	74.5	20.6	107	85.4	87.8
38	Suffolk	89.5	86.5	—	130	71.9	87.6
39	Hertfordshire	87.4	85.6	0.9	129	73.7	87.5
40	Salford	85.7	85.9	3.8	144	65.8	87.0
41	Central Lancashire	86.3	83.8	5.1	134	67.8	86.6
=42	Kent	70.7	71.1	21.0	142	75.9	86.5
=42	Kingston	94.6	93.1	2.6	125	60.9	86.5
=42	St Mary's, Twickenham	81.2	80.8	4.8	130	75.4	86.5
=42	Sheffield Hallam	83.0	80.2	8.5	133	70.9	86.5
46	Oxford Brookes	87.1	84.8	3.0	132	67.6	86.4
=47	London South Bank	66.3	62.4	35.0	126	81.6	86.3
=47	Middlesex	71.4	69.0	10.0	140	81.7	86.3
=49	Cardiff Metropolitan	81.9	83.4	7.7	137	67.8	86.2
=49	Worcester	84.2	83.4	4.9	124	72.3	86.2
51	Hull	84.9	82.6	14.2	139	59.7	85.7
52	Anglia Ruskin	89.9	87.6	—	113	69.8	85.6
=53	Brighton	83.7	80.3	10.9	130	65.9	85.5
=53	London Metropolitan	85.9	83.6	—	109	76.3	85.5
55	Leeds Beckett	83.1	83.9	12.6	126	64.3	85.2
56	York St John	87.9	85.2	5.5	125	62.9	85.1
57	Solent	81.5	80.3	0.6	130	70.6	84.8
58	Wolverhampton	82.1	79.9	5.6	120	69.7	84.4
=59	Edinburgh Napier	71.9	76.9	5.3	166	62.2	84.2
=59	Huddersfield	76.4	75.9	—	137	72.2	84.2
61	South Wales	85.1	85.2	10.8	122	59.2	83.9
=62	Bedfordshire	79.8	78.3	6.7	109	73.7	83.8
=62	Bournemouth	76.8	76.5	9.0	129	68.8	83.8
64	Wales Trinity St David	88.4	87.6	—	95	70.7	83.7
65	Derby	77.5	77.0	1.7	134	68.3	83.5
66	East London	77.5	75.5	7.6	117	71.8	83.4
67	Plymouth Marjon	85.4	82.4	—	131	59.9	83.3
68	Bolton	82.2	79.1	—	118	68.7	83.2
69	Teesside	81.8	76.8	2.4	121	67.7	83.1
70	Sunderland	83.7	82.7	2.4	129	59.2	82.9
=71	West of Scotland	75.3	72.5	9.1	136	64.2	82.7

=71 Winchester	79.1	72.8	—	110	75.5	82.7
73 Strathclyde	79.1	68.8	—	188	46.7	82.6
74 Glyndŵr	71.5	70.7	3.6	123	76.2	82.5
75 Newman	80.6	80.9	2.8	129	60.0	82.2
76 Canterbury Christ Church	85.2	81.7	19.0	113	52.6	82.0
77 Greenwich	67.0	59.7	7.4	147	68.8	81.4
78 Leeds Trinity	72.0	75.9	0.8	114	66.7	79.6
79 Northampton	86.1	79.8	—	104	48.9	77.8
80 Cumbria	66.4	66.5	3.2	112	63.4	76.6
81 Bishop Grosseteste	74.6	71.3	—	99	51.2	74.3

Employed in professional job	39%	Employed in non-professional job and Studying	4%
Employed in professional job and studying	5%	Employed in non-professional job	23%
Studying	23%	Unemployed	6%
Average starting professional salary	£19,000	Average starting non-professional salary	£16,000

Theology and Religious Studies

Just 835 students began degrees in theology or religious studies in 2018 – 175 fewer than in the previous year and about a third down on the period before higher fees were introduced. Applications have followed a similar downward path, with another 12% drop in 2018. That year saw the closure of Heythrop College, part of the University of London, after 400 years of teaching theology. There are now little more than four applications to the place nationally. There are still 36 universities in the table, however, many of which offer the subjects as part of a broader degree. Religious studies can be combined with popular music at West London, Gaelic studies at Aberdeen, or film, radio and television studies at Canterbury Christ Church.

By no means all those taking degrees in theology or religious studies go into the church, but the vocation has helped to maintain relatively healthy graduate employment records. More than 40% go on to a postgraduate course, either full or part-time, and another third go straight into professional work, taking the subjects (just) into the top half of the employment table. Even in the earnings table, the subjects are in the top 40, with average starting salaries in professional jobs of £21,500 at the end of 2017.

The top three in the table remain unchanged from last year, although Durham has closed the gap slightly on first-placed Cambridge, which has the best graduate prospects and its usual high entry standards. Oxford, in fifth place, has the highest entry grades of all, while Durham produced the best results in the Research Excellence Framework. Competition is particularly keen in Scotland, which has three universities in the top ten. They are led by St Andrews, which has the highest levels of satisfaction with the quality of teaching. South Wales, although only just in the top 30, has the best scores in the sections the National Student Survey dealing with the broader student experience.

Theology and Religious Studies

		Teaching quality %	Student experience %	Research quality %	Entry standards (UCAS points)	Graduate prospects %	Overall score
1	Cambridge	—	—	44.6	194	90.4	100.0
2	Durham	85.2	77.1	56.6	183	85.5	98.6
3	Exeter	85.6	86.4	38.9	164	87.7	95.5
4	St Andrews	95.7	90.3	28.9	189*	68.6	94.8
5	Oxford	—	—	46.7	198	77.2	93.8
6	Aberdeen	90.8	87.3	39.9	158*	73.7	93.6
7	Bristol	81.1	78.6	36.0	163	89.3	93.4
8	Lancaster	83.7	72.2	53.0	155	78.1	93.2
9	Nottingham	83.8	85.4	43.9	151	78.6	92.9
10	Edinburgh	79.6	80.7	43.2	165	75.0	91.5
11	Leeds	84.3	80.3	44.4	147	73.2	91.0
12	Glasgow	85.8	83.7	21.4	180	72.0	90.4
13	Birmingham	72.7	66.3	36.2	151	86.1	88.5
14	Sheffield	74.5	73.2	25.3	147	89.2	88.1
15	Liverpool Hope	91.8	86.7	17.7	108	82.2	87.8
16	Roehampton	87.4	86.8	24.3	123	71.4	86.7
17	Kent	79.6	73.9	44.1	128	64.6	85.7
18	King's College London	74.3	68.9	37.1	156	66.7	85.5
=19	SOAS, London	73.9	66.4	34.1	142	74.4	85.1
=19	Manchester	76.6	73.0	37.2	148	63.4	85.1
21	Winchester	93.2	87.9	18.0	107	62.0	83.9
22	Queen's, Belfast	86.2	80.3	—	138	74.3	83.6
23	St Mary's, Twickenham	84.3	80.5	9.4	103	77.5	82.5
24	Chester	89.9	87.6	11.1	114	61.7	82.4
25	Canterbury Christ Church	92.9	87.4	16.3	98	58.7	82.0
26	Newman	90.2	89.8	3.5	107	65.9	81.8
27	Cardiff	69.3	65.3	33.5	139	63.9	81.2
28	Wolverhampton	88.5	86.7	—	96	65.4	79.4
29	South Wales	95.4	91.4	—	106*	50.0	79.1
30	Bishop Grosseteste	76.5	57.4	—	108	86.1	78.9
31	Bath Spa	83.8	74.0	8.3	108	61.8	78.6
32	Wales Trinity St David	85.5	74.3	30.0	111	40.0	78.2
33	York St John	80.9	71.7	4.8	104	64.6	77.3
=34	Gloucestershire	82.4	81.4	6.9	105	52.9	76.6
=34	Leeds Trinity	81.4	74.4	9.9	99	57.6	76.6
36	Chichester	76.5	73.1	—	108*	67.3	76.4

Employed in professional job	32%	Employed in non-professional job and Studying	5%
Employed in professional job and studying	3%	Employed in non-professional job	18%
Studying	33%	Unemployed	8%
Average starting professional salary	£21,500	Average starting non-professional salary	£15,912

Town and Country Planning and Landscape

Almost two-thirds of graduates of the various courses included under the rubric of planning and landscape studies go straight into professional jobs, placing the subjects in the top 12 in the employment table. They are also in the top 20 for starting salaries in graduate-level employment. The subject table reflects these successes, with five of the top six universities seeing at least nine out of ten graduates go straight into professional jobs or further study in 2017. At University College London (UCL) and Edinburgh, the rate was 100% and only three institutions dropped below 70%.

The number of applications continued to grow in 2018, topping 4,000 for the first time in the current decade. A disappointing proportion turned into enrolments, however, as the total starting courses dropped by 8%. Many students considering a career in these areas opt for a postgraduate course.

UCL has maintained its lead over Cambridge – the perennial leader until last year – at the top of the table. Cambridge still has by far the highest entry standards, but Loughborough, in eighth place, was the top performer in the Research Excellence Framework. Ulster's students are the most satisfied with the quality of teaching, while UCL has the highest rates for the broader student experience.

Entry standards are lower on landscape and garden design courses, where there are only three applications to the place, than for planning, where the ratio is more than five per place. Just six of the 25 universities in the table average more than 160 points. More than 40 universities and colleges are offering courses in landscape or garden design in 2020, some of them as an element of a broader degree in geography or architecture. Over 70 expect to run courses in various areas of planning, including disaster management and emergency planning, rural enterprise and land management, and coastal safety management.

Town and Country Planning and Landscape	Teaching quality %	Student experience %	Research quality %	Entry standards (UCAS points)	Graduate prospects %	Overall score
1 University College London	83.1	87.0	54.1	169	100.0	100.0
2 Cambridge	–	–	49.0	204	89.7	98.5
3 Edinburgh	80.1	75.3	35.1	193	100.0	97.5
4 Sheffield	84.4	84.6	36.6	151	96.2	95.1
5 Birmingham	83.9	78.1	42.0	147	97.9	94.9
6 Queen's, Belfast	82.4	83.9	35.2	139	93.3	92.6
7 Cardiff	84.2	80.4	36.8	148	85.5	92.2
8 Loughborough	69.6	67.7	58.3	156	87.5	91.6
9 Heriot-Watt	72.2	79.7	38.1	159	89.7	91.4
10 Liverpool	85.5	84.3	26.3	132	–	90.0
11 Dundee	83.4	83.7	8.7	166	85.2	89.9
12 Glasgow Caledonian	85.2	85.4	9.1	164	80.6	89.5
13 Reading	72.2	77.6	40.0	146	–	88.2
14 Manchester	72.6	75.4	36.5	155	74.1	87.3
15 Manchester Metropolitan	85.1	85.0	9.7	–	75.0	87.0
16 Newcastle	69.3	71.1	43.7	128	85.7	86.8

Town and Country Planning and Landscape cont	Teaching quality %	Student experience %	Research quality %	Entry standards (UCAS points)	Graduate prospects %	Overall score
=17 Gloucestershire	78.3	77.1	20.6	113	91.7	86.0
=17 Ulster	86.1	84.5	28.6	117	70.2	86.0
19 West of England	81.4	79.7	10.6	115	91.4	85.6
20 Greenwich	85.3	81.2	2.0	161	66.7	85.0
21 Oxford Brookes	77.6	80.4	17.6	133	76.9	84.7
22 Leeds	60.1	66.0	32.0	162	—	83.1
23 Leeds Beckett	80.2	78.7	5.6	106	68.8	79.2
24 Birmingham City	71.3	58.6	2.7	112	77.8	76.7
25 Westminster	68.8	68.8	10.7	117	50.0	73.6

Employed in professional job	58%	Employed in non-professional job and Studying	2%
Employed in professional job and studying	6%	Employed in non-professional job	11%
Studying	16%	Unemployed	8%
Average starting professional salary	£23,000	Average starting non-professional salary	£17,000

Veterinary Medicine

Only medicine itself has higher entry standards than veterinary medicine, where successful candidates had an average of 193 points on the UCAS tariff in 2018. Applications increased by 18% and enrolments by nearly 8%, taking the number of applications to the place to seven. This is still two fewer per place than in 2013, when an eighth veterinary school opened at the University of Surrey. It has helped to swell the numbers but does not yet have enough data to be included in this table.

Most courses demand high grades in chemistry and biology, with some accepting physics or maths as one alternative subject. Cambridge and the Royal Veterinary College also set applicants a specialist aptitude test that is used by a number of medical schools. Few candidates win places without evidence of practical commitment to the subject through work experience, either in veterinary practices or laboratories. The norm for veterinary science degrees is five years, but the Cambridge course takes six years and both Bristol and Nottingham offer a "gateway" year. Edinburgh and the Royal Veterinary College (RVC) also run four-year courses for graduates. There are no degrees in the subject in Wales or Northern Ireland, or in the post-1992 universities, although a number of them and several colleges offer veterinary nursing.

Edinburgh and Glasgow have retained first and second positions in the subject table. Cambridge has the highest entry grades, but Edinburgh had the top grades in the Research Excellence Framework. Nottingham, which is up to fourth place this year, again has much the most satisfied students both for the quality of teaching and the broader student experience.

Veterinary medicine is another of the rankings in which employment scores have been removed from the calculations that determine universities' positions. The scores are still shown in the table, but the review group of academic planners consulted on the *Guide* agreed that employment rates in the subject were so tightly bunched that small differences could distort the overall ranking. Veterinary medicine is in the top three subjects for earnings in professional jobs and fourth in this year's employment table.

Veterinary Medicine	Teaching quality %	Student experience %	Research quality %	Entry standards (UCAS points)	Graduate prospects %	Overall score
1 Edinburgh	88.4	82.3	46.8	212	96.1	100.0
2 Glasgow	82.6	80.1	42.3	214	99.2	95.6
3 Cambridge	—	—	43.1	218	95.7	94.6
4 Nottingham	94.2	94.9	36.4	174	98.1	93.3
5 Royal Veterinary College	80.8	78.6	40.8	180	99.0	89.3
6 Bristol	85.1	87.5	33.2	184	98.1	88.7
7 Liverpool	83.6	81.6	32.9	175	98.2	85.8

Employed in professional job	94%	Employed in non-professional job and Studying	0%
Employed in professional job and studying	0%	Employed in non-professional job	1%
Studying	2%	Unemployed	3%
Average starting professional salary	£30,000	Average starting non-professional salary	n/a

14 Applying to Oxbridge

Oxbridge (as Oxford and Cambridge are called) not only dominates UK higher education; the two universities are recognised as among the best in the world – two of the top three, according to the *Times Higher Education* global ranking. But that is not why they merit a separate chapter in this *Guide*.

The two ancient universities have different admissions arrangements from the rest of the higher education system. Although part of the UCAS network, the deadline for applications is three months earlier than for other universities, you can only apply to one or the other, and selection is in the hands of the colleges rather than the university centrally. Most candidates apply to a specific college, although you can make an open application if you are happy to go anywhere.

There have been reforms to the admissions system at both universities in recent years, in order to make the process more user-friendly to those who do not have school or family experience to draw upon. Most significantly, Cambridge has reintroduced 'pre-interview written assessments' in most subjects, with tests on the day of interview in the rest. Oxford also has tests in about ten subject areas. In addition, both universities have changed the way applicants are matched to colleges. Candidates are now distributed around colleges more efficiently, regardless of the choices they make initially.

There is little to choose between the two universities in terms of entrance requirements, although Cambridge's are generally slightly higher, and a formidable number of successful (and even unsuccessful) applicants have the maximum possible grades. However, that does not mean that the talented student should be shy about applying: both have fewer applicants per place than many less prestigious universities, and admissions tutors are always looking to extend the range of schools and colleges from which they recruit. For those with a realistic chance of success, there is little to lose except the possibility of one wasted space out of five on the UCAS application.

Most successful candidates do not regret their choice. Research by the Higher Education Policy Unit found that Oxbridge students were more satisfied than those at other Russell Group universities. Three-quarters, compared with less than half elsewhere, felt that their course provided good value for money. They worked harder and received better and more timely feedback from academics.

Famously good career prospects and attempts both by the universities and by schools and colleges to encourage more state-educated applicants are beginning to be more successful. There were 20,155 applications to Cambridge in 2019, the first time the number has exceeded 20,000 and a 5.6% increase on the previous year. Oxford also had a small increase to 23,350 applications, both universities registering record totals despite a continuing decline in the 18-year-old population.

Overall, there are now close to six applicants to every place at Cambridge and seven at Oxford, but there are big differences between subjects and colleges. As the tables in this chapter show, competition is particularly fierce in subjects such as medicine and law, but those qualified to read earth sciences or modern languages have a much better chance of success. The pattern is similar to that in other universities, although the high degree of selection (and self-selection) that precedes an Oxbridge application means that, even in the less popular subjects, the field of candidates is certain to be strong.

Both have done their best to live down their socially exclusive image, but many sixth-formers still fear that they would be out of their depth there, socially as well as academically. In fact, the state sector produces about 60% of entrants to Oxford and 65% at Cambridge – albeit only 41% at both come from non-selective schools. The dropout rate is lower than at almost any other university. The "champagne set" is still present and its activities are well publicised, but most students are hard-working high achievers with the same concerns as their counterparts on other campuses.

Diversity

Both universities and their student organisations have put a great deal of effort into trying to encourage applications from state schools, and many colleges have launched their own campaigns. But Cambridge finished bottom of our revised widening participation table and

Cambridge: The Tompkins Table 2019

College	2019	2018	2017	2016	College	2019	2018	2017	2016
Christ's	1	1	2	3	Gonville & Caius	16	14	11	19
Trinity	2	3	1	1	Fitzwilliam	17	19	21	23
Pembroke	3	2	4	2	Magdalene	18	18	16	9
Peterhouse	4	4	10	8	Murray Edwards	19	26	29	25
Churchill	5	7	5	11	Girton	20	23	24	27
Queens'	6	13	7	6	Robinson	21	24	25	22
Emmanuel	7	9	6	4	Newnham	22	22	23	21
Selwyn	8	11	9	15	Downing	23	20	20	12
St Catharine's	9	10	19	17	Clare	24	16	13	18
Trinity Hall	10	12	15	13	Hughes Hall	25	25	26	29
Corpus Christi	11	15	12	10	Homerton	26	27	28	24
King's	12	5	8	14	Wolfson	27	29	27	20
Sidney Sussex	13	17	17	16	St Edmund's	28	21	22	28
Jesus	14	6	14	7	Lucy Cavendish	29	28	18	26
St John's	15	8	3	5					

Oxford only two places higher. Six of Cambridge's colleges admitted fewer than ten black British students between 2012-16, while a quarter of Oxford's colleges failed to admit even one such student in three years.

Some colleges set relatively low standard offers to encourage applicants from the state sector who may reveal their potential at interview. Some admissions tutors will give the edge to well-qualified candidates from comprehensive schools over those from highly academic independent schools because they consider the former to have made a greater achievement in the circumstances. Others stick with tried and trusted sources of good students. The independent sector still enjoys a degree of success out of proportion to its share of the school population.

Choosing the right college

Simply in terms of winning a place at Oxford or Cambridge, choosing the right college is not quite as important as it used to be. Both universities have got better at assessing candidates' strengths and finding a suitable college for those who either make an open application or are not taken by their first-choice college. At Oxford, subject tutors from around the university put candidates into bands at the start of the selection process, using the results of admissions tests as well as exam results and references. Applicants are spread around the colleges for interview and may not be seen by their preferred college if the tutors think their chances of a place are better elsewhere. More than a quarter of successful candidates are offered places by a college other than the one to which they applied.

Cambridge relies on the "pool", which gives the most promising candidates a second chance if they were not offered a place at the college to which they applied. Those placed in the pool are invited back for a second round of interviews early in the New Year. The system lowers the stakes for those who apply to the most selective colleges – typically around 20% of offers come via the pool. Cambridge still interviews about 80% of applicants, whereas the system at Oxford

Oxford: The Norrington Table 2019

College	2019	2018	2017	2016	College	2019	2018	2017	2016
Merton	1	4	2	1	Brasenose	16	7	7	7
New College	2	5	1	18	Pembroke	17	25	3	13
Magdalen	3	2	11	3	St Hilda's	18	=13	28	27
St Catherine's	4	3	26	10	Exeter	19	18	25	25
Mansfield	5	20	15	29	Wadham	20	8	13	6
St John's	6	1	6	12	Lincoln	21	26	30	19
Queen's	7	19	5	30	Somerville	22	22	23	16
Oriel	8	12	20	2	Keble	23	23	12	17
Balliol	9	9	10	8	Worcester	24	=13	4	9
Jesus	10	6	18	14	St Peter's	25	16	29	28
Harris Manchester	11	30	27	11	Trinity	26	10	9	5
Corpus Christi	12	15	16	15	Lady Margaret Hall	27	21	14	23
University	13	17	8	4	St Anne's	28	24	19	26
Hertford	14	27	22	20	St Edmund Hall	29	29	24	21
Christ Church	15	11	17	24	St Hugh's	30	28	21	22

Oxford applications and acceptances by course

Arts	Applications			Acceptances			Acceptances to Applications %		
	2018	2017	2016	2018	2017	2016	2018	2017	2016
Ancient and modern history	84	104	92	18	23	22	21	22	24
Archaeology and anthropology	108	94	97	26	19	18	24	20	19
Classical archaeology and ancient history	88	85	108	22	22	19	25	26	18
Classics	308	293	325	115	116	121	37	40	37
Classics and English	38	37	40	10	13	8	26	35	20
Classics and modern languages	16	28	26	6	7	6	38	28	23
Computer science and philosophy	121	82	75	12	14	10	10	17	13
Economics and management	1,449	1,317	1,116	90	80	83	6	6	7
English	983	938	1,025	236	224	235	24	24	23
English and modern Languages	132	85	100	32	20	17	24	24	17
European and Middle Eastern languages	42	63	39	13	16	11	31	25	28
Fine art	231	246	251	27	28	27	12	11	11
Geography	321	405	347	81	77	70	25	19	20
History	1,036	971	1,003	231	214	227	22	22	23
History and economics	121	121	130	16	16	15	13	13	12
History and English	91	89	81	14	16	11	15	18	14
History and modern languages	89	109	109	19	28	24	21	26	22
History and politics	383	417	355	44	52	45	11	12	13
History of art	138	126	123	12	14	14	9	11	11
Law	1,541	1,501	1,403	202	192	211	13	13	15
Law with law studies in Europe	333	278	269	31	28	25	9	10	9
Mathematics and philosophy	142	108	111	18	16	18	13	15	16
Modern languages	423	436	483	157	159	159	37	36	33
Modern languages and linguistics	79	74	90	29	26	29	37	35	32
Music	204	175	188	75	69	71	37	39	38
Oriental studies	177	155	167	40	44	44	23	28	26
Philosophy and modern languages	62	48	61	22	17	17	35	35	28
Philosophy and theology	155	141	129	28	32	29	18	23	22
Physics and philosophy	156	131	108	13	13	12	8	10	11
Philosophy, politics and economics (PPE)	2,219	1,983	1,820	239	249	248	11	13	14
Theology	110	99	93	37	30	31	34	30	33
Theology and oriental studies	8	8	9	4	2	3	50	25	33
Total Arts	**11,388**	**10,747**	**10,373**	**1,919**	**1,876**	**1,880**	**16.6**	**17.4**	**20.8**

has resulted in more immediate rejections in some subjects. Overall, fewer than half of Oxford applicants are interviewed, but there is great variation by subject.

Most Oxbridge applicants still apply direct to a particular college, however, not only to maximise their chances of getting in, but because that is where they will be living and socialising,

Sciences	Applications			Acceptances			Acceptances to Applications %		
	2018	2017	2016	2018	2017	2016	2018	2017	2016
Biochemistry	689	731	558	101	108	103	15	15	18
Biological sciences	575	568	51	109	113	114	19	20	22
Biomedical sciences	438	370	339	41	37	39	9	10	12
Chemistry	585	601	659	179	184	174	31	31	26
Computer science	592	427	384	36	36	27	6	8	7
Earth sciences (Geology)	127	122	92	38	31	31	30	25	34
Engineering sciences	1,055	904	890	169	170	177	16	19	20
Experimental psychology	395	295	251	53	51	49	13	17	20
Human science	159	185	177	31	30	28	19	16	16
Materials science (including MEM)	148	167	155	40	31	35	27	19	23
Mathematics	1,567	1,371	1,333	177	185	189	11	13	14
Mathematics and computer science	371	306	226	46	33	28	12	11	12
Mathematics and statistics	202	190	210	13	13	17	6	7	8
Medicine	1,667	1,544	1,675	150	152	154	9	10	9
Physics	1,324	1,231	1,124	181	178	186	14	15	17
Psychology and philosophy (PPL)	233	189	186	26	42	30	11	22	16
Total Sciences	10,127	9,191	8,771	1,390	1,394	1,381	13.9	15.1	17.1
Total Arts and Sciences	21,515	19,938	19,144	3,309	3,270	3,261	15.2	16.4	18.9

as well as learning. Most colleges may look the same to the uninitiated, but there are important differences. Famously sporty colleges, for example, can be trying for those in search of peace and quiet.

Thorough research is needed to find the right place. Even within colleges, different admissions tutors may have different approaches, so personal contact is essential. The tables in this chapter give an idea of the relative academic strengths of the colleges, as well as the varying levels of competition for a place in different subjects. But only individual research will suggest where you will feel most at home. For example, women may favour one of the few remaining single-sex colleges (Murray Edwards, Newnham and Lucy Cavendish at Cambridge). Men have no such option.

The applications procedure

Both universities will have a UCAS deadline of 15 October 2020 (at 6pm) for entry in 2021 or deferred entry in 2022. For Cambridge, you may then take admissions tests at the beginning of November at your school or college, or other authorised centre, while other subjects will continue to administer tests when you attend for interview. The Cambridge website lists the subjects setting the pre-interview assessments, which may include reading comprehension, problem-solving test, or thinking skills assessment, in addition to a paper on the subject itself.

Cambridge applications and acceptances by course

Arts, Humanities and Social Sciences	Applications			Acceptances			Acceptances to Applications %		
	2018	2017	2016	2018	2017	2016	2018	2017	2016
Anglo-Saxon, Norse and Celtic	47	49	65	17	19	21	36.2	38.8	32.3
Archaeology	51	56	–	18	26	–	35.3	46.4	–
Architecture	438	430	360	35	37	44	8.0	8.6	12.2
Asian and Middle Eastern studies	133	114	121	47	32	38	35.3	28.1	31.4
Classics	141	172	146	63	84	78	44.7	48.8	53.4
Classics (4 years)	54	50	32	20	18	11	37.0	36.0	34.4
Economics	1,094	1,005	1,183	167	155	164	15.3	15.4	13.9
Education	112	95	105	34	34	31	30.4	35.8	29.5
English	780	763	726	187	212	190	24.0	27.8	26.2
Geography	241	324	322	95	90	97	39.4	27.8	30.1
History	576	591	607	176	181	199	30.6	30.6	32.8
History and Mod Lang	78	77	–	23	20	–	29.5	26.0	–
History and Politics	210	195	–	44	40	–	21.0	20.5	–
History of art	120	109	102	30	23	26	25.0	21.1	25.5
Human, social and political sciences	951	932	1,070	167	166	182	17.6	17.8	17.0
Land economy	312	276	248	58	56	56	18.6	20.3	22.6
Law	1,357	1,161	1,048	202	219	217	14.9	18.9	20.7
Linguistics	112	96	113	31	33	38	27.7	34.4	33.6
Modern and medieval languages	408	404	385	158	180	176	38.7	44.6	45.7
Music	157	136	130	63	65	61	40.1	47.8	46.9
Philosophy	275	270	200	46	45	48	16.7	16.7	24.0
Theology and religious studies	99	91	100	35	39	43	35.4	42.9	43.0
Total Arts, Humanities and Social Sciences	**7,746**	**7,396**	**7,063**	**1,716**	**1,774**	**1,720**	**22.2**	**24.4**	**25.0**

Sciences	2018	2017	2016	2018	2017	2016	2018	2017	2016
Computer science	1,157	867	719	133	105	99	11.5	12.1	13.8
Engineering	2,299	2,296	2,351	330	334	337	14.4	14.5	14.3
Mathematics	1,597	1,456	1,312	234	257	256	14.7	17.7	19.5
Medical sciences	1,474	1,341	1,274	265	257	269	18.0	19.2	21.1
Natural sciences	2,810	2,809	2,943	611	629	618	21.7	22.4	21.0
Psych and behavioural sciences	461	379	497	69	75	61	15.0	15.6	15.1
Veterinary medicine	357	248	228	71	59	60	19.9	23.8	26.3
Total Science and Technology	**10,155**	**9,396**	**9,018**	**1,713**	**1,700**	**1,737**	**16.5**	**18.1**	**17.9**
Total	**17,901**	**16,792**	**16,750**	**3,429**	**3,474**	**3,457**	**18.9**	**20.7**	**20.6**

Note: the dates refer to the year in which the acceptances were made.
Mathematics includes mathematics and mathematics with physics. Medical sciences includes medicine but does not include the graduate course in medicine.

At Oxford, a number of subjects (but not all) also require applicants to take a written test, either before or at the time of interview. In addition, once Cambridge receives your UCAS form, you will be asked to complete an online Supplementary Application Questionnaire (SAQ) by 22 October in most cases. For international applications to Cambridge, you must also submit a Cambridge Online Preliminary Application (COPA), by 20 September or 15 October, depending on where interviews are held; check the Cambridge website for full details.

You may apply to either Oxford or Cambridge, but not both in the same admissions year, unless you are seeking an Organ award at both universities. Interviews take place in December for those short-listed (for international applicants, Cambridge holds some interviews overseas while Oxford holds some interviews over the internet, though medicine interviewees must come to Oxford, as must EU interviewees). Applicants will receive either a conditional offer or a rejection early in the new year.

For more information about the application process and preparation for interviews, visit **www.undergraduate.study.cam.ac.uk/** or **www.ox.ac.uk/admissions/undergraduate**.

Oxford College Profiles

Balliol

Oxford OX1 3BJ 01865 277758 www.balliol.ox.ac.uk
Undergraduates: 385 Postgraduates: 343 undergraduate@balliol.ox.ac.uk

Famous as the alma mater of many prominent post-war politicians, including Prime Minister Boris Johnson, Balliol is one of the oldest and most academic colleges at the university. It usually features in the top ten of the Norrington Table, and remains just in that group currently. Balliol has maintained a strong presence in university life and is usually well represented in the Union and most other societies. Balliol students voted unanimously to establish a scholarship for a student with refugee status. The college has surprisingly spacious grounds for its Broad Street location, with the occasional concrete block nestled in among the elegant traditional buildings. It has an impressive medieval library, which allows students 24-hour access to over 70,000 books and periodicals. Balliol has cultivated a cosmopolitan atmosphere with a thriving music and drama scene. It is also one of the few colleges with a fully functional theatre, the Michael Pilch Studio. Undergraduates are guaranteed accommodation in college for their first and final years. Graduate students are usually lodged in beautiful Holywell Manor, a ten-minute walk away. Hall food is of good quality and comparatively cheap, and the JCR has its own student-run café, Pantry. The student-run bar is a favourite across the university for its imaginative cocktails, prices and juke-box.

Brasenose

Oxford OX1 4AJ 01865 277510 (admissions) www.bnc.ox.ac.uk
Undergraduates: 360 Postgraduates: 234 admissions@bnc.ox.ac.uk

Nestled beside the Radcliffe Camera, Brasenose has a convenient city-centre position. The alma mater of David Cameron, the college was one of the first to admit women in the 1970s, and now has a near-even split. While their prestigious Boat Club is believed to be one of the oldest in the world, Brasenose's approach to sport values participation over performance. There is an annual sports day between staff and students, for instance. Diversity is also a recent focus, with Brasenose celebrating cultural events like St. David's Day & Holi and putting up portraiture of BME, LGBTQ+ and female alumni. Named after the door knocker on the 13th-century Brasenose Hall, the college has a pleasant, intimate atmosphere conducive to study, although it dropped ten places in the Norrington Table last year. Law, PPE, and History are traditional strengths, and the recently renovated library is open 24-hours – there is also a separate law library. The annexe at Frewin Court near the Oxford Union means nearly all undergraduates can live in college rooms, and postgraduates are offered accommodation at the St Cross Hollybush Row sites. Student welfare is well supported: Brasenose regularly falls at the top end of student satisfaction surveys, with morale-boosting college counsellors and yoga classes on offer, amongst other activities.

Christ Church

Oxford OX1 1DP   01865 276196 (admissions)   www.chch.ox.ac.uk
Undergraduates: 442   Postgraduates: 203   admissions@chch.ox.ac.uk

The college has hit the headlines for an apparent power struggle between the Dean and the governing body, but there has been no obvious impact so far on undergraduates. Founded by Cardinal Wolsey in 1525, Christ Church boasts the largest quad in Oxford, complete with an ornamental pond full of koi carp, donated by the Empress of Japan. Its imposing buildings attract near-permanent crowds of visiting tourists, and stern bowler-hatted porters guard the doors, setting the tone of "ChCh" as one of the most academic, traditional colleges in Oxford. Around half of offers tend to be made to state school pupils, which leaves Christ Church with one of the higher proportions of private school students. The 18th-century library is palatial (although it is a listed building, and therefore not open 24 hours a day) and is supplemented by a separate law library. Accommodation, provided for all three years, is rated by students as excellent and includes flats off Iffley Road, as well as a number of wood-panelled shared sets (double rooms), and more modern rooms in the college's Blue Boar quad. 'Oxmas', when the college places huge Christmas trees in the quads, is a highlight. A three-course dinner in the famous "Hogwarts" hall costs less than £3, providing exceptional value. Unusually there is formal dining every evening, as well as an early informal sitting for those heading off to one of many evening activities. Christ Church's chapel is the cathedral of the Diocese of Oxford, and the college backs onto the enchanting Christ Church Meadows, filled variously with walkers, college rowing teams, and a herd of English Longhorn cows.

Corpus Christi

Oxford OX1 4JF   01865 276693 (admissions)   www.ccc.ox.ac.uk
Undergraduates: 258   Postgraduates: 98   admissions.office@ccc.ox.ac.uk

Corpus is one of Oxford's smallest colleges, making it a tight-knit support network. It is naturally overshadowed by its much larger neighbour, Christ Church, but makes the most of its intimate, friendly atmosphere and exquisite beauty. Although the college has only around 350 students including postgraduates, it has an admirable 24-hour library, and its original 16th-century library is still in use. Academic expectations are high and Medicine, English and Classics are especially well-established, along with PPE, which was the course of choice for both Ed and David Miliband, who studied here. Corpus can offer accommodation to all its undergraduates, one of its many attractions to those seeking a smaller community. Because of its small size, sports teams usually pair up with other colleges. It is also one of the most generous with bursaries, giving travel, book and vacation grants at an almost unparalleled level. The MBI Al-Jaber Auditorium is a large, modern and pleasant space built into a bastion of the medieval city wall and is used for music and drama, as well as for parties, art exhibitions and film screenings. Corpus's drama club, 'The Owlets', is highly regarded. The college hosts an annual charity 'Tortoise Fair' every summer, when around 1,500 people come to hear live music and watch the famous inter-college tortoise race.

Exeter

Oxford OX1 3DP   01865 279661 (academic secretary)   www.exeter.ox.ac.uk
Undergraduates: 343   Postgraduates: 233   admissions@exeter.ox.ac.uk

Exeter boasts one of the most spectacular views of the city, from its Fellows' Garden, overlooking Radcliffe Square and All Souls' College. Nestled between the High Street and Broad Street, Exeter is right in the heart of town. Most undergraduates are guaranteed three years of college accommodation, although many second-year students currently live out. The rooms are graded in price, but tend to be of good standard. The Cohen Quad development, located offsite on Walton Street, opened in 2017 and provides 90 en-suite bedrooms in a stunning state-of-the-art building. Exeter students are known to be lively and outspoken, and the student-run charity, ExVac, is a big part of the JCR's identity. Exeter counts many prominent 20th-Century writers among its alumni including Martin Amis, Alan Bennett, Phillip Pullman and J.R.R Tolkien. The John Ford Society, which funds dramatic ventures, the Fortescue Society (law) and the PPE Society (for high-profile speakers) are just three of the many on offer. The annual arts festival, in partnership with neighbours Lincoln and Jesus, brings a week of live music, theatre and poetry to Turl Street during Hilary Term.

Harris Manchester

Oxford OX1 3TD   01865 271009 (admissions)   www.hmc.ox.ac.uk
Undergraduates: 115   Postgraduates: 150   admissions@hmc.ox.ac.uk

As the university's only college for mature students (21 or older), Harris Manchester can seem a little distant from the undergraduate community. Students are proud, however, of its close-knit, friendly atmosphere. Founded in Manchester in 1786 to provide education for non-Anglican students, Harris Manchester finally settled in Oxford in 1889 after spells in both York and London. A full college since 1996, its central location with fine buildings and grounds in Holywell Street is very convenient for the Bodleian, it also has an excellent library with the best student-to-book ratio in the university. The college also offers a number of grants of up to £18,500 for second undergraduate degrees. Due to its small size, Harris Manchester offers a more limited number of degree courses, and has fewer clubs and societies than other colleges. Students are rarely left wanting though, as they can often join larger colleges' clubs. All accommodation is on the main site and rooms are available for the first and final year. Graduate accommodation is awarded by ballot, and there is no accommodation for couples or families. Food is included in the fees, which means self-catering is not an option, but its food is excellent, if expensive. The college has renovated most of its accommodation on the main site and a new student building opened in 2017, providing a further eight en-suite rooms, a lecture hall, new music practice rooms and a gym.

Hertford

Oxford OX1 3BW   01865 279404 (admissions)   www.hertford.ox.ac.uk
Undergraduates: 410   Postgraduates: 236   undergraduate.admissions@
hertford.ox.ac.uk

Though tracing its roots to the 13th century, Hertford is determinedly modern. The college was one of the first to admit women and is popular with state school applicants, thanks to its strong commitment to access. Hertford offers a £1,000 bursary to students from low income families, the value of which is being reviewed for the 2020–21 academic year, and it was the first college to become a living wage employer. The Principal, Will Hutton, a former editor of *The Observer*, has helped foster a dynamic atmosphere since his appointment in 2011. He often invites prominent speakers for lectures and panel discussions on topics such as, Britain's Constitutional Crisis'. Hertford sits opposite the Old Bodleian Library and houses one of the university's most iconic landmarks: The Bridge of Sighs. The college can lodge undergraduates for the entire course of their study. All first years live on the main site while second and third years live in catered halls near Folly Bridge or in spacious house shares in North Oxford. Music is very strong at Hertford, with a jazz band, wind band, choir and orchestra. Hertford has a fun reputation, often hiring entire nightclubs to hold 'bops' (college parties). Open mic nights and lunchtime recitals are popular. The quality of food in hall is variable, with street food pop-ups a recent feature.

Jesus

Oxford OX1 3DW   01865 279721 (admissions)   www.jesus.ox.ac.uk
Undergraduates: 358   Postgraduates: 189   admissions.officer@jesus.ox.ac.uk

Alma mater to T.E. Lawrence and Harold Wilson, Jesus consistently ranks highly for student satisfaction. It is known for being one of the friendliest colleges in the university. Founded by Elizabeth I at the request of a Welsh churchman in 1571, the college continues to maintain strong links with the country. Welsh students take a significant share of the places, chalk drawings of Welsh dragons sit proudly at the entrances to staircases in Second Quad and Jesus is home to the only Professorship in Celtic at an English University. Since 2017 the college has run a flagship summer-school encouraging Welsh state-school students to apply to Oxford. Tucked away on a small site off Turl Street, Jesus houses a 24-hour library, music rooms, and a bar. Off-site, it has squash courts and extensive playing fields with hockey, cricket, football and rugby pitches, grass tennis courts, netball courts, a boathouse, and a sports pavilion. The college also has an orchestra shared with St Peter's, and a non-selective choir. Accommodation is almost universally excellent and relatively inexpensive. Self-catering flats in north and east Oxford have enabled every graduate to live in throughout his or her Oxford stay. The college offers a number of generous bursaries and grants, including a book grant and a vacation grant. Jesus holds a shared ball with Somerville every three years.

Keble

Oxford OX1 3PG   01865 272708 (admissions)   www.keble.ox.ac.uk
Undergraduates: 422   Postgraduates: 369   admissions@keble.ox.ac.uk

Keble is one of Oxford's most distinctive colleges, built of brick in unmistakably extravagant Victorian Gothic style. Its main quad, second only to Christ Church in scale, has been likened to a castle – and to lasagne. With over 400 undergraduates and 360 full-time graduate students, it is one of the biggest colleges in Oxford, and guarantees college accommodation for undergraduates for three years. Its vibrant community spirit provides Keble students with a coveted social life. The Duke of Edinburgh opened the long-awaited H B Allen Centre in October 2019. The state-of-the-art annexe houses new accommodation for 230 graduate students and boasts a 120-seat lecture theatre and an exhibition space. The college's sporting record remains exemplary, with rugby and rowing traditional strengths. The men's first team won the Summer Eights river headship in 2018 and came a close second to Oriel in 2019. The college also has a thriving music society and the Keble O'Reilly theatre is the largest and best equipped on any college grounds, making it sought-after by budding production teams from across the university. English is a particular strong suit in this arts-supporting college. The college hall and chapel are among the most imposing and Keble café is a hit among students from across Oxford. The annual Keble Ball is one of the most popular and best value black tie events, selling out in minutes every year.

Lady Margaret Hall

Oxford OX2 6QA   01865 274300 (admissions)   www.lmh.ox.ac.uk
Undergraduates: 405   Postgraduates: 212   admissions@lmh.ox.ac.uk

Lady Margaret Hall, Oxford's first college for women, has been co-educational since 1978 and now enjoys an equal gender balance. For many students, LMH's comparative isolation – the college is three-quarters of a mile north of the city centre – is a real advantage, providing spacious and green grounds and welcome refuge from tourists. For others it means a long journey to central facilities. The college's beautiful gardens back onto the Cherwell River, allowing LMH to have its own punt house and tennis courts. LMH also boasts a theatre and gym. It has a 24-hour library, with particularly strong collections in the arts and humanities and individual study booths prized among finalists seeking solitary working conditions. Accommodation is guaranteed for first, second and third-year students since the opening of the Pipe Partridge Building, which also houses a new JCR, dining hall and lecture theatre. The Clore Graduate centre and Donald Fothergill building, opened in 2016, provides just over 40 en-suite study bedrooms for graduate students. Former *Guardian* editor Alan Rusbridger has been Principal since 2015 and has boosted its star power. LMH's strong reputation in PPE is evident in its notable alumni and students – Benazir Bhutto, the former Prime Minister of Pakistan, and Nobel Peace Prize winner Malala Yousafzai.

Lincoln

Oxford OX1 3DR   01865 279836 (admissions)   www.lincoln.ox.ac.uk
Undergraduates: 312   Postgraduates: 302   admissions@lincoln.ox.ac.uk

Lincoln's ivy-covered medieval buildings and famous library (a converted Queen Anne church) combine to produce a delightful environment in which to spend three years. The college's relaxed atmosphere is justly celebrated and city-centre accommodation is provided for all undergraduates. Lincoln is known for having the best hall food in Oxford, and for the popular Deep Hall bar. Graduate students are housed a few minutes' walk away in Bear Lane, or at sites close to the science park and on Little Clarendon Street. Lincoln has one of the largest number of scholarships available for graduate students and rewards undergraduates who perform well in examinations. The recently refurbished Garden Building is a stylish addition to the college, providing much needed space for music practice, dining and teaching. In particular, the Oakeshott room is a popular venue for screenings and performances and hosts many of the shows in the Turl Street Arts Festival. Prominent alumni include the writers John le Carré and Dr Seuss.

Magdalen

Oxford OX1 4AU   01865 276063 (admissions)   www.magd.ox.ac.uk
Undergraduates: 390   Postgraduates: 178   admissions@magd.ox.ac.uk

Perhaps the most beautiful Oxford college, Magdalen is known around the world for its tower, its deer park and its May Morning celebrations. C. S. Lewis is said to have dreamt up Narnia whilst on a walk around the awe-inspiring grounds. In recent years, the college has worked hard to shake off its public-school image, and is taking part in various diversity initiatives, including a partnership with the House of Commons to encourage BAME leaders to stand for political office. Undergraduates tend to be studious and competitive. The college consistently performs strongly in the Norrington Table, coming third last year, and has won University Challenge a record four times. A £10.5 million refurbishment of the Longwall library at Magdalen has trebled the number of reader spaces. First-year students are accommodated in the Waynflete Building and all undergraduates can be housed in college for the full length of their course. After three years of rent freezes, accommodation prices are now more level with other colleges than in the past. Over 25% of students receive some type of financial support during their studies, ranging from travel grants to funding for creative projects. The college has had a lot of sporting success on the river in recent years and punting from Magdalen's tourist-laden punt house is popular during the season. Drama is strong, with the Magdalen Players hosting a production in the gardens every summer.

Mansfield

Oxford OX1 3TF   01865 270920 (admissions)   www.mansfield.ox.ac.uk
Undergraduates: 239   Postgraduates: 173   admissions@mansfield.ox.ac.uk

Mansfield has been celebrating its best-ever performance in the Norrington Table, jumping from 20th to fifth place in a year in which almost half of the finalists took Firsts. The college has the strongest representation of state school students in Oxford, making 96% of its offers to them in 2018. Formally becoming an Oxford college in 1995, Mansfield is fairly central, with its attractive Victorian buildings close to the science park, English faculty and social science library. Its proximity to the University Parks facilitates sporting enthusiasm. Taking less than 100 undergraduates per year, the community is close-knit and the atmosphere relaxed. All undergraduates can live in college accommodation, either on site or in an annexe in east Oxford. First-year postgraduates are also housed by the College in off-site accommodation. The College has four 24-hour libraries, an unusually high number. The JCR and Crypt Cafe are popular for socialising and casual study, as is the sun terrace during the summer months. The recently completed Hands building provides additional accommodation, a new lecture building and a home for the Law faculty's Bonavero Institute of Human Rights.

Merton

Oxford OX1 4JD   01865 286316 (admissions)   www.merton.ox.ac.uk
Undergraduates: 302   Postgraduates: 222   undergraduate.admissions@
                                                         merton.ox.ac.uk

Founded in 1264 by Walter de Merton, Bishop of Rochester and Chancellor of England, Merton is one of Oxford's oldest and most prestigious colleges. It has an enduring reputation for academic excellence – and a strict administration to go with it – reflected in its position usually at or near the top of the Norrington Table. It headed the ranking again last year. Merton houses the oldest continuously functioning library for university students and academics in the world, although unfortunately it is not open 24 hours per day. Accommodation is some of the cheapest in the university, of good standard and offered for all three years. Merton's food is well-priced and among the best; formal hall is served six times a week. The college provides generous bursaries and grants, and has a free gym. Merton's many diversions include the Merton Floats, its dramatic society, the Bodley Club for literary speakers, and an excellent Winter Ball every three years. Its choir and the organ have a growing reputation. The college recently established a scheme inviting local schoolgirls to form a choir, enabling them to participate in Merton's musical tradition.

New College

Oxford OX1 3BN   01865 279272 (admissions)   www.new.ox.ac.uk
Undergraduates: 418   Postgraduates: 295   admissions@new.ox.ac.uk

New College is very academic, finishing second in the Norrington Table last year. In spite of its name, the college is extremely old. Founded in 1379 by William of Wykeham, New is large and much more relaxed than most expect behind its daunting facade. It is a bustling place, as proud of its excellent music and its bar as of its academic prestige. Musical students flourish here with an orchestra, chamber groups and a world-class male-voice choir which sings a Choral Evensong six evenings a week during term. The new Clore Music Studios on Mansfield Road were completed in 2019. Traditionally poor at attracting state school students, the college has been making efforts to change this with its "Step Up" access initiative. All first, second and fourth-year students can live in college and most third years live out in private accommodation. Over 90% of the rooms are en-suite and many have recently been equipped for disabled access. New College boasts an enchanting common room and the walled gardens are a memorable sight, especially the other-worldly mound at their heart. The grounds provide the perfect setting for the white-tie Commemoration Ball, held every three years. Students also benefit from summer access to a chalet (shared with Balliol and University) near Mont Blanc. The college is currently planning a new tower, which has caused tension with neighbouring Mansfield College due to its height and location.

Oriel

Oxford OX1 4EW   01865 276522 (admissions)   www.oriel.ox.ac.uk
Undergraduates: 323   Postgraduates: 200   admissions@oriel.ox.ac.uk

Although it is nicknamed "Toriel" due to the strong presence of its students in the Union and Conservative Association, Oriel is a friendly, centrally located college. It is known for its unusual portico in the main quad – and more recently, for the controversial statue of Cecil Rhodes, which looks out onto the High Street. Behind this, however, are some impressive achievements. The college is traditionally described as having "a strong crew spirit", reflecting its traditions on the river; in the 2018 Torpids competition, Oriel achieved a rare Double Headship, with both the women's and men's crews coming Head of the River. Academically the college usually falls at the top end of the Norrington Table, finishing in the top ten last year. Oriel has a strong sporting reputation and facilities include a boathouse, impressive sports ground, squash courts and multiple gyms. Formal dining is popular in the college and the medieval hall provides one of the most atmospheric eating experiences in Oxford despite the fairly average food. Accommodation is banded A*– D with varying rents, which can be quite divisive, but it is guaranteed for the duration of an undergraduate course. Extensive (mainly graduate) accommodation is provided one mile away off the popular Cowley Road. Several flats have been completed recently, providing some limited facilities for couples. The annual Garden Play is a highlight of Trinity Term, with an active chapel choir and a visiting musicians fleshing out the programme of cultural activities.

Pembroke

Oxford OX1 1DW   01865 276412 (admissions)   www.pmb.ox.ac.uk
Undergraduates: 378   Postgraduates: 240   admissions@pmb.ox.ac.uk

Tucked away off St Aldate's, Pembroke is a welcoming and inclusive community with a growing state school intake. Blending traditional and modern architecture, its relaxed atmosphere contrasts with its neighbour Christ Church. History is a traditionally strong subject, with several students winning university wide prizes over the years. However, the college has a varied record in the Norrington Table, finishing just inside the top 20 last year. Pembroke has been able to accommodate all undergraduates since an elegant new quad opened in April 2013, and the Sir Geoffrey Arthur Building on the river, ten minutes' walk away, offers excellent facilities, including a large rehearsal space. Students are active in drama and music and there is a Trinity term musical each year. The college also often hosts talks and panels by high-profile figures in the media. Food is among the most expensive in Oxford and students living on site must pre-pay for a minimum of six dinners a week at a rate of £315 per term. Rowing is strong, with Pembroke men and women traditionally performing well on the river and several going on to represent the university crews.

Queen's

Oxford OX1 4AW   01865 279161   www.queens.ox.ac.uk
Undergraduates: 336   Postgraduates: 177   admissions@queens.ox.ac.uk

With its beautiful neo-Classical dome and bell-tower, Queen's is one of the more striking sights of the High Street. Its academic record is more patchy, but it is in last year's top ten in the Norrington Table. All Queen's students are offered accommodation throughout their degree, with first-years housed on the main site, and subsequent year groups housed in annexes around central Oxford. The main site is beautiful and the facilities are excellent, with many of the rooms en-suite. The two refurbished squash courts are said to be the best in Oxford and the college has a gym, and a lecture theatre used for concerts and film screenings. The Upper Library is one of the finest reading rooms in Oxford, and the New Library was completed in 2017. Queen's provides generous book and travel grants, and has active sport, drama, and music societies. The Trinity Term garden play is a highlight of the calendar. Alumni include Tim Berners-Lee and Rowan Atkinson, the masterminds behind the World Wide Web and Mr Bean respectively. Queen's is fully catered and therefore has limited kitchen access, but the food is reasonably priced. The beer cellar is one of the most popular and the JCR facilities are better than average; the daily JCR afternoon tea is a must.

St Anne's

Oxford OX2 6HS   01865 274840 (admissions)   www.st-annes.ox.ac.uk
Undergraduates: 439   Postgraduates: 352   admissions@st-annes.ox.ac.uk

Occupying a spacious site in the north of the city, St Anne's makes up in community spirit what it lacks in sandstone grandeur. The ship-shaped dining hall, with its skylight and absence of portraits, serves up some of the best food in Oxford. The new library and academic centre on Woodstock Road is an impressive sight with 2,000 books added to its shelves every year. The college coffee shop, STACS, is quaint and popular with students wanting to take a break from their studies. The college has recently had a strong presence in the university journalism scene, and its men's and women's football teams won tournaments last year. A15-minute cycle from the Bodleian, accommodation is guaranteed to undergraduates for three years, and the college also operates an equalisation scheme, giving grants to students wishing to live out. Postgraduates are housed in Summertown, a five-minute cycle away. St Anne's students benefit from a number of internships, CV clinics and career workshops organised by the college. It has its roots in the 'Society of Home Students' a 19th-century group that sought to help women achieve the education they deserve. Their progressive legacy remains today. St Anne's has the highest proportion of female undergraduates at 55%, and Tom Ilube, named the most influential British person of African-Caribbean origin in 2017, is an advisory fellow.

St Catherine's

Oxford OX1 3UJ   01865 271703 (admissions)   www.stcatz.ox.ac.uk
Undergraduates: 505   Postgraduates: 428   admissions@stcatz.ox.ac.uk

St Catherine's strikes an immediate chord with those seeking to avoid the uniformity of some other colleges. Arne Jacobsen's modernist design for "Catz", one of Oxford's youngest and largest undergraduate colleges, has attracted much attention for its spacious site (including a rare car park) and laid-back atmosphere. The student body describes itself as "Oxford without the stereotypes." Close to the Law, English and Social Science faculties, the university science park and the pleasantly rural Holywell Great Meadow, St Catherine's is a lot nearer to the city centre than it feels. The Wolfson library is open until midnight. Rooms are small but tend to be warmer than in other, more venerable, colleges, and are now available on site for first, second and third-year students. Catz has the largest bar in Oxford and their "bops" are always very popular. There is an excellent theatre, as well as an on-site boathouse, gym and squash courts. Like many of the larger colleges, sporting success is high – the men's rugby team topped the league in 2019, with the women's football team also placing highly. The College has increased welfare support with a College Counsellor and the JCR has created a gender expression fund for transgender students. Six portraits of female college members have been commissioned and are due to be hung in the library's (currently all-male) collection. The college is a hub for university drama and hosts the annual Cameron Mackintosh Chair of Contemporary Theatre, whose incumbents have included Arthur Miller, Sir Ian McKellen and Sir Tom Stoppard. With around 500 such students, St Catherine's has the highest undergraduate population in Oxford.

St Edmund Hall

Oxford OX1 4AR   01865 279009 (admissions)   www.seh.ox.ac.uk
Undergraduates: 396   Postgraduates: 296   admissions@seh.ox.ac.uk

Dating back to the 13th century, St Edmund Hall – "Teddy Hall" – has one of Oxford's smallest college sites but one of its most populous. The college offers all first year undergraduates accommodation in its medieval quads a stone's throw from the Bodleian. The sporting culture is vigorous, with the men's rugby and basketball teams securing victory in Cuppers tournaments. It is also known for creative writing, with a Writer in Residence, annual journalism prizes, weekly writers' workshops and an annual publication. High-achieving students can apply to the Masterclass Fund for up to £1,000 per year to finance advanced coaching in their area of interest. Academically, Teddy Hall tends to yo-yo between the middle and the bottom of the Norrington Table. Last year, it came 29th out of 30 colleges. Accommodation is offered for two years for undergraduates and there is an annexe at Norham Gardens, close to the University Parks. The food is more expensive than most colleges but the quality is very high.

St Hilda's

Oxford OX4 1DY   01865 286620 (admissions)   www.st-hildas.ox.ac.uk
Undergraduates: 399   Postgraduates: 183   admissions@st-hildas.ox.ac.uk

Although the college, founded in 1893, lasted more than 100 years as an all-female institution, the governing body voted in 2006 to admit men. There are now equal numbers of males and females. The college prides itself on its commitment to fostering an inclusive and laid-back atmosphere, introducing the post of 'Class Liberation Officer' to support working class students. Like the other originally female colleges, St Hilda's boasts an impressive library, which is particularly well stocked for English. The college has beautiful riverside gardens, allowing students to go punting from the college site, and is close to the lively social scene of hip Cowley Road. Some visitors mistake the college for the Magdalen School, which is next door, and there are more teenagers in the area than around other colleges. St. Hilda's has a purpose-built music building and recording studio, and the drama society puts on termly plays in the theatre. Accommodation is guaranteed for first years and finalists, and the common room and student-run bar have been renovated and enlarged. Many of the rooms offer some of the best river views in Oxford, with the city's spires as a backdrop. By Autumn 2020 phase one of a rejuvenation project should be complete with a new MCR and Porter's Lodge. St. Hilda's is known for its liberal leanings, its spacious, light-filled buildings, and its annual ball, which prides itself on being the most affordable in Oxford.

St Hugh's

Oxford OX2 6LE   01865 274910 (admissions)   www.st-hughs.ox.ac.uk
Undergraduates: 425   Postgraduates: 366   admissions@st-hughs.ox.ac.uk

St Hugh's, alma mater of former Prime Minister Theresa May, is well-liked for its relaxed atmosphere and spacious grounds. Originally founded to admit only women, St Hugh's was criticised by students in 1986 when it began admitting men, but there is now an equal male/female ratio in a large student body. St Hugh's is a bicycle ride from the city centre, or a manageable 25-30 minutes on foot, although this is far enough to make it the butt of student jokes. It is ideal for those seeking a place to live and study away from the madding crowd, and its gardens provide the perfect backdrop for a springtime outdoor cinema. Despite having one of the biggest and best libraries, open 24 hours, academic pressure remains comparatively low and it is bottom of the latest Norrington Table. St Hugh's guarantees on-site accommodation to undergraduates for the duration of their degree, although the standard of rooms is variable. The quality of food is high, with themed formal dinners on special occasions, and meals are subsidised. The college also boasts an on-site café and a comfortable JCR. The Dickson Poon Building, a recent Chinese studies centre, provides an additional place to work and socialise. As the college enjoys extensive grounds, there is space for a croquet lawn and tennis courts, as well as areas for Frisbee and football.

St John's

Oxford OX1 3JP   01865 277317 (admissions)   www.sjc.ox.ac.uk
Undergraduates: 395   Postgraduates: 236   admissions@sjc.ox.ac.uk

St John's is one of Oxford's powerhouses in academics, sport, and student life, excelling in almost every field and boasting arguably the most beautiful gardens in the university. Founded in 1555 by a London merchant, it is Oxford's wealthiest college by some distance, and makes the most of its resources by providing guaranteed accommodation at a subsidised rate for all its undergraduates as well as generous book grants and prizes. The St John's Discount Scheme, which gives students discounts at many Oxford shops and eateries, is the envy of other colleges. St John's consistently performs well on the Norrington Table, topping the ranking in 2018, although dropping to sixth last year. The college is located on a large, quiet site off the attractive St Giles'. Modernist architecture proliferates more than would be expected, tucked away behind the imposing front quads, and most students are housed in these blocks. Academic standards are high, and students benefit from the impressive library and recently renovated study spaces and attached café. The college has a strong sporting tradition especially in women's rowing, a chapel choir, drama society and orchestra. Its reputation as the most disliked or unfriendly college in the university is primarily down to envy. As befits such an all-round strong college, entry is fiercely competitive.

St Peter's

Oxford OX1 2DL   01865 278863 (admissions)   www.spc.ox.ac.uk
Undergraduates: 356   Postgraduates: 215   admissions@spc.ox.ac.uk

Opened as St Peter's Hall in 1929, St Peter's has been an Oxford college since 1961. Its eclectic mix of medieval, Georgian and 19th-century buildings are in the city centre and close to most of Oxford's main facilities, including the enormous new Westgate shopping centre. Though still young, St Peter's is well represented in university life and generally hovers in the middle of the Norrington Table. History teaching is particularly good and the Master, Mark Damazer, former controller of BBC Radio 4, regularly invites high-profile speakers. Accommodation is available for students in their first and third years, varying from traditional rooms to new purpose-built rooms a few minutes' walk away. Considering it is one of the least endowed colleges, St Peter's facilities are impressive, including a recently upgraded JCR and a popular student bar (one of the few that is entirely student run). Formal hall is held twice a week and meals are on a pay-as-you-go basis. Music is well represented with the JCR hosting popular open mic nights every two weeks, along with a roster of other cultural activities. Linton Quad and the chapel have undergone recent refurbishment, and the new Hubert Perrodo building has won multiple design awards. The college has a proud sporting heritage, being particularly strong at rugby and rowing.

Somerville

Oxford OX2 6HD   01865 270619 (admissions)   www.some.ox.ac.uk
Undergraduates: 425   Postgraduates: 209   secretariat@some.ox.ac.uk

Named after the astronomer Mary Somerville, this was one of the first two colleges at Oxford founded to admit women. Members celebrated the news that the pioneering academic would become the first woman, other than a royal, to grace a British bank note. Since 1994, Somerville has admitted men and women equally, while retaining its pioneering and inclusive ethos. Alma mater to Margaret Thatcher, Indira Gandhi and Nobel prize winner Dorothy Hodgkin, Somerville is one of the most international and diverse colleges. Standing just off the attractive St Giles' and close to the Ashmolean Museum and Taylor Institution, rooms are provided for three years to most undergraduates and all first-year postgraduates. Somerville welcomes state school applicants and drew nearly two thirds of its UK undergraduate intake from such schools last year. There are kitchens in all buildings and subsidised food in hall. There are a number of clubs, from the excellent chapel choir to a baking society and the Boat Club. There is also a new Arts Budget in place to fund various creative projects. Somerville usually ranks in the bottom half of the Norrington table. The 24-hour library is one of largest among colleges. Somerville students are often prominent in the university-wide journalism and theatre scenes. The college secured its third President of the Oxford Union in 2016.

Trinity

Oxford OX1 3BH   01865 279860 (admissions)   www.trinity.ox.ac.uk
Undergraduates: 299   Postgraduates: 135   admissions@trinity.ox.ac.uk

Architecturally impressive with enviable lawns, Trinity is one of Oxford's least populous – but most popular – colleges. It admits some 80 undergraduates each year and is among the strongest academically. It often finishes in the top ten of the Norrington Table, although it is in the bottom five in the latest edition. It is ideally located on Broad Street, next to Blackwell's bookshop and the Weston Library, a short stroll from the University Parks and the science park. It has its own debating and drama societies. The Trinity Players stage a signature garden play on Trinity lawn which is popular across the university. Facilities are impressive, with a well-stocked college gym and squash courts. Trinity Boat Club and the chapel choir are the largest societies. Journalism is popular and students produce a termly newsletter called *The Broadsheet*. Usually, all undergraduates are given a room on the main site in their first and second years, with the majority of third and fourth years living on charming Woodstock Road in the north of the city. Trinity Students rate the food highly for both its quality and price. Its lavish white-tie Commemoration Ball, held once every three years, has one of the biggest budgets in Oxford and sells out in minutes.

University

Oxford OX1 4BH   01865 276677 (admissions)   www.univ.ox.ac.uk
Undergraduates: 394   Postgraduates: 224   admissions@univ.ox.ac.uk

"Univ," as it is popularly known, was the first Oxford college to be able to boast an alumnus in the Oval Office. Bill Clinton was a Rhodes Scholar at University in the late 1960s. Centrally located on the High Street, the college is one of three claiming to be Oxford's oldest. Univ is making a significant effort to shake off its private school image and become "the friendly college" with a new 'Opportunity Programme', increasing the undergraduate intake by 10% and offering those new places exclusively to applicants from a low-income background. In 2019, Baroness Valerie Amos, Labour Life Peer and former senior UN official, was appointed as the new Master making her Oxford's first black head of house. Univ has a generous bursary scheme, and travel grants are available for study trips abroad. Academic expectations are high and the college prospers in most subjects, especially Law, PPE, and the sciences. First and third years are housed on site, with second years living in a comfortable annexe near Summertown. A newly-refurbished accommodation block provides double beds, kitchens and en-suites for students who snag rooms there (by random ballot), as well as widespread disabled access and a basement squash court. University is particularly well represented on the river, with men's and women's crews (of which there are many) doing well in recent years, and a state-of-the-art boathouse (built after an arson attack on the previous one in 1999). The college also has access to a chalet in the foothills of Mont Blanc, with reading parties welcome in the summer. Multiple 24-hour libraries and close proximity to the Bodleian make University ideal for bookish students. Beyond the libraries, the chapel choir is excellent, and the students put on a well-attended comedy Revue every Hilary Term.

Wadham

Oxford OX1 3PN   01865 277545 (admissions)   www.wadham.ox.ac.uk

Undergraduates: 466   Postgraduates: 208   admissions@wadham.ox.ac.uk

Wadham is best known among students for its progressive and liberal atmosphere and its leftist politics, although it boasts a large and imposing site to rival the most touristic of colleges. The JCR – or student union as it has rebranded itself – is famously active, although the breadth of political opinion is greater than its left-wing stereotype suggests. The college is very strong on admitting students from state schools, partly due to its successful Student Ambassador Scheme. Its gardens are beautiful and host Shakespeare performances each summer. More languages are offered here than any other college and the 24-hour library is complete with a well-stocked Persian history section. Although weekday dinners are served in the 17th-century hall, Wadham is the only college with no gowned formal hall sittings. Undergraduates are guaranteed accommodation on site in their first year and final year, and in other years they are offered accommodation in two modern college-owned complexes roughly a mile from the centre of town. Highlights in the social calendar are Queer Week, a riotous celebration of LGBTQIA culture, and Wadstock, the college's open-air spring music festival. Student welfare is a big priority at Wadham. The Student Union has four welfare officers, along with a women's officer, an LGBTQIA officer, a people of colour and racial equality officer, a disabled students officer and a trans rep. The women's and men's rowing teams perform consistently well. The college also contributes to the local community through a new scheme which delivers food that is not eaten in hall to a local homeless centre.

Worcester

Oxford OX1 2HB   01865 278391 (admissions)   www.worc.ox.ac.uk

Undergraduates: 483   Postgraduates: 179   admissions@worc.ox.ac.uk

Worcester is to the west of Oxford what Magdalen is to the east: a spacious contrast to the urban rush of the city centre. The college's subtle exterior conceals a delightful environment, including some striking Baroque architecture, extensive gardens, medieval cottages, and a lake. It is one of Oxford's most popular colleges due to its beauty, academic reputation, and student satisfaction. The college gardeners post horticultural updates to their own blog and the Buskins dramatic society makes use of the beautiful grounds, with annual summer Shakespeare performances. Worcester has a great reputation for sport; it is the only college with its sports grounds on site. Arts Week is an annual highlight and includes a delightful mix of plays, concerts and recitals. Top Shakespeare scholar Sir Jonathan Bate stepped down as provost prematurely in March 2019, and the interim Provost Dr Kate Tunstall faced a conservative backlash from students when she tried to relax dining traditions with the JCR voting to uphold the traditional Grace, and practice of standing as their tutors enter. Accommodation, guaranteed for three years and graded by price, is within the grounds, or less than 300 metres away in comfortable rooms with kitchen access. The stylish Sultan Nazrin Shah Centre opened recently, providing extra lecture theatres and rehearsal space. The college boasts good quality food, and has a formal sitting every night. Like Magdalen and New, it hosts a Commemoration Ball every three years, a highlight of the social calendar. Students hold a "Worcester in the Park" event every summer term, with music and Pimm's.

Cambridge College Profiles

Christ's

Cambridge CB2 3BU   01223 334900   www.christs.cam.ac.uk
Undergraduates 437   Postgraduates 249   admissions@christs.cam.ac.uk

Christ's, sitting on Saint Andrew's Street, lies right by Cambridge's shopping centre while also backing onto Christ's Pieces, with its tennis courts and lawns. With alumni ranging from Charles Darwin to John Milton and Sacha Baron Cohen, the college is sometimes now considered a bit of an academic hothouse, having placed first in the Tompkins Table for the last two years, with more than 40% of students awarded a first in 2019. When not in the library, however, students at Christ's can take advantage of being less than a minute's walk away from staple student nightclub, Ballare (dubbed Cindie's). Rooms are allocated on a ballot basis, but students who achieve first-class exam results are given preference, as one of the few remaining colleges to run a 'Scholar's Ballot'. Most undergraduates live in College, although a few are in row houses on King's Street and Jesus Lane. About 40% of rooms are en-suite (including small, single bedrooms in New Court and large, double bedrooms in Second Court). There are also more traditional rooms and sets (a study room and bedroom) in the college's beautiful First Court. The Visual Arts Centre, student theatre and well-attended student film group keeps Christ's culturally vibrant. On the sports front, Christ's is particularly strong on the football pitch and is one of only five Oxbridge colleges to have its own swimming pool, which is thought to be the oldest still in use in the UK. Celebrating students jump into the pool after their final exams.

Churchill

Cambridge CB3 0DS   01223 336202   www.chu.cam.ac.uk
Undergraduates 485   Postgraduates 375   admissions@chu.ac.uk

Churchill is a little way out of the city centre but is the closest to the West Cambridge Site, which houses many of the university's science departments – a fitting location for a STEM-heavy college. It has one of the largest college campuses in Cambridge and though the brutalist architecture may not be to everyone's taste, Churchill has some of the best on-site facilities: a gym, theatre-cum-cinema, music room and recording studio, squash and tennis courts, grass pitches and the largest dining hall in Cambridge. A new court, housing 68 en-suite rooms (reputed to be the university's plushest undergraduate accommodation), was completed in 2016, as was a new boathouse. More graduate accommodation opened in September and has already been shortlisted for an award. More than 40% of the college's rooms are now en-suite. Churchill is one of the least traditional Cambridge colleges: students are welcome to walk on the grass and they don't wear academic gowns when dining formally in hall. It is also one of the few colleges not to charge a fixed bill for catering in addition to meal charges – a move popular with Churchillians. While it often has one of Oxbridge's highest state undergraduate intakes – 76.5% in 2017 – this dropped to 62.2% in 2018. Male students outnumber female students by more than two to one. The college performs well academically (fifth in the most recent Tompkins Table, up from seventh the previous year), a success sometimes attributed to what students have called its 'dangerously comfortable' library.

Clare

Cambridge CB2 1TL   01223 761612   www.clare.cam.ac.uk

Undergraduates 512   Postgraduates 284   admissions@clare.cam.ac.uk

Clare is a beautiful central college, next to King's College chapel, with ornate lawns and a pretty bridge and gate opening onto the Backs. Amongst the oldest colleges in Cambridge, founded in 1326, it has a strong reputation for music, a world-renowned choir and regular recitals. The student bar is in Clare Cellars, which often plays host to DJ and live music nights that draw students from across the university. For accommodation, Old Court offers a traditional experience, while Memorial Court, across the river, is close to the University Library and both humanities and science departments. The Colony, closer to the boathouse on the slopes of Castle Hill, is made up of large houses converted into student lodgings. However, extensive renovations are taking place on Old Court, as the College tries to update the space for its 700th anniversary, with plans to build a new River Room Café with terrace views onto the Cam. All first years live in Memorial, Thirkill or Lerner Court (a modern living space opened in 2008). The college has an enthusiastic boat club, and very good sports facilities just beyond the botanic garden (a ten-minute cycle ride). The college has a good gender split – almost 50:50 among undergraduates. It fell to near the bottom of the latest Tompkins Table, however, in 26th place from 16th last year. An arts-heavy list of notable alumni includes David Attenborough and the journalist Matthew Parris.

Corpus Christi

Cambridge CB2 1RH   01223 338056   www.corpus.cam.ac.uk

Undergraduates 286   Postgraduates 262   admissions@corpus.cam.ac.uk

Corpus Christi may be one of Cambridge's smallest colleges, with an undergraduate population that hovers just below 300, but this makes it one of the most tight-knit. It is the only Oxbridge college to have been founded by townspeople (in 1352) and is home to the oldest court in either university. That said, there is plenty that is up-to-date. Corpus plans to create 30 places specifically for undergraduates from under-represented backgrounds in the next three years. The college will also provide these students with a three-week 'bridging course' before they matriculate. Accommodation is varied: some students are housed in ancient college rooms, while others are accommodated away from, but close to, the main college site, in the Beldam, Bene't Street and Botolph Court buildings. The college has its own gym, playing fields and an open-air swimming pool, located in the Leckhampton site, just over a mile away. All undergraduates are guaranteed college accommodation, although some rooms are allocated on the basis of exam results, which is not always popular. Many in Cambridge know Corpus for its unusual clock, donated by alumnus and inventor John C Taylor in 2008, which sits on the corner of Trumpington Street. It's displayed on the outside of the eponymous Taylor Library, which is housed, along with the college bar, in Kwee Court. To expand the sports offering, Corpus joins up with King's and Christ's Colleges to form collaborative 'CCK' sports teams. It also has a small but much-used theatre, the Corpus Playroom, where students from across the university stage plays and put on comedy nights. The Chaplain's ABBA parties are considered a social highlight.

Downing

Cambridge CB2 1DQ   01223 334826   www.dow.cam.ac.uk
Undergraduates 467   Postgraduates 342   admissions@dow.cam.ac.uk

Downing students enjoy vast amounts of open space for a central college, being able to walk and play on the Paddock, which hosts many a garden party when exams are finished for the summer. Tales of double beds and en-suite bedrooms make Downing accommodation the envy of students at many other colleges, although this is reflected in relatively high rents. Downing also enjoys a lively social scene, with the comfortable Butterfield Café and Bar hosting pub quizzes and live music in the evenings, while providing a relaxed study space during the day. The college was originally founded for the study of law and natural sciences, and while it is still popular with scientists, lawyers and geographers thanks to its fall-out-of-bed-and-into lectures proximity to their faculties, it is now home to an eclectic body of students studying all subjects. Extra-curricular strengths lie on the sports field (Downing is known as a fearsome opponent on both the rugby field and the river) and in the arts thanks to the Howard Theatre, a 160- seat space, a vibrant Drama Society that hosts a yearly festival of student writing, and the new Heong Gallery dedicated to modern and contemporary art that opened in 2016.

Emmanuel

Cambridge CB2 3AP   01223 334290   www.emma.cam.ac.uk
Undergraduates 512   Postgraduates 201   admissions@emma.cam.ac.uk

Students at 'Emma' are often fiercely loyal to their college, highlighting a welcoming, convivial culture. Emma regularly comes in the top ten in the Tompkins Table (seventh in the most recent ratings), however, and has fielded a couple of successful University Challenge teams. Students love it for its central location, busy and cheap bar, well-subsidised accommodation (which includes a free weekly load of washing in the rent) and the spacious grounds where ducks roam. Students are able to walk across the 'Paddock' in the centre of college, and can be found revising on the grass and hosting barbecues in the summer. The open-air swimming pool is said to be the oldest in Britain still in use. Founded by Puritans in the 1580s, Emma tries to maintain a forward-thinking and egalitarian atmosphere. It has a relatively even gender split, a female master and nearly 72% of undergraduates admitted in 2018 were from the maintained sector. Societies and sports focus more on inclusion than competition with a diverse array of activities to choose from. But Emma does enjoy sporting success too: last year it was runner-up in Cricket Cuppers, while Emma students are regularly featured in Blues teams. Its understated yet beautiful Christopher Wren chapel hosts a number of concerts organised by the music society. Other less conventional college clubs include Mountaineering Society and Emmanuel Real Ice Cream Society. As one of the better-endowed colleges, Emmanuel offers a number of bursaries and scholarships.

Fitzwilliam

Cambridge CB3 0DG   01223 332030   www.fitz.cam.ac.uk
Undergraduates 475   Postgraduates 411   admissions@fitz.cam.ac.uk

Founded in the 19th century to increase access to Cambridge, Fitzwilliam is proud of its heritage as a college committed to widening participation. It moved to its current location (in the grounds of a Regency estate) in 1963 and while it doesn't have the archetypal ancient architecture, the college gardens are some of the most beautiful and well-tended in town, and the dining hall boasts an eye-catching Lantern roof. If you climb to the top of its library, you will be standing at the highest point in the city. The atmosphere in college is one of a tight-knit community and students are accommodated throughout their degrees in one of 400 rooms in college or in houses minutes from the campus. The friendly feel is also helped by the busy coffee shop where students and staff alike indulge in the well-reputed homemade cakes. As well as extensive renovations to its Central Building and dining hall, the accommodation of 'Fitz', as the college is fondly known, has also been modernised. All first-year rooms are semi en-suite, equipped with a shower and washbasin, and most of the student kitchens contain ovens (many of the older colleges provide students with basic 'gyp rooms' that only contain fridges and hobs). On the academic front, Fitz ranges from mid-Tompkins Table to around 20th place, coming in 17th last year, and it does well on the sports field – recent success includes winning the inter-college cricket four years in a row – thanks to its well-kept pitches (five minutes away) and a new gym.

Girton

Cambridge CB3 0JG   01223 338972   www.girton.cam.ac.uk
Undergraduates 500   Postgraduates 287   admissions@girton.cam.ac.uk

Girton is as far out to the west of Cambridge as Homerton is to the east, but for some, the distance out of town is a good reason to apply there. Its grounds, which include lawns, orchards, sports pitches and courts, majestic brick buildings and an indoor swimming pool, amount to some 50 acres. Girton students either live on this tranquil campus, in rooms that range from atmospheric Victorian bedrooms to modern en-suites in Ash Court, or they live off-site in college owned houses or at the recently opened Swirles Court (located on the university's new North West Cambridge Development at Eddington), although accommodation is some of the most expensive in the University. Founded as a women's college in 1869, it was the first to go co-educational and now has an equal gender balance that recently has been slightly weighted in favour of men. There is still an all-female corridor, which female students can state a preference for in the accommodation ballot. Being out of town fosters a familial feel and many at Girton would consider themselves Girtonian first and Cambridge students second. Academically, it was at the lower end of the Tompkins Table in 20th place last year. It does have a vibrant extra-curricular scene, however. It is known for the arts and has its own museum, dark room for photography and permanent 'Peoples' Portraits' exhibition.

Gonville & Caius

Cambridge CB2 1TA   01223 332413   www.cai.cam.ac.uk
Undergraduates 593   Postgraduates 250   admissions@cai.cam.ac.uk

It is hard to believe that Gonville & Caius (pronounced 'keys') is steps away from Cambridge's main thoroughfare and market place. It is one of the university's oldest colleges, having been founded as Gonville Hall in 1348. Unlike other Cambridge colleges, Caius has Formal Hall (a three-course meal served in the ancient dining hall) every night of the week. Students who wish to attend have to wear the college's blue formal gown (though often with jeans or sports kit underneath). A unique dining policy obliges undergraduates to pay for 36 dinners a term (around four per week) up front. Unpopular with some, this tradition does create a strong community, with students generally returning to the main college site for meals. Caius has some great, functional accommodation in the Stephen Hawking Building, which offers modern, en-suite rooms (named in honour of the physicist who was a Fellow for over 52 years), and in Harvey Court, which was renovated in 2011. But there are also more traditional rooms and sets in the central, historic Old Courts, just steps away from Kings Parade. A new boathouse and gym has been welcomed by rowers and the college holds imaginative events for potential applicants such as its pioneering 'Women in Economics' day. New academic prizes for sixth formers were launched in 2017. Caius generally sits in the upper half of the Tompkins table (although 16th last year), and for those keen on study, the college library is a treat. It used to be the university library and is set under the arched roof of the Cockerell Building just outside the college. Caius elected its first female master, Dr Pippa Rogerson, in 2017.

Homerton

Cambridge CB2 8PH   01223 747111   www.homerton.cam.ac.uk
Undergraduates 570   Postgraduates 673   admissions@homerton.cam.ac.uk

The sprawling Homerton sometimes feels like its own self-contained village, due to its size and its distance from the central colleges. It is the youngest Cambridge college, gaining full college status in 2010 despite having been founded more than 250 years ago But it is the largest in Cambridge, with close to 1,500 students. Near the railway station, it is a 15-minute cycle ride from town. The benefit is space. Accommodation is made up of largely en-suite study bedrooms of a high standard. The college also has tennis courts, a gym, a squash court and a football pitch. There is an orchard and extensive lawns that can be walked on – Homerton students like the college's friendly and unstuffy atmosphere. The striking neo-Gothic Great Hall, built in 1889, is used for daily student meals and for candlelit formal dinners. It is set to be updated with a £7m project for a more capacious dining hall. Construction has also begun on a new auditorium and 18 en-suite bedrooms. Homerton's bar has been refurbished, and is well-used by students. There is a near 50:50 gender split at undergraduate level. Homerton has the largest number of students studying the education Tripos, in line with its history as a teacher training college. The arts abound and honorary fellows include Dame Carol Ann Duffy, Sir Andrew Motion and Dame Evelyn Glennie.

Hughes Hall

Cambridge CB1 2EW   01223 334898   www.hughes.cam.ac.uk
Undergraduates 138   Postgraduates 690   admissions@hughes.cam.ac.uk

Near Mill Road, the bustling street known more than anywhere else in Cambridge for its village atmosphere and independent shops and restaurants, Hughes Hall sits in a unique location. Founded in 1885, it is the oldest graduate college in the University of Cambridge. However, it also welcomes applications for undergraduate courses from students over 21 (in all subjects). Most of the students come from outside the UK, and the college has a particular flair for science, law and business. Although just around the corner from a busy high street, the college has a peaceful setting around the University's cricket ground, with the two terraces above the dining hall providing a great view. In close proximity to the main city sports centre, it's no wonder that Hughes Hall has a strong record on the sports pitch and on the river. In 2017, four students competed at the World Rowing Championships, and the year before, one of them took gold in the Rio Olympics. First-year-students are generally given rooms in the central college site. In 2016, 85 single en-suite rooms were built along with a bike store and study rooms in the new Gresham Court building. The college also has a number of flats and studios for students in established long-term relationships, but these tend to be in high demand. The Porter's Lodge is newly located in a trendy repurposed shipping container.

Jesus

Cambridge CB5 8BL 01223 339455 www.jesus.cam.ac.uk
Undergraduates 515 Postgraduates 416 undergraduate-admissions@jesus.cam.ac.uk

Jesus is the envy of many for its spacious grounds near both the river and the centre of town. Many of its red brick buildings date back to Jesus' founding in the 1500s. Its chapel is believed to be the oldest university building in Cambridge. The new buildings are not lacking in quality, however: the development at West Court has student common rooms, a games room, a swanky café that doubles as a popular bar in the evenings and a terrace. It also has on-site football, rugby and cricket pitches, as well as squash and tennis courts. As one of the biggest colleges, it is home to an eclectic student population that is as strong on the sports field as it is in music and art. All undergraduates are accommodated for every year of their degree, not just the first three (this is particularly convenient for medical students). Jesus's new master, former media executive Sonita Alleyne, is the first black woman to lead an Oxbridge college, and has stressed her wish to make Jesus feel like home for all members. The much-loved grounds are often punctuated by modern sculpture exhibitions (the college's collection contains work by the likes of Antony Gormley and John Bellany) and students are allowed to roam on most of the grass. In summer, Jesus holds a hotly touted May Ball that is especially popular with first years. Jesus saw a fair drop in its Tompkins Table position last year, however, falling to 14th place after coming sixth in 2018.

King's

Cambridge CB2 1ST 01223 331100 www.kings.cam.ac.uk
Undergraduates 418 Postgraduates 251 undergraduate.admissions@kings.cam.ac.uk

The view of King's Chapel and the Backs is the quintessential postcard image of Cambridge, although its grand buildings house one of the least traditional and most progressive colleges. Tours of the chapel (home to the famous Carol service that is broadcast on Christmas Eve) make King's extremely popular with tourists, while its central location on King's Parade appeals to students of all subjects. To current students, King's is known for a political student body, holding an 'Affair' instead of a May Ball, focused on alternative music with elaborate costumes and a left-field theme. A popular college cafe also makes an informal study space. Until recently, King's was known for a hammer and sickle hung in the college bar, but this was removed last year by student referendum. The college's state school intake (79% in the last admissions cycle) is higher than that of any college for non-mature undergraduates, aided by a campaign to seek out those from disadvantaged backgrounds. King's also has its own punts for students to rent and boasts 'Art Rooms' for their use. Accommodation ranges from the archetypally Cambridge (think mullioned windows overlooking the river) to en-suite rooms in newer hostels. The College is currently undergoing extensive renovations, however, with the traditional 'Bodley's Court' covered in scaffolding, and graduate accommodation has been repurposed for undergraduates.

Lucy Cavendish

Cambridge CB3 0BU 01223 332190 www.lucy-cav.cam.ac.uk
Undergraduates 98 Postgraduates 279 admissions@lucy-cav.cam.ac.uk

Students starting at Lucy Cavendish ('Lucy' to its members) in 2021 will be part of the first cohort to include both men and women from the age of 18. This marks a major departure from its former status as the only Oxbridge college to accept only women over the age of 21. The aim is to increase student numbers and open up places at Cambridge to more students from 'widening participation' backgrounds. Accommodation is provided for all students either in college or in nearby houses, close to those of St Edmunds, and Fitzwilliam, making for easy intermingling with these other 'hill' colleges. Students also live in an attractive apartment complex in Histon Road. The college has a growing reputation for sport, and is represented on many of the university's first teams. In recent years, it has provided two consecutive captains for Cambridge's female rugby team, players for its football team and four rowers in the Blues Boat. Internally, sport is also strong, and the Lucy Cavendish Boat Club persuades a third of the student community to give rowing a try. The college is also known for its Fiction Prize, which has helped to launch the career of many successful authors, including Gail Honeyman and Laura Marshall. It held its first Literary Festival in 2019, which sold out. Lucy is known for a slightly more staid and studious atmosphere than other colleges, but one that is highly supportive. While the college came last in the latest Tompkins Table, it also draws students from a wider range of backgrounds than many others, with at least a third of first-time undergraduates every year having undertaken Access Diplomas and qualifications other than A-levels.

Magdalene

Cambridge CB3 0AG   01223 332135   www.magd.cam.ac.uk
Undergraduates 383   Postgraduates 200   admissions@magd.cam.ac.uk

Magdalene rejoices in the longest river frontage of any Cambridge college and is renowned for its ancient and beautiful grounds. Students are often found revising on 'The Beach' during the summer exam term. It is one of the smaller colleges but this means that students tend to know each other. Magdalene has a reputation for being more traditional than some: it famously hosts one of the university's few white-tie balls every two years, and has one of the cheapest formal halls in Cambridge. It also has its own punts, which are a popular fixture in the summer term. The college's sports pitches are shared with St John's (both colleges have a sporty reputation) and Magdalene also has its own Eton Fives court on site. Students either live in the main college courts, in the 'village' on the other side of Magdalene Street, or in college-owned houses a few minutes' walk away. Students from different year groups are housed together, which helps with socialising. The college's most famous alumnus, Samuel Pepys, is immortalised in the Pepys Building that houses a collection of 3,000 of the diarist's books and manuscripts preserved on their original shelves. Magdalene tends toward the middle of the Tompkins ratings and came 18th in the last list. Its Master is the former Archbishop of Canterbury, Rowan Williams. A big fundraising campaign is under way in aid of more undergraduate bursaries, a new library and art gallery, renovation of the Pepys Building and construction of the 'New Building' that is underway.

Murray Edwards

Cambridge CB3 0DF   01223 762229   www.murrayedwards.cam.ac.uk
Undergraduates 376   Postgraduates 195   admissions@murrayedwards.cam.ac.uk

One of Cambridge's three colleges for women, Murray Edwards (often shortened to 'Medwards') is possibly the most gregarious of them. It is an informal, relaxed college whose students spend as much time mingling with students from other colleges as taking advantage of their calm and spacious campus at the top of Castle Hill. It hosts a renowned garden party during May Week, and the Saturday brunch, served up in 'The Dome' dining hall has been voted best in Cambridge. Unsurprisingly for an all-female college, it does much to promote women in the workplace, most notably running Gateway, a weekly programme on academic leadership and career development. It also has a strong population of women in STEM subjects. Its laid-back atmosphere extends to the gardens where students can grow herbs and vegetables as well as, unusually for a Cambridge college, walk on the grass. Sport is strong and everything from climbing to hockey is catered for. The college often provides Blues players to the university teams. Murray Edwards is also home to the second largest collection of women's art in the world, including work by Barbara Hepworth, Tracey Emin and Paula Rego. Murray Edwards has some of the highest rents, however, and has faced pressure from students who want to see them lowered.

Newnham

Cambridge CB3 9DF   01223 335783   www.newn.cam.ac.uk
Undergraduates 402   Postgraduates 226   admissions@newn.cam.ac.uk

Newnham has a long tradition of allowing women to find their feet at Cambridge and make the most of their potential, having been founded in 1871 so that female students could attend lectures, well before they could become members of the university. Its 'Old Labs', now an arts centre, were built in 1879 so women could study science subjects before this was a possibility in the University's labs. Alumni include Mary Beard, who is a fellow at the college and still teaches, Sylvia Plath, Diane Abbott and Emma Thompson. Last year Newnham came 22nd in the Tompkins Table – though a fifth of students still achieved a First. For arts students, it is ideally located for the Sidgwick Site and for those who like to socialise, Newnham often joins up with nearby Selwyn College for socials, formals and the choir (Newnham has no chapel). The grounds of the college stretch to 18-acres of space that includes sports pitches, and tennis courts. Newnham students can now enjoy 90 new en-suite rooms, as well as a new porters' lodge, gym, café and rooms for conferences and supervisions in the Dorothy Garrod building, named after Cambridge's first ever female professor. The new, light-filled cafe, called the Iris, is considered by many to be one of the best, meaning it is swarmed by students and fellows every lunchtime. One criticism, however, is that its rents are among the highest, with all accommodation priced the same despite large variations in quality. The college has recently made rent bursaries automatic and reduced proposed rent rises.

Pembroke

Cambridge CB2 1RF   01223 338154   www.pem.cam.ac.uk
Undergraduates 473   Postgraduates 276   admissions@pem.cam.ac.uk

Visitors to Pembroke will find Cambridge's third-oldest college situated in tranquil gardens just off busy Trumpington Street. Other students may associate Pembroke with its food – with its brunch drawing students from across the university, and formal dinner held in a pretty dining hall every night. Given its position, Pembroke is surprisingly large and is home to extensive gardens and a Christopher Wren chapel. Though most famous for its poets, including Ted Hughes and Edmund Spenser, Pembroke has seen its fair share of acting talent, including Oscar-nominated actress Naomie Harris and Tom Hiddleston. Pembroke students love the cheap rents (although reports suggest that for some rooms the rents reflect the quality), and facilities that include an on-site gym and a bowling green. The college is renovating the Mill Lane site across the road, which is expected to enlarge its footprint by a third – with plans to finish the work by 2023. Most first years live in the modern Foundress Court and in New Court, while second years tend to move further afield, with some going to Selwyn Gardens behind the Sidgwick Site, nearer to the train station on Lensfield Road and others as far as Grantchester Meadows.

Many desirable third-year rooms are in attractive terraced houses on Fitzwilliam Street. While performing well academically – in 2018 Pembroke came second in the Tompkins Table and last year it finished third – there is a strong extra-curricular ethos. There are dozens of clubs and societies, including the Music Society, the Stokes Scientific Society, Pembroke Politics, Pembroke Street magazine and the drama group the Pembroke Players, who regularly take productions to the Edinburgh Festival and are considered one of the most active drama societies.

Peterhouse

Cambridge CB2 1RD   01223 338223   www.pet.cam.ac.uk

Undergraduates 278   Postgraduates 174   admissions@pet.cam.ac.uk

The bijou Peterhouse, Cambridge's oldest college, remains home to some quirky traditions. The college welcomed its first female Master, the distinguished journalist Bridget Kendall in 2016. It is one of the richer colleges and has a roster of travel grants and academic awards available and accommodation standards are high. Students are housed either on site or not more than five minutes away for all years of their degree. Rooms are allocated on a points-based system that accounts both for academic progress and extra-curricular achievements. This rewards students for leaving the library, although it may see some students with their plates filled rather high. Though it shares a sports ground with Pembroke, Peterhouse does have its own squash court and a recently built gym. It also has one of Cambridge's wilder outdoor spaces known as 'The Deer Park' (no deer but many students roaming in summer). Every other year, the college hosts one of the few white tie balls in Cambridge. Peterhouse is well located for both the science and arts faculties and is particularly strong in the arts. It has two libraries, the Perne and the Ward, which provide plenty of quiet learning space away from the busier atmospheres of faculty libraries, and are well-used, with the college placing fourth in last year's Tompkins Table.

Queens'

Cambridge CB3 9ET   01223 335540   www.queens.cam.ac.uk

Undergraduates 532   Postgraduates 461   admissions@queens.cam.ac.uk

Queens' (make sure you get the apostrophe in the right place in comparison to its Oxford counterpart) is a bustling college that has a central location spanning both sides of the River Cam with the Mathematical Bridge, attributed to Sir Isaac Newton, joining the two. It is the third largest college by population and, especially in the new courts, has a lively, outgoing feel. Drama is popular thanks to the active BATS dramatic society and sport is strong – Queens' tends to provide a number of players to Blues teams and has sports clubs covering everything from chess to water polo. It also has a well-attended biennial May Ball that has welcomed renowned bands including Kaiser Chiefs and Bastille. An annual Arts Festival plays host to art from both inside the college and out, and features a range of events. The college has an eclectic mix of architecture that spans in date from its founding in 1448 to the present day (accommodation in the Dokett building has just been reopened with en-suite facilities). First year students are housed in the Cripps Building, while second and third year students are allocated accommodation through a ballot system, although rents are also expensive. Students have the option of sharing a set of rooms, rather than having their own single bedsit. Queens' is particularly strong in the sciences (thanks partly to a roster of bursaries and awards) and performs well at Tripos, generally ranking within the upper half of the Tompkins Table, and coming in sixth place last year.

Robinson

Cambridge CB3 9AN   01223 339143   www.robinson.cam.ac.uk
Undergraduates 405   Postgraduates 249   apply@robinson.cam.ac.uk

Students at the 'red-brick fortress' may need a bike if they want to make a quick trip to the centre of town, but an active social scene and more relaxed atmosphere makes many students fiercely loyal to Robinson. Its Brickhouse student-run theatre company is one of the most popular in Cambridge. The red-brick chapel is renowned for its fantastic acoustic and organ. It may not be the most architecturally beautiful college, but it does have a rolling programme of refurbishment that has resulted in very good facilities. There is a focus on the quality of food and 'The Garden Restaurant' (the college's canteen) is renowned. For those who want to focus on academe, Robinson is conveniently situated just behind the University Library and minutes away from the arts faculties on the Sidgwick Site and the Maths, Physics and Materials Science buildings. For those who want sport, Robinson often fields strong football, netball and rugby teams. The sports grounds, shared with Queens', Selwyn and King's, are less than a mile from the main college site. Robinson tends to rest in the bottom half of the Tompkins Table (it was 21st last year). It has recently faced criticism for having a particularly low intake of students from state schools, with only 41.3% of those accepted in 2018 coming from the maintained sector, the lowest of any college. The 2018 Big Cambridge Survey gave Robinson the dubious honour of having the highest rents of all.

Selwyn

Cambridge CB3 9DQ   01223 335896   www.sel.cam.ac.uk
Undergraduates 418   Postgraduates 239   admissions@sel.cam.ac.uk

With its own entrance to the Sidgwick Site, there isn't an easier commute to lectures than from Selwyn for arts and humanities students. Selwyn sits on the other side of the River Cam from the city centre, near Newnham and Wolfson. The only gripe about its location is that it's a ten-minute walk to the nearest cash point and supermarket. It was among the first colleges to admit women and typically has an even gender balance – there were 211 undergraduate women and 207 men at the last count. Selwyn also has a relatively large contingent of state-educated undergraduates (in the latest admissions cycle, 72% of offers were made to students from the maintained sector). All the students are accommodated for every year of their degree in what is likely to be, thanks to an extensive refurbishment programme, an en-suite room. The college bar is buzzing in the evenings and a popular study space during the day. Academically, Selwyn is doing well in the rankings, placing eighth last year after coming 11th in 2018. Music is strong and the college choir's album "The Eternal Ecstasy" was featured on Classic FM, spending three weeks in the charts. On the sports front, long-standing clubs known as the Hermes and Sirens fund grants for various teams and the college recently christened a new rowing boat. The Master of Selwyn also has a famous dog, which has featured in the QI Quiz Book and on BBC News.

Sidney Sussex

Cambridge CB2 3HU   01223 338834   www.sid.cam.ac.uk
Undergraduates 367   Postgraduates 229   admissions@sid.cam.ac.uk

Sidney Sussex, which was founded in 1596, is located, happily for students, just opposite the entrance to the city centre's main supermarket. This is not the only plus point of its situation; it's a short cycle ride in one direction to the river, a two-minute walk to the main student theatre, the ADC, and a five-minute walk to the natural science faculties. Sidney is one of the smaller colleges by population, but, because of its compact site, many students are housed in one of 11 nearby hostels. However, there are some atmospheric rooms to be had in the college's main buildings, a few of which even include en-suite facilities. Sidney is a musical college with an award-winning chapel and a recently inaugurated organ. Also in the chapel, more bizarrely, is buried Oliver Cromwell's head (he was among the college's first students). The bar is a social hub, thanks to its affordability and rowdy 'bops'. Food is well-reviewed and the college chefs scooped numerous awards in the 2017 university-wide culinary competition. Sports teams are more enthusiastic than wildly competitive and grounds are shared with Christ's, a ten-minute cycle ride away.

St Catharine's

Cambridge CB2 1RL   01223 338319   www.caths.cam.ac.uk
Undergraduates 470   Postgraduates 284   undergraduate.admissions@caths.cam.ac.uk

'Catz', as St Catharine's is fondly known, may be one of the least assuming of the colleges strung along Cambridge's famous King's Parade. It is mid-sized and has two libraries, thanks to the remit for learning instilled by its original benefactor, Robert Woodlark. St Catharine's has a high state school intake (in the last application cycle 77.6% of offers were made to students from the maintained sector). Catz students live on site in first year before moving out to the popular St Chad's complex in second year, where accommodation is split into flats with octagonal bedrooms. St Chad's is near the Sidgwick Site – useful for arts students looking to wake up as late as possible before lectures. Recent improvements to the college include the McGrath Centre, which houses an auditorium, junior common room and bar, and a refurbished boathouse and hockey pitch. St Catharine's came 10th in the Tompkins Table in 2018 and 9th in 2019, and its students are enthusiastic on the extra-curricular front. It fields strong rowing and hockey teams, and in the tradition of one of its most illustrious alumni, Sir Peter Hall, The Shirley Society (the college's drama group) is a popular troupe. It holds a May Ball every other year, and students can attend one at Corpus during the 'off' years. This year, £25 million of one of the largest donations in Cambridge's history, from the David and Claudia Harding Foundation, was made to Catz and will support postgraduates, as well as encouraging applications from students from underrepresented backgrounds. Catz is also planning major renovations of its social spaces.

St Edmund's

Cambridge CB3 0BN   01223 336086   www.st-edmunds.cam.ac.uk
Undergraduates 104   Postgraduates 449   admissions@st-edmunds.cam.ac.uk

Having recently celebrated its 50th year as a mainly graduate college, St Edmund's (called 'Eddies' by its members) enjoys a reputation as one of the most international, with a student body that, though male-heavy, hails from almost 80 different countries. Undergraduates must be 21 or more on entry. It is renowned for providing numerous sportsmen and women to the university's Blues teams and, in 2017, a team of four broke the world record for the longest continual row. St Edmund's location up on the 'hill' near Fitzwilliam and Murray Edwards gives the college a buzzing atmosphere and it is known as one of the most social of the graduate colleges. Despite climbing to 21st in the Tompkins Table in 2018, in 2019 it was back down to 28th place, however. Accommodation and food are on the expensive side as St Edmund's doesn't enjoy the big endowments of some of the larger colleges, but there are a good variety of rooms on offer from en-suites in the recently built Brian Heap building to maisonettes a short walk from college that are available to couples and small families. The new Mount

Pleasant Halls opened next door for September 2019 to meet rising demand, and provide 136 comfortable en-suite bedrooms and 64 studio flats. St Edmund's is unique among Cambridge colleges for having a Catholic chapel and takes a relaxed approach to traditions. There is no Fellows' high table in hall for example.

St Johns

Cambridge CB2 1TP	01223 338703	www.joh.cam.ac.uk
Undergraduates 637	Postgraduates 287	admissions@joh.cam.ac.uk

"I'd rather be at Oxford than St John's" is a popular refrain among the college's rivals, but for students looking for beautiful buildings on the Cam like the iconic Bridge of Sighs, John's certainly has appeal. St John's and Trinity enjoy a friendly rivalry, which sparks partly from being next-door neighbours. A large and wealthy college, it is renowned for its prowess on the sports field. The 'Red Boys' team is the dominant force in inter-college rugby – they won the league for the fourth time in five years in 2018 – and 'Maggie', as the college boat club is known, is another force to reckon with. General knowledge aficionados may be impressed that St John's won University Challenge in 2018. The size of St John's endowments means that it can support a wide range of activities from launching its own record label in aid of the strong music scene in college (The Gentlemen of St John's singers tour worldwide) to new financial initiatives which aim to help students from low income backgrounds, such as the St John's College Studentships. For the academically ambitious, first-class results are rewarded with grants. In 2018, however, only 56.3% of the undergraduate intake came from the maintained sector, one of the lowest rates in Cambridge. Accommodation standards are high and the food in the buttery is delicious and well subsidised. St John's hosts a May Week Ball that is known as one of the most fabulous. On the night, punts fill the river near the college to watch the legendary fireworks display.

Trinity Hall

Cambridge CB2 1TJ	01223 332535	www.trinhall.cam.ac.uk
Undergraduates 380	Postgraduates 218	admissions@trinhall.cam.ac.uk

Cycle up the steep Garret Hostel Bridge on your way into town and you'll see Trinity Hall students with their heads buried in books through the windows. 'Tit Hall's' Jerwood Library, overlooking the River Cam, has some of the best views in Cambridge, although the college has a less tourist-heavy river frontage than neighbours Trinity and Clare. The college's small size allows its 380 or so undergraduates to get to know each other quickly. It is also ideally located for a wander into town as well as the Sidgwick Site for the arts faculties and the University Library. Thanks to its endowments, Tit Hall is one of the richer colleges, which means that accommodation is cheap and facilities are good. All first-years are housed on the central site, where the cafeteria, coffee shop, bar, library, chapel and main music room are also located. But the college has some swanky new off-site accommodation. A block with double en-suite rooms called 'WYNG Gardens' opened recently and the rooms at the Wychfield Site (a ten-minute walk away) have been newly refurbished. The college is both sporty and musical; the chapel choir's most recent recording received gilded reviews. A sense of community is also fostered by the college's student-run Hummus Society, drawing crowds on a weekly basis. Trinity Hall rose to 10th place in the most recent Tompkins Table. Alumni include the scientists Stephen Hawking and David Thouless and the Olympic medal-winning cyclist Emma Pooley.

Trinity

Cambridge CB2 1TQ   01223 338422   www.trin.cam.ac.uk

Undergraduates 732   Postgraduates 335   admissions@trin.cam.ac.uk

The largest of all Oxbridge colleges, Trinity was established in 1546 and occupies extensive grounds that span the River Cam. The famous Wren Library contains everything from the Capell collection of Shakespeariana to the earliest manuscript of Winnie-the-Pooh. Trinity is the wealthiest of all Cambridge's colleges, which allows it to provide high quality and cheap accommodation. However, the college is one of a handful to have accepted under 60% of its students from the maintained sector in 2018. Male undergraduates outnumber females two-to-one. The college's ample resources mean that there are still lots of bursaries available to its undergraduate population. The Tudor-Gothic buildings of New Court have been renovated to provide 169 student rooms and nearly half the college's accommodation is now en-suite. Since 1997, Trinity has not come below eighth in the Tompkins Table, although its run of consistently topping the table has come to an end: it placed third in 2018, and second last year. A two-storey gym and netball, football, rugby and cricket pitches, minutes from the main gate, mean that sports are easy to enjoy (hockey pitches, badminton, tennis and squash courts are also available) and the college punts are a popular choice on summer afternoons. The chapel is home to an active choir who recently completed a tour of the United States, with Australia and Canada as upcoming destinations. In 2017 the JCR was refurbished and now has a 65-inch TV with Sky Sports and Netflix. It's a wonder work gets done, but students say that the college takes on a studious atmosphere in exam term.

Wolfson

Cambridge CB3 9BB   01223 335918   www.wolfson.cam.ac.uk

Undergraduates 180   Postgraduates 719   ugadministrator@wolfson.cam.ac.uk

Established as University College in 1965, Wolfson took its current name from a generous grant from the Wolfson Foundation just eight years after it was founded. It is, first and foremost, a college for graduate students, but also welcomes 150 or so mature undergraduates each year. All are guaranteed three years of accommodation. The community is varied with students from over 80 countries. There are students aged from 21 to those in their sixties (the average age is 25). It's a forward-thinking place with famously little distinction between fellows and students (there is no 'high table' in hall for example) and a President rather than a Master. The current President is the scientist, Professor Jane Clarke. The 1970s buildings are not the town's most beautiful, but the gardens are an oasis of calm and are close to the River Cam's picturesque banks. It is also not far from the Sidgwick Site and the University Library, though the city centre is a 20-minute walk. Wolfson's 'Howler' comedy nights take place three times a term to packed crowds and bring in professionals from the stand-up circuit as well as student talent. The college has one of the university's best gyms as well as a basketball-cum-tennis court. In celebration of its 50th anniversary in 2015, Wolfson managed to raise £7 million in donations. Students are seeing the benefit in grants and modernisation of the college.

15 University Profiles

This chapter provides profiles of every university that appears in *The Times and Sunday Time*s
league table. In addition there are profiles for Open University, the biggest supplier of part-time
degrees, and for University College Birmingham, and Birkbeck, University of London, which did
not release data for use in our main table. However, we do not have separate profiles for
specialist colleges, such as the Royal College of Music (**www.rcm.ac.uk**) or institutions that only
offer postgraduate degrees, such as Cranfield University (**www.cranfield.ac.uk**). Their omission is
no reflection on their quality, simply a function of their particular roles. A number of additional
institutions with degree-awarding powers are listed at the end of the book with their contact details.

The federal University of London (**www.london.ac.uk**) is by far Britain's biggest
conventional higher education institution, with more than 150,000 students. The majority study
at colleges in the capital, but such is the global prestige of the university's degrees that over
50,000 students in 180 different countries take University of London International Programmes.
The university, which dates back to 1836, consists of 18 self-governing colleges, the Institute in
Paris and the School of Advanced Study, which comprises ten specialist institutes for research
and postgraduate education (details at **www. sas.ac.uk**). City University joined the university in
2016. The university does not have its own entry in this chapter, but the following colleges do:
Birkbeck, City, Goldsmiths, King's College London, London School of Economics and Political
Science, Queen Mary, Royal Holloway, SOAS, St George's and University College London.
Contact details for its other constituent colleges are given on page 586.

Guide to the profiles
The profiles contain valuable information about each university. You can find contact details,
including postal address, telephone number for admission enquiries, email or web addresses
for admissions and prospectus enquiries, web addresses for the university and the students'
union, and the dates of forthcoming open days, where available. We also include data under the
heading 'Where do the students come from?' This is taken from our revamped table on social
inclusion that gives details of student recruitment and the socio-economic and ethnic mix of
each institution. The methodology for its data can be found in chapter 6. In addition, each profile
provides information under the following headings:

» ***The Times and Sunday Times*** **rankings:** For the overall ranking, the figure in bold refers to the university's position in the 2021 *Guide* and the figure in brackets to the previous year. The information is taken from the main league table (see chapter 1 for explanations and sources).

» **Undergraduates:** The number of full-time undergraduates is given first followed by part-time undergraduates (in brackets). The figures are for 2017–18, and are the most recent from the Higher Education Statistics Agency (HESA).

» **Postgraduates:** The number of full-time postgraduates is given first followed by part-time postgraduates (in brackets). The figures are for 2017–18, and are the most recent from HESA.

» **Mature students:** The percentage of undergraduate entrants who were 21 or over at the start of their studies in 2018. The figures are from UCAS.

» **International students:** The number of undergraduate overseas students (both EU and non-EU) as a percentage of full-time undergraduates. The figures are for 2017–18, and are from HESA.

» **Applications per place:** The number of applicants per place for 2018, from UCAS.

» **Accommodation:** The information was obtained from university accommodation services, and their help is gratefully acknowledged.

Tuition fees

Details of tuition fees for 2020–21 are given wherever possible. At the time of going to press, a number of universities had not published their international fees for 2020–21. In these cases, the fees for 2019–20 are given. Please check university websites to see if they have managed to give updated figures.

Although EU students have been guaranteed that UK (up to £9,250) rather than international fees will apply to them if they start in 2020, no such guarantee has yet been given for students planning to start in 2021. It is of the utmost importance that you check university websites for the latest information.

Every university website gives full details of the financial and other support the university provides to its students, from scholarships and bursaries to study support and hardship funds. Some of the support will be delivered automatically but most will not, and you must study the details on the websites, including methods of applying and deadlines, to get the greatest benefit out of your university. In addition, in England the Office for Students (**www.officeforstudents.org.uk**) publishes "Access Agreements" for every English university on its website. Each agreement outlines the university's plans for fees, financial support and measures being taken to widen access to that university and to encourage students to complete their courses.

University of Aberdeen

Our Scottish University of the Year for 2018–19 has embarked on its most ambitious programme of campus developments yet. Work has started on the £35m science teaching hub, which is due to open in the first half of 2021, and the university has committed to a massive regeneration of its Old Aberdeen campus, costing almost £100m. The facades of the historic King's buildings and the university's conservation areas will be preserved while the interior spaces are enhanced and new developments added.

The science teaching hub will provide the latest facilities and flexible teaching laboratory space to encourage collaboration between students from different disciplines. Sir George Boyne, the vice-chancellor and principal, said the subsequent projects would bring neglected spaces back to life and, through better connectivity, open up areas of the campus that would be unknown to many. The business school, which is expected to double its recruitment over the next decade, will have its own building. Elsewhere, four traditional lecture theatres last reconfigured in the 1970s are being overhauled to create two large collaborative teaching spaces.

The regeneration work follows an intensive academic recruitment drive and is part of a new strategy for the university – Aberdeen 2040 – designed to make the university "inclusive, inter-disciplinary and international in reach and quality".

Aberdeen is the fifth-oldest university in the UK, a fusion of two ancient institutions, the first of which was established in 1495. The original King's College premises are the focal point of an attractive campus, complete with cobbled main street and Georgian buildings, about a mile from the city centre. The more modern Sir Duncan Rice Library, named after the principal who commissioned it, cost £57m and has been named among the most beautiful in the world.

Aberdeen has fallen slightly in our table after last year's 14-place gain. It had to cope with three successive years of falling applications before a modest rise in the last admissions cycle. Enrolments remained more stable, even without an increased offer rate, because the proportion of applicants who take up places is higher than at most universities.

There are still fewer than 14,500 students, a third of whom come from the north of Scotland. Others come from 130 different countries. A new International Study Centre offers preparatory courses for overseas students. The university also has a joint venture with AFG College in Qatar, where it has become the first UK university to offer bachelor's degrees, initially in business management and accounting and finance. The first graduates received their degrees this year and there are plans to expand the portfolio of courses.

King's College
Aberdeen AB24 3FX
01224 272 090
study@abdn.ac.uk
www.aberdeen.ac.uk
www.ausa.org.uk
Open days 2020:
June 13 (medicine);
August 25, October 3

The Times and The Sunday Times **Rankings**
Overall Ranking: 27 (last year: 26)

Teaching quality	80.6%	=56
Student experience	81.1%	=22
Research quality	29.9%	43
Entry standards	184	11
Graduate prospects	80.9%	=39
Good honours	87.1%	13
Expected completion rate	90.2%	=37
Student/staff ratio	16.1	=75
Services and facilities	£2,445	=51

Entry standards are just outside the top ten in the UK, and this includes lower offers for applicants from schools with mainly poor results, under a contextualised admissions policy. Aberdeen also runs a Children's University programme, which provides a range of accredited activities to encourage primary and secondary school children to take part in educational and active extracurricular pursuits.

New undergraduates are paired with current students, where possible on the same course, under the Students4Students scheme, to help them settle in and get the most from university life. A menu of "enhanced study" options is designed to broaden undergraduate degrees. Students can incorporate a language, business or computing into their degree, or choose from a range of cross-disciplinary programmes.

In tune with its location, the university is particularly strong in disciplines related to the oil and gas industries. At its own underwater research facility, Oceanlab, at Newburgh, north of Aberdeen, engineers lead the world in creating systems capable of operating at depths down to 11,000 metres.

The university's expertise is spread much more widely, however. Three-quarters of the work submitted for the 2014 Research Excellence Framework was rated world-leading or internationally excellent. The university was placed top in the UK for environmental and soil science and in the top three for psychology and English.

The highly regarded medical school is based at Foresterhill, a 20-minute walk away from the main campus, where the university shares Europe's largest health campus with NHS Grampian, placing researchers, scientists, clinicians and patients together on one site. Aberdeen was awarded an additional 30 medical student places a year, specifically to train extra doctors specialising in general practice.

Aberdeen is consistently ranked among the top ten medical schools in the UK. Law, theology and civil engineering also reach our subject top-ten rankings this year.

All new undergraduates are guaranteed one of almost 2,500 residential places – an important benefit in a city with the highest rents in Scotland. The Aberdeen Sports Village offers some of the best facilities at any university in the UK, including a £22m aquatic centre with 50-metre pool and 10-metre diving board, as well as a full-size indoor football pitch and outdoor facilities.

Good travel connections make Aberdeen's location less remote than outsiders might assume. The weather is often the warmest in Scotland despite the northerly latitude.

Tuition fees

» Fees for Scottish/EU students £0–£1,820

  RUK fees £9,250 (capped at £27,750 for 4-year courses)

» Fees for International students 2020–21 £17,200–£19,700

  Medicine £43,500

» For scholarship and bursary information see www.aberdeen.ac.uk/study/undergraduate/finance.php

» Graduate salary £22,500

Student numbers

Undergraduates	9,820	(435)
Postgraduates	2,606	(1,509)
Applications/places		18,840/2,765
Applications per place		6.8
Overall offer rate		80.2%
Unconditional offers		0%
International students		33.2%

Accommodation

University provided places: 2,459
Catered costs: £147 per week
Self-catered: £89–£145 per week
First years guaranteed accommodation
www.abdn.ac.uk/accommodation

Where do the students come from?

State schools (non-grammar)	81.8%	First generation students	28.2%	Black attainment gap	-16.5%
Grammar schools	2.9%	Deprived areas	6%	Disabled	4.7%
Independent schools	15.2%	All ethnic minorities	10.2%	Mature (over 21)	26.4%

Social inclusion ranking (Scotland): 12

Abertay University

Abertay is one of the few post-1992 universities to have recorded increases in both applications and enrolments for the past two years. The numbers starting degrees rose by more than a third over that period. The university has now reviewed its portfolio of courses to try to maintain the trend, closing eight of its 43 degrees – including forensic sciences and sport and psychology, where the demand for places was low – in order to focus on its strengths in computer gaming and other digital areas.

Associated curriculum reforms have already introduced mandatory interdisciplinary courses for all undergraduates and Scotland's first accelerated degrees. The prospectus tells students: "We've never been afraid to lead the way," citing the introduction, nine years apart, of the world's first degrees in computer games and ethical hacking. The university is building a new £11.7m cybersecurity research and development centre on campus, in conjunction with the Scottish Business Resilience Centre. The aim is to marry the university's sector-leading skills in this area with the needs of the regional and national digital industries.

Seven fast-track honours degrees are offered, including ethical hacking and computer arts. These courses can be taken in three years, rather than the norm of four, north of the border. The final two years are 45 weeks long rather than the usual 30. Other subjects available in this format – unique so far in Scotland – include business studies, game design and production, sports development, and food and consumer science. All courses can be taken on a part-time basis, and many programmes aim to offer students the chance to spend at least 30% of their time in industry.

Other recent reforms have brought a guarantee of quicker responses to assessed work. Students now submit work electronically and receive feedback and marks the same way. Grading has been simplified and students have been assured that lectures and seminars will be in the same place at the same time every week..

Abertay was the first university to introduce the minimum access thresholds recommended by Scotland's Commission on Widening Access from last year's intake onwards. The scheme identifies the minimum academic standard and subject knowledge needed to complete a programme. In business management, for example, this can mean three C-grade Highers, rather than the standard offer of four Bs, if promising applicants come from a school or college with little tradition of progress to higher education, have spent significant time in care, live in an area of deprivation, or have parents or guardians who did not go to university.

The university scores well for non-selective state-school admissions and the proportion of mature learners in our social inclusion ranking. More than a third of the

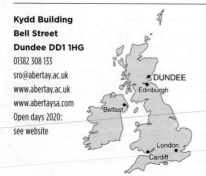

Kydd Building
Bell Street
Dundee DD1 1HG
01382 308 133
sro@abertay.ac.uk
www.abertay.ac.uk
www.abertaysa.com
Open days 2020:
see website

The Times and The Sunday Times Rankings
Overall Ranking: =98 (last year: =105)

Teaching quality	84.5%	9
Student experience	81.3%	20
Research quality	5.1%	=91
Entry standards	142	=48
Graduate prospects	73.4%	=83
Good honours	65.8%	121
Expected completion rate	77.4%	120
Student/staff ratio	19.6	121
Services and facilities	£1,919	102

undergraduates arrive from colleges rather than schools, and 94% are from some part of the state sector, almost exclusively from comprehensive schools. The new Bright Ideas programme brings pupils from disadvantaged areas to the campus to sample courses.

With fewer than 4,000 students, Abertay promises a more personal experience than undergraduates receive at most universities. It is based in the centre of Dundee, with all the teaching and learning buildings within five minutes' walk of each other. A £5m modernisation of the Bernard King library, named after a former principal, was completed last year, adding a new cafe, social area and more workstations.

Now Abertay's Centre of Excellence for Computer Games Education is being revamped to install the latest virtual and mixed reality technology, and create "student-owned" sections close to the teaching areas, with flexible space for events and conferences. The university has also opened a new centre for student enterprise, funded by the late local businessman Bill Sword, whose first business venture was a campus shop opened in the 1940s in what was then Dundee Technical College.

Abertay has a global reputation in computer arts and games design, which attracts large numbers of students from China and a number of other countries. All games students become members of UKIE (UK Interactive Entertainment) and gain access to a bespoke programme of industry mentorship and support. Graduates include David Jones, the creator of the Grand Theft Auto video game series, and Sony chose the university as the site for the largest teaching laboratory in Europe for its PlayStation consoles.

The university hosts the Dundee Academy of Sport, launched in partnership with Dundee and Angus College – a venture using sport as a vehicle for learning across the school curriculum and throughout life. There is a new strength and conditioning laboratory for sports science students, as well as an exercise studio on campus, which is also open to the public. A 580-bed student village allows all first-years who apply for accommodation to be guaranteed a place.

Dundee, a Unesco city of design, has seen considerable investment recently including the development of its waterfront, centred on the newly-opened £80m V&A Dundee design museum. *The Wall Street Journal* ranked it alongside Shanghai, Madagascar and the Faroe Islands as one of world's ten "hot destinations", and it is also among the more affordable in the UK for students.

Tuition fees

» Fees for Scottish/EU students £0–£1,820
   RUK fees £9,250
» Fees for International students 2020–21 £14,000–£15,500
» For scholarship and bursary information see
   www.abertay.ac.uk/study-apply/money-fees-and-funding/
» Graduate salary £20,500

Student numbers		
Undergraduates	3,411	(194)
Postgraduates	234	(214)
Applications/places		5,460/1,445
Applications per place		3.8
Overall offer rate		94%
Unconditional offers		0%
International students		15.6%

Accommodation
University provided places: 580 (catered 0%)
Self-catered: £64–£129 per week
First years guaranteed accommodation
www.abertay.ac.uk/life/accommodation

Where do the students come from?				Social inclusion ranking (Scotland): 3	
State schools (non-grammar)	93.8%	First generation students	45.1%	Black attainment gap	n/a
Grammar schools	0.5%	Deprived areas	19.1%	Disabled	7.1%
Independent schools	5.7%	All ethnic minorities	5.9%	Mature (over 21)	35.9%

Aberystwyth University

Aberystwyth is our Welsh University of the Year. Only one university in the UK has higher satisfaction ratings for teaching quality and the wider student experience than Aber and none can match the 91% of final-year undergraduates who say they were satisfied with their course overall.

The National Student Survey has become something of an annual triumph for Aber, and similarly high ratings have twice made it our University of the Year for Teaching Quality and have placed it top in Wales for student satisfaction for four years in a row.

The university also secured a gold rating in the Teaching Excellence Framework, after opting out in the first year of the exercise. The panel found "outstanding levels of stretch" ensuring that all students were significantly challenged to achieve their full potential. Substantial investment in e-learning was another plus point, as was the integrated approach to Welsh-language teaching.

Yet despite an offer rate (97.3%) that is among the highest in the UK, the numbers starting courses in 2018 were down by more than 10% to the lowest total in more than a decade. The drop followed a restructuring of departments and courses to address a growing deficit.

One in five of the new entrants came with an unconditional offer once they had confirmed Aber as their firm choice, but in 2020 unconditional offers will be available only to applicants who already meet Aber's entry requirements or have sat one of the university's invigilated scholarship exams.

The university has risen nearly 50 places in our league table in five years. New degrees are now being introduced: psychology and counselling; strategy, intelligence and security; and media paired with subjects such as creative writing, education or theatre studies. More new programmes are awaiting validation for 2020, including cultural heritage studies, information management and computer and information sciences.

Aber has also embarked on an ambitious programme of capital developments, including a £20m restoration of the Old College, one of Wales's most recognisable university buildings. With lottery funding, the university plans to turn the seafront grade I listed building into a gallery and performance space, a centre for entrepreneurs and new businesses, with a cafe, as well as a museum and science centre.

The university's Welsh-medium hall of residence, Pantycelyn, will reopen for the start of the academic year in 2020, following a £16.5m refurbishment. Once home to Prince Charles, in his days as an Aber student, it will provide en-suite accommodation for 200 students who want to live in a Welsh-speaking

Penglais
Aberystwyth SY23 3FL
01970 622 021
ug-admissions@aber.ac.uk
www.aber.ac.uk
www.abersu.co.uk
Open days 2020:
see website

The Times and The Sunday Times **Rankings**

Overall Ranking: 45 (last year: =48)

Teaching quality	88.3%	2
Student experience	86.1%	2
Research quality	28.1%	45
Entry standards	120	=94
Graduate prospects	78.2%	56
Good honours	69%	=104
Expected completion rate	81.6%	93
Student/staff ratio	16.9	=87
Services and facilities	£1,768	114

environment or to learn in Welsh. About a third of Aber's students are from Wales, and Welsh-medium teaching is thriving.

A £4.2m EU-backed veterinary facility will be fully operational this year. One of its research centres will be a new Centre of Excellence for Bovine Tuberculosis for Wales. Later in the year, a £40.5m Innovation and Enterprise Campus is due to open on the university's Gogerddan site, focusing on food, biorefining and agritech research and development.

Scores in the 2014 Research Excellence Framework showed improvement on the previous assessments, with the best scores in international politics, geography and earth science, and the Institute of Biological, Environmental and Rural Sciences. The institute, which serves 1,500 undergraduate and research students, gives Aber the widest range of land-related courses in the UK.

The university's strategic plan promises further improvements in the student experience. A £1m refurbishment of the Hugh Owen Library on the Penglais campus was completed last year and the Arts Centre's 300-seat theatre has reopened after a refit. The three university libraries are complemented by the National Library of Wales, which gives free access to students.

The attractive seaside location remains a draw for applicants, although travel to other parts of the UK is slow. The two campuses are about a mile apart, with teaching facilities and residential accommodation within walking distance of each other.

Aber is the first university in the world to be given Plastic Free University status. The award was made by marine conservation charity Surfers Against Sewage in recognition of Aber's campaign to reduce the use of single-use plastics.

More than 94% of the students are state-educated – a higher proportion than expected given the mix of subjects. More than a third of undergraduates receive some financial support, which includes Rashid Domingo bursaries worth £12,000 over three years open to students in biological, rural and environmental sciences who went to secondary school in Wales and require financial assistance.

All first-year students are guaranteed university-owned accommodation, which houses more than half of all Aber's undergraduates. The students' union has the largest entertainment venue in the region and sports facilities are good and well used. There is a women-only area and designated strength zone in a refurbished fitness centre, while outdoor facilities include a swimming pool, 400-metre running track, 50 acres of playing fields and specialist facilities for water sports.

Tuition fees

» Fees for UK/EU students	£9,000
» Fees for International students 2020–21	£13,600–£15,800
» For scholarship and bursary information see	
www.aber.ac.uk/en/undergrad/before-you-apply/fees-finance/	
» Graduate salary	£18,720

Student numbers

Undergraduates	6,014	(1,022)
Postgraduates	637	(514)
Applications/places	8,690/1,960	
Applications per place	4.4	
Overall offer rate	97.3%	
Unconditional offers	19.2%	
International students	17%	

Accommodation

University provided places: 3,360 (catered 4%)
Catered costs: £121–£127 per week
Self-catered: £85–£142 per week
First years guaranteed accommodation
www.aber.ac.uk/en/accommodation

Where do the students come from?

State schools (non-grammar)	89.6%	First generation students	40%	Black attainment gap	-28.4%
Grammar schools	4.4%	Deprived areas	12.0%	Disabled	10.8%
Independent schools	5.9%	All ethnic minorities	6.5%	Mature (over 21)	13.2%

Social inclusion ranking: =83

Anglia Ruskin University

The number of students starting degrees at Anglia Ruskin University (ARU) has dropped by more than 30% in two years, with applications showing an even steeper decline. The university has been looking to cut costs to ensure that it is a "world-class institution delivering innovative, inclusive and entrepreneurial education and research".

ARU was one of five universities awarded a medical school last year and has since been chosen to develop a new nursing training and education facility for the North West Anglia NHS Foundation Trust. It has moved up two places in our latest table, although it is still well outside the top 100.

ARU holds silver in the Teaching Excellence Framework, winning praise for its support for students at risk of dropping out. However, it hit the headlines earlier this year when a graduate received a £61,000 out-of-court settlement after claiming that her course in international business strategy had been a "Mickey Mouse degree" and the university had exaggerated students' career prospects. A county court ruled in ARU's favour, but its insurers' lawyers settled the £15,000 claim and paid costs when Pok Wong, who had been awarded a first-class degree in 2013, continued the litigation.

ARU has finished in the top 30 in our first two social inclusion tables and is also in the top 30 for student satisfaction with the quality of teaching, although it is in the bottom 25 for graduate prospects.

Seven new degrees have been launched this year, in addition to medicine. They range from a two-year accelerated degree in primary education to BSc programmes in artificial intelligence, professional policing, psychology with clinical psychology, and sport and exercise therapy. A new integrated master's scheme will also be introduced in the business school, with students spending two years at undergraduate level, with a further one year to complete a master's.

ARU has also been among the pioneers of degree apprenticeships, with almost 1,000 trainees on 15 programmes. The institution expects to double this number by September 2020, with new programmes for social workers, operating department practitioners, laboratory scientists, supply chain professionals, arts therapists and town planners.

The university has a history of providing innovative courses: the BOptom (Hons) was the first qualification of its kind in the UK and the hearing aid audiology course was among the first to lead directly to registration. Each undergraduate has an adviser to help compile a degree package, looking at the chosen subject from different points of view to maximise future job prospects.

The medical school is the first to open in Essex and is aiming to fill up to half of the

Bishop Hall Lane
Chelmsford CM1 1SQ
01245 686 868
answers@aru.ac.uk
www.aru.ac.uk
www.angliastudent.com
Open days 2020:
April 25

The Times and The Sunday Times **Rankings**		
Overall Ranking: 120 (last year: 122)		
Teaching quality	82.4%	=30
Student experience	79%	=51
Research quality	5.4%	=89
Entry standards	113	=115
Graduate prospects	68.3%	107
Good honours	74%	=76
Expected completion rate	78.2%	116
Student/staff ratio	18.5	=110
Services and facilities	£1,464	128

100 places each year with students from the region, who will stay to practise there when they qualify. It is already operating from a £20m building on the Chelmsford campus.

ARU has spent £115m over the past five years on campus improvements, opening a new science centre in Cambridge and two new law clinics. A further £200m will be invested over the next ten years, with the focus on improving digital learning options for all courses and providing more activities beyond the classroom. Ruskin modules will be introduced across the university, addressing employability skills and offering CV workshops.

Anglia Ruskin won an award for its work with 2,000 businesses, which aims to instil entrepreneurial values in both students and staff. The university has an innovative scheme placing graduates with the region's small firms – usually the companies least likely to take on those emerging from higher education.

There are campuses in Chelmsford, Cambridge and Peterborough, as well as in the City of London, where the focus is on business courses. There is also a partnership with University Centre West Anglia, which allows some 10,000 students to take ARU degree courses in King's Lynn, Wisbech and Milton, on the outskirts of Cambridge.

More than 93% of ARU's intake comes from non-selective state schools and more than a third of undergraduates are aged at least 21 at entry.

Some world-leading research was identified in all five faculties in the 2014 Research Excellence Framework. The best performances were in music, drama and the performing arts. Health subjects also did well, alongside media studies, geography and environmental science. The Global Sustainability Institute is building an international reputation for its research, and Anglia Ruskin is aiming to make sustainability an important part of every student's experience.

The social scene varies between campuses, all within an hour of London by train. There are residential places in Cambridge and Chelmsford, and new entrants are guaranteed accommodation if they apply in time. There is a sports centre with a well-equipped gym on the Chelmsford campus and further fitness facilities on the Cambridge campus.

Tuition fees

» Fees for UK/EU students	£9,250
» Fees for International students 2020–21	£13,500
» For scholarship and bursary information see www.aru.ac.uk/student-life/help-with-finances	
» Graduate salary	£22,000

Student numbers

Undergraduates	16,717(2,293)
Postgraduates	2,113 (2,379)
Applications/places	14,510/2,980
Applications per place	4.9
Overall offer rate	73.3%
Unconditional offers	0%
International students	13.1%

Accommodation

University provided places: 2,158
Self-catered: £103–£194 per week
First years accommodated on first-come-first-served basis
www.aru.ac.uk/student-life/accommodation

Where do the students come from?

				Social inclusion ranking: 23	
State schools (non-grammar)	93.7%	First generation students	55%	Black attainment gap	-18%
Grammar schools	2.4%	Deprived areas	16%	Disabled	6%
Independent schools	3.9%	All ethnic minorities	29.2%	Mature (over 21)	34.3%

Arts University Bournemouth

The Arts University Bournemouth (AUB) has been hovering on the verge of our top 50 for the past two years, with a gold award in the Teaching Excellence Framework (TEF) to underline its achievements. It has gone one step further now, with student satisfaction rising by a startling amount – to rank the university seventh in the UK on both our measure of teaching quality and the wider student experience.

Allied to success in the graduate jobs market, where it outperforms its peers among the specialist arts universities with a ranking in the UK top 50, AUB makes a compelling case to arts students.

The university has not been immune to the decline in demand for arts degrees nationally. Applications had dropped by more than 20% in two years when the June deadline passed in 2018. AUB remained highly selective, but offers were made to 56% of applicants, compared to just 40% in 2016 and before. However, just 4% of students secured their places through clearing.

Students starting courses will find a rapidly developing campus. A striking, orange Innovation Studio for student and alumni start-up companies is now open and new accommodation for 300 students should be available later this year. The building is arranged in eight-bed clusters with communal kitchens and dining areas centred around a landscaped courtyard.

Other recent developments include the first dedicated drawing studio to be built at a UK art school for 100 years and the Photography Building, which has flexible teaching spaces and IT suites. The Gallery showcases work by students and other contemporary artists, hosting talks, events and film nights to support the exhibition programme, while the Enterprise Pavilion helps to develop, attract and retain new creative businesses in the southwest.

Laser-cutting machinery and a 3D printer feature among the high-tech equipment available to students. The purpose-built library includes the Museum of Design in Plastics, which holds more than 12,000 artefacts of predominantly 20th- and 21st-century mass-produced design and popular culture. The items are chosen to support the courses taught at the university.

The TEF panel was impressed by the engagement of professionals from outside the university in the delivery of courses, and praised the high levels of stimulation and challenge in small classes and the regular contact with tutors. AUB also won a Queen's Anniversary Prize for "distinguished degree level education in costume design for the UK's leading creative industries" in 2018. Oscar nominations for alumni and successes in television and theatre helped to land the award.

Bournemouth Film School, which is part of the university, is the largest outside London, running nine courses covering the

Wallisdown
Poole BH12 5HH
01202 363 228
admissions@aub.ac.uk
www.aub.ac.uk
www.aub.ac.uk/life-aub/
students-union
Open days 2020:
June 6, September 26,
October 10,
November 7, December 5

The Times and *The Sunday Times* Rankings
Overall Ranking: 43 (last year: =51)

Teaching quality	84.9%	7
Student experience	82.9%	7
Research quality	2.4%	118
Entry standards	154	37
Graduate prospects	80.5%	46
Good honours	66.1%	120
Expected completion rate	90%	39
Student/staff ratio	15.1	=50
Services and facilities	£1,730	116

various aspects of filmmaking. Its students make more than 50 films a year, partly through crowdfunding. AUB as a whole has operated as a specialist institution since 1885 and also offers degrees in architecture, dance and event management, as well as art and design subjects. The university describes its courses as having a "highly practical streak" designed to give students an edge in a competitive creative world.

The university has a Skillset Media Academy in partnership with Bournemouth University, offering eight accredited courses in areas from animation to make-up for media and performance. The two institutions also bid successfully to become a Screen Academy, through which Skillset recognises excellence in film and the broader screen-based media.

A low dropout rate is a point of particular pride for AUB, with the latest projection back below 5% – around half the expected level. Seven out of ten entrants in 2019 are expected to receive some form of financial assistance. Current support for students includes refectory, bus and bicycle vouchers, funding for educational visits and hardship loans. Tuition fees include the cost of standard materials on most courses.

Only 12 staff were entered for the 2014 Research Excellence Framework, but 43% of their work was rated as world-leading or internationally excellent. Many AUB academics have links to and experience in the creative industries, while the careers service provides students with subject-specific and generic advice on future employment.

Some 700 residential places that are either run by the university or endorsed are available to current students. There is a register of approved housing at the website www.aubstudentpad.com and accommodation days in July and August help current and prospective students to find potential housemates. Priority for the allocation of a study bedroom goes to overseas students and those with disabilities or other medical conditions. Initiatives such as the recycling of coffee cups and drop-off points for clothes to be recycled brought AUB a gold EcoCampus award from the COREnvironmental Association for Universities and Colleges.

AUB has no sports facilities of its own but provides a subsidy for its students to access the extensive facilities and clubs at neighbouring Bournemouth University. The town has a large, cosmopolitan student population and one of the most vibrant club scenes outside London. The capital is less than two hours away by regular train and coach services or via good motorway links.

Tuition fees

» Fees for UK/EU students	£9,250
Foundation years £5,721	
» Fees for International students 2020–21	£16,950
» For scholarship and bursary information see	
www.aub.ac.uk/apply/funding/	
» Graduate salary	£18,000

Student numbers

Undergraduates	3,356	(9)
Postgraduates	64	(63)
Applications/places	5,850/1,120	
Applications per place	5.2	
Overall offer rate	56.3%	
Unconditional offers	0%	
International students	15.1%	

Accommodation

University provided places: 700
Self-catered: £155–£205 per week
No accommodation guarantee
www.aub.ac.uk/apply/accommodation

Where do the students come from?

State schools (non-grammar)	92.6%	First generation students	39.5%	Black attainment gap	n/a
Grammar schools	2.6%	Deprived areas	10.0%	Disabled	11.4%
Independent schools	4.8%	All ethnic minorities	12.8%	Mature (over 21)	13.8%

Social inclusion ranking: =64

University of the Arts London

University of the Arts London (UAL) is ranked by QS as the second-best place in the world (after the Royal College of Art) to study art and design.

It has followed last year's 21-place rise in our rankings with another big move upwards this year, despite student satisfaction rates for teaching quality and the wider student experience dragging UAL down, as they do at other London and arts institutions.

UAL has been addressing students' concerns, partly through an annual £3m Academic Development Fund, which will produce 55 new posts for the new academic year. A Creative Attributes Framework, drawn up in consultation with leading employers such as John Lewis, Estée Lauder and Bafta, is designed to ensure that all UAL's courses give students the qualities they need to succeed in the creative industries.

UAL has the largest careers centre in the country for art and design, while the Fashion Technology: Emerging Futures programme supports graduates early in their careers. The university also opened an enterprise programme called "not just a shop" to sell products and artwork designed by its alumni, with the profits helping to keep the scheme going to support students and graduates.

There are no new scores for graduate prospects for any institution in this year's table because the system is changing to one that measures job outcomes on a longer timescale. But a 35-place rise in our jobs rankings last year – with 72% of graduates in professional work or graduate-level study six months after leaving – suggests that UAL's innovations are having an impact.

The six constituent colleges continue to use their own names and enjoy considerable autonomy. UAL as a whole now has 15,000 undergraduates, almost 80% of whom study art and design. Entry is highly competitive: although the offer rate has risen in each of the past five years, it still stands at (fractionally) less than 40%. That is unlikely to have fallen in the latest admissions cycle, which saw a 10% rise in applications, reversing a three-year decline.

The university runs weekend classes and summer schools in an attempt to broaden the intake. It is already socially inclusive, 93% of students having attended state schools or colleges.

Campus developments have continued apace since the former London Institute became a university in 2004. A new campus is being developed for the London College of Communication near its existing premises at Elephant and Castle, while Central Saint Martins (CSM) occupies a prize-winning building at King's Cross. The £200m development brought CSM together on one site for the first time, and its grade II listed former granary was voted the world's best higher education building of the year.

272 High Holborn
London WC1V 7EY
020 7514 6000
http://enquiries.arts.ac.uk
www.arts.ac.uk
www.arts-su.com
Open days 2020:
February 5
(London College of
Communication)

The Times and The Sunday Times Rankings
Overall Ranking: =79 (last year: =94)

Teaching quality	76.3%	114
Student experience	70.1%	=127
Research quality	8.0%	72
Entry standards	137	=52
Graduate prospects	72.2%	=91
Good honours	71.3%	=91
Expected completion rate	86.2%	=62
Student/staff ratio	14.8	=45
Services and facilities	£2,397	58

Two new buildings have transformed the Camberwell College of Arts campus, adding galleries, a refectory, workshops, studios and a new library, as well as a 264-room hall of residence. Chelsea College of Arts already had a new base next to the Tate Gallery when the university was formed. Now a new waterfront campus is under construction at the Queen Elizabeth Olympic Park for the London College of Fashion (LCF). The East Bank arts quarter project, which includes the V&A and Sadler's Wells, had to be redesigned but now has approval from the mayor of London.

Wimbledon College of Arts, which has an international reputation in theatre design, is launching a Total Performance School, enabling students to train in all areas of theatre and performance, from acting and stage management to lighting, sound, special effects and robotics. Its student population is expected to triple – to 1,100 students – by 2022. Degrees in acting and contemporary theatre, both with performance, have taken their first students.

At other UAL colleges, seven new courses include virtual reality, creative computing and film and screen studies.

The new UAL Creative Computing Institute will support inter-disciplinary teaching, research and knowledge exchange, for example in human interaction with machine learning and artificial intelligence. BSc and MSc courses in creative computing offer students the chance to learn to code, build apps, create digital experiences and explore artificial intelligence. UAL is one of the 25 founding partners in the new Institute of Coding.

The university performed well in the 2014 Research Excellence Framework, when 83% of work submitted was rated world-leading or internationally excellent. All was highly rated for its external impact.

Over the years, half of all the shortlisted artists for the Turner Prize have been UAL graduates. Visiting lecturers, many of them alumni, keep students abreast of developments in their field. The university also has a celebrity chancellor – the artist Grayson Perry – who presided over this summer's graduation ceremonies in a new set of robes designed by Rachele Terrinoni, who is taking an MA costume design for performance course at the LCF. He wore a custom-made petticoat, smock dress and a Swarovski crystal-encrusted coat.

UAL has 13 halls of residence spread around the colleges and runs house-hunting workshops for those who have to rely on the scattered private housing market. The university owns no sports facilities, although it has arranged student discounts with a number of fitness providers.

Tuition fees

»	Fees for UK/EU students	£9,250
	Foundation courses from £5,420	
»	Fees for International students 2020–21	£22,920
»	For scholarship and bursary information see	
	www.arts.ac.uk/study-at-ual/student-fees-funding	
»	Graduate salary	£19,200

Student numbers

Undergraduates	14,999	(120)
Postgraduates	3,190	(660)
Applications/places	27,620/4,285	
Applications per place	6.4	
Overall offer rate	38.7%	
Unconditional offers	0%	
International students	48.4%	

Accommodation

University provided places: 3,200
Self-catered: £140–£407 per week
No accommodation guarantee
www.arts.ac.uk/study-at-ual/accommodation

Where do the students come from?

State schools (non-grammar)	91.3%	First generation students	39.9%	
Grammar schools	1.8%	Deprived areas	6.9%	
Independent schools	6.9%	All ethnic minorities	29.1%	

Social inclusion ranking: 59

Black attainment gap	-26.5%
Disabled	15.6%
Mature (over 21)	18.1%

Aston University

Aston has recovered some of the ground it lost last year when it dropped out of our top 50 for the first time. The university saw a big fall in applications in 2018 – almost 15% – and fewer students took up places, despite a much higher offer rate than normal. However, both applications and enrolments had been running at record levels in previous years, so overall numbers remain relatively healthy.

No university has a larger proportion of students from ethnic minorities. Indeed, Aston has become one of the first universities to introduce an official target to increase the recruitment of white males. It is one of the highest-placed universities established before 1992 in our social inclusion table, finishing in the top 30.

Aston has a gold rating in the Teaching Excellence Framework (TEF), partly for the way employability skills are embedded through an integrated placement year taken by seven out of ten Aston undergraduates. The TEF panel was also impressed by pre-entry masterclasses and the Aston professional mentoring scheme, as well as the involvement of professional bodies and employers in course design and delivery.

The university has an enduring reputation for success in the graduate employment market. More than 160 companies attend Aston's recruitment events and the institution has links to more than 350 international companies, many of which offer placements as well as eventual employment opportunities. Four out of five students secure professional jobs or go into graduate-level study within six months of leaving. A scheme called Languages for All allows students to learn a language alongside or as part of their degree.

A partnership with Capgemini, a global consulting, technology and outsourcing company, was responsible for the UK's first degree apprenticeships. There are now 530 students taking 11 programmes, which range from digital technology solutions to nuclear engineering and supply chain leadership and management. The numbers are expected to double by September 2020, with new programmes in transport planning, power engineering and logistics.

At the same time, Aston has launched new degree courses in business analytics, civil engineering, cybersecurity and quantity surveying. It had already added medicine at undergraduate level in 2018, having offered the subject for postgraduates for the three previous years. The aim is to make the school the most socially inclusive in the UK, taking up to 40% of students from low-income families, many of them local sixth-formers who take the Sir Doug Ellis Pathway to Healthcare programme. A £15m headquarters is planned for the school when it is operating at full capacity.

Aston Triangle
Birmingham B4 7ET
0121 204 3000
ugadmissions@aston.ac.uk
www.aston.ac.uk
www.astonsu.com
Open days 2020:
see website

The Times and *The Sunday Times* **Rankings**
Overall Ranking: 48 (last year: 56)

Teaching quality	78.3%	=93
Student experience	77.3%	=85
Research quality	25.8%	48
Entry standards	133	=60
Graduate prospects	79.1%	52
Good honours	84.4%	20
Expected completion rate	92%	28
Student/staff ratio	17.4	=95
Services and facilities	£1,983	97

A new students' union has opened at the heart of the campus, with study spaces, rooms for societies and a large auditorium, as well as a cafe, bar and kitchen where students can heat their own food. A long-running programme of improvements has opened up the campus with green spaces and a remodelled Chancellor's Lake. Located close to the centre of Birmingham, the university has replaced its 1970s buildings with modern teaching facilities and conveniently placed student accommodation.

Redevelopments have already brought an impressive library and a new home for the highly-rated business school, the base for almost half of all Aston's students. The school has a new partnership with the French business school, Kedge, to collaborate on teaching and research. Among the benefits will be access to the Kedge campus in Suzhou, in China, for Aston students.

Once a college of advanced technology, Aston also remains strong in engineering and the sciences. But the life and health sciences produced the best results in the last research assessments, when the proportion of work placed in the top two categories doubled to nearly 80%. New research centres in enterprise, healthy ageing, Europe, and neuroscience and child development have proved their worth. Another of the university's strengths – pharmacy – attracted a prestigious Regius Professorship to celebrate the Queen's 90th birthday.

Aston was one of the universities highlighted by the government for making so-called conditional unconditional offers in 2018 that required the offer holder to put Aston as their firm choice, but the only unconditional offers available in 2020 will be for candidates who already have their A-level or equivalent results.

The university has been focusing on improving the student experience. The MyAston mobile app, used regularly by 80% of students, gives access to course materials and other information.

The completion of the Aston student village brought the number of residential places on campus past the 3,000 mark, maintaining the guarantee of accommodation for all first-year students who make Aston their firm choice on their UCAS application. There are five different types of accommodation, and undergraduates have the option of a 45-week tenancy.

The Woodcock Sport Centre on campus has a grade II listed swimming pool and a sports hall with indoor courts and team sports facilities.

Tuition fees

» Fees for UK/EU students 2019–20 £9,250
» Fees for International students 2019–20 £14,600–£19,000
  Medicine £38,850
» For scholarship and bursary information see
  www.aston.ac.uk/study/undergraduate/student-finance
» Graduate salary £21,500

Student numbers

Undergraduates	10,672	(1,176)
Postgraduates	1,596	(1,171)
Applications/places		14,140/3,000
Applications per place		4.7
Overall offer rate		88.8%
Unconditional offers		7.7%
International students		16.7%

Accommodation

University provided places: 3,000
Self-catered: £133–£139 per week
First years guaranteed accommodation
www.aston.ac.uk/accommodation/

Where do the students come from?

				Social inclusion ranking: 28	
State schools (non-grammar)	84.8%	First generation students	52.1%	Black attainment gap	-11%
Grammar schools	9.2%	Deprived areas	9.5%	Disabled	4.9%
Independent schools	5.9%	All ethnic minorities	76.7%	Mature (over 21)	6%

Bangor University

Bangor is drawing up a ten-year strategy to make more efficient use of its 126 buildings and improve the experience of students, staff and visitors. Almost half of its current space is classified as requiring improvement – twice the sector average – and there is a backlog in maintenance estimated at more than £11m. Proposals have been made to close two sites and reduce the university's footprint by a quarter, refurbishing a number of the remaining buildings and creating a new student union and social hub.

The Dean Street site, which houses computer studies, would close by September 2021, while relocation from the much larger Normal site near the Menai Bridge (named after the former college there) would begin the following year. The university would then be concentrated in more sustainable buildings in better condition within Bangor itself, releasing resources to spend on teaching and research.

But these deficiencies have not held back Bangor's scores in the annual National Student Survey, where it has been consistently in or around the top 20 in the UK.

Bangor was also the only university in Wales to achieve a gold award in the first round of the Teaching Excellence Framework (TEF). Its panel commended the personalised support for students and strategic approach to assessment, as well as very good physical and virtual learning resources. Welsh/English bilingual learning also drew praise.

Bangor's Study Skills Centre helps with the transition to university and provides continuing academic support. Under a peer guiding scheme, second- and third-year students mentor new arrivals and arrange social activities for them. The university has a flourishing international exchange programme, which gives students the option of studying overseas for one extra year in a wide variety of destinations. From this year, every undergraduate will be given the option of two-week or year-long work placements. The Bangor Employability Award accredits co-curricular and extracurricular activities, such as volunteering and part-time work, that are valued by employers.

Applications have dropped by almost 20% in two years, although the decline in enrolments was only half that. Ten new degrees are being launched this year and next covering policing, politics and business, wildlife conservation, biomedical science with a foundation year, and zoology with primatology or ornithology.

Students taking Cardiff University's MBBCh programme in medicine will be able to complete their entire course at Bangor's School of Medical Sciences for the first time. Cardiff students already had the option of placements in north Wales, but the new

---

College Road
Bangor LL57 2DG
01248 383 717
applicantservices@bangor.ac.uk
www.bangor.ac.uk
www.undebbangor.com
Open days 2020:
June 27, July 4

The Times and The Sunday Times Rankings
Overall Ranking: 70 (last year: =63)

Teaching quality	83.8%	=11
Student experience	81.8%	=15
Research quality	27.2%	47
Entry standards	131	=67
Graduate prospects	67.8%	110
Good honours	71.4%	90
Expected completion rate	84.1%	=73
Student/staff ratio	17	=89
Services and facilities	£1,714	117

partnership will increase the number of young doctors with an understanding of the region.

Most of Bangor's students come from outside Wales, but about 20% speak Welsh and one of the halls of residence is for Welsh-speakers and learners of the language. The university has almost 3,000 residential places – enough to guarantee accommodation to new entrants who apply by the end of July. The 600-bed student village has a cafe, shop, laundrette, student lounges, outdoor recreation and games area, a mini cinema and performance and music space.

The university's Talent Opportunities Programme, which operates in schools across north Wales, targets potential applicants from families in lower socioeconomic groups who have little or no history of going to university. More than 96% of the students come from state schools or colleges, many in areas of low participation in higher education. A pioneering dyslexia service offers individual and group support throughout students' courses. Bangor ranks in the middle reaches of our social inclusion table overall.

In the 2014 Research Excellence Framework, Bangor finished among the top 50 universities. Half of its schools were rated in the top 20 in the UK, led by leisure and tourism, languages and psychology. The School of Ocean Sciences is highly rated and there is also a £20m science park on Anglesey, bringing together businesses from the ICT, science and research sectors with staff and students from the university.

The small coastal city is rated as one of the cheapest – and safest – places in the UK in which to study. Social life for most students is concentrated mainly on the students' union, housed in the centre. Its clubs and societies, which are free to students, were voted the best in the UK for two years in succession. The Pontio arts and innovation centre connects town and gown with a cinema, theatre and restaurants.

Bangor's main sports centre has a two-storey gym, including 50 cardiovascular machines, a six-platform Olympic lifting area, two sports halls, an aerobics studio, cycling studio, gymnastics hall, climbing wall and squash courts, and gym membership is included in accommodation fees.

The region's spectacular scenery, with its outdoor sporting opportunities from Snowdonia to the sea, is one of the university's greatest attractions.

Tuition fees

» Fees for UK/EU students £9,000

» Fees for International students 2020–21 . £14,500–£18,000

» For scholarship and bursary information see www.bangor.ac.uk/courses/undergrad/study-with-us/undergraduate-funding

» Graduate salary £20,000

Student numbers

Undergraduates	**7,966**	**(488)**
Postgraduates	**1,598**	**(1,104)**
Applications/places		**8,740/2,390**
Applications per place		**3.7**
Overall offer rate		**93.2%**
Unconditional offers		**29.2%**
International students		**22.3%**

Accommodation

University provided places: 2,809
Self-catered: £99–£195 per week
First years guaranteed accommodation
www.bangor.ac.uk/studentlife/accommodation.php.en

Where do the students come from?

State schools (non-grammar)	92%	First generation students	41.2%	Black attainment gap	-19.9%
Grammar schools	4.3%	Deprived areas	14.4%	Disabled	9.8%
Independent schools	3.7%	All ethnic minorities	7.1%	Mature (over 21)	27.5%

Social inclusion ranking: =47

University of Bath

Bath is redesigning every course, with the involvement of students, to develop "creative approaches to assessment, teaching and course delivery". The curriculum transformation is designed to produce an "inclusive academic experience", developing professional, research and academic skills while drawing on the diversity of experience of students and staff. The first courses to go through the process – mainly taught postgraduate programmes – have already been launched.

The university has a gold award in the Teaching Excellence Framework (TEF), but took part in the assessment again to ensure "continued educational excellence and a position at the forefront of the sector". The TEF panel found that students from all backgrounds achieved consistently outstanding outcomes. Employers were heavily involved and students engaged frequently with developments from the forefront of research, scholarship and professional practice.

In recent years, Bath has been a fixture on the fringes of our top ten, with consistently excellent scores for graduate prospects. Almost two-thirds of undergraduates take a work placement or study abroad as part of their degree. Student entrepreneurship is encouraged through a number of initiatives and projects. Just four universities see a greater proportion of graduates land professional jobs or progress on to further study within six months.

As well as reviewing the current curriculum, the university is introducing a number of new degrees. Chemical engineering with environmental engineering has been added and computer science and artificial intelligence will follow in 2020. Undergraduate master's degrees are also being introduced in biology, biochemistry and biomedical sciences, while Russian and Mandarin have been added to the options for modern languages and international politics and modern-language degrees.

Bath has also stepped up its efforts to broaden its intake. Ranking fourth from bottom in our social inclusion table, less than 55% of its students come from comprehensive and other non-selective state schools. The first 50 disadvantaged students to benefit from the Gold Scholarship Programme entered in 2017, receiving £5,000 bursaries and participating in an enrichment programme to enhance their experience as students and improve their employment prospects.

The university is emerging from a period in which its media coverage was dominated by controversy over the salary of Dame Professor Glynis Breakwell, the former vice-chancellor, which, at £468,000, was the highest in the country. Her successor, Professor Ian White, who was recruited from Cambridge, where he was deputy vice-chancellor, is paid £200,000 less. Drawing a line under the episode, the university

Claverton Down
Bath BA2 7AY
01225 388 388
admissions@bath.ac.uk
www.bath.ac.uk
www.thesubath.com
Open days 2020:
June 19, 20,
September 12

The Times and The Sunday Times Rankings
Overall Ranking: 11 (last year: 13)

Teaching quality	79.4%	=77
Student experience	81.8%	=15
Research quality	37.3%	24
Entry standards	182	12
Graduate prospects	87.5%	5
Good honours	88.3%	10
Expected completion rate	96.6%	3
Student/staff ratio	15.6	=62
Services and facilities	£2,541	44

also put the vice-chancellor's £3m residence up for sale, promising that the proceeds will be used to renovate a campus property to provide guest accommodation and host events.

The 200-acre Claverton Down campus is on a hillside on the outskirts of Bath. A 300-bed accommodation block and the £8.5m Milner Centre for Evolution, a research centre part-funded by an alumnus, have been added recently. A new building for the highly-rated School of Management is due to open during the 2020–21 academic year, with laboratories for student entrepreneurship and behavioural research, as well as modern teaching spaces.

After the first year, most undergraduates move into the city itself, a world heritage site and thriving social centre. In recognition of this, the university opened the £4.5m Virgil building, a student hub and professional services building in the centre of Bath, with learning spaces, a cafe and access to student support services such as the careers service, students' union and skills centre.

Bath's already considerable reputation for research has been growing. Almost a third of the university's submission to the 2014 Research Excellence Framework was judged to be world-leading, with 87% in the top two categories. Bath is the lead institution in the National Institute of Coding, which is charged with improving the digital skills of the nation.

The research grants and contracts portfolio is worth more than £130m and there are 25 international strategic partnerships with top-ranked institutions worldwide. A third of the 16,000 students are studying at postgraduate level.

The modern campus has pleasant grounds with a grass amphitheatre and lake, as well as conveniently-placed amenities. It boasts outstanding sports facilities, which have just been enhanced with a large gym extension and studios for group exercise and indoor cycling. The Sports Training Village has a 50-metre swimming pool, indoor athletics and multi-sports halls, outdoor pitches and track, indoor and outdoor tennis courts and even a bobsleigh and skeleton push-start track.

The Edge, the arts, education and events centre, has a theatre, performance studio, rehearsal studios, three galleries and a cafe for use by the university and the wider community.

The university owns or manages more than 4,700 residential places, enabling it to accommodate all new entrants and more than a quarter of all undergraduates. More than 1,000 of the places are catered – an increasingly rare option in today's universities.

Tuition fees

» Fees for UK/EU students	£9,250
Foundation courses	£7,710
» Fees for International students 2020–21	£18,000–£22,300
» For scholarship and bursary information see www.bath.ac.uk/study/ug/fees/	
» Graduate salary	£26,000

Student numbers

Undergraduates	13,185	(92)
Postgraduates	2,796	(1,481)
Applications/places		26,920/3,665
Applications per place		7.3
Overall offer rate		79.3%
Unconditional offers		0%
International students		29.8%

Accommodation

University provided places: 3,470
Catered costs: £133–£173 per week
Self-catered: £70–£188 per week
First years guaranteed accommodation
www.bath.ac.uk/student-accommodation

Where do the students come from?

State schools (non-grammar)	54.5%	First generation students	25.7%	Black attainment gap	-15.7%
Grammar schools	18.5%	Deprived areas	5.2%	Disabled	5.4%
Independent schools	27.1%	All ethnic minorities	17.2%	Mature (over 21)	1.9%

Social inclusion ranking: 112

Bath Spa University

Bath Spa has opened a new front in the controversy over unconditional offers, announcing that it will make guaranteed offers to students who impress at interview, audition or through their portfolio in arts subjects, and then give £750 scholarships to those who exceed their predicted grades to ensure that they do not neglect their studies. Once the offer has been accepted, there will also be a guarantee of accommodation.

Professor Sue Rigby, the vice-chancellor, insists offers made under the 3, 2, 1, Go! scheme will not be unconditional because they will depend on the university's assessment of the candidate's skills and attributes – but they will remove the stress from the application process.

A raft of new degrees has helped Bath Spa reverse a three-year decline in applications. Courses in microbiology, fashion marketing and management, forensic psychology, interior design and professional music, among others, had produced a 3% increase in the demand for places when the last official deadline passed. Admissions have also been falling, although even last year's reduced enrolment was bigger than at any point before 2015.

One popular innovation has been the introduction of a professional placement year option for all undergraduates. Bath

Spa is also planning a range of degree apprenticeships to supplement its existing programme in leadership, which includes an MBA. The university expects to have up to 200 apprentices in food technology and production, childcare and education, policing, and creative arts and design.

Students taking art and design subjects will be based at the new Locksbrook campus in the centre of Bath. A former factory close to the River Avon has been converted into a new home for the Bath School of Art and Design. The first phase of the refurbished grade II listed building has modern, flexible teaching facilities, workshop, studio and gallery space, and a cafe and art shop. The new campus has also led to improvements to the cycle route and pedestrian pathway that runs alongside the River Avon.

The university had already spent £6m on specialist facilities for the school at the Sion Hill campus, which is also within walking distance of the city centre and where there is a student village of 550 study bedrooms. However, Bath Spa's headquarters will remain on the Newton Park campus four miles outside the World Heritage city, in grounds landscaped by Capability Brown in the 18th century, with a handsome Georgian manor house owned by the Duchy of Cornwall as its centrepiece.

Across the campus, historic buildings blend sympathetically with modern facilities, following a £70m redevelopment that was

Newton Park
Newton St Loe
Bath BA2 9BN
01225 875 875
admissions@bathspa.ac.uk
www.bathspa.ac.uk
www.bathspasu.co.uk
Open days 2020:
see website

The Times and The Sunday Times Rankings
Overall Ranking: 110 (last year: =103)

Teaching quality	76.5%	=112
Student experience	72.2%	=123
Research quality	7.9%	=73
Entry standards	118	=100
Graduate prospects	66.9%	113
Good honours	78.8%	46
Expected completion rate	86.2%	=62
Student/staff ratio	18.7	=113
Services and facilities	£2,100	86

completed in 2014. The Creative Writing Centre is housed in the 14th-century gatehouse, a scheduled ancient monument. There is also a postgraduate centre at Corsham Court, a 16th-century manor house near Chippenham.

About 90% of the UK intake is educated in non-selective state schools, and about a third of students were from working-class homes when socio-economic background was last surveyed. Two-thirds of the students are female, reflecting the arts and social science bias in the curriculum, and about 22% of all students are over 20 at entry.

Bath Spa took silver in the government's Teaching Excellence Framework. Its panel was impressed by the personalised teaching, the availability of a personal tutor, peer mentoring, and independent study that provide "rigour and stretch". Assessors also found that the investment in physical and digital resources, supported by a team of learning technologists, demonstrably enhances student engagement.

All students have the opportunity to collect a Global Citizenship award by completing a module that covers a range of cross-cutting issues. Bath Spa also offers a pre-entry year for international undergraduates with language tuition, academic instruction and information on UK history and culture. EU students have been applying in larger numbers, and some 15% of the university's intake now comes from further afield.

Bath Spa became a university only in 2005, but its predecessor colleges date back 160 years. Famous alumni include Gruffalo books illustrator Axel Scheffler, cobbler to the stars Manolo Blahnik, Olympic gold medal athlete Jason Gardener, and the late Body Shop founder Dame Anita Roddick and Turner Prize winner Sir Howard Hodgkin.

The university enjoyed its best-ever research assessments in 2014, when more than half of a relatively small submission was rated as world-leading or internationally excellent. The university received an 86% increase in research funding as a result.

It had strengthened its research capacity in key areas such as creative writing and art and design through the appointment of high-profile professors including Fay Weldon and Gavin Turk.

The university owns or endorses more than 2,000 residential places. A new sports ground is under development close to the city and will include a cricket pitch, tennis courts and a floodlit sports pitch to supplement the main campus gym and indoor facilities

Tuition fees

» Fees for UK/EU students		£9,250
Foundation courses		£7,950
» Fees for International students 2020–21		£13,700–£15,300
» For scholarship and bursary information see		
www.bathspa.ac.uk/students/student-finance		
» Graduate salary		£18,000

Student numbers

Undergraduates	**6,224**	**(96)**
Postgraduates	**937**	**(733)**
Applications/places		**11,590/2,210**
Applications per place		**5.2**
Overall offer rate		**87.3%**
Unconditional offers		**0%**
International students		**8.4%**

Accommodation

University provided places: 2,047
Self-catered: £70–£247 per week
First years guaranteed accommodation
www.bathspa.ac.uk/accom

Where do the students come from?

State schools (non-grammar)	91.3%	First generation students	43.3%	
Grammar schools	3.2%	Deprived areas	12.9%	
Independent schools	5.5%	All ethnic minorities	7.4%	

Social inclusion ranking: 58

Black attainment gap	n/a
Disabled	11.3%
Mature (over 21)	13.3%

University of Bedfordshire

The opening of an impressive new building for Stem subjects (science, technology, engineering and maths) is part of a three-year push by Bedfordshire to improve the student experience. The university has fallen out of the top 50 in both our measures of student satisfaction, helping to drag it into the bottom ten of our main league table. Situated on the main campus in Luton, the four-storey Stem building will provide more than 6,000 square metres (64,500 sq ft) of new teaching space.

New undergraduate courses include pharmaceutical and chemical science, nutrition, biochemistry, and mechanical engineering – taught in large flexible laboratories and workshops with simulation spaces, analytical labs and a clean room facility. There is also a new outreach centre to promote the value of science and engineering to local schools and the wider community.

Other courses newly-launched include four football degrees – in business, coaching, development and science – interior design, photography, physiotherapy and behavioural science in health. There are also new higher and degree apprenticeships in quantity surveying and food science, technology and management.

The university will be hoping that the new offerings help to arrest a decline in enrolments of more than 18% in 2018. Applications have fallen for four years in a row and a much higher offer rate has not made up the difference.

Bedfordshire's strategic plan sets out to make it a leading university for expanding higher education opportunities. The targets include annual increases in the number of white working-class males enrolling as students and maintaining the university's already high participation rates for black and minority ethnic students, who account for about 60% of the intake. The university is just outside the top ten in our social inclusion ranking.

Bedfordshire also plans to expand its activities through partnerships in London, Birmingham and internationally. A link with Middle East University in Jordan has made it the first UK university to offer undergraduate degrees there. In the UK, a Community Charter sets out plans to work with partners across the region.

Bedfordshire has five campuses, by far the largest of which is in the centre of Luton, where there is a £40m student halls complex and a well-equipped media arts centre. A seven-floor library costing £46m has more than 900 study spaces, laptops for loan, 530 PCs and a cafe. A study hub offers advice and guidance on academic and study skills.

A second campus in Bedford is home to the education and sport faculty, with more than 2,000 students, making it one of the UK's largest providers of physical education teacher

University Square
Luton LU1 3JU
0300 330 0073
admissions@beds.ac.uk
www.beds.ac.uk
www.bedssu.co.uk
Open days 2020:
February 8

The Times and The Sunday Times Rankings
Overall Ranking: 128 (last year: 121)

Teaching quality	80.4%	=62
Student experience	77.4%	=83
Research quality	7.0%	=77
Entry standards	101	=130
Graduate prospects	70.6%	98
Good honours	63.9%	=125
Expected completion rate	66.3%	130
Student/staff ratio	17.1	=89
Services and facilities	£2,089	87

training, as well as a national centre for other subjects. Another 1,000 students take subjects such as performing arts, law and business management. The campus is in a leafy setting 20 minutes' walk from the town centre and has a 280-seat auditorium and a students' union, as well as accommodation for 600 students.

The Milton Keynes campus offers a range of courses from journalism to computer systems engineering and business management. The Putteridge Bury campus, a neo-Elizabethan mansion on the outskirts of Luton, doubles as a management centre and conference venue, while nursing and midwifery students are taught in Aylesbury, in Buckinghamshire.

Bedfordshire got a silver rating in the Teaching Excellence Framework. The university was praised for its successes in widening participation, not only in enrolling students from groups that are underrepresented in higher education, but also in helping them to achieve good results.

Instead of providing bursaries to only the most academically able students, as is the case in many institutions, Bedfordshire offers students who enter with fewer than 112 UCAS tariff points, or equivalent, a bursary worth £1,500 over three academic years – recognising that it is often these students who need the most support, financially and generally, to successfully complete their studies. Merit scholarships are also available, worth £2,400 over three years, for those achieving more than 112 UCAS points.

Almost all of Bedfordshire's undergraduates are state-educated and about half are 21 or over on entry. Nearly one in five students comes from outside the EU.

The university more than doubled the number of academics it entered for the 2014 Research Excellence Framework. It was rewarded with one of the biggest increases in funding for research at any university. Almost half of the work submitted for assessment was placed in the top two categories, with social work and social policy, health subjects and English producing good results.

The 1,500 residential places owned or endorsed by the university are enough to guarantee accommodation for first-year undergraduates. There are good sports facilities in Bedford and Luton.

Both Luton and Bedford have their share of pubs, clubs and restaurants, and London is 30–40 minutes away by train. Bedfordshire ranked eighth for its environmental record in the latest People & Planet League. It was the first university in England to promise not to invest in the fossil fuel industry and is Fairtrade-accredited.

Tuition fees

» Fees for UK/EU students	£9,250
Foundation courses	£6,165
» Fees for International students 2020–21	£12,650
» For scholarship and bursary information see www.beds.ac.uk/howtoapply/money	
» Graduate salary	£20,000

Student numbers

Undergraduates	8,488	(1,985)
Postgraduates	1,430	(895)
Applications/places		9,925/2,540
Applications per place		3.9
Overall offer rate		89.5%
Unconditional offers		0%
International students		18.7%

Accommodation

University provided places: 1,485
Self-catered: £100–£195 per week
First years guaranteed accommodation
www.beds.ac.uk/accommodation

Where do the students come from?

State schools (non-grammar)	97.3%	First generation students	70.7%	
Grammar schools	1.1%	Deprived areas	11.3%	
Independent schools	1.6%	All ethnic minorities	60.5%	

Social inclusion ranking: 11

Black attainment gap	-26%
Disabled	5.0%
Mature (over 21)	50.6%

Birkbeck, University of London

Birkbeck has withdrawn from our league table after only two years because it felt that, in comparison with traditional, residential universities, our measures placed it at a disadvantage. The college was surprisingly close to the bottom of the table in 2018.

The university's decision to join the table was prompted by a rapid increase in full-time courses – albeit taught in the evening – which made comparisons with other universities more valid than before. But the nature of the student experience remains part-time.

Spending on student facilities, for example, is naturally lower than in residential universities and its undergraduates are more likely to pause their education, often returning at a later date, skewing degree completion figures.

Birkbeck remains in the international rankings, where it does much better because they are based mainly on research and reputation. In the QS World University Rankings, Birkbeck is 328th – among the UK's top 40 institutions, and inside the top ten in London.

Birkbeck has a unique mission and place in British higher education, where it does more to widen participation than the vast majority of universities. (It ranked 10th last year in our inaugural social inclusion table.)

It was in the top 30 in the 2014 Research Excellence Framework, when more than 80% of its eligible academics were entered. Almost three-quarters of the work submitted was rated world-leading or internationally excellent, with psychology and environmental science in the top six.

Birkbeck was placed in the silver category in the Teaching Excellence Framework (TEF). Its assessors were impressed by the range of initiatives to help students who would not otherwise be in higher education to graduate successfully. Programmes supported students from diverse backgrounds, the TEF panel said, enabling them to achieve their full potential through a curriculum which is at the forefront of research.

Until relatively recently, all Birkbeck's courses were part-time and it still describes itself as "London's Evening University", but the option of a more intensive format enables students to complete a degree in three years and qualify for the full package of loans. Enrolments have been running at record levels.

All degrees are now available on a full-time basis and there is a range of foundation-year courses for students without the qualifications for immediate entry. Seven new degree programmes have been launched in 2019, including ancient history and archaeology, arts and media management, international business, and computing with a foundation year. A liberal arts degree and Japanese with the option of a year abroad are planned for 2020.

Malet Street
London WC1E 7HX
020 3907 0700
studentadvice@bbk.ac.uk
www.bbk.ac.uk
www.bbk.ac.uk/su
Open days 2020:
February 22

The Times and The Sunday Times **Rankings**
Overall Ranking: n/a
No data available

The switch to full-time courses was triggered by the nationwide collapse in part-time enrolments, but the option of studying for four years, rather than three, remains open. Birkbeck is also offering degree apprenticeships in chartered management and digital and technology solutions.

Founded in 1823 as a mechanics' institute, Birkbeck is part of the University of London and based near Senate House, the university's headquarters in Bloomsbury. It has its own degree-awarding powers if it chose to exercise that right but, for the foreseeable future, will continue to award University of London degrees.

Planned developments on the Bloomsbury campus include refurbishment of the library, in response to student feedback, increasing the number of study spaces and extending the silent area, as well as enabling students to access more services centrally. A new teaching building on Euston Road will house a large lecture theatre and classrooms, as well as space for students to prepare for lectures and share ideas.

The college shares a five-storey building in Stratford with the University of East London, in the first joint project of its kind in the capital. In addition, Birkbeck is part of the £40m Institute of Coding, set up in 2018 to plug the digital skills gap.

Birkbeck graduates enjoy high average starting salaries – among the best in the sector – partly because three-quarters are mature students, many of them returning to already successful careers. A professional in-house recruitment service, Birkbeck Talent, links employers with students and graduates for both employment opportunities and paid internships.

Birkbeck welcomes applications from people without traditional qualifications and continues to attract non-traditional learners of all ages and backgrounds. As mature students tend to apply late in the application process, about 45% of undergraduates arrive through clearing.

Those who have taken A-level or an equivalent qualification recently are made offers based on the UCAS tariff, but others are assessed by the college on the basis of interviews and/or short tests. The My Birkbeck student centre brings together all of the college's student support services.

Most Birkbeck students already live in the capital, but full-time students looking for accommodation have access to University of London Housing Services, as well as to places in private halls of residence run by Unite Students.

Tuition fees

» Fees for UK/EU students	£9,250
» Fees for International students 2020–21	£14,000
» For scholarship and bursary information see www.bbk.ac.uk/student-services/financial-support	
» Graduate salary	£24,960

Student numbers

Applications/places	5,130/1,465
Applications per place	3.5
Overall offer rate	n/a

Accommodation

www.bbk.ac.uk/student-services/accommodation

Where do the students come from?

No data available

University of Birmingham

Birmingham has dropped its controversial unconditional offers scheme that eliminated entry requirements in return for applicants making the university their firm choice. The Russell Group member was the highest profile advocate of the policy, which it said reduced stress for prospective students. In its place for 2020, it will introduce an "attainment offer", with minimum grade requirements for some applicants with excellent predicted grades.

Birmingham's previous strategy – which saw almost one in five receive so-called conditional unconditional offers – had served it well: applications and enrolments have been running at record levels, despite a dip in 2018. Even then, only a dozen universities recruited more undergraduates. Prospective students have access to an online offer calculator to give them the best possible idea of whether they are likely to secure a place.

Birmingham's popularity was buoyed further by a gold award in the Teaching Excellence Framework, which has proved beyond several Russell Group universities. The judging panel found an "outstanding learning environment", where the university had invested effectively in staffing and physical resources. A strategic focus on the development and delivery of relevant, research-informed teaching was said to be highly valued by employers.

There are £130m of campus developments in the pipeline, with more in years to come. A new purpose-built Teaching and Learning Building offers learning spaces for up to 1,000 students, including a 500-seat lecture theatre and interactive facilities. Construction of the National Buried Infrastructure Facility is pushing ahead and will have space for research, education and training in soil stabilisation, geophysical sensing, and tunnelling and trenchless technologies. The new School of Engineering building is due to open in September 2020, bringing together a number of related disciplines.

In recent years, the campus has been augmented by a new £60m library and a development adding 178 places to Birmingham's accommodation stock. The Green Heart programme is creating 12 acres of parkland at the centre of the campus.

Birmingham was the original "redbrick" university. The 230-acre campus in leafy Edgbaston is dominated by the 300ft Joseph Chamberlain Memorial Clock Tower, better known as Old Joe, one of the city's best-known landmarks, and has its own train station.

Dentistry courses are based in the city centre, while part of the School of Education and drama facilities are in Selly Oak, a mile from the Edgbaston campus. The BBC Drama Village, a partnership between the university and the broadcaster, is on the Selly Oak campus. A new campus in Dubai took its first students in 2018.

Edgbaston
Birmingham B15 2TT
0121 414 3344
www.birmingham.ac.uk
www.guildofstudents.com
Open days 2020:
June 26, 27;
September 12;
October 17

The Times and The Sunday Times **Rankings**
Overall Ranking: 14 (last year: 14)

Teaching quality	78.4%	92
Student experience	77.9%	=77
Research quality	37.1%	26
Entry standards	165	21
Graduate prospects	85.8%	=10
Good honours	86.6%	16
Expected completion rate	94.9%	12
Student/staff ratio	13.9	=24
Services and facilities	£3,036	14

Birmingham did well in the 2014 Research Excellence Framework, when more than 80% of its submission was rated as world-leading or internationally excellent. The university was ranked in the top five for philosophy, history, classics, theology and religion, area studies, chemical engineering, and sport, exercise and rehabilitation studies. This performance took it into the top 20 for research quality and has helped to maintain its place in our top 15 overall.

An increased focus on employability is helped by successful graduates who act as mentors, while the university provides bursaries to support work experience and internships in the UK and overseas. Three-quarters of the undergraduates undertake work experience as part of their course. The university's graduates were the third most targeted by leading employers in the High Fliers Graduate Market 2019 report, behind Manchester and Bristol.

Birmingham has introduced its first degree apprenticeships in digital technology and railway engineering, with more to come for town planners, advanced clinical practitioners and senior leaders. A range of new nursing courses has been added in 2019 and there will be new degrees in 2020 in subjects including English with Shakespeare studies, international development and politics, and mechanical engineering with a year in industry.

The numbers recruited from the poorest social groups have been rising gradually. The Pathways to Birmingham scheme encourages students whose families have little or no experience of higher education to apply. Bursaries and scholarships are available for undergraduates, as well as pastoral support. Birmingham performs better than many Russell Group universities in our social inclusion ranking, although it still ranks in the bottom 20 overall.

The university's sports facilities are some of the best in the country and include an outdoor-pursuits centre by Coniston Water in the Lake District. A £55m sport and fitness centre boasts Birmingham's first 50-metre swimming pool, a large multi-sports arena, squash courts and gym. Its 55 sports clubs attract about 4,000 students to participate.

Campus facilities include a medical practice and a comprehensive student services hub, as well as Birmingham's own nightclub. More than 7,000 residential places are owned or endorsed by the university, most of them close to the campus. The main university facilities are less than three miles from the city centre, which has become increasingly attractive to young people, and the area around the campus has plenty of shops, pubs and restaurants.

Tuition fees

» Fees for UK/EU students	£9,250
» Fees for International students 2020–21	£18,120–£24,660
Medicine & dentistry	£39,960
» For scholarship and bursary information see	
www.birmingham.ac.uk/undergraduate/fees/index.aspx	
» Graduate salary	£23,000

Student numbers

Undergraduates	21,836	(875)
Postgraduates	7,063	(5,142)
Applications/places	52,480/6,670	
Applications per place	7.9	
Overall offer rate	81.5%	
Unconditional offers	18.8%	
International students	23.6%	

Accommodation

University provided places: 7,059
Catered costs: £129–£203 per week
Self-catered: £89–£265 per week
First years guaranteed accommodation
www.birmingham.ac.uk/accommodation

Where do the students come from?

State schools (non-grammar)	66.1%	First generation students	28.3%	Black attainment gap	-15.6%
Grammar schools	15.7%	Deprived areas	6.7%	Disabled	5.3%
Independent schools	18.1%	All ethnic minorities	28.9%	Mature (over 21)	6.3%

Social inclusion ranking: 100

Birmingham City University

For applicants seeking a place in 2020, Birmingham City University (BCU) is abandoning its controversial "conditional unconditional" offer scheme. However, it is incentivising applicants who meet or exceed the required course entry grades with a £1,000 scholarship. BCU is also giving at least £150 towards course materials and other costs that might be a barrier to study.

Birmingham City thrived after changing its name from the University of Central England in 2007, with enrolments growing for seven years in a row. But both applications and enrolments dropped by about 5% in 2018.

Six out of ten students come from the West Midlands, with more than half of admissions overall drawn from ethnic minorities (53.7%) and more than 40% from the poorest socioeconomic groups. Many undergraduates enter through a network of associated further education colleges, which run foundation and access programmes.

There is also a growing portfolio of degree apprenticeships, with new programmes planned in digital technology solutions, nursing, radiography, sonography and building design engineering, which are expected to take the number of apprentices from the current 400 to about 700 by September 2020.

New honours degrees are planned for 2020 in cybersecurity, visual effects, building services engineering and design management, as well as a four-year integrated master's in nursing and a foundation degree in popular music. The School of Jewellery, one of BCU's best-known features, has also embarked on further expansion after opening a new building close to its existing base.

One of the most striking elements of a £260m development programme is the new home for the Royal Birmingham Conservatoire, which has five performance spaces including a 500-seat concert hall.

Specialist laboratories have been added for new courses in sport and life sciences, as well as an experimental learning space and a new building for education.

The university has now concentrated most of its activities onto two campuses in the city centre and nearby Edgbaston. The City Centre campus, close to the proposed HS2 rail terminus, houses all student support services as well as business, law, social sciences and English. Courses in art and design and media are also based there, and the university occupies part of the Millennium Point building, helping to create the Eastside Learning Quarter.

The City South campus, in Edgbaston, has a prize-winning library, IT suites, recreational space and teaching facilities enhanced by features such as an altitude chamber and anti-gravity treadmill.

University House
15 Bartholomew Row
Birmingham B5 5JU
0121 331 6295
admissions@bcu.ac.uk
www.bcu.ac.uk
www.bcusu.com
Open days 2020:
March 21

The Times and The Sunday Times **Rankings**

Overall Ranking: =96 (last year: =87)

Teaching quality	81%	=49
Student experience	77.3%	=85
Research quality	4.3%	=98
Entry standards	123	=86
Graduate prospects	76.8%	63
Good honours	71.6%	89
Expected completion rate	82.6%	86
Student/staff ratio	17.9	=102
Services and facilities	£2,123	=82

The Bournville campus hosts a college offering preparatory courses for overseas students to support the university's international ambitions. These took on a new dimension with the establishment of the Birmingham Institute of Fashion and Creative Art in Wuhan, China, in partnership with Wuhan Textile University.

All BCU's degrees were "refreshed" in 2017 to give students the most relevant practical experience to boost their prospects in the graduate employment market. Work placements are available on most courses and employability skills are built into the curriculum through the Graduate+ scheme.

BCU has appointed the world's first professor of blockchain, the record-keeping technology behind online currencies. New undergraduate degrees in event and experience management, and global sport management were the first of their kind to be accredited by the Chartered Management Institute. The university has also been selected as the region's provider for the new National Centre for Computing Education, which will train the next generation of IT teachers.

There are strong links with business and the professions, including pioneering work in green technology, which is attracting support from national and regional partners. The STEAMhouse centre, which opened in 2018 to facilitate collaboration between the science, technology, engineering, arts and maths (Steam) sectors, is already being extended. A Victorian factory building is to be transformed into a £60m innovation centre for start-ups and other small companies by 2021.

BCU made a relatively small submission to the Research Excellence Framework in 2014, but 60% of the work reached the top two categories and almost 90% delivered "outstanding" or "very considerable" external impact.

The university offers a number of scholarships and bursaries to encourage undergraduates to stay on to take a postgraduate course. The student inquiry service, Ask, has a helpdesk or answers questions over the phone or online. Students have access to learning tools such as Shareville – a virtual learning environment where students can engage with real-life scenarios.

BCU owns or manages more than 2,700 residential places – enough to guarantee accommodation for first-years whose homes are more than ten miles away, if they apply before the deadline. The city's student scene is highly rated and has become a draw for many young applicants.

Tuition fees

- » Fees for UK/EU students £9,250
- » Fees for International students 2020–21 £12,800–£20,300
- » For scholarship and bursary information see www.bcu.ac.uk/student-info/finance-and-money-matters
- » Graduate salary £21,000

Student numbers

Undergraduates	17,860	(1,930)
Postgraduates	2,545	(2,240)
Applications/places	32,665/6,235	
Applications per place	5.2	
Overall offer rate	73.1%	
Unconditional offers	39.9%	
International students	11.9%	

Accommodation

University provided places: 2,709
Self-catered: £128–£149 per week
First years guaranteed accommodation
www.bcu.ac.uk/student-info/accommodation

Where do the students come from?

State schools (non-grammar)	97.7%	First generation students	55.5%	
Grammar schools	0.5%	Deprived areas	12.5%	
Independent schools	1.7%	All ethnic minorities	53.7%	

Social inclusion ranking: =30

Black attainment gap	-18.5%
Disabled	5.2%
Mature (over 21)	21.3%

Birmingham, University College (UCB)

University College Birmingham (UCB) is unique among UK universities in having a third of its students taking further education programmes, some of them enrolling at 16. It believes that would place it at a disadvantage in league tables such as ours, so it has again instructed the Higher Education Statistics Agency not to release its data. As a result, UCB does not appear in our main league table or any of the subject tables.

Nevertheless, it was around average for overall satisfaction in the 2019 National Student Survey after an improvement on the previous year and was placed in the Silver category in the Teaching Excellence Framework (TEF). The TEF panel was impressed by the strong vocational focus in UCB's curriculum design, with work placements and professional accreditation a common feature on many courses. It found that students were stretched and there were "appropriate" contact hours, personalised learning through individual and group tutorials, and effective support services.

The numbers starting degrees were stable in 2018, but applications were down sharply – by almost 30% – for the third year in a row. Over 93% of applicants were offered places, seven percentage points up on 2016.

UCB chose not to change its name when full university status arrived in 2013, in order to preserve its identity. It was the largest of a dozen colleges to become universities then, with more than 5,000 higher education students and nearly 2,500 taking further education courses. The university traces its history back more than 100 years to the foundation of a Municipal Technical School offering cookery and household science courses. It has had degree awarding powers since 2007, although many degrees are still accredited by the University of Birmingham.

The core subjects are hospitality, tourism, business, sport and education. The most recent Ofsted inspection rated the further education provision as outstanding. UCB has an international reputation in hospitality and tourism, with about a third of the students coming from outside the UK. Two restaurants staffed by the university's students are open to the public, as well as to students and staff.

Based in the city centre, UCB is located close to the International Convention Centre, Symphony Hall and the Library of Birmingham, as well as the main shopping areas. The main campus is at Summer Row, five minutes' walk from New Street station. UCB is investing £100m in new teaching and residential facilities. The first phase of development in Birmingham's historic Jewellery Quarter –a short walk from the main campus – opened in 2014. The second phase, costing £42m, will follow during the current academic year. The new red brick building, designed to celebrate the

---

University College Birmingham
Summer Row
Birmingham B3 1JB
0121 604 1000
admissions@ucb.ac.uk
international@ucb.ac.uk
www.ucb.ac.uk
www.ucbguild.co.uk
Open days 2020:
March 28, June 27

The Times and The Sunday Times **Rankings**
Data not supplied

architectural heritage of the area, includes three lecture theatres, modern teaching spaces, a high performance strengthening and conditioning suite for sports studies, a gym and a student diner.

Specialist teaching facilities include high-quality training kitchens, a full bakery and a £2million Food Science and Innovation Suite. Many courses include full or half-year industrial placements, including overseas opportunities in the USA, Hong Kong, Canada and Europe. As well as arranging placements, the expanded careers and employability team, hired@UCB, helps students to develop skills such as communication, teamwork, problem solving and time management.

A new financial trading suite is one of the largest at any UK university and will be used by students at UCB's Business School and other finance-related modules across the university, as by industry partners. With 21 workstations, two large wall screens and a scrolling ticker providing real-time global market information, the trading suite will be a key component of a new Finance and Accounting BSc starting in September 2020.

Aviation students will also benefit from new simulation facilities, including a mock plane cabin. The facilities will also include check-in areas and Galileo GDS system for training students on UCB's aviation and airport management foundation and bachelor's degree, as well as other courses in travel and tourism.

UCB has one of the most socially diverse student bodies in the country – more than half are from a black or minority ethnic background. Student ambassadors promote further and higher education to young people from a range of backgrounds. Almost all the undergraduates are state-educated and more than half come from the four poorest socio-economic groups. Retention rates have been improving, but the TEF panel commented on the below-benchmark rates for some groups.

More than 1,000 students can be accommodated in UCB's two halls of residence, and accommodation can be offered to all years and programmes of study. The Maltings halls are ten minutes' walk from UCB and Cambrian Hall is only 150 yards from the main campus. Both offer among the best value in the Midlands. The Spa offers hairdressing salons, beauty therapy suites, a sports therapy clinic, a multi-gym, and a fitness assessment suite. There is also a gym and sports hall at The Maltings site, as well as a multipurpose community hub with specialised work and dining spaces.

Tuition fees

» Fees for UK/EU students 2019–20	£9,250
» Fees for International students 2020–21	£11,500
Foundation course	£8,600
» For scholarship and bursary information see www.ucb.ac.uk/our-courses/undergraduate/ fees-funding-and scholarships/	

Student numbers

Total	7,500
International	900

Accommodation

University provided places: 1,000+ (0% catered)
Self-catered: £106–£126 per week
No guarantee but all first years offered accommodation
www.ucb.ac.uk/student-life/accommodation/
accommodation.aspx

Where do the students come from?

Data not supplied

Bishop Grosseteste University

Bishop Grosseteste (BGU) was planning to have 4,500 students by 2019, but is barely halfway to that target, and still one of the UK's smallest universities. Applications for courses beginning in that year dropped by 9%, the fourth annual decline in succession, although the numbers actually enrolling have risen slightly for the past two years. Nine out of ten applicants were offered places in 2018, compared with only 58% five years earlier.

The university managed a gold award in the first round of the government's Teaching Excellence Framework (TEF). The panel found that students of all backgrounds were challenged to achieve excellent outcomes, frequently engaging with developments from the forefront of research, scholarship or working practice. The learning environment was said to be outstanding.

BGU is in the top ten for the proportion of academics holding a teaching qualification – three quarters, compared with the national average of less than half. But previous stellar ratings for student satisfaction with teaching declined in 2018 and 2019's slight improvement was not sufficient to lift the university back into our top 100.

The university has an attractive, leafy campus in uphill Lincoln, not far from the cathedral and castle, where teachers have been trained since 1862. Named after a theologian and scholar who was bishop of Lincoln in the 13th century, BGU is still proudly associated with the Church of England, although it welcomes students of all faiths and none. It describes itself as a church university within the Anglican tradition.

The portfolio of courses now stretches well beyond teacher training, although this remains the largest area. Ofsted rates the courses for early years, primary and secondary teachers as "good". The introduction of courses leading to Early Years Teacher Status has meant that, for the first time, Bishop Grosseteste is training teachers of every age group, including adults.

Other degrees range from applied drama and archaeology to health and social care, sport and theology. A new degree in military history was launched in 2019, alongside an MSc in mental health and wellbeing. The portfolio of courses covers a range of arts and social sciences, with more new subjects planned in the next few years.

The campus has been gearing up for a larger intake, with new teaching and learning facilities attached to one of the two on-campus halls of residence. The former college canteen and dining room had already been turned into teaching accommodation, with an award-winning £2.2m extension doubling the available space and creating a new landmark building for the university.

Longdales Road
Lincoln LN1 3DY
01522 583 658
enquiries@bishopg.ac.uk
www.bishopg.ac.uk
www.bgsu.co.uk
Open days 2020:
see website

The Times and *The Sunday Times* **Rankings**
Overall Ranking: =102 (last year: 113)

Teaching quality	81.2%	=45
Student experience	75.8%	=103
Research quality	2.1%	120
Entry standards	112	=119
Graduate prospects	72.9%	=85
Good honours	69%	=104
Expected completion rate	90.2%	=37
Student/staff ratio	20.2	=104
Services and facilities	£2,212	76

Other developments have seen the campus theatre upgraded to double as a cinema. The Venue is home to the Lincoln Film Society and is open to staff, students and the public. The library has been extended and now houses the student advice and learning development teams.

BGU claims to be the top university for widening participation among those with a gold rating in the TEF, based on the Higher Education Statistics Agency's measures for entrants from state schools and low participation neighbourhoods – and it ranks second in the UK in our new social inclusion ranking.

More than 60% of BGU's students come from the East Midlands, 44% from Lincolnshire. Their backgrounds reflect the socio-economic make-up of the county, with eight out of ten fitting one or more of the government's "widening participation" categories. Almost a quarter come from an area with little tradition of higher education. The expansion of the university was intended to include more such students, as well as more mature students taking work-based courses and more postgraduates and research students.

Only 11 staff entered the 2014 Research Excellence Framework, but some work was classed as "world-leading" in education, English and history, the three subjects in which the university was assessed. BGU has since opened the Lincolnshire Open Research and Innovation Centre (Loric) to assist local business, the public and third-sector organisations. An executive dean heads up the centre and is responsible for extending the university's research capability and capacity.

BGU has a total of 215 residential places of its own on campus and another 150 elsewhere that it manages or endorses. Rooms are allocated on a first come first served basis, but the university guarantees to find approved accommodation for all first-year and international students.

The Sport and Fitness Centre can cater for a variety of different activities and has a well-appointed fitness suite. Ten acres of sports fields are close by.

The city of Lincoln is one of the fastest growing in the UK, with relatively low living costs. It may not compete with the big conurbations for youth culture, but it has a growing student population (thanks to two universities) and a range of bars and nightclubs.

Tuition fees

» Fees for UK/EU students	£9,250
Foundation courses	£6,935
» Fees for International students 2020–21	£11,820
» For scholarship and bursary information see www.bishopg.ac.uk/fees-funding/	
» Graduate salary	£22,000

Student numbers

Undergraduates	1,689	(15)
Postgraduates	392	(157)
Applications/places		1,565/725
Applications per place		2.2
Overall offer rate		92.9%
Unconditional offers		0%
International students		0.5%

Accommodation

University provided places: 365
Self-catered: £85–£139 per week
First years guaranteed accommodation
www.bishopg.ac.uk/student/accommodation/

Where do the students come from?

State schools (non-grammar)	95.3%	First generation students	66.6%	Black attainment gap	n/a
Grammar schools	3.0%	Deprived areas	24.2%	Disabled	13.4%
Independent schools	1.6%	All ethnic minorities	4.2%	Mature (over 21)	40.7%

Social inclusion ranking: 2

University of Bolton

While its peer institutions were struggling to attract applicants, Bolton enjoyed an increase of almost 10% – among the largest of any university – in the 2019 admissions cycle. The university had already seen record numbers start courses the previous year, having doubled its intake in little more than a decade. It hopes to have 20,000 students taking its courses this year, partly through collaboration with other institutions in the region.

The university merged with Bolton College in 2018 and has formed a strategic alliance with Alliance Learning, which provides apprenticeships, foundation degrees and training courses. Bolton is also establishing its first university centre in Manchester after forming a partnership with another private training provider.

Almost half of the offers made in 2018 were unconditional, but not of the type criticised by ministers for requiring students to make the university their first choice.

New degrees will be introduced in 2020 in social work, physiotherapy, and screenwriting and media production, and the university is adding foundation years to existing degrees in photography, graphic design and screenwriting. There will also be new degree apprenticeships in physiotherapy, advanced clinical practice, facilities management, social work, laboratory science and construction engineering, adding to the 20 existing programmes.

In recent campus developments, the university has opened a new flagship building in the centre of Bolton, home of the recently established Institute of Management. The National Centre for Motorsport Engineering opened in 2017 and hosts the renowned Cape training facility (the Centre for Advanced Performance Engineering). Bolton has its own professional motor racing team, run in conjunction with a motorsports company, and offers degrees in automotive performance engineering and motorsport technology. Students work and learn alongside engineers and mechanics from the team, as well as academics.

A £40m village for 850 students, replacing two existing halls that are out of the town centre campus and have a smaller capacity is planned. There are only 384 residential places now, but the predominantly local intake means accommodation is guaranteed to first-years who want it.

A collaboration with the council and local NHS produced the Bolton One development, a £31m health, leisure and research centre on the main campus. It boasts a multi-sports hall, climbing wall and a sports and spinal injuries clinic, as well as a 25-metre competition swimming pool and a therapeutic hydrotherapy pool, fitness suite and community gym. The former sports

Deane Road
Bolton BL3 5AB
01204 903 903
study@bolton.ac.uk
www.bolton.ac.uk
www.boltonsu.com
Open days 2020:
March 21

The Times and The Sunday Times Rankings
Overall Ranking: 125 (last year: 126)

Teaching quality	85.6%	5
Student experience	82.1%	=13
Research quality	2.9%	114
Entry standards	116	108
Graduate prospects	57.4%	130
Good honours	60.8%	=129
Expected completion rate	72.8%	128
Student/staff ratio	14.2	=30
Services and facilities	£1,488	=126

hall is being transformed into a Creative Technologies Research Centre.

Bolton received a silver rating in the Teaching Excellence Framework. The panel commended it on an institutional culture that facilitates, recognises and rewards excellent teaching, as well as providing excellent support for students from disadvantaged backgrounds. While Bolton is still near the bottom of our academic league table, it is close to the top of our social inclusion ranking. Its students rate their experience highly, placing Bolton in the top five for student satisfaction with the quality of teaching and the top 15 for the wider student experience.

General engineering was one of two subject areas to see a majority of its work rated as world-leading or internationally excellent in the 2014 Research Excellence Framework. The best results were in English and almost a third of the university's submission reached the top two categories overall. Among the distinctive research features is a Centre for Islamic Finance. The criminological and forensic psychology degree, which includes the opportunity to take counselling certificates, received the top award for innovative programmes from the British Psychological Society.

The university traces its roots back 194 years to the establishment of one of the country's first three mechanics institutes. Bolton exceeds all the access measures designed to widen participation in higher education: the proportion of undergraduates coming from areas without a tradition of higher education is among the highest, at 22%. More than a third of undergraduates study part-time – a significant proportion when part-time numbers have plummeted. The downside is that the projected dropout rate is also one of the highest, at 20%.

Bolton has increased its international activity in recent years. There are partner colleges in several Asian countries and a branch campus in the United Arab Emirates, at Ras al-Khaimah. The campus offers a range of undergraduate and postgraduate courses identical to those taught in the UK and is designed to take 700 students. Those at Bolton have the opportunity to study in the UAE for part of their course, while more than 100 Saudi students came to Bolton in 2018 to study environmental sciences as part of the Saudi 2030 Vision project.

The town of Bolton has a growing range of student-oriented facilities and is only 20 minutes from Manchester by train. The university has also acquired an outdoor residential activity centre for young people, the Anderton Centre, on Lower Rivington Reservoir, seven miles outside Bolton.

Tuition fees

» Fees for UK/EU students	£9,250
» Fees for International students 2020–21	£12,450
» For scholarship and bursary information see www.bolton.ac.uk/study/undergraduate/feesfunding/	
» Graduate salary	£18,500

Student numbers

Undergraduates	4,417	(923)
Postgraduates	469	(735)
Applications/places		4,870/1,735
Applications per place		2.8
Overall offer rate		69.6%
Unconditional offers		0%
International students		7.8%

Accommodation

University provided places: 384
Self-catered: £80 per week
First years guaranteed accommodation
www.bolton.ac.uk/study/undergraduate/accommodation/

Where do the students come from?

State schools (non-grammar)	97.9%	First generation students	57.9%	Black attainment gap	-30%
Grammar schools	1.0%	Deprived areas	22.1%	Disabled	11.9%
Independent schools	1.1%	All ethnic minorities	37%	Mature (over 21)	47%

Social inclusion ranking: 12

University of Bournemouth

Every Bournemouth undergraduate has the option of a work placement, either in the UK or abroad, as part of their course. Most take it up, and almost three in ten end up working at their placement firm after graduating. More than 1,000 students took the international route in 2017, with placements lasting anything from four to 30 weeks. More than 2,500 students from 120 countries come in the opposite direction, underlining Bournemouth's growing international activity.

The successful placement system was one of the factors behind the university's silver award in the Teaching Excellence Framework. Assessors also found strong support for peer-assisted learning, offering all first-year undergraduates advice and mentoring from students who are further along in their chosen course.

Yet applications have dropped by more than 20% since 2016. A higher offer rate has helped to keep the decline in enrolments to more manageable proportions.

Bournemouth was among the ten universities to issue the most "conditional unconditional" offers in 2018, requiring students to make the university their firm choice – more than 3,400 in the first year it had used the process. Despite criticism of this type of offer from the government, Bournemouth stuck to its guns for the 2020 admissions process, offering a £1,000 Academic Excellence Scholarship to unconditional offer holders who go on to achieve at least AAA at A-level.

The university is about to embark on a five-year programme of investment totalling £100m, having already spent £200m on its two campuses. A £38m building for science and technology students is planned alongside the Poole Gateway development under construction on the Talbot campus. The latest plans feature computing and psychology laboratories, lecture theatres, seminar rooms and research facilities, bringing together disciplines that are currently split between the Talbot and Lansdowne campuses. Other developments include accommodation for almost 1,000 students in two new blocks.

The new Bournemouth Gateway building, on the Lansdowne campus, will house the faculty of health and social sciences – an expanding area. Degrees in biomedical sciences, cyberpsychology, operating department practice, medical science and psychology with forensic investigation took their first students in September 2019. New degree courses in accounting, finance, sport coaching and sport and exercise science will start in 2020. Bournemouth is also expanding its small portfolio of degree apprenticeships in nursing and engineering, with the aim of having about 100 students by September 2020.

Media courses are Bournemouth's

Fern Barrow
Talbot Campus
Poole BH12 5BB
01202 961 916
futurestudents@bournemouth.ac.uk
www.bournemouth.ac.uk
www.subu.org.uk
Open days 2020:
February 19; March 7;
April 8

The Times and The Sunday Times **Rankings**

Overall Ranking: 94 (last year: 78)

Teaching quality	77.3%	=104
Student experience	75.4%	=108
Research quality	9.0%	=64
Entry standards	122	92
Graduate prospects	68.7%	=105
Good honours	76.4%	=54
Expected completion rate	85.3%	67
Student/staff ratio	17	=89
Services and facilities	£2,325	65

best-known feature and are impressively resourced. A motion capture facility for real-time animation is used in teaching and is available for use by outside companies. The university hosts the National Centre of Computer Animation and large numbers of its graduates have worked on award-winning films such as *Rogue One: A Star Wars Story*, *Fantastic Beasts and Where to Find Them*, *Ex Machina*, and the Disney movie *Moana*.

Tourism and hospitality management is another successful area. The department, which works with the United Nations World Tourism Organisation, has been designated an Institute of Travel & Tourism Centre of Excellence.

In the 2014 Research Excellence Framework, 60% of the university's entry was assessed as world-leading or internationally excellent – one of the biggest proportions at any post-1992 university.

The university has been increasing its use of education technology, for example to enable part-time students to study from home or the workplace and reduce the amount of time they need to spend on campus. It invested £6m in a new virtual learning environment, which gives all students access to a range of services and enables academics to track the performance of undergraduates.

These initiatives have not translated into high levels of student satisfaction, however. Students' scores for satisfaction with teaching quality and their wider experience have fallen back in 2019 to rank Bournemouth outside the top 100 on both measures, contributing to a fall in the university's overall ranking in our league table.

The subject mix and an increasingly fashionable seaside location, between the World Heritage Jurassic Coast and the New Forest National Park, attract more middle-class students than most post-1992 universities, although more than 90% of undergraduates attended non-selective state schools. Applicants from low-income families and/or areas with little tradition of higher education are made offers below the published tariff and the university sits in the middle reaches of our new social inclusion table.

Sports facilities have been improving following a refurbishment of the gym and the addition of a large multipurpose studio.

The university does not own any residential accommodation, but controls or approves nearly 4,000 places, enough to guarantee accommodation to first-year undergraduates who apply by early July.

Tuition fees

» Fees for UK/EU students	£9,250
Foundation courses	£8,200
» Fees for International students 2020–21	£14,100–£15,000
» For scholarship and bursary information see	
www.bournemouth.ac.uk/study/undergraduate/fees-funding	
» Graduate salary	£21,909

Student numbers

Undergraduates	13,487	(1,934)
Postgraduates	1,548	(1,717)
Applications/places		20,030/4,535
Applications per place		4.4
Overall offer rate		84.4%
Unconditional offers		39.3%
International students		12.4%

Accommodation

University provided places: 3,964
Self-catered: £118–£198 per week
First years guaranteed accommodation
www.bournemouth.ac.uk/why-bu/accommodation

Where do the students come from?

State schools (non-grammar)	90.5%	First generation students	49%	Black attainment gap	-24.6%
Grammar schools	4.6%	Deprived areas	10.5%	Disabled	7.7%
Independent schools	4.9%	All ethnic minorities	15.1%	Mature (over 21)	19.2%

Social inclusion ranking: 66

University of Bradford

Bradford is our University of the Year for Social Inclusion, the only pre-1992 institution in the top 20 of our ranking that measures social diversity on campus. But at the same time it has slipped out of the top 100 in our main academic league table.

The university has one of the largest proportions of ethnic minority students of any UK institution (accounting for 72.5% of 2018's intake) and more than half of its UK undergraduates come from the four poorest socioeconomic groups.

Many honours degrees offer work experience or placements, which has long placed Bradford in our top 30 for graduate prospects. The university is also developing a portfolio of degree apprenticeships, with seven already in health roles, outside broadcasting, chemistry and management.

Professor Shirley Congdon, the new vice-chancellor and the first woman to hold the role, has made it a priority to place the university at the heart of the region's economic and social regeneration.

Awarding Bradford silver, the assessment panel for the Teaching Excellence Framework (TEF) praised the "strategic and systematic commitment to diversity and social mobility that enables the majority of students, including a very high number from black, Asian and minority ethnic backgrounds, to achieve excellent outcomes". The TEF panel commended the university for stretching students to achieve their full potential and acquire the knowledge, skills and understanding most highly valued by employers.

These findings are at odds with our main academic ranking, however, where Bradford is hampered once again by a poor showing in the National Student Survey, with students rating the quality of teaching in the bottom ten in the UK and their wider university experience in the bottom 20.

But enrolments have held up better at this university than at many of its rivals: there was a small increase in 2018 in spite of a 10% decline in applications. A quarter came through clearing and 11% received unconditional offers. The university believes that they relieve the pressure on candidates and allow them to focus on achieving excellent grades.

Originally one of the ten colleges of advanced technology, Bradford now markets itself as the only technology university in the north of England. It has chosen three strategic themes – advanced healthcare, innovative engineering and sustainable societies – but is perhaps best known for its highly-rated School of Management, which has moved to the main campus in the centre of the city.

Richmond Road
Bradford BD7 1DP
0800 073 1225
enquiries@bradford.ac.uk
www.bradford.ac.uk
www.bradfordunisu.co.uk
Open days 2020:
see website

The Times and The Sunday Times **Rankings**
Overall Ranking: 105 (last year: 98)

Teaching quality	74.3%	=122
Student experience	74.3%	=114
Research quality	9.2%	=62
Entry standards	132	=64
Graduate prospects	82.8%	25
Good honours	80.2%	38
Expected completion rate	83%	=83
Student/staff ratio	17.2	=92
Services and facilities	£2,076	89

New degrees have been introduced in finance and management with business analytics, as well as international relations, politics and security studies, and politics, peace and development. The Division of Peace Studies and International Development, created after an internal merger in 2018, is another of the university's best-known features and the largest department studying peace and conflict in the world.

Campus developments so far include new and upgraded teaching facilities. A recent library refurbishment won a Green Gown award for its insulation and natural ventilation. The university's "ecoversity" programme addresses issues of sustainable development, including the curriculum, and Bradford is the only university in the world with three buildings rated Breeam Outstanding.

The university has led a £13m Digital Health Enterprise Zone partnership aiming to deliver innovative solutions for the health and care sectors with a focus on long-term health conditions and improvements to quality of life. New facilities for physiotherapy and optometry have opened while the Wolfson Centre for Applied Healthcare Research, a joint project with Leeds University and Bradford Teaching Hospitals NHS Foundation Trust, is under construction.

Bradford entered fewer than a quarter of eligible academics for the 2014 Research Excellence Framework, but almost three-quarters of the work submitted reached the top two categories. Allied health, management and archaeological science led the way.

An online portal is available to applicants and new students to smooth their transition to higher education. Computer-assisted learning is increasing in many subjects, making use of unusually extensive IT provision and a new wireless network. The university also has particularly good provision for disabled students, who account for almost 10% of the university population.

Bradford remains a small university, with only 11,000 students, but its degrees are taught in partner institutions in Singapore, Brunei, Malaysia, Pakistan and India. The compact, lively campus is an integral part of the city centre.

Sports facilities are conveniently placed and include a gym and climbing wall, and an improved sports hall. Bradford invested £500,000, awarded by the Premier League and the Football Association, in a sports hub for students and the local community with a floodlit 3G football pitch, four tennis courts, refurbished changing pavilion and conditioning suite.

Tuition fees

- » Fees for Scottish/EU students   £9,250
- » Fees for International students 2019–20   £15,320–£18.901
  Foundation   £12,190
- » For scholarship and bursary information see
  www.bradford.ac.uk/money/fees/
- » Graduate salary   £20,020

Student numbers

Undergraduates	7,155	(539)
Postgraduates	811	(1,610)
Applications/places		11,155/2,505
Applications per place		4.5
Overall offer rate		87.8%
Unconditional offers		0%
International students		14.9%

Accommodation

University provided places: 1,026
Self-catered: £86–£108 per week
First years guaranteed accommodation
www.bradford.ac.uk/accommodation/the-green/

Where do the students come from?

Social inclusion ranking: 3

State schools (non-grammar)	92.8%	First generation students	67.3%	Black attainment gap	-3%
Grammar schools	5.5%	Deprived areas	13.6%	Disabled	9.1%
Independent schools	1.7%	All ethnic minorities	72.5%	Mature (over 21)	26.3%

University of Brighton

Brighton has bowed to government pressure and stopped making "conditional unconditional" offers – which made up 40% of the total in 2018. The university denied "pressure-selling" and said such offers were made only to students who would benefit and were not accompanied by financial incentives.

Applications have dropped by almost 20% in two years, despite a rising offer rate. The decline in enrolments has been less steep, but the numbers arriving in 2018 were still down on 2015, when recruitment restrictions were lifted.

Professor Debra Humphris, the vice-chancellor, had already ruled out increasing student numbers beyond the current 21,500, partly to ease the pressure on local housing. Five new student accommodation blocks are being built at the Moulsecoomb campus, the university's largest base, ranging from eight to 18 floors and providing another 800 bedrooms as well as students' union and fitness facilities. The development will be completed in 2021.

A new academic building will also open at Moulsecoomb in 2020–21 as part of a £300m development masterplan for the university. The Centre for Contemporary Arts has opened in the centre of Brighton, with a programme of exhibitions, projects and commissions from emerging and established international artists. The £14m Advanced Engineering Building opened in 2018 and the university is spending £1.5m a year upgrading its other teaching and learning spaces.

Brighton holds silver in the government's Teaching Excellence Framework. The judging panel praised its close working relationships with professional bodies, employers and local community groups and its personalised learning and support, particularly for first-year students.

The university has been dropping in our league table, however, finishing in the bottom ten for the first time in 2018 and staying there this year. Student satisfaction has recovered, however, with the score for teaching quality up more than 30 places. Its final-year students' assessment of their wider experience has also made a (smaller) recovery – although not enough to lift it more than one place overall. About one in seven students drops out.

Ten new degree courses have been introduced, such as animation, computer science with cybersecurity, games art and design, psychology with counselling studies, nutrition, and international event management. Brighton is also expanding its portfolio of degree apprenticeships, adding another ten programmes in 2020, which will double the number of places to more than 400.

At least nine out of ten degree programmes feature a work placement or the option of a sandwich year. Four-year degrees

---

Mithras House
Lewes Road
Brighton BN2 4AT
01273 644 644
enquiries@brighton.ac.uk
www.brighton.ac.uk
www.brightonsu.com
Open days 2020:
June 6, 13, 20; July 4

The Times and The Sunday Times Rankings
Overall Ranking: 122 (last year: 123)

Teaching quality	79.8%	=69
Student experience	75.8%	=103
Research quality	7.9%	=73
Entry standards	117	=104
Graduate prospects	67.2%	111
Good honours	72.2%	86
Expected completion rate	81.3%	95
Student/staff ratio	18.5	=110
Services and facilities	£1,587	124

in fashion and textiles, for example, offer placements in America and Europe. For a wide range of courses, the university's teaching facilities are designed to build real-life skills and students have access to a radio station and TV studio, flight simulator, rapid prototyping facilities and industrial textile rooms. Nursing students can practise in clinical skills and simulation suites and the university has its own podiatry hospital and physiotherapy clinic.

Beyond Brighton, the university has a campus in Eastbourne with a modern library, extensive leisure and sports facilities and 354 en-suite rooms. A new teaching and research gym is designed to allow students to work in elite sport and rehabilitation.

Brighton, winner of our inaugural University of the Year award in 1999, has a longstanding partnership with the University of Sussex, running one of the first medical schools to be awarded to a post-1992 university. The medical school has increased its intake by 50 to accept 200 trainee doctors each year at the Falmer campus, on the outskirts of Brighton, where courses in education and applied social sciences are also based.

Brighton's submission to the 2014 Research Excellence Framework was rated in the top quarter of British universities. Two-thirds of its work was placed in one of the top two categories – a big improvement on 2008, when it was already among the most

successful of the post-1992 universities. Brighton is also in the top tier of the People and Planet league of environmental performance, ranked 25th in the UK in 2019.

The fashionable seaside location is a draw for students, who revel in Brighton's famously lively social scene. The university has a cosmopolitan atmosphere, with more international students than most post-1992 universities. Although its UK student profile is more middle-class than most, almost nine out of ten undergraduates enrol from non-selective state schools and colleges.

Efforts to widen the intake further include well-established progression partnerships with schools in the region and cash bursaries of £500 a year for those with a household income of less than £25,000, with larger awards for care leavers. About 40% of undergraduates qualify for one or more of the bursaries and scholarships on offer.

Tuition fees

- » Fees for UK/EU students   £9,250
- » Fees for International students 2020–21   £13,384–£14,460
  Medicine   £32,886
- » For scholarship and bursary information see
  www.brighton.ac.uk/studying-here/fees-and-finance/index.aspx
- » Graduate salary   £22,000

Student numbers

Undergraduates	15,035 (2,665)
Postgraduates	1,570 (2,286)
Applications/places	28,235/4,595
Applications per place	6.1
Overall offer rate	79.5%
Unconditional offers	40%
International students	12.7%

Accommodation

University provided places: 2,701
Catered costs: £165–£185 per week
Self-catered: £80–£170 per week
First years guaranteed accommodation
www.brighton.ac.uk/accommodation-and-locations/Index.aspx

Where do the students come from?

State schools (non-grammar)	87.9%	First generation students	46.9%
Grammar schools	5.7%	Deprived areas	11.2%
Independent schools	6.4%	All ethnic minorities	21%

Social inclusion ranking: 68

Black attainment gap	-24.3%
Disabled	9.8%
Mature (over 21)	19.8%

University of Bristol

Bristol has increased its intake of undergraduates by more than every university except Exeter since restrictions on recruitment were lifted in 2015. The 730 additional places for new entrants represent a rise of 14% and applications were up by another 6% when the official deadline passed for courses beginning last autumn.

Entry standards remain near the top ten despite further development of the contextual admissions policy it has operated for two decades. Those from schools with below-average results or living in areas with little tradition of higher education can now expect offers two grades lower than the standard offer for their course.

The university has spent heavily on other measures designed to broaden the intake, including bursaries of up to £2,000 a year for those from families earning less than about £43,000. A new scheme will provide extra support for black, Asian and minority ethnic (Bame) students, whose results have lagged behind those of others – although the 8.4% gap between Bame and white students attaining firsts and 2:1s is by no means the worst.

However, the university remains in the bottom ten in our social inclusion table for England and Wales. Barely half the students come from non-selective state schools and only around one in 20 are recruited from the most deprived parts of the country.

Wellbeing and mental health has been a key priority for the university following the deaths of 12 students in the past three years (eight recorded as suicides and two with narrative verdicts from the coroner, with two inquests still to take place). There has been substantial investment in a school-based Student Wellbeing Service as well as university-wide health and counselling services. All staff are now urged to "reach out to help our students rather than wait to be asked". Some of the new strategies have been developed with the support and input of parents of students who died.

Bristol is introducing almost 50 new degree programmes over the next two years. Most of the latest additions are joint honours programmes featuring a modern language paired with English, history or music, but the list also includes criminology with quantitative research methods, marketing and dental hygiene and therapy.

Foundation programmes in medicine and dentistry and the arts and humanities are available for those who need more preparation for degree study. In 2020, the first students will start integrated master's courses in childhood studies and innovation, neuroscience, pharmacology and physics with scientific computing.

The new courses follow a wider overhaul of the curriculum. Under the Bristol

Senate House
Tyndall Avenue
Bristol BS8 1TH
0117 928 9000
choosebristol-ug@bristol.ac.uk
www.bristol.ac.uk
www.bristolsu.org.uk
Open days 2020:
see website

The Times and The Sunday Times **Rankings**
Overall Ranking: 15 (last year: =19)

Teaching quality	78.7%	=89
Student experience	77.2%	=87
Research quality	47.3%	6
Entry standards	177	14
Graduate prospects	80.6%	=44
Good honours	89.8%	=5
Expected completion rate	95.8%	=7
Student/staff ratio	13.5	=19
Services and facilities	£2,309	67

Futures initiative undergraduates can study innovation and enterprise, global citizenship or sustainable futures at the same time as acquiring core academic skills

In the Teaching Excellence Framework, the panel was pleased to see Bristol encouraging independent learning but the university had to settle for silver. Low levels of student satisfaction with assessment and feedback were the university's undoing – not uncommon in our table – although Bristol has been moving up our top 20 recently, assisted this year by notable improvements in students' scores for teaching quality and their wider experience.

Results in the 2014 Research Excellence Framework were outstanding: the university was ranked fourth equal alongside Oxford. Bristol was rewarded for entering more than 90% of its eligible staff – a higher proportion than Oxford – with 83% of its research rated as world-leading or internationally excellent. Geography, sport and exercise sciences were judged the best in the country overall. Bristol's whole submissions in clinical medicine, health subjects, economics and sport and exercise sciences were placed in the top categories for their impact.

Now Bristol is planning a new campus in the heart of the city to focus on digital technologies. The £300m Temple Quarter Enterprise Campus, next to Temple Meads station, is scheduled to open in 2022 and will include a new student village and a hub for intercultural activities, where international students can meet and mingle. The main Clifton campus is to be transformed with a new library, more teaching, study and shared spaces, a student resource centre and improved sports facilities.

The university already has 6,200 residential places for undergraduates, who must apply by July 31 and have Bristol as their firm choice to be guaranteed a room. Some first-years were disappointed in 2019 and were offered accommodation as far away as Newport in South Wales.

An impressive sports complex with a well-equipped gym has been developed at the heart of the university precinct, where the careers centre has also been refurbished. The students' union houses one of the city's biggest live music venues as well as a cafe, bars, theatre and swimming pool.

As one of Britain's most prosperous cities, Bristol offers job opportunities to students and graduates alike. The university's famous gothic tower dominates the skyline, and there is a vibrant youth culture. Bristol topped the list in *The Sunday Times* Best Places to Live in 2017. Many students stay on after graduation, although the high cost of living can be a drawback.

Tuition fees

» Fees for UK/EU students £9,250

» Fees for International students 2020–21 £19,500–£24,000
Dentistry £37,100; Medicine £33,500; Veterinary science £29,900

» For scholarship and bursary information see www.bristol.ac.uk/fees-funding/

» Graduate salary £25,000

Student numbers

Undergraduates	17,915	(353)
Postgraduates	5,220	(1,364)
Applications/places		49,245/6,120
Applications per place		8.0
Overall offer rate		72.6%
Unconditional offers		0%
International students		23.6%

Accommodation

University provided places: 6,200
Catered costs: £180–£205 per week
Self-catered: £90–£201 per week
First years guaranteed accommodation
www.bristol.ac.uk/accommodation/undergraduate/

Where do the students come from?

State schools (non-grammar)	52.9%	First generation students	21.9%		
Grammar schools	13.0%	Deprived areas	4.6%		
Independent schools	34.1%	All ethnic minorities	16.0%		

Social inclusion ranking: 110

Black attainment gap	-8.4%
Disabled	4.9%
Mature (over 21)	5.0%

Brunel, University of London

Despite a long-term aspiration to be the leading technological university in the UK and in the top tier worldwide, Brunel dropped into the bottom half of our main table in 2018 and remains there after scores for student satisfaction slipped further. It has been a startling decline: in five years Brunel has sunk from the top 20 to the bottom three in the UK for satisfaction with the overall student experience.

These poor scores have yet to impact Brunel's application rate. It was one of the few universities to see a significant increase in applications in 2019 – up almost 6% at undergraduate level and 21% for taught postgraduate degrees. It follows a small drop in enrolments in 2018, when many competitors suffered a more serious decline. Seven out of ten students come from black and ethnic minority backgrounds – many from local Asian communities in northwest London –helping to place Brunel in the top three pre-1992 universities in our social inclusion table.

The judging panel in the government's Teaching Excellence Framework admired Brunel's analytical approach to addressing attainment gaps within the diverse student body and awarded a silver rating. It is aided by the Brunel Educational Excellence Centre, which provides students with opportunities to enhance their academic skills and encourages innovative teaching.

Graduate employability has been Brunel's greatest strength over the years despite its current low ranking on this measure. The award-winning Professional Development Centre brings together a careers service with modern foreign language classes and an innovation hub. The Brunel+ award recognises non-academic activities well regarded by employers.

A business degree specialising in entrepreneurship and innovation is one of several courses that took its first students in 2019 and fully online master's degrees, now offered in partnership with InterActive Pro, include public health and health promotion as well as engineering management. There is also a transnational degree in communications engineering, in partnership with Chongqing University of Posts and Telecommunications, where students spend two years in China and two in the UK. A new department of chemical engineering has opened.

Since 2014 the university has pumped £150m into its Uxbridge campus, where striking new buildings and landscaping contrast with original 1960s architecture. Engineering and sports facilities account for most of the latest round of spending and a £50m seven-storey learning and teaching centre is planned. The Stem Centre uses the latest green technology for temperature regulation and rainwater harvesting.

Kingston Lane
Uxbridge
UB8 3PH
01895 265 265
admissions@brunel.ac.uk
www.brunel.ac.uk
https://brunelstudents.com/
Open days 2020:
see website

The Times and The Sunday Times **Rankings**
Overall Ranking: 100 (last year: 76)

Teaching quality	73.1%	126
Student experience	73.4%	120
Research quality	25.4%	49
Entry standards	125	=81
Graduate prospects	70.9%	=94
Good honours	75.7%	=59
Expected completion rate	86.5%	60
Student/staff ratio	18	=104
Services and facilities	£2,418	54

The sports facilities are among the best at any university and some of the world's top athletes, including the Jamaican sprinters, Usain Bolt and Yohan Blake, have visited to train here. The centrepiece is the multi-million-pound Indoor Athletics Centre with a 130-metre sprint straight, pole vault, high jump and long/triple jump facilities. There is also a bespoke strength and conditioning gym for elite student athletes.

The Sports Park, just outside the campus, boasts a 400-metre athletics track with tennis and netball courts, space for football, rugby and hockey, and an FA-registered 3G pitch. The university encourages casual use of the facilities, rather than reserving them for elite sport. Brunel has become the first UK university to introduce a sports hijab for its Muslim sportswomen, long underrepresented in competitive sport.

Brunel has become one of 12 founder members of ProtectED, a pioneering scheme that aims to improve student safety, security and wellbeing. The initiative requires measures such as safe-guarding mental health and promoting the welfare of international students.

Brunel has increased its research funding since performing well in the 2014 Research Excellence Framework. More than 60% of a large submission was rated world-leading or internationally excellent, with sports sciences achieving the best results and ranking in the top five in the UK. Brunel did particularly well on the impact of its research.

Well-known figures on staff include Benjamin Zephaniah as chair of creative writing, and the author Will Self, professor of contemporary thought. Brunel alumni Jo Brand and Lee Mack have helped to establish the first Centre for Comedy Studies Research.

Following the refurbishment of existing halls of residence and some construction, there are now more than 4,600 places for new first-year, full-time students – enough to enable Brunel to be among the few universities to guarantee accommodation even to those from the local area and those arriving through clearing, as long as they apply by the end of August.

The university is little more than an hour from the West End by public transport. The self-contained campus is a rarity in London and serves as the centre of many students' social lives. A cycle hire scheme has four docking stations on campus and one at Uxbridge Tube station.

Tuition fees

» Fees for UK/EU students	£9,250
» Fees for International students 2020–21	£15,860–£19,280
» For scholarship and bursary information see	
www.brunel.ac.uk/study/undergraduate-fees-and-funding	
» Graduate salary	£23,000

Student numbers

Undergraduates	10,319 (228)
Postgraduates	2,445 (920)
Applications/places	20,125/3,620
Applications per place	5.6
Overall offer rate	88.1%
International students	26.2%

Accommodation

University provided places: 4,626
Self-catered: £114–£160 per week
First years guaranteed accommodation
www.brunel.ac.uk/life/accommodation

Where do the students come from?

State schools (non-grammar)	88.7%	First generation students	50.2%	Black attainment gap	-15%
Grammar schools	5.6%	Deprived areas	4%	Disabled	6.6%
Independent schools	5.7%	All ethnic minorities	72.2%	Mature (over 21)	9.8%

Social inclusion ranking: 27

University of Buckingham

Buckingham has fewer than 3,000 students, but its popularity has soared in recent years. The two-year degree that it pioneered more than 40 years ago as the UK's only private university has helped to draw twice as many applications since 2016 – with another 25% increase in 2019, as other institutions have struggled to recruit students.

One of Buckingham's biggest draws is the medical school programme, which has now received full accreditation from the General Medical Council. As the UK's first private not-for-profit medical school, it had catered mainly for international students. But there was a 30% increase in applicants in 2019 from all sources. The course is 4½ years long, modelled on Leicester University's MB ChB programme, and a new £8m clinical training centre opened at Milton Keynes Hospital last year.

Fees for medicine are £37,000 a year, but in other subjects UK and EU undergraduates pay a total of £25,200 for their two-year course – marginally less than three-year degrees in other universities, while also saving a year's living costs and entering the labour market sooner.

The extended academic year, which makes the university's accelerated degrees possible, consists of four nine-week terms and still allows for 12–13 weeks off. Undergraduates can begin courses in January or September. Just over half of the students are from overseas, but the proportion from Britain is growing.

Undergraduates have the option of a three-year degree in the humanities, and other schools are beginning to follow suit. Economics and business economics are now available in this format, both with an integrated foundation programme for those who need an introduction to the subject before they decide which degree course to pursue. Students are already able to take French or Spanish as minor options in degree programmes ranging from accounting to psychology. A new two-year degree in security, intelligence and cyber was also launched in 2019.

Students from the five closest counties – Buckinghamshire, Bedfordshire, Northamptonshire, Hertfordshire and Oxfordshire – receive an automatic reduction of £1,100 a year on their fees. Others who take out government maintenance loans of more than £5,000 qualify for bursaries of up to £2,000 and high achievers with at least AAB at A-level are eligible for £2,000 scholarships, excluding medical students. Buckingham students qualify for larger student loans, worth up to £900 annually, because they are studying for 40 weeks a year.

Until this year, the university has featured at or near the top for student satisfaction and

Hunter Street
Buckingham MK18 1EG
01280 820 313
admissions@buckingham.ac.uk
www.buckingham.ac.uk
Open days 2020:
April 25

The Times and The Sunday Times Rankings		
Overall Ranking: =92 (last year: =43)		
Teaching quality	80.6%	=56
Student experience	80.5%	26
Research quality	n/a	
Entry standards	121	93
Graduate prospects	81.5%	33
Good honours	69.7%	=101
Expected completion rate	84%	=75
Student/staff ratio	15.8	=66
Services and facilities	£1,926	101

secured gold in the first Teaching Excellence Framework. It is a former winner of our University of the Year for Teaching Quality. Students value the tutorials of no more than ten undergraduates and the open access to academics and teaching staff. However, this year's student satisfaction scores slumped into the middle of the rankings for teaching quality, and fell outside the top 20 for the quality of the wider student experience.

Still the only private university in our main league table, Buckingham has been a regular in our overall top 50 before this year's exceptional fall of almost 50 places, triggered by the decline in student satisfaction, a hefty drop in services and facilities spend, and a big increase in the student-staff ratio. It would finish higher if it had been eligible for the Research Excellence Framework, which it hopes to enter in future.

Buckingham is aiming to become the country's first drug-free university, fostering a culture which emphasises educating students about safety and encourages alternatives to drugs and excessive alcohol for relaxation and enjoyment.

It has declared itself Europe's first "positive university" – using positive psychology to improve mental health. All tutors are trained in positive psychology and every student will complete a module on how to apply it to find meaning in their lives beyond their studies.

A £70m fundraising programme will allow the university to expand. The £8m Vinson Building, opened in 2018, houses the university's biggest lecture theatre as well as an Enterprise Hub for the region and a coffee shop.

The university also expects to construct 150 new student rooms on campus to maintain its guarantee of accommodation for first-year students as numbers grow. There are currently 548 rooms, allocated on a first come, first served basis.

The leafy main campus is the safest in the southeast according to a study in 2016. There is a bar and fitness facilities, with the Radcliffe Centre, which hosts university and external events, nearby. The School of Education is based at Whittlebury Hall, near Towcester, and the university also has a base in London for humanities research students.

The town of Buckingham is a pretty, rural, county town, with a good selection of pubs and restaurants. The bright(er) lights of Milton Keynes are a 20-minute drive away.

Tuition fees

» Fees for UK/EU students (Two-year courses)	£12,600
» Fees for International students 2020–21	£17,800
Medicine	£37,000
» For scholarship and bursary information see	
www.buckingham.ac.uk/admissions/fees	
» Graduate salary	£20,000

Student numbers

Undergraduates	**1,406**	**(61)**
Postgraduates	**1,250**	**(144)**
Applications/places		**925/145**
Applications per place		**4**
Overall offer rate		**n/a**
Unconditional offers		**n/a**
International students		**31.8%**

Accommodation

University provided places: 548
Self-catered: £95–£237 per week
First years guaranteed accommodation
www.buckingham.ac.uk/life/accommodation

Where do the students come from?

State schools (non-grammar)	73.8%	First generation students	33.2%	Black attainment gap	n/a
Grammar schools	3.1%	Deprived areas	6.9%	Disabled	4.2%
Independent schools	23.1%	All ethnic minorities	n/a	Mature (over 21)	20%

Social inclusion ranking: 106

Buckinghamshire New University

Bucks New is introducing almost 50 new degrees over two years, as it recasts its portfolio of courses. At least a third of the new offerings have the option of a foundation year for its three-year degrees. But the variety of new programmes, from acting to data science, law, songwriting and paramedic science, is a considerable undertaking for a university where applications have halved over the past two years.

The first tranche of new courses helped to increase applications by 3% in the 2019 admissions cycle. But this follows a 40% drop in the number of students starting courses in 2018 compared with the previous year, in spite of a sharp rise in the offer rate. More than 20% of offers were unconditional, but not of the controversial strings-attached variety.

The institution is also expanding the range of its degree apprenticeships and expects to treble the number of trainees by 2020. Six new programmes will be added to the existing ten – some in healthcare, including district nursing and operating department practitioners, as well as digital marketing and project management. Thames Valley Police will add to the total with "blended" programmes allowing students to learn in the classroom, online and on the job.

The university was one of six to have an initial bronze rating upgraded to silver in the second round of the Teaching Excellence Framework. The judging panel was impressed by Bucks New's small class sizes and individual action plans to help students into work, as well as "live briefs" where students examined real-world problems.

Awarded university status in 2007, Bucks New has its main campus in High Wycombe and a second base in Uxbridge, northwest London. Its newest campus is in Aylesbury, where nursing and other healthcare courses are taught. More than £100m has been invested in the High Wycombe campus over ten years and its prize-winning Gateway Building dominates the town centre.

Bucks New's focus is on serving the public sector as well as the creative and cultural industries. The university was one of the first to offer a degree in policing and is also among the leading providers of nursing qualifications in the southeast, offering adult, child and mental health pre-qualifying nursing, as well as post-registration courses. The social work academy is run in partnership with Buckinghamshire county council, where the university's academics support the continuing professional development of qualified social workers and managers.

The university prides itself on its links with local business and private sector employers, who help to shape the curriculum

---

Queen Alexandra Road
High Wycombe HP11 2JZ
0330 123 2023
advice@bucks.ac.uk
www.bucks.ac.uk
www.bucksstudentsunion.org
Open days 2020: March 14;
June 13 Nursing (Uxbridge)
March 28; June 20

The Times and The Sunday Times Rankings
Overall Ranking: 113 (last year: 117)

Teaching quality	81.9%	36
Student experience	79.7%	39
Research quality	1.5%	123
Entry standards	117	=104
Graduate prospects	68.8%	104
Good honours	60.4%	131
Expected completion rate	79.3%	109
Student/staff ratio	15.8	=66
Services and facilities	£2,647	37

as well as providing placement opportunities. Undergraduate programmes for the film and television industries are based at nearby Pinewood Studios, where students work alongside industry professionals. Travel and aviation courses provide the opportunity to study for a professional pilot's licence while working towards a degree.

Although Bucks New aspires to lead the way in applied research, it entered only 24 staff for the 2014 Research Excellence Framework and is ranked in the bottom three in our research quality table.

A new Life Sciences Innovation Centre will have bases at Stoke Mandeville Hospital and High Wycombe, supporting the development of innovative products focused around a range of clinical areas, including health and wellbeing, prevention and public health.

Almost two-thirds of the 9,000 students are over 21 and the university scores well for social inclusion across all of our measures. Ranking in the top 20 in England and Wales, just over half of the intake is drawn from ethnic minorities and just under half are first generation students, whose parents did not attend university.

Under the students' union's Big Deal programme, everyone receives a package of freebies to use in entertainment, recreation and sport. However, there are only 100 means-tested bursary scholarships because the university prioritises widening

participation through other means. It runs outreach programmes in "hard-to-reach" communities and focuses on helping its diverse student body to get ready to enter the jobs market.

Bucks New runs one of only five swimming performance centres approved by Swim England. There are 30 sports clubs and links with professional clubs in the region. The university gym is one of the best in the area with app-based cardio machines and interactive exercise equipment. The Human Performance, Exercise and Wellbeing Centre has a three-lane running track with 3D motion-capture technology, with sports injury and physiotherapy clinics.

High Wycombe has a range of student pubs and clubs and is within easy reach of London. The campus has a student village of more than 400 en-suite bedrooms a short walk from the campus. This has brought the total accommodation stock to 885 residential places, ensuring that new students are guaranteed a hall place even if they come through clearing.

Tuition fees

» Fees for UK/EU students £9,250
» Fees for International students 2020–21 £12,000–£16,000
» For scholarship and bursary information see www.bucks.ac.uk/applying-to-bucks/undergraduate/fees-and-funding
» Graduate salary £22,000

Student numbers

Undergraduates	6,662	(1,366)
Postgraduates	360	(699)
Applications/places		6,025/1,745
Applications per place		3.5
Overall offer rate		97.9%
Unconditional offers		0%
International students		8.6%

Accommodation

University provided places: 885
Self-catered: £114–£190 per week
First years guaranteed accommodation
www.bucks.ac.uk/life-at-bucks/accommodation

Where do the students come from?

				Social inclusion ranking: 19	
State schools (non-grammar)	93.5%	First generation students	48.8%	Black attainment gap	-9%
Grammar schools	1.9%	Deprived areas	9.4%	Disabled	3%
Independent schools	4.7%	All ethnic minorities	52.7%	Mature (over 21)	62.5%

University of Cambridge

At the top of our league table for its seventh year in a row, Cambridge received a record £100m donation in 2019 to attract the most talented students of the future. About £1m of the £100m donation from the David and Claudia Harding Foundation – at the time, the largest ever made to a UK university – has been earmarked for developing new approaches to attracting undergraduate students from underrepresented groups. A further £79m will fund 100 PhD scholarships, with £20m to be spent on student support and to encourage more Cambridge graduates to donate money.

Social inclusion has long been a difficult nut to crack for this elite institution. It has sunk to the bottom of our ranking in this area, despite successive increases in the proportion of state school entrants. Only 41% of students come from comprehensives and non-selective colleges. Students with a household income of less than £42,620 are eligible for bursaries of £3,500 a year.

The university has fallen behind Oxford in several international rankings, which emphasise research, but remains ahead on measures that matter most to undergraduates – with the highest proportion of firsts and 2:1s awarded, the highest entry standards and the most spending on student facilities. Cambridge is top in 27 of our 67 subject tables.

For applicants, competition doesn't get much tougher. Even to get through the first stage of the selection process, applicants must be predicted A*AA at A-level in arts subjects and A*A*A in the sciences – although lower offers may be made where a candidate's school or personal circumstances may disadvantage them. Cambridge also sets its own entrance tests, taken either on the day of an interview or in advance.

Cambridge never takes part in clearing. But in 2019, for the first time, those who did not receive an offer but went on to meet or exceed their offer from another university were reconsidered under the adjustment process, as long as they met Cambridge's criteria for widening participation: 67 students were admitted in this way.

Applications must be in by October 15. At that point candidates receive a supplementary application questionnaire seeking greater detail on their academic record. For those unfamiliar with the collegiate system, choosing the right college is an added complication – and it matters, in order to maximise your chances of getting in and to ensure a good university experience if you do. A minority of students make an open application to any college, statistically no less likely to succeed.

Unlike most Russell Group institutions, Cambridge has not expanded its undergraduate intake significantly, with just over 2,500 places

Cambridge Admissions Office
Student Services Centre
New Museums Site
Cambridge CB2 3BT
01223 333 308
admissions@cam.ac.uk
www.cam.ac.uk
www.cusu.co.uk
Open days 2020:
July 2, 3

The Times and The Sunday Times **Rankings**
Overall Ranking: 1 (last year: 1)

Teaching quality	n/a	
Student experience	n/a	
Research quality	57.3%	1
Entry standards	224	1
Graduate prospects	86.8%	7
Good honours	93.4%	2
Expected completion rate	98.3%	2
Student/staff ratio	11.2	5
Services and facilities	£3,854	1

available each year. Although there are fewer than five applicants for each place, only three in ten received an offer in 2018. Nine out of ten entrants have at least three A grades at A-level, or the equivalent.

For the few who are offered a place, the workload is high, with a demanding schedule crammed into eight-week terms.

Cambridge received a gold rating in the Teaching Excellence Framework. Its tutorial system enabled students to engage with world-leading scholars, said the judging panel, and to receive personalised feedback on their academic progress.

The university's £1bn North West Cambridge development will provide private housing and open the door to a bigger post-graduate intake. Postgraduate degree apprenticeships are on the way in conjunction with Lloyds Bank, Greggs Bakery and British Airways.

Renowned worldwide for its research, Cambridge entered 95% of eligible academics for the Research Excellence Framework – the highest proportion of any institution in the UK – and 87% of their work was rated as world-leading or internationally excellent. The university got the best results in the country for aeronautical and electronic engineering, business and management, chemistry, classics and clinical medicine.

Cambridge has some of the most ancient and iconic buildings of any university in the world and huge sums have been spent on modernising the facilities. Fundraising schemes will create new professorships and continue the development of a biomedical campus and the West Cambridge site, where research scientists from industry will occupy laboratory and desk space alongside Cambridge research groups.

Sports facilities are excellent at individual colleges and at the university's £16m sports centre, which features a large sports hall and a strength and conditioning wing.

Most students have college rooms for all three years of their degree. Satisfaction rates have been high in the past, but successive Oxbridge boycotts of the National Student Survey have made it impossible to tell exactly how high in the past three years. Cambridge's score in our table is derived from the 2016 survey, the last one where at least 50% of students bothered to respond.

Tuition fees

»	Fees for UK/EU students	£9,250
»	Fees for International students 2020–21	£21,168–£32,214
	Medicine and veterinary science	£55,272
»	For scholarship and bursary information see	
	www.undergraduate.study.cam.ac.uk/fees-and-finance	
»	Graduate salary	£27,000

Student numbers

Undergraduates	12,184	(358)
Postgraduates	6,722	(1,246)
Applications/places		18,590/3,445
Applications per place		5.4
Overall offer rate		29.4%
Unconditional offers		0%
International students		34.3%

Accommodation

See: http://www.undergraduate.study.cam.ac.uk/
why-cambridge/student-life/accommodation
College websites provide accommodation details

See Chapter 14 for individual colleges

Where do the students come from?

Social inclusion ranking: 115

State schools (non-grammar)	41%	First generation students	14.2%	Black attainment gap	-14.8%
Grammar schools	22.4%	Deprived areas	4.7%	Disabled	4.1%
Independent schools	36.6%	All ethnic minorities	22.8%	Mature (over 21)	4.5%

Canterbury Christ Church

A raft of new courses helped Canterbury Christ Church to reverse a three-year decline in applications in 2018, and there are plenty more new offerings in the pipeline. They will include medicine, with the first students joining the new joint medical school with the University of Kent in 2020.

The numbers starting degrees rose by almost 9% in 2018, as a new building opened for the schools of media, art and design, and music and performing arts, with specialist teaching facilities, including performance space and design studios. The project marked the start of a £150m plan to develop its main campus in Canterbury over 15 years.

Canterbury Christ Church has adopted the internationally recognised CDIO (conceive, design, implement and operate) curriculum that fosters creativity in engineering as part of a drive to rebalance the intake. If successful, the makeup of the next engineering cohort will be 35% women and 40% from disadvantaged areas – and a new centre for science, engineering, technology and health will greet their arrival in 2020. The Kent and Medway Engineering, Design, Growth and Enterprise (Edge) Hub will set up shop there, and there will be specialist health facilities, too

The new Kent and Medway medical school will be the first in the county, offering 100 places on five-year bachelor of medicine and bachelor of surgery programmes. It is expected that many of the students will come from local communities.

Degrees in chemical, biomedical, mechanical and software engineering, creative music and production, arts education and product design took their first students in autumn 2019. New courses this year include animation production, criminal investigation, international business management, and terrorism and transnational crime.

Christ Church is also expanding a portfolio of higher and degree apprenticeships which currently covers nursing and allied health professions, and management. New apprenticeship routes are planned in life sciences, engineering, accountancy, law, computing, teaching, coaching and mentoring, leisure and tourism, policing and journalism.

The university has campuses in Chatham and Broadstairs, and a postgraduate centre in Tunbridge Wells. The purpose-built campus at Broadstairs offers subjects ranging from commercial music to digital media, photography, and early childhood studies, while the recently expanded Chatham site specialises in education and health programmes.

In addition, a life sciences industry liaison laboratory at Discovery Park in Sandwich provides students with first-class facilities for

North Holmes Road
Canterbury CT1 1QU
01227 767 700
courses@canterbury.ac.uk
www.canterbury.ac.uk
https://ccsu.co.uk
Open days 2020:
see website

Edinburgh
Belfast
Cardiff London
CANTERBURY

science and research, and acts as an added resource for local businesses.

The majority of the students, however, are in Canterbury, on a world heritage site where Christ Church has a prize-winning library and student services centre. All campuses are interconnected by a high-speed data network.

The former Church of England college achieved university status in 2005, and is one of the region's largest providers of courses and research for the public services, with teacher training courses that are highly rated by Ofsted, and strong programmes in health and social care, nursing and policing.

Christ Church has a silver rating in the Teaching Excellence Framework, recognising the gains made by students from disadvantaged backgrounds, ethnic minority communities and those with disabilities, who achieve good degrees at the same rate as other students and have good long-term employment prospects.

The university was in the top 30 in our first table measuring social inclusion but slipped to 57th in our second edition. Just under 92% of the undergraduates come from non-selective state schools or colleges and more than a third are at least 21 on entry.

Two-thirds of the undergraduates are female, partly reflecting the subject mix, with its emphasis on health subjects and education. There are now 14,500 students, more than half of whom come from Kent. The university remains a Church of England foundation and has the Archbishop of Canterbury as its chancellor, but it admits students of all faiths and none.

Almost half of Christ Church's submission to the 2014 Research Excellence Framework was placed in the top two categories, resulting in one of the biggest increases in funding. It has since established the UK Institute for Migration Research and the Institute of Medical Sciences, which focuses on stem cell research and minimally invasive surgery.

Bucking the trend of recent years, Christ Church moved from three terms to a semester-based system with teaching spread over two extended periods.

Sports facilities are good for those on the Canterbury campus and there is enough residential accommodation to guarantee a place for first-years who apply by the end of July. Canterbury is now a thriving student centre, and Christ Church contributes to the cultural life of the city with the Sidney Cooper gallery and St Gregory's Centre for Music, a historic concert venue.

Tuition fees

»	Fees for UK/EU students	£9,250
	Foundation courses	£7,050
»	Fees for International students 2020–21	£13,000
»	For scholarship and bursary information see www.canterbury.ac.uk/study-here/fees-and-funding/ undergraduate-fees-and-funding/	
»	Graduate salary	£22,000

Student numbers

Undergraduates	9,931	(1,836)
Postgraduates	1,133	(1,557)
Applications/places		11,250/3,650
Applications per place		3.1
Overall offer rate		87.1%
Unconditional offers		0%
International students		5%

Accommodation

University provided places: 1,825
Self-catered: £118–£167 per week
First years guaranteed accommodation
www.canterbury.ac.uk/accommodation

Where do the students come from?

State schools (non-grammar)	91.7%	First generation students	58.3%	
Grammar schools	5.9%	Deprived areas	15.9%	
Independent schools	2.4%	All ethnic minorities	26.2%	

Social inclusion ranking: 57

Black attainment gap	-42.2%
Disabled	6.2%
Mature (over 21)	33.7%

Cardiff University

There is good news and bad news at the research-led Russell Group's only Welsh member. New enrolments reached record levels in 2018 and applications increased in 2019, with Cardiff remaining just outside our top 30. But Swansea has taken over the mantle of top-ranked university in Wales, buoyed by considerably better scores for student satisfaction.

Applications to Cardiff are still well below the peak years of 2014–16 and a £22.8m deficit opened up in 2017–18, prompting plans to cut 380 full-time equivalent staff over the next five years.

The university's five-year strategy aims to establish Cardiff as one of the top 20 universities in the UK and in the world's top 100 – although it has just dropped out of the top 150 in the QS rankings. The strategy, called The Way Forward, expresses a renewed focus on the university's civic mission and a desire to be seen as the home of innovation, as well as improving the student experience.

Work has started on the Centre for Student Life, at the heart of the Cathays Park campus, which will open during the 2020–21 academic year. It is designed to transform the way the university supports students, including their mental health and wellbeing. As well as a central hub for student services, there will be flexible social learning spaces, a 550-seat lecture theatre and shops.

Work has also begun on Cardiff's new innovation campus, which will house start-up companies, spin-outs and partnerships, as well as hosting two of the university's most successful research centres, the Institute for Compound Semiconductors and Cardiff Catalysis Institute.

A new home has already opened for the highly-regarded School of Journalism, Media and Culture, next door to BBC Cymru Wales, in the latest phase of a £600m development plan

Cardiff was rated silver in the government's Teaching Excellence Framework, thanks in part to the support provided by personal tutors and the direct engagement of students with developments at the forefront of research, scholarship and professional practice.

The university achieved excellent results in the 2014 Research Excellence Framework, but entered only 62% of eligible staff – much the lowest proportion at any Russell Group university. This depressed its position in our research ranking, but 87% of the submission was rated as world-leading or internationally excellent, and Cardiff was in the UK's top three for the impact of its research. Civil and construction engineering was rated top in the exercise.

Subsequent developments have seen the launch of a £20m Dementia Research Institute, as part of a UK-wide initiative, and a £14m Medicines Discovery Institute to

Cardiff
CF10 3AT
029 2087 4455
enquiry@cardiff.ac.uk
www.cardiff.ac.uk
www.cardiffstudents.com
Open days 2020:
April 1

The Times and The Sunday Times **Rankings**

Overall Ranking: 34 (last year: 32)

Teaching quality	78.2%	95
Student experience	77.5%	82
Research quality	35.0%	34
Entry standards	159	=27
Graduate prospects	81.7%	=30
Good honours	83.3%	26
Expected completion rate	91.8%	=29
Student/staff ratio	14	=28
Services and facilities	£2,379	60

develop new drugs for mental health and central nervous system conditions.

Cardiff has also been selected to host a new £5m Climate Change and Social Transformations hub. The centre is a collaboration with the universities of Manchester, York and East Anglia and the charity Climate Outreach. Further developments include a new partnership with the University of Bremen to strengthen European relations through collaborative research.

Cardiff is encouraging more students to spend time abroad during their studies. The Global Opportunities Programme provides study, work and volunteering options across the world to enhance the student experience.

Some 15% of undergraduates come from an independent school – the highest proportion in Wales – but there are extensive efforts to widen participation. Although Cardiff performs better than many Russell Group institutions, it is ranked in the bottom 15 in England and Wales for social inclusion. Bursaries of £1,000 are available to undergraduates from low-income families, and an additional £3,000 is paid to care leavers. More than 5,000 students received some support in 2018.

The Residences Life programme helps students to transition smoothly to higher education, ensuring that they feel part of their new community, while the Student Mentoring Scheme matches new entrants with established undergraduates from the same academic school to discuss topics including study techniques, budgeting and module choices.

The university is based in Cardiff's civic complex around Cathays Park. The five healthcare schools share a 53-acre campus at Heath Park with the University Hospital of Wales. The £18m Cochrane Building provides teaching and learning facilities for all healthcare schools based there. The dental education clinic offers students some of the UK's most modern training facilities, including a new simulation suite.

The university has 5,350 residential places for undergraduates, enabling it to guarantee a place to those making Cardiff their first choice. The main residential site at Talybont boasts a sports training village, and there is also a city-centre dance studio and fitness suite, as well as 33 acres of outdoor facilities. The university's Cardiff Half Marathon is the second largest such event in the UK. Beyond the campus, Cardiff is a popular student city, relatively inexpensive and with a good range of nightlife and cultural venues.

Tuition fees

» Fees for UK/EU students	£9,000
» Fees for International students 2020–21	£16,950–£20,950
Dentistry £38,059; Medicine £33,000	
» For scholarship and bursary information see www.cardiff.ac.uk/fees	
» Graduate salary	£22,000

Student numbers

Undergraduates	19,412 (3,673)
Postgraduates	5,239 (3,273)
Applications/places	34,590/5,500
Applications per place	6.3
Overall offer rate	79.0%
International students	23.8%

Accommodation

University provided places: 5,346
Catered costs: £126–£161 per week
Self-catered: £102–£142 per week
First years guaranteed accommodation
www.cardiff.ac.uk/residences

Where do the students come from?

State schools (non-grammar)	75%	First generation students	32.3%	Black attainment gap	-20.6%
Grammar schools	9.8%	Deprived areas	9.4%	Disabled	4.6%
Independent schools	15.2%	All ethnic minorities	17.4%	Mature (over 21)	11.8%

Social inclusion ranking: 101

Cardiff Metropolitan University

Cardiff Met is launching 37 new degrees in 2019 and 2020, in a significant broadening of its offer to undergraduates. Courses ranging from brand and marketing management to computer security, data science and primary education have taken their first students. Those to follow include aviation management, community theatre, digital health and robotics engineering.

Much of the activity centres on the new Cardiff School of Technologies, which was launched in 2018 on the university's Llandaff campus and is due to transfer to a new campus in the city centre by 2022, attracting another 2,000 students. It will focus on the digital media and smart technology, data sciences, design technology, and the engineering needs of Wales and the wider world.

As part of a commitment to improve its students' experience the main teaching rooms at Llandaff have been partially refurbished, modernising the facilities and providing social learning spaces. The overall masterplan involved £600m of developments.

Summer 2019 also saw the addition of a new, larger gym, studio and wellbeing facilities on the Cyncoed campus, the smaller of Cardiff Met's two existing bases. Student residences on the campus have been refurbished, ensuring that the majority of Cardiff Met's bedrooms are en-suite.

Cardiff Met's ranking for teaching quality is up more than 40 places, while satisfaction with student experience has seen a similar rise to stand just outside the UK top 30 – all of which, unusually, has not been enough to improve Cardiff Met's overall ranking.

Llandaff hosts the School of Art and Design and the School of Management, as well as design, engineering, food science and health courses. Education and sport – the university's best-known feature – are at Cyncoed, which has a modern student centre and is the main centre of social activity, particularly for first years. Construction of a 25-metre swimming pool, fitness suite, sports hall and squash courts is under way there.

Cardiff Met is one of Britain's leading centres for university sport, with team performances that do justice to some excellent facilities. In recent years, the university has had British university champions in sports ranging from archery and gymnastics to squash, weightlifting and judo. More than 300 past or present students are internationals in 30 sports.

The £7m National Indoor Athletics Centre is the university's pride and joy, but other facilities are also of high quality. Around 2,000 students take sport and dance related courses.

A new partnership for education, which includes Oxford and Cardiff universities in a consortium with its associated schools, was launched last year. Cardiff Met is the only

---

200 Western Avenue
Llandaff
Cardiff CF5 2YB
029 2041 6010
askadmissions@cardiffmet.ac.uk
www.cardiffmet.ac.uk
www.cardiffmetsu.co.uk
Open days 2020:
April 4 (Cyncoed),
April 25 (Llandaff)

The Times and The Sunday Times **Rankings**
Overall Ranking: 112 (last year: 108)

Teaching quality	80.7%	=53
Student experience	80%	=32
Research quality	3.9%	107
Entry standards	123	=86
Graduate prospects	65.9%	115
Good honours	67.4%	=113
Expected completion rate	79.6%	=107
Student/staff ratio	18.8	=115
Services and facilities	£2,565	40

provider in southeast Wales to be accredited by the Education Workforce Council.

The university is aiming to break into the UK's top 50 by 2022–23 and to attract more students. The number of new entrants was steady in 2018, when many of its peers saw declining recruitment, but the university dropped out of our top 100, with a big decline in student/staff ratio.

The Cardiff Global initiative, launched last year, is expected to add to the 8,500 international students, most of whom are taught in partner institutions overseas. The scheme also encompasses Cardiff Open Colleges, which will extend the university's partnerships with schools and further education colleges to deliver clear progression routes to university entry.

Cardiff Met was one of just four Welsh universities to be awarded silver in the government's Teaching Excellence Framework (TEF). The panel found that personalised learning, including Welsh medium content and delivery, secures high levels of engagement and commitment to learning and study from students.

An enhanced personal tutor system gives students greater access to academic support, advice and guidance. The TEF panel noted that course design was informed by a significant focus on employability, producing good outcomes for a range of student groups, including those from black and minority ethnic communities, disadvantaged and mature students.

Each academic school now has its own careers consultants with sector-specific knowledge. In addition, the Centre for Entrepreneurship assists with the growing number of start-ups.

The university entered only 35 academics for the 2014 Research Excellence Framework out of 381 who were eligible – only two universities entered a smaller proportion. But the small submission scored well, with 80% of the work rated in the top two categories. The university has since received a Queen's Anniversary Prize for the use of design and related 3D digital scanning technologies as applied to maxillofacial reconstructive surgery.

Students from Wales account for two-thirds of the 10,000 Cardiff-based students. The campuses are close to the city centre and linked by the Met Rider bus service during termtime. The halls of residence are a mile from the main campus and have enough rooms to guarantee accommodation to international students and those from outside the city who make Cardiff Met their firm choice and apply by the end of March.

Tuition fees

» Fees for UK/EU students	£9,000
» Fees for International students 2020–21	£12,500
» For scholarship and bursary information see www.cardiffmet.ac.uk/study/finance/	
» Graduate salary	£19,000

Student numbers

Undergraduates	7,703	(628)
Postgraduates	1,298	(804)
Applications/places		8,860/2,945
Applications per place		3
Overall offer rate		93.5%
Unconditional offer rate		0%
International students		12.6%

Accommodation

University provided places: 1,556
Catered costs: £164–£185 per week
Self-catered: £103–£132 per week
www.cardiffmet.ac.uk/accommodation/Pages/default.aspx

Where do the students come from?

State schools (non-grammar)	92.3%	First generation students	48.3%	Black attainment gap	-42.9%
Grammar schools	1.6%	Deprived areas	17.7%	Disabled	6.5%
Independent schools	6.1%	All ethnic minorities	14.4%	Mature (over 21)	25.5%

Social inclusion ranking: 86

University of Central Lancashire

The University of Central Lancashire (UCLan) returns to our top 100 this year after significant improvement in student satisfaction scores for teaching quality and the wider university experience. The institution gained silver in the government's Teaching Excellence Framework.

That may help to stem a fall in applications, which have dropped by a third since 2015, when recruiting restrictions were lifted. The numbers of students starting courses fell by almost 1,000 in that time, although its undergraduate enrolment of more than 5,000 was still close to the top 20 in the country.

The university is not shy about trumpeting accolades: its prospectus tells students, "You'll be joining one of the top universities in the world." The evidence for this is that the Centre for World University Rankings (CWUR) places it in the top 3.7% of universities, although it does not appear among the 1,000 listed on CWUR's website for 2018-19. In the QS World Rankings it continues to hold four out of five stars – just outside the top 800 – and has five stars for teaching quality.

UCLan dominates its home town of Preston and is expanding in nearby Burnley, where there is a collaboration with Cisco Systems for advanced manufacturing. A £200m campus masterplan encompasses a new Engineering and Innovation Centre – where more women will be encouraged to enter the industry. Work has begun on a £60m student centre and pedestrianised civic square in the heart of Preston. In Burnley, where the student population is intended to bloom from 400 to 4,000 by 2025, new accommodation and car parking is planned.

The Westlakes campus in West Cumbria focuses on nursing and other health subjects and UCLan has an outpost in Cyprus, which has a wide range of courses and offers the opportunity of a year abroad for UK students, although without access to student loans for that period.

More than 20 new degrees are now on stream in subjects ranging from occupational therapy to cyberpsychology, professional policing and creative advertising. They will be followed in 2020 by multimedia journalism and transatlantic studies. The university is also extending its already extensive programme of degree apprenticeships and expects to have up to 2,000 apprentices by September 2020.

The first UK students were admitted to study medicine at UCLan in 2019. The School of Medicine opened four years previously, but government quotas restricted the early intakes to self-funded international students. They continue to be charged the full cost – £40,500 in 2020–21 – but their British

Preston PR1 2HE
01772 201 201
cenquiries@uclan.ac.uk
www.uclan.ac.uk
www.uclansu.co.uk
Open days 2020:
see website

The Times and The Sunday Times Rankings
Overall Ranking: 75 (last year: =105)

Teaching quality	81.3%	=42
Student experience	78.7%	=59
Research quality	5.6%	=86
Entry standards	133	=60
Graduate prospects	76.9%	62
Good honours	71.8%	=87
Expected completion rate	79.6%	=107
Student/staff ratio	14.2	=30
Services and facilities	£2,241	72

counterparts pay standard £9,250 fees.

UCLan offers an unusually wide range of subjects, including astrophysics, which benefits from a longstanding collaboration with Nasa. The Dental School was one of the few to open in 100 years, while the architecture degree was the first to be introduced at a British university for a decade.

World-leading research was found in all 16 subject areas assessed in the 2014 Research Excellence Framework. UCLan academics have been involved in sector-leading stroke research with the Department of Health and work on nutritional science with the Bill and Melinda Gates Foundation. The undergraduate research internship scheme enables students from all disciplines to work on research projects for up to ten weeks.

UCLan is best known, however, for a longstanding commitment to widening participation in higher education and it is in our top 20 for social inclusion. Every undergraduate programme includes the option of a foundation year for those without the necessary qualifications for degree-level study, while large numbers take external programmes delivered in further education colleges. About 45% of first-year undergraduates are eligible for a £2,000 bursary.

There is also a strong focus on entrepreneurship, with a range of business incubation facilities for students and graduates. The university claims the largest number of start-up companies which remain active after three years of trading. In the 12 months covered by the latest national survey, UCLan's Propeller team helped to establish 33 new businesses. All students can take advantage of work placements and other opportunities to enhance their employability.

A partnership with a car recycling business won a Times Higher Education award for the most innovative contribution to business-university collaboration in 2018.

New students who want accommodation are guaranteed one of 1,630 residential places.

Facilities for sport are excellent, both on campus and at the UCLan Sports Arena, two miles away. Preston offers a generally safe student environment and lower cost of living than Liverpool or Manchester, but is within 50 minutes of either city by public transport.

Tuition fees

» Fees for UK/EU students	£9,250
Foundation courses	£5,550
» Fees for International students 2020–21	£12,700–£13,700
Medicine	£40,500
» For scholarship and bursary information see	
www.uclan.ac.uk/study_here/fees_and_finance/index.php	
» Graduate salary	£20,000

Student numbers

Undergraduates	15,976 (2,046)
Postgraduates	1,804 (3,176)
Applications/places	18,630/5,375
Applications per place	3.5
Overall offer rate	83.1%
Unconditional ofers	0%
International students	9.9%

Accommodation

University provided places: 1,630
Self-catered: £75–£121 per week
First years guaranteed accommodation
www.uclan.ac.uk/accommodation/index.php

Where do the students come from?

				Social inclusion ranking: 17	
State schools (non-grammar)	96.7%	First generation students	52.5%	Black attainment gap	-16.5%
Grammar schools	1.5%	Deprived areas	19.2%	Disabled	6.8%
Independent schools	1.8%	All ethnic minorities	23.3%	Mature (over 21)	38.7%

University of Chester

Chester introduced 18 new degree programmes in 2019 and is planning at least eight more this year as it tries to stimulate demand for places. Applications have dropped by a third in four years – from more than 25,000 in 2014 to less than 18,000 in 2018 – and were down again at the deadline for 2019 courses.

New offerings range from cell and molecular biology to economics, music production and digital marketing and further additions will include business enterprise, artificial intelligence in finance, creative and cultural industries management, and marine biology.

The university has already expanded its portfolio of degree apprenticeships and expects to add programmes for advanced clinical practitioners, social workers and police constables in 2020, taking the number of apprentices from about 300 to 700–800. It has also opened new facilities in Birkenhead, on the Wirral, to educate student nurses and midwives in skills laboratories simulating hi-tech hospital wards, with virtual reality equipment.

Professor Eunice Simmons has taken over as the university's vice-chancellor – only the second to hold the post – after Professor Tim Wheeler retired following more than 20 years at the helm. He oversaw the step up to university status in 2005 and a rise in the student population from 4,000 to 18,300.

Another 2,400 students take Chester's qualifications at partner institutions.

When Chester was awarded silver in the Teaching Excellence Framework, the judging panel praised the university for helping students to develop employability skills. About two-thirds of undergraduates take work-based learning modules. The panel said Chester had an "embedded culture of valuing, recognising and rewarding good teaching". More than two-thirds of the academic staff hold Higher Education Academy fellowships.

One in four undergraduates is at least 21 on entry and two-thirds are female. Nearly all are state-educated, and more than half come from families where neither parent has gone to university. Progression agreements guarantee interviews to students at a number of local colleges, subject to certain conditions, but there is no reduction in entry requirements.

Completion rates had been improving but have now slipped back below the national average for Chester's courses and entry qualifications. The university more than doubled the number of submissions made to the 2014 Research Excellence Framework compared with 2008. Some research was judged to be world-leading in all but one of the 15 subject areas.

Chester's parent institution was a Church of England college established in 1839 as the first purpose-built college for teacher training. William Gladstone was among the founders

Parkgate Road
Chester CH1 4BJ
01244 511 000
admissions@chester.ac.uk
www.chester.ac.uk
www.chestersu.com
Open days 2020:
see website

The Times and The Sunday Times **Rankings**
Overall Ranking: =79 (last year: 73)

Teaching quality	82.7%	24
Student experience	79.1%	=48
Research quality	4.1%	=101
Entry standards	114	=112
Graduate prospects	70.1%	102
Good honours	69.7%	=101
Expected completion rate	80.5%	101
Student/staff ratio	15.5	=59
Services and facilities	£2,803	=20

of the college, which pre-dated all the English universities apart from Oxford, Cambridge, London and Durham. The link with the church remains – two of the campuses have chapels and there are other faith spaces – and Chester's teacher training has been rated outstanding by Ofsted. These days the institution has expanded its course provision to cover more than 20 subject areas.

The university has been spreading out geographically, opening a base in Shrewsbury to add to its campuses in Warrington and Thornton, and four in its home city. The Queen's Park Campus in Chester, once the wartime headquarters of the army's Western Command, now houses the Chester Business School, which won Business School of the Year at the Educate North awards in 2018.

The university had already opened the UK's first new engineering faculty for two decades, in the former Shell research facility at the Thornton Science Park campus, near Ellesmere Port. The Energy Centre there brings industry and academia together to work on new intelligent energy technologies.

The Parkgate Road campus, the original headquarters, is only a short walk from the centre of Chester on a 32-acre site with manicured gardens, where recent developments include an upgraded library, new sports facilities and biology laboratories.

The adjacent Riverside Innovation Centre serves new and growing businesses, some run by entrepreneurial students and graduates. Health and social care, education and children's services are also based at the Riverside campus in the former County Hall. The Kingsway campus houses arts and media courses.

The Warrington campus focuses on the creative industries and public services, with high-quality production facilities and links with the BBC in Salford. The university owns 1,800 residential places in Warrington and Chester and endorses another 910 private rooms. Accommodation guarantees vary between campuses but, with many students living at home, new students seeking accommodation almost always get it.

There are extensive sports facilities at Warrington and especially on the Parkgate Road campus, which has tennis courts, a 100-metre sprint track and a floodlit 3G multi-use sports pitch.

The quaint walled city of Chester also has plenty to offer students – and came second in *The Sun*'s top 50 student-friendly cities in the UK last year.

Tuition fees

» Fees for UK/EU students		£9,250
Foundation courses		£7,850
» Fees for International students 2020–21		£12,450
» For scholarship and bursary information see		
http://www1.chester.ac.uk/study/undergraduate/finance		
» Graduate salary		£20,000

Student numbers

Undergraduates	9,654 (1,293)
Postgraduates	1,259 (3.204)
Applications/places	17,740/3,210
Applications per place	5.5
Overall offer rate	84.2%
Unconditional offers	0%
International students	5.8%

Accommodation

University provided places: 2,710
Catered costs: £125–£150 per week
Self-catered: £88–£149 per week
www.chester.ac.uk/accommodation

Where do the students come from?

State schools (non-grammar)	93.6%	First generation students	54.4%	Black attainment gap	-28.7%
Grammar schools	3.6%	Deprived areas	19.1%	Disabled	7.4%
Independent schools	2.8%	All ethnic minorities	8%	Mature (over 21)	24%

Social inclusion ranking: 45

University of Chichester

Chichester claims to be carrying out a "revolution on the south coast" with the expansion of its degree apprenticeships and the opening of a £35m Tech Park in Bognor Regis in 2018. Supported by more than 40 companies and funded by the Local Enterprise Partnership, the park brings together courses in engineering with the creative and digital technologies to form an academic area labelled Steam – science, technology, engineering, arts and mathematics.

Since the Duke and Duchess of Sussex unveiled a plaque on the Tech Park's opening day, the university has moved closer to its goal of trebling the number of degree apprenticeships by 2020. Apprenticeships for social workers and business analysts in digital technology are being added to the ten existing programmes ranging from postgraduate teaching to cybersecurity analysis.

Some of the apprenticeship programmes will be based at the new facility and will allow the university to take an additional 500 students a year. Chichester has introduced degrees in audio production and music technologies, counselling psychology, e-sports, law, and musical theatre and cabaret performance, and will add seven more in 2020, in subjects ranging from games design to physiotherapy and law, philosophy and ethics.

Applications have dropped by about 1,000 since 2016, and the numbers starting courses fell by nearly 20% over the same period. But the broader range of options may help the university to achieve its plans for gradual growth. New engineering degrees, for example, which took their first students in 2018, have an industry-led curriculum on the CDIO (conceiving, designing, implementing, operating) model that is being adopted by a growing number of universities.

Students will have access to a welding floor, fabricating laboratory, 3D printers and an engineering centre. The Tech Park also houses the Department of Creative and Digital Technologies, which has one of only three sound stages in the UK big enough to hold a professional orchestra. There is also a television production studio, special effects room and media operation centre.

The university traces its history back to 1839 as a teacher training college set up in memory of William Otter, Bishop of Chichester, for whom the development of education was a passion. In 1873 it became a women-only college and although male students were accepted from 1957, women still hold two-thirds of the places.

Awarded silver in the government's Teaching Excellence Framework, the university was commended for its outstanding support for disadvantaged students. Chichester has recovered all of its recently

Bishop Otter Campus
College Lane
Chichester PO19 6PE
01243 816 002
admissions@chi.ac.uk
www.chi.ac.uk
www.ucsu.org
Open days 2020:
see website

The Times and The Sunday Times **Rankings**
Overall Ranking: 71 (last year: =94)

Teaching quality	83.3%	=18
Student experience	79.9%	=35
Research quality	6.4%	81
Entry standards	123	86
Graduate prospects	64.6%	120
Good honours	73.1%	=81
Expected completion rate	88%	53
Student/staff ratio	14.4	35
Services and facilities	£1,833	108

lost ground in our academic rankings, following an upturn in results from the annual National Student Survey. Its scores for student satisfaction with teaching quality returned to the UK top 20 this year (up from 63rd last year), while the wider student experience climbed 19 places.

About a third of the students qualify for financial aid, which includes cash bursaries of £500 a year for those from households with an annual income of £25,000. Two bridging courses are being developed – health and social care, and maths for engineering – for students who lack the qualifications to begin a degree.

The university is also running the first programme in the UK to prepare homeless people for higher education. The ten-week module utilises the students' life experiences to develop academic reading, writing and research skills, self-confidence and self-esteem.

The university entered a quarter of its eligible staff for the Research Excellence Framework and did well in music, drama and performing arts, English and sport. The Mathematics Centre has an international reputation and has become a focal point for curriculum development in England and elsewhere.

The 1,142 residential places are roughly equally divided between the two campuses, enabling Chichester to guarantee accommodation to anyone who has been offered a place and made the university their first choice. There is a university bus service linking the two centres, and students' union bars at each.

A £2m investment programme has matched the university's excellent sports provision with world-class facilities. A programme for gifted athletes will use a new running track on the Chichester campus. A multi-use sports dome has been built as part of the Tudor Hale Centre for Sport, which allows for all-weather teaching for sports courses. As well as tennis and netball courts the centre has laboratories and a sports injury clinic.

The small cathedral city of Chichester is best known for its theatre and as a yachting venue, while along Bognor's coast all types of water sports are available. Both offer a good supply of private housing and some student-oriented bars.

Much of the surrounding countryside has been designated an area of outstanding natural beauty. It is an appealing combination: very few students drop out and its projected non-completion rate of 6.6% is roughly half the expected level.

Tuition fees

» Fees for UK/EU students	£9,250
» Fees for International students 2019–20	£13,000
» For scholarship and bursary information see www.chi.ac.uk/study-us/fees-finance	
» Graduate salary	£19,200

Student numbers

Undergraduates	4,064	(400)
Postgraduates	414	(640)
Applications/places		6,360/1,325
Applications per place		4.8
Overall offer rate		77.1%
Unconditional offers		0%
International students		3.1%

Accommodation

University provided places: 1,142
Catered costs: £161–£177 per week
Self-catered: £118–£152 per week
First years guaranteed accommodation
www.chi.ac.uk/accommodation

Where do the students come from?

State schools (non-grammar)	93.1%	First generation students	49.7%	Black attainment gap	n/a
Grammar schools	3.1%	Deprived areas	18.2%	Disabled	8.9%
Independent schools	3.8%	All ethnic minorities	6.7%	Mature (over 21)	18.9%

Social inclusion ranking: =47

City, University of London

The numbers starting degrees at City have risen for six years in a row, and applications were up last year. More than half of all applicants now receive offers, compared with barely a third at the start of that period, and one in five enters through clearing.

City is planning to continue its expansion over ten years, while also improving the quality of its teaching and research. The university hopes that its London location and international approach will help position it "well within" the top 300 universities in the world and the top 30 in the UK – but so far it falls short of these targets. A five-place fall in our academic ranking has reversed 2018's modest gains. Considerable improvements in student satisfaction and graduate prospects would be required for it to make up ground.

City is much closer to the top 30 in our social inclusion ranking, no mean feat considering the competition for places on so many of its courses. Seven out of eight students come from non-selective state schools, half are the first in their family to go to university and almost three-quarters are drawn from ethnic minorities. Just five pre-1992 universities rank higher than City on these terms.

The outreach team was named Higher Education Institute of the Year by the professional organisation for widening access, for its wide range of subject masterclasses. The university has introduced a Sanctuary Scholarship for asylum-seekers, which consists of full tuition fee support and a grant for living and study costs. Other scholarships include the City Education Grant, an award offering £3,000 per academic year for new undergraduates depending on their household incomes.

City joined the University of London in 2016. It has a silver rating in the Teaching Excellence Framework, thanks to strong engagement with students, excellent assessment and feedback.

In 2020, history and politics, and data analytics and actuarial science will be new offerings. City also expects to have 50 degree apprentices beginning health programmes in September 2020, as well as twice that number of nursing associates.

Once a college of advanced technology, City now offers a wide range of subjects, including journalism, law and the arts. The university's law school was the first in the capital to offer a one-stop shop for legal training, from undergraduate to professional courses. A new seven-storey home for the law school will open this year, with facilities including a technology-led mock courtroom, law library and legal advice clinic.

More than £140m has been invested in new developments since 2012, most of them on the main campus at Northampton Square, in Islington. A new main entrance complex

Northampton Square
London EC1V 0HB
020 7040 8716
ugadmissions@city.ac.uk
www.city.ac.uk
www.citystudents.co.uk
Open days 2020:
June 27; October 3

The Times and The Sunday Times Rankings
Overall Ranking: 73 (last year: 68)

Teaching quality	76.2%	=115
Student experience	77.1%	=91
Research quality	22.6%	51
Entry standards	145	=44
Graduate prospects	73.4%	=83
Good honours	73.1%	=81
Expected completion rate	88.5%	=49
Student/staff ratio	17.8	=99
Services and facilities	£2,495	47

was added last year, with social spaces, a coffee shop, seating areas and exhibition space. It includes a 240-seat lecture theatre, students' union, cafeteria and multi-faith area.

The highly regarded Cass Business School has been given an extra floor for open plan space and meeting rooms. The Cass school is one of City's greatest strengths, ranking among the top 50 such institutions in the world. Based in the heart of the financial district, it offers an MBA that is ranked fifth globally for entrepreneurship by the *Financial Times*, and has built up an impressive cadre of visiting lecturers who find it easy and convenient to visit.

City's commitment to business and entrepreneurship is encapsulated in the City Launch Pad, an incubation space for students and entrepreneurs, which accommodates 50 companies. City ranks fifth in the UK for external investment in graduate start-ups, at £11.23m.

About 400 professionals – most of them City graduates – take part in the prize-winning mentoring scheme each year. Many courses offer the chance to spend a year at a partner university in places such as Singapore, South Korea, Australia and the United States.

The university entered little more than half of its eligible academics in the 2014 Research Excellence Framework, but three-quarters of its submission was rated as world-leading or internationally excellent. The best results were in music and business.

City has only 741 privately operated residential places, but guarantees accommodation for new entrants who accept an offer by the end of June.

The redeveloped sports centre, between the campus and the business school, is the largest university sports facility in central London. The 3,000 square metres of floor space at CitySport is available to students, staff and the local community. At its heart is the Saddlers sports hall, which meets Sport England standards and has seating for up to 400 spectators. CitySport has been the training base for visiting NBA basketball teams for three consecutive years.

Tuition fees

» Fees for UK/EU students	£9,250
» Fees for International students 2020–21	£15,090–£19,000
» For scholarship and bursary information see www.city.ac.uk/study/fees-and-funding	
» Graduate salary	£25,000

Student numbers

Undergraduates	9,454	(1,185)
Postgraduates	6,810	(2,331)
Applications/places		24,095/3,670
Applications per place		6.6
Overall offer rate		75.3%
Unconditional offers		10.9%
International students		37.3%

Accommodation

University provided places: 741
Catered costs: £268–£276 per week
Self-catered: £156–£223 per week
First years guaranteed accommodation
www.city.ac.uk/accommodation/undergraduate

Where do the students come from?

					Social inclusion ranking: =30	
State schools (non-grammar)	87.5%	First generation students	51.2%	Black attainment gap	-21%
Grammar schools	6.3%	Deprived areas	4.2%	Disabled	3.7%
Independent schools	6.2%	All ethnic minorities	74.3%	Mature (over 21)	14.2%

Coventry University

Spreading its wings beyond Coventry, Scarborough and London, the university has opened a new base in Wroclaw, southwest Poland – one of the first UK campuses in Europe. The first 300 students will take Coventry degrees in business management and leadership, cybersecurity, digital and technology solutions, and tourism and hospitality management. More subjects will follow soon.

Expansion in the UK helped to make Coventry one of the few post-1992 universities to see applications and enrolments rise in 2018. Fees of between £6,200 and £7,500 are obvious attractions at the university's "no frills" colleges in Scarborough and Dagenham, east London. Students sacrifice some facilities for a lower-cost degree, while those at the original university pay the full £9,250.

The original Coventry site continues to thrive following a £500m investment programme and now has a £33m new campus, a ten-minute walk away.

New facilities include a science and health building, with healthcare simulation facilities and a biomedical superlab. Undergraduates can use a £55m engineering and computing building which features an ethical hacking lab, while aerospace students can simulate flights in an ex-RAF Harrier jump jet and test theory in a wind tunnel built by the Mercedes F1 team.

Student satisfaction ratings for teaching quality and the wider university experience are frequently in the top 20, although they have fallen back somewhat this year. Coventry was our University of the Year for the student experience in the last edition of this guide and has since become a founding member of the ProtectED scheme, which aims to improve student safety, security and wellbeing.

Coventry was awarded gold in the government's Teaching Excellence Framework. The judging panel found "consistently outstanding" student support services, especially for those from disadvantaged backgrounds, which aid retention and progression.

The university scores well in our social inclusion ranking with more than 91% of students from non-selective state schools and more than half drawn from ethnic minorities. Just under half of the students are the first in their family to go to university.

The Centre for Academic Writing offers advice on essays and theses, while the Maths Support Centre provides specialist support for dyslexics. Employability skills are improved through the Add+vantage scheme and the university's International Centre for Transformational Entrepreneurship helps students and small firms to start up and grow a business.

Priory Street
Coventry CV1 5FB
024 7765 7688
studentenquiries@coventry.ac.uk
www.coventry.ac.uk
www.coventry.ac.uk/cuc/ – for
University Colleges
www.cusu.org
Open days 2020:
see website

The Times and The Sunday Times **Rankings**
Overall Ranking: 50 (last year: =46)

Teaching quality	82.3%	32
Student experience	81.5%	=18
Research quality	3.8%	=108
Entry standards	126	=77
Graduate prospects	80.9%	=39
Good honours	76.1%	57
Expected completion rate	83.9%	77
Student/staff ratio	14.6	=41
Services and facilities	£2,411	57

Seven new degree programmes took their first students last autumn on the main campus, including languages for global communications and forensic psychology. At Scarborough an acting course is being introduced and applied global marketing, and financial economics and banking is now offered at the university's second London campus, near Liverpool Street station, which caters mainly for international students.

The university is also bringing in many more degree apprenticeships, tripling available places to more than 1,500 by September 2020. Training will be offered for physiotherapists, engineers and police constables, among other specialities.

Coventry also provided more overseas opportunities for students than any other university for three years in a row, according to a government study in 2017. Almost 3,500 went abroad for up to a year in 2016–17, an increase of 23% on the previous year. It has also established a partnership with Deakin University, in Australia, to offer online courses, beginning with a postgraduate degree in entrepreneurship.

Only 13% of the university's eligible academics were entered for the 2014 Research Excellence Framework, although 60% of the submission was rated world-leading or internationally excellent. The university has since invested heavily to increase its research capacity and performance.

The Institute for Advanced Manufacturing and Engineering, for example, is a "faculty on the factory floor" where university researchers and Unipart engineers work together on product development. The university has also collaborated with global engineering specialists FEV to develop the Centre for Advanced Low-Carbon Propulsion Systems.

Applicants who make Coventry their firm choice and request accommodation by mid-June are guaranteed one of the 5,200 rooms owned or endorsed by the university. Coventry has a relatively low cost of living and the city is not short of student-oriented nightlife. On campus, the hub contains the students' union, a music venue, plenty of informal study space, shops and restaurants. Other recent projects have included an arts centre and a sports centre.

Tuition fees

» Fees for UK/EU students	£9,250
(£6,200–£7,329 at University Colleges)	
» Fees for International students 2019–20	£15,600
Foundation	£11,000
» For scholarship and bursary information see	
www.coventry.ac.uk/study-at-coventry/finance/	
» Graduate salary	£22,000

Student numbers

Undergraduates	25,339	(2,557)
Postgraduates	3,873	(2,356)
Applications/places		35,780/8,525
Applications per place		4.2
Overall offer rate		82.9%
Unconditional offers		0%
International students		33.1%

Accommodation

University provided places: 5,201
Catered costs: £150 per week
Self-catered: £116–£199 per week
First years guaranteed accommodation
www.coventry.ac.uk/accommodation

Where do the students come from?

					Social inclusion ranking: 46	
State schools (non-grammar)	91.2%	First generation students	47.2%	Black attainment gap	-17.7%
Grammar schools	5.1%	Deprived areas	10.5%	Disabled	3.8%
Independent schools	3.7%	All ethnic minorities	56.4%	Mature (over 21)	19.5%

University for the Creative Arts

Some of the features that made the University for the Creative Arts (UCA) our Modern University of the Year for 2018–19, have seen it upgraded to gold in the latest round of the Teaching Excellence Framework. UCA's teaching provides "outstanding levels of stretch" to challenge students, according to the judging panel.

UCA jointly held the highest position ever achieved by a post-1992 institution in our last edition and remains the highest-placed specialist arts university. Student satisfaction with teaching quality lies just outside the top ten – unheard of among specialist arts institutions.

Scores for student satisfaction with the overall experience have slipped this year, largely accounting for its fall of nine places in our rankings.

It is the top-ranked specialist arts institution in our social inclusion rankings, however, placed just inside the top 40. More than nine in ten undergraduates are recruited from non-selective state schools, with half of the intake classified as first generation students, whose parents did not attend university. One in eight students comes from the most deprived postcodes in the country.

Enrolments held up well in 2018, despite a second successive fall in applications, but the university has begun a staffing review in anticipation of testing times ahead. Investment continues, however: the £4m Film and Media Centre is now open on the Farnham campus with industry-standard film and sound studios, editing suites, rehearsal spaces and a 260-seat lecture theatre. UCA has built a strong reputation in the film world, producing a slew of Oscar and Bafta winners.

The emphasis is on turning out highly employable graduates with an entrepreneurial outlook. Many staff are practitioners as well as academics, and UCA can point to many success stories such as the artist Tracey Emin and the fashion designers Karen Millen and Zandra Rhodes, its former chancellor.

Although the university's submission to the Research Excellence Framework was small, almost two thirds was rated world-leading or internationally excellent and 90% reached the top two categories for its impact.

Plenty of new degrees are in the pipeline on UCA's four campuses – in Farnham, Epsom, Canterbury and Rochester – ranging from industrial design to make-up and hair design. UCA has a unique Business School for the Creative Industries in Epsom, capitalising on the university's links with diverse business and cultural institutions, offering courses such as event and promotion management, and international buying and merchandising.

Farnham is the largest campus, with more than 2,000 students taking subjects

UCA Farnham
Falkner Road
Farnham GU9 7DS
01252 892 960
admissions@uca.ac.uk
www.uca.ac.uk
http://ucasu.com
Open days 2020:
see website

The Times and The Sunday Times Rankings
Overall Ranking: 42 (last year: =33)

Teaching quality	83.8%	=11
Student experience	78%	=72
Research quality	3.4%	112
Entry standards	143	47
Graduate prospects	72.7%	89
Good honours	75.1%	=65
Expected completion rate	80.1%	103
Student/staff ratio	12.9	13
Services and facilities	£2,666	34

ranging from advertising, animation and computer games technology to film production, journalism, music composition and technology. An acting and performance course is based at Farnham Maltings, where students have access to a network of theatre professionals, as well as performance and rehearsal spaces.

The Epsom campus specialises in fashion, graphics and music courses as well as business, and offers further education courses in general art, design and media. At Rochester, where the purpose-built campus overlooks the River Medway, there is a full range of art and design courses, covering fashion, photography, computer animation and jewellery-making. Students taking UCA's popular television production course are based at Maidstone TV Studios, the largest independent studio complex in the UK.

On a modern site close to the city centre, the Canterbury School of Architecture is one of only two such faculties remaining within a specialist art and design institution, encouraging collaboration between student architects, designers and fine artists. The Canterbury campus also hosts degree courses in fine art, interior design, graphic design, and illustration and animation.

UCA offers some four-year degrees incorporating a foundation year. Students can also take a two-year extended diploma that can be topped up to produce an honours degree. All students are encouraged to develop an international perspective and to collaborate with students from parallel disciplines.

A Creative Enterprise and Development Team helps students to become employable, entrepreneurial in their outlook and equipped to become freelancers or to start a business within their chosen sector.

For those who want to study at a pace to suit them, UCA also offers distance learning degree and diploma courses through the Open College of the Arts, which became part of the university in 2016. A wide range of subjects includes painting and art history.

There are no sports facilities but the students' union operates a variety of clubs using outside facilities. Almost 1,000 residential places are available, housing 45% of first-years who apply.

Tuition fees

» Fees for UK/EU students	£9,250
» Fees for International students 2020–21	£16,250
Foundation	£14,800
» For scholarship and bursary information see www.uca.ac.uk/life-at-uca/fees	
» Graduate salary	£18,000

Student numbers

Undergraduates	4,544	(1,718)
Postgraduates	185	(174)
Applications/places		6,165/1,605
Applications per place		3.8
Overall offer rate		69.2%
Unconditional offers		0%
International students		12.8%

Accommodation

University provided places: 979
Self-catered: £109–£166 per week
www.uca.ac.uk/life-at-uca/accommodation

Where do the students come from?

State schools (non-grammar)	92.7%	First generation students	50.5%	Black attainment gap	-25%
Grammar schools	3.9%	Deprived areas	12.4%	Disabled	10.8%
Independent schools	3.4%	All ethnic minorities	23%	Mature (over 21)	15.3%

Social inclusion ranking: 39

University of Cumbria

It has been a challenge for Cumbria to fill its places since competition for students intensified following the end of restrictions on recruitment. Both applications and the numbers starting courses at the university have fallen by a third since 2014. New enrolments fell by 14% in 2018 alone.

A nationwide fall in the demand for teaching and nursing courses – two key areas for Cumbria – has contributed to the decline. But Professor Julie Mennell, the vice-chancellor, has said that Cumbria met its student targets in 2019 and has a new strategic plan that will leave it well placed to respond to both the challenges and opportunities it faces.

The university has moved (just) out of the bottom ten in our league table, after a rise of four places. Student satisfaction with the quality of teaching, entry standards and the proportion achieving good honours have all improved since the last edition.

Cumbria is just outside the top 25 in our new social inclusion table. More than half of its undergraduates are the first in their family to go to university and the proportion from areas of low participation in higher education is in the top ten in England and Wales.

The university has the only campus in the UK located in a national park – at Ambleside, in the Lake District. One of seven bases, Ambleside offers the country's biggest programme of outdoor education courses and hosts conservation and forestry degrees. The Institute for Leadership and Sustainability, part of the business school, is developing a portfolio of short courses and research specialisms at Ambleside.

The institution's largest campus is in Lancaster, where there is a new teaching block with a 220-seat lecture theatre, communal study space and classrooms. The parkland campus, a short walk from the city centre, has a gymnastics centre and fitness suite, as well as a student centre, library and extensive accommodation.

Cumbria is now focusing on improving its two sites in Carlisle, where the university has its headquarters. It has extended the library at its Institute of Arts and expanded IT capacity, following the opening of new laboratories for Stem subjects (science, technology, engineering and maths).

The larger of the two Carlisle campuses, Brampton Road, is in parkland close to the River Eden. The second, Fusehill Street, is closer to the city centre and features an innovative multimedia learning resource centre and sports facilities such as a four-court sports hall and well-equipped fitness room.

Established in 2007, Cumbria now also has campuses in London, Workington and Barrow-in-Furness. There are only 7,600 students, and the gender balance is heavily female: fewer than 2,500 students are male.

Head Office
Fusehill Street
Carlisle CA1 2HH
01228 616 234
enquirycentre@cumbria.ac.uk
www.cumbria.ac.uk
www.ucsu.me
Open days 2020: March 18,
April 22, June 26,
August 15/16 (Lancaster);
June 5 (Carlisle)

The Times and The Sunday Times Rankings
Overall Ranking: 121 (last year: 125)

Teaching quality	78.9%	85
Student experience	73.8%	119
Research quality	1.2%	124
Entry standards	126	=77
Graduate prospects	73.6%	=77
Good honours	67.4%	=113
Expected completion rate	82.7%	85
Student/staff ratio	16.8	=85
Services and facilities	£1,611	123

Foundation years are offered in games development, professional policing, working with children and families, business management with marketing, psychology, microbiology, film and television, and law, with fees set at £6,000 for 2019–20.

The Workington campus has dedicated facilities for the nuclear graduate programme. The university is a partner in both the National College for Nuclear and the Project Academy for Sellafield, helping to provide specialist education and training in delivering decommissioning, reprocessing and nuclear waste management. The university's base in Barrow is at Furness College, specialising in nursing and health practitioner courses. The London campus, in the East End, is now in its 12th year and provides training for teachers, police officers and health professionals.

Cumbria promises students a high level of personal support and employs mental health case workers on its campuses in Ambleside, Carlisle and Lancaster. It offers training on suicide prevention and awareness for all staff working with students. A network of student ambassadors who are studying mental health nursing, or who have an interest in the issue, also work to increase awareness.

Cumbria is one of 11 universities rated bronze in the government's Teaching Excellence Framework (TEF). It suffered for a low graduate employment rate in highly-skilled jobs, although it pointed out that these are in short supply regionally, compared with the national average. Cumbria also noted that 76% of its academics hold teaching qualifications, compared with 44% nationwide, reflecting the university's commitment to excellence in teaching and learning.

The creative arts produced by far the best results in the 2014 Research Excellence Framework, with 90% of the submission judged to have world-leading or internationally excellent impact. Overall, however, Cumbria is just two places off the bottom of our research ranking, having entered only 27 academics (8% of those eligible) for assessment. Almost 30% of the work of this small group was placed in the top two categories, however.

Cumbria was granted the power to award its own research degrees in 2019. The Quality Assurance Agency said the university had proved that it met the highest standards. The award came as Cumbria prepared to open two new research institutes, for health and wellbeing, and leadership, business and industrial skills.

Tuition fees

»	Fees for UK/EU students	£9,250
	Foundation courses	£6,000
»	Fees for International students 2020–21	£10,500–£15,500
	Foundation years	£7,500
»	For scholarship and bursary information see www.cumbria.ac.uk/study/student-finance/undergraduate/	
»	Graduate salary	£22,000

Student numbers

Undergraduates	4,434	(1,426)
Postgraduates	786	(936)
Applications/places		5,240/1,275
Applications per place		4.1
Overall offer rate		80.2%
Unconditional offers		0%
International students		3.1%

Accommodation

University provided places: 1,100+
Self-catered: £74–£120 per week
First years guaranteed accommodation
www.cumbria.ac.uk/student-life/accommodation/

Where do the students come from?

State schools (non-grammar)	95.7%	First generation students	53.8%
Grammar schools	2.5%	Deprived areas	21.5%
Independent schools	1.8%	All ethnic minorities	11.6%

Social inclusion ranking: =25

Black attainment gap	-21%
Disabled	7.8%
Mature (over 21)	33.6%

De Montfort University

De Montfort has pledged to build on its success in serving a diverse student community, spending £85m on its Leicester campus over the next five years. Its new strategy promises a "stimulating, accessible and award-winning environment for our students and staff" starting with a flexible new library that supports physical and digital study.

As our inaugural University of the Year for Social Inclusion for 2018–19, DMU continues to enjoy high levels of satisfaction from its student body – more than half from black, Asian and ethnic minority (Bame) backgrounds and more than half from families where neither parent went to university – and to offer good graduate prospects. DMU is determined to reduce the attainment gap between Bame students and their white peers and is one of seven institutions chosen to take part in a national project to tackle the issue. It also has a strong reputation for supporting disabled students.

All undergraduates and postgraduates will be given the chance to spend time abroad or develop language skills on campus through the ground-breaking #DMUglobal programme, already said to offer the UK's most extensive network of overseas study opportunities. The university has an innovative partnership with the United Nations, acting as an ambassador for its 17 sustainable development goals and incorporating them in its teaching, research and student activities.

DMU is also committed to furthering its #DMUworks scheme to help students "think, feel and get work-ready while they're still at university". The programme combines work placements, internships and volunteering with training and visits from business insiders – and promises lifelong support for graduates in the workplace.

The university's successful graduate employment record contributed to a gold rating in the government's Teaching Excellence Framework. DMU has also been making steady progress in our main league table, breaking into the top half in 2018, before falling back nine places in this new edition.

Enrolments were up by 11% in 2018 despite a 6.4% decline in applications. More than 20% of DMU's offers were unconditional but applicants were not required to make it their first choice.

Student satisfaction scores in this year's National Student Survey have slipped during a year of administrative turmoil at the university, when vice-chancellor Dominic Shellard resigned over an investigation by the Office for Students (OfS). The university's chairman of governors and several other members of the governing body have also quit their roles and investigators have since reported "significant and systemic" failings in governance.

The Gateway
Leicester LE1 9BH
0116 250 6070
enquiry@dmu.ac.uk
www.dmu.ac.uk
www.demontfortsu.com/
Open days 2020:
February 15, March 14

The Times and The Sunday Times **Rankings**
Overall Ranking: 74 (last year: 65)

Teaching quality	79.9%	=66
Student experience	80%	=32
Research quality	8.9%	=67
Entry standards	111	=122
Graduate prospects	83.8%	=20
Good honours	75.1%	=65
Expected completion rate	85%	69
Student/staff ratio	19.9	=122
Services and facilities	£2,246	71

Opened in 1870 as the Leicester School of Art, later Leicester Polytechnic, DMU has already invested heavily in reshaping its city centre campus. The Vijay Patel Building, which brought all art and design courses together for the first time and includes the city's largest display space, was named the region's best new educational building. In addition, a new business school has opened in the Great Hall of Leicester Castle.

New degree courses in paramedicine, diagnostic radiography, aeronautical engineering, professional policing and English with creative writing are among those which welcomed their first students in 2019. There are plans to double the number of higher and degree apprentices – currently about 160 – through multiple intakes and bespoke employer cohorts. Its seven existing programmes cover cybersecurity, policing, chartered management and digital and technology solutions.

Everyone is encouraged to volunteer in the award-winning Square Mile programme, which aids community projects locally, across the UK and overseas. About 2,500 students and staff have participated so far.

Almost 60% of the university's research was rated world-leading or internationally excellent in the 2014 Research Excellence Framework. Longstanding partnerships with Hewlett-Packard and Deloitte illustrate strong links with business and industry, which feed into innovative training and research collaborations. The Stephen Lawrence Research Centre is one recent example, established to promote social justice on a local, national and global scale.

The university has 4,600 residential places in 14 halls of residence, but only international students are guaranteed accommodation, if they apply by the end of July.

The campus boasts extensive sports facilities, including a 25-metre swimming pool and an £8m leisure centre. Outdoor pitches, five miles to the north and served by free buses, have had a £3.4m upgrade. Almost £1m has been spent on coaching and support for DMU's sports teams and there are partnerships with Leicester City football club, Leicester Tigers rugby club, Leicestershire County Cricket Club and Leicester Ladies Hockey Club.

In the past ten years £3bn has been lavished on regeneration projects in Leicester, one of the UK's most diverse cities. Its vibrant atmosphere makes it popular with most students and private sector rents are low.

Tuition fees

»	Fees for UK/EU students	£9,250
	Foundation courses	£6,165
»	Fees for International students 2020–21	£13,750–£14,950
»	For scholarship and bursary information see www.dmu.ac.uk/study/undergraduate-study/ fees-and-funding/index.aspx	
»	Graduate salary	£20,000

Student numbers

Undergraduates	**19,496**	**(1,357)**
Postgraduates	**2,770**	**(2,074)**
Applications/places		24,815/7,160
Applications per place		3.5
Overall offer rate		87.8%
Unconditional offers		0%
International students		18.3%

Accommodation

University provided places: 4,600
Self-catered: £97–£191 per week
www.dmu.ac.uk/study/undergraduate-study/
accommodation/index.aspx

Where do the students come from?

State schools (non-grammar)	95.2%	First generation students	51.7%	Black attainment gap	-19.6%
Grammar schools	2.4%	Deprived areas	14.3%	Disabled	11.1%
Independent schools	2.3%	All ethnic minorities	50.1%	Mature (over 21)	13.4%

Social inclusion ranking: =20

University of Derby

Derby wants to be an "applied university of today and tomorrow" and to build on a gold award in the Teaching Excellence Framework (TEF), although its ranking has slipped significantly this year.

Numbers have been running at record levels, but applications and enrolments fell in 2018, despite a big increase in unconditional offers. Some 17% of those were so-called "conditional unconditional" offers, requiring students to make Derby their first choice – a practice criticised by the government.

Derby won the Times Higher Education Teaching and Learning Strategy Award last year and was praised by the TEF panel for its personalised learning and support. A new Centre for Excellence in Learning and Teaching has a brief to lead further improvements in assessment and feedback, invariably a bone of contention in student satisfaction surveys. The university's overall rankings for student satisfaction with teaching quality and their wider university experience have slipped 26 and 21 places respectively this year.

The university has taken the lead on a national Education for Mental Health project to better design the curriculum and assessment processes to improve student wellbeing. All undergraduates have access to their personal tutor whenever they need it and Derby guarantees that 85% of its classes contain fewer than 30 students.

Students are attracted by an emphasis on "real-world learning". Facilities include a hospital simulation suite for healthcare students; a crime scene house for forensic science students; industry-standard kitchens and a fine dining restaurant for those on hospitality courses. The university also offers computer games suites; a commercial spa and salon; a crown court replica and a 58-acre Outdoor Leadership Centre. More mock wards and other facilities for nurse training have been added recently.

The College of Health and Social Care has been restructured to give nursing a school of its own, in Chesterfield, to reflect the growing demand for places and ensure that teaching reflects changing employment demands. A new degree in children's nursing has taken its first students.

Derby also offers degree apprenticeships in more than 20 subject areas and is developing 16 more courses for roles such as paralegals, higher education researchers, chartered surveyors and sports analysts. By 2020, the university is expecting to fill 460 places, and ultimately aims to expand to 1,000 places.

There are three university bases in Derby, linked by free shuttle buses. The Kedlestone Road campus, two miles from the city centre, is the largest, hosting most teaching subjects

Kedleston Road
Derby DE22 1GB
01332 590 500
admissions@derby.ac.uk
www.derby.ac.uk
www.derbyunion.co.uk
Open days 2020:
February 22

The Times and The Sunday Times **Rankings**

Overall Ranking: 91 (last year: 75)

Teaching quality	81.6%	=39
Student experience	78.6%	=61
Research quality	2.5%	117
Entry standards	123	=86
Graduate prospects	76.2%	65
Good honours	65.7%	122
Expected completion rate	79.1%	110
Student/staff ratio	14.5	=36
Services and facilities	£2,042	92

including business, computing, science, humanities, education and law. The students' union, multi-faith centre and main sports facilities are all here, as well as clinical skills facilities such as a full-body iDXA scanner.

The Markeaton Street site hosts arts, design, engineering and technology courses, while courses including fine art and social care are based at Britannia Mill, ten minutes' walk away.

The 550-seat Derby Theatre is in the city centre and there are ambitious plans to create a university quarter, perhaps by developing a new business school on a car park site purchased in 2018.

In Buxton, the university's operations are based in the Devonshire Dome, formerly the Devonshire Royal Hospital. Teaching facilities for hospitality management include a beauty salon and health spa. A former girls' school in Chesterfield provides a second centre for nursing, engineering and IT, as well as an innovation centre.

Links with local industry help to prepare students for the workplace with placements available at Microsoft and IBM and internships at car manufacturers including Porsche, Bentley, Rolls-Royce and the locally-based Toyota. The university's Institute for Innovation in Sustainable Engineering gives small businesses access to research and technology, backed by Rolls-Royce, Toyota and the aircraft manufacturer Bombardier.

Only 19% of Derby's eligible academics were entered for the 2014 Research Excellence Framework. Nearly 30% of the university's submission was placed in the top two categories.

Local students who come from Derbyshire or have graduated from a local college qualify for a £1,000 bursary. All full-timers get £100 to buy books or other study resources and about half are eligible for a bigger payout.

All first-years are guaranteed accommodation following a £30m, five-year investment to offer more than 3,000 places. The sports centre has a 70-station fitness gym, squash courts, sports hall, climbing wall and adjacent outdoor pitches.

Tuition fees

»	Fees for UK/EU students	£9,250
»	Fees for International students 2019–20	£13,250–£14,250
»	For scholarship and bursary information see www.derby.ac.uk/undergraduate/fees-and-finance/	
»	Graduate salary	£20,800

Student numbers

Undergraduates	11,527 (3,068)
Postgraduates	1,372 (2,521)
Applications/places	17,835/3,605
Applications per place	4.9
Overall offer rate	87.9%
Unconditional offers	17.2%
International students	8.3%

Accommodation

University provided places: 3,005
Self-catered: £110–£155 per week
First years guaranteed accommodation
www.derby.ac.uk/life/accommodation/

Where do the students come from?

State schools (non-grammar)	96.6%	First generation students	51.7%
Grammar schools	1.7%	Deprived areas	21%
Independent schools	1.7%	All ethnic minorities	25.6%

Social inclusion ranking: =20

Black attainment gap	-16.3%
Disabled	9.7%
Mature (over 21)	27.2%

University of Dundee

Outstanding student satisfaction scores helped Dundee to win our University of the Year for Student Experience award this year and it took gold in the Teaching Excellence Framework (TEF), winning praise for its focus on employability.

Dundee's strength in the life sciences is bringing the university extra income of £40m from the Scottish and UK governments to promote growth in the region under the Tay Cities Deal. Two projects – a biomedical cluster and institute for innovation in forensic science – have won funding.

The top university for biological sciences in the Research Excellence Framework in 2014, Dundee attracts students from all over the world in this area – offering a joint degree with the National University of Singapore. But the university's appeal is broader than that. Its research was rated in the top three in the UK for civil engineering and the top ten for maths and general engineering.

Applications from international students were up by more than 20% in 2019, following a 7% rise in the previous year. The International College on the main campus offers preparatory courses for degree study. A quarter of all students are from outside Scotland, and Dundee was sixth in the world for overall satisfaction in the 2018 International Student Barometer.

Domestically, the demand for places is flat, with both applications and enrolments about the same as in 2018 – although this is a good result when many universities are seeing sharp falls in both. The university is fifth for student satisfaction with the overall experience, according to the latest National Student Survey, helping the institution to achieve another top-30 place in our rankings overall. A partnership agreement with the students' association commits the university to enhancing student engagement, employability and representation.

Dundee was one of only three Scottish universities to be rated gold by the TEF panel. Dundee claims to send more graduates into the professions than any other institution in Scotland. Most degrees include a career planning module and an internship option.

A new business school, previously part of the School of Social Science, has received key professional accreditations for its courses. Humanities students follow a liberal arts model, allowing them to gain a broad-based education.

Scotland's first graduate entry medical course has been introduced at Dundee and St Andrews, with a focus on rural general practice. For those hoping to change career and qualify as a teacher, there is a new masters-level diploma open to graduates in

---

Nethergate
Dundee DD1 4HN
01382 383 838
contactus@dundee.ac.uk
www.dundee.ac.uk
www.dusa.co.uk
Open days 2020:
August 31,
September 26

The Times and The Sunday Times **Rankings**

Overall Ranking: 24 (last year: 27)

Teaching quality	83.5%	15
Student experience	83.8%	5
Research quality	31.2%	41
Entry standards	172	=15
Graduate prospects	81.7%	=30
Good honours	78.9%	45
Expected completion rate	88.5%	=49
Student/staff ratio	13.9	=24
Services and facilities	£2,517	46

chemistry, physics, home economics, maths and engineering.

The university is also expanding its graduate-level apprenticeships by 30%. They are available in business management, civil engineering, IT management for business, software development and engineering, design and manufacturing. By 2021 Dundee hopes to have 150 trainees a year.

Fees for students from the rest of the UK taking four-year degrees are capped at a total of £27,750 in 2019–20. Bursaries of £2,000 a year are available for students from low-income families and there is a scholarship offered for refugees.

Dundee has a proud record in widening participation in higher education and has set itself the target of recruiting 350 students a year from the 20% most deprived postcodes in Scotland. More than one-third of the intake is drawn from families where neither parent attended university. Two-thirds of the undergraduates are from Scotland and nearly one in ten from Northern Ireland.

Applicants have access to the online portal MyDundee and the university claims its online learning resources are among the best in the UK. It invested £6m in a campus-wide network refresh, boosting wi-fi capability. Responding to student feedback, the new network has brought superfast connection to university accommodation for many gaming and streaming devices.

Dundee has spent £200m redeveloping its campus, partly designed by the leading architect, Sir Terry Farrell. The £50m Discovery Centre encourages interaction between different disciplines. Away from the city centre, the medical school is on a 20-acre site, while nursing and midwifery students are 35 miles away in Kirkcaldy.

The highly-rated design courses are taught at the Duncan of Jordanstone College of Art, which has become one of the university's nine schools.

The university is a lead participant in the V&A Dundee project to improve design in Scotland, which celebrated the opening of the museum's branch in the city in 2018. The cost of living is among the lowest in the UK and the university has one of Scotland's most active students' unions. Sports facilities are excellent and the nightlife is lively.

Tuition fees

- » Fees for Scottish/EU students   £0–£1,820
  RUK fees (capped at £27,750 for four-year courses)   £9,250
- » Fees for International students 2020–21   £18,150–£21,950
  Medicine £44,650; Dentistry £46,885 (clinical years)
- » For scholarship and bursary information see
  www.dundee.ac.uk/study/tuition-fees/
- » Graduate salary   £22,200

Student numbers

Undergraduates	**9,481**	**(1,233)**
Postgraduates	**1,852**	**(2,538)**
Applications/places		**22,610/2,970**
Applications per place		**7.6**
Overall offer rate		**54.3%**
International students		**13.8%**

Accommodation

University provided places: 1,587
Self-catered: £125–£155 per week
First years guaranteed accommodation
www.dundee.ac.uk/accommodation

Where do the students come from?

State schools (non-grammar)	83.9%	First generation students	37.3%	
Grammar schools	6.4%	Deprived areas	15.8%	
Independent schools	9.7%	All ethnic minorities	10.5%	

Social inclusion ranking (Scotland): 6

Black attainment gap	-6.5%
Disabled	4.8%
Mature (over 21)	29%

Durham University

Durham is opening its 17th college – the first new one in Durham City for almost 20 years – in time to bring in new courses for students starting in 2020. South College will open at Mount Oswald, where John Snow College is also relocating. There is room to accommodate 1,000 students and facilities will include a yoga and dance studio, games area and faith room.

Durham is planning to expand from 18,000 students to 21,500 – and should have no trouble filling the extra places, with applications hitting a new high in 2018 at nearly 30,000. The third-oldest in England, Durham is determined to maintain its character as one of the few collegiate universities in the UK.

The mixed colleges range in size from 500 to 1,500 students and provide a focal point for social life, although all teaching takes place in central departments. There are significant differences in atmosphere and student profile, from the historic University College, in Durham Castle, to Collingwood College's modern buildings on the outskirts of the city.

At least two more colleges are planned and by 2027 at least half of all the students will be able to live in college accommodation, reducing the pressure on private rented accommodation.

A ten-year, £1bn project is in the works to make sure the quality of staffing and physical resources keeps up with the expansion. A £40m Teaching and Learning Centre opened in time for the 2019–20 academic year, where students can share courses in real time with others from peer institutions around the world. A new building for maths and computer science is due to be ready in 2020 and the Assembly Rooms theatre, renovated at a cost of £2.4m, is set to reopen. The business school will relocate to a riverside site in a later phase of the estate masterplan.

Durham's Encore system means lectures are recorded for students to replay at their convenience and £25m is being spent to upgrade the university's IT programmes.

Durham was the highest-ranked of six universities upgraded to a gold award in the Teaching Excellence Framework (TEF) in 2018. The TEF panel noted that rates of continuation and progression to highly-skilled employment or further study were exceptionally high – and the university is in our top 20 for both. Durham also won praise for "rigorous monitoring" in a culture which "facilitates, recognises and rewards excellent teaching".

The university slipped out of the top five in our rankings last year, dropping two places, and has not made up the ground this year after poor results in the National Student Survey. Durham's student satisfaction scores this year are its worst yet, with satisfaction for the overall student experience sinking into the bottom 20.

The Palatine Centre
Stockton Road
Durham DH1 3LE
0191 334 1000
study@durham.ac.uk
www.dur.ac.uk
www.durhamsu.com
Open days 2020:
June 29, July 4,
September 18/19

The Times and The Sunday Times **Rankings**
Overall Ranking: 7 (last year: 7)

Teaching quality	78.8%	=86
Student experience	75%	112
Research quality	39.0%	16
Entry standards	195	7
Graduate prospects	84.9%	17
Good honours	92.1%	3
Expected completion rate	96.4%	5
Student/staff ratio	15	=48
Services and facilities	£3,052	12

The institution's global reputation is holding up, however: Durham is 78th in the QS World University Rankings 2020. Its planned expansion is intended to ensure that it remains competitive, especially in its strongest subjects, and maximises its contribution to the region. An independent report found the university contributes £1.1bn to the UK economy each year.

Seven new degrees were launched in 2019, including archaeology of the historic world, and visual arts and film. Behavioural science will follow in 2020, as well as accounting and education studies, if they receive approval.

A member of the research-led Russell Group since 2012, Durham reached the top five in a quarter of the subject areas submitted to the Research Excellence Framework – English, classics, chemistry, law, anthropology, archaeology, education, physics, theology and music – and 80% of its academics' work was judged world-leading or internationally excellent.

The university's blueprint for expansion promises a more diverse student intake. The proportion of undergraduates recruited from independent schools stands at 38.7% – more than at Cambridge and behind only Oxford and St Andrews. Students with a household income of less than £25,000 receive £2,000 bursaries, and there is some support up to an income of almost £43,000.

One of the UK's leading sports universities, Durham is opening a new complex at Maiden Castle, on the banks of the River Wear, in a £31m sports park. A new rubber crumb pitch and upgraded hockey zone will be available and indoor facilities will be added later. As well as Durham's successful national competitors, three-quarters of all students – and 2,500 local people – use the university's sports facilities regularly. There are national centres of excellence in cricket, fencing, lacrosse, rugby union, tennis and rowing.

The university dominates the small and picturesque cathedral city. Newcastle is a short train ride away for those in search of serious clubbing or shopping, but most students find enough entertainment in Durham.

Tuition fees
- » Fees for UK/EU students   £9,250
- » Fees for International students 2020–21   £20,500–£26,500
- » For scholarship and bursary information see www.dur.ac.uk/study/ug/finance/
- » Graduate salary   £25,000

Student numbers

Undergraduates	13,649	(187)
Postgraduates	3,385	(1,110)
Applications/places		29,890/4,390
Applications per place		6.8
Overall offer rate		75.7%
Unconditional offers		0%
International students		28.2%

Accommodation

University provided places: 6,710
Catered costs: £197–£209 per week
Self-catered: £138–£150 per week
First years guaranteed accommodation
www.dur.ac.uk/undergraduate/experiencee/colleges/

Where do the students come from?

					Social inclusion ranking: 109	
State schools (non-grammar)	46.5%	First generation students	23.5%	Black attainment gap		-3.7%
Grammar schools	14.8%	Deprived areas	5.6%	Disabled		5.5%
Independent schools	38.7%	All ethnic minorities	12.2%	Mature (over 21)		4%

University of East Anglia

A tranche of new degree programmes has helped to reverse a decline in applications of more than 20% over the past two years at the University of East Anglia (UEA). Applications were up by 16% in 2019 when many other universities were struggling. The first 20 new degrees have taken students already, most adding the option of a year abroad, a foundation year or a placement year to existing programmes.

More degrees will be added in 2020, including drama and creative writing, computational psychology, marketing and management, and medicine with a gateway year. The university has 270 apprentices following programmes in nursing and leadership and hopes to have up to 500 trainees by September 2020.

A new £30m teaching building for Stem subjects (science, technology, engineering and maths) is up and running and another is due to open in 2022 for the arts, humanities and some social sciences.

A total of £250m is being invested in facilities for staff and students on UEA's Norwich campus. The £80m Quadram Institute opened in 2018 to investigate the links between diet and disease, alongside clinicians working in the bioscience cluster on the Norwich Research Park.

After two successive falls in our rankings, including an eight-place drop this year, UEA has lost its spot in the top 15 institutions. It was upgraded to gold in the government's Teaching Excellence Framework (TEF), and praised for its "strategic approach to personalised learning, which secures high levels of commitment to studies".

The TEF panel also found that investment in high-quality physical and digital resources have had a demonstrable impact on the learning experience. These include a media suite in the arts and humanities faculty with recording studios, a radio drama studio and edit suites, and the new £19m Biomedical Research Centre for medical students. The Enterprise Centre helps to develop students' entrepreneurial skills.

Most undergraduates have the opportunity to take work experience as part of their course. The university has sharpened its focus on employability in the curriculum and introduced an internship programme for recent graduates to work for between four weeks and a year at a business in the eastern region.

But satisfaction with the student experience has recovered only slightly this year following a sharp fall in 2018. Almost 5,000 people signed a petition calling for better mental health services after the deaths of four students in less than a year. The university has increased the budget for mental health services by 63%, pledging to spend £1.4m in the present academic year.

Norwich Research Park
Norwich NR4 7TJ
01603 591 515
admissions@uea.ac.uk
www.uea.ac.uk
www.uea.su
Open days 2020:
see website

The Times and The Sunday Times **Rankings**
Overall Ranking: 23 (last year: 15)

Teaching quality	79.1%	=83
Student experience	79%	=51
Research quality	35.8%	32
Entry standards	147	=42
Graduate prospects	77.1%	60
Good honours	87.2%	12
Expected completion rate	90.7%	=35
Student/staff ratio	13.6	21
Services and facilities	£2,842	19

Environmental science is traditionally UEA's flagship subject area. The institution's Climatic Research Unit and the Tyndall Centre for Climate Change Research, funded by a consortium of universities and the Chinese government, are among the leading investigators of climate change. Social work and pharmacy led UEA's results in the 2014 Research Excellence Framework, when 82% of all the work submitted by the university was placed in one of the top two categories.

The Sainsbury Centre for the Visual Arts houses a priceless collection of modern and tribal art in a building designed by Sir Norman Foster. Many of the original 1960s buildings on campus are listed, including the iconic Denys Lasdun-designed Ziggurat accommodation blocks.

The #AskUEA online platform gives prospective students the chance to prepare for university life. Once at UEA, students can bring any inquiries to four learning and teaching hubs; one for postgraduates, one for nursing and two for other undergraduates.

About a quarter of UEA students receive financial help from scholarships and bursaries. The university is one of the more socially inclusive among the top 30 institutions in our academic ranking, with almost four in five students recruited from non-selective state schools and two in five from homes where neither parent went to university.

The 320-acre campus with rolling parkland on the outskirts of Norwich was awarded a Green Flag in 2018 for the third year running for its high environmental standards.

UEA's Sportspark has an Olympic-sized swimming pool and fitness centre, five sports halls, 20 badminton courts, five squash courts, a martial arts and dance studio, and a climbing wall.

First-year students are guaranteed one of the university's 4,600 rooms. Norwich, with its mixture of ancient architecture and contemporary culture, has been listed as one of *The Sunday Times* Best Places to Live.

Tuition fees

» Fees for UK/EU students	£9,250
» Fees for International students 2020–21	£15,900–£20,200
Medicine	£31,200
» For scholarship and bursary information see www.uea.ac.uk/study/undergraduate/finance	
» Graduate salary	£21,909

Student numbers

Undergraduates	12.724	(261)
Postgraduates	3,127	(1,844)
Applications/places		19,035/4,365
Applications per place		4.4
Overall offer rate		82%
Unconditional offers		0%
International students		21.8%

Accommodation

University provided places: 4,593
Self-catered: £76–£168 per week
First years guaranteed accommodation
www.uea.ac.uk/study/undergraduate/accommodation

Where do the students come from?

State schools (non-grammar)	92.8%	First generation students	67.3%	Black attainment gap	-3%
Grammar schools	5.5%	Deprived areas	13.6%	Disabled	9.1%
Independent schools	1.7%	All ethnic minorities	72.5%	Mature (over 21)	26.3%

Social inclusion ranking: 81

University of East London

The University of East London (UEL) shows signs that it can bounce back from slipping into the bottom five of our academic ranking. Enrolments climbed more than 20% in 2018, partly due to the introduction of nursing at degree level and grew again ahead of the current academic year. International recruitment, mainly from India, has been strong.

Student satisfaction has fallen significantly, alongside lower spending on facilities, but UEL has adopted a ten-year strategy to become the UK's leading careers-focused university. It is one of the few universities with no debts and it is raising over £100m from the securitisation of its residences to drive its strategy forward.

A ground-breaking partnership with Amazon Web Services (AWS) enabled the university to switch to cloud technologies and benefit from the company's expertise in artificial intelligence. The agreement includes the creation of a career zone and innovation loft and the establishment of an industry research institute.

AWS will also support UEL's new Professional Fitness and Mental Wealth programme, introduced in September 2019, designed to equip UEL graduates with the competencies sought by employers and lifelong resilience to flourish in the digital economy. The university's Career Passport will be a digital repository, giving employers evidence of the skills and experience the graduate has developed. AWS will help students to qualify for the company's certification digital badges to add to their passport.

Professor Amanda Broderick, appointed UEL's vice-chancellor in 2018, is determined to make the most of the university's docklands location in London's only enterprise zone. Another agreement has been signed with Tongji University of Shanghai to establish a design-led innovation hub.

The portfolio of degree courses is being transformed, with placement years added in more than 30 subjects for 2019 and foundation years in 12 subjects. In addition, there are three new degrees in journalism and others in media production and professional policing. UEL also expects to have 200 degree apprentices in 2020, in areas such as management, civil engineering, digital technology, nursing and teaching.

UEL is now one of only 11 universities in our table rated bronze, the lowest rung in the Teaching Excellence Framework, having failed in a bid to be upgraded to silver. Low graduate employment rates were the main stumbling block.

The university is in the top five in our new table for widening participation in higher education, however. Two-thirds of its undergraduates are drawn from East London's large ethnic minority populations and more than half are the first in their family to go to university.

Docklands Campus
University Way
London E16 2RD
020 8223 3333
study@uel.ac.uk
www.uel.ac.uk
www.uelunion.org
Open days 2020:
see website

Overall Ranking: 127 (last year: =115)

Teaching quality	78%	=96
Student experience	76.1%	100
Research quality	7.2%	76
Entry standards	111	=122
Graduate prospects	65.3%	116
Good honours	68.1%	109
Expected completion rate	75.5%	124
Student/staff ratio	18.9	117
Services and facilities	£2,018	94

Almost half of UEL's undergraduates are 21 or older on entry – many choosing to start courses in February rather than in the autumn. A guidance unit advises local people considering returning to education. New Beginnings courses, up to ten weeks long, show prospective mature students what study involves and allow successful participants to move on to a range of degree courses.

Every undergraduate receives a free Samsung tablet, pre-loaded with core e-textbooks. The student charter urges undergraduates to adopt the "35-hour attitude", which means studying for at least 35 hours a week and handing in assignments on time. Helpdesks in the student support hubs at both the Docklands and Stratford campuses provide advice on academic and other problems.

UEL puts civic engagement at the heart of its strategic vision, giving students the opportunity to get involved in real-life projects. The Noon Centre for Equality and Diversity in Business helps black, Asian, and minority ethnic students to prepare for a successful career in business. Almost 1,000 businesses take part in mentoring programmes and/or offer accredited placements.

World-class research doubled in the 2014 Research Excellence Framework compared with the 2008 assessments: 62% of the work submitted reached the top two categories. UEL was ranked first equal in England for the impact of its research in psychology.

UEL's waterside campus, in the shadow of Canary Wharf, was the first new campus in London for 50 years. Stratford, the original headquarters, has been the focus of recent development and is now the location for a joint venture with Birkbeck, University of London, offering subjects including law, performing arts, dance, music and information technology as daytime or evening courses.

There are almost 1,200 bed spaces, with more to come in Stratford – enough to guarantee accommodation to all new students who live more than an hour away. Social life for many students revolves around the Docklands campus, although Stratford has more to offer since its post-Olympics transformation.

UEL, too, has built on the legacy of the 2012 London Olympics, when it hosted the United States team at SportsDock, a £21m centre at the Docklands campus. The institution's high-performing sports programme offers £2m in scholarships and bursaries, and has trained competitors including sprinter Adam Gemili, who graduated from UEL in 2015 with a BSc in sport and exercise science with human biology.

Tuition fees

» Fees for UK/EU students	£9,250
» Fees for International students 2020–21	£12,100
» For scholarship and bursary information see www.uel.ac.uk/fees-and-funding	
» Graduate salary	£20,020

Student numbers

Undergraduates	**8,976**	**(721)**
Postgraduates	**1,932**	**(1,460)**
Applications/places		**15,765/3,945**
Applications per place		**4**
Overall offer rate		**79.4%**
Unconditional offers		**0%**
International students		**10.1%**

Accommodation

University provided places: 1,169
Self-catered: £148–£193 per week
www.uel.ac.uk/accommodation

Where do the students come from?

State schools (non-grammar)	96.6%	First generation students	54.7%	
Grammar schools	1.4%	Deprived areas	9.4%	
Independent schools	2.0%	All ethnic minorities	68.2%	

Social inclusion ranking: 5

Black attainment gap	-19%
Disabled	6.4%
Mature (over 21)	47.7%

Edge Hill University

Edge Hill's new medical school will take its first trainee doctors in 2020, some of whom will already have started on a foundation year in medicine. The foundation course is aimed at students from below-average schools in the northwest of England. Its entry requirements are three grades lower than for direct entry onto the five-year MBChB degree, in recognition that applicants may have had access to less support than their peers. The university has promised that the school will be distinctive, with a strong focus on widening access, community medicine, general practice and psychiatry.

Medical students will study alongside others taking health and social care courses in a new Simulation and Skills Education Centre, which is part of a £300m investment in new facilities over the past decade. The focal point is the £27m Catalyst building, opened in 2018, housing library, careers and student services under one roof, increasing the number of study spaces by half.

Creative Edge, a £17m complex, has industry-standard equipment and resources for students on media, film, animation, advertising and computing degree courses. It serves as a base for the Institute for Creative Enterprise, an interface between academic research and the creative industries, which gives students the opportunity to work on live TV and secure work placements. Performing arts students now have access to a unique performance space, after the conversion of a 1930s swimming pool.

Edge Hill was one of only three universities in the northwest of England to take gold first time around in the Teaching Excellence Framework. The panel noted that "students from diverse backgrounds achieve consistently outstanding outcomes". Almost all the students are state-educated and the projected dropout rate (8.6%) is substantially better than the university's benchmark (11.8%). Edge Hill has performed well in our first two social inclusion rankings and offers an award-winning £1.1m financial support package that rewards achievement, rather than simply offering incentives to enrol. Edge Hill expects 1,000 students to benefit from financial aid each year.

A university since 2005, Edge Hill has been moving up our league table and is now among the ten leading post-1992 institutions. It has scored particularly well in recent years in the National Student Survey, but this year its rankings have fallen from the top 25 into the top 35 for student satisfaction with teaching quality and to the top 50 for the overall student experience.

Much of the university's capital spending has been on new residences to ensure that all first-years can be guaranteed accommodation

---

St Helens Road
Ormskirk L39 4QP
01695 650 950
admissions@edgehill.ac.uk
www.edgehill.ac.uk
www.edgehillsu.org.uk
Open days 2020:
June 13

The Times and The Sunday Times **Rankings**
Overall Ranking: 55 (last year: 59)

Teaching quality	82.1%	35
Student experience	79.1%	=48
Research quality	4.9%	=93
Entry standards	134	=58
Graduate prospects	77.2%	59
Good honours	74%	=76
Expected completion rate	85.1%	68
Student/staff ratio	14	=28
Services and facilities	£2,230	73

and more senior students can also be housed on campus. A £13m Technology Hub boasts facilities such as big data servers and a virtual reality suite, available to employers and students alike. The latest addition is a £6m law and psychology building with a 265-seat lecture theatre, specialist laboratories, seminar and tutorial rooms and social learning space.

Edge Hill has been training teachers since the 19th century and remains one of the UK's largest providers of secondary teacher training and courses for classroom assistants. Its portfolio has become broader – growing again with the addition of degrees in global public health, sports therapy, robotics and artificial intelligence, and politics and criminology.

As well as medicine, new degree courses to be introduced in 2020 will include computer engineering, systems automation, biomedical science and religion. There is also a limited range of degree apprenticeships in healthcare.

All undergraduates on arts and science programmes have the option of a sandwich year in industry or a year studying abroad to enhance their learning and boost employability. Every student has a personal tutor, as well as access to counsellors and financial advice. The Solstice e-learning centre promotes excellence in teaching and learning. Three-quarters of all graduates leave with professional accreditation.

Applications and enrolments have both fallen in 2017 and 2018 – but Edge Hill has resisted the step of making unconditional offers. Applications were down again in the last admissions cycle, but the numbers accepting places are up by 11%.

English, sport and media produced the best results in the 2014 Research Excellence Framework. Scores for all six areas in which the university submitted work showed improvement compared with the previous assessments, although Edge Hill is only just in our top 100 on this measure.

A £30m sports centre has an eight-court sports hall, 25-metre swimming pool, 80-station fitness suite, aerobics studio and health suite with sauna and steam rooms. The outdoor facilities include a competition standard running track, rugby, hockey and football pitches, an athletics field, netball and tennis courts, and a trim trail with exercise stations.

Tuition fees

» Fees for UK/EU students	£9,250
Foundation courses	£6,165
» Fees for International students 2020–21	£12,250
» For scholarship and bursary information see	
www.edgehill.ac.uk/studentservices/moneyadvice	
» Graduate salary	£22,000

Student numbers

Undergraduates	9,891	(1,160)
Postgraduates	1,159	(2,046)
Applications/places		16.275/3,340
Applications per place		4.9
Overall offer rate		79.6%
Unconditional offers		0%
International students		2%

Accommodation

University provided places: 2,489
Self-catered: £76–£127 per week
First years guaranteed accommodation
www.edgehill.ac.uk/study/accommodation

Where do the students come from?

State schools (non-grammar)	96.7%	First generation students	55.8%	Black attainment gap	-21.3%
Grammar schools	2.3%	Deprived areas	20.3%	Disabled	6.8%
Independent schools	1.%	All ethnic minorities	6.5%	Mature (over 21)	21.4%

Social inclusion ranking: 41

University of Edinburgh

Still Scotland's most prestigious university, even if it is no longer our top-ranked institution north of the border, Edinburgh is deliberately losing its exclusivity. It has met government targets for greater diversity three years early, recruiting 11% of 2018's undergraduate intake from the most deprived parts of Scotland.

Edinburgh attributes the sharp increase to a new strategy using school partnerships, part-time access routes for adult learners and extra funding for students who commute from home. Such initiatives should begin to feed through into our social inclusion ranking in the coming years. Although still in the bottom three of our Scottish social inclusion ranking, it fares better than St Andrews and Glasgow.

Overall applications and enrolments were down in 2018, but they recovered in the most recent admissions cycle. Six new degrees, including agricultural economics, anatomy and development, and a Portuguese masters course were introduced in 2019, with a degree in politics, philosophy and economics to follow. The university already has by far the largest intake of undergraduates in Scotland and is ranked in the top 15 in the UK. But such is the demand for places that only 52% of applicants receive offers.

Edinburgh continues to finish higher in world rankings than it does in our league table, where it is hampered by poor scores for student satisfaction. The university remains stubbornly in the bottom ten once again for student satisfaction with teaching quality and the wider student experience. However, it is in the top 20 in the QS World University Rankings, which place a greater emphasis on research.

The university plans to invest £1.5bn over the next decade on new buildings and other improvements, aiming to produce a "highly satisfied student body with a strong sense of community". An £82m redevelopment of the students' union facilities is on the way. An £8m wellbeing centre will allow counselling and disability services to be based alongside the medical practice and pharmacy.

The university has announced a new personal tutor system and a peer support scheme, as well as introducing the Edinburgh Teaching Award, a two-year qualification for staff.

Most of the university's buildings border the historic Old Town. The law school is returning to Old College after comprehensive refurbishment and the addition of new facilities. Two miles to the south, the BioQuarter is a collaboration between the university and public bodies, consolidating Scotland's reputation as a world leader in biomedical science. The £100m Rosalind Franklin Institute will bring together scientists and engineers from across the UK to develop new treatments for chronic disease. The

---

33 Buccleuch Place
Edinburgh EH8 9J
0131 650 4360
https://www.sra.is.ed.ac.uk/
comms/enquiry/
www.ed.ac.uk
www.eusa.ed.ac.uk
Open days 2020:
June (see website)

EDINBURGH
Belfast
London
Cardiff

The Times and The Sunday Times Rankings
Overall Ranking: 25 (last year: 28)

Teaching quality	73.3%	125
Student experience	72.6%	121
Research quality	43.8%	10
Entry standards	190	8
Graduate prospects	77.5%	57
Good honours	89.5%	8
Expected completion rate	92.1%	=25
Student/staff ratio	11.9	=9
Services and facilities	£2,169	78

Easter Bush campus is to accommodate a new £79m national supercomputer.

The leading Scottish university in the 2014 Research Excellence Framework, with 80% of its large submission rated world-leading or internationally excellent, Edinburgh led the field in the UK for sociology, earth systems and environmental sciences, including geography, as well as computer science and informatics.

Edinburgh's strategic vision includes a commitment to enable undergraduates to develop as researchers and to give them the opportunity to draw on expertise outside their core discipline.

There is a growing emphasis on innovation and entrepreneurship, reflected in £5,000 awards for the best student projects. As part of the Edinburgh and South East Scotland Region Deal, the university will establish five data innovation hubs, using high-speed data analytics to help industry and local groups.

More than a quarter of Edinburgh's undergraduates come from outside the UK, and there is a joint institute in China with Zhejiang University. Efforts to broaden the UK intake include a large summer school programme and support for students in the transition to higher education. There is also a range of bursaries, some worth up to £8,500 a year, to reduce the costs to English, Welsh or Northern Irish undergraduates, who must pay the full £9,250 fee for all four years of their degrees.

Edinburgh's sports programmes are among the best in the UK, producing past Olympic champions such as the cyclist Sir Chris Hoy and the rower Dame Katherine Grainger. The university has an outdoor centre 80 miles distant from Edinburgh in a beautiful setting in the southern Highlands. In and around the city there is a network of gyms for student use, where membership packages start at just £15 a year. Students have a choice of 65 sports clubs and can take part in the full range of fixtures from informal games to competitive tournaments.

There are 9,500 residential places – more than enough to guarantee a room for first-year students. Students thrive in the world-renowned cultural capital. The university has appointed its first director of festival, cultural and city events to strengthen its ties with arts events such as the venerated Edinburgh Festival and Fringe.

Tuition fees

» Fees for Scottish/EU students 2019–20 £0–£1,820
   RUK fees £9,250
» Fees for International students 2020–21 £19,800–£32,100
   Medicine £49,900 Veterinary; £32,850 (clinical years)
» For scholarship and bursary information see
   www.ed.ac.uk/student-funding
» Graduate salary £22,510

Student numbers

Undergraduates	21,434	(660)
Postgraduates	8,203	(2,590)
Applications/places		60,905/6,575
Applications per place		9.3
Overall offer rate		51.8%
Unconditional offers		0%
International students		36.5%

Accommodation

University provided places: 9,500
Catered costs: £193–£258 per week
Self-catered: £96–£160 per week
First years guaranteed accommodation
www.accom.ed.ac.uk/

Where do the students come from?

State schools (non-grammar)	58.6%	First generation students	22.4%	
Grammar schools	7.7%	Deprived areas	8.1%	
Independent schools	33.7%	All ethnic minorities	11.6%	

Social inclusion ranking (Scotland): 13

Black attainment gap	4%
Disabled	5.4%
Mature (over 21)	12.5%

Edinburgh Napier University

Edinburgh Napier has jumped almost 20 places in our table but is still (just) outside the top 100. Markedly higher rates of student satisfaction have made the difference, although the university remains in the bottom 15 in the sections of the National Student Survey covering the quality of teaching.

The university has been streamlining its portfolio of courses, most recently withdrawing a number of joint honours programmes in the business school. The result has been a 5% drop in applications in 2019, the fifth successive decline.

There are only 13,000 students on the three campuses in Edinburgh. But the university's successful international activities may take it close to its target of 20% growth over five years. Edinburgh Napier is the largest UK provider of higher education in Hong Kong, and now has 4,500 students taking its courses around the world, with another 1,300 learning online. It has partners in Switzerland and several Asian countries, including China and India.

New degrees have been launched in digital design and marketing and mass communications, paired with advertising or public relations. Edinburgh Napier is also offering its first teacher education degrees in biology, chemistry, maths and physics, having committed to developing education at all levels in Stem (science, technology, engineering and maths) subjects.

In addition, the university has doubled the number of places available for graduate apprenticeships, expanding into two new areas – data science, and engineering: design and manufacture – in the present academic year.

Edinburgh Napier is investing £84m in new teaching and research facilities. The aim is to create spaces that are more fluid than traditional classrooms to accommodate different styles of learning and teaching.

The Merchiston campus, home to a Cyber Academy, cyber-attack simulation suite and expanded computer games laboratory, also houses a hub for computing and the creative industries, with fully soundproofed music studios and a broadcast journalism newsroom. The university's degree in cybersecurity and forensics has become the first undergraduate course in the UK to be fully certified by the National Cyber Security Centre, whose parent organisation is GCHQ, the Government Communications Headquarters.

There are also plans to extend the Sighthill campus, which is the base for the schools of nursing, midwifery and social care, and life, sport and social sciences. It has a five-storey learning resource centre, an environmental chamber and biomechanics laboratory, and a large simulation and clinical skills centre with mock hospital wards and a high-dependency unit simulator suite.

Sighthill Court
Edinburgh EH11 4BN
0333 900 6040
ugadmissions@napier.ac.uk
www.napier.ac.uk
www.napierstudents.com
Open days 2020:
see website

The Times and The Sunday Times **Rankings**
Overall Ranking: 101 (last year: 120)

Teaching quality	76.2%	=115
Student experience	75.9%	102
Research quality	4.6%	=95
Entry standards	148	=40
Graduate prospects	73.8%	=74
Good honours	75.7%	=59
Expected completion rate	82.2%	88
Student/staff ratio	17.9	=102
Services and facilities	£2,136	81

The university has recently added dedicated qualifying programmes in occupational therapy, social work and physiotherapy. A number of collaborative modules are shared across all three subjects, allowing students to gain a deeper understanding of the links between the roles.

Edinburgh Napier runs Screen Academy Scotland in partnership with Edinburgh College of Art (now part of the University of Edinburgh), reflecting the institution's strong reputation in film education. The creative arts produced the most successful of Edinburgh Napier's entries for the 2014 Research Excellence Framework.

The business school is at the Craiglockhart campus, once a hospital for shell-shocked First World War soldiers. The building blends history and modernity, featuring a glass atrium and cybercafe and displaying the War Poets Collection, by Siegfried Sassoon and Wilfred Owen.

Many of Edinburgh Napier's courses include a work placement. The Confident Futures programme uses workshops to improve students' faith in their own abilities and help them to develop skills, attributes and attitudes that will enhance their chances of being successful both while at university and in their careers.

For the growing numbers choosing to start their own businesses, Bright Red Triangle, the university's student enterprise service, offers free office space and advice to students and alumni. Edinburgh Napier has supported 500 start-ups in 11 years.

New students are mentored by student volunteers. Support begins with pre-term introductions to staff and continues with workshops in employability skills and personal development.

Widening participation is high on the list of priorities. One third of the undergraduates are aged over 21 at entry and just under 40% are the first in their family to go to university. More than 2,000 students join Edinburgh Napier through "articulation routes", using their college qualifications to gain direct entry into year two or three of a degree course.

Each campus has fully networked libraries and a multimedia language laboratory and adaptive learning centre for students with special needs.

Integrated sports facilities feature a well-equipped fitness centre and a sports hall, as well as the BT Sport Scottish Rugby Academy. There are 1,200 university study bedrooms and all first-years from outside Edinburgh are guaranteed a place.

Tuition fees

» Fees for Scottish/EU students   £0–£1,820

    RUK fees   £9,250 (capped at £27,750 for 4-year courses)

» Fees for International students 2020–21   £13,360–£15,522

» For scholarship and bursary information see www.napier.ac.uk/study-with-us/undergraduate/fees-and-finance

» Graduate salary   £22,440

Student numbers

Undergraduates	9,235	(1,047)
Postgraduates	1,600	(1,232)
Applications/places		20,540/3,300
Applications per place		6.2
Overall offer rate		69%
Unconditional offers		0%
International students		19.7%

Accommodation

University provided places: 1,240

Self-catered: £98–£156per week

First years guaranteed accommodation

www.napier.ac.uk/study-with-us/accommodation

Where do the students come from?

State schools (non-grammar)	90.8%	First generation students	39.1%	Black attainment gap	-30.8%
Grammar schools	2.5%	Deprived areas	10.9%	Disabled	5.3%
Independent schools	6.7%	All ethnic minorities	10%	Mature (over 21)	37.2%

Social inclusion ranking (Scotland): 7

University of Essex

While other universities were declaring redundancies last year in the face of mounting uncertainty over funding and student recruitment, Essex announced plans to employ another 150 staff to facilitate its biggest expansion yet. Professor Anthony Forster, the vice-chancellor, said the move was a response to record applications – which have almost doubled in a decade. He hoped it would further enhance students' educational experience and boost the university's research power.

New enrolments have grown for six years in succession and are also running at record levels. By 2025, Essex is hoping to increase its student population by a third, to 20,000. At the same time, the university has set itself the target of holding down a place in the top 25 in our table. It met that goal two years ahead of schedule but has since slipped back.

Essex is a university on the rise, however. Shortlisted for our University of the Year award in 2017, it won the University of the Year title awarded by *Times Higher Education* last year and took gold in the Teaching Excellence Framework. The panel was impressed that student feedback was being used to develop "rigorous and stretching teaching that is tailored to student needs". It said: "Students from all backgrounds achieve outstanding outcomes with regard to continuation and progression to highly skilled employment or further study, notably exceeding the university's benchmark."

The university's employability intiatives have won plaudits. The award-winning Frontrunners scheme arranges paid work experience for students on campus. There is also an extensive internship programme, and work placements are integral to many courses. The Big Essex employability award recognises students' extracurricular and volunteering activities. Language tuition is free and Essex discounts or exempts tuition fees for a full year abroad or a placement year.

On the 200-acre parkland campus near Colchester, the original 1960s buildings are gradually being refurbished or replaced. The Bertrand Russell Tower, the first of the university's iconic residences, has had a refit. The £13m Stem Centre includes a versatile, 180-seat wet laboratory for the biological sciences and a 200-seat exploratory space to encourage science and health students to collaborate.

A new £12m Sports Arena and 634 rooms in a new residential development opened in 2018, along with a "zero carbon" business school. Now Essex has opened the Innovation Centre, where 2,000 people are expected to work in start-up businesses.

Essex's student population is unusually diverse for a pre-1992 university. There are high proportions of mature and international students and 95% of the UK undergraduates

Wivenhoe Park
Colchester CO4 3SQ
01206 873 333
admit@essex.ac.uk
www.essex.ac.uk
www.essexstudent.com
Open days 2019:
June 15 (Colchester)

The Times and The Sunday Times **Rankings**

Overall Ranking: 37 (last year: 29)

Teaching quality	79.5%	=73
Student experience	80.3%	=29
Research quality	37.2%	25
Entry standards	111	=122
Graduate prospects	74.3%	72
Good honours	74.5%	71
Expected completion rate	85.4%	=65
Student/staff ratio	15.9	=71
Services and facilities	£3,521	4

are state-educated. Almost half are the first in their family to go to university. More than 44% of students are drawn from ethnic minorities. An active outreach team works with schools to encourage progression.

These initiatives have helped to depress the university's average UCAS tariff point score, now among the lowest in the UK. Widening participation inevitably means admitting students who are less well qualified, making it harder to score highly in one of our key league table measures – so Essex should not be too disappointed with this year's fall in our rankings.

Degrees in cognitive science, event management, mechatronic engineering, human biology, and sociology with data science are among new courses introduced in 2019. The university is planning to expand its portfolio of degree apprenticeships with the number of trainees expected to double to 300 by 2020.

The social sciences are Essex's greatest strength, putting the institution among the world's top 50 in the QS rankings for both politics and sociology. It achieved the best results in the 2014 Research Excellence Framework in politics and was in the top ten for economics and art history. Essex is in the top 25 in our research ranking, with almost 80% of its large submission rated world-leading or internationally excellent.

Wivenhoe House, the original campus centrepiece, is now a four-star hotel run by the Edge Hotel School. A modern campus in Southend-on-Sea offers courses in business, health and the arts and its accommodation complex houses a gym and fitness studio. The Forum at the heart of the Southend campus houses a public and academic library, learning facilities, cafe and gallery – with a floor reserved for student use. The East 15 Acting School has a theatre in Southend and a campus in Loughton, which will have a new double-height studio in time for the 2020–21 academic year.

There is plenty to do thanks to an active students' union and a 40-acre sports area that includes an 18-hole golf course, all-weather tennis courts and room for five-a-side futsal. The £12m Essex Sports Arena opened in 2018, with seating for 1,655 spectators and courts for badminton, basketball, volleyball and netball. All the facilities are also open to the public.

All first-years are guaranteed a place in university accommodation, which has been voted some of the best in the UK. Some ground-floor flats have been adapted for disabled students. All the campuses are within easy access of London.

Tuition fees

» Fees for UK/EU students   £9,250
» Fees for International students 2020–21   £16,050–£18,730
» For scholarship and bursary information see
   www1.essex.ac.uk/fees-and-funding/
» Graduate salary   £20,000

Student numbers

Undergraduates	10,753	(618)
Postgraduates	2,161	(1,229)
Applications/places		20,855/4,455
Applications per place		4.7
Overall offer rate		79.4%
Unconditional offers		0%
International students		29.5%

Accommodation

University provided places: 2,063
Self-catered: £99–£191 per week
First years guaranteed accommodation
www1.essex.ac.uk/life/accommodation

Where do the students come from?

State schools (non-grammar)	88.7%	First generation students	47.8%	Black attainment gap	-18.9%
Grammar schools	6.2%	Deprived areas	11.8%	Disabled	4.2%
Independent schools	5%	All ethnic minorities	44.3%	Mature (over 21)	14.1%

Social inclusion ranking: 87

University of Exeter

Exeter has doubled its undergraduate admissions in 12 years, taking advantage of the abolition of recruitment restrictions more than any other university. Applications have dropped for three years in a row, but almost nine out of ten candidates receive an offer – one of the highest rates in the UK, partly because the university has been attracting better-qualified applicants since joining the Russell Group of research-led universities in 2012.

Despite this expansion, however, Exeter ranks in the bottom five in our social inclusion table with a less diverse intake than many universities, even within the highly selective Russell Group. More than a third of its places go to students from independent schools and little more than 7% come from areas of low participation in higher education. Students from disadvantaged backgrounds and schools with poor results are made lower offers to encourage fair access, however, as the university tries to address the issue.

Exeter holds gold in the Teaching Excellence Framework, attracting praise for "optimum" contact hours and class sizes and for involving business, industry and professional experts in its teaching.

The university remains on the fringes of our top ten, despite losing some of its lustre in the National Student Survey, where it was formerly among the leaders. While it remains just outside the top 30 for satisfaction with the overall student experience, its teaching quality score has slipped into the bottom half of the rankings.

Exeter has lavished about £380m on campus improvements. Hubs where students can eat, socialise and study have been built on all four campuses. Additional accommodation is due to open on the main campus in September 2020 and more the following year – 1,182 extra rooms in total.

Much of the expansion has come at the £100m Penryn campus in Cornwall, which Exeter shares with Falmouth University. There is a joint students' union and a helpdesk for students at either institution at the Exchange, a £10m learning, teaching and research hub, as well as a £4m sports centre.

A new building for the recently established business school and the highly regarded Camborne School of Mines opened in 2019, also providing space for law, energy and mathematics, as well as the Centre for Ecology and Conservation.

The main Streatham campus is one of the most attractive settings for any UK university. The majority of students are based there, served by the £48m Forum building, which features an extended library, student services centre, technology-rich learning areas and auditorium, as well as social space and shops.

The nearby St Luke's campus houses the medical school, which also has a health

The Old Library
Prince of Wales Road
Exeter EX4 4SB
0300 555 6060 or 01392 723 044
https://www.exeter.ac.uk/enquiry/
www.exeter.ac.uk
www.exeterguild.org
Open days 2020:
June 29/30 (Exeter);
May 28 (Penryn)

The Times and The Sunday Times Rankings
Overall Ranking: 12 (last year: 12)

Teaching quality	79.3%	=79
Student experience	80.1%	31
Research quality	38%	18
Entry standards	172	=15
Graduate prospects	85.5%	13
Good honours	87.9%	11
Expected completion rate	95.8%	=7
Student/staff ratio	15.5	=59
Services and facilities	£2,987	16

education and research centre at the Royal Devon and Exeter Hospital and a smaller base in Truro, Cornwall. The Graduate School of Education and the sport and health sciences school are also based at St Luke's.

Exeter recorded much-improved results in the Research Excellence Framework in 2014. More than 80% of its large submission was rated as world-leading or internationally excellent, with the best results in clinical medicine, psychology and education. A £10m donation from *Sunday Times* Rich Listers Dennis and Mireille Gillings will fund a neuroimaging centre at the medical school to accelerate the diagnosis and treatment of dementia.

Neuroscience is one of nine new degrees to be launched by the university in 2020. Others include data science, archaeological science, and politics courses with English or geography.

The university is also adding to its degree apprenticeship programmes, which train nearly 300 students in civil engineering, digital and technology solutions, applied finance, senior leadership and chartered management. A master's in data science is planned for 2020.

For sport, geography and mining engineering, Exeter is ranked in the top 20 in the world, according to the QS rankings. It has a research partnership with the University of Queensland focusing on environmental sustainability, healthy ageing, and physical activity and nutrition. Students can choose three and four-year courses with a year abroad or international study options, and all are offered tuition in foreign languages.

The university's Career Zone scheme helps boost student employability and access to internships, while the Exeter Award provides official recognition of extracurricular activities. The university has one of the highest numbers of student volunteers in the UK.

Even before the new accommodation comes on stream, Exeter had enough residential places – more than 5,400 for undergraduates – to guarantee a room to first-years, although an over-running private development left hundreds of students in costlier accommodation when the current academic year started.

More than £20m has been invested in sports facilities. The Sports Park on the main campus includes a 200-station gym, and Exeter is one of the few UK universities to have indoor tennis facilities to national competition standards. Student-oriented bars and clubs dot the city.

Tuition fees

» Fees for UK/EU students	£9,250
» Fees for International students 2020–21	£18,500–£22,950
Medicine	£35,750
» For scholarship and bursary information see www.exeter.ac.uk/undergraduate/money/scholarships/	
» Graduate salary	£23,000

Student numbers

Undergraduates	18,242	(240)
Postgraduates	3,823	(1,740)
Applications/places		38,510/6,745
Applications per place		5.7
Overall offer rate		91.7%
Unconditional offers		0%
International students		25%

Accommodation

University provided places: 5,951
Catered costs: £173–£261 per week
Self-catered: £106–£259 per week
First years guaranteed accommodation
www.exeter.ac.uk/undergraduate/life/accommodation

Where do the students come from?

State schools (non-grammar)	51.6%	First generation students	27.8%	Black attainment gap	-19.7%
Grammar schools	14.3%	Deprived areas	7.2%	Disabled	7.2%
Independent schools	34.1%	All ethnic minorities	10.2%	Mature (over 21)	6.2%

Social inclusion ranking: 111

Falmouth University

Twelve new degree courses will be introduced over the next two years building on Falmouth's roots as a school of art – and embracing cutting-edge technology. Immersive computing and creative virtual reality are two examples of its trademark blend of creativity and innovation.

The Teaching Excellence Framework panel awarded Falmouth gold, commending its ability to stretch students with personalised teaching, and to provide skills and understanding highly valued by employers.

Falmouth still regards itself as a specialist art institution, although the curriculum now embraces business entrepreneurship and marketing, journalism, game development and architecture. Both applications and enrolments have declined recently, as they have at most arts-based universities. But the numbers starting undergraduate courses are still higher than at any point before 2015 – and twice what they were a decade ago.

The university has two campuses: Falmouth and Penryn, where £100m has been spent in the past decade. The Falmouth campus is near the town centre and has subtropical gardens and a popular cafe. It claims some of the best teaching facilities for photography in Europe and an in-house photo agency helps students and graduates to make their way in a fast-changing industry.

The campus at Penryn is shared with the University of Exeter, featuring a unique joint students' union, FXU. It is the base for Falmouth's performing arts courses, added to the university's portfolio following a merger with Dartington College of Arts, in south Devon, more than a decade ago.

The Academy of Music and Theatre Arts at Penryn attracts performers from all over the world and gives students access to exceptional facilities such as a 117-seat cinema, motion capture studio, video editing suites and specialist animation software, fully sprung dancefloors, rehearsal studios and theatre space.

The animation and visual effects department is part of the Cross Channel Film Lab, which aims to develop innovative visual effects for use in low-budget feature film production.

Falmouth's submission to the Research Excellence Framework gained its best results in music, dance, drama and the performing arts, with a third of its work emerging as world-leading or internationally excellent. Almost a quarter of its art and design submission was placed in the top two categories.

There are still only about 5,000 students at the university, about 60% female at undergraduate level – although male applicants are just as likely to receive an offer. Each new arrival is offered a student mentor

Woodlane
Falmouth TR11 4RH
01326 254 350
futurestudies@falmouth.ac.uk
www.falmouth.ac.uk
www.thesu.org.uk
Open days 2020:
March 13, April 8

The Times and The Sunday Times **Rankings**

Overall Ranking: 72 (last year: 84)		
Teaching quality	81.1%	48
Student experience	76.5%	=96
Research quality	4.6%	=95
Entry standards	131	=67
Graduate prospects	77.0%	61
Good honours	78%	=49
Expected completion rate	86.8%	=56
Student/staff ratio	18.3	109
Services and facilities	£1,488	=126

for a year to support them during their transition to university life. The university has an internal teaching qualification for staff to promote high standards.

More than nine out of ten undergraduates are state-educated. Those with a family income of less than £25,000 receive up to £200 a year to spend on course materials. Students from Cornwall qualify for up to £1,500 a year towards equipment, internships and end-of-year shows.

Students are encouraged to set up a business while they study under the Team Academy scheme, to tap in to Cornwall's unrivalled leisure market.

The Launchpad postgraduate scheme brings together teams of highly skilled software, creative digital and business minds to develop high-growth, high-value digital companies to meet identified market demand in just one year. The programme, based in a new building, upends the usual start-up model. Instead of participants coming up with their own idea, they are offered challenges by business partners such as Amazon, the BBC and Sony Interactive Entertainment.

The Launchpad scheme has been named as one of only 20 new University Enterprise Zones by UK Research and Innovation, recognising its importance in supporting the growth of the Cornish economy. The award, announced in September, includes £1m of match funding in the current year, which is expected to unlock a further combined funding package of £8m.

There are residential places on both campuses, enabling the university to guarantee accommodation to all full-time first-years who apply in time.

The sports centre on the Penryn campus has a four-court sports hall, fitness studio and gym, as well as multi-use outdoor pitches. There's no excuse not to try watersports on Cornwall's coastline and paid work in the tourist trade helps to offset the cost of study.

Tuition fees

» Fees for UK/EU students	£9,250
» Fees for International students 2020–21	£16,000
» For scholarship and bursary information see www.falmouth.ac.uk/tuition-fees	
» Graduate salary	£18,000

Student numbers

Undergraduates	**5,586**	**(18)**
Postgraduates	**104**	**(294)**
Applications/places		**5,980/1,810**
Applications per place		**3.3**
Overall offer rate		**72.7%**
Unconditional offers		**0%**
International students		**10.9%**

Accommodation

University provided places: 1,367
Catered costs: £192
Self-catered: £110–£197 per week
First years guaranteed accommodation
www.falmouth.ac.uk/accommodation

Where do the students come from?

State schools (non-grammar)	91.3%	First generation students	34.6%	
Grammar schools	2.2%	Deprived areas	9.8%	
Independent schools	6.5%	All ethnic minorities	6.2%	

Social inclusion ranking: 73

Black attainment gap	n/a
Disabled	11.1%
Mature (over 21)	13.5%

University of Glasgow

Hot on the heels of Glasgow's ambitious £1bn Western Infirmary campus development, the university has announced plans for a hi-tech innovation campus in the former shipyards of Govan, on the banks of the Clyde.

A new learning hub for 3,000 students will open on the infirmary site during the current academic year. Later, there will also be new buildings for arts, social sciences, the health and wellbeing institute, and the science and engineering college, as the university invests £430m over four years. It is promising a "new, vibrant piece of city" woven into the social, cultural and economic fabric of the West End of Glasgow.

Glasgow was the first university in Britain to have a school of engineering and the first in Scotland to have a computer. Carrying on the tradition of innovation, the new Govan campus, part-funded from the Glasgow City Region Deal, will focus on nanotechnology and precision medicine, with academics working alongside partners from industry. The eventual cost is expected to reach £80m and it will include "invention rooms" for use by local school pupils and young people, to inspire a culture of innovation and entrepreneurship.

The university is in our UK top 20 despite a poor showing in the annual National Student Survey. Student satisfaction with teaching quality slumped so far that it has dumped the university out of the UK top 100 on this measure in our table.

However, across all nine of our league table measures, only St Andrews is ranked higher in Scotland. The numbers starting courses at Glasgow in 2018 dropped slightly, but only after a record enrolment in the previous year. The intake has grown by almost 1,000 in three years and applications were up again in the 2019 admissions cycle.

Seven new degrees have taken their first students, six featuring international relations, which can now be paired with social and public policy, quantitative methods, central and eastern European studies, economic and social history or sociology. The other addition is a graduate apprenticeship in software engineering.

Last summer's graduates were able to toast their success with the university's branded gin, created by a former arts student, named 1451 after the year of the university's establishment by papal bull.

Since 1871, the institution has been based on the Gilmorehill campus in the city's fashionable West End, where fundraising continues for a £110m expansion. At the redeveloped Kelvin Hall, £35m teaching and learning facilities have been created with room for collections from the university's museum, the Hunterian.

University Avenue, Glasgow G12 8QQ
0141 330 2000
ruk-undergraduate-enquiries@glasgow.ac.uk;
scot-undergraduate-enquiries@glasgow.co.uk;
student.recruitment@glasgow.ac.uk
www.gla.ac.uk
www.guu.co.uk
Open days 2020: June 18

The Times and The Sunday Times Rankings
Overall Ranking: 16 (last year: 17)

Teaching quality	77.4%	103
Student experience	78.2%	=70
Research quality	39.9%	12
Entry standards	200	=5
Graduate prospects	85.3%	16
Good honours	84.8%	19
Expected completion rate	89.9%	=40
Student/staff ratio	13.7	=22
Services and facilities	£2,549	43

Extensive work has also taken place on the Garscube campus, four miles out of the city, which houses the veterinary school and outdoor sports facilities. At Dumfries, where liberal arts and teaching courses are based, more than £13m has been spent on better sporting and social facilities.

Unusually for a university of its type, Glasgow exceeds its benchmarks for widening participation, although it is next to bottom in our Scottish social inclusion table (which does not take account of subject, student or location-adjusted benchmarks). Almost two-thirds of the students still come from Scotland – many from Glasgow and the surrounding area. Pioneering access schemes such as the Top-Up programme, running for 20 years with schools in the west of Scotland, combine with talent scholarships of £1,000 a year to academically able Scottish applicants from poor backgrounds. Four out of five students come from non-selective state schools with about 16% recruited from private schools.

One of Scotland's two representatives in the Russell Group, the university is in the top 100 in both the Times Higher Education and QS world rankings. It moved into the top dozen universities in the UK for research after a much-improved performance in the 2014 Research Excellence Framework, ranking in the top ten in 18 subjects. The best results came in architecture, agriculture, veterinary science and chemistry.

More than a quarter of undergraduates are from outside the UK and Glasgow has a branch campus in Singapore, working with the Singapore Institute of Technology, and a joint graduate school with Nankai University in China.

Glasgow has a popular flexible system that allows students to delay choosing a specialism until the end of their second year. Almost half of the university's applications are for broad arts or sciences degrees. Managed by the internship hub, there are more than 350 paid opportunities each year, including 150 on campus.

There are more than 3,400 residential places, enough to guarantee accommodation for new undergraduates. Most revel in the combination of campus and lively city life, where the relatively low cost of living is a plus. Glasgow's sports union supports more than 50 clubs and activities with purpose-built facilities..

Tuition fees

» Fees for Scottish/EU students   £0–£1,820
   RUK fees   £9,250 (capped at £27,750 for 4-year courses)
» Fees for International students 2020–21   £18,370–£21,920
   Medicine £47,900 (clinical years); dentistry £45,170;
   Veterinary £30,500
» For scholarship and bursary information see
   http://www.gla.ac.uk/study/undergraduate/fees/
» Graduate salary   £22,800

Student numbers

Undergraduates	**18,171**	**(2,636)**
Postgraduates	**7,293**	**(1,626)**
Applications/places		**35,135/5,440**
Applications per place		**6.5**
Overall offer rate		**68.8%**
Unconditional offers		**0%**
International students		**29.7%**

Where do the students come from?

State schools (non-grammar)	78.3%	First generation students	27%	Black attainment gap	-33%
Grammar schools	6.0%	Deprived areas	12.3%	Disabled	3%
Independent schools	15.7%	All ethnic minorities	9.1%	Mature (over 21)	23.9%

Accommodation

University provided places: 3,419
Catered costs: £161–£178 per week
Self-catered: £98–£161 per week
First years guaranteed accommodation
www.gla.ac.uk/undergraduate/accommodation

Social inclusion ranking (Scotland): 14

Glasgow Caledonian University

Glasgow Caledonian (GCU) has been attracting undergraduates in record numbers, exceeding 4,000 new students for the first time in 2018 after a third successive rise in enrolments. The university's increased popularity has coincided with a small rise in student satisfaction, which has helped to push it back into our top 100.

Like other universities north of the border, GCU benefits from the conversion rate for Scottish secondary qualifications in the UCAS tariff – putting it in the top 25 for entry grades, above the likes of Nottingham and Loughborough. The university has also improved its ranking for graduate prospects, which has been a strong focus. More than half of the undergraduate programmes are accredited by professional bodies and most include work placements.

Glasgow School for Business and Society pioneered subjects such as entrepreneurial studies and risk management and offers specialist degrees, such as tourism management and consumer protection. The School of Engineering and Built Environment teaches three-quarters of Scotland's part-time construction students.

There are seven graduate apprenticeships ranging from mechanical engineering and software development for business to quantity surveying. It has been awarded £5.4m by Skills Development Scotland to offer another 194 apprenticeships in civil engineering, construction, cybersecurity and software development, making it one of Scotland's biggest providers.

GCU describes itself as the University for the Common Good, a philosophy which extends into the curriculum. There is a focus on active and global citizenship, an entrepreneurial mindset, responsible leadership and self-confidence to equip students to serve their communities effectively.

The university is part of the Changemaker Campus network set up by entrepreneurs Ashoka to deliver social impact through education, research and innovation. It has been chosen to lead a government scheme to set up Scotland's first migrant and refugee skills recognition and accreditation hub, addressing the country's skills gap as well as helping migrants to fulfil their potential.

GCU helped to set up the African Leadership College in Mauritius, where the first students embarked on GCU degrees in 2017. It also co-founded the Grameen Caledonian College of Nursing in Bangladesh, and has links with institutions in Oman, China, India and South America.

GCU's greatest coup, however, was to become the first foreign university to be granted a charter to award its own degrees (in fashion and business) in New York. Despite some criticism over the costs associated with

---

Cowcaddens Road
Glasgow G4 0BA
0141 331 8630
admissions@gcu.ac.uk
www.gcu.ac.uk
www.gcustudents.co.uk
Open days 2020:
see website

The Times and The Sunday Times Rankings
Overall Ranking: =96 (last year: 101)

Teaching quality	78.7%	=89
Student experience	76.5%	=96
Research quality	7.0%	=77
Entry standards	167	=18
Graduate prospects	73.7%	76
Good honours	79.9%	=39
Expected completion rate	83.7%	=78
Student/staff ratio	20.2	=124
Services and facilities	£1,651	121

the project, the university is increasing its loan facility to £15m to expand its campus in the Big Apple. GCU was also the first from Scotland to open a campus in London, again for fashion postgraduates.

The university is best known for its fashion courses and its British School of Fashion has a partnership with Marks & Spencer, which has a design studio on the London campus and funds a scholarship programme. There are also courses in fashion business creation, luxury brand marketing and management, luxury retail management and international fashion marketing.

GCU is one of the largest providers of graduates to the NHS in Scotland, training 90% of the country's eyecare specialists. Its health building includes a virtual hospital and health was one of GCU's strengths in the 2014 Research Excellence Framework, when half its submission attained the top two categories. GCU was in the top 20 in the UK for allied health research and did well in social work and social policy, and the built environment.

Ranking fourth this year among Scottish universities in our new measure of social inclusion, widening participation in higher education has always been a main aim, and it has recruited some heavy hitters behind the project. Sir Alex Ferguson has pledged £500,000 to a bursary programme, while Annie Lennox is GCU's chancellor. Just under half the students are the first in their family to go to university, while almost all come from non-selective state schools, one of the highest proportions in the UK.

The university's Caledonian Club works with children as young as three years old and their families in Glasgow and London. The Advanced Higher Hub offers students in their final year at schools across Glasgow specialist teaching, access to GCU's facilities and preparation for university life. The university also gives academic, social and financial support to those at risk of dropping out – a policy that is bearing fruit as the dropout rate (about 9%) is now below the expected level.

GCU was named the first cycle-friendly campus by Cycle Scotland and is also a platinum-award winning eco campus. The centrepiece of a £32m redevelopment is the Heart of the Campus, which has a striking glass reception area.

Student facilities include the Arc sports centre and 24-hour computer labs. There are only 654 residential places, so international or disabled students, and those under 19, get first dibs. Glasgow has a large student population and the cost of living is reasonable.

Tuition fees

»	Fees for Scottish/EU students	£0–£1,820
	RUK fees £9,250 (capped at £27,750 for 4-year courses)	
»	Fees for International students 2020–21	£12,250
»	For scholarship and bursary information see www.gcu.ac.uk/study/tuitionfees/	
»	Graduate salary	£21,500

Student numbers

Undergraduates	11,240 (2,337)
Postgraduates	1,770 (1,104)
Applications/places	21,505/4,035
Applications per place	5.3
Overall offer rate	66.1%
International students	12.2%

Accommodation

University provided places: 654
Self-catered: £100–£118 per week
www.gcu.ac.uk/study/undergraduate/accommodation/

Where do the students come from?

State schools (non-grammar)	96.2%	First generation students	45.2%
Grammar schools	0.9%	Deprived areas	23.5%
Independent schools	2.9%	All ethnic minorities	11.1%

Social inclusion ranking (Scotland): 4

Black attainment gap	46.8%
Disabled	2.4%
Mature (over 21)	40.9%

University of Gloucestershire

Gloucestershire claims to offer undergraduates more time with academic staff than almost any other university. In most subjects, students are said to spend at least a quarter of their time in lectures, seminars or other supervised activities.

More than half of the academics have formal teaching qualifications, one of the highest proportions for any university. The strategic plan promises to push that proportion even higher, as well as pledging greater use of technology to provide online content, wherever possible, to support face-to-face teaching.

The university holds silver in the Teaching Excellence Framework, winning praise for its integrated approach to careers, volunteering and placements, which enhances student employability.

Gloucestershire has completed a number of campus developments, and there are plans to increase the numbers taking its degrees by a third. Many of the additional students will study at partner colleges, online or through work-based learning. The university is launching 20 new honours degrees and a similar number of degree apprenticeship programmes in 2019 and 2020.

The changes may be affecting student satisfaction, which has dropped significantly for the second year in a row. With the university's scores for completion and the proportion of

first-class or 2:1 degrees also falling, Gloucestershire is down 14 places in our latest table.

Enrolments are down as well: the numbers starting degrees in 2018 had fallen by 16% compared with two years earlier. There was an even steeper decline in applications over the same period.

Among the new options for last year's entrants were physiotherapy, law with business, mechatronics engineering and criminology and criminal justice. Among 2020's additions will be applied artificial intelligence, education, inclusion and special educational needs, stage management and international relations.

At the same time, Gloucestershire expects to almost double the numbers taking degree apprenticeships. Programmes in development include project management, manufacturing engineering, schools business management and social work.

New facilities include a business school with a live trading room and moot court on the Oxstalls campus in Gloucester. The building also hosts the growth hub, a partnership between the university and the Gloucestershire Local Enterprise Partnership, allowing students to gain practical experience with local companies.

In Cheltenham, there is a new design centre and an engineering suite, while facilities for art and design, engineering and social sciences have been added on the

The Park
Cheltenham GL50 2RH
03330 141 414
enquiries@glos.ac.uk
www.glos.ac.uk
www.yourstudentunion.com
Open days 2020:
see website

The Times and The Sunday Times Rankings
Overall Ranking: 95 (last year: =81)

Teaching quality	81%	=49
Student experience	78%	=72
Research quality	3.8%	=108
Entry standards	123	=86
Graduate prospects	72.9%	=85
Good honours	71.3%	=91
Expected completion rate	80.9%	=97
Student/staff ratio	18.7	=113
Services and facilities	£2,055	91

Francis Close Hall site. Other improvements include a large sports park, with an international standard arena and 3G pitches, and 1,100 extra residential places.

The main Park campus is a mile from the centre of Cheltenham, and houses the business, education and professional studies faculty. Art and design facilities, and the education and public services institute are closer to the town centre at Francis Close Hall.

The purpose-built Oxstalls campus caters for sport and exercise sciences, leisure, tourism, hospitality and event management. It also houses the Countryside and Community Research Institute, the largest rural research centre in the UK, which produced the best results in the 2014 Research Excellence Framework. Overall, 44% of the submission was rated as world-leading or internationally excellent, but fewer than 20% of eligible staff took part.

In 2001, Gloucestershire was the first with formal links to the Church of England to achieve university status for more than a century. Originally a teacher training college, its primary and secondary training courses are rated "outstanding" by Ofsted. A third of all undergraduates take work placements.

At the top of the 2019 People & Planet league of universities' environmental performance, Gloucestershire has long championed green issues. Students are invited to allow themselves to be "seeduced" to sign up with the allotment society, where they can take a break from their studies to grow potatoes, onions, pumpkins and chillies. Diplomas are offered in environmentalism, as well as sustainability research and development projects that bring together researchers from around the world, undertaking work for agencies such as Unesco.

As well as its conventional degrees, the university offers a range of two-year "fast-track" degrees in subjects such as biology, events management and law. The institution's intake is more diverse than many, with 92.5% of undergraduates coming from non-selective state schools and just under half from homes where parents did not attend university.

Gloucestershire has a strong sporting tradition. Students can get involved with more than 80 sporting activities – for fun or at competitive level.

All first-year applicants are guaranteed housing in university halls or managed accommodation if they make Gloucestershire their first choice and apply by the deadline. The options include an 800-bed student village in Cheltenham, opened in 2017, and 300 places in the centre of Gloucester.

Tuition fees

» Fees for UK/EU students	£9,250
» Fees for International students 2020–21	£14,680
» For scholarship and bursary information see www.glos.ac.uk/life/finance/Pages/default.aspx	
» Graduate salary	£19,200

Student numbers

Undergraduates	6,737	(342)
Postgraduates	543	(870)
Applications/places		8,040/2,310
Applications per place		3.5
Overall offer rate		87.4%
Unconditional offers		0%
International students		4.9%

Accommodation

University provided places: 1,900
Self-catered: £123–£197 per week
First years guaranteed accommodation
www.glos.ac.uk/life/accommodation/pages/accommodation.aspx

Where do the students come from?

State schools (non-grammar)	92.5%	First generation students	47.7%	Black attainment gap	-36%
Grammar schools	3.8%	Deprived areas	14.7%	Disabled	9.8%
Independent schools	3.7%	All ethnic minorities	10.9%	Mature (over 21)	22.3%

Social inclusion ranking: 77

Goldsmiths, University of London

Goldsmiths has appointed its first female warden, Professor Frances Corner, who headed the London College of Fashion and was responsible for its digital developments. She has set the college some inspiring challenges, urging it to think radically about students' changing needs and expectations, as well as becoming involved in the big questions about inequalities, climate change and increasingly polarised communities.

Applications have risen for the past three years, but the numbers starting courses fell in 2018. The college is just outside the top ten universities in the world for art and design and in the top 50 for the performing arts in the QS subject rankings. It is up three places in our league table this year and has a bronze rating in the Teaching Excellence Framework (TEF).

The TEF panel conceded that students had access to high-quality resources and benefited from connecting with local communities, and conducting research of relevance to them. But the college was dragged down by low student satisfaction levels, a common problem in London, and poor graduate employment, also a challenge in arts-dominated institutions.

Student satisfaction has improved slightly this year, still leaving it in the bottom 20 for teaching quality and the bottom ten for the broader student experience. Goldsmiths is also near the bottom of the list for graduate prospects.

New facilities should help to secure Goldsmiths' place as one of the leading universities for the creative arts. The Goldsmiths Centre for Contemporary Art opened in autumn 2018, an art gallery in a redeveloped listed building that once housed public baths. It followed the opening of a £2.9m performance and teaching space for student and public use, containing studios and a 200-seat theatre.

The portfolio of degrees includes management, economics, politics and computing. A new law degree was launched in 2019, featuring practical skills like public speaking, the drafting of legal documents, and the use of social media, big data and analytics, alongside traditional legal education. A separate pathway in 2020 will allow students to specialise in criminal justice and human rights. Goldsmiths is also about to embark on degree apprenticeships for the first time.

The arts remain Goldsmiths' greatest strength, however. In recent years, the director Steve McQueen scooped the best picture Oscar for 12 Years a Slave, James Blake took the Mercury prize for his album Overgrown and Charlotte Prodger won the Turner prize in 2018 – the eighth former student or staff member to receive the award, alongside Damien Hirst and Sir Antony Gormley.

Goldsmiths did well in the 2014 Research Excellence Framework, with 70% of its

New Cross
London SE14 6NW
020 7078 5300
info@gold.ac.uk
www.gold.ac.uk
www.goldsmithssu.org
Open days 2020:
June 20

The Times and The Sunday Times Rankings		
Overall Ranking: 68 (last year: 71)		
Teaching quality	76.5%	=112
Student experience	72%	124
Research quality	33.4%	36
Entry standards	131	=67
Graduate prospects	58.3%	129
Good honours	81.9%	30
Expected completion rate	78.5%	112
Student/staff ratio	15.1	=50
Services and facilities	£2,902	18

submission judged world-leading or internationally excellent. The best results came in communication and media studies, and the college did particularly well in terms of the impact of its research. The entire submission in music was considered world-leading for its impact.

With only 6,000 undergraduates, Goldsmiths remains small for a multi-faculty university and intends to grow further in the next few years. It is based on a single campus that has a mixture of traditional and modern buildings.

Located in New Cross, southeast London, Goldsmiths is committed to increasing recruitment from the boroughs of Lewisham, Greenwich and Southwark. The Alchemy project, for example, provides music tuition for teenagers at risk of exclusion to try to develop their listening, communication and collaboration skills. About half of the undergraduates are from black, Asian and ethnic minority (Bame) communities and one in five are at least 21 on entry.

A peer-assisted learning scheme helps new arrivals to settle in with weekly sessions run by second- and third-year students. There are integrated work placements on many degrees, while workshops help students to develop entrepreneurial skills. The university's Gold award encourages students to develop the skills and experience that employers are looking for.

The campus has a thriving music scene. A varied events programme includes recitals, exhibitions, public lectures and readings. The students' union has a strong tradition in volunteering and has won awards for ethical and environmental campaigns.

Protesters staged more than 100 days of action, including a lengthy occupation, to demand a new strategy to combat racism after a black election candidate's poster was defaced. The college appointed a senior academic to investigate the significant gap between the proportions of Bame and white students awarded a first or 2:1 degree in 2017–18, but protesters argued that she was not given sufficient resources to address the problem. Our new social inclusion ranking records that gap at 23 percentage points, one of the widest in the country: 89% of white students leave with a first or 2:1, compared with 66% of black students.

There are almost 1,600 rooms available in halls of residence, many of which are in New Cross, and all are within a 30-minute commute of the campus. Priority for places is given to international students and new undergraduates from outside the London area. There is a well-equipped and affordable gym on campus, but the outdoor pitches are half an hour away.

Tuition fees

» Fees for UK/EU students	£9,250
» Fees for International students 2020–21	£16,390–£22,590
» For scholarship and bursary information see www.gold.ac.uk/fees-funding/	
» Graduate salary	£20,000

Student numbers

Undergraduates	6,389	(158)
Postgraduates	2,292	(1,163)
Applications/places		12,905/2,615
Applications per place		4.9
Overall offer rate		78.5%
Unconditional offers		0%
International students		25.3%

Accommodation

University provided places: 1,483
Self-catered: £144–£318 per week
www.gold.ac.uk/accommodation/

Where do the students come from?

State schools (non-grammar)	87.5%	First generation students	44.3%	Black attainment gap	-23%
Grammar schools	3.3%	Deprived areas	5%	Disabled	8.4%
Independent schools	9.2%	All ethnic minorities	51%	Mature (over 21)	20.7%

Social inclusion ranking: 29

University of Greenwich

The university has been modernising the World Heritage site that it occupies overlooking the Thames. The historic Dreadnought building reopened in November 2018 after a £23m refurbishment which has brought together the library and students' union with student and academic services under one roof at the heart of the campus. An enclosed courtyard houses a cafe, gymnasium and basement bar.

In the same month, hi-tech forensic crime suites opened, equipped to cover all aspects of forensic work. The forensic science department is led by Linda Brownlow, who was formerly head of crime scene training for the Metropolitan Police.

The employment-related theme is one that the university has pursued consistently. The prize-winning Stockwell Street development, in Greenwich, is another example. Designed partly by the university's own specialists in architecture, it includes 14 landscaped roof terraces and has a large architecture studio, a model-making workshop, and TV and sound studios, plus the main library and other facilities.

Greenwich has almost trebled the number of undergraduates taking work placements and is the only university in the country to have an on-campus strategic relationship with a recruitment firm. The service aims to place final-year undergraduates or recent graduates in full-time,

graduate-level jobs that are suited to their skills, as well as finding them high-quality internships and other opportunities along the way.

New degrees for 2020 include digital media design and development, games design and development, and a degree apprenticeship in midwifery. The university has approved 22 degree apprenticeship programmes and expects to have 400 trainees by 2022.

Applications have dropped by a third since 2014, but the university has managed to keep the numbers starting courses relatively stable without compromising on entry standards.

Student satisfaction with both teaching quality and the student experience has risen further this year, cementing Greenwich's place back in our top 100. The university took silver in the Teaching Excellence Framework, attracting accolades for course design and assessment practices that stretch students. Assessors said personalised provision secures good engagement and commitment to learning from most students, and that the university had invested in high-quality physical and digital resources.

Greenwich has scored well in our first two social inclusion tables, taking more than half of its undergraduates from ethnic minorities and a similar proportion from households where parents are not educated to degree level. There is an unusually wide range of scholarships and bursaries, and those who do not qualify for them receive an

---

Maritime Greenwich Campus
Old Royal Naval College
Park Row
London SE10 9LS
020 8331 9000
courseinfo@gre.ac.uk
www.gre.ac.uk
www.greenwichsu.co.uk
Open days 2020:
February 29, June 27

The Times and The Sunday Times **Rankings**
Overall Ranking: 84 (last year: 100)

Teaching quality	79.9%	=66
Student experience	78.4%	65
Research quality	4.9%	=93
Entry standards	137	=52
Graduate prospects	70.3%	101
Good honours	77%	53
Expected completion rate	82%	89
Student/staff ratio	17.4	=95
Services and facilities	£2,329	64

Aspire@Greenwich smart card worth £200 to spend on learning resources.

Redevelopment is about to start on one of the university's three campuses, Avery Hill, a Victorian mansion on the outskirts of southeast London, which is the base for education, health and the social sciences. Part of the campus has been sold to house a school, allowing teaching and learning facilities to be improved. There is already a £14m sports and teaching centre, and laboratories for health courses that replicate NHS wards. The campus also contains a student village of 1,300 rooms.

At Chatham, in Kent, the Medway campus houses the schools of pharmacy, science and engineering in the Natural Resources Institute, as well as nursing and some business courses. The campus, which is shared with the University of Kent, also has a student hub featuring study spaces plus a restaurant, bar and nightclub.

A new international college on the main campus, run jointly with a private company, will add to the 5,000 students from around the world by preparing others to take Greenwich degrees.

Greenwich has a rising number of staff with accredited teaching qualifications. A special programme to encourage innovation in its teaching and learning is designed to produce graduates who not only have good academic knowledge but also the skills sought by employers such as a high level of digital literacy, familiarity with new technology and expertise in social media.

The university has also been investing in research. It secured £20.7m of research and enterprise income in 2017–18, among the largest at any post-1992 institution. More than 200 academics entered the 2014 Research Excellence Framework – a considerable increase on 2008 – and 42% of their work was placed in the top two categories. The new Institute of Lifecourse Development will bring together the university's research and practice across education, health and human sciences.

Greenwich was in the top 15 in the 2019 People & Planet University League for environmental performance, partly due to progress towards a longstanding commitment to cut carbon emissions.

Sports facilities include two all-weather pitches at the Avery Hill campus. Record numbers are engaging with sports clubs and societies.

The residential stock has also been expanded. All new entrants who apply in time are guaranteed accommodation, although those who apply by the end of June have priority for room selection.

Tuition fees

»	Fees for UK/EU students	£9,250
	Foundation courses	£6,165
»	Fees for International students 2019–20	£13,000
»	For scholarship and bursary information see www.gre.ac.uk/study/finance	
»	Graduate salary	£22,500

Student numbers

Undergraduates	12,358 (2,382)
Postgraduates	1,591 (2,474)
Applications/places	23,545/4,555
Applications per place	5.2
Overall offer rate	78.9%
Unconditional offers	0%
International students	18.8%

Accommodation

University provided places: 2,541
Self-catered: £116–£280 per week
First years guaranteed accommodation
www.gre.ac.uk/accommodation

Where do the students come from?

State schools (non-grammar)	91.3%	First generation students	55.8%	
Grammar schools	5.3%	Deprived areas	8.9%	
Independent schools	3.5%	All ethnic minorities	55.2%	

Social inclusion ranking: 37

Black attainment gap	-21.1%
Disabled	5%
Mature (over 21)	31%

Harper Adams University

A purple patch for Harper Adams is set to continue in 2020 with the opening of the UK's ninth veterinary school, in partnership with Keele University. Harper Adams is runner-up for our overall University of the Year award, as well as being named Modern University of the Year for the second time in four years. It tops our rankings of modern universities for the fourth successive year, breaking into our elite top 20 to boot – a first for a university created since 1992.

Harper Adams is one of only two institutions to strike gold in successive years in the Teaching Excellence Framework (TEF). Although the institution was not required to be reassessed, vice-chancellor David Llewellyn said the university wanted to test its performance against the latest measures.

The new veterinary school will marry the excellence in animal health found at Harper Adams with Keele's strength in basic science and medicine. Students on the five-year programme will have a "home" campus but will have access to new facilities and support at both.

Both applications and enrolments were steady in 2018. Improved scores in the National Student Survey this year have further bolstered Harper Adams's reputation.

The university is based on a single campus in the Shropshire countryside, with a course portfolio that extends far beyond agriculture to business, veterinary nursing and physiotherapy, land and property management, engineering and food studies. Veterinary science is the latest of a number of new subjects to be introduced as Harper Adams widens its scope.

Degree apprenticeships are in development for 2020 in geospatial mapping and for environmental practitioners and professional advisers in agriculture and horticulture. There is also a new five-week course, split between the UK and Holland, for people in the agricultural industry to adopt precision technology.

The university is also introducing a range of extended degree programmes in 2019 and 2020, leading to standard or honours degrees, subject to students' performance. The extra year will prepare students who lack the necessary qualifications for immediate entry to degree courses.

There are more than 4,500 students, but little more than half of them are on campus at any one time. The rest are on placement years or accredited part-time programmes in industry. Contrary to the stereotypes associated with its agricultural specialisms, the majority of entrants to degree courses – and an even bigger majority of the applicants – are female.

Harper Adams is investing £700,000 over three years in teaching and learning

Edgmond
Newport
Shropshire TF10 8NB
01952 815 000
admissions@harper-adams.ac.uk
www.harper-adams.ac.uk
www.harpersu.com
Open days 2020:
March 21 (Animal & Veterinary Science);
March 25 (Land & Property management)

The Times and The Sunday Times Rankings
Overall Ranking: 17 (last year: =33)

Teaching quality	83.4%	=16
Student experience	82.4%	11
Research quality	5.7%	85
Entry standards	134	=58
Graduate prospects	72.9%	=85
Good honours	74.4%	=72
Expected completion rate	91.3%	32
Student/staff ratio	13.7	=22
Services and facilities	£3,793	2

initiatives, including the provision of more e-learning and the appointment of teaching fellows in each department.

The university's work on agri-technologies persuaded the government to designate the local area as one of three pilot High Potential Opportunity locations, the only one focused on agritech. A hub for the development, testing and sharing of technologies to boost productivity in farming and the food supply chain opened in 2018. Harper Adams is also a partner in a world-leading agritech research and innovation facility to be built in nearby Newport.

A commercial farm outside the town includes the Ancellor Yard, a redevelopment of the original courtyard of the home of Thomas Harper Adams, after whom the university is named. The university has now bought 239 acres of neighbouring land, bringing its farmed acreage to over 1,500. The long-term strategy is to develop teaching and applied research activities, which range from dairy and poultry production to arable farming and horticulture.

The university achieved a world first with its Hands Free Hectare, where a crop was grown and harvested without human hands touching it, demonstrating the automation of agricultural technology. The project won the Future Food prize at the BBC's Food and Farming awards in 2018 and was recognised by a Queen's Anniversary prize for higher and further education.

Harper Adams entered only 17 staff for the 2014 Research Excellence Framework – two fewer than in 2008 – but more than half of their work was considered internationally excellent or world-leading. There are links with four agricultural universities in China and, since February, one in Holland.

The students' union, careers service and cafe are all under one roof at the heart of the campus, where open access computers allow students to work and socialise in the same area. The Bamford library holds one of the largest specialist land-based collections.

Sports facilities include a shooting ground as well as a gymnasium, heated outdoor swimming pool, rugby, cricket, football and hockey pitches, tennis courts and an all-weather sports pitch. There is a dance/fitness studio and even a 4x4 club, as well as a rowing club that operates from nearby Shrewsbury. The social scene is strong despite the rural setting.

There are more than 800 residential places on campus, with first-years taking priority. A shuttle bus runs at key times of the day for students living in Newport to get to the campus.

Tuition fees

» Fees for UK/EU students	£9,250
» Fees for International students 2020–21	£10,800
» For scholarship and bursary information see www.harper-adams.ac.uk/apply/finance/	
» Graduate salary	£21,000

Student numbers

Undergraduates	2,337	(2,470)
Postgraduates	96	(408)
Applications/places		2,805/665
Applications per place		4.2
Overall offer rate		70.5%
Unconditional offers		0%
International students		3.7%

Accommodation

University provided places: 830
Catered costs: £105–£162 per week
Self-catered: £120 per week
First years given priority for accommodation
www.harper-adams.ac.uk/university-life/accommodation

Where do the students come from?

State schools (non-grammar)	80.1%	First generation students	38.7%	Black attainment gap	n/a
Grammar schools	5.8%	Deprived areas	6.5%	Disabled	16.3%
Independent schools	14.1%	All ethnic minorities	2.3%	Mature (over 21)	5.3%

Social inclusion ranking: 88

Heriot-Watt University

Heriot-Watt has campuses in Dubai and Malaysia, as well as its native Edinburgh, and encourages students to take advantage of all of them through its Go Global programme. Undergraduates can explore new horizons during an inter-campus transfer for a semester, full academic year or even longer and the system earned Heriot-Watt our inaugural award for International University of the Year in 2017.

Little more than a third of the university's 30,000 students are based on the Riccarton campus, Heriot-Watt's main administrative headquarters on the outskirts of Edinburgh. Others are studying with "collaborative partners" in 150 countries, as well as on the two international campuses. There are also two smaller bases in Scotland, in Orkney and Galashiels, but even a third of those studying in Scotland come from abroad, making the university one of the most global institutions in the UK.

Heriot-Watt has been moving gradually up our top 40 and is the leading university in Scotland for graduate salaries six months after graduation. But applications are down by more than one fifth since 2015 and the numbers starting courses dropped by more than 15% in 2018.

The university is gradually renewing the 1970s buildings on its attractive main campus, adding several hundred study spaces in a phased refurbishment of the main library, which now has more space for digital learning and collaborative study. Last summer the Grid (Global Research, Innovation and Discovery) building opened, designed with open learning spaces to encourage collaboration. Its enterprise hub supports business innovation and promotes emerging technology and inventions, encouraging staff and students to pursue the commercial potential of their ideas.

Close links with business and industry have helped the university to secure one of the largest allocations of graduate apprenticeships for three years in a row. Skills Development Scotland awarded it more than 200 funded places for the 2019–20 academic year – 50 more than last time. The seven existing programmes cover engineering, design and management, and there are plans to extend the range by September 2020. Statistical data science and computer science have been added to the portfolio of traditional degrees.

The university traces its history back to 1821, when it was the world's first mechanics' institute. Its name honours George Heriot and James Watt, two giants of industry and commerce. The current strategic plan stresses that the university's ambitions will require all academic staff to perform at internationally competitive levels of creativity in research, scholarship and teaching. The panel awarding

Edinburgh EH14 4AS
0131 451 3376
ugadmissions@hw.ac.uk
www.hw.ac.uk
www.hwunion.com
Open days 2020:
see website

EDINBURGH
Belfast
London
Cardiff

***The Times* and *The Sunday Times* Rankings**
Overall Ranking: 33 (last year: =35)

Teaching quality	77.9%	=98
Student experience	77.9%	=77
Research quality	36.7%	28
Entry standards	163	=22
Graduate prospects	79.3%	51
Good honours	79.7%	41
Expected completion rate	86.8%	=56
Student/staff ratio	17.8	=99
Services and facilities	£3,217	9

Heriot-Watt silver in the Teaching Excellence Framework praised its course design "directly informed by research activity".

More than 80% of the work submitted for the 2014 Research Excellence Framework was rated world-leading or internationally excellent, and Heriot-Watt was among the leaders in the UK in mathematics, general engineering and architecture, planning and the built environment, where it made joint submissions with the University of Edinburgh. Heriot-Watt did particularly well in the assessments of the impact of research, and features in the top 30 of our research ranking.

The £20m Lyell Centre is a main research facility for geological, petroleum and marine sciences, staffed by the university and the British Geological Survey, which has its Scottish headquarters there.

The main campus hosts Oriam, Scotland's national centre for performance in many sports, where world-class facilities are available to Heriot-Watt students. The £33m complex features a Hampden Park replica pitch, outdoor synthetic and grass pitches, a nine-court sports hall, a 3G indoor pitch and a fitness suite, plus medical facilities.

Heriot-Watt has a professional director of music and offers a number of music scholarships, as well as a varied programme of events. The Edinburgh halls of residence are conveniently placed and house more than 2,000 students. Regular bus services link the campus to the city centre and its wide range of nightlife and cultural events.

The Orkney campus caters exclusively for postgraduates and specialises in renewable energy, while the Scottish Borders campus, 35 miles south of Edinburgh in Galashiels, specialises in textiles, fashion and design. It offers one of the few degrees in the world in menswear and the only course in Scotland in fashion communication. Heriot-Watt and Borders College share the merged campus, in a region that has been poorly served for higher education.

The Dubai campus, which opened 14 years ago, has almost 4,000 students taking business, engineering, science and technology, or textiles and design courses, and numbers are expected to rise further. The five-year-old £35m Malaysian campus in the administrative capital of Putrajaya, near Kuala Lumpur, has space for up to 4,000 students to take degrees in science, engineering, business, mathematics and design.

Tuition fees

- » Fees for Scottish/EU students   £0–£1,820
  RUK fees   £9,250 (capped at £27,750 for 4-year courses)
- » Fees for International students 2020–21   £15,080–£19,400
- » For scholarship and bursary information see
  www.hw.ac.uk/study/fees-funding.htm
- » Graduate salary   £24,500

Student numbers

Undergraduates	**7,255**	**(404)**
Postgraduates	**2,018**	**(1,232)**
Applications/places		**10,845/1,800**
Applications per place		**6**
Overall offer rate		**85.4%**
Unconditional offers		**13.7%**
International students		**28.8%**

Accommodation

University provided places: 2,039
Self-catered: £115–£210 per week
First years guaranteed accommodation
www.hw.ac.uk/uk/edinburgh/accommodation.htm

Where do the students come from?

State schools (non-grammar)	80.5%	First generation students	31.8%	
Grammar schools	7.8%	Deprived areas	11.2%	
Independent schools	11.7%	All ethnic minorities	14.5%	

Social inclusion ranking (Scotland): 8

Black attainment gap	-10%
Disabled	5.7%
Mature (over 21)	18.3%

University of Hertfordshire

Hertfordshire's upgrade to gold in the Teaching Excellence Framework (TEF) came too late to save it from a 16% drop in applications in 2018. A slightly higher offer rate helped to keep the decline in enrolments to manageable proportions, but the university has been reviewing its provision and considering cuts in some areas.

About a third of offers in 2018 were "conditional unconditional" – the type criticised by ministers because they require the applicant to make the university their first choice. The university has said offers of this sort will not be made for courses starting in 2020.

Students arriving then will have access to a £12m business and social hub on the de Havilland campus, in Hatfield. It will include social space, an area dedicated to business incubation and more teaching space for degree apprentices and MBA students. Hertfordshire was the original "business-facing" university.

The TEF panel was impressed by a strong emphasis on work-based learning, entrepreneurship and enterprise, with employability and transferable skills embedded in the curriculum. It noted high levels of investment in physical and digital resources and said courses benefited from "vocationally informed pedagogy supported by the university's educational research network".

Degree apprenticeships have been at the heart of the university's recent development, with each of the ten schools asked to develop programmes. There are now 14, and four more in development covering data science, advanced clinical practice, applied biomedical science and public sector management. The university expects to have 750 apprenticeship students by September 2020, three times the current total.

This should help broaden the intake further. Hertfordshire is one of the more socially inclusive universities in the UK and few can beat its recruitment from non-selective state schools, which stands at 94%. Half of Hertfordshire's students are the first in their family to go to university and nearly 60% of students come from ethnic minorities.

Hertfordshire's original College Lane campus is linked by cycle ways, footpaths and free shuttle buses to the £120m purpose-built de Havilland base, a 15-minute walk away. One of the UK's largest teaching observatories is to be found at Hertfordshire's third campus at Bayfordbury, featuring seven large optical telescopes, four radio telescopes and a high-definition planetarium. Astronomers from the university were credited in 2018 with the discovery of a new planet orbiting a distant star.

Hertfordshire has a strategic plan to deliver a "distinctive campus experience for students, staff and visitors, in which the dynamism of the university is embodied in its physical estate". It has spent £300,000 on quiet zones in its

---

College Lane
Hatfield AL10 9AB
01707 284 800
ask@herts.ac.uk
www.herts.ac.uk
www.hertfordshire.su
Open days 2020:
see website

The Times and The Sunday Times **Rankings**
Overall Ranking: 88 (last year: 90)

Teaching quality	78.8%	=86
Student experience	78.3%	=66
Research quality	5.6%	=86
Entry standards	115	=109
Graduate prospects	80.6%	=44
Good honours	64.9%	123
Expected completion rate	83.7%	=78
Student/staff ratio	16	=73
Services and facilities	£2,700	28

learning resource centres and the library has study rooms and small study pods.

The Hutton Hub on the College Lane site houses the students' union, a counselling centre, a pharmacy, banking facilities and a juice bar. The campus has a £50m science building, an art gallery in the media centre and the £38m Forum, which has three entertainment spaces, a restaurant, cafe and multiple bars. The Automotive Centre on College Lane delivers up-to-date engineering teaching and many Formula One teams include Hertfordshire graduates.

The university launched a new nursing simulation laboratory and ward last summer, with the help of a £165,000 grant from Hertfordshire Local Enterprise Partnership.

The Herts Mobile app provides personalised notifications and other information, such as the availability of computers by building, floor and zone. A £2m wi-fi improvement project is under way, installing high-capacity access points. More than 400 different software applications are available for student use, including a Microsoft Office 365 account for the duration of their studies.

More than half the academic staff hold a teaching qualification and more than 85% of single honours students leave Hertfordshire with a degree that has professional accreditation or approval. Most courses offer work placements and study abroad. The Go Herts award, which attracted praise from the TEF panel for its links with degree programmes, gives students formal recognition for extracurricular activities.

The university plays an important role in the regional economy. It runs seven subsidiary companies including the independent Uno regional bus service, which has expanded to run urban bus networks in St Albans and Northampton as well as routes between Milton Keynes, Bedford and Flitwick for Cranfield University.

In the 2014 Research Excellence Framework, more than half the work submitted by Hertfordshire was placed in one of the top two categories. The best results were in history: 45% of the submission was assessed as world-leading and all achieved the top grade for external impact.

The £15m Hertfordshire Sports Village includes a 110-station health and fitness centre, 25-metre pool, physiotherapy and sports injury clinic and a large, multipurpose sports hall. The university has 4,800 study bedrooms on its books, having added 2,500 residential places since 2015 at a cost of £120m and refurbished 500 more. The campus is just 20 minutes from London by train.

Tuition fees

»	Fees for UK/EU students	£9,250
	Foundation courses	£6,165
»	Fees for International students 2020–21	£13,000
»	For scholarship and bursary information see www.herts.ac.uk/study/fees-and-funding	
»	Graduate salary	£22,000

Student numbers

Undergraduates	**15,899**	**(2,939)**
Postgraduates	**1,787**	**(3,777)**
Applications/places		**21,995/4,960**
Applications per place		**4.4**
Overall offer rate		**79.2%**
Unconditional offers		**30.3%**
International students		**16.4%**

Accommodation

University provided places: 4,800
Self-catered: £96–£197 per week
www.herts.ac.uk/life/student-accommodation

Where do the students come from?

State schools (non-grammar)	94%	First generation students	50%	Black attainment gap	-28.6%
Grammar schools	3.1%	Deprived areas	7.5%	Disabled	4.7%
Independent schools	2.9%	All ethnic minorities	58.5%	Mature (over 21)	19.1%

Social inclusion ranking: 52

University of the Highlands and Islands

The University of the Highlands and Islands (UHI) is a federation of 13 colleges and research institutions spread across hundreds of miles in the Scottish Highlands and islands, with more than 70 local learning centres and large numbers of part-time staff and further education students. As such, it is a key resource for the region and unique in its mission – but it does not feature in our league tables because its structure does not lend itself to comparison with traditional universities.

Setting up the university was a difficult process over a number of years, but there is no doubting the success of the project. Both applications and enrolments have risen every year for the past decade and did so again in 2019. The undergraduate intake has increased by more than a third in the current decade.

More provision in nursing and education has boosted the demand for places, and there has even been growth on part-time courses, which have been in decline nationally. More than half of UHI's students are over 21 at the start of their course.

More than 70% of the students are drawn from the Highlands and Islands. But the university has begun to attract greater numbers from the rest of Scotland, other parts of the UK and overseas. It has been adding residential places accordingly, and now has more than 630 rooms in nine colleges. Teaching is increasingly through "blended" learning, combining online and face-to-face tuition with small class sizes and extensive use of video conferencing, although some courses are available entirely online.

UHI has taken over the pre-registration programmes in mental health nursing and adult nursing previously delivered by the University of Stirling in Inverness and Stornoway, adding 40 staff and 300 students. A £19m health, social care and life sciences school was established in 2017 with the aim of further extending UHI's work in these areas.

This includes collaboration with Dundee and St Andrews universities on the development of Scotland's first graduate entry medical programme (ScotGem) to enhance remote and rural training and the supply of GPs. The first 55 ScotGem students started in September 2018.

The university has since received £3.75m from the European Regional Development Fund to enhance its facilities at a new building on the Inverness campus for a life sciences innovation centre. The centre will be part of a larger custom-built facility supported by the Inverness and Highlands City-Region Deal to promote engagement between the health service, the academic sector and commercial partners.

New degrees in sports therapy and rehabilitation, philosophy and bioscience

---

Executive Office
12b Ness Walk, Inverness IV3 5SQ
01463 279 180
info@uhi.ac.uk
www.uhi.ac.uk
www.uhi.ac.uk/en/students/get-involved/students-association/
Open days 2020: February 20,
March 26, May 16
(nursing, Inverness);
August 4 (open evening, Inverness College)

***The Times and The Sunday Times* Rankings**
Overall Ranking: n/a
No data available

were launched in 2019, with optometry, creative writing, financial services, software development and theology, philosophy and education for intending teachers to come in 2020. There are now nearly 10,000 higher education students and 30,000 taking further education courses.

The university offers one accelerated degree in geography, taught over three years rather than the usual four, but has not so far extended the option to other subjects. Entry requirements on other courses are not high: university policy is to pitch offers at the minimum level required to complete the course.

UHI's colleges spread from Dunoon in western Scotland to the village of Scalloway, the ancient capital of the Shetland Islands, in the north. The university's network of campuses is much wider, however. Argyll College, for example, has 13 sites on the mainland and on islands such as Arran, Islay and Mull.

Some colleges are relatively large and located in the urban centres such as Perth, Elgin and Inverness, while others are smaller institutions, including some whose primary focus is research.

The federation operates from some spectacular locations. Lews Castle College UHI in Stornoway in the Outer Hebrides, is set in 600 acres of parkland and UHI claims that its harbourside Lochmaddy campus in North Uist is "possibly the UK's most attractive location to study art". North Highland College

UHI has an equestrian centre in Caithness, with international-sized outdoor and indoor arenas.

Sabhal Mor Ostaig UHI is the only Gaelic-medium college in the world, set in breathtaking scenery on the Isle of Skye. Across the university, many courses can be studied in the language. UHI was the first in Scotland to produce a Gaelic Language Plan, now on its third edition, which includes proposals to enhance the Gaelic curriculum, produce more bilingual resources for students and hold more Gaelic events. Donnie Munro, the former Runrig frontman, is director of development here.

There are a dozen specialist research facilities and an enterprise and research centre on the Inverness campus. They helped to produce some extremely good results in the 2014 Research Excellence Framework. Almost 70% of the research submitted for review was classified as world-leading or internationally excellent.

Tuition fees

» Fees for Scottish/EU students   £0–£1,820
  RUK fees   £9,000 (capped at £27,000 for 4-year courses)
» Fees for International students 2019–20   £11,650–£12,800
» For scholarship and bursary information see
  www.uhi.ac.uk/en/studying-at-uhi/first-steps/
  how-much-will-it-cost/
» Graduate salary   £19,000

Student numbers

Undergraduates	**5,421**	**(3,051)**
Postgraduates	**279**	**(572)**
Applications/places		**4,325/2,910**
Applications per place		**1.5**
Overall offer rate		**69.5%**
Unconditional offers		**0%**
International students		**3.2%**

Accommodation

University provided places: 632
Self-catered: £76–£144 per week
www.uhi.ac.uk/en/studying-at-uhi/first-steps/accommodation/

Where do the students come from?

State schools (non-grammar)	98.8%	First generation students	44.4%	Black attainment gap	n/a
Grammar schools	0%	Deprived areas	8.3%	Disabled	5.3%
Independent schools	1%	All ethnic minorities	5%	Mature (over 21)	53.1%

Social inclusion ranking (Scotland): 5

University of Huddersfield

Seven out of ten students leave Huddersfield with a professional qualification. Every undergraduate does some work experience as part of their degree course and a third take extended placements in business or industry, putting the university in the top 15 in the UK on this measure.

Many students now develop their own businesses for the work placement component of their course, taking advantage of the advice and facilities available at the university's Young Entrepreneur Centre. Nominations for a new chancellor were being sought after Prince Andrew stepped down last year.

A consistent and effective focus on teaching quality has paid off for Huddersfield with a series of awards and steady progress up our league table. It has the UK's highest proportion of staff with a postgraduate teaching qualification (94%), a gold rating in the Teaching Excellence Framework (TEF) and in 2017 won the first Global Teaching Excellence Award.

The TEF panel complimented the university on the way that the effective use of learning analytics allowed targeted and timely interventions to boost students' results. It also commended an institution-wide strategy for assessment and feedback, which ensures that all students are challenged to achieve their full potential.

However, the university's successes are still not fully reflected in admissions. The numbers starting degrees fell slightly in 2018. Applications were also down, by 8%, and declined again in the 2019 admissions cycle. They are down about 30% from their 2011 peak.

Last September's intake had a number of new degrees to choose from, including textiles, business data analytics, events management with digital marketing, sport and physical education, and sociology with social policy. Huddersfield has also been expanding its range of degree apprenticeships, adding advanced clinical practice and podiatry for 2019. Paramedic science is expected to begin in 2020.

The university is investing heavily on teaching and research facilities and is redeveloping a former industrial site and neighbouring land into the new Western Campus. A £30m home for the study of art, design and architecture has taken its first students. Named after Barbara Hepworth, the West Yorkshire-born sculptor, its main frontage will overlook the Huddersfield Narrow Canal, which runs through the heart of the Queensgate campus.

Another £18.2m has been spent on a new science block. The Joseph Priestley Building includes a laboratory for sixth-formers and college students to carry out practical work in areas such as DNA analysis, microbiology, chemical synthesis and forensics.

Queensgate
Huddersfield HD1 3DH
01484 472 625
study@hud.ac.uk
www.hud.ac.uk
www.huddersfield.su
Open days 2020:
see website

The Times and The Sunday Times Rankings
Overall Ranking: 61 (last year: 62)

Teaching quality	81.2%	=45
Student experience	78.3%	=66
Research quality	9.4%	61
Entry standards	131	=67
Graduate prospects	80%	48
Good honours	74.6%	70
Expected completion rate	84.2%	72
Student/staff ratio	1750	98
Services and facilities	£2,417	55

Huddersfield has always had a proud record for widening participation in higher education. One undergraduate in six comes from an area without a tradition of higher education, and the university has a growing focus on supporting as well as recruiting such students. The last cohort of graduates included 120 who were admitted with three Ds or less at A-level – 5% of the total. Fifty of them left with a first.

The prize-winning Flying Start scheme helps all new undergraduates find their feet. Its two-week timetable of special sessions is designed to stimulate academic interest, develop good study habits and provide opportunities for students to work and engage socially. Students take part in quizzes and debates, subject-based film clubs, lab skills workshops, campus orienteering and trips, as well as meeting successful alumni and discussing their career goals. Huddersfield's seminars, as well as lectures, are filmed so students can revisit them later online.

Some of the most successful subject areas for Huddersfield in the 2014 Research Excellence Framework were in the arts and social sciences. The university did well overall, entering almost a third of its academics for assessment. Nearly 60% of their work was rated world-leading or internationally excellent. There were particularly good results in music, drama and performing arts, as well as in English, social work and social policy.

Huddersfield has close relations with local business and industry. It is in the top ten universities for the scale of its knowledge transfer partnerships.

The university does not own any accommodation, but its preferred provider, Digs, has enough places – more than 1,600 – to guarantee a room to new entrants. Most are in the Storthes Hall Park student village, with additional housing available at Ashenhurst, just over a mile from the campus.

The Student Central building has a good range of sports facilities, including an 80-station gym, and the town's leisure centre is within a ten-minute walk of campus. Town-and-gown relations are good, although students tend to base their social life around the students' union. Public transport provides easy access to Leeds and Manchester, which offer nightlife on a different scale.

Tuition fees

» Fees for UK/EU students	£9,250
» Fees for International students 2020–21	£14,500–£17,400
» For scholarship and bursary information see www.hud.ac.uk/undergraduate/fees-and-finance	
» Graduate salary	£20,000

Student numbers

Undergraduates	12,940	(1,223)
Postgraduates	1,991	(2,091)
Applications/places	17,415/3,915	
Applications per place	4.4	
Overall offer rate	86.7%	
Unconditional offers	0%	
International students	18.6%	

Accommodation

University provided places: 1,666
Self-catered: £70–£110 per week
First years guaranteed accommodation
www.hud.ac.uk/uni-life/accommodation

Where do the students come from?

State schools (non-grammar)	95.4%	First generation students	56.4%	Black attainment gap	-21.1%
Grammar schools	3.3%	Deprived areas	16.5%	Disabled	8.5%
Independent schools	1.3%	All ethnic minorities	38.7%	Mature (over 21)	21.3%

Social inclusion ranking: 15

University of Hull

Hull may have to cut its costs by £20m – roughly 10% – over four years after a review found that the university's financial position was "unsustainable" and its league table position "untenable". It dropped out of our top 100 for the first time last year – and despite leaping up 26 places this year it remains among the lowest-ranked of the pre-1992 generation of universities.

Professor Susan Lea, the vice-chancellor, has told staff that Hull's future is as a smaller university of higher quality. It is in the throes of a £300m investment programme to boost the student experience, teaching and research, but the numbers starting degrees have dropped by 25% from their peak. Recruitment to language degrees, apart from Chinese, was suspended in 2019 and some philosophy courses were cut.

The university said its plans, which include high-quality, on-campus accommodation and a six-year agreement to be an official partner of Team GB for activities surrounding the summer and winter Olympic Games, would benefit students and help to attract more applicants.

Hull is expanding the medical school it shares with the University of York, after being awarded another 90 places for doctors, a 69% increase in capacity. In the £25m Allam medical building, opened by the Queen and substantially bankrolled by local businessman Assem Allam, medical students can work alongside nursing, midwifery and allied health undergraduates, as well as PhD students, advanced nurse practitioners and physician associates.

Industry-standard recording and performance facilities have been installed in the redeveloped Middleton Hall, while a £28m upgrading of the Brynmor Jones library has added an art gallery and provided a new centrepiece for the university.

A £4.5m redevelopment of the students' union is due to be complete by September 2020 and a £16m enhancement of the sports facilities is under way.

Hull applied without success to have its silver rating in the Teaching Excellence Framework (TEF) upgraded, arguing that initiatives such as its Curriculum 2016+ strategy for teaching and learning were improving the student experience, but were too recent to be reflected in the data considered in the original assessment. The upgrade was refused but the panel praised Hull's course design and assessment practices for stretching and challenging students, and was impressed by investment in physical and digital infrastructure.

Hull won a Queen's Anniversary prize for its research into slavery and played a key role in shaping the UK's Modern Slavery Act. The university's strength in politics is reflected in a steady flow of graduates into the House of Commons. The Westminster-Hull internship programme offers a year-long placement for British politics and legislative studies students.

Cottingham Road
Hull HU6 7RX
01482 466 100
admission@hull.ac.uk
www.hull.ac.uk
www.hullstudent.com
Open days 2020:
see website

The Times and The Sunday Times Rankings
Overall Ranking: 77 (last year: =103)

Teaching quality	80.8%	52
Student experience	77.1%	=91
Research quality	16.7%	54
Entry standards	126	=77
Graduate prospects	76.0%	=66
Good honours	70.4%	=97
Expected completion rate	83%	=83
Student/staff ratio	16.2	=77
Services and facilities	£2,370	62

The Curriculum 2016+ programme seeks to develop a distinctive "vision for teaching and learning", integrating teaching skills with subject knowledge and technology to produce highly employable graduates. Undergraduates have the option of taking a 20-credit module on career management skills. The careers service approaches undergraduates early in their studies and the Enterprise Centre has a successful record with those who would rather start their own businesses.

More than a third of Hull's undergraduates are local, while 22% come from areas of low participation in higher education – significantly more than the national average for Hull's courses and entry qualifications. The university expects two-thirds of new undergraduates to qualify for a bursary or scholarship. They include merit scholarships of £2,000 in the first year for students, regardless of income, who manage at least 120 UCAS tariff points.

New degrees planned for 2020, pending validation, include physiotherapy, cybersecurity, mathematics with statistics, and geology.

Some include a foundation year, extended placement or year abroad. The university is also expanding its provision for degree apprentices, and expects to have 350 by September 2020, with new programmes in computer science and healthcare.

More than 60% of the work entered for the 2014 Research Excellence Framework was rated as world-leading or internationally excellent, although Hull made a relatively small submission for a pre-1992 university. The best results were in the allied health category, where 87% of the research was awarded three or four stars, while geography and computer science also did well.

The university's new Olympic partnership will involve students in a range of subjects, from sports science to marketing, logistics, healthcare and engineering. There will also be opportunities to volunteer and participate in Team GB events. New sports facilities will include a 12-court sports hall, 120-station fitness suite and floodlit 3G pitches, as well as a fitness and conditioning suite.

Another 1,450 residential places are being developed by the University Partnerships Programme to supplement the existing 2,850 study bedrooms and meet "rising student expectations", helping to maintain the university's guarantee of accommodation to new entrants.

The city now has plenty of student-orientated nightlife and is less than an hour from Leeds by train.

Tuition fees

»	Fees for UK/EU students	£9,250
	Foundation courses	£7,195
»	Fees for International students 2020–21	£14,500–£17,200
	Medicine	£33,000
»	For scholarship and bursary information see www.hull.ac.uk/money	
»	Graduate salary	£21,500

Student numbers

Undergraduates	**12,077**	**(1,311)**
Postgraduates	**1,509**	**(690)**
Applications/places		**13,400/3,770**
Applications per place		**3.6**
Overall offer rate		**90%**
Unconditional offers		**0%**
International students		**12.4%**

Accommodation

University provided places: 2,761
Catered costs: £125–£160 per week
Self-catered: £79–£195 per week
First years guaranteed accommodation
www.hull.ac.uk/choose-hull/student-life/accommodation/accommodation.aspx

Where do the students come from?

State schools (non-grammar)	91%	First generation students	49.2%	
Grammar schools	3.5%	Deprived areas	22%	
Independent schools	5.5%	All ethnic minorities	11.9%	

Social inclusion ranking: 34

Black attainment gap	-10.1%
Disabled	5.6%
Mature (over 21)	33.1%

Imperial College London

All 106 undergraduate programmes at Imperial have been reviewed as part of a new learning and teaching strategy that seeks to make courses more interactive and prepare students more effectively for the world of work and the global challenges of the future. Laboratory exercises have been restructured, digital technologies will be used more often, and there will be greater opportunities to collaborate, for example in multidisciplinary projects.

To facilitate this radical change, more than 100 classrooms, lecture theatres and other learning spaces have been refurbished to make them brighter and more flexible. Timetables are being developed between departments, which have also promised to work more closely with central support services to aid students' wellbeing and to offer more staff-student social events.

Imperial has created a number of projects aimed at making studying and research more collaborative. The StudentShapers programme pairs students with staff on projects to improve curricula and teaching methods.

All undergraduates now take an I-Explore module in their second or third year in a subject other than their specialism. They can be multidisciplinary, or in the humanities or social sciences, business, or a different Stem subject (science, technology, engineering and maths) in order to broaden students' knowledge.

The college hopes the changes will improve student satisfaction, which has been a major focus for consultation. Scores in the National Student Survey have fallen further ahead of the changes: Imperial is still in the bottom ten in the UK for the sections of the survey devoted to teaching quality, while scores for the wider student experience have slipped back again, leaving the university in the bottom half of our rankings on that measure.

Overall, however, Imperial has never been out of the top five in our league table and features in the top ten of both the QS and Times Higher Education world rankings. It was named by Reuters as the third most innovative university in Europe – and top in the UK.

Imperial won gold in the government's Teaching Excellence Framework (TEF), with the panel praising an "exceptionally stimulating and stretching academic, vocational and professional education that challenges students to achieve their full potential".

This success followed even greater plaudits in the 2014 Research Excellence Framework, when Imperial was found to have greater impact on the economy and society than any other university – 90% of its submission was rated as world-leading or internationally excellent overall, bettered only by Cambridge.

Imperial's new 23-acre campus is taking shape in White City, west London, where a

South Kensington Campus
Exhibition Road
London SW7 2AZ
020 7589 5111
www.imperial.ac.uk/study/ug/
apply/contact/
www.imperial.ac.uk
www.imperialcollegeunion.org
Open days 2020:
June 24/25; September 19

The Times and The Sunday Times Rankings
Overall Ranking: 4 (last year: 4)

Teaching quality	75.1%	120
Student experience	77.9%	=77
Research quality	56.2%	2
Entry standards	206	4
Graduate prospects	90.4%	2
Good honours	89.2%	9
Expected completion rate	96.5%	4
Student/staff ratio	11.4	7
Services and facilities	£3,767	3

community of research-focused businesses is in place at the Translation & Innovation Hub (I-Hub). The Molecular Sciences Research Hub opened in April 2019 – at £167m, the most expensive new university building in London this century. The full White City development will cost a total of £3bn.

The college now has nine sites in London, with teaching bases attached to a number of hospitals in central and west London. The faculty of medicine is one of Europe's largest in terms of its staff and student numbers, while the UK's first Academic Health Science Centre (AHSC), run in partnership with Imperial College Healthcare NHS Trust, aims to translate research advances into patient care. Imperial is also a partner in a new medical school in Singapore, run jointly with Nanyang Technological University.

Undergraduates in most subjects are based at the original South Kensington campus, which includes the business school and the Dyson School of Design Engineering, funded through a £12m donation from the inventor's James Dyson Foundation. Imperial is unique in the UK for providing teaching and research in the full range of engineering disciplines. It describes itself as the only UK university to focus exclusively on science, medicine, engineering and business.

Only Cambridge, Oxford and St Andrews have higher average entry standards. Both applications and enrolments were steady in 2018, when barely more than four out of ten applicants received offers. Female applicants were more likely to secure an offer than their male counterparts in 2018, almost two-thirds of the undergraduates are men.

More than a third of the undergraduates are from independent schools – outnumbering recruits from comprehensives this year. The independent school contingent at Imperial is one of the biggest at any university and considerably more than the benchmark calculated by the Higher Education Statistics Agency (HESA). Another 23.6% of undergraduates are from grammar schools.

A bursary scheme provides support on a sliding scale for UK undergraduates with annual household incomes of up to £60,000. Four out of ten undergraduates qualified for some support.

Imperial is London's top sporting university, on the basis of results in the British Universities and Colleges Sports leagues. Outdoor sports facilities are remote, but there is a well-equipped campus sports centre with a swimming pool. New entrants are guaranteed one of the 2,700 residential places if they apply by the deadline.

Tuition fees

» Fees for UK/EU students	£9,250
» Fees for International students 2020–21	£31,750-£33,000
Medicine	£44,000
» For scholarship and bursary information see www.imperial.ac.uk/study/ug/fees-and-funding	
» Graduate salary	£30,000

Student numbers

Undergraduates	9,732	(0)
Postgraduates	7,192	(1,451)
Applications/places		21,310/2,805
Applications per place		7.6
Overall offer rate		46.2%
Unconditional offers		0%
International students		52%

Accommodation

University provided places: 2,700
Self-catered: £105–£288 per week
First years guaranteed accommodation
www.imperial.ac.uk/study/campus-life/accommodation/halls/

Where do the students come from?

State schools (non-grammar)	38.2%	First generation students	22.6%	
Grammar schools	23.4%	Deprived areas	3.8%	
Independent schools	38.3%	All ethnic minorities	50%	

Social inclusion ranking: 114

Black attainment gap	n/a
Disabled	3.5%
Mature (over 21)	2.1%

Keele University

Keele's biggest-ever investment in teaching and learning is taking shape on the UK's biggest campus, as the university prepares for a larger student population. Sir David Attenborough opened the new life sciences laboratories in May 2019 and the new Keele Business School building followed, providing new spaces for undergraduates and graduates, a big data laboratory and a business incubator.

Next comes a new veterinary school, to open this year in collaboration with Harper Adams University. The five-year bachelor of veterinary medicine and surgery degree will be delivered on both campuses, in partnership with local clinical providers and industry. It will provide new veterinary services on the campus, including a veterinary hospital and clinical skills centre.

Other developments taking shape include new central science laboratories, part of a £45m investment in the faculty of natural sciences. The four-floor building will feature open-plan teaching and research laboratories and social learning spaces.

Keele has declared an intention to grow by a third over five years, with postgraduates accounting for many of the new places. The target is beginning to look ambitious, however. Although the numbers starting first degrees grew by 5% in 2018, applications were down by 13.5% at the official deadline for courses starting last autumn.

Eight new degree courses admitted their first students in 2019. The latest offerings included health and wellbeing, psychology and education, and economic degrees twinned either with marketing or international business.

Keele achieved gold in the Teaching Excellence Framework (TEF). The panel said there was an institutional culture that "demonstrably values teaching as highly as research", with outstanding levels of student engagement and excellent teaching and assessment practices resulting in a commitment to learning.

The Keele Curriculum, introduced in 2012, attracted particular praise in the TEF assessment. It covers voluntary and sporting activities, as well as the academic core, contributing to the Keele University Skills Portfolio – the only such scheme in the UK to be accredited by the Institute of Leadership and Management.

The university's student charter identifies ten "graduate attributes" such as independent thinking, synthesising information, creative problem-solving, communicating clearly, and appreciating the social, environmental and global implications of all studies and activities. Keele has also been at the forefront of moves to record in more detail what graduates have achieved through a Higher Education Achievement Report.

Keele ST5 5BG
01782 734 010
admissions@keele.ac.uk
www.keele.ac.uk
www.keelesu.com
Open days 2020:
see website

The Times and The Sunday Times Rankings
Overall Ranking: 46 (last year: =48)

Teaching quality	82.5%	=26
Student experience	82.5%	10
Research quality	22.1%	53
Entry standards	127	=75
Graduate prospects	82.1%	=27
Good honours	74.2%	75
Expected completion rate	88.7%	47
Student/staff ratio	14.1	=26
Services and facilities	£2,087	88

It has generally been among the leaders on student satisfaction, this year ranking in the top 30 in the UK for satisfaction with teaching quality and 10th for the wider student experience enjoyed by undergraduates. Keele is a former winner of our University of the Year for Student Experience.

Nearly all undergraduates have the option of spending a semester abroad at a partner university. Nine out of ten undergraduates are state-educated, almost a third of them from black, Asian and minority ethnic backgrounds. The university has been trying to broaden its intake further by offering special projects and masterclasses in local schools. There is also an Excellence Scholarship, worth £1,000 in cash, paid to students who achieve the highest grades at A-level (or the equivalent), regardless of household income.

Keele's results in the 2014 Research Excellence Framework showed considerable improvement on the 2008 assessments. More than 70% of the work submitted was placed in the top two categories. Research in primary care and health sciences, pharmacy, chemistry, science and technology, the life sciences, and history scored particularly well.

The university has since launched the New Keele Deal, in which public and private sector partners support programmes to boost the local economy and provide opportunities for students and graduates. In its first two years, the university has worked with more than 300 local organisations, helping to generate employment opportunities worth £14.5m. The Keele Deal/Culture was launched in 2019 to make similar use of the university's cultural resources and assets.

Keele's 600 acres of parkland are located in the heart of England, near Stoke. A new hall of residence opened in 2018, the first of a series planned across the campus. A third of all undergraduates, as well as many postgraduates and even some staff, live on campus and their surroundings, which include an arboretum, have won a clutch of environmental awards. Students can grow their own fruit and vegetables on campus, and all undergraduates can take a module in sustainability or environmental studies.

The recently refurbished students' union organises entertainment on campus every night of the week during term and won the Best Bar None Gold Award for responsible drinking and a safe environment for six years in a row.

Sports facilities include a full-size 3G football pitch suitable for all-weather play in a variety of sports to supplement the indoor facilities.

Tuition fees

» Fees for UK/EU students £9,250
» Fees for International students 2020–21 £14,750–£24,000
  Medicine £32,000 (2019–20)
» For scholarship and bursary information see
  www.keele.ac.uk/study/undergraduate/tuitionfeesandfunding/
» Graduate salary £21,500

Student numbers

Undergraduates	7,821	(687)
Postgraduates	722	(1,639)
Applications/places		16,110/2,750
Applications per place		5.9
Overall offer rate		82.4%
Unconditional offers		9.9%
International students		10.2%

Accommodation

University provided places: 2,800
Self-catered: £87–£166 per week
www.keele.ac.uk/discover/accommodation/

Where do the students come from?

State schools (non-grammar)	82.6%	First generation students	43.5%	Black attainment gap	-14.3%
Grammar schools	9%	Deprived areas	16.7%	Disabled	7%
Independent schools	8.4%	All ethnic minorities	34.6%	Mature (over 21)	15.1%

Social inclusion ranking: 44

University of Kent

Kent has set itself the target of being one of the leading civic universities by 2025, aiming to balance its portfolio of courses to include more science and engineering as well as a larger cultural, creative and digital offer. Professor Karen Cox, the vice-chancellor, said there was no reason why Kent should not be in the top ten for education and the student experience, while raising its research profile.

The university has also been consulting the public on a new campus masterplan, which aims to make the 300-acre estate more sustainable and better organised, with the capacity to take more students. A new central university square has been proposed as a focal point, as well as a hotel and conference centre, but the low-rise parkland character of the original 1960s campus will be retained with a four-storey height limit on developments.

Kent was shortlisted for our University of the Year award in 2015, when its overall ranking rose as high as 23, well above its present level, which is only marginally up on last year.

More than 20 new degrees are being launched at Kent in 2019 and 2020, some adding a placement year or year abroad to existing programmes. Attention will focus on medicine, which takes its first students in 2020 at the new Kent and Medway Medical School, shared with Canterbury Christ Church. It will be the first medical school in the county, serving a rising population, and will work in partnership with the Brighton and Sussex Medical School.

Enrolments have held up well but departments have been asked to find savings, and voluntary redundancies are being sought in anticipation of an increasingly competitive climate for student recruitment and the possibility of lower tuition fees.

Kent is one of a handful of universities in the UK to operate a college system, one of the factors that secured gold in the Teaching Excellence Framework (TEF). The panel saw the system as a vital element underpinning a "flexible and personalised" approach to academic support and praised Kent's "outstanding" Student Success Project, which identifies trends in results and completion rates and acts to help those likely to fall behind.

Every student is attached to a college, although they do not select it themselves. Colleges are the focus of social life – especially in first year – and include academic as well as residential facilities.

Since the addition of the 800-bed Turing College in 2015, there have been six colleges in Canterbury and one on the university's Medway campus, at the old Chatham naval base, which is shared with Greenwich and Canterbury Christ Church universities. The site houses the university's newly refurbished

---

Canterbury CT2 7NZ
01227 768 896
information@kent.ac.uk
www.kent.ac.uk
www.kentunion.co.uk
Open days 2020:
see website

The Times and The Sunday Times **Rankings**
Overall Ranking: 54 (last year: 55)

Teaching quality	76.8%	110
Student experience	76.6%	95
Research quality	35.2%	33
Entry standards	135	=55
Graduate prospects	78.3%	55
Good honours	79.1%	43
Expected completion rate	89%	45
Student/staff ratio	18	=104
Services and facilities	£1,827	109

business school, the £50m School of Pharmacy and the purpose-built Centre for Music and Audio Technology.

The latest addition to the main campus overlooking Canterbury is an £18.8m economics building opened in time for the 2019–20 academic year, giving students on the popular course their own space for the first time. A £3m hub opened in 2018 in the Park Wood student village, which includes a shop, cafe/bar and dance studios.

Kent markets itself as "the UK's European university" and is perhaps the UK's most active participant in EU programmes. It has postgraduate sites in Brussels, Paris, Athens and Rome, as well as giving many undergraduates the option of a year abroad. Almost 40% of the academic staff are EU nationals and there are partnerships with more than 100 European universities. Brexit may be felt harder here than elsewhere, although the vice-chancellor has insisted the university's European outlook will not change.

"Europe is not the European Union," she said. "We are still the UK's European university. Europe is part of our DNA and we are determined to remain outward-looking. Our education and research reflects the expertise and knowledge of our European experts, and we embrace our collaborations with our European partners. That will not change."

Almost three-quarters of the work submitted for the 2014 Research Excellence Framework was judged world-leading or internationally excellent. Social work and social policy, music and drama, and modern languages, helped achieve its highest-ever ranking.

The university exceeds its benchmarks for widening access to higher education. About 750 students benefit from the Kent financial support package, which is worth £1,500 a year to state-educated students whose household income is below £42,875, if they meet other criteria, such as living in social housing.

Kent is one of the best-provided universities for accommodation, with 5,400 residential places in Canterbury and a further 1,100 at Liberty Quays in Medway. Campus security is good and the leisure facilities in Canterbury feature a well-equipped sports centre and multipurpose fitness and dance studio. The university is also a partner in the Medway Park sports centre, which has gym and swimming facilities..

Tuition fees

»	Fees for UK/EU students	£9,250
»	Fees for International students 2019–20	£16,200–£19,800
	Medicine	£55,000 (2020–21)
»	For scholarship and bursary information see www.kent.ac.uk/finance-student/fees/index.htm	
»	Graduate salary	£21,000

Student numbers

Undergraduates	15,332	(573)
Postgraduates	2,617	(1,302)
Applications/places	27,620/5,065	
Applications per place	5.5	
Overall offer rate	89.6%	
Unconditional offers	8.7%	
International students	22.9%	

Accommodation

University provided places: 5,379
Catered costs: £135–£251 per week
Self-catered: £119–£193 per week
First years guaranteed accommodation
www.kent.ac.uk/accommodation/

Where do the students come from?

State schools (non-grammar)	91.1%	First generation students	45.6%	
Grammar schools	2.3%	Deprived areas	10.3%	
Independent schools	6.6%	All ethnic minorities	37.6%	

Social inclusion ranking: =69

Black attainment gap	-27.4%
Disabled	7.2%
Mature (over 21)	9%

King's College London

King's enjoyed an increase of more than 12% in applications for courses beginning in September 2019, which was among the biggest rises at any university. New degrees in accounting and management, and social sciences helped to swell the numbers, but two-thirds of the increase came on existing courses.

The intake of new undergraduates has expanded by almost 50% over the course of this decade, although there was a dip in 2018. Almost three-quarters of all applicants now receive an offer, compared with less than 40% five years ago. Much of the expansion preceded the lifting of the government cap on student numbers.

In common with other London research universities, however, King's has struggled with student satisfaction and dropped down our league table as a result. Scores in the National Student Survey have improved this year from last year's nadir – contributing to a small rise in this year's overall ranking – but the university still ranks in the bottom ten for satisfaction with both teaching quality and the wider student experience.

In the QS World University Rankings, which are driven mainly by research and academic reputation, it occupies a position just three places lower than in our domestic table.

Professor Edward Byrne, the president and principal at King's, has said that education and the student experience will be the top priority in its strategy for the years running up to its 200th anniversary in 2029. The plans acknowledge growing demands for increased flexibility – from student time management to academics delivering world-class education alongside world-class research.

New degrees for 2020 include culture, media and creative industries, psychology and neuroscience, and general engineering.

Opportunities for students to engage with employers contributed to a silver award in the government's Teaching Excellence Framework. The panel commented approvingly on the "excellent" extent to which students were stretched academically and on a "strong research-led culture" that requires research staff to teach.

One of the oldest and largest colleges in the University of London, King's has more than 30,000 students, a third of them from outside the UK. More than half of its undergraduates are from ethnic minorities, but little more than 60% came from comprehensive schools and colleges. Overall, however, only Liverpool and Queen Mary, University of London, are more socially inclusive among the highly-selective Russell Group universities.

King's has a variety of schemes to broaden its intake and support those from low-income families. The Access to Medicine course, which attracts talented students from low-performing schools into medical degrees, has now been replicated for dentistry.

Strand
London WC2R 2LS
020 7848 5454
Admissions@kcl.ac.uk
www.kcl.ac.uk
www.kclsu.org
Open days 2020:
see website

The Times and The Sunday Times **Rankings**
Overall Ranking: 30 (last year: =35)

Teaching quality	74.3%	=122
Student experience	72.5%	122
Research quality	44.0%	9
Entry standards	169	17
Graduate prospects	84.5%	18
Good honours	86.7%	15
Expected completion rate	91.8%	29
Student/staff ratio	12.4	11
Services and facilities	£2,670	32

Four of the five campuses are within a single square mile around the banks of the Thames. The most recent addition was Bush House, former headquarters of the BBC World Service, opposite the original Strand campus, where the business school is based, with some student services and the faculty of social science.

The Strand site and the Waterloo campus house most of the non-medical departments. KCL had already expanded into the East Wing of Somerset House, providing impressive premises for the Dickson Poon School of Law.

Nursing and midwifery and some biomedical subjects are based at Waterloo, while medicine and dentistry are mainly at Guy's Hospital, near London Bridge, and the St Thomas' Hospital campus, across the river from the Houses of Parliament. The Denmark Hill campus, in south London, is home to the Institute of Psychiatry, Psychology and Neuroscience, as well as facilities for dentistry.

King's has a unique partnership with the Technische Universitat Dresden. The Transcampus programme, which is focused on biomedicine, is based in Dresden but allows for free movement of students and researchers between the two institutions, guarding against the possible impact of Brexit. King's already has one overseas degree: nursing, at the Ngee Ann Academy, in Singapore.

The university is in our top ten for research after 85% of the work submitted to the 2014 Research Excellence Framework was judged to be world-leading or internationally excellent.

Law, education, clinical medicine and philosophy all ranked in the top three in the country and there were good results in general engineering, history, psychology and communication and media studies. This led to the biggest increase in research funding at any university.

Today's researchers follow in a tradition that has seen King's play a part in many of the advances that shape modern life, including the discovery of DNA and the development of radar. Twelve alumni or academics have won Nobel prizes.

There are more than 5,600 residential places, including about 400 in intercollegiate halls run by the University of London.

Some of the outdoor sports facilities are a long train ride from the campuses, but there are facilities for all the main sports, as well as rifle ranges, two gyms and a swimming pool. Alumni include the elite athlete Dina Asher-Smith, who won three sprint gold medals in the 2018 European championships after graduating in history the previous year. She followed this up by winning a gold and two silvers at last year's World Championships in Doha.

Tuition fees

»	Fees for UK/EU students	£9,250
»	Fees for International students 2020–21	£19,800–£26,700
	Medicine £38,850; Dentistry £43,500	
»	For scholarship and bursary information see www.kcl.ac.uk/study/undergraduate	
»	Graduate salary	£26,000

Student numbers

Undergraduates	17,265 (1,662)
Postgraduates	8,305 (5,038)
Applications/places	46,535/5,860
Applications per place	7.9
Overall offer rate	72.9%
Unconditional offers	0%
International students	34.6%

Accommodation

University provided places: 5,612
Catered costs: £280–£293
Self-catered: £150–£399 per week
First years guaranteed accommodation
www.kcl.ac.uk/study/accommodation

Where do the students come from?

State schools (non-grammar)	63.5%	First generation students	29.2%
Grammar schools	14.2%	Deprived areas	3.8%
Independent schools	22.3%	All ethnic minorities	54.4%

Social inclusion ranking: =79

Black attainment gap	-12.2%
Disabled	5.5%
Mature (over 21)	14.7%

Kingston University

Applications have more than halved and the number of students starting degrees at Kingston has dropped by about 40% since the start of the decade. But the university has reduced its recruitment targets having "refocused" its course portfolio, and a small drop in applications in the 2019 admissions cycle was restricted to a few subjects, notably education and nursing.

At the same time, the university joined the rush towards unconditional offers. UCAS analysis showed that 46.8% of all offers in 2018 were unconditional – all except 20 of the most controversial "conditional unconditional" variety, requiring students to make Kingston their firm choice. The practice continued for the 2019 admissions cycle.

The pace of change for Kingston's degree portfolio has now slowed, with just two new honours programmes introduced in 2019: pharmaceutical science with regulatory affairs, and environmental science with hazards and disasters. But the institution is planning to almost quadruple the numbers taking degree apprenticeships. Construction management, a master's in senior leadership and a foundation degree for nursing associates have all been added for 2019–20.

Kingston is in the middle of an extensive programme of campus developments. A new "flagship" building is due to open in 2020, with a learning resources centre, covered courtyard and cafes at the front of the campus. Almost 900 students have taken part in the construction work. Studios and workshops on the School of Art's Knights Park campus were being refurbished to provide more flexible space for some of Kingston's most successful courses.

Art subjects achieved some of the university's best results in the 2014 Research Excellence Framework, alongside history and English. The university entered relatively few academics – just 16% of the eligible staff – but 60% of Kingston's submission reached the top two categories and there was some world-leading research in each of the nine areas assessed.

Kingston has the lowest (bronze) rating in the Teaching Excellence Framework, however. The panel complimented the university on its award-winning focus on black and ethnic minority students, and a completion rate which is in line with the national average for Kingston's courses and student profile.

The student population is one of the most diverse in the UK. More than 60% of undergraduates are from ethnic minorities and more than 30% of the places go to mature students. The university ranks 25th in our table for social inclusion this year.

The university offers unique incentives to its graduates' family members to take courses. The children of alumni qualify for a 10%

Holmwood House
Penrhyn Road
Kingston upon Thames
KT1 2EE
020 3308 9932
admissionsops@kingston.ac.uk
www.kingston.ac.uk
www.kingstonstudents.net
Open days 2020:
June 3 (Knights Park)

KINGSTON
UPON THAMES

Edinburgh
Belfast
Cardiff
London

The Times and The Sunday Times Rankings		
Overall Ranking: 106 (last year: =110)		
Teaching quality	79.3%	=79
Student experience	78.3%	=66
Research quality	5.1%	=91
Entry standards	124	=84
Graduate prospects	64.5%	121
Good honours	72.5%	84
Expected completion rate	84.1%	=73
Student/staff ratio	16.6	83
Services and facilities	£2,559	42

reduction in fees, as do the spouses of current students or alumni and the siblings of students or graduates.

Kingston has been among the top two universities for graduate start-up companies for nine years in a row and was the most successful in the latest survey. The well-established enterprise department gives advice to would-be entrepreneurs in any subject and the possibility of financial support with start-ups. Students and staff also link with local companies through a new HackCentre, which addresses real-world business challenges.

Marketing its location as "lively, leafy London", Kingston makes a virtue of its suburban, riverside location – and its relative proximity to the bright lights. Two of its four campuses are close to Kingston town centre; another, two miles away and close to Richmond Park, is at Kingston Hill. The fourth campus is in Roehampton Vale, where a one-time aerospace factory now contains a technology block. Kingston is the UK's largest provider of undergraduate aerospace education, with its own Learjet and flight simulator.

The health, social care and education faculty is run jointly with St George's, University of London. There is a link with the Royal Marsden School of Cancer Nursing and Rehabilitation, enabling some students to spend up to half of their course on clinical placements working in hospital, primary care and community settings.

Kingston and St George's have also launched Gibraltar's first social work degree, while the business school offers postgraduate degrees in Hanover, under a partnership with Gisma (the German International School of Management and Administration).

As part of the university's outreach activities, laboratories are open to the public to show how science and technology can make an impact on daily life. Kingston also runs Head Start events each summer to prepare applicants, including a residential option for those who want to experience hall life.

Good outdoor sports facilities are only three miles from the main campus, and there is a gym on the Penrhyn Road campus. The university is working with Fulham Football Club on a range of sport and education initiatives, including internships.

Kingston has spent more than £20m extending and upgrading its student accommodation, and all new entrants are guaranteed one of its 2,400 residential places. Most students like the university's location – but complain about the high cost of living.

Tuition fees

» Fees for UK/EU students   £9,250
     Foundation courses   £7,800
» Fees for International students 2020–21   £13,100–£15,600
» For scholarship and bursary information see
     www.kingston.ac.uk/undergraduate/fees-and-funding/
» Graduate salary   £22,000

Student numbers

Undergraduates	12,701	(922)
Postgraduates	2,281	(1,727)
Applications/places		22,025/4,820
Applications per place		4.6
Overall offer rate		79.8%
Unconditional offers		46.4%
International students		16.8%

Accommodation

University provided places: 2,436
Self-catered: £124–£338 per week
First years guaranteed accommodation
www.kingston.ac.uk/undergraduate/accommodation/

Where do the students come from?

State schools (non-grammar)	93.6%	First generation students	56.8%
Grammar schools	3.1%	Deprived areas	8%
Independent schools	3.3%	All ethnic minorities	61.9%

Social inclusion ranking: =25

Black attainment gap	-19.2%
Disabled	7.3%
Mature (over 21)	31%

Lancaster University

THE TIMES / THE SUNDAY TIMES
GOOD UNIVERSITY GUIDE 2020
INTERNATIONAL UNIVERSITY OF THE YEAR

Lancaster has pumped more than £170m into its campus since 2013 and our International University of the Year plans to spend another £250m over the next five years. The spending will go on a new Health Innovation campus, a four-storey extension to the library, a second sports hall and work on the management school.

It has set itself the target of becoming a "global player" in both teaching and research. It is the only UK university with a presence in sub-Saharan Africa, having opened a campus in Ghana, and there is a joint institute in China, with Beijing Jiaotong University. Now it has announced a new campus in Leipzig, Germany, initially offering four BScs and a foundation programme.

Lancaster is becoming a fixture in our top ten and enjoyed a 4% increase in admissions in the 2019 round. Awarded a gold rating in the Teaching Excellence Framework (TEF), the university was said to make students feel valued, supported and challenged academically. The TEF panel said its "culture of research-stimulated learning" provided the knowledge, skills and understanding that is most highly valued by employers.

In 2018, when Lancaster was named our University of the Year, it set a new record with a fourth successive increase in enrolments. More than a quarter of its 2018 offers were unconditional, nearly all requiring applicants to make Lancaster their first choice.

Lancaster is the highest ranked of the universities to embrace so-called "conditional unconditional" offers, criticised for carrying a risk of demotivating young people. It was one of the 23 institutions rebuked by Damian Hinds, then education secretary, but Lancaster insisted that the beneficiaries outperformed those receiving the normal conditional offers by 12 UCAS points on average, adding that it would not be in the university's interests to encourage or accept poorer performance.

Already in the top three for graduate prospects, Lancaster is hoping for further improvement by introducing placement years in a wide range of subjects including social sciences, maths and art. Hundreds of Lancaster students already spend part of their courses in America, Asia, Australia or Europe.

New degrees have been added in German or Spanish with Chinese, economics, zoology and fine art and design. A BA in architecture is planned for 2020, subject to validation. The majority of undergraduates make their final choice of degree only at the end of the first year.

Expansion of the medical school with another 60 places will coincide with the opening of the £41m first phase of the Health Innovation campus, developed in

Bailrigg
Lancaster LA1 4YW
01524 592 208
ugadmissions@lancaster.ac.uk
www.lancaster.ac.uk
www.lancastersu.co.uk
Open days 2020:
see website

The Times and The Sunday Times Rankings
Overall Ranking: 8 (last year: 6)

Teaching quality	79.5%	=73
Student experience	79.3%	=42
Research quality	39.1%	15
Entry standards	157	=32
Graduate prospects	89.1%	3
Good honours	78.7%	47
Expected completion rate	93.6%	15
Student/staff ratio	12.6	12
Services and facilities	£3,427	5

collaboration with business and the NHS, alongside the university's main Bailrigg site. In 2020, Lancaster's largest lecture theatre will open, with a capacity of 400.

Undergraduates join one of eight residential colleges, which become the centre of most students' social lives. Most colleges house between 800 and 900 in self-catering accommodation.

The 560-acre campus features eco-friendly student residences, which have won awards in the National Student Housing Survey six times. With almost 10,000 rooms owned or endorsed by the university, all first-years and many others can be accommodated.

The university has usually done well in the annual National Student Survey, although scores have slipped this year, placing it in the middle reaches of our ranking for student satisfaction with teaching quality and accounting for a small fall in overall ranking..

The university's research grades improved substantially in the 2014 Research Excellence Framework, when 83% of its work was considered world-leading or internationally excellent. There were particularly good results in business and management, sociology, English, and maths and statistics.

Lancaster is more successful than most research universities in widening participation among underrepresented groups. Just less than 40% of 2018's recruits had parents who did not go to university and 79% attended non-selective state schools. Among Lancaster's outreach activities, staff run summer schools, masterclasses and mentoring schemes for teenagers, and the university has come up with an adaptation of the Minecraft computer game to teach children more about science.

The university hosts a thriving live arts scene for everyone in the region, not just students. It has brought together art, design and theatre studies with a public art gallery, concerts and theatre, and invested heavily in design. Lancaster has also been among the most successful universities at reducing carbon emissions, winning a string of environmental awards for its facilities.

The historic town of Lancaster is a ten-minute bus ride away, and both the campus and town have been rated among the safest in the UK. Some of the nation's most unspoilt countryside, including the Lake District, is on the doorstep. Sports facilities are good and conveniently placed, with a £20m sports centre on campus, as well as a boathouse on the River Lune. Road and rail communications are good, but Lancaster is limited for off-campus nightlife.

Tuition fees

- » Fees for UK/EU students   £9,250
- » Fees for International students 2020–21   £18,700–£22,550
  Medicine £34,700
- » For scholarship and bursary information see
  www.lancaster.ac.uk/study/undergraduate/fees-and-funding
- » Graduate salary   £24,000

Student numbers

Undergraduates	10,213	(6)
Postgraduates	2,563	(1,429)
Applications/places	19,045/3,590	
Applications per place	5.3	
Overall offer rate	91%	
Unconditional offers	26.2%	
International students	32.9%	

Accommodation

University provided places: 9,807
Catered costs: £142–£198 per week
Self-catered: £92–£167 per week
First years guaranteed accommodation
www.lancaster.ac.uk/accommodation/

Where do the students come from?

State schools (non-grammar)	78.8%	First generation students	38%	Black attainment gap	-25.8%
Grammar schools	11.2%	Deprived areas	10.2%	Disabled	5.7%
Independent schools	10%	All ethnic minorities	17.3%	Mature (over 21)	4.2%

Social inclusion ranking: 91

University of Leeds

Leeds is one of the most popular universities in the country and remains close to the top ten despite a second successive fall in our table. It was in the top five for the number of entrants to degree courses in 2018, when only Manchester attracted more applications. New enrolments were down slightly, but only compared with a record crop in the previous year.

The university is nearing the end of a £520m investment programme designed to maintain its standing. Developments have included the significant refurbishment of its libraries and lecture theatres, and the addition of new sports facilities.

The £40m Nexus innovation centre is the latest project to be completed to foster collaboration between business and the university's researchers, students and graduates. Next will come new laboratories and teaching space for engineering and the physical sciences, as well as an expansion of the Leeds Business School.

The £26m Laidlaw Library was designed specifically for undergraduates and there has been a £17m transformation of the students' union, improving its social spaces and performance venues, and extending the facilities for its 300 clubs and societies.

Leeds secured gold in the Teaching Excellence Framework (TEF), impressing the panel with a strong emphasis on education inspired by "discovery, global and cultural insight, ethics and responsibility, and employability". The assessors found that students take charge of their experiences with academic and co-curricular opportunities while preparing them for the world beyond university. Leeds was our University of the Year in 2017.

More than 80% of the research assessed in the 2014 Research Excellence Framework was considered world-leading or internationally excellent, placing Leeds in the top ten in the UK in 30% of its subject areas. It is also in the top 100 in the QS World University Rankings, one of a minority of UK institutions not to drop down its list this year.

The university occupies a 98-acre site within walking distance of the city centre, although much of the accommodation is further out. Park Lane and Headingley are particularly popular with students living out. The student population is highly cosmopolitan, with 9,000 international students from 170 countries among a total of more than 38,000.

Like most highly-selective Russell Group universities, Leeds does not fare well in our social inclusion rankings and sits in the bottom ten in England and Wales. About two-thirds of the intake comes from non-selective state schools, with one in five educated privately. Barely 8% come from the most deprived parts of the country, but one in three are the first in their family to go to university

---

Woodhouse Lane
Leeds LS2 9JT
0113 343 2336
study@leeds.ac.uk
www.leeds.ac.uk
www.luu.org.uk
Open days 2020:
June 19/20;
September 12;
October 3

The Times and The Sunday Times **Rankings**

Overall Ranking: 13 (last year: 11)

Teaching quality	79.8%	=69
Student experience	80.4%	=27
Research quality	36.8%	27
Entry standards	166	20
Graduate prospects	81.2%	36
Good honours	86.9%	14
Expected completion rate	92.4%	23
Student/staff ratio	13.4	=17
Services and facilities	£3,043	13

– a higher proportion that at most similar universities.

There are more than 500 undergraduate programmes, with students encouraged to take courses outside their main subject. The Leeds Curriculum scheme requires undergraduates to undertake a research project in their final year, which is intended to be the "pinnacle of their academic achievement" and is weighted accordingly.

Leeds has one of the largest lecture capture and multimedia management systems in Europe and upgraded it last year to improve user experience. Students can access lectures and other teaching facilities through the virtual learning environment, enabling them to study at their own pace. Twenty-five of the university's academics have been awarded National Teaching Fellowships.

The financial support fund at Leeds is one of the largest of any institution, benefiting about a third of UK and EU undergraduates. An innovative Alternative Entry Scheme takes account of mature students' work and life experiences if they lack the formal qualifications to secure a degree place.

The LeedsforLife service provides students with academic and careers advice, as well as helping with work placements and volunteering opportunities. It is available for five years after graduation.

Leeds is among the top ten recruiting grounds of leading UK companies, according to the 2019 High Fliers survey. The university has also created more spin-out companies than any other institution – more than 100 – six of them listed on the Aim (Alternative Investment Market). An annual business plan competition offers prizes of up to £3,000 for the most entrepreneurial students.

Sports and social facilities are first-rate, and Leeds teams regularly excel in competition. The university hosts one of six centres of cricketing excellence. It has more playing field space than any other higher education institution, while The Edge sports centre includes a 25-metre swimming pool and a huge fitness suite.

The university's Brownlee Centre, named after the triathlete brothers and Leeds alumni Jonny and Alistair, is the UK's first purpose-built triathlon training centre.

The rise of Leeds as a shopping and clubbing centre has added to the attractions of the university. Some 3,500 students volunteer in the local community and 400 are trained as mentors and tutors, supporting schools in the region. There are 8,500 residential places, so new entrants are guaranteed accommodation.

Tuition fees

» Fees for UK/EU students	£9,250
» Fees for International students 2020–21	£19,500–£23,750
Medicine £34,500	
» For scholarship and bursary information see	
www.leeds.ac.uk/undergraduatefees	
» Graduate salary	£22,000

Student numbers

Undergraduates	25,043	(387)
Postgraduates	7,064	(1,928)
Applications/places		61,220/8,115
Applications per place		7.5
Overall offer rate		73.2%
Unconditional offers		0%
International students		23.5%

Accommodation

University provided places: 8,500
Catered costs: £91–£210 per week
Self-catered: £91–£159 per week
First years guaranteed accommodation
www.accommodation.leeds.ac.uk/

Where do the students come from?

State schools (non-grammar)	68.9%	First generation students	33.8%	Black attainment gap	-28.9%
Grammar schools	11.9%	Deprived areas	8.3%	Disabled	5.2%
Independent schools	19.2%	All ethnic minorities	18.5%	Mature (over 21)	7.5%

Social inclusion ranking: 107

Leeds Arts University

The former Leeds College of Art made a spectacular debut in our league table last year, on the verge of the top 50 and among the top ten modern universities. Some decline was to be expected in the latest edition, particularly after a significant fall in student satisfaction.

Improvements are being made to the university's already impressive facilities, however. A £22m development opened in 2019, expanding the Blenheim Walk campus and adding a 230-seat auditorium, music, film, and photography studios and a larger specialist arts library. An open-plan atrium-style entrance includes a coffee bar and a gallery, which opened with an exhibition by Yoko Ono.

Leeds Arts became the city's fourth university in 2017 and immediately reaped the benefits. Applications rose by a third in a single year and the numbers starting degrees by almost a quarter. The demand for places fell a little in the 2019 admissions cycle, but by no more than the average at specialist arts universities.

The university, which is ten minutes' walk from the centre of Leeds, has been expanding its range of courses into the wider creative arts, launching degrees in film and popular music performance, as well as comic and concept art. A new degree in creative writing took its first students in the current academic year.

Founded in 1846 as the Leeds Government School of Art and Design, Leeds Arts now markets itself as the only specialist arts university in the north of England. Former students include Henry Moore, Barbara Hepworth, Damien Hirst, film director Danny Sangra and London-based designer Omar Kashoura.

There were only 1,600 higher education students in 2017–18, including just 125 from outside the UK. The university also offers a range of further education courses in art and design and the visual arts, delivered in the original art school building, in the city centre.

As Leeds College of Art, the institution was placed in the silver category in the Teaching Excellence Framework. The awards panel was impressed that a significant number of teaching staff were practising artists or designers, enhancing the students' exposure to the creative industries. The panel also praised the "highly valued" student support services, which include dedicated advice for mature students and those with disabilities.

Group tutorials on degree courses are conducted in sessions of between four and eight, while individual personal progress tutorials are timetabled at key points in the year, providing an opportunity to discuss general progress across all modules. The student engagement strategy, which was developed largely by the students' union, commits to involving students in strategic decision-making and operational processes.

Blenheim Walk
Leeds LS2 9AQ
0113 202 8039
admissions@leeds-art.ac.uk
www.leeds-art.ac.uk
www.leedsartsunion.org.uk
Open days 2020:
June 10

The Times and The Sunday Times **Rankings**
Overall Ranking: =56 (last year: 54)

Teaching quality	83.1%	=20
Student experience	79%	=51
Research quality	n/a	
Entry standards	158	=29
Graduate prospects	57.1%	131
Good honours	79.9%	=39
Expected completion rate	88.8%	46
Student/staff ratio	11.9	=9
Services and facilities	£1,287	131

Leeds Arts was our University of the Year for Student Retention in the last edition. Although its dropout rate had risen in the latest survey, it was still only 5.6%, compared with the national average of 8.6% for the university's courses and entry qualifications.

Widening participation is encouraged through a range of activities with partner schools throughout the year, including Easter and summer schools, an after-school taster course, workshops for all stages from primary, secondary, further education to mature learners, as well as providing mentoring, campus tours and presentations. Some 98% of students are state educated — significantly more than average for the courses and entry qualifications.

Bursaries of £250 in the first year, £350 in the second and £500 in the third are available for undergraduates whose family income is below £25,000 a year. There is also a £500 scholarship, for the first year only, for those who progress from one of the university's further education courses to a degree. All final-year undergraduates receive £75 towards the cost of materials for their creative arts projects.

Leeds College of Art did not enter the 2014 Research Excellence Framework but will join the next exercise.

There are strong links with industry, which provide placements and allow students to attend trade fairs featuring their work, as well as studios and galleries in the UK and abroad. The university has a Creatives in Residence scheme, providing selected graduates with access to campus facilities and a support network. Internationally renowned guest practitioners visit to critique work and run workshops. Speakers have included Jake Chapman, Andrew Graham Dixon and Jeff Banks. Other graduates can apply for studio or creative office space in Leeds.

All students are given free membership to the Association of Independent Professionals and the Self-Employed to enable them to explore freelancing as a career option. Leeds Arts is bottom of our graduate prospects measure, however.

Leeds Arts does not own its own accommodation, but most new entrants are offered one of the 555 places in university-endorsed private halls. Only international students who apply by the end of June are guaranteed a place. The city has become a magnet for students, with its famously lively culture and nightlife.

Tuition fees

» Fees for UK/EU students	£9,250
» Fees for International students 2019–20	£15,400–£16,400
» For scholarship and bursary information see www.leeds-art.ac.uk/apply/finance/	
» Graduate salary	£17,000

Student numbers

Undergraduates	1,570	(0)
Postgraduates	6	(30)
Applications/places		4,820/795
Applications per place		6.1
Overall offer rate		37.3%
Unconditional offers		0%
International students		7.9%

Accommodation

University provided places: 555
Self-catered: £127–£145 per week
First years given priority
www.leeds-art.ac.uk/life-in-leeds/accommodation

Where do the students come from?

State schools (non-grammar)	96.6%	First generation students	41.6%
Grammar schools	1.2%	Deprived areas	10.5%
Independent schools	2.2%	All ethnic minorities	11.7%

Social inclusion ranking: 78

Black attainment gap	n/a
Disabled	12%
Mature (over 21)	7%

Leeds Beckett University

Campus developments costing £125m are due to open before Leeds Beckett students arrive for courses beginning in 2020. A teaching and research building for the School of Sport is due to open, with world-class facilities including an indoor sprint track and the UK's largest hypoxic chambers for altitude training.

It will be followed by the £80m creative arts building with a theatre and 220-seat Dolby Atmos cinema, as well as professional-standard music studios. This is part of a seven-year, £200m plan to create distinct academic "homes" for the university's 13 schools. Almost £1m has also been invested in libraries, with open-plan learning spaces, advice counters and a disability resource area.

Leeds Beckett is aiming to halve its drop-out rate – at one in five students, way above the expected level – and to ensure that nine out of ten are satisfied with their course over the same period. With student satisfaction rates down slightly (although still in the top half of our rankings for satisfaction with teaching quality and the wider student experience), the target remains some way off.

Professor Peter Slee, the vice-chancellor, describes Leeds Beckett as "world-class" because it features among the 1,000 institutions in the QS World University Rankings. The university has been in the bottom ten in our league table for the past three years, however, and this year's one-place rise keeps it there once more.

The launch of six new degrees in 2019, in subjects ranging from housing studies to creative writing and event marketing, will help to swell the numbers. Another ten are planned for 2020, including an accelerated (two-year) degree in inclusive education, and others in sport performance and management, games art, data science, occupational therapy, and marketing and public relations.

New degree apprenticeships are on the way, too, adding to the 16 already offered in areas ranging from building services engineering to social work, nursing and advanced clinical practice.

Leeds Beckett's silver rating in the Teaching Excellence Framework (TEF) came with praise for its employability strategies for students, who can learn real-world skills through live project briefs, case studies, practice-related assessments, and placements. Students were stretched, the TEF panel said, and developed transferable and personal skills.

Graduates are expected to leave the university with three attributes: to be enterprising, digitally literate and have a global outlook. All undergraduate courses were redesigned with this in mind and all include at least two weeks' work-related learning each year.

Applications fell for the fourth year in a row in 2018, but an increased offer rate

---

Portland Way
Leeds LS1 3HE
0113 812 3113
admissionenquiries@
leedsbeckett.ac.uk
www.leedsbeckett.ac.uk
www.leedsbeckettsu.co.uk
Open days 2020:
see website

The Times and The Sunday Times Rankings
Overall Ranking: 123 (last year: 124)

Teaching quality	80.4%	=62
Student experience	79.3%	=42
Research quality	4.1%	=101
Entry standards	112	=119
Graduate prospects	63.2%	127
Good honours	70.3%	99
Expected completion rate	76.4%	123
Student/staff ratio	19.3	=118
Services and facilities	£1,954	99

helped to ensure that almost 500 more students took up places than in the previous year. More than a fifth received unconditional offers, although not of the type criticised by ministers for requiring applicants to make the university their first choice.

Leeds Beckett and its predecessor institutions have acquired a reputation for success in widening participation in higher education. It has increased its proportions of mature students, those with disabilities and entrants from low-participation neighbourhoods over the past three years. It runs a range of summer schools and attracts some 30,000 young people to outreach events each year.

The university almost doubled the number of academics it entered for the 2014 Research Excellence Framework compared with the 2008 assessments. Just over a third of their work was rated as world-leading or internationally excellent, with architecture and sports studies producing the best results. Leeds Beckett's reputation is mainly for applied research: three inter-disciplinary research institutes focus on health, sport and sustainability, and there are ten centres in more specialist fields.

Leeds Beckett is split between the City campus, in the centre of Leeds, and the Headingley campus, three miles away in 100 acres of park and woodland. The focal point of the City campus is the futuristic Rose Bowl lecture theatre complex next to Leeds Civic Hall, where the business school and the site of the new arts building are to be found. At Headingley, there are outstanding sports facilities, and teaching accommodation for education, informatics, law and business.

More than 7,000 students take part in some form of sporting activity, and there is a range of sports scholarships. The Athletic Union hosts 41 clubs and 80 university teams are among the most successful in national competitions.

In the first developments of their kind, a new stand was built at the Headingley rugby ground, with classrooms, coaching facilities and social space for use by the university and the two professional clubs. A pavilion at the adjacent Test and county cricket ground has similar multi-use facilities.

Leeds Beckett is benefiting from the city's growing reputation for nightlife – while making its own contribution with a famously lively entertainments scene. With more than 4,000 bed spaces, those who make it their firm choice are guaranteed accommodation.

Tuition fees

»	Fees for UK/EU students	£9,250
»	Fees for International students 2020–21	£12,000
	Foundation courses	£11,000
»	For scholarship and bursary information see www.leedsbeckett.ac.uk/undergraduate/ financing-your-studies/	
»	Graduate salary	£19,000

Student numbers

Undergraduates	**16,183**	**(2,434)**
Postgraduates	**1,708**	**(3,246)**
Applications/places		**26,710/6,650**
Applications per place		**4**
Overall offer rate		**86.5%**
Unconditional offers		**0%**
International students		**5.9%**

Accommodation

University provided places: 4,250
Self-catered: £96–£200 per week
First years guaranteed accommodation
www.leeds-beckett.ac.uk/our-university/accommodation/

Where do the students come from?

					Social inclusion ranking: 95	
State schools (non-grammar)	91.6%	First generation students	39%		Black attainment gap	-30.4%
Grammar schools	3%	Deprived areas	17.3%		Disabled	4.9%
Independent schools	5.4%	All ethnic minorities	19.7%		Mature (over 21)	13.1%

Leeds Trinity University

A big decline in student satisfaction is the main factor behind a second successive fall in our league table for Leeds Trinity. The university was on the verge of the top ten in both of our student satisfaction measures derived from the National Student Survey but is now nearly 100 places lower. Having dropped 20 places overall in the last edition, the university has now fallen out of the top 100 in our rankings with a fall of even greater magnitude.

After a sharp fall in applications and enrolments in 2017, Leeds Trinity saw a 17% increase in numbers starting courses in 2018 against a pattern of falling recruitment among peer institutions.

Starters in 2019 had the option of a new foundation year in all subject areas if they lacked the necessary qualifications for immediate entry. There were also new degrees in business and enterprise, and criminology and law. In 2020, journalism and creative media, digital marketing and professional policing will be added.

Degree apprenticeships are expanding rapidly under the aegis of a dedicated Centre for Apprenticeships. The university expects to add to the seven existing programmes and to have more than 500 apprentices by September 2020.

Leeds Trinity claims to be the only UK university to include at least two professional work placements, totalling 11 weeks of relevant experience, as part of every degree. Relationships with more than 3,000 employers give undergraduates a range of options.

More than 60% of students continue to work or volunteer with their placement provider during the remainder of their degree, and 11% find jobs there as graduates. Students have their own placement adviser and undergo an intensive two-week preparation programme. Overseas placements are encouraged, and all form part of an assessed module towards final degree classification.

The scheme contributed to a silver rating for Leeds Trinity in the Teaching Excellence Framework (TEF). Assessors commented on the supportive educational culture, innovative assessment and feedback, excellent use of technology, and professional input.

Three senior teaching fellows work with staff to pilot and evaluate new approaches to teaching and learning. The university's strategy for teaching and learning stresses student-led enquiry, placing more onus on students to develop and lead their own learning in order to be more employable. Undergraduates receive personalised support from the Learning Hub.

Leeds Trinity is one of two institutions with Catholic foundations that were given university status in 2012. It "promotes dialogue and teaching of the Catholic Church" but is not controlled by the church and welcomes students of all faiths and

Brownberrie Lane
Horsforth
Leeds LS18 5HD
0113 283 7100
admissions@leedstrinity.ac.uk
www.leedstrinity.ac.uk
www.ltsu.co.uk
Open days 2020:
see website

The Times and The Sunday Times Rankings
Overall Ranking: 117 (last year: =87)

Teaching quality	77.1%	108
Student experience	74.8%	113
Research quality	2.0%	121
Entry standards	109	=127
Graduate prospects	68.1%	109
Good honours	79.3%	42
Expected completion rate	82.4%	87
Student/staff ratio	19.9	=122
Services and facilities	£1,940	100

none. The university grew out of two teacher training colleges established in the 1960s. Education is still the biggest subject, but there are also schools of arts and communication and social and health sciences.

The university is in Horsforth, six miles northwest of Leeds city centre. Some £15m has been invested in campus improvements, and further developments worth £25m are on the way. New photography studios have opened, following the launch of a degree in the subject. The student bar and dining room have been refurbished, with an industrial-style look, while there are also new fitness and sports therapy suites and a motion capture analysis lab.

Students also have access to the Trinity Enterprise Centre if they are considering launching their own business. Its advice and facilities are available to local businesses as well as students, who receive more general careers advice from the myFuture team.

Only 20 academics were entered for the 2014 Research Excellence Framework, but there were good results in communication, cultural and media studies, and library and information management. The flagship research group, the Leeds Centre for Victorian Studies, has a national and international reputation.

Two-thirds of the students are female, and Leeds Trinity exceeds all its national benchmarks for widening participation: one undergraduate in five comes from an area with little tradition of sending students to university – one of the highest proportions in the country. Among the outreach activities is a Children's University, based on campus, which offers high quality, innovative learning activities outside normal school hours to children aged seven to 14, and a Junior University for those approaching GCSEs.

It is the highest placed of the city's four universities in our social inclusion ranking: more than 60% of students are the first in their family to go to university.

The university has nearly 800 residential places – enough to guarantee accommodation to first-years. Sports facilities are good and include a 3G pitch and recently upgraded changing facilities. The sports centre caters for elite athletes as well as casual users, with specialist strength and conditioning equipment, and a functional training rig.

The city of Leeds is regularly voted one of the most popular destinations for students, with plentiful part-time work and well-established nightlife, shopping and cultural events.

Tuition fees

» Fees for UK/EU students	£9,250
» Fees for International students 2019–20	£12,000
» For scholarship and bursary information see www.leeds-trinity.ac.uk/student-life/student-finance	
» Graduate salary	£17,680

Student numbers

Undergraduates	2,701	(23)
Postgraduates	405	(235)
Applications/places		5,880/995
Applications per place		5.9
Overall offer rate		90.1%
Unconditional offers		0%
International students		1.4%

Accommodation

University provided places: 796
Catered costs: £123–£139 per week
Self-catered: £96–£129 per week
First years guaranteed accommodation
www.leeds-trinity.ac.uk/student-life/accommodation

Where do the students come from?

State schools (non-grammar)	97.2%	First generation students	61.3%	
Grammar schools	1.7%	Deprived areas	20.1%	
Independent schools	1.1%	All ethnic minorities	22.2%	

Social inclusion ranking: 18

Black attainment gap	n/a
Disabled	7%
Mature (over 21)	17.6%

University of Leicester

Several years of rising enrolments ended abruptly in 2018 when the numbers starting degrees at Leicester dropped by 18%. There was an 8% fall in applications in 2019 but the university resisted the route of making unconditional offers to students who made it their firm choice as a means of bolstering flagging numbers.

It has dropped out of our top 40 this year. Although student satisfaction has risen a little in the latest National Student Survey, Leicester is still outside the top 100 in the sections relating to teaching quality.

Leicester has projects under way, however, that are designed to improve the student experience. Academics can only be promoted to professor or assistant professor, for example, if they have a qualification from Advance HE (formerly the Higher Education Academy), an organisation that recognises academics' commitment to teaching, learning and the student experience.

A redevelopment of the students' union building will double the amount of social learning space, creating a new façade and entrance that improves accessibility and includes a spacious food court. The business school has a new home and contracts have been agreed for a new teaching and learning centre and seven accommodation blocks providing another 1,164 student rooms.

Leicester has a silver rating in the Teaching Excellence Framework (TEF), drawing favourable comments for putting in place a system to film lectures, in response to student feedback. The TEF panel also congratulated the university on engaging students with current research on all its courses.

New degrees have been launched in human resource management, journalism, marketing and physiotherapy. Creative writing with English or journalism, English with English language, creative computing and data science will all take their first students in 2020.

Leicester provides one of the most flexible curriculums in the UK, in response to strong demand among current and prospective students for more choice in degree options. Undergraduates can choose single, joint or major/minor programmes. Those taking the major/minor route are able to combine a wide range of subjects, spending three-quarters of their time studying their principal subject and a quarter on the minor element.

The university has also introduced employability initiatives, including an undergraduate internship programme with up to 500 places available each year.

The university has received planning permission for the first phase of the new National Space Park, which is due to open late in 2020. Recognising Leicester's longstanding commitment to space research, it will house companies in space-related industries as well

University Road
Leicester LE1 7RH
0116 252 5281
study@le.ac.uk
www.le.ac.uk
www.leicesterunion.com
Open days 2020:
June 6, July 3

Edinburgh
Belfast
LEICESTER
London
Cardiff

The Times and The Sunday Times Rankings
Overall Ranking: 41 (last year: =38)

Teaching quality	77.7%	101
Student experience	78%	=72
Research quality	31.8%	=37
Entry standards	133	=60
Graduate prospects	75.4%	=68
Good honours	78.4%	48
Expected completion rate	92.3%	24
Student/staff ratio	14	=26
Services and facilities	£2,749	25

as hosting postgraduate teaching and research. There are also plans for a life sciences park at Charnwood, near Loughborough.

Three-quarters of the work submitted to the 2014 Research Excellence Framework was rated as world-leading or internationally excellent, with the School of Museum Studies producing the best results, as it did in 2008. Results were also good in clinical medicine, biology, earth science and general engineering.

The main campus and much of the residential accommodation is concentrated in a leafy suburb a mile from the centre of Leicester. The university's first overseas venture – the Leicester International Institute/Dalian University of Technology – opened in China in 2017. Based in Panjin, it offers degrees taught in English in chemistry, mechanical engineering and mathematics.

The undergraduate population is more socially diverse than at most pre-1992 universities: almost 40% of students are the first in their family to go to university and more than half are from ethnic minorities. Four out of five undergraduates attended non-selective state schools or colleges.

About a quarter of Leicester's undergraduates receive financial support. The Centenary Scholarship has been introduced in the run-up to the 100th anniversary of the university's foundation. It will provide 100 awards of £1,000 to recognise students who have overcome adversity or made sacrifices in pursuit of their goals, ideally in service of something greater than themselves.

New entrants are guaranteed one of the 3,700 bed spaces, as long as they apply by the end of August. Facilities at Oadby Student Village include study areas, social spaces, a cinema room and bar.

The university has two modern sports centres. Both have a gym, swimming pool, spa, sauna and steam room, and studios. There are also flood-lit tennis courts, all-weather courts and rugby pitches at Oadby. Students pay a basic membership fee of £160 a year to use the facilities, or £5 a session for pay-as-you-go.

The city of Leicester's ethnic diversity provides a rich cultural experience, and in term-time the student body represents 12% of the population. Last year the NatWest Student Living Index ranked Leicester as the third most affordable student city in the UK after Cardiff and Hull, taking account of rents, entertainment prices and other expenses. The city has top-class sports teams, attracts big-name bands and has the biggest Diwali celebrations outside India.

Tuition fees

» Fees for UK/EU students	£9,250
» Fees for International students 2020–21	£17,450–£21,515
Medicine	£40,140 (clinical years)
» For scholarship and bursary information see www.le.ac.uk/fees	
» Graduate salary	£20,800

Student numbers

Undergraduates	12,184	(373)
Postgraduates	3,261	(1,592)
Applications/places		21.205/3,430
Applications per place		6.2
Overall offer rate		86.2%
Unconditional offers		0%
International students		24.6%

Accommodation

University provided places: 3,770
Catered costs: £102–£174 per week
Self-catered: £85–£180 per week
First years guaranteed accommodation
www.le.ac.uk/study/undergraduates/accommodation

Where do the students come from?

State schools (non-grammar)	80.4%	First generation students	39.3%	Black attainment gap	-18.7%
Grammar schools	11.2%	Deprived areas	9.7%	Disabled	5.3%
Independent schools	8.4%	All ethnic minorities	52%	Mature (over 21)	12.5%

Social inclusion ranking: 62

University of Lincoln

Lincoln's popularity has been growing impressively at a time when many of its peers have had to cope with smaller intakes. A fourth successive rise in enrolments meant that almost 1,000 more students started courses in 2018 than three years previously, an increase of nearly 27%.

Almost 40% of Lincoln's offers in 2018 were "conditional unconditional", requiring students to make the university their first choice – a sharp rise on previous years and enough to earn a rebuke from Damian Hinds, then education secretary. Lincoln has since said it will no longer make such offers.

Sixteen new degree courses took their first students in 2019. The additions include law for business, games and visual effects, three branches of engineering, and architectural science and technology. Sports therapy, Chinese studies, international accounting and biomedical engineering are all due to start in 2020. Foundation years have been added in science and the arts for those without the qualifications for immediate entry to degree courses.

Lincoln's new £21m medical school welcomed its first 80 entrants last September. Run in partnership with the University of Nottingham, whose BMBS (bachelor of medicine, bachelor of surgery) degree the students will take, it is a first for the county. At full capacity, the school will train 400 undergraduates a year and offer a foundation year for students without the necessary qualifications for immediate entry to the five-year course.

The university has also been chosen to lead one of the UK's first institutes of technology. Backed by the government and employers, the Lincolnshire Institute of Technology will specialise in agritech and food manufacturing, energy and engineering.

Lincoln runs the National Centre for Food Manufacturing in Holbeach, south Lincolnshire, where it offers part-time degrees for workers in the industry and carries out research. It also offers apprenticeships at three levels in food-related areas. The university's portfolio is expanding, with degree apprenticeships in nursing and social work now available.

Although it has slipped almost ten places in this year's rankings, Lincoln remains just outside the top five modern universities in our table, a far cry from the days when a predecessor institution (the University of Lincolnshire and Humberside) finished bottom of our rankings.

The university has a gold rating in the Teaching Excellence Framework, whose assessors praised a strong approach to personalised learning through highly engaged personal tutors, with access to analytics to monitor students' progress proactively. It found that students were involved in the design of courses, which enabled them to develop their independence, understanding and skills to reflect their full potential.

Brayford Pool
Lincoln LN6 7TS
01522 886 644
enquiries@lincoln.ac.uk
www.lincoln.ac.uk
www.lincolnsu.com
Open days 2020:
see website

The Times and The Sunday Times **Rankings**
Overall Ranking: 51 (last year: 42)

Teaching quality	79.5%	=73
Student experience	79.3%	=42
Research quality	10.3%	58
Entry standards	128	=73
Graduate prospects	81.4%	34
Good honours	75.1%	=65
Expected completion rate	88.1%	52
Student/staff ratio	14.7	=43
Services and facilities	£2,123	=82

Having added geography and engineering to its range of subjects in recent years, the university will have spent more than £100m on new facilities when its development programme is complete. It extended its engineering hub after securing a formal partnership with Siemens, joining Cambridge, Manchester and Newcastle among 16 universities worldwide to hold global "principal partner" status with the company.

More than half of a large submission to the 2014 Research Excellence Framework was rated internationally excellent or world-leading. Lincoln was in the top ten in the health category for the quality of its outputs. Research in the fields of agriculture, veterinary and food science got Lincoln's best results.

The university occupies an attractive, purpose-built campus next to Brayford Pool near the centre of Lincoln. There are more than 14,000 students, almost one in five of whom comes from an area of low participation in higher education – significantly exceeding expectations based on its courses and student profile.

About half of all new undergraduates qualify for support through the Access and Participation Plan. Lincolnshire has a variety of "cold spots" for participation in higher education, where the university focuses its outreach activities.

Lincoln runs an expanded graduate internship scheme and a popular summer placement programme. Several degrees can be taken as work-based programmes, with credit awarded for relevant aspects of the job, and the university was the first to win a Charter Mark for exceptional service. As well as the courses offered with Siemens, pharmacy undergraduates study in industry-standard laboratories at the £22m Science and Innovation Park in Lincoln.

The university sports centre is based on the main campus and has a wide range of facilities, including a sports hall and outdoor space for football and hockey pitches. A £6m performing arts centre on campus contains a 450-seat theatre and three large studio spaces, and there is a popular venue in a former railway engine shed.

Lincoln owns, manages or endorses almost 6,500 residential places, including 1,772 on campus, and guarantees accommodation to new entrants who apply by the end of June with Lincoln as their first choice. The campus is next to a marina and the city caters well to students, while the students' union is successful both socially and politically.

Tuition fees

- » Fees for UK/EU students   £9,250
- » Fees for International students 2020–21   £14,100–£15,900
- » For scholarship and bursary information see www.lincoln.ac.uk/home/studywithus/ undergraduatestudy/feesandfunding/
- » Graduate salary   £20,000

Student numbers

Undergraduates	11,157	(1,489)
Postgraduates	1,184	(1,142)
Applications/places	19,020/4,675	
Applications per place	4.1	
Overall offer rate	91.9%	
Unconditional offers	38.3%	
International students	8%	

Accommodation

University provided places: 6,455
Self-catered: £70–£366 per week
First years guaranteed accommodation
www.lincoln.ac.uk/home/studentlife/accommodation/

Where do the students come from?

State schools (non-grammar)	93%	First generation students	52.3%	Black attainment gap	-26.1%
Grammar schools	4.2%	Deprived areas	18.1%	Disabled	6.7%
Independent schools	2.8%	All ethnic minorities	10.3%	Mature (over 21)	10.6%

Social inclusion ranking: 63

University of Liverpool

Liverpool is back in the top 30 in our league table for the first time in eight years, continuing a run of improvements. Its rise of two places is driven by higher spending on student facilities and an improved completion rate, as well as the strong graduate prospects for which it has become known.

The university has been consulting on a £1bn estates masterplan to take it through the next 15 years. It includes a £23m building for the School of Architecture, a new £42m electrical engineering and electronics facility, significant enhancements to the Veterinary Institute and the creation of a new university park opposite Liverpool Metropolitan Cathedral.

Liverpool has already invested heavily in its city-centre campus to make room for more undergraduates and improve the student experience. A new teaching hub was completed in 2018, providing social study space, more formal teaching areas and new PC suites. The first phase of a new home for the School of Law and Social Justice is due to open. The department has an agreement with the University of Law (ULaw) to offer its legal practice course so law graduates are now able to remain at the university for their professional training. Those enrolled in other subjects can take ULaw's graduate diploma in law.

The management school has been extended and the Guild of Students building can host live drama, comedy and music in its own theatre. It also has a cinema, four bars and shops. A partnership with Unilever, co-founder of the £68m Materials Innovation Factory, aims to accelerate research and reduce development times for products across a range of sectors. Interdisciplinary research facilities for the health and life sciences can better focus on the leading challenges of the 21st century thanks to a £70m project.

The numbers starting courses at Liverpool fell in 2018 but enrolment was still more than 700 higher than before recruiting restrictions were lifted in 2015. Applications were back up in the 2019 admissions cycle.

A new degree in finance, with a year in industry, was launched last year. For 2020, avionic systems, computer science and electronic engineering, electrical and electronic engineering, and mechatronics and robotic systems will be added – all with a year in industry.

Liverpool was upgraded from bronze to silver in the Teaching Excellence Framework in 2018, but is still outside the top 75 on our measure of student satisfaction with teaching quality, drawn from the National Student Survey. It fares better in the sections on the broader student experience, approaching the top 30 this year.

The university is among the best performing of the research-led Russell Group universities

Foundation Building
Brownlow Hill
Liverpool
L69 3BX
0151 794 5927
ugrecruitment@liverpool.ac.uk
www.liverpool.ac.uk
www.liverpoolguild.org
Open days 2020:
June 19/20,
September 26, October 17

The Times and The Sunday Times Rankings
Overall Ranking: 29 (last year: 31)

Teaching quality	79.4%	=77
Student experience	80%	=32
Research quality	31.5%	40
Entry standards	147	=42
Graduate prospects	85.4%	=14
Good honours	80.6%	35
Expected completion rate	92.9%	=18
Student/staff ratio	14.3	34
Services and facilities	£2,445	=51

in our table on social inclusion. Up to 11,000 young people in disadvantaged areas from primary-school age to sixth form take part in a programme of long-term engagement with the university. Almost a third of students qualify for the Liverpool Bursary of between £750 and £2,000 a year, which can be taken as a cash bursary or a fee waiver.

More than £2m went into making the university's Career Studio one of the largest such centres in the UK. Peer-to-peer mentoring and "boot camps" give new graduates opportunities to network with employers and to develop world-of-work skills. Liverpool is inside the top 20 for graduate prospects and ranks 24th in the High Fliers Graduate Market report for the number of large leading employers targeting its students.

For a Russell Group institution, Liverpool entered a relatively low proportion of its eligible academics for the 2014 Research Excellence Framework. This holds it back in our research ranking even though 70% of the work was judged to be world-leading or internationally excellent. More than half of its chemistry research was considered world-leading. Computer science and general engineering also scored particularly well.

Liverpool has a campus in the Chinese city of Suzhou, run in partnership with Xi'an Jiaotong University. It also offers joint courses with the Singapore Institute of Technology and links with universities in Chile, Mexico and Spain allow students to complete part of their degree abroad.

Closer to home, there is a site for postgraduates in London which is now the base for third-year undergraduates in architecture, industrial design or urban planning who want to connect with industry and build contacts in the capital.

About £250m has been spent to bring the number of rooms owned or endorsed by the university to 4,400. New entrants are guaranteed a study bedroom if they make Liverpool their first choice. A new accommodation discount will be worth £800 to those in receipt of a Liverpool Bursary.

The Guild of Students is the centre of social activity on campus, but the city is as lively as ever with a thriving music and club scene. The indoor and outdoor sports facilities are good and include a 25-metre swimming pool that is open to the public.

Tuition fees

» Fees for UK/EU students	£9,250
Foundation courses	£5,140
» Fees for International students 2020–21	£17,050–£21,800
Dentistry £36,300; Medicine £34,550;	
Veterinary Science £34,550	
» For scholarship and bursary information see	
www.liverpool.ac.uk/study/undergraduate/finance/fees	
» Graduate salary	£22,000

Student numbers

Undergraduates	21,527	(545)
Postgraduates	3,843	(2,880)
Applications/places	39,455/5,635	
Applications per place	7	
Overall offer rate	85.9%	
Unconditional offers	0%	
International students	27.7%	

Accommodation

University provided places: 4,400
Catered costs: £212–£213 per week
Self-catered: £138–£212 per week
First years guaranteed accommodation
www.liverpool.ac.uk/accommodation/

Where do the students come from?

State schools (non-grammar)	76.2%	First generation students	42.8%	Black attainment gap	-4.5%
Grammar schools	11.9%	Deprived areas	10%	Disabled	5.3%
Independent schools	11.9%	All ethnic minorities	15.7%	Mature (over 21)	9.2%

Social inclusion ranking: =69

Liverpool Hope University

Liverpool Hope has fallen ten places and is out of our top 50 after a surprisingly large tumble in student satisfaction. It was in the top five for both of our measures derived from the National Student Survey only two years ago. Nonetheless, Liverpool Hope remains among the leading dozen post-1992 universities overall and its top-50 positions for student satisfaction would be the envy of many of its peers. The university boycotted league tables for several years but admitted that its success in them may have been one of the factors behind a rise in applications after its return.

Liverpool Hope was the only higher education institution in the city to achieve gold in the Teaching Excellence Framework (TEF). Assessors commented on "outstanding levels of stretch provided through judicious partnerships, good curriculum design and extracurricular activities". The panel also acknowledged a strategic approach to ensuring outstanding outcomes for all students, and recognition of the value of an inclusive community of diverse learners.

The university's purpose-built Creative Campus, close to the city centre, was expanded in 2018. The development houses an arts centre, food court, new study spaces and additional library facilities. There are new studios for students taking fine and applied art courses, group study rooms and a hub for the student support, wellbeing and students' union teams, as well as two theatres, a recording studio and dance studios.

The main campus, Hope Park, is four miles from the centre of Liverpool in the suburb of Childwall. More than £60m has been spent improving facilities, producing an £8.5m health sciences building, housing laboratories for nutrition, genomics, cell biology and psychology, along with facilities for sport and exercise science that include a 25-metre biomechanics sprint track.

The result of a 1980 merger of two Catholic and one Church of England teacher training colleges, Liverpool Hope sponsors an academy with the same dual-faith character. It became a university in 2005 and accepts students of all religions and none, although "taking faith seriously" remains one of its key values.

Most students opt for combined-subject degrees, deciding after the first year whether to give them equal weight or to choose a major/minor weighting. For most degrees there is an option to spend a semester abroad at a partner university.

Undergraduates are guaranteed small-group tutorials with a named tutor each week, and the university pledges to ensure that all the teaching they receive should be informed by research. Postgraduate students act as mentors to help undergraduates to develop their writing style. Students are

Taggart Avenue
Hope Park
Liverpool L16 9JD
0151 291 3111
enquiry@hope.ac.uk
www.hope.ac.uk
www.hopesu.com
Open days 2020:
see website

The Times and The Sunday Times Rankings
Overall Ranking: 60 (last year: 50)

Teaching quality	82.5%	=26
Student experience	79.3%	=42
Research quality	9.2%	=62
Entry standards	117	=104
Graduate prospects	83.8%	=20
Good honours	68%	=110
Expected completion rate	79.9%	104
Student/staff ratio	14.5	=36
Services and facilities	£2,103	85

encouraged to register for the Service and Leadership Award, which runs alongside their degree work. Anyone can volunteer locally, within the region or internationally as part of Global Hope, the university's award-winning overseas charity.

More than half the university's eligible staff were entered for the 2014 Research Excellence Framework – far more than at most post-1992 universities – and there were good results in theology and education. There are research-led seminars in the final year of degree courses to introduce undergraduates to a research culture, and all students produce a dissertation or advanced research project.

Nearly 60% of students at Liverpool Hope come from beyond Merseyside but the university is proud of its strong commitment to the region. A university centre has opened in Blackburn, mainly offering degrees in business and education, in partnership with St Mary's College. The Network of Hope takes university courses to sixth-form colleges in parts of the region with limited higher-education provision.

Hope comfortably exceeds all the official benchmarks for widening participation in higher education and is just outside the top 50 in our latest league table for social inclusion. Almost all its undergraduates are state-educated and one in five is from an area with little tradition of higher education. No university bursaries are currently offered, but there are performance scholarships worth £3,000 in music, dance, drama and sport.

A mile-long running track was first used in 2018, along with a new 3G pitch and tennis courts, adding to already impressive indoor sports facilities. The university also has a residential outdoor education centre in Snowdonia.

Most of the 1,100 residential places are at Aigburth Park, three miles from the main Hope Park campus – enough to guarantee accommodation for new entrants who apply before clearing. Liverpool is a magnet for students and its rich cultural offering continues through university partnerships with the Royal Liverpool Philharmonic Orchestra, Liverpool Tate, the National Museums Liverpool and Liverpool Sound City.

Tuition fees

» Fees for UK/EU students	£9,250
» Fees for International students 2020–21	£11,400
» For scholarship and bursary information see www.hope.ac.uk/undergraduate/feesandfunding/	
» Graduate salary	£19,000

Student numbers

Undergraduates	3,774	(134)
Postgraduates	797	(493)
Applications/places		8,795/1,555
Applications per place		5.7
Overall offer rate		89.5%
Unconditional offers		0%
International students		3.6%

Accommodation

University provided places: 1,145
Self-catered: £90–£125 per week
First years guaranteed accommodation
www.hope.ac.uk/halls

Where do the students come from?

State schools (non-grammar)	87.7%	First generation students	54.1%	Black attainment gap	n/a
Grammar schools	10.6%	Deprived areas	20%	Disabled	8.8%
Independent schools	1.7%	All ethnic minorities	10.1%	Mature (over 21)	18.6%

Social inclusion ranking: 54

Liverpool John Moores University

Liverpool John Moores (LJMU) is hoping 2020 will see the opening of the first phase of the city centre development that will eventually enable the university to concentrate all its activities on a single area with two campuses. The £100m Copperas Hill project was hit by delays but a five-storey Student Life Building and a separate two-storey Sports Building are now under construction, with a second phase to follow. The IM Marsh campus, four miles from the city centre, will then close.

Based near the Sensor City hub for industrial research, development and commercialisation – a joint venture with the University of Liverpool – Copperas Hill will be a key part of the city's new Knowledge Quarter. The Student Life centre will provide a meeting point for students on the City and Mount Pleasant campuses, with an atrium, rooftop terrace and sports facilities, as well as teaching and learning spaces.

Responding to feedback from the students' union, LJMU has already invested £1.5m to create social spaces in six buildings across the university conducive to relaxing, socialising and "casual study" by putting in indoor lawns and trees, IT facilities and phone-charging docks.

The numbers starting courses in 2018 dropped a little, but only in comparison with a record figure in the previous year.

Applications also fell but LJMU's total was still among the top 25 universities.

Eleven new degrees offered in 2019 include interior architecture, international relations and politics, professional policing, and mechatronics and autonomous systems. LJMU has also added the option of a foundation year to existing programmes. A degree in biotechnology with that option will be introduced in 2020.

The university was among the pioneers of degree apprenticeships and offers them in 13 areas, including civil engineering, construction management, quantity surveying, and digital and technology solutions. More programmes may be added in 2020.

Placing LJMU in the silver category in the Teaching Excellence Framework, the awarding panel complimented it on a "highly effective institutional strategic drive to improve satisfaction with assessment and feedback", strong recognition of teaching excellence and a consistent commitment to student engagement.

Perhaps the university's best-known feature is its highly-rated World of Work (WoW) programme. LJMU was a pioneer of the employment-focused curriculum that has since become common in higher education. The WoW initiative involves leading companies and business organisations and encourages undergraduates to become expert in eight transferable skills, applicable to a wide range of careers. All students are offered extensive work-related opportunities, both

Exchange Station
Tithebarn Street
Liverpool L2 2QP
0151 231 5090
courses@ljmu.ac.uk
www.ljmu.ac.uk
www.jmsu.co.uk
Open days 2020:
see website

The Times and The Sunday Times **Rankings**
Overall Ranking: 78 (last year: 74)

Teaching quality	80.5%	=59
Student experience	79.1%	=48
Research quality	8.9%	=67
Entry standards	142	=48
Graduate prospects	74.9%	71
Good honours	73.8%	78
Expected completion rate	84.7%	70
Student/staff ratio	16.9	=87
Services and facilities	£1,802	111

paid and voluntary, some of them overseas.

The Centre for Entrepreneurship supports students and graduates who want to start up in business, become self-employed or work freelance. The Teaching and Learning Academy offers assistance from leaving school, through university and into the workplace.

Students arrive at work well qualified. Almost three-quarters of graduates – 73.8% – left with a first or 2:1 compared with 76% the previous year. Even with these slightly lower figures, LJMU is one of the five universities to have increased its proportion of top-class degrees by the greatest amount – up 80% since 1998.

LJMU has spent £180m on improved facilities in little more than a decade. These include the award-winning John Lennon Art and Design Building and the £25.5m life sciences building, where the facilities include an indoor 70-metre running track and labs for testing cardiovascular ability, motor skills and biomechanics. The £37.6m Redmonds Building houses the Liverpool Screen School, with its industry-standard television and radio studios, the Liverpool Business School and the School of Law.

Named after a football pools millionaire, LJMU draws more than 40% of its students from the Merseyside area. Nearly all its undergraduates are state-educated and almost 19% come from low-participation neighbourhoods. A wide range of scholarships and bursaries include the John Lennon Imagine Awards, match-funded through a gift of £260,000

from Yoko Ono, helping students who have been in care or are estranged from their parents.

A growing research reputation is a source of pride at the university. More than 60% of the work submitted for the 2014 Research Excellence Framework was rated world-leading or internationally excellent, with the proportion topping 80% in physics which includes astronomy, where researchers and students use the university's robotic telescope in the Canary Islands. LJMU was ranked second in the UK for sports science and fourth among post-1992 universities for law and education.

The new Sports Building will provide an eight-court sports hall, three multipurpose halls and a gym. Students have free off-peak access to 11 Lifestyles fitness centres across Liverpool and eight swimming pools, squash and badminton courts, an athletics track and two golf courses. LJMU does not have its own accommodation but endorses 3,800 privately-operated places – enough to guarantee accommodation to all first-years who want it.

Liverpool is a popular city and one of the UK's most affordable for students.

Tuition fees

»	Fees for UK/EU students	£9,250
»	Fees for International students 2020–21	£15,600–£16,100
	Foundation years	£11,000
»	For scholarship and bursary information see www.ljmu.ac.uk/discover/fees-and-funding/	
»	Graduate salary	£20,000

Student numbers

Undergraduates	17,685	(1,192)
Postgraduates	2,094	(2,257)
Applications/places		31,385/6,730
Applications per place		4.7
Overall offer rate		86.3%
Unconditional offers		0%
International students		7.0%

Accommodation

University provided places: 3,800
Self-catered: £85–£166 per week
First years guaranteed accommodation
www.ljmu.ac.uk/discover/your-student-experiencee/
accommodation

Where do the students come from?

State schools (non-grammar)	89.9%	First generation students	55.3%	Black attainment gap	-28.7%
Grammar schools	7.7%	Deprived areas	18.9%	Disabled	6.9%
Independent schools	2.4%	All ethnic minorities	12.1%	Mature (over 21)	15.8%

Social inclusion ranking: 61

London Metropolitan University

The number of students at London Met has almost halved since the introduction of £9,000 fees and recent restructuring has left it with a deficit of £20m. But Professor Lynn Dobbs, the new vice-chancellor, has assured doubters that the university will not be the "Northern Rock of the higher education sector".

Dobbs acknowledges that a possible cut in tuition fees and increased competition for students represent serious challenges, but she insists that London Met has enough money in the bank to weather a storm. Much of the deficit is due to a rationalisation of the university's estate to focus almost entirely on Islington, eventually reducing running costs.

London Met emerged from the merger of London Guildhall University and the University of North London in 2002, although its origins date from the mid-19th century. The transfer of the Guildhall School of Business and Law to the university's Holloway Road headquarters in summer 2019 represented the latest phase of the reorganisation.

Soon only the Sir John Cass School of Art, Architecture and Design will remain in Aldgate, exploiting the university's strong links with east London's "Tech City", where it provides workshops, boot camps and an incubator programme for students thinking of setting up their own businesses.

The concentration on Holloway Road, which is costing £125m, was driven by student feedback. The Science Centre's Superlab – one of the largest teaching laboratories in Europe – has audiovisual systems that enable it to transmit 12 practical lectures simultaneously for different groups of students. A new social learning hub opened in 2018, after the conversion of a building used for administration, with high-spec classrooms and a cafe.

So far, London Met remains in the bottom 30 for student satisfaction with teaching quality and the wider student experience, and close to the bottom of our overall league table, despite a small improvement this year. It is one of the ten most socially inclusive universities in the country, according to our new ranking on this measure. London Met has the highest proportion of black students and fifth-highest presence of mature students at any university.

Undergraduates take year-long modules consisting of 30 weeks of timetabled teaching. Over a year, students will typically study four modules and receive a minimum of 60 teaching hours per module. The university expects first-year students to have 12 hours of teaching a week. However, Dobbs, whose own research has focused on social exclusion, would like first-years to have two days when they are not expected to study, to allow them to work and travel. Lectures would not start before 10am, so they can take their children to school.

166–220 Holloway Road
London N7 8DB
020 7133 4200
courseenquiries@londonmet.ac.uk
www.londonmet.ac.uk
www.londonmetsu.org.uk
Open days 2020:
March 14, April 1,
July 3, August 15

The Times and The Sunday Times **Rankings**
Overall Ranking: 128 (last year: 131)

Teaching quality	77.9%	=98
Student experience	75.7%	=105
Research quality	3.5%	111
Entry standards	101	=130
Graduate prospects	70.7%	=96
Good honours	60.8%	=129
Expected completion rate	65.7%	131
Student/staff ratio	17.8	=99
Services and facilities	£3,129	11

Student support services include the Pass (peer-assisted student support) scheme in which successful second- and third-year students coach first-years on their course.

The Programme for Improved Student Outcomes guarantees accredited, work-related learning opportunities for all students, to provide real-world experience in preparation for the graduate jobs market. Another aim is to create a better sense of community in a university with a particularly diverse student body.

Many courses with low recruitment closed as the university began its reorganisation. But 19 new degrees will take their first students in 2019 and 2020, the subjects including digital business management, games programming, toxicology and youth justice. The university is reviewing its portfolio of degree apprenticeships, which currently cover social work, early years education, accounting, finance and law, policing and data analysis.

London Met is in the bronze category in the government's Teaching Excellence Framework. An unusually negative assessment by the panel said students' achievement was "notably below benchmark across a range of indicators". It acknowledged a range of positive and appropriate strategies to address student satisfaction, but was concerned that comparatively few students continue their studies after graduating.

The university entered far fewer academics for the 2014 Research Excellence Framework than it did in the 2008 assessments – only 15% of those eligible. As a result, it slipped down our research ranking, even though half of its submission was rated as world-leading or internationally excellent. English and health subjects scored well.

A new cybersecurity research centre opened in autumn 2018. The hub for innovation and collaboration is the first of its kind in a UK university and will bring together students and businesses. Languages are another strength: London Met is one of only 22 universities globally to be a member of the UN Language Careers Network.

The university does not own any residential accommodation but works with private hall providers to ensure that new entrants have suitable housing. Many of London Met's students live at home. There are fitness centres on the main campuses, and outdoor sports facilities a short Tube ride away. The competitive teams are successful and the social scene is lively.

Tuition fees

»	Fees for UK/EU students	£9,250
»	Fees for International students 2020–21	£12,700
»	For scholarship and bursary information see www.londonmet.ac.uk/applying/funding-your-studies/undergraduate-tuition-fees/	
»	Graduate salary	£21,600

Student numbers

Undergraduates	6,853	(1,066)
Postgraduates	1,012	(1,364)
Applications/places	12,160/2,605	
Applications per place	4.7	
Overall offer rate	87.8%	
Unconditional offers	0%	
International students	9.9%	

Accommodation

University provided places: 0
Self-catered: £144–£346 per week (private providers)
www.londonmet.ac.uk/services-and-facilities/accommodation/

Where do the students come from?

State schools (non-grammar)	95.7%	First generation students	50.6%	Black attainment gap	-27%
Grammar schools	0.6%	Deprived areas	8.8%	Disabled	6.6%
Independent schools	3.7%	All ethnic minorities	67.4%	Mature (over 21)	58.3%

Social inclusion ranking: 6

London School of Economics and Political Science

A new strategy for the LSE promises a focus on educating for global impact, with students developing analytical, digital and entrepreneurial skills to tackle complex social questions. This will involve "inquiry-based learning and research practice at every level", as well as consistently excellent student services, with an emphasis on wellbeing.

Dame Minouche Shafik, the school's director, has set the LSE a target of being the world's leading social science institution, with the greatest global impact. It is already second only to Harvard in the QS world rankings for social science, although low student satisfaction rates have hampered it in our rankings in recent years.

Scores in the National Student Survey have improved since 2018, when it finished rock bottom on both our student satisfaction measures, but the LSE remains in the bottom two for perceptions of the broader student experience and in the bottom three for teaching quality. The LSE 2030 strategy addresses many of the assumed causes of such scores and commits to continuing investment to upgrade teaching, learning and social spaces.

The completion in spring 2019 of the school's largest ever building project is an important step in this direction. The Centre Buildings scheme has seen the reopening of the traditional heart of the campus, providing students with more tailored lecture facilities, study spaces and areas in which to eat and relax.

The small improvements in student satisfaction contributed to the LSE's rise of three places in our overall ranking, the biggest move of any university in our elite top ten, earning it a shortlisting for our University of the Year award.

Despite the school receiving a bronze rating in the Teaching Excellence Framework, applications and enrolments have been running at record levels. The official deadline for courses starting in September saw another increase of 7.5%. With 8.5 applications for every place in 2018, it was already among the most selective universities in the country.

The launch of four new degrees, in criminology, psychological and behavioural science, language, culture and society, and international relations and Chinese, accounts for some of the latest increase in the demand for places. But there have been increases across a range of subjects.

Low levels of student satisfaction were the primary reason for the poor TEF rating, although completion rates and graduate employment were also included in the process – areas where LSE is among the top-performing institutions. The school is first in

---

Houghton street
London WC2A 2AE
020 7955 6613
www.lse.ac.uk/ask-LSE
www.lse.ac.uk
www.lsesu.com
Open days 2020:
see website

The Times and The Sunday Times **Rankings**

Overall Ranking: 6 (last year: 9)

Teaching quality	72.3%	127
Student experience	68.5%	128
Research quality	52.8%	4
Entry standards	189	9
Graduate prospects	86.2%	8
Good honours	90.5%	4
Expected completion rate	95.4%	9
Student/staff ratio	11.1	=3
Services and facilities	£2,968	17

the UK for graduate earnings in law, based on a study conducted over the past three years by the Chambers Student guide, while the Institute for Fiscal Studies concluded in 2018 that the prestige of having studied at the LSE boosted men's wages by 49% and women's by 37%, compared with the average graduate.

The school introduced greater diversity of assessment and resits for first-year students for the first time after a review of all undergraduate programmes, in collaboration with student representatives and it committed to investing an additional £11m in teaching and learning over a three-year period. This included the creation of LSE Life (praised by the TEF panel), which offers students a single source of support for their academic, personal and professional development.

Efforts to widen access to the LSE have been stepped up, with the school spending more of its fee income on student support and other activities to widen participation than any other university. Our social inclusion table shows that because of the large intake from grammar schools, as well as the private sector, fewer than half of the undergraduates (48%) come from non-selective schools or colleges. The LSE ranks just outside the bottom ten for social inclusion across a range of measures.

The school is extending its network of graduates to encourage active involvement with the LSE and help to maintain lifelong relationships. More than 30 past or present heads of state have either been LSE students or academics, as have 16 winners of the Nobel prize in economics, literature and peace. The school has a long history of political involvement, from its foundation by Beatrice and Sidney Webb, pioneers of the Fabian movement.

The LSE had more "world-leading" research than any university in the 2014 Research Excellence Framework. It was the clear leader in the social sciences, with particularly good results in social work and social policy, and communication and media studies. A £10m donation from alumnus Firoz Lalji has since created an academic centre focused on Africa.

The portfolio of courses is already much wider than the school's name suggests, and includes maths, law and environmental policy. Its international character not only gives the LSE global prestige, but also an unusual degree of financial independence.

Almost 2,800 residential places for less than 5,000 full-time undergraduates enable the LSE to guarantee accommodation to all new entrants, as well as giving others the opportunity to avoid central London's notoriously high private-sector rents.

Tuition fees

»	Fees for UK/EU students	£9,250
»	Fees for International students 2020–21	£21,570
»	For scholarship and bursary information see	
	www.lse.ac.uk/study-at-lse/undergraduate/fees-and-funding	
»	Graduate salary	£29,000

Student numbers

Undergraduates	**4,788**	**(45)**
Postgraduates	**6,399**	**(390)**
Applications/places		19,725/1,790
Applications per place		11
Overall offer rate		39.6%
Unconditional offers		0%
International students		67.8%

Accommodation

University provided places: 2,768
Catered costs: £107–£291 per week
Self-catered: £151–£406 per week
First years guaranteed accommodation
www.lse.ac.uk/accommodation

Where do the students come from?

					Social inclusion ranking: 104	
State schools (non-grammar)	48%	First generation students	29.2%	Black attainment gap	-10%
Grammar schools	20.7%	Deprived areas	6.7%	Disabled	3.7%
Independent schools	31.2%	All ethnic minorities	53.2%	Mature (over 21)	2.8%

London South Bank University

LSBU was our University of the Year for Graduate Employment in 2018, for the second year in a row, an accolade which the university thinks may have helped it to a 4.7% increase in applications in the 2019 admissions round. The number of applications had dropped considerably over the previous three years, but enrolments held up well.

The university ranks fourth for graduate prospects, beaten only by St George's, London (predominantly a medical school), Imperial College and Lancaster, all universities with a very different student profile. It also challenges the most prestigious institutions on the salaries secured by its graduates, who earn thousands of pounds more than the national average. More than half have been mature students, many returning to well-paid careers.

LSBU operates its own employment agency to help students find part-time work while they study. About 1,000 students are sponsored by employers, either on degree apprenticeships or traditional degrees.

The university expects to continue to expand its course portfolio based on the demand for skills, job growth and its own strengths in academic and professional practice. It is one of the top universities for knowledge transfer partnerships and has dedicated facilities to help students and graduates with start-up companies. LSBU plans to have 2,000 degree apprentices – more than double the current number – by the end of 2020, adding new programmes in construction and chartered town planning.

LSBU received a silver rating in the government's Teaching Excellence Framework. The expert panel was impressed by the "appropriate" contact hours and consistently high levels of personalised learning for a diverse student population, provided by specialist staff and interactive education. This produces high levels of engagement and commitment to learning and study, it said.

Three core principles – student success, real-world impact and access to opportunity – underpin the university's offering. Three-quarters of the students are from London and just under 60% are drawn from ethnic minorities, helping to place the university in the top ten of our social inclusion rankings.

It has also moved into the top 100 of our main academic ranking after an impressive turnaround in student satisfaction in the past 12 months, which has seen the university rise by 43 places in our teaching quality rankings and only slightly less in satisfaction with the student experience.

LSBU's main campus is in Southwark, not far from the Southbank arts complex. The site includes the Centre for Efficient and Renewable Energy in Buildings, the UK's first

103 Borough Road
London SE1 0AA
0800 923 8888
admissions@lsbu.ac.uk
www.lsbu.ac.uk
www.lsbsu.org
Open days 2020:
March 7, June 20

The Times and The Sunday Times **Rankings**

Overall Ranking: 86 (last year: 107)

Teaching quality	80.4%	=62
Student experience	77.9%	=77
Research quality	9.0%	=64
Entry standards	114	=112
Graduate prospects	87.7%	4
Good honours	69.5%	103
Expected completion rate	77.5%	119
Student/staff ratio	15.6	=62
Services and facilities	£2,156	79

inner-city green technology research centre. A redevelopment project launched in 2019 will transform the main London Road building into a learning hub for students and the community, improving the library and sports facilities by September 2021.

The university entered more academics for the 2014 Research Excellence Framework than for previous assessments and scored well on the external impact of its research, with almost three-quarters of the submission placed in the top two categories on this measure.

Some health students are based in hospitals in Romford and Leytonstone in east London and there is a smaller satellite campus in Havering. The health and social care school works with more than 50 NHS partner organisations and is one of ten institutions with the highest rating from the Nursing & Midwifery Council.

Widening participation has always been a priority at LSBU and it seeks to diversify the intake further with initiatives that include after-school and Saturday clubs and a summer festival to help local people upgrade their qualifications.

The projected dropout rate for undergraduates remains high, however, and there is concern over the attainment gap between Bame (black, Asian and ethnic minority) students and the rest. LSBU allocates a good proportion of its fee income to supporting students to complete their education in the expected time and helping those who work to manage their studies.

LSBU is the only UK university to hold four accreditations from the Institute of Customer Service (ICS) for excellent service across its accommodation service, library and learning resources, centre for student life and sports academy. It uses the ICS business benchmarking services not just within the university's sector of public services but also to compare its performance with leading private-sector organisations including John Lewis and Marks & Spencer.

The students' union and many support services were brought together to make them more convenient and accessible and a £1m makeover of the sports centre equipped it with a multi-purpose hall, therapy services and facilities that include a 40-station fitness suite, dance studio and injury clinic. Southwark council contributed £300,000 to improve the facilities and guarantee public access.

All 1,400 rooms are less than ten minutes' walk away. International students are guaranteed accommodation and priority for the remaining places goes to those who live furthest away.

Tuition fees

» Fees for UK/EU students	£9,250
» Fees for International students 2019–20	£13,780–£17,155
» For scholarship and bursary information see www.lsbu.ac.uk/study/undergraduate/fees-and-funding	
» Graduate salary	£26,000

Student numbers

Undergraduates	**8,059**	**(4,261)**
Postgraduates	**1,862**	**(2,946)**
Applications/places	**19,205/3,690**	
Applications per place	**5.2**	
Overall offer rate	**81.4%**	
Unconditional offers	**0%**	
International students	**9.3%**	

Accommodation

University provided places: 1,405
Self-catered: £127–£213 per week
First years given priority
www.lsbu.ac.uk/student-life/accommodation

Where do the students come from?

State schools (non-grammar)	94.9%	First generation students	51.2%	Black attainment gap	-16%
Grammar schools	2%	Deprived areas	7.5%	Disabled	10.8%
Independent schools	3.1%	All ethnic minorities	59%	Mature (over 21)	46.7%

Social inclusion ranking: 9

Loughborough University

Record numbers started degrees at Loughborough in 2018 as the university reached fifth place, its highest position in our table, and was named our University of the Year for a second time. Now student satisfaction, always its greatest strength, has improved again and Loughborough has not only maintained its ranking in our table, but moved considerably closer to Imperial College, London, which is ranked one place higher.

Students rate their experience at Loughborough the third best in the UK, a product of the outstanding campus experience and a strong brand loyalty to one of higher education's recent success stories. No university has been shortlisted more for our University of the Year award over the past 20 years.

Loughborough has a gold rating in the Teaching Excellence Framework (TEF) to add to its attractions. The TEF panel found that students from all backgrounds achieve consistently outstanding outcomes, thanks to a culture of personalised learning.

A dozen degree courses have been launched in 2019, five adding a foundation year to an existing programme plus entirely new degrees including English with creative writing; English with digital humanities; physics with theoretical physics; mathematics and physics; and psychology with communication. Seven more

will start in 2020 including philosophy, politics and economics; urban planning; marketing and management; and business analytics.

Most subjects are available either as three-year full-time or longer sandwich degrees, which include a year in industry. The university is also a leader in the use of computer-assisted assessment, offering students the chance to gauge their progress online.

There is a small portfolio of degree apprenticeships. Systems engineering was added in 2019.

Loughborough is a significant centre of engineering, with more than 2,800 students in a £20m integrated complex. The Science and Enterprise Park, which is home to at least 70 companies, has the £59m BAE-sponsored Systems Engineering Innovation Centre as its centrepiece. The National Centre for Combustion and Aerothermal Technology is due to open this year, training aerospace engineers in a critical area for the UK.

The university is best known for its unparalleled sporting pedigree, however. The medal haul of its students, graduates and campus-based athletes would have placed it 10th in the 2018 Commonwealth Games table.

There are facilities to match. Loughborough claims that it has the best integrated training environment in Europe and "arguably" the best square mile of facilities anywhere in the world, the result of a £60m investment over the past 15 years.

Epinal Way
Loughborough LE11 3TU
01509 223 522
admissions@lboro.ac.uk
www.lboro.ac.uk
www.lsu.co.uk
Open days 2020:
June 26/27;
September 18/19

The Times and The Sunday Times Rankings
Overall Ranking: 5 (last year: 5)

Teaching quality	83.4%	=16
Student experience	85.8%	3
Research quality	36.3%	=30
Entry standards	162	24
Graduate prospects	86.9%	6
Good honours	83.8%	24
Expected completion rate	92.1%	=25
Student/staff ratio	13.4	=17
Services and facilities	£3,286	7

They include a 50-metre swimming pool, a stadium that holds 3,500 people, the National Cricket Performance Centre and the High Performance Athletes Centre.

Loughborough's programme of sports scholarships is the largest in the UK. It was the 2019 winner of the Bucs (British Universities and Colleges Sport) championships for an incredible 40th year in a row.

Loughborough's growing popularity has been achieved without the aid of so-called "conditional unconditional" offers. Professor Robert Allison, the vice-chancellor, led the opposition to the practice, saying it can be "tantamount to bribery".

The expanded intake has not brought equivalent increases in diversity, however. Despite a generous package of bursaries and a variety of outreach activities, the university misses its access benchmarks and is in the bottom 20 in England and Wales in our latest social inclusion table.

Only eight universities entered such a high proportion of their eligible staff – 88% – for the 2014 Research Excellence Framework. Almost three-quarters of their research was judged to be world-leading or internationally excellent, with sport and exercise sciences producing the best results in the UK and six other subject areas featuring in the top ten.

Loughborough's 216-acre campus has seen further improvements in the past year. A four-star elite athlete centre and hotel was opened by Lord Coe, the university's chancellor, last November. The facilities include 20 rooms that mirror the effects of high-altitude training. This was followed by the completion of a new development of ten accommodation blocks providing 600 en-suite rooms.

Loughborough also has a campus for postgraduates at the Queen Elizabeth Olympic Park in east.

About 44% of all Loughborough-based students live on campus, which is the centre of most students' social life. Its arts facilities include a 266-seat theatre, a separate auditorium for concerts and film screenings and a dance studio. The prize-winning students' union is among the most popular in the country. Its community activities received the Queen's award for voluntary service.

First-year students from the UK and European Union are guaranteed one of the 6,200 residential places, while those from outside the EU can stay in the same hall for two years. A £40m student accommodation block being built will be named after Claudia Parsons, one of the UK's first female engineers, who attended the university from 1919 to 1922.

Tuition fees

» Fees for UK/EU students   £9,250
» Fees for International students 2020–21   £18,650–£23,100
» For scholarship and bursary information see www.lboro.ac.uk/study/undergraduate/fees-funding/
» Graduate salary   £25,000

Student numbers

Undergraduates	12,961	(148)
Postgraduates	3,109	(1,096)
Applications/places		29,715/4,310
Applications per place		6.9
Overall offer rate		79.2%
Unconditional offers		0%
International students		22.1%

Accommodation

University provided places: 6,196
Catered costs: £155–£193 per week
Self-catered: £96–£170 per week
First years guaranteed accommodation
www.lboro.ac.uk/study/undergraduate/accommodation/

Where do the students come from?

State schools (non-grammar)	71.5%	First generation students	34.8%	
Grammar schools	12.9%	Deprived areas	7.1%	
Independent schools	15.6%	All ethnic minorities	26.4%	

Social inclusion ranking: 96

Black attainment gap	-25%
Disabled	8.3%
Mature (over 21)	2.2%

University of Manchester

Manchester has moved another place up the top 20 to occupy its highest position in our league table for 15 years. Spending on student facilities and the proportion achieving good honours have both risen, helping the university to jump 14 places in the past three years.

Its progress would be even more dramatic if student satisfaction improved. The university is still outside the top 100 in the sections of the National Student Survey (NSS) that focus on teaching quality and only just inside the top 90 for the broader student experience, stubbornly poor ratings in both instances that nevertheless seem to have little impact on Manchester's application rate, which remains the highest in the UK.

Among other initiatives to address the poor scores in the NSS, Manchester is investing in digital services to improve the experience of all students, from first contact through to graduation.

The university has a silver award in the Teaching Excellence Framework, with the panel acknowledging its investment in facilities and commenting favourably on the way that students were stretched, enabling them to progress and develop transferable and professional skills.

All undergraduates explore three "ethical grand challenges", one for each year of their degree. Sustainability is addressed from the start of Welcome Week, with units on the crisis of nature, global citizenship, innovation and leadership. It is followed by social justice in the second year and workplace ethics in the third.

The programme is part of Manchester's Stellify package of extracurricular activities that is designed to make its graduates socially responsible and highly employable. The institution was once again the favourite recruiting ground of employers in this year's High Fliers survey of *The Times* top 100 graduate employers and wins our University of the Year for Graduate Employment title.

Manchester is much the biggest university in our table – the only one with more than 40,000 students. But, unusually among the leading institutions, numbers starting degrees have declined since restrictions were lifted in 2015. The university puts a 10% decline down to the increasingly competitive market in student recruitment. It has compensated by taking more international students.

More than £750m has been spent in recent years on improvements, with £1bn more to come by 2022 as part of a strategy to create a single "world-class" campus that Manchester hopes will help it to secure a place among the top 25 research universities in the world. It has only two places to go in the QS World

---

Oxford Road
Manchester M13 9PL
0161 275 2077
study@manchester.ac.uk
www.manchester.ac.uk
www.manchesterstudentsunion.com
Open days 2020:
June 19/20; October 3, 10

The Times and *The Sunday Times* Rankings		
Overall Ranking: 18 (last year: =19)		
Teaching quality	77.3%	=104
Student experience	77.2%	=87
Research quality	39.8%	13
Entry standards	167	=18
Graduate prospects	80.7%	=42
Good honours	83.1%	28
Expected completion rate	92.9%	=18
Student/staff ratio	13.3	16
Services and facilities	£3,144	10

University Rankings, although a little more in other international exercises.

Current projects in the scheme include the flagship Manchester Engineering Campus Development (MECD), one of the largest construction projects undertaken by a UK university. The £400m-plus building will bring the university together along Oxford Road and house Manchester's four engineering schools and two research institutes. Other facilities in the pipeline include the £235m Sir Henry Royce Institute for Advanced Materials Research.

Several projects have been completed such as the Manchester Cancer Research Centre, the National Graphene Institute, the renovation of the Whitworth art gallery and the refurbishment of the Alliance Manchester Business School and its library, with further teaching and learning spaces added. Brunswick Park, a stretch of green space for students and staff was opened in autumn 2018, as was the Lume, a 19-storey hotel on campus. Students and staff are offered preferential rates.

Outstanding teaching is part of the university's strategy. The £24m Alan Gilbert Learning Commons, named after the former vice-chancellor, provides more than 1,000 flexible learning spaces, high-quality IT facilities and a hub for student-centred activities and learning support services.

More than 80% of the work submitted to the 2014 Research Excellence Framework was considered world-leading or internationally excellent, although the university entered a lower proportion of its academics than several of its peers in the Russell Group. Manchester has had 25 Nobel laureates.

Manchester has been trying to broaden its intake, with a focus on increasing recruitment from the city and its surrounds. The university admits more low-income students than most in the Russell Group and has surpassed its national benchmarks for widening participation. More than a third of the intake comes from homes where neither parent attended university.

The city's famed youth culture, plentiful accommodation and the university's position at the heart of a huge student population remain great attractions for applicants. Manchester owns or endorses 8,000 residential places, enough to guarantee accommodation for all new entrants. There are first-rate sports facilities and the university's teams frequently rank near the top of the British Universities & Colleges Sport league.

Tuition fees

» Fees for UK/EU students   £9,250
» Fees for International students 2020–21   £19,000–£24,000
    Medicine (clinical years) £44,000; Dentistry £44,000
» For scholarship and bursary information see
    www.manchester.ac.uk/study/undergraduate/student-finance/
» Graduate salary   £22,000

Student numbers

Undergraduates	27,295	(208)
Postgraduates	9,357	(3,281)
Applications/places	65,060/8,425	
Applications per place	7.7	
Overall offer rate	68.3%	
Unconditional offers	0%	
International students	34.2%	

Accommodation

University provided places: 8,000
Catered costs: £141–£194 per week
Self-catered: £77–£155 per week
First years guaranteed accommodation
www.accommodation.manchester.ac.uk

Where do the students come from?

State schools (non-grammar)	72.4%	First generation students	34.2%	Black attainment gap	-11.6%
Grammar schools	12.1%	Deprived areas	8.8%	Disabled	7.5%
Independent schools	15.4%	All ethnic minorities	30.1%	Mature (over 21)	7.9%

Social inclusion ranking: 85

Manchester Metropolitan University

Universities often experience a drop in student satisfaction while big construction projects are under way. Not so Manchester Met, which has moved up about 20 places on our two measures derived from the National Student Survey while implementing a £400m programme of campus improvements.

An eight-storey building for the arts and humanities in the city centre is due to open in 2020. It will include a poetry library and the writing school and language centre, as well as a 180-seat auditorium for the Manchester School of Theatre.

The new School of Digital Arts (Soda) follows in 2021. It will produce more than 1,000 graduates a year in disciplines such as film, animation, games design, artificial intelligence and photography, as well as housing the proposed International Screen School Manchester, backed by director Danny Boyle.

Future projects will include a £4m technology hub for companies in the city working on carbon-neutral hydrogen fuel cells and a new institute of sport with leading-edge facilities for academic, performance and participation sport.

Only Nottingham Trent recruits more undergraduates than Manchester Met – more than 8,600 in 2018. It is still outside the top 50 on both measures of student satisfaction (teaching quality and student experience), but the improvement has helped the university to move further up our overall league table and into the top half.

Manchester Met was one of the pioneers of degree apprenticeships and now has around 1,500 working with over 240 employers in positions such as chartered manager, digital marketer and laboratory scientist at undergraduate level and senior leader and advanced clinical practitioner at masters level.

Professor Malcolm Press, MMU's vice-chancellor and a member of the board of the Institute for Apprenticeships, has forecast "exponential growth".

Any expansion will be undertaken with sustainability in mind. MMU is second in the latest People & Planet league, comparing universities' all-round environmental performance. It has been in the top three for six years in a row and was the top university in 2017.

The university was given a silver rating in the Teaching Excellence Framework. An unusually brief commentary by the judging panel praised the inclusive curriculum for providing high levels of support for the diverse student population, the use of learning analytics and high levels of engagement with employers.

MMU offers postgraduate medicine in partnership with NHS trusts but proposals for an independent and international Greater Manchester Medical School, to be run in concert with Manchester and Salford universities, were

---

All Saints Building
All Saints
Manchester M15 6BH
0161 247 2000
courses@mmu.ac.uk
www2.mmu.ac.uk
www.theunionmmu.org
Open days 2020:
see website

The Times and The Sunday Times Rankings
Overall Ranking: =62 (last year: 69)

Teaching quality	80.7%	=53
Student experience	78.9%	=56
Research quality	7.5%	75
Entry standards	133	=60
Graduate prospects	70.7%	=96
Good honours	73.2%	80
Expected completion rate	83.5%	81
Student/staff ratio	15.5	=59
Services and facilities	£2,719	27

stood down last year after the venture was not allocated any training places by the Higher Education Funding Council for England.

The Manchester School of Architecture is rated in the world's top ten by QS, while fashion is another successful area for the university. The multidisciplinary Manchester Fashion Institute covers undergraduate and postgraduate training in design, business, promotion, fashion buying and technology.

MMU has been concentrating its activities on the city after closing its Cheshire campus in Crewe, where 800 trainee teachers and 3,000 other students studied contemporary arts and sports science. The two Manchester campuses border Hulme and Moss Side. A £75m business school and science and engineering buildings were added at All Saints, while the Brooks building at Birley Fields, which hosts the education and health faculties, won a prize for regeneration.

Many courses offer the opportunity for overseas study in Asia, Australia, Europe or America. Academics are encouraged to take a teaching qualification but less than a quarter were entered for the 2014 Research Excellence Framework. Almost two-thirds of the work submitted was rated world-leading or internationally excellent, with health, art and design, and English producing the best results. The former poet laureate, Professor Carol Ann Duffy, is creative director of the English department's writing school.

There is a long-standing commitment to extending access to higher education and MMU ranks just outside the top 50 in our social inclusion table, with more than half the intake being the first in their family to go to university. MMU's First Generation scheme targets young people in this category, providing financial, professional and personal support throughout their studies and into their careers. The university offers financial support to about 38% of undergraduates and 250 students with a household income of less than £25,000 have their fees waived during work placements.

Almost two-thirds of MMU graduates stay and work in the northwest. The Talent Match service, run in partnership with the Greater Manchester Chamber of Commerce, helps to match skilled graduates to the needs of local employers.

All first-years who request accommodation by mid-July are guaranteed a place.

The Sugden Sports Centre, was redeveloped in 2018, and Manchester Aquatics Centre, with three gyms and a 50-metre pool, is also on the doorstep.

Tuition fees

» Fees for UK/EU students	£9,250
» Fees for International students 2020–21	£15,000–£16,500
Architecture	£24,000
» For scholarship and bursary information see www2.mmu.ac.uk/study/undergraduate/money-matters	
» Graduate salary	£19,000

Student numbers

Undergraduates	24,738	(1,869)
Postgraduates	3,229	(3,245)
Applications/places	49,875/8,645	
Applications per place	5.8	
Overall offer rate	81.8%	
Unconditional offers	0%	
International students	7.4%	

Accommodation

University provided places: 4,257
Self-catered: £112–£218 per week
First years guaranteed accommodation
www2.mmu.ac.uk/accommodation/

Where do the students come from?

State schools (non-grammar)	94.3%	First generation students	52.1%	Black attainment gap	-29.8%
Grammar schools	3%	Deprived areas	15.8%	Disabled	5.3%
Independent schools	2.8%	All ethnic minorities	31.4%	Mature (over 21)	14.8%

Social inclusion ranking: 53

Middlesex University

Middlesex brands itself as a "university for skills", promising distinctive practice-based learning and embracing the value and power of diversity. Its strategy focuses on a combination of academic rigour and meeting practical needs.

One example of the university's "learning through doing" approach is the UK's first Cyber Factory training facility, which opened in 2017 to prepare students to be at the forefront of emerging smart technology. Another is the new augmented reality equipment for midwifery courses. This approach extends to all areas of the curriculum.

The tailored employability support system for Middlesex's diverse student body helped to earn the university silver in the Teaching Excellence Framework (TEF). Employability is embedded within and alongside programmes of study, said the TEF panel, with the result that students progress to highly skilled employment.

Middlesex is outside our top 80 for graduate prospects but the university has stepped up its employability services to offer work experience and start-up support.

The numbers starting degrees have dropped by almost a quarter in two years and applications were down by another 5% at the start of the 2019–20 academic year. Middlesex has gone up three places in our latest table but is still outside the top 100.

One of the university's main selling points is its network of global campuses, where students can spend part of their degree if they choose. There are campuses in Dubai and Mauritius, but last year Middlesex announced the closure of its base in Malta in 2022. Existing students can complete their courses there.

Middlesex also has long-established and extensive links in Europe, with almost 1,400 undergraduates from other EU countries. Another 3,000 students are based in Dubai, with 1,000 in Mauritius, where the campus opened in 2017.

The university has spent more than £200m on its impressive main campus in Hendon, northwest London, as it concentrated its activities there. It has an upgraded library, technology labs and a well-resourced £80m art, design and media centre. The centre includes Sony-designed, equipped and built television studios and a newsroom, and flexible performance and exhibition spaces.

Eight new degrees introduced in 2019 include creative writing and journalism, dance practice, medical physiology, and cybersecurity and digital forensics. Most come with the option of a foundation year for those who lack the qualifications for immediate entry. From 2020, two new degrees in theatre will be offered, together with one in sport and exercise science, specialising in football.

The Burroughs
Hendon
London NW4 4BT
020 8411 5555
enquiries@mdx.ac.uk
www.mdx.ac.uk
www.mdxsu.com
Open days 2020:
February 26

The Times and The Sunday Times **Rankings**
Overall Ranking: 107 (last year: =110)

Teaching quality	75.5%	=117
Student experience	74%	117
Research quality	9.7%	60
Entry standards	123	=86
Graduate prospects	73.5%	=81
Good honours	67.2%	116
Expected completion rate	78.9%	111
Student/staff ratio	16.7	84
Services and facilities	£3,030	15

Middlesex trains police constables, social workers, teachers and nursing associates through degree apprenticeships in these fields, among others, and will expand its portfolio in 2020 to include accountancy, construction site and design management, quantity surveying and civil engineering site management. The university has a Centre for Apprenticeships and Skills to bring academics and businesses together and ensure that programmes meet the needs of both employers and apprentices.

The highly flexible course system allows students to start some courses in January if they prefer not to wait until autumn, and offers the option of an extra five-week session in the summer to try out new subjects or add to their credits with work-based programmes. Many conventional degrees include work placements or the option of a sandwich year.

More than a third of the eligible staff were entered for the 2014 Research Excellence Framework and 58% of their work reached one of the top two categories. Art and design produced the best results, with three-quarters of the research assessed as world-leading or internationally excellent.

Almost all the British students are state-educated and Middlesex ranks just outside the top 20 in our social inclusion table. More than two-thirds of the students are drawn from ethnic minorities with just under 60% from homes where parents have not attended university. Having previously abandoned

bursaries and scholarships in the belief that outreach and retention activities did more for students from poor households, Middlesex has now reintroduced a variety of awards, as well as hardship funds.

There are 1,400 residential places on or near the campus, including 630 in a privately run development near Wembley stadium, with more to come in the next few years. New entrants are guaranteed accommodation if they apply by the end of June, or mid-August for international students.

On campus, there is a bouldering wall and fitness pod for sporting types as well as floodlit multipurpose outdoor courts and a real tennis court. The West End and London's other attractions are a Tube journey away.

Tuition fees

» Fees for UK/EU students	£9,250
» Fees for International students 2020–21	£13,400
» For scholarship and bursary information see www.mdx.ac.uk/courses/undergraduate-funding	
» Graduate salary	£23,000

Student numbers

Undergraduates	**13,820**	**(1,100)**
Postgraduates	**2,114**	**(2,658)**
Applications/places		**23,485/4,245**
Applications per place		**5.5**
Overall offer rate		**82%**
Unconditional offers		**18.7%**
International students		**22.9%**

Accommodation

University provided places: 1,399
Self-catered: £148–£186 per week
First years guaranteed accommodation
www.mdx.ac.uk/student-life/accommodation

Where do the students come from?

State schools (non-grammar)	96.5%	First generation students	58.5%	Black attainment gap	-17%
Grammar schools	1.3%	Deprived areas	5.4%	Disabled	5.5%
Independent schools	2.2%	All ethnic minorities	68.2%	Mature (over 21)	26.9%

Social inclusion ranking: 22

Newcastle University

A decline in student satisfaction has cost Newcastle ground in our latest league table and it is in danger of losing its place in the top 30. The university is only just in the top 100 for student perceptions of teaching quality, although it remains among the leaders for completion and graduate prospects.

Newcastle has a gold rating in the government's Teaching Excellence Framework. The panel was impressed by "exceptional" support for students, including tailored help for disabled students, and consistently engaging undergraduates with developments from the forefront of research and scholarship.

The fourth successive rise in the numbers starting degrees left the annual intake of new entrants more than 1,000 higher in 2018 than it was in 2014.

Developments costing £350m are under way on the edge of the main campus, at the Cochrane Park sports ground and at Newcastle Helix, the inner-city site it is regenerating in partnership with the city council and Legal & General Capital. They follow new buildings for physics, music and medicine, which has expanded considerably with the transfer of all 2,000 students from Durham's School of Medicine, Pharmacy and Health.

All three university buildings at Newcastle Helix (previously Science Central) should be open when the academic year starts in 2020. The £58m urban sciences building, which houses the highly-rated school of computing, has been in operation since 2017. A £35m learning and teaching centre, with a 750-seat auditorium, is due to open, and the £50m national innovation centre will follow in 2020. It will focus on ageing, data and research innovation.

A six-storey building for clinical teaching and learning, which is under construction near the dental hospital, will provide a 300-seat lecture theatre, social learning spaces and seminar rooms.

Other developments include £30m investment in sports facilities, including three artificial-turf pitches and a rowing training centre. The new sports centre has teaching and research spaces, an eight-court sports hall, four squash courts and a spinning studio.

Newcastle's growing international agenda includes a new research and innovation institute in Singapore, focusing mainly on environmental and energy issues. Its medical school in Johor, Malaysia, was the first such venture by a UK university. There is also an association with the Singapore Institute of Technology, offering engineering and nutrition degrees under the rubric of Newcastle University International Singapore.

Nearer home, the university has a campus in London, in partnership with INTO, a company that also runs a teaching and accommodation complex in Newcastle to prepare international

Newcastle upon Tyne
NE1 7RU
http://www.ncl.ac.uk/enquiries/
www.ncl.ac.uk
www.nusu.co.uk
Open days 2020:
see website

Belfast · Edinburgh · NEWCASTLE UPON TYNE · London · Cardiff

The Times and The Sunday Times Rankings
Overall Ranking: 28 (last year: 21)

Teaching quality	77.9%	=98
Student experience	78.7%	=59
Research quality	37.7%	=21
Entry standards	159	=27
Graduate prospects	85.8%	=10
Good honours	81.3%	34
Expected completion rate	95.1%	=10
Student/staff ratio	14.2	=30
Services and facilities	£2,304	68

students for undergraduate and graduate courses. Newcastle University London offers courses from the triple-accredited business school for the international market.

A new degree in archaeology was launched in 2019 and international relations, with or without politics, will follow in 2020. The university took its first degree apprentices in power engineering in September 2019, and is developing a programme at masters level for digital and technology solutions.

Nearly all of Newcastle's degrees provide an opportunity to spend up to a year in the workplace. The award-winning ncl+ initiative encourages students to develop employability skills through extracurricular activities. Students commit to at least 70 hours of activity and the award will appear on their Higher Education Achievement Report.

Almost 80% of the research entered for the 2014 Research Excellence Framework was judged to be world-leading or internationally excellent. Neuroscience, English and computing science were rated as leading departments in the UK. Among the university's subsequent research initiatives have been the opening of the Tyne Subsea centre of excellence for hyberbaric testing, and the Emerson Cavitation Tunnel research centre, which tests propellers and turbine blades for the marine industries.

Unusually for a Russell Group university, Newcastle has a long-standing reputation for agriculture. It owns two farms in Northumberland.

Newcastle is popular with students from independent schools, who took almost a quarter of the places in 2016. The university has long-established programmes to attract more students from non-traditional backgrounds and leads a national access programme but is in the bottom 15 overall in our table on social diversity. Just one in 11 students is recruited from a deprived area of low participation in higher education, with about a third of students being the first in their family to attend university. Four out of five students come from outside the northeast.

The main campus, which opens onto the busy Haymarket shopping area, close to the Civic Centre, hosts an independent theatre, museum and art gallery, which has had a £3.7m refurbishment.

The £75m Park View Student Village opened in 2018, adding 1,300 rooms and lifting the total to more than 5,000 rooms, ensuring that all first-years continue to be guaranteed accommodation.

The city is frequently rated the UK's best for student life and has good transport links.

Tuition fees

»	Fees for UK/EU students	£9,250
»	Fees for International students 2020–21	£18,000–£22,800
	Dentistry £36,400; Medicine £33,600	
»	For scholarship and bursary information see www.ncl.ac.uk/undergraduate/finance	
»	Graduate salary	£22,500

Student numbers

Undergraduates	19,807	(52)
Postgraduates	5,182(1,431)	
Applications/places	33,785/6,465	
Applications per place	5.2	
Overall offer rate	88.3%	
Unconditional offers	0%	
International students	25.7%	

Accommodation

University provided places: 5,000
Catered costs: £141–£175 per week
Self-catered: £84–£154 per week
First years guaranteed accommodation
www.ncl.ac.uk/undergraduate/accommodation

Where do the students come from?

Social inclusion ranking: 105

State schools (non-grammar)	65.2%	First generation students	34.7%	Black attainment gap	-16.9%
Grammar schools	11.5%	Deprived areas	9.1%	Disabled	4.3%
Independent schools	23.2%	All ethnic minorities	13.2%	Mature (over 21)	6.1%

Newman University

A big rise in student satisfaction helped Newman move away from the basement of our league table. The small Catholic university is now in the top 30 in both of our measures derived from the National Student Survey, jumping more than 30 places on its combined scores for the two indicators.

Newman has been reorganising its portfolio of courses, dropping a number of joint honours degrees in education and the humanities, and some single honours programmes – replacing them with others in the arts and humanities, business and social sciences. The latest offerings are in law and computer science.

All full-time degrees include work placements of at least 100 hours, some of which are abroad, and undergraduates can opt to study at a partner university in Europe or further afield. There is a range of part-time courses and foundation degrees, most of which are taught at Newman rather than in partner colleges.

The university had been expanding but the reorganisation, possibly combined with the effects of discontinuing academic achievement scholarships, prompted a 12% decline in applications in 2019. Newman also has to compete with the opening of a rival campus nearby, and the decline in the number of 18-year-olds.

Newman received a silver rating in the Teaching Excellence Framework, whose panel noted that students were "acquiring knowledge, skills and attributes that are valued by employers through work placements, volunteering support and enterprise opportunities, and which proactively embed career skills into the curriculum".

The university is ranked in the top 15 in England and Wales for diversity, in our table measuring social inclusiveness in recruitment and performance. Nearly half of the undergraduates come from ethnic minorities, more than a third were at least 21 on entry and 8% had disabilities. Three-quarters of students come from homes where their parents did not attend university – the highest proportion in the UK. But Newman is close to the bottom ten for immediate graduate prospects.

The campus is in a quiet residential area eight miles southwest of Birmingham city centre, with views over the Bartley reservoir and the Worcestershire countryside. Its modern buildings are arranged around quadrangles of lawns and trees. About £22m has been invested in upgrades that include new halls of residence opened in 2018, adding almost 100 en-suite bedrooms and open-plan living spaces. Teaching facilities were redeveloped to facilitate interactive learning and one of the main teaching buildings was completely refurbished.

Newman was one of three Catholic foundations awarded university status in 2012.

Genners Lane
Bartley Green
Birmingham B32 3NT
0121 476 1181
admissions@newman.ac.uk
www.newman.ac.uk
www.newmansu.org
Open days 2020:
March 7, June 10, July 4

The Times and The Sunday Times Rankings

Overall Ranking: 115 (last year: 119)

Teaching quality	82.5%	=26
Student experience	81.2%	21
Research quality	2.8%	115
Entry standards	118	=100
Graduate prospects	64.7%	=118
Good honours	60.9%	128
Expected completion rate	76.6%	122
Student/staff ratio	14.5	=36
Services and facilities	£1,696	118

It takes its name from John Henry Newman, the author of The Idea of the University and a Catholic cardinal in the 19th century. He was made a Saint by the Pope last year. His vision of a community of scholars still guides the university, which was established in 1968 as a teacher training college but now has a wider portfolio of degrees, mainly in the social sciences and humanities.

The university claims that the cardinal's influence is apparent in the small class sizes and interactive teaching style it offers. Newman stresses its Catholic affiliation but also a commitment to be inclusive in its recruitment and subsequent activities.

A higher than average proportion of the academic staff have teaching qualifications. The university received one of eight national awards to improve the use of technology in learning and teaching. The successful bid drew on a project designed to boost the digital literacy of the university's students, part of a larger initiative, Newman in the Digital Age.

Although only 23 academics were entered for the Research Excellence Framework, that was twice as many as in the previous assessments. Education and history produced the best results, but less than a third of the research submitted was placed in the top two categories. Newman does not employ staff for research alone, in order to ensure that students have regular contact with active researchers.

Three-quarters of the undergraduates are female, almost all of them state-educated. One in five entered through clearing in 2018. There will be no bursaries or scholarships for students joining the university in 2020, but student support payments of up to £1,750 can be awarded and the university issues supermarket and travel vouchers to those who can demonstrate hardship.

Newman is part of the West Midlands Consortium supporting students from disadvantaged backgrounds. The university has partnered five schools and further education colleges, as well as running outreach programmes.

First-year students have no guarantee of a place in university-owned accommodation, although they are given priority in the allocation of rooms. The halls of residence are close to the teaching areas and library.

A refurbished fitness suite and performance room improved sports facilities that include a 3G sports pitch, sports hall, gymnasium and squash courts.

Birmingham city centre, with its cultural attractions and student-oriented nightlife, is within easy reach.

Tuition fees

» Fees for UK/EU students — £9,250
» Fees for International students 2019–20 — £11,250
» For scholarship and bursary information see www.newman.ac.uk/fees
» Graduate salary — £21,000

Student numbers

Undergraduates	1,840	(381)
Postgraduates	258	(310)
Applications/places		3,220/760
Applications per place		4.2
Overall offer rate		94.5%
Unconditional offers		0%
International students		0.7%

Accommodation

University provided places: 290
Self-catered: £100–£190 per week
www.newman.ac.uk/accommodation

Where do the students come from?

State schools (non-grammar)	99.4%	First generation students	74.8%	Black attainment gap	-21%
Grammar schools	0.2%	Deprived areas	17.7%	Disabled	8.3%
Independent schools	0.4%	All ethnic minorities	46%	Mature (over 21)	34.6%

Social inclusion ranking: 13

University of Northampton

Every full-time undergraduate entering Northampton for the 2019–20 academic year was offered a free laptop to keep, a discount on hall fees or weekly credit to spend on campus. They also have the benefit of the £330m Waterside campus, which opened in 2018, providing residential accommodation for 1,000 students and leisure facilities that are shared with the local community.

The new campus did not prove an immediate draw – applications dropped in 2018 and remained considerably below earlier years of the decade. But a higher offer rate helped to increase the numbers starting courses by 10%.

Nor have the excellent new facilities translated into high scores in the National Student Survey. The verdicts of final-year undergraduates, who endured the disruption of moving from the old campuses, left Northampton close to the bottom ten in the sections dealing with the student experience. The university has dropped more than 30 places on student satisfaction with teaching quality.

However, Professor Nick Petford, the vice-chancellor, is optimistic that the campus will win over students with its teaching and learning space for the 21st century, rather than lecture theatres for 200–300, where students are "spouted at". Instead, classrooms for up to 40 people and smaller lecture theatres

accommodate "flipped learning", in which students prepare digital material in advance and interact with other students and staff.

Northampton was given a gold rating in the government's Teaching Excellence Framework before the opening of the new campus, despite falling below its benchmark for highly-skilled graduate employment. The panel welcomed "an embedded approach to the involvement of students in research, scholarship and professional practice, with strengths in community-based research and scholarship, and sector-leading work on social enterprise".

The 58-acre campus, a few minutes' walk from the town centre, has been funded mainly through a £231.5m bond guaranteed by the Treasury, the first time the government made such a guarantee. Its centrepiece is the four-storey Learning Hub, where most teaching takes place. The Senate building includes flexible learning spaces and accommodation for guest lectures and exhibitions, while a grade II-listed engine shed was restored to house the students' union.

Northampton was the first UK university to be named a Changemaker Campus by the Ashoka global network of social entrepreneurs and has since been ranked top in the country for social enterprise. Every student has the opportunity to work in a social enterprise as part of their course, developing entrepreneurial skills.

The university ranks in the top 40 of our table assessing the social inclusiveness of

Waterside Campus
University Drive
Northampton NN1 5PH
0300 303 2772
study@northampton.ac.uk
www.northampton.ac.uk
www.northamptonunion.com
Open days 2020:
see website

The Times and The Sunday Times **Rankings**

Overall Ranking: 116 (last year: 99)

Teaching quality	78.8%	=86
Student experience	73.9%	118
Research quality	3.2%	113
Entry standards	105	129
Graduate prospects	68.2%	108
Good honours	68%	=110
Expected completion rate	80.6%	=99
Student/staff ratio	16.8	=85
Services and facilities	£2,728	26

universities across a range of measures covering the educational background of students, ethnicity, disability, opportunities given to mature students and the proportion of students who are the first in their families to attend university. Almost all the undergraduates are state-educated in non-selective schools, although the proportion from areas of low participation in higher education is below the university's benchmark.

#AspireMe days bring young people onto campus for a programme of visits, lectures and activities to show them what life is like at university. The Changemaker student award recognises engagement with primary and secondary schools.

Northampton co-sponsors a University Technical College at the nearby Silverstone motor racing circuit. It also works with the Northamptonshire Growth Hub, assisting businesses and highlighting opportunities for student placements and part-time jobs.

Northampton traces its history from the 13th century when Henry III dissolved the original institution, allegedly because his bishops thought it posed a threat to Oxford. The modern institution, which was awarded university status in 2005, was the ultimate result of an amalgamation of the town's colleges of education, nursing, technology and art. It has a focus on training for the region's public services and is the area's largest provider of teachers and healthcare professionals.

In the 2014 Research Excellence Framework only 30% of its research was placed in the top two categories, but the university had entered just a quarter of its eligible staff. There was an outstanding result in history, where two-thirds of the work was considered world-leading or internationally excellent.

Northampton has five research centres, focusing on subjects from contemporary fiction to anomalous psychological processes and transitional economics in China.

It is one of only two universities in the UK to offer all students free access to sports facilities. The sports dome is used for teaching as well as recreation, and is supplemented by a pavilion, outdoor games areas and an artificial pitch.

The student village contains a mix of flats and four-storey town houses, as well as a hotel and community facilities, including a multi-faith chaplaincy, bank, convenience store and health centre. New entrants are guaranteed accommodation if they apply by the end of April.

The town itself has bars popular with students and the new campus will add to the leisure facilities. The Platform, a students' union venue in the town centre, houses a nightclub, a bar and cafe.

Tuition fees

» Fees for UK/EU students	£9,250
» Fees for International students 2020–21	£12,900–£15,750
» For scholarship and bursary information see www.northampton.ac.uk/study/fees-and-funding/	
» Graduate salary	£21,000

Student numbers

Undergraduates	8,598	(1058)
Postgraduates	811	(1,501)
Applications/places		14,415/3,185
Applications per place		4.5
Overall offer rate		85%
Unconditional offers		0%
International students		13.4%

Accommodation

University provided places: 2,260
Self-catered: £82–£162 per week
First years guaranteed accommodation
www.northampton.ac.uk/student-life/accommodation

Where do the students come from?

State schools (non-grammar)	96.6%	First generation students	51.1%	
Grammar schools	1.1%	Deprived areas	12.7%	
Independent schools	2.2%	All ethnic minorities	44.1%	

Social inclusion ranking: 40

Black attainment gap	-19.8%
Disabled	6.1%
Mature (over 21)	25%

Northumbria University

A decline in student satisfaction has cost Northumbria some of the gains the university made in our table last year. It has now dropped into the bottom half on both measures derived from the National Student Survey, for student satisfaction with the quality of teaching and the wider experience.

The university has a silver rating in the government's Teaching Excellence Framework. The panel praised Northumbria for helping students to enjoy their studies and achieve high attainment through a range of academic and personal support services, plus graduate start-up and careers assistance. High-quality physical and digital resources are used effectively both in teaching and by students, it said.

A £52m investment in the City campus to improve the student experience has brought together services such as careers, welfare and international support in the Student Central zone around the students' union. The library has also been upgraded.

A £7m building for computing and information sciences and an extension of the 18th-century Sutherland Building to create new studio spaces for students taking architecture programmes are open. Students across all disciplines are also benefiting from the opening of the 24/7 Digital Commons IT space, which provides access to software usually only found in specialist labs through a cloud-based AppsAnywhere service.

Yet applications have dropped by more than 10% in the last two years and another fall of 5% came in 2019. Changes in the portfolio of courses are partly responsible, along with the decline in the number of 18-year-olds. A higher offer rate has helped to keep the fall in the number of students to manageable proportions.

New degrees in computer games programming and American studies, with history or English literature, are planned for 2020. There will also be a new music degree, bucking the trend elsewhere in higher education, which will allow students who have not had opportunities to develop their passion at school to go on to take music at university through the option of a foundation year. The vice-chancellor Professor Andrew Wathey is a professor of music history.

Northumbria has also been among the pioneers of degree apprenticeships, running programmes in chartered surveying, chartered managership and digital and technology solutions. It launched the UK's first 18-month nursing degree apprenticeship in 2018, in partnership with Newcastle upon Tyne Hospitals NHS Foundation Trust. Now it has launched a police constable degree apprenticeship with Northumbria Police.

For three years running, Northumbria has been the top university for graduate start-ups,

Sutherland Building
Newcastle upon Tyne
NE1 8ST
0191 227 4646
ask4help@nurthumbria.ac.uk
www.northumbria.ac.uk
www.mynsu.co.uk
Open days 2020:
June 26/27

The Times and The Sunday Times Rankings

Overall Ranking: =65 (last year: 61)

Teaching quality	79.7%	71
Student experience	78.3%	=66
Research quality	9%	=64
Entry standards	145	=44
Graduate prospects	75.4%	=68
Good honours	77.3%	=51
Expected completion rate	84%	=75
Student/staff ratio	16.3	80
Services and facilities	£2,224	74

based on estimated turnover. Since 2009, it has supported more than 370 new companies, which employ over 1,100 staff and have a combined turnover of more than £81m. It is now developing a purpose-built incubator hub offering office space and a range of support for graduate enterprise.

More than 560 employers sponsor undergraduate programmes – one of the highest rates in the UK – and accreditation comes from 60 professional bodies. Northumbria's Business Clinic has received government funding to develop a digitally-enabled service offering free student-led consultancy to small firms.

The biggest university in northeast England, Northumbria has a longstanding agreement with St George's University in Grenada in the West Indies to offer its medical students the opportunity to undertake part of their course in Newcastle. This is being extended so that students spend two years, rather than one, at Northumbria.

In 2018, Northumbria became the first UK university to start training nurses on Malta to help address the shortage of nurses there. An exchange partnership with the Amsterdam University of Applied Sciences began at the same time to deliver courses there.

About half of the students are from the northeast, but the proportion drawn from other parts of the UK has been rising. Free one-day taster courses run throughout the year to give prospective students an idea of what university life would be like and there are bursaries for applicants from the poorest homes.

The university more than doubled the number of academics entered for the 2014 Research Excellence Framework compared with the 2008 assessments – and results improved – 60% of the work was judged to be world-leading or internationally excellent, attracting one of the biggest increases in research funding.

The £30m Sport Central hub, based on the main City campus, has a swimming pool, multiple laboratories, a climbing wall and a 3,000-seat indoor arena. Students pay a heavily subsidised fee to use the facilities, which are also open to the public.

A second sports centre with outdoor pitches is located on the Coach Lane campus, a few miles out of the city centre. A new partnership is bringing US students to the university to take a degree at the same time as a high-level football training programme.

The city of Newcastle is a renowned student honeypot. First-year undergraduates are guaranteed en-suite accommodation.

Tuition fees

» Fees for UK/EU students	£9,250
» Fees for International students 2020–21	£15,500
» For scholarship and bursary information see www.northumbria.ac.uk/study-at-northumbria/fees-and-scholarships/	
» Graduate salary	£21,500

Student numbers

Undergraduates	18,254	(2,895)
Postgraduates	3,181	(2,315)
Applications/places	24,635/6,100	
Applications per place	4	
Overall offer rate	91.5%	
Unconditional offers	0%	
International students	13.8%	

Accommodation

University provided places: 3,281
Catered costs: £118 per week
Self-catered: £80–£171 per week
First years guaranteed accommodation
www.northumbria.ac.uk/study-at-northumbria/accommodation/

Where do the students come from?

State schools (non-grammar)	89.7%	First generation students	52%	Black attainment gap	-28.5%
Grammar schools	4%	Deprived areas	18.7%	Disabled	6.1%
Independent schools	6.3%	All ethnic minorities	10.1%	Mature (over 21)	17%

Social inclusion ranking: =79

Norwich University of the Arts

Norwich University of the Arts is our University of the Year for Student Retention with a projected dropout rate of 5.6%, which is less than half the expected level. Students have every reason to want to stay on board, with the latest new building – the third in as many years – having just come on stream, providing a new base for the students' union, a cafe and lounge, laboratories and other teaching facilities for courses including film and moving image production, photography, and fashion communication and promotion.

Planning consent has already been granted for the next development: a seven-storey teaching and accommodation building due to open in 2021.

The new facilities should benefit Norwich University of the Arts (NUA) in our league table since satisfaction scores relating to the student experience have been one of the elements holding the university back from an even higher ranking than it has achieved in the five years since first entering our tables. It remains in the top 40 for satisfaction with teaching quality, but 40 places lower in the sections of the National Student Survey covering other areas.

Applications have dropped for the past two years, in common with most arts-based institutions, but the number of students starting degrees rose in 2018. The intake is twice what it was a decade ago, and the university has ambitions to double in size again.

NUA has a gold rating in the Teaching Excellence Framework (TEF). The panel found that course design and assessment practices encouraged experimentation, creative risk-taking and team-working, providing "outstanding levels of stretch for students".

The Ideas Factory, which was praised by the TEF panel, provides supported facilities to help graduates with the development of new digital businesses. It also hosts the university's Digital User Research Lab and its creative agency, which provides opportunities for students to work on commercial projects with local, national and international organisations.

Norwich has been widening its portfolio of courses, adding "year 0" for students without the necessary qualifications for immediate entry to all remaining courses from 2020. The option already exists for photography, film, graphic design, fine art and illustration. A new degree in acting is also being introduced.

The university makes a virtue of focusing entirely on the arts, design and media, rather than venturing into business or the humanities and social sciences, as other former art schools have done.

Recent investment of £10m in facilities includes the John Hurt Studio, named after the late actor and NUA chancellor. The cinema

---

Francis House
3-7 Redwell Street
Norwich NR2 4SN
01603 610 561
admissions@nua.ac.uk
www.nua.ac.uk
www.nuasu.co.uk
Open days 2020:
see website

NORWICH
London
Cardiff
Edinburgh
Belfast

The Times and The Sunday Times Rankings
Overall Ranking: =62 (last year: 66)

Teaching quality	81.6%	=39
Student experience	77.7%	81
Research quality	5.6%	=86
Entry standards	137	=52
Graduate prospects	60.6%	128
Good honours	71.8%	=87
Expected completion rate	88.6%	48
Student/staff ratio	15	=48
Services and facilities	£2,638	38

complex is housed in a renovated grade-II listed building that is also home to the school of architecture and won an award from the Royal Institute of British Architects.

Such initiatives should help address graduate prospects at NUA, which are in the bottom five in the UK. The university has also been trying to develop graduate pathways in non-creative sectors, demonstrating to firms how creative thinking can lead to growth.

The university traces its history to 1845, when the Norwich School of Design was established by the artists and followers of the Norwich school of painters, known for its landscape painting. Former tutors at the university include the artists Lucian Freud, Lesley Davenport and Michael Andrews.

The campus is concentrated on the pedestrianised centre of Norwich. The public art gallery enables students to showcase their work and gain experience curating and organising exhibitions, while the library has a large art, design and media collection.

Almost all the undergraduates are state-educated and one in six is from an area of low participation in higher education. Both exceed the national average for NUA's courses and entry qualifications.

Up to half the entrants in 2020 are expected to qualify for financial support. Philanthropic support has boosted the range of scholarships and bursaries available to undergraduates, which include a contribution towards the cost of materials, equipment and other expenses for those whose household income is below £25,000.

Norwich Arts has an art materials shop which sells basic and specialist art supplies at discounted prices. Individual studio space is provided for all full-time students in the faculties of art and design and media students can access digital media workstations. Experienced professionals, artists and graduates staff workshops that provide resources for everything from digital video editing to laser cutting.

More than half of the work submitted to the 2014 Research Excellence Framework was judged to be world-leading or internationally excellent, with 90% placed in the top two categories for its impact on the broader cultural and economic landscape.

NUA does not have its own sports site but its students have access to the University of East Anglia's Sportspark, which includes an Olympic-sized swimming pool.

The city of Norwich is popular with students and is one of the safest and greenest in the UK. In addition to its own stock in the city centre, the university keeps a register of more than 1,000 student-friendly private residential places.

Tuition fees

» Fees for UK/EU students	£9,250
» Fees for International students 2020–21	£15,000
» For scholarship and bursary information see www.nua.ac.uk/study-at-nua/fees-funding/	
» Graduate salary	£17,000

Student numbers

Undergraduates	2,114	(0)
Postgraduates	51	(52)
Applications/places	2,765/850	
Applications per place	3.3	
Overall offer rate	70.6%	
Unconditional offers	0%	
International students	7.4%	

Accommodation

University provided places: 800
Self-catered: £99–£153 per week
www.nua.ac.uk/university-life/accommodation/

Where do the students come from?

State schools (non-grammar)	94.3%	First generation students	45.4%	
Grammar schools	3.2%	Deprived areas	17%	
Independent schools	2.5%	All ethnic minorities	11.4%	

Social inclusion ranking: 50

Black attainment gap	n/a
Disabled	11.9%
Mature (over 21)	13%

University of Nottingham

Winner of our International University of the Year award and Sports University of the Year in 2018, Nottingham saw a 3.5% increase in applications for courses in the current academic year. But the demand for places was not evenly spread: medicine, veterinary medicine, sciences, pharmacy and engineering were all up; arts, cultures, languages, humanities and social sciences down.

Nottingham had seen an even bigger increase in applications – 10% – in 2018, when more than 3,000 of the 35,000 offers subsequently made to candidates were unconditional. However, the university's High Achievers scheme has been discontinued for 2020.

The university has a gold rating in the Teaching Excellence Framework (TEF) rating, with the panel praising high levels of contact time, which are prescribed and monitored; a culture of personalised learning that ensures all students are challenged to achieve their full potential; and exceptionally high student engagement with advanced technology-enhanced learning.

The TEF assessors also commented favourably on the preparation of students for future employment. Undergraduates across the full range of disciplines are able to undertake a placement year as part of their studies and Nottingham features among big employers' top ten recruiting grounds in the latest High Fliers survey.

Nottingham boasts one of the most attractive campuses in the UK, the 330-acre University Park, which has won several environmental awards. But much of the recent development has been on the Jubilee campus, the university's second base in the city, where the new Advanced Manufacturing Building, hosting collaboration with the likes of Rolls-Royce and Siemens, opened in 2019. The campus also includes the Centre for Sustainable Chemistry, part-funded by GlaxoSmithKline, housed in a carbon-neutral building claimed to be the first of its kind in the UK.

A third campus, 12 miles south of the city, at Sutton Bonington, focuses on the biosciences and veterinary medicine. The veterinary school has ambitious expansion plans, adding 150 places a year with a second intake in April. Students are promised smaller teaching groups and more hands-on practical learning as a result.

Nottingham is also helping to launch a new medical school which took its first students in September 2019, in partnership with the University of Lincoln, where it will be based. Students will take the Nottingham curriculum from its Queen's Medical Centre, close to University Park. A £4.5m facility for nursing is at Derby Hospital.

The university is by no means restricted to the East Midlands, however – one of the key reasons behind the awarding of the international

---

University Park
Nottingham NG7 2RD
0115 951 5559
nottingham.ac.uk/
studywithus/enquiry.aspx
www.nottingham.ac.uk
www.su.nottingham.ac.uk
Open days 2020:
June 26, 27;
September 11, 12

The Times and The Sunday Times **Rankings**
Overall Ranking: 21 (last year: 16)

Teaching quality	78%	=96
Student experience	78%	=72
Research quality	37.8%	20
Entry standards	161	25
Graduate prospects	86%	9
Good honours	84.1%	22
Expected completion rate	93.8%	14
Student/staff ratio	14.5	=36
Services and facilities	£2,663	35

university title last year. It has long-established campuses in China and Malaysia, which are both centres of research as well as teaching. There are more than 6,600 students at Ningbo, in China, and almost 5,000 an hour's drive from Kuala Lumpur, taking Nottingham's total student population to 45,000.

Undergraduates are encouraged to transfer between campuses and, with more than 7,000 international students coming to Nottingham, the university markets itself as a global institution. It is in the top 100 universities in the world in the QS rankings, with 16 subjects in the top 100.

Among the recent developments is a central teaching and learning hub on the University Park campus, which has a 300-seat lecture theatre and performing arts space. There is also a new health centre for the UK's biggest register of patients, which serves local people, students and staff.

More than 80% of the work entered for the 2014 Research Excellence Framework was rated as world-leading or internationally excellent. The university was in the UK's top ten in half of the 32 subject areas in which it made submissions, with pharmacy, chemistry and physics producing particularly good results.

Nottingham launched a £200m research fund in 2017. The investment over five years is expected to leverage more funding from industry, government and philanthropists. It will focus on six diverse areas: modern slavery, future food, green chemicals, precision engineering, propulsion and smart industrial systems.

About a third of UK undergraduates receive a Core Bursary, part of a wide range of initiatives to broaden the university's intake further. But Nottingham is only just outside the bottom 15 in our social inclusion table, with more than a third of the students coming from independent or selective state grammar schools. However, more than a quarter of the intake are drawn from ethnic minorities and almost a third are from homes where parents have not gone to university, which puts Nottingham ahead of 13 of its Russell Group rivals for diversity.

The David Ross Sports Village, a £40m complex with an indoor sprint track, hydrotherapy pool and 200-station fitness suite, is at the centre of sporting activity. Inspired by the new facilities, Nottingham's students ousted Durham as the second-ranked university in the 2018–19 BUCS inter-university leagues.

The university owns or endorses almost 10,000 residential places, enough to guarantee accommodation to new entrants.

Tuition fees

»	Fees for UK/EU students	£9,250
»	Fees for International students 2020–21	£18,420–£23,760
	Medicine £24,990–£40,500 (clinical years);	
	Veterinary science £35,220	
»	For scholarship and bursary information see	
	www.nottingham.ac.uk/fees/index.aspx	
»	Graduate salary	£22,500

Student numbers

Undergraduates	24,213	(392)
Postgraduates	6,188	(2,306)
Applications/places	52,415/7,800	
Applications per place	6.7	
Overall offer rate	80.9%	
Unconditional offers	11.2%	
International students	23%	

Accommodation

University provided places: 9,940
Catered costs: £154–£179 per week
Self-catered: £105–£179 per week
First years guaranteed accommodation
www.nottingham.ac.uk/student-experiencee/
accommodation.aspx

Where do the students come from?

State schools (non-grammar)	66%	First generation students	31.9%	Black attainment gap	-18.2%
Grammar schools	15.1%	Deprived areas	7.1%	Disabled	5.3%
Independent schools	19%	All ethnic minorities	26.4%	Mature (over 21)	7.3%

Social inclusion ranking: 99

Nottingham Trent University

Nottingham Trent University (NTU) became the largest recruiter of undergraduates in the UK in 2018, when enrolments grew by 18% and left the university within touching distance of being the first to welcome 10,000 new students in a single year. With applications up another 11% by March 2019, it may well have reached this milestone by now.

The university believes that being *The Times and Sunday Times* Modern University of the Year for 2017–18 contributed to its increased popularity. It has also been named University of the Year by both *The Guardian* (this year) and *THE* (Times Higher Education) magazine (in 2017) in recent times.

However, Nottingham Trent was one of the 23 universities accused by Damian Hinds, then the education secretary, of unethical recruitment practices because almost 40% of offers in 2018 were unconditional as long as candidates held NTU as their first choice. The system continued in the latest admissions cycle but, at the time of writing, no announcement had been made about 2020.

NTU has a gold rating in the Teaching Excellence Framework (TEF) and has been making great strides up our league table. A rise of ten places took NTU into the top 40 last year for the first time, with only two modern universities ahead of it. A small decline in student satisfaction has caused the progress to stall in our new edition, although NTU remains in the top 20 in the sections of the National Student Survey dealing with the broad student experience, and only just outside it for teaching quality.

The TEF panel acknowledged the "considerable" investment in the university's employability team and the provision of high-quality work placements for all students. There was exemplary engagement with employers, it said.

NTU ranks in the top ten among universities for the number of students on year-long work placements, a format it is keen to promote since establishing that it transforms the job prospects of students from poor backgrounds in particular. Most courses include placements of at least four weeks and a dedicated employment team can help students to find international opportunities to widen their skill set.

Six degrees have been added for the 2019–20 academic year, in subjects as diverse as games art, music performance, equine behaviour and medicinal chemistry. Apprenticeships are a strategic priority, with more than 175 employers training more than 500 apprentices. This figure is expected to double in 2020.

NTU has spent £350m on its campuses in the past ten years, producing a £9m digital media hub; the Contemporary Music Hub with its learning and performance studios; and Netronome, a 350-seat popular culture centre with bar, six recording studios and rehearsal

50 Shakespeare Street
Nottingham NG1 4FQ
0115 941 8418
applications@ntu.ac.uk
www.ntu.ac.uk
www.trentstudents.org
Open days 2020:
see website

The Times and The Sunday Times Rankings		
Overall Ranking: 40 (last year: 37)		
Teaching quality	83%	=22
Student experience	81.7%	17
Research quality	6.5%	80
Entry standards	135	=55
Graduate prospects	81.7%	=30
Good honours	74.4%	=72
Expected completion rate	87.6%	55
Student/staff ratio	14.5	=36
Services and facilities	£2,434	53

rooms. There is also a new engineering building and £175m has been earmarked for facilities in the next five years.

Plans have also been submitted for a dual-site £23m medical technologies innovation facility, which will integrate the work of scientists, engineers, clinicians and med-tech entrepreneurs to develop innovative products and materials for future healthcare.

At the Brackenhurst campus, a country estate 14 miles from Nottingham and home to NTU's Ares (animal, rural and environmental sciences teaching) facilities, a multi-million-pound reception and environmental centre is being built that will include teaching and learning spaces for geography, ecology and conservation. The campus already houses one of the country's best-equipped equestrian centres, where the Great Britain eventing team trains. A further 191 study bedrooms have also opened at Brackenhurst.

The Clifton campus, just outside Nottingham, is home to arts and humanities, and science and technology, as well as the Nottingham Institute of Education. A £20m transformation has produced the £13m ISTeC (Interdisciplinary Science and Technology Centre) facility as well as the Clifton Pavilion, a landscaped green zone and a sports village with an Olympic-standard hockey pitch. The Clifton campus is also home to the Lee Westwood Sports Centre with a freshly refurbished gym, sports halls, studios and more.

NTU is best known for fashion and other creative arts, but also has one of the UK's biggest law schools, offering legal practice courses for solicitors and barristers, as well as degrees.

Almost a third of undergraduates receive bursaries or scholarships. Among its efforts to broaden its intake, NTU places 300 undergraduates in local schools to work with more than 30,000 pupils. The university was chosen in 2019 to co-lead the National Social Mobility Research Centre.

More than half the work submitted to the 2014 Research Excellence Framework was considered world-leading or internationally excellent. In health subjects and general engineering, more than 80% of the work was placed in the top two categories.

There is residential accommodation on every campus, and new entrants who pay their booking fee by the end of May are guaranteed a place. The university has a strong sporting reputation, frequently reaching the top 20 in the BUCS (British Universities & Colleges Sport) leagues. Its latest ranking is 13th overall. Social life varies between campuses, but all have access to the city's lively cultural and clubbing scene.

Tuition fees

» Fees for UK/EU students	£9,250
» Fees for International students 2020–21	£14,500
» For scholarship and bursary information see www.ntu.ac.uk/fees	
» Graduate salary	£20,000

Student numbers

Undergraduates	**23,489**	**(1,031)**
Postgraduates	**3,260**	**(3,111)**
Applications/places		**40,595/9,725**
Applications per place		**4.2**
Overall offer rate		**87.5%**
Unconditional offers		**39.9%**
International students		**13.4%**

Accommodation

University provided places: 5,954
Self-catered: £101–£179 per week
First years guaranteed accommodation
www.ntu.ac.uk/life-at-ntu/accommodation

Where do the students come from?

State schools (non-grammar)	88.9%	First generation students	45.7%	Black attainment gap	-23.2%
Grammar schools	3.9%	Deprived areas	13.3%	Disabled	6.2%
Independent schools	7.2%	All ethnic minorities	23.6%	Mature (over 21)	9.3%

Social inclusion ranking: 76

The Open University

The Open University (OU) has been celebrating its 50th anniversary at a time of great strain for the university. While it is proud to have empowered more than 2m students across 157 countries to "transform their lives through learning" over the past half century, student numbers have dropped by more than a third since higher fees were introduced.

Professor Tim Blackman, the new vice-chancellor, faced a projected deficit of £30m when he took office last October. His predecessor resigned after failing to win backing from the OU's governing council for his plans to cut the budget.

Blackman held the post in an acting capacity before becoming vice-chancellor of Middlesex University in 2015. It is safe to say that he "gets" what the OU is about, saying at the time of his appointment: "The OU is one of the UK's best inventions. It ranks with the NHS and the national parks as a visionary idea, bringing the opportunity to learn and study to anyone, whatever their circumstances." He has also described the OU as "a social movement as much as a place of higher learning".

The university expects cost-cutting measures –which have included a cull of the least popular courses and the departure of more than 400 staff – to have balanced the books by the end of the next academic year. With about 175,000 students, the OU is still twice as big as any university in our league table, but the national decline in part-time education has raised concerns for its future.

A recent campaign targeted 14 markets overseas, including the European Union, aiming to increase the number of students – more than 7,000 – signed up from outside the UK.

Our rankings have never included the OU because the absence of campus-based undergraduates would place it at a disadvantage in comparisons with traditional universities. There are no entrance requirements, for example, and no need for physical facilities for students.

On those measures where comparisons are possible, the OU generally performs well. It is in the top 20 for student satisfaction with the broader experience, and 72% of the OU's submission for the 2014 Research Excellence Framework was considered world-leading or internationally excellent. Music was outstanding, with 94% in the top two categories, and work in art and design and electronic engineering also did well. It is world-ranked by QS in nine subjects.

Embodying the concept of widening participation even before the term had been invented, the OU remains the model for distance-learning universities around the world. Based in Milton Keynes,

---

Walton Hall
Milton Keynes
MK7 6AA
0300 303 7444
general-enquiries@open.ac.uk
www.open.ac.uk
www.oustudents.com

The Times and The Sunday Times **Rankings**
Not applicable

Buckinghamshire, the university employs thousands of part-time tutors around the country to guide students through their degrees. Its "supported open learning" system allows students to work where they choose: at home, in the workplace or at a library or study centre. They have contact with fellow students at tutorials, day schools or through online forums and social networks and their work is monitored by continual assessment, examination or assignment.

As well as degrees in a named subject, the OU awards "Open" bachelor's degrees, where students can combine modules in a variety of subjects. Except in fast-moving areas such as computing, there is no limit on the time taken to complete a degree.

Over its half century in operation, the OU has evolved from relying on late-night television broadcasts to much more provision online – and it is not standing still. Three new degrees were launched in 2019: religion, philosophy and ethics; data science; and criminology and sociology. The university is also offering degree and higher apprenticeships in a wide range of subjects in England, Scotland and Wales and expects to expand the programme in 2020, adding to its total of 1,500 apprentices so far.

In an attempt to revitalise part-time higher education, the university has introduced the online information service Pearl (Part Time Education for Adults Returning to Learn)

and runs a joint programme with the consultant KPMG to advise employers about apprenticeship programmes.

Undergraduate fees are £6,024 for the equivalent of full-time study, the cheapest at any university and eligible for a tuition fee loan. The OU provides fee waivers for students from poor backgrounds through its Widening Access and Success programme. Some 2,000 access students were expected to receive a free place for the 2019–20 academic year.

Although more than a third of new OU students are less than 25 years old, three-quarters of its students combine their studies with full- or part-time work. More than 60% of undergraduates are female. The OU is the largest provider of higher education to disabled people, offering special support to nearly 25,000 current students with disabilities.

Tuition fees

»	Fees for English/EU students 2020–21	£6,024
	Scotland, Wales and Northern Ireland	£2,016
»	Fees for International students 2020–21	£6,024
»	For scholarship and bursary information see www.open.ac.uk/courses/fees-and-funding	
»	Graduate salary	n/a

Students

Undergraduates	175 (83,126)
Postgraduates	300 (7,527)

Accommodation

Not applicable

Where do the students come from?

Not available

University of Oxford

Oxford is ahead of Cambridge in two of the three main international rankings – and the top university in the world, according to the *Times Higher Education* magazine – but it remains second in our league table, which is focused on the concerns of undergraduates, rather than on research.

The dark blues lead the latest table on completion and on the proportion achieving good honours – only 6% missed out on a first or 2:1 in 2018. It has also risen two places from the foot of our first social inclusion table, despite taking just 41% of its entrants from non-selective state schools and colleges.

Professor Louise Richardson, the vice-chancellor, is promising a "sea change" in the numbers admitted from ethnic minorities and disadvantaged areas, with the launch in 2019 of two new access schemes. By 2023, the aim is to add 250 state school applicants to the intake, taking the proportion of undergraduates from underrepresented backgrounds from the current 15% to 25%.

Opportunity Oxford will provide a programme of home study and a fortnight at the university for up to 200 students who have applied in the normal way and are on course to gain the required grades, but need additional support to transition successfully from school to Oxford. The second scheme will see the introduction of a foundation year for students who have experienced severe disadvantage or educational disruption, enabling them to reach the standard required for Oxford entrance.

Oxford already offers the most generous financial support in UK higher education for students from poor backgrounds. Nearly a quarter of all students receive some support, with those from the lowest-income families receiving £6,700 a year – a £3,700 bursary and £3,000 fee waiver.

Applications have risen for the past four years and are running at record levels, but there have been barely any more places available. Less than a quarter of 18-year-olds applying to Oxford receive an offer, the lowest proportion in the UK and significantly less than at Cambridge.

There are written admissions tests for certain subjects and you may be asked to submit samples of work. Some courses now demand two A* grades and an A at A-level and 99% of successful candidates achieve at least three As at A-level or their equivalent.

Selection is in the hands of the 30 undergraduate colleges, which vary considerably in their approach. Sound advice on the colleges' academic strengths and social flavour is essential for applicants to give themselves the best chance of winning a place and finding a setting in which they can thrive. Most colleges can accommodate undergraduates for two of their three years at Oxford, if not more. (See chapter 14)

A minority of candidates opt to go straight

University Offices
Wellington Square
Oxford OX1 2JD
01865 288 000
study@ox.ac.uk
www.ox.ac.uk
www.oxfordsu.org
Open days 2020:
July 1/2, September 18

***The Times and The Sunday Times* Rankings**
Overall Ranking: 2 (last year: 2)

Teaching quality	n/a	
Student experience	n/a	
Research quality	53.1%	3
Entry standards	215	2
Graduate prospects	83.5%	23
Good honours	94%	1
Expected completion rate	98.6%	1
Student/staff ratio	10.4	1
Services and facilities	£3,354	6

into the admissions pool without expressing a preference for a particular college. The choice of college is particularly important for arts and social science students, however, whose tuition is based in-college. Science and technology are taught mainly in central facilities.

The gap in our table between Oxbridge and their nearest challengers cannot be precise while the two universities' undergraduates continue to boycott the National Student Survey, which students at all other universities see fit to participate in. Oxford's satisfaction levels are based on 2016 responses, but the ancient rivals remain well clear of the rest overall on all our other league table measures, which are current.

Oxford has a gold rating in the Teaching Excellence Framework. The panel praised its collegiate system and the small group tutorials, as well as the opportunities for students to engage as active researchers with the possibility, in some cases, of co-publishing with world-leading academics. The only negative comments concerned satisfaction levels among disadvantaged students and the immediate prospects for black and ethnic minority graduates holding A-levels.

In the 2014 Research Excellence Framework Oxford achieved the best results in the UK in nine subject areas and 87% of its submission was rated as world-leading or internationally excellent, but it entered 87% of eligible staff, compared with 95% at Cambridge, leading to a slightly lower overall score in our research

ratings. Over the years, it has produced more than 50 Nobel prize-winners as well as 28 British prime ministers, including Boris Johnson.

The university has begun a £1.5bn programme of improvements. These include a new neuroscience research facility at the John Radcliffe Hospital. Another new development, provisionally called the Life and Mind Building, will be the university's largest-ever construction project, transforming space for the psychological and biological sciences.

Oxford has also received a £150m gift from Stephen A Schwarzman, the co-founder of Blackstone, the world's largest alternative investment firm, to create a centre for innovation in teaching and research in the humanities. The centre will also be home to a new Institute for Ethics in Artificial Intelligence.

Sports facilities are first-class. The Iffley Road sports complex has been upgraded with a new gym and sports hall.

The deadline for applications to Oxford is October 15, and it is not possible to apply to both Oxford and Cambridge in the same year.

Tuition fees

» Fees for UK/EU students	£9,250
» Fees for International students 2020–21	£25,740–£36.065
Medicine	£44,935 (clinical years)
» For scholarship and bursary information see www.ox.ac.uk/admissions/undergraduate/ fees-and-funding?wssl=1	
» Graduate salary	£27,040

Student numbers

Undergraduates	11,542 (3,097)
Postgraduates	7,791 (2,484)
Applications/places	21,905/3,320
Applications per place	6.6
Overall offer rate	22.2%
Unconditional offers	0%
International students	32.9%

Accommodation

College websites provide accommodation details
See chapter 14 for individual colleges

Where do the students come from?

Social inclusion ranking: 113

State schools (non-grammar)	41.3%	First generation students	13.8%	Black attainment gap	-5.7%
Grammar schools	16.9%	Deprived areas	4.1%	Disabled	7.5%
Independent schools	41.8%	All ethnic minorities	18.1%	Mature (over 21)	3.2%

Oxford Brookes University

Student satisfaction has fallen away at Oxford Brookes. The university's scores in the National Student Survey have taken one of the biggest tumbles of any institution this year, coming to rest outside the top 100 for student satisfaction with teaching quality and near that level for the wider student experience. The drop is largely responsible for a halt to the university's progress in our overall rankings over the past two years, back towards the position it traditionally occupied a decade or more ago.

Applications dropped by 23% in 2018, but a second successive rise in the offer rate helped to ensure that the numbers starting courses did not fall significantly. More than a quarter of the 2018 entrants were made unconditional offers that required them to make Oxford Brookes their first choice, putting the university in the frame as one of 23 rebuked by Damian Hinds, then education secretary. Oxford Brookes said it would hold its normal review of the practice but had not announced any change at the time of writing.

The university has been responding to some of the students' concerns evidenced in the annual National Student Survey. The library and student centre was redesigned after feedback from students and staff, adding recreational space and a gym. An updated Academic Framework will be launched in 2020, speeding up some elements of module registration and timetable delivery, after a consultation on programmes and structures.

Oxford Brookes was given a silver rating in the Teaching Excellence Framework. The panel noted that there had been high levels of investment in physical and digital resources, which are valued by students. It also saw a "developing" focus on graduate prospects for employment or further study.

New degree courses introduced in 2019 include design, photography, robotic engineering and electro-mechanical engineering. For 2020, physical activity and health promotion will be added, as well as a foundation course in law.

Plans for 2020 also include the expansion of degree apprenticeships to include six more programmes, for social workers, chartered surveyors, midwives, digital technology solutions, teachers and health and science practitioners.

Oxford Brookes is the UK's only representative in QS's world ranking of the top 50 universities that are less than 50 years old. There has been a growing emphasis on its international profile, notably through a global partnership with the Association of Chartered Certified Accountants, which gives Oxford Brookes far more students than any other UK university – more than 200,000 – taking its qualifications in other countries.

Closer to home, a campus for nursing, on a business park in Swindon, is in its fifth year. An innovative collaboration combines education, clinical practice and research across the nursing,

Headington Campus
OX3 0BP
01865 741 111
admissions@brookes.ac.uk
www.brookes.ac.uk
www.brookesunion.org.uk
Open days 2020:
see website

The Times and The Sunday Times Rankings
Overall Ranking: 64 (last year: =63)

Teaching quality	77.3%	=104
Student experience	77%	93
Research quality	11.4%	57
Entry standards	131	=67
Graduate prospects	77.4%	58
Good honours	75.7%	=59
Expected completion rate	89.6%	43
Student/staff ratio	15.1	=50
Services and facilities	£2,248	70

midwifery and allied health professions in a partnership between the university, Oxford University Hospitals NHS Foundation Trust and Oxford Health NHS Foundation Trust.

Oxford Brookes offers one of the most valuable bursaries at any UK university, in the shape of the Tessa Jane Evans bursary for nursing, worth £30,000 over three years to three candidates from low-income households.

There is a tradition of innovation that dates back to its time as a polytechnic, when it pioneered the modular degree system that has swept British higher education. In addition to providing the traditional degree classification it uses the grade point average (GPA) system – favoured by many overseas universities – that takes into account all a student's marks from the first year onwards.

In the latest phase of a £220m development programme, a new "making hub" will provide practical teaching and research facilities for the Faculty of Technology, Design and Environment, bringing together a number of disciplines serving the creative industries.

The university is popular with independent schools, which provide almost 30% of the undergraduates – much the highest proportion among the non-specialist post-1992 universities and three times the national average for the institution's subjects and entry grades. Oxford Brookes has been trying to attract more students from state schools and has targeted areas in Oxfordshire and the wider region with subject-specific summer schools and online mentoring.

Oxford Brookes excelled in the 2014 Research Excellence Framework, entering more academics than most of its peer group and still having almost 60% of its work rated as world-leading or internationally excellent. There were particularly good results in architecture, English and history. The overall performance produced a 41% rise in research funding, among the top ten increases in England.

Applicants who make Oxford Brookes their firm or insurance choice are guaranteed one of the 5,300 rooms owned or endorsed by the university. However, as 17% of entrants come through clearing, only 60% of those who would like to live in are able to be accommodated.

Impressive sports facilities include a 25-metre swimming pool and nine-hole golf course. Oxford Brookes is especially strong in rowing, and Dame Katherine Grainger, a medallist at the Rio and London Olympics, is chancellor of the university. The cricketers combine with the University of Oxford to take on county teams.

The students' union runs one of the biggest entertainment venues in Oxford.

Tuition fees

» Fees for UK/EU students	£9,250
Foundation courses	£7,350
» Fees for International students 2020–21	£13,900–£14,800
» For scholarship and bursary information see www.brookes.ac.uk/studying-at-brookes/finance/	
» Graduate salary	£22,000

Student numbers

Undergraduates	12,061	(1,057)
Postgraduates	1,822	(2,232)
Applications/places		19,245/4,655
Applications per place		4.1
Overall offer rate		87.5%
Unconditional offers		28.5%
International students		17.5%

Accommodation

University provided places: 5,302
Catered costs: £158 per week
Self-catered: £85–£184 per week
First years guaranteed accommodation
www.brookes.ac.uk/studying-at-brookes/accommodation/

Where do the students come from?

State schools (non-grammar)	64.4%	First generation students	40.2%		
Grammar schools	5.8%	Deprived areas	6.1%		
Independent schools	29.7%	All ethnic minorities	16.2%		

Social inclusion ranking: 90

Black attainment gap	-20.4%
Disabled	11.3%
Mature (over 21)	20.9%

Plymouth University

Plymouth is planning to be a "smaller, higher-quality institution, building on its core strengths including its research excellence, its strong reputation for teaching and its pivotal role in the city and wider region". The university is expecting a 17% drop in its student numbers over three years, having already experienced a similar decline in new entrants in 2018, and is cutting more than 100 jobs to address "significant financial challenges".

Following the arrival of Professor Judith Petts as vice-chancellor, Plymouth has been developing a "ten-year vision". Petts has promised students a university that is "just a little bit different" and approved a new school of nursing in Exeter. A new building for engineering and design is planned.

However, applications have dropped by more than a quarter in five years and the vice-chancellor has told staff she is acting now to ensure that the university is sustainable and has the potential for a highly successful future.

Expansion is continuing in some areas. More than 40 new degrees took their first students last September, most of them adding a foundation year to an existing programme. Fourteen are in nursing, mainly specialising in child or adult mental health. There are new offerings on the Cornwall and Exeter campuses, as well as in Plymouth itself, in subjects ranging from art and photography to maritime business and law with logistics.

Plymouth has dropped four places in this year's league table, but this follows a rise of 14 places in 2018. It is in the top 30 for student satisfaction with the quality of teaching and not far outside for the wider student experience.

The university has a silver rating in the Teaching Excellence Framework, having argued successfully that its initial bronze rating should be upgraded. The 2018 panel found that students were sufficiently challenged and benefited from sustained investment in learning resources. The panel noted that although progression to highly-skilled employment was still below the university's benchmark, this was being addressed.

Plymouth is also expanding its portfolio of degree apprenticeships, planning for 400 additional apprentices in engineering to add to its new programmes introduced in 2019 for civil engineering, social work, town planning and construction.

The university has spent more than £200m on its main campus. A £17m medical, dental and biomedical research laboratory opened in May 2019, attached to the city's Derriford Hospital. The university is the largest provider of nursing, midwifery and health professional education and training in the region, with nursing provision in Plymouth and Truro, as well as the new venture in Exeter.

A Sustainability Hub opened on campus in summer 2019, a collaborative space for

Drake Circus
Plymouth PL4 8AA
01752 585 858
admissions@plymouth.ac.uk
www.plymouth.ac.uk
www.upsu.com
Open days 2020:
June 24

The Times and The Sunday Times **Rankings**
Overall Ranking: 76 (last year: 72)

Teaching quality	82.4%	=30
Student experience	79.9%	=35
Research quality	15.9%	56
Entry standards	132	=64
Graduate prospects	73.6%	=77
Good honours	70.9%	95
Expected completion rate	83.6%	80
Student/staff ratio	16.2	=77
Services and facilities	£2,020	93

sustainable research, education and partnership. Work has begun, too, on a new facility for the most advanced brain research in the region, which will open in spring 2020.

Another innovation was the launch of the Plymouth Conservatoire, a joint project with the Theatre Royal Plymouth to teach acting, dance and theatre and performance at undergraduate level. Students divide their time between the university's performing arts building, the House, and theatre.

Only two post-1992 universities produced better results in the 2014 Research Excellence Framework. Plymouth entered a far larger proportion of its academics than most of its peer group and still managed to have nearly two-thirds of its research judged world-leading or internationally excellent. Much of the research is focused on business and industry in the region.

Plymouth was the first university to be awarded Regional Growth Fund money to promote economic development and now has one of the country's top ten business incubation facilities — part of a managed portfolio of £100m worth of innovation assets. It focuses on small and medium-sized enterprises in the southwest.

Some 12,000 students undertake work-based learning or placements with employability skills embedded throughout the curriculum, while the Plymouth Award recognises extracurricular achievements. There are 13 partner colleges across the southwest and the Channel Islands delivering the university's

degrees, as well as others overseas.

The undergraduate intake reflects Plymouth's position as the working-class hub of the region, with 88% of students educated in non-selective state schools and 45% who are the first in their family to go to university. About four in ten students receive some form of financial support. A range of funds includes one named after a previous vice-chancellor, which provides awards of up to £1,500 to help meet the cost of extracurricular activities.

Student facilities include the £3m health and wellbeing centre and almost 2,000 residential places, many privately operated. Applicants holding Plymouth as their firm choice are guaranteed a place in one of the managed halls or in an accredited private hall if they apply by the end of May.

On campus there is a sports hall, fitness centre, dance studio and squash courts. The university has upgraded its facilities for water sports and sessions are run exclusively for students at the city's international-standard swimming and diving centre. The city centre is not short of student-oriented nightlife.

Tuition fees

» Fees for UK/EU students	£9,250
» Fees for International students 2020–21	£13,800
Dentistry £38,040; Medicine £39,900 (clinical years)	
» For scholarship and bursary information see www.plymouth.ac.uk/fees	
» Graduate salary	£22,000

Student numbers

Undergraduates	15,857	(1,882)
Postgraduates	1,542	(1,486)
Applications/places		17,670/4,520
Applications per place		3.9
Overall offer rate		87.9%
Unconditional offers		0.3%
International students		9.9%

Accommodation
University provided places: 1,989
Self-catered: £97–£175 per week
First years guaranteed accommodation
www.plymouth.ac.uk/student-life/services/accommodation

Where do the students come from?

State schools (non-grammar)	88.3%	First generation students	45.3%	Black attainment gap	-15.2%
Grammar schools	6.2%	Deprived areas	14.8%	Disabled	8%
Independent schools	5.4%	All ethnic minorities	11.1%	Mature (over 21)	24.9%

Social inclusion ranking: 55

Plymouth Marjon University

Plymouth Marjon might have expected a dip in student satisfaction after unprecedented increases in the last edition of the guide. Instead, the rates in our two measures taken from the National Student Survey have nudged even higher. Only two universities have students who are more satisfied with the quality of teaching, and the university ranks in the top ten for student experience overall.

The numbers starting courses rose by almost 10% in 2018, following a 30% rise in applications – one of the biggest at any university in a year when the demand for places fell nationally. Half of the entrants received unconditional offers, but not on condition that they made Marjon their firm choice. While the university therefore avoided censure by the government, it has confirmed that only a limited number of unconditional offers will be available in 2020 following a "robust review of statements and programme team discussions, in many cases with interviews or conversations".

Popular new degree programmes in subjects such as coaching and physical education, commercial music, sport, and music journalism helped to boost the demand for places in 2018. There was another, much smaller, increase in applications in 2019.

The university has gone up 17 places in our table over the past two years, but is still just outside the top 100. Marjon has a silver rating in the Teaching Excellence Framework. The awards panel found "appropriate levels of contact time on courses, and a personalised approach to delivery that promotes good engagement".

A number of initiatives to improve the student experience may have played their part in the improved satisfaction levels. Every student now has a personal development tutor to help with academic skills, careers advice, one-to-one mentoring, confidence-building and resilience.

A new student bar and a student hub, with social working space and an information centre, opened in 2018. The hub acts as a one-stop shop for student support services such as learning support, employability and career development, and counselling.

The university has also been investing in teaching and learning technology, introducing a new Moodle virtual learning environment in 2019 and installing 30 interactive TV screens in the main lecture rooms. All lectures are filmed for later viewing by students.

Teaching is now live from a new TV and radio broadcasting facility, part of the BBC studio building in Plymouth. Almost all courses have some form of placement for students, some in NHS hospitals and local football clubs, as well as media outlets.

More than 97% of the undergraduates are state-educated and one in five comes

Derriford Road
Plymouth PL6 8BH
01752 636 890
admissions@marjon.ac.uk
www.marjon.ac.uk
www.marjonsu.com
Open days 2020:
June 5/6

The Times and The Sunday Times **Rankings**
Overall Ranking: =102 (last year: 109)

Teaching quality	86.7%	3
Student experience	82.7%	9
Research quality	0%	127
Entry standards	125	=81
Graduate prospects	63.7%	=122
Good honours	77.1%	52
Expected completion rate	78.4%	=113
Student/staff ratio	22.2	129
Services and facilities	£1,996	96

from an area of low participation in higher education. Marjon has two sponsored schools and progression arrangements with a further five, where there are targeted interventions and advice and guidance sessions to raise awareness of higher education. Bursary programmes include one that awards up to £500 to help students to afford an international experience.

Established in 1840 as a Church of England teacher training college in London, with the son of poet Samuel Taylor Coleridge as its first principal, the university describes itself as "arguably the third oldest higher education institution in England". The College of St Mark and St John only moved to Plymouth in 1973.

Still officially a Church of England voluntary institution, its Chaplaincy Centre is at the heart of the campus, but there is limited emphasis on religion in the university's promotional material.

Teacher training remains a strength. Ofsted has rated its courses outstanding for leadership and management. Courses are available in six counties, as well as in Cyprus and Germany. A new apprenticeship for teacher training has been approved.

However, Marjon lists sport as its top specialism. The teaching facilities include sports science labs with a climate chamber, bod pod and an anti-gravity treadmill. A sports scholarship scheme extends to sports not currently covered by the national Talented Athlete Scholarship Scheme.

The university's excellent sports facilities are all available to the public. They include a floodlit 3G pitch for rugby, lacrosse and football, two further floodlit all-weather lacrosse and hockey pitches, a climbing wall, 25-metre indoor swimming pool and gym, as well as a rehabilitation clinic and sports science lab.

Marjon suffers in our table for a decision not to take part in the 2014 Research Excellence Framework, which leaves it in last place for research quality. A subsequent research strategy has reversed the policy.

The campus is located on the expanding north side of Plymouth, close to the Dartmoor National Park and the sea. On campus, students can seek peace at a duck pond and nature trail.

There are residential places on campus for 456 students in seven halls of residence and 38 village houses. First-year students are guaranteed places, and those whose offers become unconditional have first choice of accommodation. Those living on campus may only bring a car in exceptional circumstances, but the lively city centre is a short bus ride from the campus.

Tuition fees

»	Fees for UK/EU students	£9,250
	Foundation courses	£6,000
»	Fees for International students 2020–21	£12,000
»	For scholarship and bursary information see www.marjon.ac.uk/courses/fees-and-funding/	
»	Graduate salary	£18,000

Student numbers

Undergraduates	1,965	(177)
Postgraduates	311	(183)
Applications/places		3,110/835
Applications per place		3.7
Overall offer rate		84%
Unconditional offers		0%
International students		2.7%

Accommodation

University provided places: 456
Self-catered: £95–£115 per week
First years guaranteed accommodation
www.marjon.ac.uk/student-life/accommodation/

Where do the students come from?

State schools (non-grammar)	93.8%	First generation students	59.2%	
Grammar schools	3.5%	Deprived areas	20.9%	
Independent schools	2.7%	All ethnic minorities	4.4%	

Social inclusion ranking: =7

Black attainment gap	n/a
Disabled	15.1%
Mature (over 21)	31.1%

University of Portsmouth

"Optimum levels of student engagement and commitment to learning" gained Portsmouth gold in the government's Teaching Excellence Framework. But falling scores in the National Student Survey in 2019 have helped to bring an end to a sustained period of progress in our league table. The university had been in the top 30 for the student experience, but has dropped 16 places on this measure and is down five places overall in our latest ranking.

Close to record enrolment in 2018 after reversing a one-year decline, Portsmouth's greatest strength remains in graduate employment. It is in the top 20 for graduate prospects across all universities, and second among modern universities created since 1992. In 2017 *The Economist* named Portsmouth the top UK university for boosting graduate salaries when background, qualifications and subjects were taken into account.

To ensure this trend continues, the university is investing in "real-life" work scenarios – both real and simulated. The latest example is the recently opened Portsmouth Eye Clinic, staffed by qualified optometrists who supervise second and third-year optometry students, helping them to gain essential clinical experience. Elsewhere, student pharmacists learn to dispense medicines for a high-street pharmacy, while forensic scientists work alongside police officers, and dental nurses and hygienists treat patients in the university's dental clinic.

The TEF panel also praised the university for excellent, integrated teaching and assessment practices, and industry-leading physical and digital resources used by students to develop their independence and confidence.

In July 2019, the university opened a £12m Future Technology Centre, where students on the new BEng (Hons) and MEng Innovation Engineering courses will be able to get to grips with real world problems in health, humanitarianism and the environment through specialist technology.

Other new degrees introduced for 2019–20 include mental health nursing, financial management, virtual and augmented reality, and science with a foundation year for those without the necessary qualifications for immediate entry to a degree course. BSc courses in nutritional therapy, music technology, and economic crime and compliance come on stream in 2020.

Portsmouth also plans to have 1,000 students taking degree apprenticeships by September 2020 – more than three times the current total. There will be new programmes in adult nursing and practical policing and for cybersecurity technical professionals.

Well over 90% of school leavers who apply to Portsmouth receive offers and those with unconditional offers are eligible for a

Academic registry
University House
Winston Churchill Avenue
Portsmouth PO1 2UP
023 9284 5566
admissions@port.ac.uk
www.port.ac.uk
www.upsu.net
Open days 2020:
July 1, 4; October 3, 31;
November 28

The Times and The Sunday Times **Rankings**
Overall Ranking: =56 (last year: =51)

Teaching quality	80.5%	=59
Student experience	79.3%	=42
Research quality	8.6%	70
Entry standards	115	=109
Graduate prospects	85.4%	=14
Good honours	75%	68
Expected completion rate	85.4%	=65
Student/staff ratio	15.4	=56
Services and facilities	£2,222	75

£1,000 vice-chancellor's scholarship if they meet their predicted grades. In the face of recent criticism over unconditional offers, the university insists the scholarship incentive helps to avoid demotivation.

Health subjects gained the best results in the university's Research Excellence Framework submission in 2014. Dentistry, nursing and pharmacy academics did best, with about 90% of their research reaching the top two categories for world-leading or internationally excellent work. Almost two-thirds of the university's submission was judged in the top two categories overall.

Portsmouth has one of the largest language departments, teaching six languages to degree level and offering free language courses to all students. About 1,000 students go abroad for part of their course, and as many come from the Continent to study here.

The university has pioneered new approaches to student well-being. Academic staff, including personal tutors, are trained in mental health awareness and how best to support their students. Portsmouth was the first university to use WhatsUp?, an app that promotes communication between students and pastoral services.

The Guildhall campus is in the centre of Portsmouth with most residential accommodation nearby. It has undergone extensive redevelopment, including remodelling the library to provide more access to study spaces and IT equipment.

Students have access to almost 900 personal computers and laptops in the library, with 1,000 more dotted around the campus.

Portsmouth paid £5.7m in 2018 for Highbury College's City Learning Centre to provide additional high-quality teaching facilities at the heart of the campus.

A £6.5m student centre includes alcohol-free areas. A £50m sports facility is due to open in 2021, with an eight-lane 25m swimming pool, an eight-court sports hall, a 175-station fitness suite and a ski simulator. The university's seaside location provides an excellent base for water sports and outdoor sports facilities include an all-weather 3G pitch suitable for football, rugby, lacrosse and American football.

Many students live in Southsea, which has a vibrant social scene and quirky shops. The university has 4,000 residential places – enough to guarantee accommodation to all new students who apply by the deadline and make Portsmouth their firm choice. However, some 250 students were left without accommodation at the start of the current academic year because a development by a private provider was not ready.

Tuition fees

»	Fees for UK/EU students	£9,250
»	Fees for International students 2020–21	£14,300–£16,400
»	For scholarship and bursary information see www.port.ac.uk/study/undergraduate/undergraduate-fees-and-student-finance	
»	Graduate salary	£21,840

Student numbers

Undergraduates	18,083 (2,223)
Postgraduates	2,140 (1,951)
Applications/places	25,600/6,040
Applications per place	4.2
Overall offer rate	96%
Unconditional offers	0%
International students	16.3%

Accommodation

University provided places: 4,062
Catered costs: £130–£169 per week
Self-catered: £96–£159 per week
First years guaranteed accommodation
www.port.ac.uk/study/accommodation

Where do the students come from?

State schools (non-grammar)	90.9%	First generation students	48.4%	Black attainment gap	-25.8%
Grammar schools	5.1%	Deprived areas	13%	Disabled	8.7%
Independent schools	4.0%	All ethnic minorities	28.4%	Mature (over 21)	12%

Social inclusion ranking: 49

Queen Margaret University Edinburgh

QMU has jumped another 15 places in our league table after returning to the top 100 last year. The strongest factor was improved student satisfaction: in the bottom ten as recently as 2017 after students took a dim view of teaching quality, QMU is now approaching the top 50 on this measure.

Applications increased in 2019 by a healthy 5% after a fall in the demand for places in 2018. Two new degrees in education studies and a broad-based social science degree are partly responsible, according to the university.

The first students have also started new degree courses in media and communications, and public relations and marketing communications. An integrated master's degree in dietetics will follow in 2020.

Since 2015, the university's Scottish Centre for Food Development and Innovation has supported teaching and research for its food and drink courses. A partnership with the Edinburgh New Town Cookery School, run by a QMU graduate, helps students gain practical experience during their degree studies in international hospitality management.

A "student-centred approach" with a culture of personalised support has been adopted in the university's strategy to prepare for its 150th anniversary in 2025. Nearly a quarter of the workforce has been trained in mental health first aid – offering a bigger network than any other university in Scotland.

The university's efforts have been recognised with rising student satisfaction scores for their overall experience as well as their assessment of teaching quality. QMU has the best results across both measures of any university in Edinburgh.

Queen Margaret has a highly successful employer mentoring scheme, matching third- and fourth-year students with experienced professionals who have relevant industry experience.

A business innovation zone supports the creation of student and staff start-up businesses. QMU is the only university in Scotland to host a Business Gateway on campus, offering guidance for new and established local businesses. In partnership with East Lothian council, the university is developing Edinburgh Innovation Park on land next to the university campus.

The university is named after Saint Margaret, the 11th-century wife of King Malcolm III of Scotland, and was originally a school of cookery for women, set up in 1875. It moved to its purpose-built campus, designed in consultation with the students, in the seaside town of Musselburgh 12 years ago when it gained university status. The campus, which won a string of awards, is one of the most

University Drive
Edinburgh EH21 6UU
0131 474 0000
admissions@qmu.ac.uk
www.qmu.ac.uk
www.qmusu.org.uk
Open days 2020:
see website

The Times and The Sunday Times Rankings
Overall Ranking: 82 (last year: 97)

Teaching quality	80.7%	=53
Student experience	76.5%	=96
Research quality	6.6%	79
Entry standards	151	39
Graduate prospects	72.9%	=85
Good honours	79%	44
Expected completion rate	81.9%	90
Student/staff ratio	18.6	112
Services and facilities	£1,775	113

environmentally sustainable in the UK and still exceeds current standards.

Of only 3,100 undergraduates, three-quarters are women and two-thirds are from Scotland. QMU has the broadest range of allied health courses in Scotland, from dietetics, podiatry and audiology to art therapy, music therapy and health psychology.

QMU ranks second in the country in our new Scottish social inclusion table. Almost 97% of the students are state-educated, with applicants from disadvantaged groups eligible for an offer at the minimum entry requirements for their desired course. More than four in ten students are the first in their family to go to university. However, the university has a completion rate well below the UK average for its subjects and entry grades.

Although only 22% of the eligible staff were entered in the 2014 Research Excellence Framework, results showed great improvement and almost 60% of the submission was considered world-leading or internationally excellent. Its work in speech and language sciences is well regarded and 92% of its submission in this area rated in the top two categories, placing the university second in the UK and first in Scotland.

QMU has since launched new centres for research and knowledge exchange, which place academics in direct contact with business, industry and the health profession. The university also introduced its first graduate apprenticeship in 2018 and will offer another 30 places in business management in 2020.

From campus, next door to Musselburgh train station, Edinburgh can be less than a ten-minute journey. There are 800 residential places on campus, which also hosts all the sports facilities. The university does not guarantee accommodation for new entrants, although 92% of those who wanted one were offered a place in 2018.

As part of its accommodation service, QMU runs the ResLife programme in partnership with the sports centre and students' union. This includes a range of social, educational, recreational and cultural activities to help students settle in and feel welcomed and supported.

Tuition fees

» Fees for Scottish/EU students £0–£1,820
  RUK fees £9,250 (capped at £27,750 for 4-year courses)
» Fees for International students 2020–21 £13,000–£14,500
» For scholarship and bursary information see
  www.qmu.ac.uk/current-students/
  current-students-general-information/
  fees-and-charges/202021-undergraduate-fees/
» Graduate salary £20,280

Student numbers

Undergraduates	2,917	(513)
Postgraduates	604	(1,140)
Applications/places	5,655/1,015	
Applications per place	5.6	
Overall offer rate	69.7%	
Unconditional offers	0%	
International students	20.8%	

Accommodation

University provided places: 800
Self-catered: £114–£137 per week
www.qmu.ac.uk/campus-life/accommodation/

Where do the students come from?

State schools (non-grammar)	95.4%	First generation students	41.4%
Grammar schools	1.1%	Deprived areas	19.1%
Independent schools	3.5%	All ethnic minorities	8.4%

Social inclusion ranking (Scotland): 2

Black attainment gap	n/a
Disabled	9.7%
Mature (over 21)	39.4%

Queen Mary, University of London

Queen Mary's new strategy, adopted this year, aims to make it "the most inclusive university of its kind, anywhere". It is already 18 places ahead of the next Russell Group institution in our social inclusion table, with two-thirds of its undergraduates from ethnic minorities and 46% the first in their family to go to university.

The strategy promises a world-leading learning experience, co-created with students and employers, promoting new approaches to teaching using bespoke technological advances. Extra support will be available for students who lack the confidence and networks to fulfil their potential. There will also be efforts to raise QMUL's profile and provide more courses in partner institutions.

QMUL had already introduced a new degree structure to improve students' networking and communication skills and provide experience outside their subject. The QMUL Model accounts for 10% of a student's degree, covering activities such as work experience, volunteering in the community, overseas travel, project work with local businesses and other organisations, learning a language, or taking modules from other subjects.

As in other research universities in London, student satisfaction remains an obstacle for Queen Mary in our main league table.

It is well outside the top 100 in both of the measures (of teaching quality and the wider student experience) derived from the National Student Survey and only just in the top 50 institutions overall.

However, QMUL does not suffer from the dispersed nature of other London institutions, with most of its 13,600 undergraduates both taught and housed on a self-contained campus in the fashionable East End. Its large medical school, Barts and the London School of Medicine and Dentistry, is based in nearby Whitechapel.

QMUL was given a silver rating in the government's Teaching Excellence Framework. The panel was impressed by the quality of coaching programmes, mentoring schemes and employer engagement that help students gain highly skilled employment.

The launch of a raft of new degrees – many of them existing offerings with the addition of a year abroad – helped to boost applications to Queen Mary in 2018. The trend continued in the 2019 admissions round, with the option of a professional placement or a year abroad added to a number of programmes and applications rising by almost 6%.

Another 22 degrees will take their first students in 2020, most of them incorporating a year abroad. At the same time, the small portfolio of degree apprenticeships will expand into data science, aerospace engineering and digital and technology solutions following QMUL's successful bid to

Mile End Road
London E1 4NS
020 7882 5511
admissions@qmul.ac.uk
www.qmul.ac.uk
www.qmsu.org/
Open days 2020:
June 26/27

The Times and The Sunday Times **Rankings**
Overall Ranking: 49 (last year: =46)

Teaching quality	73.5%	124
Student experience	74.3%	=114
Research quality	37.9%	19
Entry standards	144	46
Graduate prospects	78.7%	=53
Good honours	83.2%	27
Expected completion rate	89.9%	=40
Student/staff ratio	13.1	15
Services and facilities	£2,352	63

be the site of one of the government's 12 new institutes of technology.

Medicine and the other health subjects did well in the 2014 Research Excellence Framework, but the best results came in the humanities. About 95% of the research in linguistics and in music, drama and the performing arts was rated as world-leading or internationally excellent. More than 85% of QMUL's entire submission reached the top two categories.

The new strategy includes the establishment of interdisciplinary research institutes, centres and networks – both physical and virtual – in areas such as global health and inequalities, the digital environment, ethics and governance, and the creative industries. There will be a focus on medical research, especially on haemophilia.

More than £100m has been spent in five years on campus improvements, which have included a new graduate centre, a new dental school and redevelopment of the engineering and maths buildings.

The medical school, which is ranked just outside the top 50 in the world by the QS 2020 guide, is based in the £45m Blizard building. Its dentistry institute moved into the first new dental school to be built in the UK for 40 years, when it occupied new facilities in the Royal London Hospital.

The undergraduate intake has grown by more than a third since QMUL joined the Russell Group in 2012. The international options include QMUL's medical school in Malta, where there is a five-year degree taught by staff from Barts and local clinicians trained by the school.

The award-winning Queen Mary Careers and Enterprise Centre provides a range of short-term consultancy, enterprise and project opportunities for students. The university expects to place more than 1,000 students with a range of employers in 2019–20.

More than two-fifths of all undergraduates receive financial support from QMUL. The new strategy targets further increases in diversity, both among home and international students.

The Mile End campus has a refurbished students' union and a subsidised health and fitness centre. Students welcome the relatively low prices (for the capital) in east London and their proximity to the lively youth culture of Shoreditch, Brick Lane and Spitalfields. QMUL students can use the sports facilities at the nearby Queen Elizabeth Olympic Park, including the Copper Box indoor arena and the Aquatic Centre's swimming pool.

Tuition fees

» Fees for UK/EU students	£9,250
» Fees for International students 2020–21	£18,000–£22,500
Dentistry, Medicine	£38,000
» For scholarship and bursary information see	
www.qmul.ac.uk/undergraduate/feesandfunding/	
» Graduate salary	£25,000

Student numbers

Undergraduates	13,932	(3)
Postgraduates	4,725	(1,412)
Applications/places	32,155/4,875	
Applications per place	6.6	
Overall offer rate	80.9%	
Unconditional offers	0%	
International students	33.4%	

Accommodation

University provided places: 2,983
Self-catered: £131–£180 per week
First years guaranteed accommodation
www.qmul.ac.uk/study/accommodation

Where do the students come from?

State schools (non-grammar)	79.3%	First generation students	46%	
Grammar schools	11.5%	Deprived areas	4.6%	
Independent schools	9.2%	All ethnic minorities	68.1%	

Social inclusion ranking: 51

Black attainment gap	-15%
Disabled	7.5%
Mature (over 21)	9.2%

Queen's University, Belfast

Queen's has moved three places further up our top 40 this year, but it could have been more if the university had not dropped out of the top 100 for student satisfaction with teaching quality. The university also slipped five places in the National Student Survey section on the broader student experience.

Investment of £350m in capital projects – with the same amount pledged over the next ten years – may help to turn the tide. A £7.5m advanced manufacturing technology facility and a new cybersecurity lab opened in 2018 and a £39m School of Biological Sciences the following spring to expand the university's life sciences sector in areas such as agriculture, food science and the environment. As part of a partnership, the university has also opened Queen's Precision Medicine Centre of Excellence, which hopes to develop artificial intelligence solutions to enable early, rapid and precise diagnoses of cancers.

A member of the Russell Group and well inside the top 200 in the QS World University Rankings, Queen's is recognised as Northern Ireland's premier university, with graduates in senior positions in most of its top companies. Enrolments are nearing record levels in spite of marginal declines in applications in 2019 and in the previous two years.

More than 60% of the undergraduates come from grammar schools, which educate a much larger proportion of the population in Northern Ireland than elsewhere in the UK.

Queen's takes inclusiveness seriously, with 30% of undergraduates receiving financial support from a £3.8m pool of funds for widening participation. A Pathway Opportunity Programme helps Northern Irish students living in disadvantaged areas who may require additional financial support and encouragement. The latest programme has 187 participants, who are guaranteed a conditional offer which may be two grades lower than the norm for their chosen course.

The university charter has guaranteed student representation, equal rights for women and non-denominational teaching since 1908. Queen's was one of four university colleges for the whole of Ireland in the 19th century, and still draws students from all over the island of Ireland. However, the vast majority come from Northern Ireland, and Queen's suffers somewhat in our main league table from the comparison of entry grades because relatively few sixth-formers in the province take four A-levels.

Queen's intends to double its 10% international contingent of students enrolled in 2017–18. More than half of the international students received scholarships in the last academic year.

The IT facilities are good: Queen's was the first institution to meet the national target

University Road
Belfast BT7 1NN
028 9097 3838
admissions@qub.ac.uk
www.qub.ac.uk
www.qubsu.org.uk
Open days 2020:
see website

The Times and The Sunday Times **Rankings**
Overall Ranking: 35 (last year: =38)

Teaching quality	77.5%	102
Student experience	77.4%	=83
Research quality	39.7%	14
Entry standards	152	38
Graduate prospects	82.4%	26
Good honours	84%	23
Expected completion rate	91.8%	=29
Student/staff ratio	15.9	=71
Services and facilities	£2,416	56

of providing at least one computer workstation for every five undergraduates. Students are encouraged to complete online language programmes.

Queen's ranks first in the UK for establishment of knowledge transfer partnerships. With Warwick, it runs a national programme to promote the commercialisation of university research, helping to determine whether there is a market for products or services. The university won a Queen's Anniversary Prize for research and technology transfer in cybersecurity, and was awarded Northern Ireland's first Regius Professorship in electronics and computer engineering.

The university is in our top 20 for research after entering 95% of its academics for the 2014 Research Excellence Framework, a proportion matched only by Cambridge. Of the large submission, 77% of the research was considered world-leading or internationally excellent and 14 subject areas were ranked in the UK's top 20.

There are four global research institutes in food security; health sciences; electronics, communications and information technology; and global peace, security and justice.

Queen's has a cinema, an art gallery and theatre, all of which are open to the wider community as well as students. The city centre now has plenty of nightlife, but the social scene is mainly concentrated on the students' union and the surrounding area.

Most of the 4,000 residential places are at the Elms Student Village, close to the university, on the south side of the city, but a new development of 1,200 rooms with its own services, including pastoral care, security and social activities opened in September 2019 in the city centre. The additional places have enabled Queen's to guarantee accommodation to all first-year students.

The sports facilities, which include Mourne Cottage in the mountains, benefited from a £20m programme of investment. There is an arena pitch which can host football, rugby or Gaelic sport, another 14 pitches, a recreational trail and conference facilities.

The Physical Education Centre includes two swimming pools, and there is a £1.2m boathouse on the River Lagan. An Elite Athlete programme offers up to £8,000 of support for those at the top of their game.

Tuition fees
» Fees for Northern Ireland/EU students £4,275
  Students from England, Scotland and Wales £9,250
» Fees for International students 2020–21 £16,900–£20.800
  Medicine £41,850
» For scholarship and bursary information see
  www.qub.ac.uk/Study/scholarshipsandfunding/
» Graduate salary £21,500

Student numbers

Undergraduates	15,013	(3,618)
Postgraduates	3,705	(2,152)
Applications/places		28,360/4,400
Applications per place		6.4
Overall offer rate		86%
Unconditional offers		0%
International students		14.8%

Where do the students come from?

State schools (non-grammar)	36.1%	Other data	n/a
Grammar schools	61.9%		
Independent schools	2.1%		

Accommodation
University provided places: 4,024
Catered costs: £113–£156 per week
Self-catered: £75–£165 per week
First years guaranteed accommodation
www.qub.ac.uk/accommodation

Social inclusion ranking: n/a

Ravensbourne University, London

Ravensbourne is spending its second year in our table – like the first – rooted to the bottom. It is not the first to do so, and the new university is hampered by the absence of a score for research quality because in its pre-university days it did not enter the 2014 Research Excellence Framework.

The specialist design and digital media institution occupies a striking, purpose-built, open-plan building, next to the O2 Arena, on London's Greenwich Peninsula. It was awarded university status in 2018, only a few months after securing the right to award its own degrees.

Ravensbourne has fewer than 2,600 students, but a record number entered in 2018 – almost twice as many as a decade ago. In contrast to most specialist arts universities, male students are in a narrow majority.

Even before university status arrived, Ravensbourne's graduates enjoyed higher starting salaries than those at any of the universities specialising in creative art and design. There is also a strong track record for business creation. The incubation unit has hosted more than 100 creative technology businesses, from award-winning production companies and digital agencies to internationally recognised fashion labels.

Ravensbourne was given a silver rating in the Teaching Excellence Framework (TEF). The panel was impressed by the high level of practice-based learning linked to excellent digital resources, as well as by the highly valued employer input to course design and extensive industry collaboration.

This year's table sees a leap in the official projection for the completion of degrees – one of the TEF measures. The new rate is almost 90%, taking the university up 74 places on this measure. However, Ravensbourne finishes bottom of our ranking for both student satisfaction with the student experience and staffing levels, and next to bottom for satisfaction with teaching quality.

Established only in 1962, Ravensbourne was located on Bromley Common and then Chislehurst, Kent, before moving to its current home nine years ago. Its degrees were validated by the University of Arts London until 2018.

New degrees were introduced in games design, illustration for communication, music and sound design, user-experience and user-interface (UX/UI) design, and digital television technology. There is also a range of pre-degree courses that combine practical studio projects, workshops and traditional academic learning.

More than 40% of students taking foundation programmes progress to degree courses. As in other similar institutions, admission decisions hinge on applicants' portfolio or showreel as much as on their academic grades.

---

6 Penrose Way
Greenwich Peninsula
London SE10 0EW
020 3040 3500
admissions@rave.ac.uk
www.ravensbourne.ac.uk
www.ravesu.co.uk
Open days 2020:
February 22,
March 18, June 20

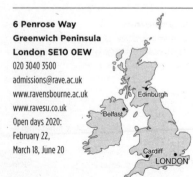

***The Times and The Sunday Times* Rankings**
Overall Ranking: 131 (last year: 132)

Teaching quality	72.1%	128
Student experience	66.1%	129
Research quality	n/a	
Entry standards	113	=115
Graduate prospects	68.7%	=105
Good honours	63.9%	=125
Expected completion rate	89.7%	42
Student/staff ratio	31.6	131
Services and facilities	£1,460	129

Widening participation is among Ravensbourne's priorities, although it is in the bottom half of our latest social inclusion table. Almost 40% of the undergraduates are from ethnic minorities and more than 93% attended non-selective state schools or colleges. There is a range of bursaries for low-income students, the main one being the Ravensbourne Bursary of £500 a year for those with a household income of less than £25,000. All new students receive a £300 laptop bursary, going up to £500 for those from low-income households.

There is also a programme of free meals for the most disadvantaged students, covering those in receipt of, or having parents who are in receipt of, one or more of a number of benefits.

A new partnership with Berghs School of Communication, in Stockholm, allows students there who successfully complete one semester to be accepted into the first year at Ravensbourne, and stay on to complete their degrees. The first cohort of students from Berghs arrived at Ravensbourne in January 2019.

The single-building campus requires the university to manage its student numbers, room use and teaching model carefully, but the strategic plan envisages gradual growth, increased commercial activity and more research in the longer term.

Ravensbourne aims to be recognised as a national and international leader in creative industries education and training. It is already in the top 150 in the QS global ranking for art and design, which relies on academic and employer reputation.

Ravensbourne's best-known alumni include fashion designers Clare Waight Keller of Givenchy, who designed the dress Meghan Markle wore for her wedding to Prince Harry; Stella McCartney; Bruce Oldfield; Kevin Carrigan, the senior vice-president and creative director at Ralph Lauren; literary scholar Robert Hewison; handbag designer Emma Hill, sculptor Alison Wilding and the co-designer of the Olympic 2012 torch, Jay Osgerby.

The university does not own halls of residence, but it works with a number of private providers to offer accommodation. No guarantees are given, but first-year students who request accommodation are usually found a room.

There is discounted membership for students of a gym within 200 yards of the university building and good transport into central London. Ravensbourne students also enjoy discounts at restaurants, bars and shops in the neighbouring O2 arena.

Tuition fees

»	Fees for UK/EU students	£9,250
	Foundation courses	£5,421
»	Fees for International students 2019–20	£14,500
	Foundation courses	£9,500
»	For scholarship and bursary information see www.ravensbourne.ac.uk/study-here/ bursaries-and-scholarships/	
»	Graduate salary	£20,000

Student numbers

Undergraduates	2,474	(0)
Postgraduates	47	(7)
Applications/places		3,205/965
Applications per place		3.3
Overall offer rate		64.2%
Unconditional offers		0%
International students		10.8%

Accommodation

University provided places: 0
Self-catered: £149–£310 per week (through private providers)
www.ravensbourne.ac.uk/study-here/accommodation/

Where do the students come from?

State schools (non-grammar)	93.5%	First generation students	45.8%	
Grammar schools	2.2%	Deprived areas	6.1%	
Independent schools	4.4%	All ethnic minorities	39.9%	

Social inclusion ranking: 72

Black attainment gap	-25%
Disabled	6.8%
Mature (over 21)	14.6%

University of Reading

By 2020, Reading wants one new graduate in five to spend part of their degree abroad – and is determined to increase the proportion to one in three by its centenary year in 2026. Summer schools at its own branch campus in Malaysia, as well as at longstanding partner institutions in Moscow and Nanjing, China, will be among the options.

Many of the 24 new degrees welcoming their first students in 2019 incorporate a year abroad or a placement year into existing programmes such as geography and archaeology. Another seven new degrees are planned for 2020, including archaeology and anthropology, architectural engineering and chemistry with cosmetic science.

The remodelling of undergraduate options has contributed to swings in the numbers starting courses in recent years. New admissions were up by 15% in 2017 and down by a similar amount in 2018 – but still 1,000 more than in the years before £9,000 fees were introduced.

More change is on the way to mark Reading's centenary with its 2026: Transform programme, designed to make the university a "larger, vibrant and more sustainable institution" by pumping £200m into its three campuses. Many of the ideas being put into practice have been shaped by student feedback.

The main library has been undergoing a £40m three-year upgrade, increasing study space and improving key facilities, and a £55m health and life sciences building is set to open in spring 2020, housing one of the largest teaching labs in the UK and bringing together a school that is currently spread over six buildings.

Lecture theatres across the campus have been refurbished, and £2m has been spent on the student union's popular nightclub, 3sixty. A £1m capital fund has been set up to pay for projects suggested by staff or students, selected by the students' union. The first projects include more storage lockers, a 3G sports pitch and further investment in the filming of lectures, as well as a new "relaxation zone" with massage chairs, bean bags and sleeper pods.

Reading gained silver in the Teaching Excellence Framework on the basis of its high-quality physical and digital resources, particularly for consistent use of virtual learning tools and the effective integration of student support services with academic provision. It noted that students were consistently engaged with developments at the forefront of research, scholarship and practice.

The university has moved up two places in our table this year, consolidating its membership of the top 40. However, Reading remains outside the top 100 in both of our measures of student satisfaction, which holds back its overall ranking.

Reading brought in a new academic tutor system in 2018 to enhance students'

Whiteknights
PO Box 217
Reading RG6 6AH
0118 378 8372
www.reading.ac.uk/question
www.reading.ac.uk
www.rusu.co.uk
Open days 2020:
June 19/20;
October 3, 10

The Times and The Sunday Times **Rankings**
Overall Ranking: =38 (last year: 40)

Teaching quality	77.3%	=104
Student experience	75.2%	110
Research quality	36.5%	29
Entry standards	132	=64
Graduate prospects	76.0%	=66
Good honours	81.7%	=31
Expected completion rate	93%	17
Student/staff ratio	15.8	=66
Services and facilities	£2,785	23

professional development and work in partnership with the student welfare team. The university also runs an award-winning career mentoring programme, which connects students for a year with successful alumni.

Reading was one of only two universities established between the two world wars. Originally the University of Oxford's extension college, its main campus is set in 320 acres of parkland on the outskirts of Reading and has won four Green Gown environmental awards in a row. The university has another campus in town and 2,000 acres of farmland at nearby Sonning and Shinfield, where the Centre for Dairy Research is based. A global reputation for courses and research in agriculture and development attracts many of the international students, who now make up 20% of the total.

The university's business school, formerly Henley Management College, has an attractive site on the banks of the River Thames for postgraduate and executive programmes.

All undergraduates can take work placements as part of their course, and career management skills modules contribute five credits towards their degree classification. There are also plans to expand the single degree apprenticeship programme in applied management by adding three more in management, financial services and digital solutions. The university is aiming for up to 600 degree apprentices, with the possibility of more in early-years education.

Reading entered more academics for assessment in the 2014 Research Excellence Framework than most of its peers and still had almost 80% of its research rated as world-leading or internationally excellent. Real estate, planning and construction management were among the top-performing subject areas.

More than 5,000 residential places are either on the main campus, Whiteknights, or within easy walking distance. A place in halls is guaranteed for all new entrants.

The SportsPark, on the edge of the campus, has extensive indoor and outdoor facilities including dance and yoga studios, three floodlit 3G five-a-side football pitches, plus courts for badminton, squash and tennis. There are also boathouses on the Thames and a sailing and canoeing club nearby.

Reading has plenty of nightlife and is within easy reach of London. The town boasts an award-winning shopping centre, although the cost of living is high.

Tuition fees

» Fees for UK/EU students   £9,250
» Fees for International students 2020–21   £16,890–£20,315
» For scholarship and bursary information see
   www.reading.ac.uk/ready-to-study/study/
   fees-and-funding.aspx
» Graduate salary   £22,000

Student numbers

Undergraduates	**12,280**	(98)
Postgraduates	2,972	(1,646)
Applications/places		20,225/3,970
Applications per place		5.1
Overall offer rate		90.1%
Unconditional offers		0%
International students		25.7%

Accommodation

University provided places: 4,984
Catered costs: £128–£194 per week
Self-catered: £130–£221 per week
First years guaranteed accommodation
www.reading.ac.uk/ready-to-study/accommodation.aspx

Where do the students come from?

State schools (non-grammar)	73.8%	First generation students	36.8%	Black attainment gap	-25.3%
Grammar schools	10.5%	Deprived areas	6.3%	Disabled	6.2%
Independent schools	15.7%	All ethnic minorities	29.5%	Mature (over 21)	7.9%

Social inclusion ranking: 98

Robert Gordon University

A big rise in student satisfaction has lifted RGU into the top 30 in both of our measures derived from the National Student Survey and moved the university 13 places up the overall league table, almost reversing the decline it suffered in the last edition.

Applications were up a little during the 2019 admissions cycle, but remain almost 18% lower than they were five years ago. The university has been developing new, more flexible course models focusing on employability.

With many graduates now choosing to start their own businesses, RGU is embedding entrepreneurship and innovation across the university. Innovation@RGU gives students the opportunity to develop their entrepreneurial skills, learn from industry experts and take part in valuable networking events. A new start-up accelerator is the first funded programme of its kind in the northeast of Scotland, helping students, staff and recent alumni to turn their business dreams into reality.

RGU gained gold in the Teaching Excellence Framework and has developed a strategy to be an "innovative, disruptive force in higher education". The TEF panel was impressed by the range of opportunities for students to develop knowledge, understanding and skills that are most highly valued by employers, and to engage "consistently and frequently" with developments at the forefront of professional practice.

High graduate employment levels have been RGU's greatest strength since the start of the decade, when it was the leading post-1992 university in our table. In the top 20 for graduate prospects until 2016, during the peak years of the North Sea oil and gas industry, it is still in the top 40 on this measure.

The university remains best known for its links with the offshore industries, both in the North Sea and abroad. The RGU Oil and Gas Institute offers drilling and advanced rig training and has the world's only decommissioning simulator.

RGU introduced 13 new degrees in 2018 and another five took their first students in 2019: sports coaching for health, digital marketing, accounting and management, and electronic or mechanical biomedical technology.

There are also new graduate apprenticeships in data science and accountancy. The university is the only institution in Scotland to offer a five-year degree and professional qualification in accountancy.

Degree students are attracted by the work placements that have become the norm and can last for up to a year. The university's Employability Hub launched the eHub mobile app this year, which offers career management tools including access to coaching.

The Garthdee campus, where all teaching is based, overlooks the River Dee on the

Garthdee House
Garthdee Road
Aberdeen AB10 7QB
01224 262 728
UGOffice@rgu.ac.uk
www.rgu.ac.uk
www.rguunion.co.uk
Open days 2020:
September 19,
November 7

The Times and The Sunday Times Rankings
Overall Ranking: 83 (last year: 96)

Teaching quality	83%	=22
Student experience	80.4%	=27
Research quality	4.0%	=104
Entry standards	157	=32
Graduate prospects	81.1%	37
Good honours	69.9%	100
Expected completion rate	86.8%	=56
Student/staff ratio	20.4	126
Services and facilities	£1,449	130

south side of Aberdeen. RGU, named after an 18th-century philanthropist, has a pedigree in education that goes back 250 years and its landmark green glass library tower, with views over the city, symbolises its future ambitions following a £135m capital programme.

The university made a relatively small submission to the 2014 Research Excellence Framework, but more than 40% of the work was placed in the top two categories. Health subjects and communication and media studies provided the best results. RGU's current strategy promises investment in sustainable transportation, data and analytics, pharmacy, smart cities and biomedical toxins.

Efforts to extend access beyond the normal higher education catchment have produced a diverse student population, and Robert Gordon ranks in the top ten in our new Scottish social inclusion table. A third of the intake are first generation students whose parents did not go to university and 95% have been educated in non-selective state schools.

The university has a particularly high rate of transfer from colleges in the region via its Degree Link programme, allowing students to take a two-year Higher National Diploma at a college, followed by two years at RGU to gain a degree.

A new Student Mental Health Agreement commits the university to improving the mental wellbeing of all students and staff, challenging negative attitudes. The student-led Peer Support group backs up RGU's efforts.

The university has invested more than £11m in its sports facilities, which include a centre of excellence for hockey. As well as providing a social hub at Garthdee, RGU provides regional facilities for cycling, netball, volleyball, gym and fitness classes, and a 25-metre swimming pool. There is a climbing wall with bouldering courses for students and Aberdeen schools in term time.

Aberdeen may seem a long way to go, but train and air links are excellent, and the city regularly features in top-ten lists for quality of life. RGU cannot guarantee accommodation for first-years, but its 900 residential places have been enough to house everyone who applied in recent years.

Tuition fees

» Fees for Scottish/EU students	£0–£1,820
RUK fees	£5,000–£8,240
» Fees for International students 2019–20	£14,000–£17,700
» For scholarship and bursary information see www.rgu.ac.uk/study/finance-funding	
» Graduate salary	£22,000

Student numbers

Undergraduates	7,882	(1,294)
Postgraduates	1,216	(2,137)
Applications/places		9,675/2,405
Applications per place		4
Overall offer rate		78.5%
Unconditional offers		0%
International students		17%

Accommodation

University provided places: 905
Self-catered: £98–£160 per week
www.rgu.ac.uk/life-at-rgu/accommodation

Where do the students come from?

State schools (non-grammar)	94.8%	First generation students	33.7%		
Grammar schools	0.2%	Deprived areas	6.5%		
Independent schools	5%	All ethnic minorities	10%		

Social inclusion ranking (Scotland): 9

Black attainment gap	-16.9%
Disabled	5.5%
Mature (over 21)	32.6%

University of Roehampton

Two-thirds of the entrants to Roehampton in 2018 were made unconditional offers, provided they made the university their first choice – the highest proportion in the country. It topped the list of 23 institutions rebuked over the practice by then education secretary Damian Hinds. But the university had already decided to abandon unconditional offers for fear of demotivating candidates, and none will be available for courses beginning in 2020.

Roehampton is enjoying its third successive rise in our table and is now on the cusp of the top half. Student satisfaction with the quality of teaching has shown particular improvement.

Applications grew in 2019, partly because the university is offering nursing degrees for the first time. It is a welcome trend: the numbers starting courses fell by 20% in 2018, dropping below 2,000 new entrants for the first time in more than 12 years.

The offer rate has gone up by 11 percentage points since £9,000 fees were introduced, so that more than nine out of ten applicants now receive an offer. The rate is even higher for male applicants, as the university tries to regain a gender balance. Two-thirds of entrants in 2018 were female, reflecting the domination of education, the arts and social sciences in the degree portfolio.

A new degree in computer science will start in 2020, alongside another in media and communications, taught in Roehampton's new media hub, which will feature film studios and editing suites, newsrooms, resources for photography and digital media, and a cinema. The media hub is on the former library site, vacated when a £35m purpose-built library opened in 2017, with 300,000 books and 1,200 study places. The prize-winning development has become the centrepiece of the university's parkland campus in southwest London.

Roehampton was one of two universities upgraded to silver in the Teaching Excellence Framework in 2019. The panel complimented the university on the reduction in the attainment gap for Bame (black, Asian, minority ethnic) students, and for support to find work experience.

More than half the students are the first in their families to go to university, with a similar proportion recruited from ethnic minorities – both among the highest proportions of any university. Almost all of the undergraduates are state-educated.

The university does not offer bursaries to students from poor backgrounds, other than for care-leavers, so only those winning scholarships will receive financial support unless they qualify for help from the student hardship fund.

The university's four colleges retain some of the original ethos of their religious foundations, but students need not follow any denomination to join them. The Anglican

Grove House
Roehampton Lane
London SW15 5PJ
020 8392 3232
ug.information@roehampton.ac.uk
www.roehampton.ac.uk
www.roehamptonstudent.com
Open days 2020:
February ??, April 15

The Times and The Sunday Times Rankings
Overall Ranking: 69 (last year: 70)

Teaching quality	79.2%	=81
Student experience	77.2%	=87
Research quality	24.5%	50
Entry standards	111	=122
Graduate prospects	72.2%	=91
Good honours	68.7%	107
Expected completion rate	74.3%	126
Student/staff ratio	14.2	=30
Services and facilities	£2,759	24

Whitelands college was the first in the country to open higher education to women. Digby Stuart was established by French Catholic women, Southlands by Methodists, and Froebel follows the humanist teachings of Frederick Froebel. Roehampton also has a Jewish resource centre and Muslim prayer rooms.

A quarter of Roehampton students take education courses. The university's degrees are also taught in Birmingham and Manchester by the private firm QA Higher Education, while international partnerships include an agreement with the EU Business School to offer Roehampton-accredited degrees to students across Europe.

Two-thirds of Roehampton's eligible academics submitted work in the 2014 Research Excellence Framework and 66% was rated world-leading or internationally excellent. The university outperformed all post-1992 universities and had the most highly rated dance department in the UK, with 94% of research placed in the top two categories. The results in education and English were among the best in London. These successes produced a 40% increase in funding for research.

The university guarantees accommodation for UK students who make Roehampton their firm choice and apply by the end of May, and international applicants who apply by the end of July. The options include a development at Vauxhall, 20 minutes from the main campus by public transport, which has a swimming pool and other facilities. Among the 2,200 residential places are some described as "quieter, more study-focused accommodation" where students are expected to keep the noise down and stick to a "moderated lifestyle" in terms of alcohol and parties.

There is a new gym on campus, with football pitches, a running track and multi-use games area. The sport performance and rehabilitation centre provides well-equipped laboratory facilities and performance coaching. The university is a high-performance centre for British fencing and sitting volleyball.

Roehampton also introduced the UK's first e-sports (video gaming) scholarships. Open to undergraduates or postgraduates, the awards are worth up to £1,500 a year, like the university's other sports scholarships, and require a continued commitment to e-sports as well as good academic progression.

Private sector rents are not cheap, but the suburbs are lively and central London is close at hand.

Tuition fees

» Fees for UK/EU students	£9,250
» Fees for International students 2020–21	£13,145
» For scholarship and bursary information see www.roehampton.ac.uk/undergraduate-courses/tuition-fees/	
» Graduate salary	£21,000

Student numbers

Undergraduates	9,765	(392)
Postgraduates	966	(785)
Applications/places		7,250/1,915
Applications per place		3.8
Overall offer rate		95.4%
Unconditional offers		65.8%
International students		9.5%

Accommodation

University provided places: 2,200
Self-catered: £120–£182 per week
First years guaranteed accommodation
www.roehampton.ac.uk/accommodation

Where do the students come from?

State schools (non-grammar)	94.3%	First generation students	52.7%	Black attainment gap	-26%
Grammar schools	1.7%	Deprived areas	5.5%	Disabled	5%
Independent schools	4%	All ethnic minorities	57.3%	Mature (over 21)	20.1%

Social inclusion ranking: =64

Royal Agricultural University

The Royal Agricultural University (RAU) took the biggest fall in our table in 2018, but has recovered most of the lost ground after what may be the greatest year-on-year rise in student satisfaction, up by more than six percentage points in both our measures drawn from the National Student Survey assessing teaching quality and the wider student experience. On student satisfaction with teaching quality, the university has risen nearly 80 places to reach the top 40, while its scores for the student experience have leapt to 12th place after languishing below the top 100 in 2018.

The RAU's aim is to become the leading small, specialist institution in the UK but in our overall rankings it is 72 places behind Harper Adams, the other largely agricultural university, which this year achieves the highest ever ranking for a modern university. It is also well behind several of the art specialists.

Leadership has been strengthened with a number of senior appointments and the RAU is adding two new undergraduate courses this year in food and sustainability, following the introduction of postgraduate programmes along the same lines in 2019. An accelerated two-year degree in business and innovation, in relation to food and farming, has been co-designed with industry to address skills shortages, while a three-year BSc in environment, food and society will combine teaching with work-based modules.

New enrolments dropped a little in 2018 and course closures hit applications subsequently, but numbers are still more than a third up on the previous decade. With fewer than 1,200 students, the RAU is the UK's smallest publicly funded university, but the proportion of female students has been rising consistently and has almost reached parity with the men.

Established in 1845 as the Royal Agricultural College, the institution was the first of its type in the English-speaking world. It was set up following a meeting of the Fairford and Cirencester Farmers' Club, which expressed concern at the lack of government support for education, particularly in relation to agriculture. Since then, every monarch since Queen Victoria has visited at least once.

Today's RAU has been described as the "Oxbridge of the countryside" because of its privileged intake and beautiful Cotswolds campus. Its proportion of entrants from independent schools is one of the highest in the country, although almost a third also came from the four poorest socioeconomic groups when last surveyed. The RAU also delivers degree courses in Hong Kong and China.

The RAU gained silver in the government's Teaching Excellence Framework, winning praise for its specialist facilities. The panel was impressed by the employer-informed course

Stroud Road
Cirencester GL7 6JS
01285 889 912
admissions@rau.ac.uk
www.rau.ac.uk
www.rausu.co.uk
Open days 2020:
April 22

The Times and The Sunday Times **Rankings**

Overall Ranking: =89 (last year: =115)

Teaching quality	81.8%	=37
Student experience	82.3%	12
Research quality	1.1%	125
Entry standards	118	=100
Graduate prospects	63.5%	=124
Good honours	63.5%	127
Expected completion rate	91.2%	33
Student/staff ratio	20.9	=127
Services and facilities	£2,803	=20

design, work placements and extracurricular opportunities for students to develop skills and attributes valued by employers.

The university scores less well for research, however, with one of the lowest scores. Only 12 staff were entered for the 2014 Research Excellence Framework – a quarter of those holding research contracts – and just 7% of their work was placed in the top two categories.

Many RAU courses include a 20-week work placement. There is an extensive network of student placement sponsors in the UK and overseas, and part-time work is available both in the university and in nearby Cirencester. It became the first specialist university to be made a centre of excellence by the Institute of Enterprise and Entrepreneurs in 2019.

Close to the campus, two university farms totalling 1,200 acres provide working examples of arable farming (Coates Manor) and integrated livestock and cropping (Harnhill). There is an equestrian centre providing stabling and livery facilities, and students also have access to a large dairy complex.

The university is opening the Cultural Heritage Institute, in Swindon this year, focusing on archaeology, applied heritage and historic environment management. A two-year accelerated degree in archaeology and heritage will be available there, as well as taught masters and MBA programmes.

A £4.2m building opened in 2018 on the main campus to strengthen links with agritech companies. One floor is used by the Farm491 project, named after the number of hectares available for research and testing in sustainable food production here. The building also houses the Cirencester Growth Hub, helping local businesses of all kinds.

On campus, the small numbers and countryside setting encourage a collegiate atmosphere. Four balls are held each year and the campus is the centre of social activities. There are eight halls of residence on campus for undergraduates with 334 rooms – enough for about 80% of first-years to be offered a place. Private rentals are available in Cirencester and the surrounding area.

Sport plays an important part in student life. Clubs include polo, clay pigeon shooting, beagling and team chasing – a cross-country equestrian sport. There are ample opportunities to explore the Cotswolds countryside and London is only 90 minutes away by train.

Tuition fees

» Fees for UK/EU students	£9,250
» Fees for International students 2020–21	£10,200
» For scholarship and bursary information see www.rau.ac.uk/study/undergraduate/ funding-your-time-at-university	
» Graduate salary	£21.000

Student numbers

Undergraduates	1,019	(25)
Postgraduates	126	(18)
Applications/places	1,190/380	
Applications per place	3.1	
Overall offer rate	n/a	
International students	11.6%	

Accommodation

University provided places: 334
Catered costs: £154–£219 per week
Self-catered: £146 per week
www.rau.ac.uk/university-life/accommodation

Where do the students come from?

State schools (non-grammar)	59.6%	First generation students	34.4%	Black attainment gap	n/a
Grammar schools	3.2%	Deprived areas	0.5%	Disabled	12.9%
Independent schools	37.2%	All ethnic minorities	n/a	Mature (over 21)	17.1%

Social inclusion ranking: 102

Royal Holloway, University of London

Royal Holloway has been moving up our league table and this year breaks into the top 20, earning a shortlisting for our University of the Year award. Based on an attractive single campus in leafy Egham, it has not suffered the same problems with student satisfaction as other members of the University of London and it is in the top 25 for completion.

This year's scores in the National Student Survey were sharply up on last, lifting Royal Holloway nearly 20 places on our measure for satisfaction with teaching quality and 45 places for satisfaction with the broad student experience on offer. Its satisfaction ratings are by far the best in the University of London and largely explain Royal Holloway's rise into the overall top 20 in our league table.

It claims to have one of the most beautiful university settings anywhere, offering students the best of both worlds: a safe environment in Surrey, but only 40 minutes by train from central London. The 135-acre woodland campus close to Windsor Castle and Heathrow is dominated by the Founder's Building, which was modelled on a French chateau and opened by Queen Victoria. Facilities are being upgraded as part of a £150m development plan.

A new science building, which opened in 2018, is intended to attract more female students into science and engineering – an appropriate brief for a university that incorporates a college (New Bedford) that was founded for women only. SuperFab, a world-class clean room, opened in April 2019 and houses advanced electronic nanofabrication equipment for research and development of the technology needed for medical imaging and quantum computers.

Just under 30% of the total intake in 2018 received so-called "conditional unconditional" offers, requiring them to make Royal Holloway their first choice in return for the unconditional offer of a place. This high proportion placed Royal Holloway on the list of universities accused by Damian Hinds, the then education secretary, of unethical practice, but the university has confirmed that such offers will not be made in 2020.

Unconditionals may have helped Royal Holloway increase the numbers starting degrees in 2018, clearing the 3,000 mark for the first time. The university set itself a target of 10,500 undergraduate and postgraduate students by 2020, and has already reached this level.

Applicants had nine new degrees to choose from in 2019, and a dozen more that had been given the option of a foundation year for those lacking the necessary qualifications for immediate entry. Video games art and design, economics and econometrics, and drama with dance were among the latest additions, with

Egham TW20 0EX
01784 414 944
study@royalholloway.ac.uk
www.royalholloway.ac.uk
www.su.rhul.ac.uk
Open days 2020:
June 19/20;
September 26,
October 17

The Times and The Sunday Times **Rankings**

Overall Ranking: 19 (last year: 24)

Teaching quality	80.3%	=60
Student experience	78.3%	=70
Research quality	36.3%	=30
Entry standards	142	=49
Graduate prospects	73.5%	=81
Good honours	80.0%	=32
Expected completion rate	93.0%	=16
Student/staff ratio	15.2	=50
Services and facilities	£2,530	32

modern languages, politics and international relations, and a new degree in social sciences due to start in 2020.

All Royal Holloway's degrees are sufficiently flexible to allow undergraduates to take an additional year, which can be spent studying abroad. The options include universities in Japan, Singapore, Australia, South Korea, Canada and the United States. The portfolio of degrees has been widening, with the addition of a new department of engineering with degrees focusing on areas such as the internet of things, as part of a BEng in computer systems engineering.

Royal Holloway was given a silver rating in the government's Teaching Excellence Framework. The awards panel was impressed by the level of investment in e-learning facilities and said students were engaged with developments from the forefront of research, scholarship and professional practice.

About 16% of the undergraduates come from independent schools, but there is a range of bursaries for undergraduates from low-income households and some for postgraduates, so that students who graduate with large debts are not deterred from continuing their studies.

More than 80% of the work assessed in the 2014 Research Excellence Framework was judged to be world-leading or internationally excellent, placing Royal Holloway in the top 30 institutions on this measure in our table.

Geography achieved the best results in England, while earth sciences, psychology,

mathematics, music, media arts, and drama and theatre were all in their respective top tens. Royal Holloway was chosen as an academic centre of excellence in cybersecurity research by the UK.

The Royal Holloway Passport, which is intended to enhance graduates' employability, recognises the additional skills that students gain from many extracurricular activities. An advanced skills programme, covering information technology, communication skills and foreign languages, further encourages breadth of study.

More on-campus accommodation has opened recently, ensuring that new entrants are guaranteed a residential place, as long as they apply by early June with the university as their firm choice. The students' union is the centre of most social life, putting on entertainment and activities seven days a week.

Sports facilities are good and Royal Holloway has had considerable success with its "student talented athlete recognition scheme" (Stars). It has become one of the University of London's top sporting colleges, with more than 80 sports teams. There is a fitness studio and multi-use sport hall and outdoor facilities.

Tuition fees

- » Fees for UK/EU students 2019–20   £9,250
- » Fees for International students 2020–21   £18,300–£20,900
- » For scholarship and bursary information see www.royalholloway.ac.uk/ugfeesandfunding
- » Graduate salary   £20,000

Student numbers

Undergraduates	7,328	(309)
Postgraduates	1,985	(705)
Applications/places		15,560/2,270
Applications per place		6.9
Overall offer rate		90.8%
International students		28.2%

Accommodation

University provided places: 3,501 (catered 29%)
Catered costs: £115–£184 per week
Self-catered: £161–£184 per week
First years guaranteed accommodation
www.royalholloway.ac.uk/studyhere/accommodation/home.aspx

Where do the students come from?

State schools (non-grammar)	74.1%	Working-class homes	28.4%	Black ethnic minority	5.6%
Grammar schools	11.4%	Deprived areas	5.1%	Disabled	6.1%
Independent schools	14.6%	All ethnic minorities	36.3%	Mature (over 21)	6.1%

Social inclusion ranking: 71

University of St Andrews

Our University of the Year is within a whisker of breaking the Oxbridge duopoly at the top of our rankings. Just 18 points shy of Oxford this year, it has closed the gap from 73 points in 2018. Student satisfaction lies behind the sustained success: this year's results from the National Student Survey put St Andrews top of the tree for both teaching quality and the wider student experience.

Big changes are afoot following the adoption of a new university strategy which, "for the first time in six centuries, [has] made a clear commitment to social responsibility". St Andrews has pledged to promote equality and diversity, build environmental leadership and support the local community. There is a long way to go as St Andrews sits at the bottom of our social inclusion ranking for Scottish universities at present.

Just under 40% of British undergraduates come from independent schools and the proportion from non-selective state schools has dropped from 54% to 52.2% since last year. However, there are already signs of a change in admissions. Although still a relatively small minority, the number of entrants from the most deprived areas last year more than doubled compared with 2016.

Professor Sally Mapstone, principal and vice-chancellor of St Andrews, led the Scotland-wide work on contextual admissions which proposed that applicants from disadvantaged areas should be given offers at no more than the minimum grades needed to complete their chosen course. Now Scottish government policy, the scheme has been embraced by St Andrews, which published two sets of standard offers in 2019, depending on the background of the applicant. The university is pledging £13m to support bright candidates who would otherwise be unable to attend St Andrews.

The strategy also guarantees the involvement of students and staff in governance and decision-making. In the academic sphere, it has added a new interdisciplinary area – behaviour, evolution, and environment – and emphasised a commitment to digital innovation and to supporting staff and students with disabilities.

Almost a dozen new degrees have been launched in 2019, ranging from data science to a series of joint honours degrees pairing sustainable development with management or a language. There is a new part-time evening master's course in combined studies.

St Andrews remains well ahead of the other Scottish universities in our table. International students make up about 45% of the intake, with the largest grouping coming from the United States, a legacy that endures from the time when the Duke of Cambridge was a student here from 2001 to 2005.

St Katharine's West
16 The Scores
St Andrews KY16 9AX
01334 462 150
admissions@st-andrews.ac.uk
www.st-andrews.ac.uk
www.yourunion.net
Open days 2020:
April 1, 8, 15

The Times and The Sunday Times Rankings
Overall Ranking: 3 (last year: 3)

Teaching quality	88.5%	1
Student experience	87.9%	1
Research quality	40.4%	11
Entry standards	208	3
Graduate prospects	79.6%	=49
Good honours	89.8%	=5
Expected completion rate	96.3%	6
Student/staff ratio	11.7	8
Services and facilities	£3,220	8

One of a handful of universities north of the border to enter the Teaching Excellence Framework in its first year, St Andrews seized gold. The panel praised "exemplary" teaching and said "a culture of rigour and stretch within a research-intensive environment" stimulated students' enthusiasm.

Applications are running at record levels, now 50% higher than a decade ago. The number of places available to undergraduates has not kept pace, so about ten applicants chase every place.

Many students come from other parts of the UK, even though, like Edinburgh, St Andrews charges undergraduates from England, Wales or Northern Ireland £9,250 a year for the full four years of a degree. Nearly a third of such students received bursaries in 2018. Scots and other EU students still pay nothing.

About 450 professional services staff have relocated to the University's new Eden campus, creating additional teaching space in the heart of St Andrews. Nicola Sturgeon, Scotland's First Minister, opened the new Scottish Oceans Institute building last September and the Laidlaw Music Centre will follow shortly.

Scotland's oldest higher education institution and the third oldest in the English-speaking world, St Andrews boasts Europe's first Centre for Syrian Studies, an Institute of Iranian Studies and a Centre for Peace and Conflict Studies.

It has also invested heavily in the sciences, which produced some of the best results in the 2014 Research Excellence Framework. More than 90% of work submitted in joint submissions with Edinburgh in chemistry and physics was rated world-leading or internationally excellent. Classics and history of art scored well and more than 70% of the overall submission reached the top two categories.

In the town of St Andrews, renowned as a golfing centre, more than half the 17,000 residents are students and nearly half of them live in university-owned accommodation. First-years are guaranteed a place if they apply by the end of June. Two new halls opened in 2018, part of a £70m programme to add 900 student beds to the 3,600 already owned or endorsed by the university.

Traditionally, third- or fourth-year students help new arrivals, known as "bejants" and "bejantines", adjust to university life. Students enjoy a lively social life in a tight-knit community.

A £14m redevelopment of the sports centre was completed in 2019, providing a new sports hall, a larger and better-equipped fitness suite and an indoor tennis centre.

Tuition fees

»	Fees for Scottish/EU students	£0–£1,820
	RUK fees	£9,250
»	Fees for International students 2020–21	£23,910
	Medicine	£31,950
»	For scholarship and bursary information see	
	www.st-andrews.ac.uk/study/fees-and-funding/undergraduate	
»	Graduate salary	£23,000

Student numbers

Undergraduates	7,677	(948)
Postgraduates	1,822	(290)
Applications/places		18,565/1,680
Applications per place		11.1
Overall offer rate		49.2%
Unconditional offers		0%
International students		45.7%

Accommodation

University provided places: 3,635
Catered costs: £164–£249 per week
Self-catered: £139–£227 per week
First years guaranteed accommodation
www.st-andrews.ac.uk/study/accommodation/

Where do the students come from?

State schools (non-grammar)	52.2%	First generation students	17%	Black attainment gap	n/a
Grammar schools	8.2%	Deprived areas	7.5%	Disabled	5.2%
Independent schools	39.6%	All ethnic minorities	12.1%	Mature (over 21)	6.6%

Social inclusion ranking (Scotland): 15

St George's, University of London

St George's has been a pioneer in broadening access to medicine, one of the most socially exclusive subjects in higher education. It was the first medical school to advertise places in clearing.

Across all courses, which include other health and science programmes, St George's recruits a third of its undergraduates through clearing. Less than 40% of applicants receive offers through the normal route so the demand for places is strong, but St George's considers clearing the fairest way to find high-quality candidates. However, despite such access policies the university has slipped from its top-60 ranking in our inaugural social inclusion table last year to rank 75th in England and Wales this year.

The Adjusted Criteria Scheme reduces the entry requirements by two A-level grades for anyone applying from a non-selective state school whose results are in the bottom 20% nationwide. The scheme applies to medicine, biomedical science, physiotherapy and healthcare science. About 40% of entrants have qualified for financial assistance over the past two years.

St Georges offered its first merit-based scholarships for undergraduates in 2019, but they were restricted to candidates for the new clinical pharmacology BSc, the first of its kind. Scholarships in other subjects are only available for postgraduate courses.

St George's has the highest employment rating in our table. While that might not be surprising for the only freestanding medical school in the University of London – and the only one in our table – the portfolio now extends to biomedical science and healthcare science degrees covering respiratory and cardiac physiology and sleep physiology, while paramedic science and radiography degrees are also taught in partnership with Kingston University.

There are interviews for all undergraduate courses except biomedical science and clinical pharmacology. Applications were down by almost 8% overall in the 2019 admissions cycle, continuing a gradual decline, but this is attributed to the demographic downturn in the number of 18-year-olds.

St George's is one of only 11 universities in our table to hold the (lowest) bronze rating in the government's Teaching Excellence Framework. Although the panel gave the university credit for an "embedded institutional culture that rewards excellent teaching, and promotes inclusivity among staff and students", low student satisfaction with assessment and feedback held it back, as did comparisons with other largely medically-based institutions with even higher employment rates.

This year, students rated teaching quality at St George's lower than at any other institution in the UK, while they ranked the university fifth lowest for the broader student experience.

Cranmer Terrace
Tooting
London SW17 0RE
020 3897 2032
study@sgul.ac.uk
www.sgul.ac.uk
www.sgsu.org.uk
Open day 2020:
June 27

The Times and The Sunday Times **Rankings**
Overall Ranking: 67 (last year: 80)

Teaching quality	71.9%	129
Student experience	71.9%	125
Research quality	22.2%	52
Entry standards	158	=29
Graduate prospects	93.8%	1
Good honours	80.3%	37
Expected completion rate	93.3%	16
Student/staff ratio	11.1	=3
Services and facilities	£2,560	41

Despite this, it has managed a 13-place rise in our rankings this year, due in large part to a better completion rate, an improved staff to student ratio, and an increased proportion of firsts and 2:1s awarded.

The original medical school opened in 1868 at St George's hospital, which had been established in 1733 at Hyde Park Corner, in central London, when it was open countryside. Edward Jenner trained there before inventing the smallpox vaccination and the hide of Blossom the cow, the subject of his experiments, can be seen in the library of St George's Hospital in Tooting, south London, the institution's home since the 1970s. The university shares clinical facilities with the hospital, one of London's busiest. A new 200-seat lecture theatre opened for the 2019–20 academic year for teaching in a range of courses and to host public events.

St George's was the first UK institution to launch the MBBS Graduate Entry Programme, a four-year fast-track medical degree open to graduates in any discipline, which has become an increasingly popular route into the medical profession. There are now nearly 5,000 students across all subjects and levels. A shadowing scheme offers sixth-formers from Wandsworth and Merton state schools the opportunity to accompany a doctor or other healthcare professional at St George's or Queen Mary's Hospital.

A preparatory centre for international students is based on the campus. St George's also offers a four-year, graduate-entry bachelor of surgery degree at the University of Nicosia in Cyprus, where the first intake graduated in 2015.

A strong research record at St George's led to historic developments in cardiac pacemakers and IVF, and the university was second only to Imperial College London for the impact of its work in the 2014 Research Excellence Framework. Overall, 70% of its submission reached the top two categories for world-leading and internationally excellent research.

The university's strategic plan to 2022 commits it to immersing students in research and healthcare practice, as well as providing opportunities to broaden their horizons.

There is an active students' union with 120 clubs, societies and community projects. The sports centre is on campus and competitive teams play in regional and national competitions. Students have use of a rowing club on the River Thames and can also take advantage of University of London facilities for sport.

Applicants who have accepted St George's as their firm offer before the end of June are guaranteed one of the 500 residential places.

Tuition fees

» Fees for UK/EU students	£9,250
» Fees for International students 2020–21	£16,000–£18,000
Medicine	£36,000
» For scholarship and bursary information see	
www.sgul.ac.uk/study/undergraduate/fees-and-funding	
» Graduate salary	£26,600

Student numbers

Undergraduates	2,939	(997)
Postgraduates	283	(754)
Applications/places		5,825/835
Applications per place		7
Overall offer rate		59.2%
Unconditional offers		0%
International students		8.6%

Accommodation

University provided places: 486
Self-catered: £168–£178 per week
Undergraduates and international students get priority
www.sgul.ac.uk/study/accommodation

Where do the students come from?

State schools (non-grammar)	65.2%	First generation students	35.5%	Black attainment gap	-20%
Grammar schools	20.1%	Deprived areas	5.9%	Disabled	7.2%
Independent schools	14.7%	All ethnic minorities	61.8%	Mature (over 21)	25.9%

Social inclusion ranking: 75

St Mary's University, Twickenham

St Mary's has dropped eight places in our table, largely because it could not quite repeat last year's outstanding student satisfaction scores. It is still close to the top 30 in the sections of the National Student Survey related to teaching quality and just outside the top 50 for the overall experience, but St Mary's can no longer claim to have the most satisfied students in London.

The university is still 30 places higher in our overall ranking than it was three years ago. It gained silver in the Teaching Excellence Framework and enrolments were stable in 2018, when many similar institutions saw numbers fall. The TEF panel cited high-quality resources and good staffing levels which allowed personalised and small-group learning.

In the prospectus, Professor Francis Campbell, the vice-chancellor, tells prospective applicants they are choosing a home away from home as well as a university. St Mary's markets itself as offering the best of both worlds: a location in the leafy suburb of Twickenham, only half an hour from dynamic central London.

With 5,000 students, St Mary's is the largest of three Catholic universities in the UK. It admits students of all faiths and none, but its first stated objective is to provide "a unique experience for our students and staff by virtue of our values and identity as a Catholic university".

Founded in Hammersmith in 1850 by the Catholic Poor Schools Committee to meet the need for teachers for the growing numbers of poor Catholic children, St Mary's has retained its focus on training teachers, who still make up a third of the student body.

St Mary's sporting prowess is well established and its athletics track is named after Sir Mo Farah, a graduate who has set up a scholarship programme for promising young competitors. At the Rio Olympics in 2016, 22 St Mary's students and alumni won six medals – including three gold – and if it had been a country, it would have finished 25th in the medals table, ahead of South Africa and Poland.

The £8.5m sports centre on the main campus attracted teams from Japan and China during the London-hosted World Athletics Championships in 2017. There are more outdoor sports facilities not far from the main campus in Teddington.

Degrees in sport and exercise nutrition and sport psychology were introduced in 2019, alongside a course in creative media. Drama with education or creative writing will take their first students in 2020. There are about 500 undergraduate degree combinations across four schools covering sport, health and applied science; education, theology and

---

Waldegrave Road
Strawberry Hill
Twickenham TW1 4SX
020 8240 2394
apply@stmarys.ac.uk
www.stmarys.ac.uk
www.stmaryssu.co.uk
Open days 2020:
February 22, March 21,
April 25

The Times and The Sunday Times **Rankings**
Overall Ranking: 85 (last year: 77)

Teaching quality	82.2%	=33
Student experience	79%	=51
Research quality	4%	=104
Entry standards	119	=98
Graduate prospects	72.6%	90
Good honours	75.3%	64
Expected completion rate	81%	96
Student/staff ratio	16	=73
Services and facilities	£1,741	115

leadership; management and social sciences; and the arts and humanities.

St Mary's has appointed a series of high-profile visiting professors including Dr Mary McAleese, the former president of Ireland; Sir Vince Cable, former leader of the Liberal Democrats; Cherie Blair; and Sir Clive Woodward, who coached England to the 2003 Rugby World Cup. Ruth Kelly, education secretary under Tony Blair, is the pro vice-chancellor for research and enterprise.

The campus occupies 35 acres of gardens and parkland near the River Thames. Its centrepiece is the restored Strawberry Hill House, a Gothic fantasy designed by Horace Walpole, the son of Britain's first prime minister. The university also has a community building in the centre of Twickenham, with theatre space, studio rooms and a large conservatory area with a cafe. The Exchange offers training courses for local residents and firms, as well as providing more teaching space for students.

St Mary's has a small cohort of international students and has opened an international college on campus, in partnership with an Australian higher education firm, to attract more. Pathway courses started last year, leading to 30 degree programmes.

A number of outreach schemes are designed to make the intake of undergraduates more diverse, including mentoring school pupils throughout the academic year. Foundation years, with additional pastoral and learning support, are available in most subjects for those who lack the qualifications needed for immediate entry to degrees. More than half of St Mary's students have parents who did not go to university and a third are from ethnic minorities, placing it well inside the top half of our social inclusion table.

Other initiatives provide academic support and monitor the progress of under-represented groups once they begin courses. There is financial support for targeted groups, such as students with children, homeless and final-year students who meet certain criteria.

The 778 residential places were enough to guarantee accommodation to this year's new entrants if they applied by the end of May.

Tuition fees

»	Fees for UK/EU students	£9,250
	Foundation courses	£5,140–£8,660
»	Fees for International students 2020–21	£12,250
»	For scholarship and bursary information see	
	www.stmarys.ac.uk/student-finance/overview.aspx	
»	Graduate salary	£21,000

Student numbers

Undergraduates	3,671	(191)
Postgraduates	610	(840)
Applications/places		5,020/1,165
Applications per place		4.3
Overall offer rate		90.5%
Unconditional offers		20.3%
International students		7%

Accommodation

University provided places: 778
Catered costs: £151–£243 per week
Self-catered: £170–£180
First years guaranteed accommodation
www.stmarys.ac.uk/accommodation

Where do the students come from?

State schools (non-grammar)	92.5%	First generation students	51.6%	Black attainment gap	-17%
Grammar schools	2.7%	Deprived areas	6.7%	Disabled	10.8%
Independent schools	4.8%	All ethnic minorities	34.1%	Mature (over 21)	20.2%

Social inclusion ranking: 35

University of Salford

A fall of 30 places has sent Salford tumbling out of our top 100 universities, reversing its recent progress, but demand for places remains strong. Record enrolment in 2018 was more than 50% higher than in 2012, and applications were up by another 6% at the deadline for courses beginning in September 2019.

New foundation year programmes and additional nursing places were partly responsible for the latest increase, but the university appears to be reaping the rewards of a controversial reshaping of its course portfolio. It has narrowed the range of subjects to focus on its strengths, creating four Industry Collaboration Zones in engineering and environments, health and wellbeing, digital and creative, and sport. Salford describes the move as a "bold departure from traditional structures and models of learning" allowing students to apply their skills to real-world environments through industrial partners.

Such changes are yet to win over current undergraduates, however. Salford has dropped more than 50 places for student satisfaction with teaching quality, and only slightly less for their wider experience. Poor student satisfaction scores are the main reason for Salford's fall in our rankings this year.

Big changes are afoot on Salford's campus, however. An £800m plan agreed between the university and the local authority will create a new city district linking Manchester's Central Business District and the MediaCity UK area. The university's share will be £300m of investment split into three zones within and around the existing campus.

The first regeneration projects are already under way. New student residences adjacent to the campus opened in September 2019 and life sciences laboratories have been expanded and upgraded. A new engineering building is due to open in 2020–21 and the library will be refurbished.

The university managed only bronze in the Teaching Excellence Framework, after an appeal to upgrade the assessment was rejected in 2018. Despite good links with employers and a commitment to learning by students, the panel found that progression to employment or further study remained "exceptionally low". In our table, Salford ranks equal 77th out of 131 universities for progression to graduate-level work.

Having rethought its traditional degree offer, the university is establishing a substantial portfolio of degree apprenticeships. A dozen programmes launched in 2019, from business and management to civil engineering and biomedical science, will be joined in 2020 by housing management, with master's programmes including leadership and management in health.

Maxwell Building
43 The Crescent
Salford
Greater Manchester
M5 4WT
0161 295 4545
enquiries@salford.ac.uk
www.salford.ac.uk
www.salfordstudents.com
Open days 2020:
see website

The Times and The Sunday Times **Rankings**
Overall Ranking: 111 (last year: =81)

Teaching quality	78.5%	91
Student experience	76.8%	94
Research quality	8.3%	71
Entry standards	130	72
Graduate prospects	73.6%	=77
Good honours	73.7%	79
Expected completion rate	78.3%	115
Student/staff ratio	16.2	=77
Services and facilities	£1,980	98

Salford opened the British University of Bahrain in 2018, the first UK-linked institution in the kingdom. It is offering Salford degrees in engineering and the built environment, business, and information and communication technology, with the option of splitting study time between Bahrain and the UK.

At home, there are opportunities to work with BBC staff and other media professionals at the £30m MediaCityUK building in Salford Quays. The university has also invested more than £80m in the Peel Park Quarter, with impressive student facilities and 1,367 residential places. The £55m New Adelphi teaching centre serves art, performance, and design and technology students.

Salford entered only a third of its eligible academics for the 2014 Research Excellence Framework, but more than half of their work was found to be world-leading or internationally excellent. The School of Health Sciences has an international reputation for the treatment of sports injuries.

Salford does well on the government's access measures: about one undergraduate in five comes from an area that sends few students to higher education. The university ranks 38th in our latest social inclusion table, with more than 95% of its students drawn from comprehensive schools, one third from ethnic minorities, and nearly half from homes where parents did not go to university. From 2019, under the Inspire scheme, all new UK and EU undergraduates receive a £150 credit bursary for study materials. More credit is available for those from poor families.

Two squash courts were refurbished in 2018 and there is also a swimming pool, five fitness suites and a multi-use sports hall. Membership packages started at £143 a year in 2018–19, but facilities can be used on a pay-as-you-go basis. There are three grass football pitches and one rugby pitch on the adjacent David Lewis playing fields and students can use the separate Albert Park facility of a 3G full-sized 11-a-side football pitch.

Manchester is a draw for students and both main campuses are within walking distance of the city centre, by the River Irwell. University accommodation, administered by the private operator, Campus Living Villages, is within a ten-minute walk of the main campus. First-years are not guaranteed accommodation, but they are allocated most of the rooms.

Tuition fees

»	Fees for UK/EU students	£9,250
	Foundation course	£8,250
»	Fees for International students 2020–21	£12,660–£18,450
»	For scholarship and bursary information see www.beta.salford.ac.uk/undergraduate/fees	
»	Graduate salary	£21,600

Student numbers

Undergraduates	15,218	(768)
Postgraduates	2,182	(2,121)
Applications/places	24,305/6,040	
Applications per place	4	
Overall offer rate	81.7%	
Conditional offers	0%	
International students	9.8%	

Accommodation

University provided places: 2,111
Self-catered: £93–£154 per week
www.beta.salford.ac.uk/accommodation

Where do the students come from?

State schools (non-grammar)	95.6%	First generation students	46.3%	Black attainment gap	-13.8%
Grammar schools	2.5%	Deprived areas	18%	Disabled	5.7%
Independent schools	1.9%	All ethnic minorities	33.8%	Mature (over 21)	26%

Social inclusion ranking: 38

University of Sheffield

Sheffield has committed to including Education for Sustainable Development in all its courses in the next five years to educate the 'change makers for a sustainable future'. The university says the change, part of a wider sustainability strategy, reflects the desire of students to learn more about environmental issues and how they can improve practices in their own lives and future workplaces.

The university is among the most socially inclusive in the Russell Group, ranking fifth among the 21 members in England and Wales in our new social inclusion table. The proportion of students from state schools and areas of low participation in higher education are significantly higher than average for its courses and entry qualifications, the result of a push to widen participation.

The university's Discover programme helps to raise aspirations among disadvantaged local sixth-formers, offering successful participants up to two grades off the standard offer for subjects including medicine, law, science and the humanities.

Hundreds of apprentices work at the university's Advanced Manufacturing Research Centre with partners such as Boeing and Rolls-Royce, and have the option of taking undergraduate and master's degrees. Six degree apprenticeship programmes run at the university itself, ranging from manufacturing to management, social work and strategic leadership.

Applications were up in 2019, as they were in 2018, and are approaching record levels. More than 20 new degree programmes will have helped, nine of them adding the option of a foundation year for students who do not yet meet the entry requirements. Others are adding a year abroad or a placement year in business or industry.

However, the numbers starting degrees at Sheffield have dropped by 10% since 2015, when recruiting restrictions were lifted, in contrast to other Russell Group institutions. The university says it has not been willing to compromise on entry standards in a competitive market, refusing to join the rush towards unconditional offers, although one in eight students won a place in 2018 through clearing.

Although Sheffield has dropped one place in our league table, it has registered a big increase in student satisfaction. The university has moved up more than 35 places in the National Student Survey for teaching quality and is now in the top 15 for the wider student experience. The students' union has been voted the best in the country for 11 years in a row.

Rated silver in the Teaching Excellence Framework, Sheffield is 78th= in the latest QS World University rankings, with 17 subjects in the top 100. The TEF panel commended "high levels of stretch and challenge" to develop skills valued by employers.

Western Bank
Sheffield S10 2TN
0114 222 8030
study@sheffield.ac.uk
www.sheffield.ac.uk
http://su.sheffield.ac.uk
Open days 2020:
June 27, July 11,
September 12,
October 17

The Times and The Sunday Times **Rankings**

Overall Ranking: 26 (last year: 25)

Teaching quality	80.6%	=56
Student experience	82.1%	=13
Research quality	37.6%	23
Entry standards	157	=32
Graduate prospects	84.4%	19
Good honours	81.5%	33
Expected completion rate	92.8%	=20
Student/staff ratio	15.2	=53
Services and facilities	£2,290	69

The main university precinct stretches for a mile, ending near the city centre. The £23m Information Commons operates 24-hours throughout the year and was refurbished in 2018.

A £81m Diamond engineering building – the university's biggest single development – caters for the growing number of students in one of Sheffield's key strengths. The aluminium-clad hub has 19 specialist laboratories and 1,000 study spaces. Work on the commercialisation of engineering research will be housed in the new Royce Discovery Centre from 2020.

A social sciences building due to open in 2021 will bring together a range of subjects for the first time, with collaborative teaching and social space, encouraging more interdisciplinary work to tackle global societal challenges. Sheffield has also been awarded £21m for a new Translational Energy Research Centre to support the UKs transition to a low-carbon economy, reflecting the university's growing focus on climate change.

In the 2014 Research Excellence Framework, about 85% of the university's submission was considered world-leading or internationally excellent. Biomedical sciences, control and systems engineering, history and politics were all in the top three in the UK. But Sheffield entered a smaller proportion of its academics than most of its peers, keeping it just outside the top 20 in our research table.

The university attracts more than 8,000 students from outside the UK. It is also among the dozen universities most favoured as recruiting grounds by *The Times*'s 100 leading employers, according to the 2019 graduate market survey by High Fliers.

Most of university's 6,200 student beds are within walking distance of lectures, in the suburbs on the affluent west side of Sheffield. New entrants are guaranteed accommodation.

Excellent sports facilities close to the main university precinct include five floodlit synthetic pitches, a large fitness centre with more than 150 pieces of equipment, a swimming pool with sauna and steam rooms, sports hall, fitness studio, four squash courts and a bouldering wall.

Outdoor pitches for rugby, football and cricket are a bus ride away. Sheffield has one of the biggest programmes of internal leagues at any university and elite sport is thriving. Three alumnae brought home either a gold or silver medal from the Rio Olympics in 2016.

The famously lively social scene is based mainly on the students' union. The city has plenty of student-orientated bars and clubs, and town-gown relations are much better here than in most of the main university centres.

Tuition fees

» Fees for UK/EU students £9,250
» Fees for International students 2020–21 £17,600–£22,600 Dentistry £35,880; Medicine £33,500 (clinical years)
» For scholarship and bursary information see www.sheffield.ac.uk/undergraduate/fees-funding/
» Graduate salary £22,800

Student numbers

Undergraduates	**19,180**	**(580)**
Postgraduates	**7,384**	**(2,533)**
Applications/places		**35,780/5,165**
Applications per place		**6.9**
Overall offer rate		**86.1%**
Unconditional offers		**0%**
International students		**30.2%**

Accommodation

University provided places: 6,200
Catered costs: £137 per week
Self-catered: £102–£174 per week
First years guaranteed accommodation
www.sheffield.ac.uk/accommodation

Where do the students come from?

State schools (non-grammar)	74.6%	First generation students	33.1%	Black attainment gap	-15.8%
Grammar schools	13%	Deprived areas	9.3%	Disabled	7.5%
Independent schools	12.4%	All ethnic minorities	19.1%	Mature (over 21)	10.8%

Social inclusion ranking: 92

Sheffield Hallam University

Sheffield Hallam, whose mission is to be the world's leading university for applied learning, is our University of the Year for Teaching Quality. Ranked 14th in the UK on our measure, based on the latest outcomes of the National Student Survey, the university has steadily climbed our teaching rankings in recent years, rising from 30= last year and 36th in 2017. It is rare for such a large institution to perform so well on student satisfaction with teaching quality.

The award comes as the university launches a 15-year campus plan that includes in its first phase new facilities for business and social science students, a refurbished students' union and the creation of a university green as a focal point for the institution, as part of a £220m spend. The plan will produce new teaching and learning facilities in the city centre and at the Collegiate campus in the western suburbs.

The university found itself at the centre of controversy in early 2019, when it was revealed that more than 40% of offers made to applicants the previous year were so-called 'conditional unconditional', requiring candidates to make Sheffield Hallam their first choice. It was among those rebuked by Damian Hinds, then education secretary, over the practice. It has since confirmed that it will not be making this type of offer in future.

Sheffield Hallam is one of the largest in the country, with more than 30,000 students. Applications have dropped by more than 17% since 2015, when recruitment restrictions were lifted, but a higher offer rate has helped to keep the fall in enrolments manageable.

A report in 2019 found that Hallam was the UK's biggest recruiter of poor, white students – a group whose educational underperformance is a cause of growing concern to policy-makers. Almost half of the undergraduates come from the Yorkshire and Humber region, and even more stay and work there after graduation.

The university scores well in our social inclusion ranking, finishing in the top half of the table, with more than 50% of students recruited from families where the parents have not gone to university. Almost 94% are educated in non-selective state schools.

Hallam exceeds all of its access benchmarks and the projected dropout rate is significantly lower than the national average for its courses and entry qualifications.

Nine new degrees launched in 2019 include nutrition, game design and marketing with public relations or psychology. From 2020 the university will be offering a degree in e-sports.

Hallam is one of the largest providers of degree apprenticeships and collaborates with the University of Sheffield to offer the qualification in engineering. More than 800

City Campus
Howard Street
Sheffield S1 1WB
0114 225 5555
admissions@shu.ac.uk
www.shu.ac.uk
www.hallamstudentsunion.com
Open days 2020:
see website

Edinburgh
Belfast
SHEFFIELD
London
Cardiff

The Times and The Sunday Times Rankings
Overall Ranking: =65 (last year: 67)

Teaching quality	83.7%	14
Student experience	81.1%	=22
Research quality	5.4%	=89
Entry standards	119	=98
Graduate prospects	73.8%	=74
Good honours	74.7%	69
Expected completion rate	85.7%	64
Student/staff ratio	17.2	=92
Services and facilities	£2,318	66

apprentices are spread across 31 programmes, ranging from digital technology solutions to surveying and professional practice in food technology, physiotherapy and social work. It expects to double this number by 2020, with programmes in health, social care and sciences.

In addition, Hallam has a new £14m Advanced Wellbeing Research Centre (AWRC), the centrepiece of Sheffield's Olympic Legacy Park, a joint venture between the university, the city council and Sheffield Teaching Hospitals NHS Foundation Trust. Hallam claims that the AWRC will be the most up-to-date research and development centre for physical activity in the world.

The university's National Centre of Excellence for Food Engineering is also open. Only 16% of eligible academics entered the 2014 Research Excellence Framework, but 65% of their work was considered world-leading or internationally excellent.

More than 200 "specialist flexible courses" mix part-time study, distance learning and work-based education. Business and industry are closely involved in the development of courses and more than half of the undergraduates take work placements.

Hallam's employability activities helped it to a silver rating in the government's Teaching Excellence Framework (TEF), which was chaired by Professor Sir Chris Husbands, the university's vice-chancellor. He was not involved in the decision, but the TEF panel complimented the institution on an exemplary commitment to the region and support for students to be retained in the region.

The university also has a growing international dimension, with large cohorts taught in partner institutions in Malaysia and other Asian countries, to add to the 2,700 who come to Sheffield from outside the UK.

International students and new entrants are guaranteed accommodation, although the large local intake means that many students live at home. The university does not own accommodation, but offers some 4,800 rooms through private providers.

Hallam manages Sheffield's only athletics stadium, which was among the venues hosting the 6,000-plus students competing in the 10th annual Bucs (British Universities & Colleges Sport) Championships last year.

Sports provision is supplemented by those provided by Sheffield for the World Student Games in 1991 with the swimming complex, on the university's doorstep. The city's well-run bus and tram services help students get to and from lectures by day and, later, to sample the wide range of nightlife on offer.

Tuition fees

» Fees for Scottish/EU students	£9,250
» Fees for International students 2020–21	£13,650
» For scholarship and bursary information see www.shu.ac.uk/study-here/fees-and-funding	
» Graduate salary	£21,909

Student numbers

Undergraduates	22,149	(2,171)
Postgraduates	3,105	(3,304)
Applications/places		31,860/7,675
Applications per place		4.2
Overall offer rate		81.3%
Unconditional offers		40.8%
International students		7.7%

Accommodation

University provided places: 4,787
Self-catered: £84–£205 per week
First years guaranteed accommodation
www.shu.ac.uk/study-here/accommodation

Where do the students come from?

State schools (non-grammar)	93.7%	First generation students	51.6%	Black attainment gap	-32.6%
Grammar schools	3.3%	Deprived areas	20%	Disabled	7.5%
Independent schools	3%	All ethnic minorities	19.6%	Mature (over 21)	19%

Social inclusion ranking: 56

SOAS University of London

As an international institution with a long tradition of student protest and a focus on many former colonies, it is no surprise to find SOAS (the School of Oriental and African Studies) in the vanguard of moves to "decolonise" the curriculum. The school has committed itself to challenging Eurocentrism and developed a toolkit for making teaching more inclusive and redressing disadvantage associated with racism and colonialism.

There has been a student working group on the subject since 2016, prompted partly by SOAS's own colonial origins. The process has not involved rules on teaching or research, but is producing change across the school.

A related campaign has encouraged moves by SOAS to close the attainment gap between black students (72% of whom get firsts or 2:1s) and their white counterparts (87%), a figure that forms part of our new social inclusion ranking. Baroness Amos, the school's director and the first Afro-Caribbean woman to lead a UK university, led a national study of the question and has asked a senior academic to examine the position at SOAS and propose improvement.

Overall, SOAS is one of the more socially inclusive members of the University of London, with three-quarters of its students educated in non-selective state schools, 55% drawn from ethnic minorities and 42% the first in their families to go to university.

SOAS successfully appealed against a second successive bronze rating in the Teaching Excellence Framework in 2018 and was upgraded to silver. The panel praised an emphasis on personalised learning and small-group teaching, as well as a comprehensive student engagement system and outreach initiatives.

However, the university again ranks near the bottom nationally in our two league table indicators derived from the annual National Student Survey (NSS). In common with several London-based institutions, SOAS has poor levels of student satisfaction with both teaching quality (where it ranks in the bottom 15 in the UK) and the wider student experience (where it ranks fourth bottom).

The school has been restructuring to improve the student experience. For the first time, the library opened 24 hours a day during Ramadan, for example, and more breakout spaces have been created for students.

Despite the NSS outcomes, SOAS has fashioned a nine-place rise in our overall ranking this year, based on improvements in several other indicators, including an increased spend on student services and facilities, an improved staff-to-student ratio, better qualified entrants and more top-class degrees.

Applications rose for five years in a row to 2018 but, unlike most universities, SOAS has reduced the proportion of candidates who receive offers. The numbers starting courses

Thornhaugh Street
Russell Square
London WC1H 0XG
020 7898 4700
study@soas.ac.uk
www.soas.ac.uk
http://soasunion.org
Open days 2020:
June 13

The Times and The Sunday Times Rankings
Overall Ranking: 44 (last year: 53)

Teaching quality	75.5%	=117
Student experience	71.2%	126
Research quality	27.9%	46
Entry standards	156	=35
Graduate prospects	70.9%	=94
Good honours	81.7%	=31
Expected completion rate	81.4%	94
Student/staff ratio	11.3	6
Services and facilities	£2,608	39

are down by more than a third in two years.

The only specialist institution in the UK for the study of Asia, Africa and the Middle East, SOAS enjoys global prestige. More than 40% of the 6,300 students are from outside the UK and the school is ranked by QS close to the top 50 in the world for the arts and humanities. Music, drama and the performing arts produced the best results in the Research Excellence Framework, when two-thirds of the work was rated world-leading or internationally excellent.

Degrees are available in areas such as law, history and the social sciences, but with a specialist emphasis. There is a limited portfolio of foundation programmes and language courses.

About 45% of undergraduates take a language as part of their degree and the school has introduced a language entitlement programme that offers one term of a non-accredited SOAS language centre course free of charge. The £6.5m project to transform the library added more language laboratories, music studios, discussion and research rooms.

The school celebrated its centenary in 2016 by moving into the north block of Senate House, the Bloomsbury headquarters of the University of London, which adjoins the SOAS precinct. The five-floor development brought the school together on a single site for the first time in many years. It includes a student hub, hosting services such as accommodation, counselling, student finance.

A £20m gift from a graduate with a passion for southeast Asian art is funding new posts, building developments and scholarships for Asian students. More than 40% of degree programmes offer the opportunity to spend a year at partner universities in Africa or Asia.

Almost a fifth of the British undergraduates come from independent schools, but the school devotes much of its fee income to outreach activities and bursaries. Those who are the first in their family to go to university, or are over 21, or from a low-participation neighbourhood, are invited to a free, week-long bridging course so that they can make a flying start to their studies. Those with household incomes below £25,000 are eligible for the SOAS Excellence Bursary, worth at least £4,500.

There is no separate students' union building, although the students do have their own bar, social space and catering facilities. The former University of London Union, is close at hand, with a swimming pool, gym and bars.

More than 1,100 residential places are available within 20 minutes' walk of the school. SOAS has few of its own sports facilities and the outdoor pitches are remote. For most students, however, sport is not a priority.

Tuition fees

» Fees for UK/EU students	£9,250
» Fees for International students 2019–20	£17,750
» For scholarship and bursary information see www.soas.ac.uk/registry/funding	
» Graduate salary	£22,700

Student numbers

Undergraduates	3,124	(30)
Postgraduates	2,010	(1,107)
Applications/places		6,325/735
Applications per place		8.6
Overall offer rate		72.5%
Unconditional offers		0%
International students		43.2%

Accommodation

University provided places: 1,093
Catered costs: £221–£280 per week
Self-catered: £148–£290 per week
www.soas.ac.uk/accommodation

Where do the students come from?

State schools (non-grammar)	74.6%	First generation students	42.4%	Black attainment gap	-15%
Grammar schools	5.6%	Deprived areas	3.9%	Disabled	8.7%
Independent schools	19.9%	All ethnic minorities	55.2%	Mature (over 21)	18.9%

Social inclusion ranking: =93

Solent University

Solent is introducing a new learning analytics programme to utilise big data to identify students at risk of failing their course or dropping out and give them targeted support to increase their engagement and achievement. This should address an area of weakness with the university in the bottom 20 for completion in our rankings, dropping further in the latest table.

Overall, Solent has dropped four places, but that was after a big rise last year that took the university to its highest-ever position. Student satisfaction rates have continued to rise in the new table, as have entry standards, but it has seen a small fall in spending on student facilities.

Solent, which dropped Southampton from its name in 2018, has been upgraded to the silver category in the Teaching Excellence Framework. The new panel was impressed by students' high levels of engagement and commitment to learning, and by the substantial investment in learning resources and successful integration of research and professional practice into the curriculum.

It accepted that the low graduate employment rate – the main factor in the university's bronze rating in 2017 – was being addressed, although it remained below Solent's benchmark.

Applications were not affected by the initial assessment, but enrolments dropped a little. The numbers starting degrees remain 1,000 lower than in the final year before £9,000 fees were introduced – a drop of more than a quarter. But Solent is launching 14 new degrees and several programmes below degree level in 2019 and 2020, as well as expanding its portfolio of degree apprenticeships.

Digital design and web development, international design tourism management and popular music production are among the new degree subjects. There is even a new degree in body art, which will explore the anthropological rationale for body art in different cultures, as well as providing practical skills.

The new higher and degree apprenticeships are planned in project management, cybersecurity, software engineering, digital and technology solutions, broadcast production, social work and healthcare science, potentially taking the number of apprentices from 550 to 900 by September 2020.

Solent's main campus is close to the city centre, with the £33m Spark building at its heart, containing 40 high-tech teaching spaces accommodating 1,500 students at any one time. A £28m sports building provides two sports halls, gymnasiums, fitness suites and teaching facilities. It will be used by students in subjects such as media, journalism and photography, as well as sport.

A £12.5m refurbishment of two buildings on the main campus has produced specialist maritime simulation facilities and new

---

East Park Terrace
Southampton SO14 0YN
023 8201 5066
admissions@solent.ac.uk
www.solent.ac.uk
www.solentsu.co.uk
Open days 2020:
February 1, March 14,
April 18

The Times and The Sunday Times **Rankings**

Overall Ranking: =89 (last year: =85)

Teaching quality	82.2%	=33
Student experience	79%	=51
Research quality	0.5%	126
Entry standards	118	=100
Graduate prospects	70.4%	=99
Good honours	71.3%	=91
Expected completion rate	77.9%	118
Student/staff ratio	15.6	=62
Services and facilities	£2,112	84

classrooms. Work will begin at Warsash in 2020 to provide upgraded facilities for maritime safety training, including open water rescue boat and survival craft, fire school, helicopter underwater escape training and medical facilities.

Solent is UK higher education's premier yachting institution, with a world champion student team and alumni who have gone on to win Olympic and Paralympic gold medals. The world-renowned maritime and superyacht academies serve the training and research needs of the superyacht, shipping and offshore oil industries.

The university is frequently among the leaders for graduate start-ups. Students wishing to set up their own businesses or become freelancers can join the institution's Sparks society and the Enactus social enterprise organisation, which operates nationwide. Solent is proud of the fact that 40% of the ventures its students launch are still in business three years later.

Students have access to the university's creative agency, Solent Creatives, and Re:So store – the first fully student-operated retail outlet in a UK shopping centre. The university's support for students, which includes a scheme providing employment for 50 recent graduates, was identified as an example of best practice by the Quality Assurance Agency.

Solent recruits mainly in London and the south of England, a quarter of the higher education students coming from Hampshire.

The university's outreach work focuses particularly on progression rates for white males from disadvantaged backgrounds.

The university plans to bring student support facilities together in 2020, with access to advice desks for areas such as finance, accommodation and assessment to provide a more efficient service. The students' union is also being moved to the centre of the campus.

The university finished bottom of those that entered the 2014 Research Excellence Framework. It entered the lowest proportion of eligible academics, at only 7%, and none of its research was placed in the top two categories for its external impact.

Facilities accredited by the Football Association are used by the city's Premier League team, while other options include outdoor pitches, tennis and netball courts four miles away.

There are 2,000 places in halls – including one that is newly refurbished – enough to guarantee accommodation to first-years who apply by the end of June.

Tuition fees

» Fees for UK/EU students	£9,250
» Fees for International students 2019–20	£12,875
Foundation	£11,330
» For scholarship and bursary information see www.solent.ac.uk/finance/tuition-fees	
» Graduate salary	£18,000

Student numbers

Undergraduates	8,960	(1054)
Postgraduates	292	(269)
Applications/places		12,575/2,840
Applications per place		4.4
Overall offer rate		88.2%
Conditional offers		0%
International students		17.3%

Accommodation

University provided places: 2,054
Self-catered: £110–£158 per week
First years guaranteed accommodation
www.solent.ac.uk/studying-at-solent/accommodation

Where do the students come from?

State schools (non-grammar)	96.3%	First generation students	50.3%	
Grammar schools	1%	Deprived areas	15.3%	
Independent schools	2.7%	All ethnic minorities	16.2%	

Social inclusion ranking: 60

Black attainment gap	-24.4%
Disabled	6.1%
Mature (over 21)	18.5%

University of South Wales

The number of undergraduates starting courses at USW has fallen by more than 22% – almost 1,000 students – since the merged university had its first intake in 2014. Further decline seems inevitable with the loss of the university's large teacher training intake last September. While the university's completion rate has improved, entry standards and spending on student facilities have declined.

USW has fallen four places in our rankings and lies in the bottom 20, despite stellar student satisfaction scores that improved even on last year's excellent results. The university is in the top 30 for students' assessment of teaching quality and the top 40 for the wider student experience – up more than 30 places. It is worth noting that the final-year undergraduates who responded to the National Student Survey were there for the controversy surrounding the closure of the Carleon campus, outside Newport, which might have been expected to bring down satisfaction rates.

The university was the product of a merger between Glamorgan and Newport universities. The largest campus is in Pontypridd, ten miles outside Cardiff, where two sites cater mainly for science, engineering and health subjects. Recent developments there have included a new Law School and upgraded laboratories, as well as a £6m Learning Resource Centre.

USW's greatest investment has been at the Cardiff campus for the creative industries, where the new ATRiuM building replicates workplace facilities for advertising, TV and film set design and fashion. It also has room for dance studios, rehearsal spaces and photographic studios. USW's other simulated learning facilities include a trading room, hospital wards and a scene-of-crime house.

The £35m Newport City Campus opened in 2011 and is the base for professional and executive courses. Part of USW's remit is to attract inward investment and strengthen the local economy. Newport was rated the top university in Wales for enterprise education by the Knowledge Exploitation Fund for three years in a row.

Education degrees are still taught in Newport – another two are being launched in 2020 – but accreditation for the teacher education programmes has been withdrawn. USW has introduced new courses in business, a new centre for counselling and therapies, and the National Cybersecurity Academy on the campus. The money from the sale of the Carleon campus is being reinvested in a planned Knowledge Quarter for Newport.

Across the university, a dozen new degrees took their first students in 2019, some with the option of a foundation year for those without the necessary qualifications for immediate entry. They include natural history and media, automotive engineering and forensic investigation.

Pontypridd
CF37 1DL
03455 760101
www.southwales.ac.uk/contact-us
www.southwales.ac.uk
www.uswsu.com
Open days 2020:
March 28, July 4

The Times and The Sunday Times **Rankings**
Overall Ranking: 114 (last year: =110)

Teaching quality	82.5%	=26
Student experience	79.5%	=40
Research quality	4.0%	=104
Entry standards	128	=81
Graduate prospects	63.4%	126
Good honours	67.3%	115
Expected completion rate	79.8%	=105
Student/staff ratio	15.6	=62
Services and facilities	£1,580	125

The university has 400 degree apprentices in policing and digital and technology solutions, and is expanding into mechanical and electrical engineering. It also runs the Network 75 programme, in which students work in a local business for three days a week and attend university for two. Employers pay the fees for the five-year programme.

USW is one of the two largest universities in Wales and belongs to the University of South Wales Group, which includes the Royal Welsh College of Music and Drama and Merthyr Tydfil College, and a strategic alliance bringing in further education colleges throughout southeast Wales.

The university opened a campus in Dubai in 2018, initially offering courses in aircraft maintenance engineering – one of its strengths in Wales. USW is the only UK university to have a partnership with British Airways which enables students to graduate with a European Aviation Safety Agency licence as well as a degree.

Three-quarters of USW students are from Wales and more than a fifth come from areas of low participation in higher education. The university offers a range of bursaries, including three scholarships of £1,000 for undergraduates who study in the Welsh language.

Like most universities in Wales, USW has not entered the Teaching Excellence Framework. Of its relatively small submission in the 2014 Research Excellence Framework, half of the work was considered world-leading or internationally excellent. The best results came in a joint submission with Cardiff Metropolitan and Trinity St David universities in art and design. Results were also good for sport and exercise science, and social work and social policy.

Leisure facilities have improved with a recreation centre, new students' union and more halls. USW owns or endorses 1,700 rooms but does not guarantee accommodation for new entrants.

USW Sport Park provides a high-performance setting for elite athletes and regular users. It includes a specialist centre for strength and conditioning with 12 lifting platforms and a full-size 3G indoor football pitch, the only one in Wales and one of five in the UK.

USW has a good record in student competitions, especially in rugby, football and golf and participates in one of six centres of excellence for cricket. A foundation degree in rugby coaching and development was launched in 2018, run in partnership with the Welsh Rugby Union, Cardiff Blues and the Dragons.

Tuition fees

» Fees for UK/EU students	£9,000
» Fees for International students 2020–21	£13,200-£13,500
Foundation courses	£10,000
» For scholarship and bursary information see www.southwales.ac.uk/study/fees-and-funding/undergraduate/	
» Graduate salary	£20,046

Student numbers

Undergraduates	**14,360**	**(4,001)**
Postgraduates	**1,808**	**(2,690)**
Applications/places	12.925/3,240	
Applications per place	4.1	
Overall offer rate	81.9%	
Unconditional offers	0%	
International students	13.1%	

Accommodation

University provided places: 1,700
Self-catered: £94–£170 per week
www.southwales.ac.uk/student-life/accommodation

Where do the students come from?

State schools (non-grammar)	97%	First generation students	43.9%
Grammar schools	0.8%	Deprived areas	21.1%
Independent schools	2.2%	All ethnic minorities	10.3%

Social inclusion ranking: 36

Black attainment gap	-19.5%
Disabled	7.4%
Mature (over 21)	25.5%

University of Southampton

Southampton has dropped two places in our league table but remains in the top 20. However, it is also the Russell Group university that has seen the biggest decline in new enrolments – 29% – since recruitment restrictions were lifted in 2015.

The university says that it has "strategically reduced acceptances" in order to safeguard the student experience. The offer rate was reduced slightly under the previous vice-chancellor, Sir Christopher Snowden, but Southampton's applications were down by almost 15% in 2018, after two record years.

Applications were back up in the 2019 admissions round, which followed the upgrading of the university from bronze to silver in the Teaching Excellence Framework (TEF). Computer science, mechanical engineering, maths, allied health, nursing and history have all recruited strongly.

The flexible undergraduate curriculum sees some subjects offering a "major-minor" structure that allows students to spend a quarter of their time on a subject other than their original degree choice. There are also interdisciplinary modules that are designed to give students a broader perspective.

Most subjects – if not all individual degree programmes – now offer the option of a year in employment. Leading employers

participating in the scheme range from Marks & Spencer to IBM, Nationwide and the Royal National Lifeboat Institution.

The TEF panel noted that satisfaction with academic support was still below the university's benchmark, but it complimented the institution on a strategic commitment to enhancing the quality of teaching and a learning environment in which students participate actively in research. Our analysis of the latest National Student Survey shows satisfaction with teaching quality still in the bottom half of the table.

Developments include a new teaching and learning centre and the £36.5m National Linear Infrastructure Laboratory. A £300m public bond will allow the university to invest further in infrastructure.

Recent additions are the £25m cancer immunology centre – the first of its kind in the country and funded entirely through donations – and the £140m Boldrewood Innovation campus, which was developed jointly with Lloyd's Register and reported to be the largest business-university relationship of its kind in the UK.

The university's business accelerator unit, Future Worlds, has invested more than £500,000 in student and graduate start-ups chosen from its own Dragons Den-style investment event.

The university has campuses in Southampton and Winchester, and one in Malaysia dedicated to engineering. The main Highfield campus is in an attractive green location two miles from the city centre. The nearby Avenue campus is

University Road
Highfield
Southampton SO17 1BJ
023 8059 9699
enquiry@southampton.ac.uk
www.southampton.ac.uk
www.susu.org
Open days 2020:
see website

The Times and The Sunday Times Rankings
Overall Ranking: 20 (last year: 18)

Teaching quality	79.1%	=83
Student experience	78.6%	=61
Research quality	44.9%	7
Entry standards	160	26
Graduate prospects	82.1%	=27
Good honours	84.9%	18
Expected completion rate	89.3%	44
Student/staff ratio	13.5	=19
Services and facilities	£2,454	50

home to most of the humanities departments, while clinical medicine is based at Southampton General Hospital.

Winchester School of Art has been part of the university since 1996, while other sites include the National Oceanography Centre Southampton, based in the revitalised dock area. Southampton researchers led the first mission of the autonomous submarine vehicle Autosub Long Range (better known as Boaty McBoat-face) which, for the first time ever, has shed light on a key process linking increasing Antarctic winds to rising sea temperatures.

The university performed well in the 2014 Research Excellence Framework. It is in the top seven for research quality after entering nine out of ten eligible academics for assessment with more than 80% of their work rated world-leading or internationally excellent.

The best results came in health subjects, environmental science, psychology, physics, chemistry, electronic engineering and music, drama and performing arts. There are also strengths in computer science: Sir Tim Berners-Lee, inventor of the web, is a professor and Dame Wendy Hall is a Regius professor in the subject.

Southampton is in the top 100 in the QS global rankings and the proportion of income derived from research is among the highest in Britain. The university has 8,000 international students and a growing number of those from the UK spend time at one of the partner institutions in 54 countries.

The new India Centre for Growth and Sustainable Development was launched in 2019, with the target of becoming a globally recognised think tank for innovation and knowledge sharing. Part of the centre's programme of activities will include undergraduate student exchanges and placements with partners in India.

The university has a more diverse intake than most of its peers in the Russell Group, but just scrapes into the top 100 in our social inclusion ranking. Only six of the 24 members recruit more students educated in non-selective state schools. Students act as ambassadors, associates and mentors in local schools and colleges as part of efforts to broaden the intake further.

Sports facilities are first-class, with an indoor complex next to the students' union and a 25-metre pool. Sport and Wellbeing membership, for which a basic pass starts at £99 a year, provides access to numerous gyms on campus and across the city, while the outdoor sports complex has multiple grass and synthetic pitches.

Southampton has more than 7,000 residential places, enough for all new entrants who apply by the deadline – and most others.

Tuition fees

» Fees for UK/EU students		£9,250
» Fees for International students 2020–21		£17,560–£21,580
» For scholarship and bursary information see www.southampton.ac.uk/uni-life/fees-funding.page		
» Graduate salary		£23,000

Student numbers

Undergraduates	16,869	(132)
Postgraduates	6,158	(1,464)
Applications/places		33,995/4,405
Applications per place		7.7
Overall offer rate		80%
Unconditional offers		0%
International students		29.2%

Accommodation

University provided places: 7,000
Catered costs: £145–£195 per week
Self-catered: £112–£320 per week
First years guaranteed accommodation
www.southampton.ac.uk/uni-life/accommodation.page

Where do the students come from?

State schools (non-grammar)	71.5%	First generation students	35.8%	Black attainment gap	-10.6%
Grammar schools	14.7%	Deprived areas	7.7%	Disabled	6%
Independent schools	13.8%	All ethnic minorities	22.9%	Mature (over 21)	10.9%

Social inclusion ranking: =93

Staffordshire University

Staffordshire was shortlisted for our University of the Year award, finishing in its highest position for the third year in a row, representing a rise of nearly 40 places. The university is now close to the top 50 and is in the top 20 for student satisfaction with the quality of teaching, despite a slight decline in the rate this year.

The university was also one of two upgraded to gold in 2019 in the Teaching Excellence Framework. The panel said students from all backgrounds achieve outstanding outcomes and it complimented the university on high rates of progression to highly skilled employment or further study (Staffordshire ranks just outside our top 40 on this measure), as well as its strong commitment to supporting students' personal and professional development.

There was praise for projects and initiatives which have smoothed students' paths into university and supported them during studies. The Student Journey scheme – which was co-created by students and staff to address disadvantage – was given special mention, as was the Quiet Induction, which offers a calm, personalised registration and welcome for students on the autistic spectrum.

Its connected university strategy commits Staffordshire to widening participation in higher education, promoting social mobility and connecting with its communities. The university is just outside the top 30 in our social inclusion table, with almost all the undergraduates coming from non-selective state schools and colleges – just three universities have a bigger proportion. More than 57% of students have parents who have not gone to university.

A longstanding focus on computer science and games design has encouraged Staffordshire to open a new Digital Institute London, in the Queen Elizabeth Olympic Park, offering degrees in games PR and community management, e-sports, and computer games design. A degree in cybersecurity will be added in 2020.

On the home campus, nine new degrees were introduced in 2019, including automotive and motorsport engineering, artificial intelligence and robotics, and criminology. Nine more will be added to the portfolio in 2020, including e-law, acting for stage and screen, games cultures and augmented and virtual realities.

Staffordshire has also been among the pioneers of degree and higher apprenticeships, working with employers such as Vodafone and the NHS. A planned £40m Catalyst Building, part-funded by the Office for Students, will be a hub for apprentices and digital skills. Scheduled to open in 2021, it will be the base for 6,500 apprentices by 2030 and be a centre of excellence for the region.

There are currently ten degree-

College Road
University Quarter
Stoke-on-Trent ST4 2DE
01782 294 400
enquiries@staffs.ac.uk
www.staffs.ac.uk
www.staffsunion.com
Open days 2020:
March 28 (Stoke-on-Trent);
March 21 (Stafford);
March 14, June 24 (Shrewsbury)

The Times and The Sunday Times **Rankings**

Overall Ranking: 53 (last year: 57)		
Teaching quality	83.3%	=18
Student experience	79.8%	38
Research quality	16.5%	55
Entry standards	120	=94
Graduate prospects	80.8%	41
Good honours	72.3%	85
Expected completion rate	78.4%	=113
Student/staff ratio	15.4	=56
Services and facilities	£2,484	48

apprenticeship programmes and eight for higher apprenticeships. New options are being developed for 2020 in business administration, health and science, and childcare and education.

The numbers starting degrees were down in 2018, but by less than 5%, and there has been an equivalent increase in applications in the latest round. More than eight out of ten applicants received an offer in 2018, compared with less than two-thirds in 2014.

Staffordshire's campus transformation project has concentrated most of its activities in Stoke. Closing the Stafford campus was intended to improve the student experience and create an award-winning, teaching-led university, with a focus on employability, enterprise and entrepreneurialism, as well as saving money. Only the highly-rated nursing and midwifery programmes and other health-related courses are now taught in the town.

The strategy seems to be working: the university is in the top 40 in the UK for student satisfaction with their experience once again this year.

The main campus is at the heart of Stoke's University Quarter project, which forms a gateway to the city for anyone arriving at the main train station. An £80m investment programme is upgrading buildings, expanding the university library, extending student accommodation and improving public spaces.

Two satellite campuses have survived the reorganisation. Primary teacher training programmes are based at Lichfield, where there is an integrated further and higher education centre, developed in partnership with South Staffordshire College. Nursing and midwifery students are based in the Royal Shrewsbury Hospital. There are also 15,000 students taking Staffordshire courses outside the UK.

Staffordshire increased the size and scope of its submission to the 2014 Research Excellence Framework, compared with previous assessments, but entered just 91 academics. Best results were in sport and exercise sciences, although all of the research in psychology was placed in the top two categories for external impact.

Sports facilities are good and will see more investment as numbers on the Stoke campus rise. Team Staffs Sports Elite scholarships are available and a recent £1.25m refurbishment of the sports centre added studio spaces and tripled the capacity of the gym. There are 1,250 residential places – enough to guarantee accommodation for first-years.

Stoke is not the liveliest city of its size, but the University Quarter is attracting more social and leisure facilities, and there is an active students' union.

Tuition fees

» Fees for UK/EU students	£9,250
» Fees for International students 2020–21	£14,000–£15,000
» For scholarship and bursary information see www.staffs.ac.uk/courses/undergraduate/fees-and-funding	
» Graduate salary	£20,600

Student numbers

Undergraduates	8,413	(3,890)
Postgraduates	619	(1,425)
Applications/places	12,010/3,420	
Applications per place	3.5	
Overall offer rate	87.8%	
Unconditional offers	39.1%	
International students	3.1%	

Accommodation

University provided places: 1,247
Self-catered: £95–£130 per week
www.staffs.ac.uk/student-life/accommodation

Where do the students come from?

State schools (non-grammar)	98.6%	First generation students	57.2%	Black attainment gap	-29.8%
Grammar schools	0.3%	Deprived areas	26.4%	Disabled	9.5%
Independent schools	1.1%	All ethnic minorities	18.4%	Mature (over 21)	33.5%

Social inclusion ranking: 33

University of Stirling

Stirling is our Sports University of the Year, punching well above its weight in inter-university competition (ranking 11th in the UK this year) and enjoying some of the finest sports facilities to boot. Designated Scotland's University for Sporting Excellence as long ago as 2008, the campus is home to national swimming and tennis centres, a nine-hole golf course and a football academy.

A new £20m sports centre is nearing completion, which will include purpose-built fitness studios, a gym, a three-court sports hall, an indoor cycling studio and strength and conditioning areas. The university runs an international sports scholarship programme and manages Winning Students, the national sport scholarship programme across Scotland.

Athletes and alumni from the university won 11 medals at the Gold Coast Commonwealth Games in 2018 to go with the three won at the Rio Olympics two years before. The university's tennis courts hosted the young Murray brothers, Andy and Jamie, as they were growing up at a time when their mother Judy, worked there as Scotland's national tennis coach from 1995–2004.

This year's award from *The Times* and *The Sunday Times* also recognises the academic reputation of Stirling's sports degrees, ranked 18th in our latest sport science subject table. Degrees in sport and exercise science, sports studies and sport business management are among those on offer.

Applications to study at Stirling have been running at record levels, but they are down by more than 8% in 2019. The university blames Brexit uncertainty and increased competition for students.

Stirling has 2,500 students from outside the UK, 1,000 of them from the EU – 20% of the total numbers. Those from other EU countries enrolling in 2019 – and 2020 – have been assured they will continue to pay no fees.

The university has fallen three places in our new table, following a slight decline in student satisfaction with their university experience. Although it is still in the top 50 overall, it is a long way from its target of becoming one of the top 25 universities by 2021.

Satisfaction with the student experience, as measured by the National Student Survey, is now outside the top 100. But the university has been upgrading the facilities on its famously attractive campus. Alongside the new sports centre, a £21m Campus Central development is due to open, with retail, catering, events space and student support services facilities, as well as more social learning and study space.

Like most Scottish universities, Stirling did not enter the Teaching Excellence Framework. But the university was awarded the maximum five stars in the QS global rating system,

Stirling
FK9 4LA
01786 467 044
admissions@stir.ac.uk
www.stir.ac.uk
www.stirlingstudentsunion.com
Open days 2020:
June 6, September 19,
October 24

The Times and The Sunday Times **Rankings**
Overall Ranking: 47 (last year: =44)

Teaching quality	79.5%	=73
Student experience	75.6%	107
Research quality	30.5%	42
Entry standards	163	=22
Graduate prospects	78.7%	=53
Good honours	76.3%	56
Expected completion rate	86.7%	59
Student/staff ratio	16.4	=81
Services and facilities	£1,865	105

which covers teaching, graduate employability, internationalisation and inclusiveness.

The main campus – 330 acres of parkland, set around a loch at the foot of the Ochil Hills – invariably features in lists of the most beautiful places to study. There is also a campus for nurses and midwives in Inverness, and a Western Isles campus in Stornoway.

Stirling was the UK pioneer of the semester system, which has now become popular throughout higher education. The academic year is divided into two blocks of 15 weeks with short mid-semester breaks. Students have the option of starting courses in January or September and can choose subjects from across five faculties.

Undergraduates can switch the whole direction of their studies, in consultation with their academic adviser, as their interests develop. They can also speed up their progress on a summer academic programme, which squeezes a full semester's teaching into July and August. Full-time students are not allowed to use the programme to reduce the length of their course, but part-timers can.

The virtual learning environment has improved students' access to course and campus information. All lectures are filmed to make them accessible online for use with lecture notes.

Two-thirds of the students are from Scotland. Applicants from the 40% of Scottish postcodes that are classified as the most deprived are eligible for reduced offers.

There is an international study hub – the INTO Academic Centre – on the main campus, offering preparatory courses for students hoping to take degrees at Stirling. International exchanges are common, with many of Stirling's students taking part of their degree at an American, Asian or European university.

Almost three-quarters of the work submitted to the 2014 Research Excellence Framework was judged to be world-leading or internationally excellent. The best results were in agriculture, veterinary and food science, where Stirling was ranked fourth in the UK. It was top in Scotland for health sciences and third for psychology.

There are 2,894 residential places, following a £38m expansion of accommodation. Rooms are guaranteed for first-year students living more than 20 miles away. A centralised Student Hub provides services including support for mental and emotional health.

A lively social scene is based on the award-winning students' union. The Macrobert Arts Centre offers a full programme of cultural activities, while the surrounding countryside attracts walkers and climbers.

Tuition fees

» Fees for Scottish/EU students   £0–£1,820
    RUK fees   £9,250 (capped at £27,750 for 4-year courses)
» Fees for International students 2020–21   £13,100–£15,600
» For scholarship and bursary information see
    www.stir.ac.uk/study/fees-funding/
» Graduate salary   £22,000

Student numbers		
Undergraduates	8,138	(609)
Postgraduates	2,396	(1,440)
Applications/places		17,710/2,390
Applications per place		7.4
Overall offer rate		65.3%
Unconditional offers		0%
International students		20.3%

Accommodation
University provided places: 2,894
Self-catered: £84–£175 per week
First years guaranteed accommodation
www.stir.ac.uk/student-life/accommodation

Where do the students come from?					
State schools (non-grammar)	88.4%	First generation students	37.7%	Black attainment gap	-51.9%
Grammar schools	5.2%	Deprived areas	15.9%	Disabled	6.4%
Independent schools	6.4%	All ethnic minorities	6.4%	Mature (over 21)	24.9%

Social inclusion ranking (Scotland): 11

University of Strathclyde

 Strathclyde is our Scottish University of the Year, after an eight-place rise in our table pushed it into the top 40, its highest ranking since 2013. It has the best overall student satisfaction rates of any university in Glasgow with scores for teaching quality up 16 places this year. Student satisfaction with the wider student experience falls just outside the top 50.

In our new rankings, it is the high entry standards at Strathclyde that really stand out, placing the university fifth in the UK, behind only Cambridge, Oxford, St Andrews and Imperial College London. While this ranking is undoubtedly aided by the high conversion rate for Scottish secondary qualifications in the UCAS tariff system (which also benefits other Scottish institutions), it is indicative of the calibre of the intake here.

The university is in the midst of a £1bn building programme – often the cause of temporarily lower student satisfaction. A £31m sport centre opened in autumn 2018 and a £60m learning and teaching building will follow in 2020. It will provide a new base for the students' union and other services at the heart of the campus, as well as study spaces.

Other projects include upgraded facilities for biomedical engineering and a £20m combined heat and power network that will improve sustainability. The ten-year programme included an £89m technology and innovation centre, the largest in the UK.

Four years of rising applications, during which demand rose by almost 60%, came to an end in 2018. However, the decline was minimal and there was still a small increase in enrolments.

Strathclyde was established in 1796 to be a "place of useful learning", which is still central to its mission today. It is the third-largest university in Scotland and is aiming to be one of the world's leading technological universities.

All courses are taught on the John Anderson campus, in the city centre, which has the humanities and social sciences faculty at its heart. The engineering faculty is the largest in Scotland, and home to one of Europe's biggest university electrical power engineering and energy research groupings.

The business school, rated among the top 40 in Europe by *The Financial Times*, is considered Strathclyde's greatest strength. It is among the largest in Europe and one of just 88 in the world to be "triple accredited" by the main international bodies. It has seven well-established centres in Europe, the Gulf and Southeast Asia.

Like most Scottish universities, Strathclyde did not enter the Teaching Excellence Framework, but it excelled in the 2014 Research Excellence Framework, taking it near the top 20 in our research rankings. Almost 80% of an exceptionally large submission was rated

---

McCance Building
16 Richmond Street
Glasgow G1 1XQ
0141 548 4400
study-here@strath.ac.uk
www.strath.ac.uk
www.strathunion.com
Open days 2020:
September 1, October 3

GLASGOW
Edinburgh
Belfast
London
Cardiff

The Times and The Sunday Times Rankings
Overall Ranking: 36 (last year: =44)

Teaching quality	78.3%	=93
Student experience	78.9%	=56
Research quality	37.7%	=21
Entry standards	200	=5
Graduate prospects	79.6%	=49
Good honours	83.4%	25
Expected completion rate	88.5%	=49
Student/staff ratio	19.5	120
Services and facilities	£1,867	104

world-leading or internationally excellent.

The university was top in the UK for physics and top in Scotland for business, among a clutch of eye-catching performances. Since then, Strathclyde has launched the Advanced Forming Research Centre, a research partnership with international engineering firms, and become the European partner for South Korea's global research and commercialisation programme.

More than nine out of ten undergraduates are state-educated – far above the UK average for its courses and entry grades – and Strathclyde ranks 10th in Scotland in our social inclusion table. Scholarships and bursaries are available for all students. Just over a third of students have parents who did not go to university.

Strathclyde delivers both Scotland's graduate apprenticeships and, from 2019, degree apprenticeships validated in England. The university expects the number of apprentices to double by September 2020, with a blended learning approach allowing apprentices to spend minimal time away from the workplace.

The university has also launched a new route into teaching technical education and home economics, with a BSc in education and curricular studies.

Strathclyde's enterprise pathway allows students to develop, enhance and test their transferable skills, while alumni and businesses in the Strathclyde 100 Network support emerging entrepreneurs. Since 2005, the university has helped to launch more than 260 spin-out companies. Students can take a degree in Business Enterprise at the Hunter Centre for Entrepreneurship, a unit endowed by the Scottish businessman and philanthropist Sir Tom Hunter that is one of Europe's leading centres for the study of entrepreneurship, innovation and strategy.

The recently opened Strathclyde Sport building has a six-lane, 25-metre swimming pool; two sports halls; squash courts; a cafe and specialist health facilities – and student membership costs just £145 a year.

There are 1,500 residential places in a student village on the main campus and nearby in the Merchant City – enough to guarantee new entrants accommodation. The existing ten-storey students' union building attracts students from all over Glasgow.

The latest *Time Out* magazine guide ranks Glasgow as one of the top ten cities in the world, and first for friendliness and affordability. It is the UK's first Unesco City of Music and has the largest civic art collection in Europe. There are theatres, comedy clubs and cabaret venues galore – plus more than 700 bars and clubs.

Tuition fees

- » Fees for Scottish/EU students   £0–£1,820
  RUK fees   £9,250 (capped at £27,750 for 4-year courses)
- » Fees for International students 2020–21   £15,300–£21,500
- » For scholarship and bursary information see
  www.strath.ac.uk/studywithus/feesfunding/
- » Graduate salary   £22,216

Student numbers

Undergraduates	13,362	(1,497)
Postgraduates	4,853	(2,581)
Applications/places		28,505/4,220
Applications per place		6.8
Overall offer rate		60.1%
Unconditional offers		0%
International students		18.8%

Accommodation

University provided places: 1,500
Self-catered: £105–£145 per week
www.strath.ac.uk/studywithus/accommodation/

Where do the students come from?

State schools (non-grammar)	87.9%	First generation students	36.3%
Grammar schools	2%	Deprived areas	16.6%
Independent schools	10.1%	All ethnic minorities	10.8%

Social inclusion ranking (Scotland): 10

Black attainment gap	-35.9%
Disabled	2.9%
Mature (over 21)	33.1%

University of Suffolk

The number of students starting degrees at Suffolk shot up by almost 1,000 in 2018, an increase of 64% in a single year. But fewer than half of them had been placed with the university by the June deadline, with 30% coming through clearing.

Almost 20 new degrees, in key subjects such as law and architecture, helped to boost applications. The university has hung on to most of the increase in the latest admissions round, which has seen more new degrees, in English literature, biomedical science, software engineering and network engineering.

There will be another ten new offerings in 2020, in subjects ranging from economics and human geography to professional policing, marketing and film studies. Suffolk is also expanding its portfolio of degree apprenticeships, with new programmes in social work and policing planned in the next two years. The blended learning model, mixing workplace learning with online and campus tuition, is expected to be suitable for other occupations.

The Ipswich-based university has climbed one place further up the table this year, but is still in the bottom three. It is hampered by the absence of a research rating because the 2014 Research Excellence Framework pre-dated its establishment as an independent institution.

Suffolk, founded in 2007 as University Campus Suffolk, a satellite of East Anglia (UEA) and Essex universities, was expected to take 20 years to become independent. But it was granted the power to award degrees in 2015 and the Privy Council conferred the full university title shortly afterwards. UEA and Essex continue to work with the new university, which has developed an academic strategy and set up a foundation board with a philanthropic role.

However, the university was given a bronze rating in the Teaching Excellence Framework (TEF) because it was "substantially" below its benchmarks for student satisfaction and graduate employment. The panel did acknowledge the contribution of employers to course design and found a "developing approach to the creation of research and practice-based communities of staff enabling students to benefit by exposure to scholarship, research and professional practice".

The university is only just below halfway for satisfaction with teaching quality in our new table, having moved up 46 places on this measure. But it is well outside the top 100 for graduate prospects and in the bottom three for completion, another of the TEF criteria.

There are more than 5,000 students on the Waterfront Campus and at smaller bases in Bury St Edmunds, Lowestoft, Great Yarmouth and Otley. Nearly 60% of applicants are over 20 when they start their courses, most of them coming from the region. The university's target is between 6,500 and 7,000 students by 2020.

Waterfront Building
Neptune Quay
Ipswich IP4 1QJ
01473 338 833
admissions@uos.ac.uk
www.uos.ac.uk
www.uosunion.org
Open days 2020:
April 25

The Times and The Sunday Times Rankings
Overall Ranking: 129 (last year: 130)

Teaching quality	80%	65
Student experience	76%	101
Research quality	n/a	
Entry standards	117	=104
Graduate prospects	65.0%	117
Good honours	66.8%	118
Expected completion rate	72.2%	129
Student/staff ratio	18.8	=115
Services and facilities	£2,387	59

Founded in a part of the country poorly served for higher education, it is no surprise that Suffolk does so well in our new social inclusion ranking, standing in 14th position this year and drawing more than a quarter of its undergraduates from areas of low participation, among the highest proportions in the country. Almost 60% of students come from homes where parents are not educated to degree level and 98.5% of them attended non-selective state secondary schools.

A larger-than-average share of Suffolk's fee income is allocated to student support, with more than half of its spending going on cash bursaries for students from under-represented backgrounds.

Having completed a £2.5m renovation of the library, Suffolk has refurbished one of its main teaching buildings, adding specialist facilities for psychology, computer games design, network and software engineering. The Atrium also houses the Ipswich Waterfront Innovation Centre for business and innovation activities. Its 3D Productivity Suite contains a range of 3D printers.

Support for student and graduate entrepreneurship is central to the university's five-year business and engagement strategy, and internships and placements with industry are becoming the norm.

Suffolk is committed to a strategy of being a distinctive "community impact" university, with a focus on Stem (science, technology, engineering and mathematics) subjects. A £10.3m lottery grant will enable the university to host The Hold, a heritage centre for the county, which will also contain teaching areas. Other research centres already focus on areas such as sustainability, health and wellbeing, heart research, and the study of children and childhood.

A partnership with Ipswich Town Football Club is typical of the university's community approach. A suite of football sports science courses cover coaching, performance analysis, sports performance physiology, sports psychology, and strength and conditioning. The four-year masters courses include placements at the club.

Many students live at home but there is a privately-operated hall of residence for 700 students close to the campus in Ipswich. The university offers no guarantees of accommodation and the allocation of places is on a first come, first served basis.

The students' union coordinates a range of competitive and social sporting activities. Students have access to the sports facilities of neighbouring Suffolk New College and there are student discounts at private and council-run gyms.

Tuition fees

»	Fees for UK/EU students	£9,250
	Foundation courses	£8,220
»	Fees for International students 2020–21	£11,790–£13,330
»	For scholarship and bursary information see www.uos.ac.uk/content/student-finance	
»	Graduate salary	£21,909

Student numbers

Undergraduates	4,077	(834)
Postgraduates	70	(394)
Applications/places	4,375/2,540	
Applications per place	1.7	
Overall offer rate	79.8%	
Unconditional offers	0%	
International students	2.6%	

Accommodation

Available places: 708
Self-catered: £90–£171 per week
www.uos.ac.uk/accommodation

Where do the students come from?

Social inclusion ranking: 14

State schools (non-grammar)	98.5%	First generation students	59.6%	Black attainment gap	-17%
Grammar schools	0.6%	Deprived areas	27.1%	Disabled	7.7%
Independent schools	1%	All ethnic minorities	9.3%	Mature (over 21)	65.3%

University of Sunderland

Students at Sunderland have the option of spending part of their degree at the university's London campus, in Canary Wharf, and the Student Mobility programme may soon be extended to include the branch campus in Hong Kong.

Sunderland's three successive rises up our table have come to an abrupt end this year, with the university dropping 16 places and out of the top 100. Big declines in student satisfaction have seen Sunderland drop 31 and 29 places respectively in our two measures on teaching quality and university experience drawn from the latest National Student Survey.

The numbers starting degrees rose spectacularly in 2018, following the opening of the Hong Kong campus, after four years of decline. They may rise again in 2019 following the opening of a new medical school, which has taken its first 50 students. Its specialisms will address the need for more GPs and psychiatric specialists, providing exposure to real-life clinical settings and making use of the university's simulation suites in its Living Lab.

The award of the school recognises Sunderland's successes in other health subjects, such as pharmacy and nursing, as well as its leading record in widening participation in higher education. The medical intake will rise to 100 in September 2020, with a target of recruiting 20% from areas of low participation in higher education.

The university ranks in the top five in our new social inclusion table, with almost 90% of students in one or more of the government's target groups for widening participation. More than 30% come from areas with little tradition of higher education, the biggest proportion in the country, and nearly 60% come from homes where parents have not been to university. About 85% of British undergraduates are from the northeast of England, although there is a surprisingly large cohort – one in five – from outside the UK.

Sunderland-born singer Emeli Sandé is the university's new chancellor, and has pledged to use her time in the role to help others realise their potential and break down barriers, real or imagined.

A dozen new degrees were launched in 2019, in addition to medicine, most of them with an integrated foundation year for those lacking the necessary qualifications for immediate entry. They include film production, occupational health, social media management and physiotherapy.

The university has a silver rating in the Teaching Excellence Framework. The panel said students' academic experiences were tailored to the individual, with personalised support available. It also praised the exposure of students to professional practice through engagement with industrial and community

Edinburgh Building
City Campus
Chester Road
Sunderland SR1 3SD
0191 515 3000
student.helpline@sunderland.ac.uk
www.sunderland.ac.uk
www.sunderlandsu.co.uk
Open days 2020:
see website

The Times and The Sunday Times Rankings
Overall Ranking: 109 (last year: 93)

Teaching quality	79.9%	=66
Student experience	77.2%	=87
Research quality	5.8%	=83
Entry standards	115	=109
Graduate prospects	67.1%	112
Good honours	64.7%	124
Expected completion rate	80.4%	102
Student/staff ratio	15.8	=66
Services and facilities	£2,657	36

partners, and the engagement with employers in course development.

There are two campuses in Sunderland, one in the city centre and the other on the banks of the River Wear, built around a 7th-century abbey described as one of Britain's first universities and incorporating the National Glass Centre. The London campus focuses on business, tourism and nursing degrees, which already accounts for 12% of the students and is scheduled for expansion.

Sunderland's Hong Kong campus, which opened in 2017, has room for 1,000 students. Undergraduates in a growing range of subjects will spend a half year in the UK.

The university invested £15m in projects in the past academic year. This included the School of Medicine, the final phase of the Sciences Complex, and teaching, gateway and social spaces in Sunderland.

All new international students receive a fee reduction of £1,500 and nearly all UK and EU full-time students receive the Get There Scholarship, which provides free public transport costs or offers discounts on university rents. Home students get at least £150 to spend on textbooks and other study essentials.

Disabled students benefit from excellent support, with trained staff in the libraries and in every academic school and special modules to help dyslexics. The North East Regional Assessment Centre on the main campus assesses the requirements of students with disabilities and specific learning difficulties.

Many students take work placements with multinational companies that have been attracted to the northeast and now have links with the university. The Centre of Excellence for Sustainable Advanced Manufacturing, for example, has been developed with Nissan.

Less than a third of the work submitted for the 2014 Research Excellence Framework reached the top two categories, but the university entered almost 40% of the eligible academics, a much higher proportion than most of its peers.

More places were added in 2018 in the £12m Forge U-Student Village, bringing the total stock to 1,328 rooms. Applicants are guaranteed a room if they make Sunderland their firm choice, as are all international students.

The city of Sunderland is fiercely proud of its identity and has the advantage of a riverside and coastal location. Leisure facilities are good: the city has the northeast's only 50-metre swimming pool and dry ski slope, as well as Europe's biggest climbing wall and a theatre. A short journey away is the culture and legendary nightlife of Newcastle.

Tuition fees

»	Fees for UK/EU students	£9,250
	Foundation courses	£8,200
»	Fees for International students 2020–21	£12,000
»	For scholarship and bursary information see www.sunderland.ac.uk/about/your-finances/	
»	Graduate salary	£18,200

Student numbers

Undergraduates	9,783	(1,537)
Postgraduates	1,696	(1,053)
Applications/places		7,765/3,520
Applications per place		2.2
Overall offer rate		88.8%
Unconditional offers		0%
International students		18.6%

Accommodation

University provided places: 1,328
Self-catered: £78–£154 per week
www.sunderland.ac.uk/about/accommodation/

Where do the students come from?

State schools (non-grammar)	97.2%	First generation students	59.2%	Black attainment gap	-26.4%
Grammar schools	0.3%	Deprived areas	30.6%	Disabled	5.1%
Independent schools	2.5%	All ethnic minorities	27.5%	Mature (over 21)	59%

Social inclusion ranking: 4

University of Surrey

Surrey has fallen nine places, dropping out of our top 30. A second successive big drop in student satisfaction is the main cause. Student satisfaction scores taken from the National Student Survey have seen the university topple at least 20 places this year – falling out of the top 100 for teaching quality and down to 70= for the broader student experience.

The survey coincided with controversy over proposed staffing cuts to address a projected budget shortfall of £15m, largely blamed on reduced tuition fee income. Although Surrey was only marginally short of its all-time record intake in 2018 after making more offers than ever before, it still had 185 fewer new students.

The university was awarded gold in the Teaching Excellence Framework. A glowing reference from the panel described "innovative and personalised provision", "high levels of teaching excellence" and "an effective approach to the development of professional skills and employability".

Fifteen new degrees were launched in 2019, many with a physics or electronic engineering core, plus international tourism management with transport, chemical and petroleum engineering, and computer and internet engineering. A first intake of 50 degree apprentices is planned for 2020, subject to validation, to include a course in hospitality, tourism and events.

Surrey's two campuses are ten minutes' walk from the centre of Guildford, and the separate Surrey Research Park is one of the largest in the UK still to be owned, funded and managed by its host university. The university has spent more than £400m on development since 2000.

Surrey has also opened a branch campus in Dalian, China, in partnership with the Dongbei University of Finance and Economics. Professor Max Lu, the vice-chancellor, is keen to develop the university's international reputation.

A new school of health sciences has opened on the Manor Park campus in a building adapted for teaching nursing, midwifery and paramedic science courses.

The 5G Innovation Centre, where Surrey's researchers work with global players in mobile telecommunications, received £58m from an international consortium. The university has taken a lead role in projects collaborating with two other university partners, and has already demonstrated Europe's first autonomous car and started the world's first 5G digital gaming initiative.

More than a quarter of Surrey's students come from outside the UK – and more than half of the university's research publications have an international partner. All students are encouraged to take a free course in a

Senate House
Guildford GU2 7XH
01483 682 222
admissions@surrey.ac.uk
www.surrey.ac.uk
www.ussu.co.uk
Open days 2020:
see website

The Times and The Sunday Times **Rankings**
Overall Ranking: 32 (last year: 23)

Teaching quality	76.9%	109
Student experience	78.2%	=70
Research quality	29.7%	44
Entry standards	156	=35
Graduate prospects	81%	38
Good honours	85%	17
Expected completion rate	92.6%	22
Student/staff ratio	16.1	=75
Services and facilities	£2,678	=29

European language alongside their degree, under the Global Graduate Award.

More than 90% of the UK students are state-educated (78% from non-selective schools). The university targets particular schools, rather than areas, where the progression rate to higher education is low. A new one-stop shop for all student support – MySurrey Hive – opened in the centre of the main Stag Hill campus in 2019.

Undergraduates in most subjects undertake year-long work placements or several shorter periods, often abroad. As a result, most degrees are four years long at Surrey.

Engineering and science subjects dominate the numbers but the university has other strengths, notably in business and the top-ten School of Hospitality and Tourism Management. Lecturers set coursework on SurreyLearn, the virtual learning environment, where students can also take part in discussions and blogs.

Almost 80% of the work submitted by Surrey academics to the 2014 Research Excellence Framework was assessed as world-leading or internationally excellent. The best results were in nursing and other health subjects. Surrey's research is organised around "grand challenges" such as global wellbeing, sustainable cities and communities, and connecting societies and cultures.

There are more than 6,000 residential places, 650 of which opened in 2019 on the Manor Park campus. New entrants are guaranteed accommodation if they apply by July 25 and everyone is allocated a student life mentor to provide support and assistance.

The £36m Surrey Sports Park has extensive indoor and outdoor facilities which have played host to elite athletes and sports teams, including Harlequins rugby club and Surrey Storm Netball.

The main campus is the centre of social life, although Guildford has plenty of retail, cultural and recreational diversions. The proximity of London (35 minutes by train) is an attraction to many students, although it also helps to account for the high cost of renting in the private sector.

Tuition fees

» Fees for UK/EU students	£9,250
» Fees for International students 2020–21	£16,800–£21,700
Veterinary Medicine	£33,400
» For scholarship and bursary information see www.surrey.ac.uk/fees-and-funding	
» Graduate salary	£24,000

Student numbers

Undergraduates	12,351	(873)
Postgraduates	2,572	(1,150)
Applications/places	32,275/4,115	
Applications per place	7.8	
Overall offer rate	74.7%	
Unconditional offers	0%	
International students	29.1%	

Accommodation

University provided places: 6,190
Self-catered: £72–£225 per week
First years guaranteed accommodation
www.surrey.ac.uk/accommodation

Where do the students come from?

State schools (non-grammar)	78.3%	First generation students	42.8%	Black attainment gap	-16.2%
Grammar schools	11.5%	Deprived areas	7.3%	Disabled	4.6%
Independent schools	10.2%	All ethnic minorities	37.5%	Mature (over 21)	8.6%

Social inclusion ranking: 82

University of Sussex

Sussex has adopted a seven-year strategy to "reimagine the pioneering spirit of the original purpose of our university" for new times and a new generation. Students have been promised "meaningful participation" in decisions on the physical shape of the university, the curriculum and even academic appointments.

Among the promised developments will be increased opportunities for placements and internships, to be recognised in a new accreditation scheme along with voluntary work. There will also be a nationally recognised programme to promote positive physical and mental health and wellbeing.

Sussex has moved up three places to re-enter our top 40 but is still a far cry from its top-20 finish only three years ago. The main cause has been a big fall in student satisfaction, although the university has seen scores improve in 2019. For student satisfaction with teaching quality, Sussex remains in the bottom 20 and is only just in the top 100 for the wider student experience.

The numbers starting degrees were up by 8% in 2018, however. The intake of new undergraduates has increased by almost 1,500 in four years.

A new attraction for 2019 was the UK's first undergraduate degree in finance and technology to offer the option of a year in industry. Another popular feature is the growing range of four-year undergraduate master's degrees, which carry an entitlement to student loans beyond the normal three years.

Sussex has also introduced its first online degree, an MSc in international marketing. Master's courses in energy policy and sustainable development are to follow.

The university gained silver in the Teaching Excellence Framework, winning praise for its "outstanding" employment strategy, designed to help students develop transferable employment skills.

Since 2007, the university has invested £150m regenerating the campus in the Brighton suburb of Falmer and expects the total to reach £500m eventually. The Attenborough Centre has become an interdisciplinary arts hub for the university and the wider community, with a 350-seat auditorium, studios and exhibition space and a cafe bar.

A successful joint medical school is shared with neighbouring Brighton University, and split between the Royal Sussex County Hospital and the two universities' Falmer campuses.

An interdisciplinary approach has been the university's hallmark since the 1960s and Sussex has pledged to renew efforts to provide opportunities for a more diverse student body. Extensive bursary and scholarship schemes have been brought in to broaden its intake, focusing on candidates with no family experience of higher education.

Sussex House
Falmer
Brighton BN1 9RH
01273 876 787
ug.enquiries@sussex.ac.uk
www.sussex.ac.uk
www.sussexstudent.com
Open days 2020:
see website

The Times and The Sunday Times **Rankings**
Overall Ranking: =38 (last year: 41)

Teaching quality	76.6%	111
Student experience	76.4%	99
Research quality	31.8%	=37
Entry standards	148	=40
Graduate prospects	80.4%	47
Good honours	75.6%	62
Expected completion rate	90.7%	=35
Student/staff ratio	15.8	=66
Services and facilities	£2,678	=29

A prize-winning scheme supports them with rent reductions and scholarships. Sussex performs respectably in our new social inclusion ranking, placing 84th and well ahead of many of its immediate academic rivals.

Three-quarters of the work submitted for the 2014 Research Excellence Framework was assessed as world-leading or internationally excellent and Sussex was among the leaders in history, English, psychology and geography. The university has launched a new centre for Jewish studies, with backing from the German government, to address the rise in anti-semitism.

The university has topped the QS world ranking for development studies for three years in a row and has a sustainability research programme headed by the former chief scientist at the UN Environment Programme, Professor Joseph Alcamo. Sussex has joined the international affairs think tank Chatham House in setting up the UK Trade Policy Observatory, which draws on the largest concentration of scholars in economics, law and international relations to consider post-Brexit options.

Undergraduates are encouraged to study outside their core area unless they are constrained by professional accreditation requirements. They can take a language or an elective in another subject, leading to a major/minor degree and opening up opportunities to study abroad. Two 12-week teaching periods are punctuated by mid-year assessment – a pattern that the university believes improves learning.

A work-study programme helps students to earn as they learn, providing funded work placements and three years' aftercare for graduates looking for a suitable career. The Sussex Plus programme makes sure extracurricular skills can be credited on a CV, while Startup Sussex supports students' creative business ideas and social projects.

A new student village has added 1,000 residential places over the past two years, bringing the current total to 5,370 rooms and enabling Sussex to continue to guarantee accommodation to new entrants. The village has its own social hub and laundry room, and will provide another 2,000 places by early 2021.

The campus boasts a well-equipped sports centre and a separate sports complex, with indoor and outdoor facilities.

Transport links are excellent and there is no shortage of social events on campus or in Brighton – always a magnet for students.

Tuition fees

- » Fees for UK/EU students — £9,250
- » Fees for International students 2020–21 — £18,500–£22,500
  Medicine 2019–20 — £32,886 (clinical years)
- » For scholarship and bursary information see www.sussex.ac.uk/study/fees-funding
- » Graduate salary — £20,400

Student numbers

Undergraduates	12,998	(0)
Postgraduates	3,890	(910)
Applications/places	24,750/5,025	
Applications per place	4.9	
Overall offer rate	92.7%	
Unconditional offers	3.1%	
International students	31.3%	

Accommodation

University provided places: 5,370
Self-catered: £91–£162 per week
First years guaranteed accommodation
www.sussex.ac.uk/study/accommodation

Where do the students come from?

State schools (non-grammar)	78.5%	First generation students	42%		
Grammar schools	10.4%	Deprived areas	8.2%		
Independent schools	11.1%	All ethnic minorities	22.1%		

Social inclusion ranking: =83

Black attainment gap	-24.8%
Disabled	7.7%
Mature (over 21)	11%

Swansea University

Swansea is down one place in our rankings, dropping out of the top 30. But, perhaps more importantly, it maintains its bragging rights as the top-ranked university in Wales, staying ahead of Cardiff. The points margin between the two institutions is statistically insignificant – both are fine universities – but top is top.

The university has endured a fraught year in the run-up to its centenary in 2020, with the suspension of the former vice-chancellor Professor Richard Davies in November 2018 over a property deal. He retired as planned at the end of the 2018–19 academic year and has been succeeded by Professor Paul Boyle, who began his career at Swansea and has had success leading the University of Leicester.

He has assumed responsibility for a £522m capital plan which has already seen the opening of a second campus. The university is now redeveloping the original Singleton Park campus. More than £70m has been invested in new facilities there, and the new programme includes improvements to the library, upgraded laboratories and flexible learning spaces.

The new Bay campus is a 65-acre site with direct access to the beach, five miles along the coast from Singleton Park. It is the base for the College of Engineering and School of Management and a £31m "computational foundry" as well as housing about 1,500 students in new halls of residence.

The new campus was expected to herald a larger student population. The numbers starting degrees rose for five years in a row, but were down nearly 12% in 2018, when almost a quarter of the intake came through clearing. There has been a further decline in the 2019 admissions round as the university has rationalised courses and switched international foundation programmes to a private provider based on the Bay campus.

Under Prof Davies' 15-year tenure, the university was transformed – physically and aspirationally – to become our Welsh University of the Year in the previous edition of this guide and runner-up for the UK title. For all its turmoil in governance, student satisfaction remains a strong point: Swansea has moved into the UK top 20 for student satisfaction with the wider experience this year, and gained nearly ten places to break back into the top 50 for student satisfaction with teaching quality.

Eleven new degrees took their first students in 2019, two in early childhood studies and another two combining Welsh language with law and policy, one with a year in industry. Applied linguistics and English, philosophy, and Egyptology and ancient history with a year abroad are among the other courses coming onstream.

Swansea also launched its first degree apprenticeship in 2018, in applied software engineering, and now has 190 apprentices,

---

Singleton Park
Swansea SA2 8PP
01792 205 678
admissions@swansea.ac.uk
www.swansea.ac.uk
www.swansea-union.co.uk
Open days 2020:
February 15

The Times and The Sunday Times Rankings
Overall Ranking: 31 (last year: 30)

Teaching quality	81.2%	=45
Student experience	81.5%	=18
Research quality	33.7%	35
Entry standards	135	=55
Graduate prospects	85.6%	12
Good honours	78%	=49
Expected completion rate	90.8%	34
Student/staff ratio	15.4	=56
Services and facilities	£2,372	61

introducing advanced manufacturing engineering and aeronautical courses.

The university's greatest strength in our table is graduate prospects, where it is now in the top dozen in the UK. The Swansea Employability Academy provides paid internships and co-ordinates programmes for career development.

Swansea holds gold in the Teaching Excellence Framework, thanks to its clear employability strategy and strong staff-student partnerships. Undergraduates are encouraged to take modules outside their specialist area in their first year. Many degrees include opportunities to work abroad or study at one of more than 100 partner institutions worldwide.

Outreach activities are mainly in southwest Wales, but from 2020, the new Swansea Outreach Unit will widen targets to include a range of underrepresented groups from primary school age to adults across Wales. There is good provision for disabled students, whose needs are addressed through a dedicated assessment and training centre, and the projected dropout rate is close to half the expected level at 5.2%.

Four-fifths of the work submitted for the 2014 Research Excellence Framework was assessed as world-leading or internationally excellent, with health subjects, English and general engineering getting Swansea's best results. A new £35m research institute at the Bay campus will focus on innovative materials, processing and numerical technologies, supporting the engineering industry in Wales and worldwide with collaborative, fundamental research.

The law school has been re-named after Hillary Rodham Clinton, who received an honorary degree in 2017. She is supporting a postgraduate scholarship programme intended to produce a generation of leaders committed to addressing challenges, including the rights and protection of children online, the climate crisis and cybersecurity.

The £20m Sports Village has an athletics track, grass and all-weather pitches, squash and tennis courts, plus an indoor athletics training centre and 80-station gym. The adjacent Wales National Pool has 50-metre and 25-metre pools. The 360° Beach and Water Sports Centre is the only university-operated centre of its kind, while at Fairwood, five miles away, there are grass and 3G pitches, built in partnership with Swansea City Football Club.

The university has just over 5,000 residential places – enough to guarantee accommodation for new entrants who apply by the end of June. The city has good leisure facilities and is close to the beautiful Gower Peninsula.

Tuition fees

- » Fees for UK/EU students — £9,000
- » Fees for International students 2020–21 £14,950–£22,000
  Medicine — £36,750 (clinical years)
- » For scholarship and bursary information see
  www.swansea.ac.uk/undergraduate/scholarships
- » Graduate salary — £22,000

Student numbers

Undergraduates	15,256	(1,592)
Postgraduates	2,576	(991)
Applications/places	17,835/4,530	
Applications per place	3.9	
Overall offer rate	92.5%	
Unconditional offers	0%	
International students	17.8%	

Accommodation

University provided places: 5,097
Catered costs: £139–£144 per week
Self-catered: £93–£202 per week
First years guaranteed accommodation
www.swansea.ac.uk/accommodation

Where do the students come from?

State schools (non-grammar)	85.4%	First generation students	37.6%		
Grammar schools	5.5%	Deprived areas	9.9%		
Independent schools	9%	All ethnic minorities	16.3%		

Social inclusion ranking: 89

Black attainment gap	-17.1%
Disabled	4.6%
Mature (over 21)	15.2%

University of Teesside

Teesside has ambitions to rise into the top half of our league table. Although it has fallen back marginally overall this year, further improvements in student satisfaction suggests those hopes are not without foundation. In the assessment and feedback section of the National Student Survey, Teesside ranked eighth in the UK this year, its best ever performance in the lowest scoring part of the annual survey of student opinion.

The university recruits about 60% of its students from the immediate area, so its relative lack of student halls is less of a problem than it might otherwise be. The £21m Cornell accommodation block of 300 en-suite rooms, being built at the heart of the main campus, will help the university to widen its recruitment net geographically as its league table ranking improves. A further 400 rooms are planned on recently acquired land adjoining the main site.

The pace of development under vice-chancellor Professor Paul Croney shows no sign of abating, fuelled by some of the healthiest accounts in British higher education. Teesside currently has no debts and recently reported a post-tax operating surplus of more than £8.5m. A new students' union building is in the pipeline to follow the opening of the £12.5m Student Life building in September 2019, a one-stop shop for support on mental health, finance and accommodation, among other services.

The numbers starting degrees in 2018 fell by 8% despite a raft of new degrees for applicants to choose from. However, the decline followed a record enrolment and was still high compared with most previous years.

Another 14 new offerings are being launched in 2019 and 2020. They include construction management, journalism for music and events, sport and exercise science, and table-top game design. Nearly all come with the option of a foundation year for those who lack the necessary qualifications for immediate entry.

Degree apprenticeships are offered in each of the five schools, and the numbers taking them have doubled in the past year. Ofsted rated Teesside's programmes as outstanding, in one of its first full inspections of degree apprenticeships. More are being developed in areas such as health, social work and supply chain management.

A strong culture of partnership with students was cited by assessors for the Teaching Excellence Framework (TEF), who awarded Teesside a silver rating. The TEF panel was also impressed by innovative and well-resourced support for the development of employability.

Teesside considers itself an "anchor institution" for its region with a commitment

---

Middlesbrough
TS1 3BX
01642 218 121
enquiries@tees.ac.uk
www.tees.ac.uk
www.tees-su.org.uk
Open days 2020:
February 29

The Times and The Sunday Times **Rankings**		
Overall Ranking: 87 (last year: =85)		
Teaching quality	83.1%	=20
Student experience	79.5%	=40
Research quality	3.6%	110
Entry standards	120	=94
Graduate prospects	81.3%	35
Good honours	68%	=110
Expected completion rate	79.8%	=105
Student/staff ratio	18	=104
Services and facilities	£2,464	49

to social impact and civic engagement. It is in the top 40 for graduate prospects – no mean feat when many alumni continue to live in the area, where there is relatively high unemployment, after graduating.

Support for graduates continues for a minimum of two years after they leave university through paid internship and training opportunities. Second-year students undertake summer work placements.

A longstanding commitment to widening access to higher education is evident in Teesside's top-ten finish in our social inclusion table. Three undergraduates in ten come from areas of low participation in higher education – twice the national average for its courses and entry qualifications.

Almost 7,000 of the 18,400 students are part-time – a much larger proportion than at most universities given the national decline of part-time higher education – and 5,400 are taking courses below degree level. The Teesside Advance Scheme provides all first-year, full-time undergraduates with an iPad, a compatible keyboard and selected apps, as well as £100 credit each year to buy learning resources and textbooks.

Only 14% of Teesside's eligible academics were entered for the 2014 Research Excellence Framework, but almost 60% of their work was considered world-leading or internationally excellent – twice as much as in the previous round. Social work and social policy, history and health subjects produced the university's proudest results.

Teesside is pouring £300m into campus development over the next ten years, mainly at its base in Middlesbrough town centre. The first phase of an expanded business school opened in 2018, and the £22m National Horizons Centre, for biomedical teaching and research, took its first students in 2019 at the university's second campus in Darlington.

For now, there are 1,000 residential places on campus and rents in the private sector are among the cheapest in the UK.

Sports tournaments are held at the Olympia sports complex, where there is room for 500 spectators. There is a £2.75m health and fitness centre, and the university also has a water sports centre on the River Tees, featuring a world-class white-water rafting course. An all-weather pitch and other facilities are within a few minutes' walk of campus.

Tuition fees

»	Fees for UK/EU students	£9,250
	Foundation courses	£6,150
»	Fees for International students 2020–21	£13,000
	Foundation courses	£9,750
»	For scholarship and bursary information see www.tees.ac.uk/sections/fulltime/fees.cfm	
»	Graduate salary	£21,909

Student numbers

Undergraduates	10,348 (5,482)
Postgraduates	1,175 (1,372)
Applications/places	11,765/3,695
Applications per place	3.2
Overall offer rate	79.6%
Unconditional offers	0%
International students	5.7%

Accommodation

University provided places: 1,001
Self-catered: £58–£115 per week
www.tees.ac.uk/sections/accommodation

Where do the students come from?

State schools (non-grammar)	98.1%	First generation students	56.9%	Black attainment gap	-13.9%
Grammar schools	0.5%	Deprived areas	29.2%	Disabled	10.3%
Independent schools	1.4%	All ethnic minorities	13.4%	Mature (over 21)	42.4%

Social inclusion ranking: 10

University of Wales, Trinity St David

A 13-place fall has taken the University of Wales, Trinity Saint David (UWTSD) out of our top 100 overall – reversing its progress last year, when it was one of the biggest risers in our table. Although it remains in the top ten for student satisfaction with teaching quality, growing dissatisfaction with other aspects of the broader experience has combined with a small decline in spending on student facilities to drag the university down our list.

A new range of courses and the opening of a new campus in Swansea have boosted the demand for places, however. Applications rose by 7% in 2019, well above the average for Wales and the rest of the UK.

The £350m SA1 campus, on Swansea's waterfront, opened in September 2018. The first phase has allowed businesses to share the space, encouraging close working relationships between students and industry – leading to job opportunities upon graduation. There is a new library and facilities for architecture, education, computing and engineering. A second phase of the development is due for completion in 2021.

UWTSD was one of six Welsh universities to enter the Teaching Excellence Framework (TEF) in 2017 and the only one to emerge with a bronze rating. Having resubmitted without success in 2018, it has finally persuaded the TEF panel to raise the grade to silver. Levels of contact time were described as "optimal", leading to outstanding personalised provision, and UWTSD had a strong sense of regional and civic mission. Graduates' progress to highly-skilled employment was still below the university's benchmark, but the panel was satisfied that this was being addressed.

Five new degrees were launched in 2019, in advocacy, law and legal practice, music performance and production, professional policing, and sociology. The university is also rapidly expanding its apprenticeship programme – at higher and degree level – and expects to have more than 600 apprentices in eight subject areas by the end of 2020, three times the current total.

Already divided between Swansea, Carmarthen and Lampeter, in mid-Wales, the university has now opened a learning centre in Birmingham as well. Based in the city's Sparkhill neighbourhood, it has been established to provide opportunities for people of all backgrounds to study a higher education programme in their own community, with flexible courses that enable students to balance their studies with family and work commitments.

The university was established from two mergers in three years: the first brought together the former Trinity University College, Camarthen, and the University of

---

Carmarthen Campus, College Road
Carmarthen SA31 3EP

0300 500 5054
admissions@uwtsd.ac.uk
www.uwtsd.ac.uk
www.tsdsu.co.uk
Open days 2020:
May 9 (Cardiff);
June 20 (Carmarthen
& Lampeter);
June 27 (Swansea);

The Times and The Sunday Times **Rankings**
Overall Ranking: =102 (last year: 89)

Teaching quality	84.6%	8
Student experience	78.6%	=61
Research quality	2.6%	117
Entry standards	109	=127
Graduate prospects	66%	114
Good honours	72.9%	83
Expected completion rate	77.2%	121
Student/staff ratio	15.2	=53
Services and facilities	£1,779	112

Wales Lampeter, 23 miles away. The former Swansea Metropolitan University was added in 2013.

There are further satellite campuses in London, where international students take business, management and IT degrees, and Cardiff, where the Wales International Academy of Voice is based. In addition, a group structure connects UWTSD with two large further education colleges, Coleg Ceredigion and Coleg Sir Gar.

Yet UWTSD's student population is only a little over 10,000, with more than a third of the 2018 entrants arriving through clearing. The Lampeter campus makes a virtue of its small size by emphasising its friendly atmosphere and intimate teaching style. Based on an ancient castle and modelled on an Oxbridge college, it offers subjects including anthropology, archaeology, Chinese, classics and philosophy.

The Carmarthen campus, established in 1848 to train teachers, offers programmes in the creative and performing arts, as well as a growing portfolio within the school of sport, health and outdoor education. Canolfan S4C Yr Elgin, headquarters of the Welsh broadcaster S4C, opened in 2018 on the campus and will house creative and digital companies where media students can gain valuable experience. A mile from the campus, the university has a centre for outdoor education on the All Wales coastal walking path.

The original Swansea campus began as a college of art, but its automotive engineering courses – especially those focused on motor sport – are now its most well-known. UWTSD hosts half of Yr Athrofa, the Institute of Education, in Carmarthen, sharing responsibility with partner schools for the construction and delivery of teacher training programmes.

UWTSD ranks just outside the top 20 in our table measuring social inclusion. Almost all its undergraduates are educated at comprehensive schools or colleges and a high proportion are aged 21 or older on admission. Only one Welsh university (Wrexham Glyndŵr) has a more socially diverse student population.

First-year undergraduates are guaranteed accommodation. Sports are available at the Carmarthen, Lampeter, and Swansea campuses, offering plenty of indoor and outdoor facilities. A 40ft climbing wall at Carmarthen is a good place to start before venturing up the crags of Pembrokeshire.

Tuition fees

» Fees for UK/EU students	£9,000
Foundation courses	£4,500
» Fees for International students 2020–21	£11,500
Foundation courses	£10,250
» For scholarship and bursary information see www.uwtsd.ac.uk/finance/tuition-fees/	
» Graduate salary	£18,000

Student numbers

Undergraduates	6,989	(1,506)
Postgraduates	805	(980)
Applications/places		3,710/1,495
Applications per place		2.5
Overall offer rate		86.9%
Unconditional offers		0%
International students		5.3%

Accommodation

University provided places: 807
Catered costs: £109 per week
Self-catered: £70–£140 per week
First years guaranteed accommodation
www.uwtsd.ac.uk/accommodation

Where do the students come from?

				Social inclusion ranking: 24	
State schools (non-grammar)	97.7%	First generation students	34.7%	Black attainment gap	-34.4%
Grammar schools	0.8%	Deprived areas	14.1%	Disabled	20.3%
Independent schools	1.5%	All ethnic minorities	7.2%	Mature (over 21)	44.5%

Ulster University

A £250m campus development – claimed to be among the largest in Europe – is taking shape in Belfast, with the next phase due to open this year. Students who started degrees in 2019 on the Jordanstown campus – currently Ulster's largest base, seven miles north of the city – were warned they would be moving mid-course.

That prospect seems not to have deterred prospective students unduly. Applications fell in 2019, but by little more than the UK average. The numbers starting courses held up well in 2018, although the total was still almost 1,000 down on 2014 – largely the result of course closures to cope with budget cuts.

The new campus in Belfast's Cathedral Quarter, where art and design, architecture, hospitality, event management, photography and digital animation courses are already based, will have room for students in business and management, the built environment, computing and engineering, health and sport sciences, and social sciences, who will relocate from Jordanstown.

Ulster is also expanding on the Magee campus in Londonderry. An £11m central teaching block attached to Magee's library opened in 2018, and a graduate medical school will take its first students in 2020. At Coleraine, on the north coast, a £5m sports centre has opened and a new psychology building is planned.

The university also has branch campuses in London and Birmingham, where a postgraduate school of dentistry is scheduled to open in 2020. The two campuses focus mainly on business, computing and engineering and are operated in partnership with QA Higher Education, a private organisation that also delivers apprenticeships and training programmes.

Ulster has moved up two places to 58th= in our latest league table, despite declines in student satisfaction. It is still in the top 40 in both of our measures derived from the National Student Survey and has improved its scores on entry standards and spending on student facilities.

Five new degrees were introduced for 2019–20. An honours course in personalised medicine reflects one of the university's key research interests, to improve diagnostics and target treatments in an ageing population. The first financial technology, games design, screen production and music, sound and technology courses are also up and running. Ulster is also increasing the number of higher level apprenticeships that it offers from six to nine, catering for about 450 apprentices by September 2020.

Almost all the undergraduates are from state schools, but the university does not feature in our social inclusion ranking because the education system in Northern Ireland is radically different to the rest of the UK, with

Cromore Road
Coleraine BT52 1SA
028 9036 6565
study@ulster.ac.uk
www.ulster.ac.uk
http://uusu.org
Open days 2020:
see website

COLERAINE
Edinburgh
Belfast
London
Cardiff

The Times and The Sunday Times Rankings
Overall Ranking: =58 (last year: 60)

Teaching quality	81.8%	=37
Student experience	80.3%	=29
Research quality	31.8%	=37
Entry standards	128	=73
Graduate prospects	71.9%	93
Good honours	76%	58
Expected completion rate	83.3%	82
Student/staff ratio	17.4	=95
Services and facilities	£2,143	80

selective grammar schools making up a significant proportion of state secondary schools. Our ranking measures recruitment from non-selective state schools, a figure that is unduly depressed at Ulster and Queen's, Belfast.

Ulster has an extensive outreach programme and a variety of bursaries and fee waivers, although it remains well below its benchmark for recruitment from neighbourhoods with low participation in higher education.

Although neither of the universities in Northern Ireland entered the Teaching Excellence Framework, Ulster features in *Times Higher Education* magazine's top 200 universities in the world less than 50 years old.

Ulster cultivates links with thousands of businesses. Each year more than 2,000 students take work placements, some for a year. Under the Ulster Edge Award, sponsored by PwC, 1,000 students gain accreditation for extracurricular activities to boost their career prospects.

The Centre for Molecular Biosciences, at Coleraine, produced the university's most highly rated work in the 2014 Research Excellence Framework. More than 70% of Ulster's submission was considered world-leading or internationally excellent, notably in law, nursing and health science. The university has since been awarded almost £20m in research funding from an EU cross-border scheme for projects in health and life sciences and renewable energy.

Northern Ireland's emergence as a leading film and television centre has inspired many students, who gain insight into the industry at a £6.5m media centre opened three years ago at Coleraine. It has a BBC television studio at its heart, with a multimedia newsroom and editing suites. At Magee, the focus is on the creative and performing arts, nursing and social work, computing, business and management, and social sciences. Its expansion will be mainly in computer science, engineering and creative technologies.

In the long term, only the High Performance Sports Centre, which houses the Sports Institute, will remain in Jordanstown. Its outdoor and indoor sprint tracks, sports science and sports medicine facilities will remain available to students. All three campuses have sports facilities and the university has a longstanding and award-winning sports outreach programme encouraging people to get active in the wider community.

Accommodation is guaranteed for all first-year students and private sector rents are low by UK standards.

Tuition fees

» Fees for Northern Irish/EU students		£4,275
RUK fees		£9,250
» Fees for International students 2020–21		£14,060
» For scholarship and bursary information see www.ulster.ac.uk/finance/student		
» Graduate salary		£20,000

Student numbers

Undergraduates	15,395 (2,972)
Postgraduates	1,921 (3,427)
Applications/places	28.940/5,285
Applications per place	5.5
Overall offer rate	83.1%
Unconditional offers	0%
International students	8.9%

Accommodation

University provided places: 2,014
Self-catered: £75–£150 per week
First years guaranteed accommodation
www.ulster.ac.uk/accommodation

Where do the students come from?

State schools (non-grammar)	62.9%	Working-class homes	n/a	**Social inclusion ranking: n/a**	
				Black attainment gap	n/a
Grammar schools	37.1%	Deprived areas	n/a	Disabled	n/a
Independent schools	0%	All ethnic minorities	n/a	Mature (over 21)	n/a

University College London

Work has started on a new campus for UCL on the Queen Elizabeth Olympic Park in Stratford, six miles east of the main campus in Bloomsbury. The development, which will be part of the East Bank cultural and educational quarter, will involve all eight faculties in interdisciplinary teaching and research, with the first phase opening in 2022.

Two new buildings will cater for 4,000 students and house laboratories and research space, student accommodation and designated areas for working with schools, charities and local groups. The intended areas of study include robotics, smart cities, culture and conservation.

The college's Transforming UCL programme involves an investment of £1.2bn over ten years. It has seen a new student centre open in 2019 with 1,000 extra study seats, group collaboration areas and space for other forms of social learning. Another £1.4m was invested in 2018 in better-quality library spaces, at the behest of students, and the law faculty was redeveloped with improved teaching and research facilities.

The UCL Institute of Education (rated the best in the world for its subject by QS) was refurbished in 2019 as well, with 930 new teaching seats and social study space for 100 students. A hall of residence was upgraded and extended in time for the start of the 2019–20 academic year. Overall, the college has risen two places to eighth in the global QS table, one of just two top-ten institutions to buck a UK-wide trend that saw others slide down the table.

After languishing near the bottom on our measures of student satisfaction, UCL has finally seen scores in the National Student Survey improve this year, although it is still in the bottom ten for teaching quality and only just outside the bottom 20 for satisfaction with the wider student experience. The results were not good enough to prevent a slip of one place in our overall league table.

In addition to the capital investment programme, the UCL ChangeMakers scheme has helped address engagement levels in departments with low scores for student satisfaction by establishing new types of assessment and a more agile response to undergraduate feedback. Every student gets the opportunity to engage in research as part of the connected curriculum framework.

Applications are running at record levels, with another increase in the 2019 admissions round. More than 2,000-plus places have been added for new entrants since the last year before £9,000 fees were introduced.

Five new degrees were launched in 2019, including medical innovation and enterprise, sport and exercise medical sciences, and international social and political studies. Professional policing is due to be added in 2020.

Low satisfaction scores contributed to UCL being placed in the silver category in the

Gower Street
London WC1E 6BT
020 3370 1214
(020 3108 8520 International)
study@ucl.ac.uk;
international@ucl.ac.uk
www.ucl.ac.uk
http://studentsunionucl.org
Open days 2020:
June 19, 20; September 12

The Times and The Sunday Times Rankings
Overall Ranking: 9 (last year: 8)

Teaching quality	74.7%	121
Student experience	75.4%	=108
Research quality	51.0%	5
Entry standards	187	10
Graduate prospects	83.8%	=20
Good honours	89.7%	7
Expected completion rate	94.5%	13
Student/staff ratio	10.5	2
Services and facilities	£2,671	31

government's Teaching Excellence Framework. The panel found a "wide array of exceptional learning resources, both physical and digital" and complimented UCL on a highly successful approach to supporting students into employment or further study.

There is no doubting UCL's research strength, with 29 Nobel prize-winners among its staff, researchers and graduates. Such was the quality and quantity of its submission to the 2014 Research Excellence Framework that only Oxford subsequently received a higher research grant. More than 90% of the eligible academics were entered for assessment and at least 80% of their work was rated as world-leading or internationally excellent.

UCL had the most world-leading research in medicine and the biological sciences, the largest volume of research in science, technology, engineering and maths, and the biggest share of top grades in the social sciences.

The medical school, with several associated teaching hospitals, is among the largest in Europe. UCL was a founding partner in the Francis Crick Institute that is undertaking leading-edge research in health and disease. Other developments have included a management school in Canary Wharf.

Already comfortably the biggest of the University of London's colleges, there were more than 50,000 applications to UCL in 2018 with just under 6,000 gaining places. Summer schools, outreach activities and campus-based programmes try to make the intake more diverse, but the share of places going to independent school students remains one of the highest in Britain, at 30%.

A contextual offer scheme was launched in 2019. Applicants may be asked for two A-level grades less than the standard UCL offer if they come from areas of low progression to higher education, less advantaged backgrounds or low-performing schools.

Students are required to have a foreign language at grade C for GCSE or the equivalent, although they are allowed to reach this standard during their degree if they have not taken a language at school.

Close to the West End and with its own theatre and recreational facilities, UCL offers plenty of leisure options. Almost 7,000 residential places are owned or endorsed by the college, enough to guarantee accommodation for new entrants who apply by the end of June. Indoor sports and fitness facilities are close at hand, but the main outdoor pitches are a (free) coach ride away in Hertfordshire.

Tuition fees

- » Fees for UK/EU students   £9,250
- » Fees for International students 2020–21   £19,720–£29,220
  Medicine   £34,660 (2019–20)
- » For scholarship and bursary information see www.ucl.ac.uk/prospective-students/undergraduate/fees-funding
- » Graduate salary   £26,000

Student numbers

Undergraduates	18,286	(1,418)
Postgraduates	14,423	(5,887)
Applications/places		50,090/5,885
Applications per place		8.5
Overall offer rate		60.1%
Unconditional offers		0%
International students		44.9%

Accommodation

University provided places: 6,890
Catered costs: £152–£243 per week
Self-catered: £99–£306 per week
First years guaranteed accommodation
www.ucl.ac.uk/prospective-students/accommodation

Where do the students come from?

State schools (non-grammar)	54%	First generation students	26.9%		
Grammar schools	15.8%	Deprived areas	4%		
Independent schools	30.2%	All ethnic minorities	47.5%		

Social inclusion ranking: 108

Black attainment gap	-13.7%
Disabled	3.4%
Mature (over 21)	5%

University of Warwick

The new £150m National Automotive Innovation Centre (NAIC) exemplifies the collaboration with business for which Warwick has become known over the past 50 years. The centre is a partnership between the Warwick Manufacturing Group (part of the university), the government and local car manufacturers Jaguar Land Rover and Tata Motors. More than 1,000 designers, engineers and researchers will work closely on key projects such as the reduction of carbon emissions and driverless technology.

The NAIC is part of a £250m investment programme under way on the university's campus, three miles south of Coventry. A new mathematical sciences building is under construction and the Arts Centre is being extended and refurbished in time to play a vital role in Coventry's year as City of Culture in 2021. The university is funding community projects and a year of events is planned to boost the reputation of a city said to have "constantly reinvented itself to survive".

A £49m sports hub opened in April 2019, followed by a new Materials Engineering Centre in June. Engineering is the main focus of Warwick's seven degree apprenticeship programmes. The university is expanding into training for research scientists and economics professionals in 2020, tripling the numbers to 750 apprentices.

Warwick is one of the Russell Group of research-led universities that has taken most advantage of the lifting of recruitment restrictions. New enrolments have risen by almost 12% since 2015 and the trend seems likely to continue. Applications were up another 8% when the official deadline passed for courses beginning last September.

The university has never been out of our top ten and remains tenth this year. It is also among the top four recruiting grounds for *The Times* top 100 employers and is 62nd in the QS World University Rankings, driven by research strength and reputation.

However, Warwick was restricted to silver in the 2017 Teaching Excellence Framework (TEF), and failed to persuade the panel to upgrade it the following year. It has not tried again. The university argued that consistent high achievement by its students and staff, excellent completion and employment rates and exceptional employer feedback met the criteria for a gold award. It is in our top ten for completion and the top 25 for good honours and graduate prospects.

The TEF panel was impressed by the culture of research-stimulated learning that challenged students, but said Warwick had missed its benchmarks for student satisfaction and continuation rates among some groups of students. Its scores in the National Student Survey have improved this year, although in common with many Russell Group

Admissions Office
University House
Coventry CV4 8UW
024 7652 3723
ugadmissions@warwick.ac.uk
www.warwick.ac.uk
www.warwicksu.com
Open days 2020:
see website

The Times and The Sunday Times **Rankings**
Overall Ranking: 10 (last year: 10)

Teaching quality	79.6%	72
Student experience	79.2%	47
Research quality	44.6%	8
Entry standards	180	13
Graduate prospects	83.2%	24
Good honours	84.3%	21
Expected completion rate	95.1%	=10
Student/staff ratio	13	14
Services and facilities	£2,537	45

institutions, it is still outside the top 70 for student satisfaction with teaching quality.

Almost 90% of the work submitted for the 2014 Research Excellence Framework was rated as world-leading or internationally excellent, confirming Warwick's place among the top eight universities for research. English and computer science produced the best results, and Warwick ranked in the top ten in 14 different areas.

Under the Global Research Priorities programme, Warwick has begun to focus on the themes of energy, connecting cultures, food security, global governance, individual behaviour and innovative manufacturing. The Cancer Research Unit, established in 2016, brings together experts in maths, physics and engineering to research new treatments using digital technologies.

Warwick became a founder member of the Eutopia alliance in 2019, which unites universities in France, Spain, Belgium, Slovenia and Sweden to address global and local challenges, and has received a €5m grant from the Erasmus+ organisation to develop a university of the future.

Warwick also has a library and teaching rooms in Venice for third-year history students who spend the autumn term there. The university's large business school has a London base in the Shard, which delivers part-time programmes. Undergraduates taking global sustainable development courses can spend part of their second year at Monash University – either in Melbourne, in Australia, or in Kuala Lumpur, in Malaysia.

At 24%, Warwick's proportion of independent school students is smaller than that at most Russell Group universities – although a large contingent from grammar schools means that only 58% come from non-selective schools.

The university has introduced a "student lifecycle" approach to widening participation, helping non-traditional students from primary school age to the application stage through to employment or postgraduate study. Successful participants receive offers below the norm to offset their background. The scheme includes bursaries of up to £3,000 a year for those educated in a state school and from families with income of £35,000 or less.

The 750-acre campus has almost 7,000 residential places. There is a study facility for students living in nearby Leamington Spa.

The new multipurpose sports and wellness hub is said to have the "wow" factor, with a 240-station gym and 12-lane, 25-metre swimming pool. There is a running track, indoor climbing and tennis centres.

Tuition fees

- » Fees for UK/EU students £9,250
  Foundation courses £6,750
- » Fees for International students 2020–21   £20,210–£25,770
  Medicine £44,110 (clinical years)
- » For scholarship and bursary information see
  www.warwick.ac.uk/study/undergraduate/studentfunding/
- » Graduate salary £26,500

Student numbers

Undergraduates	15,178	(1,342)
Postgraduates	6,123	(3,064)
Applications/places		38,780/5,370
Applications per place		7.2
Overall offer rate		79.3%
Unconditional offers		0%
International students		35%

Accommodation

University provided places: 9,205
Self-catered: £75–£189 per week
First years guaranteed accommodation
www.warwick.ac.uk/study/undergraduate/campuslife/accommodation/

Where do the students come from?

State schools (non-grammar)	57.7%	First generation students	31.9%	Black attainment gap	-13.8%
Grammar schools	18.4%	Deprived areas	6.5%	Disabled	5.1%
Independent schools	23.9%	All ethnic minorities	38.2%	Mature (over 21)	5.9%

Social inclusion ranking: 97

University of West London

Huge swings in student satisfaction rates are behind the erratic performance of the University of West London (UWL) in our league table. In 2017 student satisfaction went up more than three percentage points; fell by four points last year and has risen more than six percentage points this year.

This year's improvement, allied to higher scores for entry standards, staffing levels and an improved completion rate, has propelled UWL 31 places up our league table, more than compensating for last year's 27-place fall. It is the biggest rise for any university in our new ranking and takes UWL close to its target of a top-50 position by 2020.

UWL achieved silver in the government's Teaching Excellence Framework (TEF). A dozen new degrees, ranging from interior design and computer games technology to leisure management and aviation with a commercial pilot's licence, are designed to address a long-term fall in applications, which are down almost 20% since 2013.

The university is also expanding an already substantial range of degree apprenticeships, moving into new areas such as chartered surveying, social work, midwifery and policing. It expects to have 500 apprentices by September 2020, compared with 110 at the end of the 2018–19 academic year.

The TEF panel complimented the university on its investment in high-quality physical and digital resources, with students fully involved in the design of the new facilities. It also commented favourably on peer mentoring and targeted financial support programmes to improve the engagement of those most at risk of dropping out.

On its well-equipped Ealing campus, UWL has been developing a reputation for a focus on career-building. The £50m Future Campus, with the HeartSpace at its centre, is popular with students. The Paul Hamlyn Library stretches across all four floors of the campus and has a 24-hour social learning area. The project also added music practice rooms, a new performance space, an architecture studio and a concrete testing lab.

UWL is in the top 40 for spending on student facilities, which include a Boeing 737 flight simulator, opened in 2018 for aviation management students.

All students have a personal tutor, as well as access to a team of mentors to advise on non-academic issues. Undergraduates are guaranteed work placements on every course.

The university now concentrates most of its activities in Ealing and Brentford, west London, having closed its campus in Slough. The landmark Paragon Building in Brentford remains the headquarters of one of the largest healthcare faculties in Britain, with top ratings for nursing and midwifery. There is also an

St Mary's Road
Ealing
London W5 5RF
0208 231 2220
undergraduate.admissions@uwl.ac.uk
www.uwl.ac.uk
www.uwlsu.com
Open days 2020:
March 28, June 24, July 4

The Times and The Sunday Times Rankings
Overall Ranking: 52 (last year: 83)

Teaching quality	85.7%	4
Student experience	84.7%	4
Research quality	1.6%	122
Entry standards	124	=84
Graduate prospects	74%	73
Good honours	74.3%	74
Expected completion rate	78.1%	117
Student/staff ratio	14.8	=45
Services and facilities	£2,669	33

outpost in Reading, which houses the Berkshire Institute of Health, and also has nursing and midwifery students.

UWL's first overseas venture opened in 2018, with a centre at Hong Kong Nang Yan College, where university staff will teach a range of undergraduate and postgraduate courses.

Many degrees include the option of a foundation year for those without conventional entry qualifications. All students taking these courses receive a bursary of £500 a year for the full four years as an undergraduate.

Almost 30 degrees offer the option of a January start as an alternative to September. They include a range of business programmes with specialisms such as airline and airport management, and four in psychology, including one dealing with substance use and misuse.

UWL is in the top 20 of our new widening participation table, with about half of its undergraduates receiving some form of financial support. The university's Aspire programme gives all UK and EU full-timers free books worth £100 in their first year and £100 of credit in subsequent years for books or other resources, or catering. Part-time students qualify for half these amounts. Half of the undergraduates are from homes where parents did not go to university, and mature students (21 or over) make up an even larger proportion. More than six out of ten are from ethnic minorities.

The modern students' union was voted the best in the UK in 2017 for representing its members in academic areas. However, the university is in the bottom ten of our research ranking after entering only 13% of eligible academics for the 2014 Research Excellence Framework. A quarter of its submission was judged to be world-leading or internationally excellent, led by exemplary results in communication and media studies.

The university has now launched the UK's first research centre focusing on urban street gangs to tackle growing problems of youth violence and gang culture across the country.

The sites in Ealing and Brentford are linked by a free bus service, and are within easy reach of central London. The Paragon has more than 800 residential places, but private housing in west London is prohibitive. There is a new gym in Ealing and the new Gunnersbury Park leisure centre will be open to the public.

Tuition fees

»	Fees for UK/EU students	£9,250
»	Fees for International students 2020–21	£12,500
»	For scholarship and bursary information see www.uwl.ac.uk/courses/undergraduate/fees-and-funding	
»	Graduate salary	£21,999

Student numbers

Undergraduates	7,794	(1,190)
Postgraduates	737	(1,047)
Applications/places	12,910/2,890	
Applications per place	4.5	
Overall offer rate	78.7%	
Unconditional offers	12%	
International students	14%	

Accommodation

University provided places: 949
Catered costs: £185–£255
Self-catered: £168–£238 per week
www.uwl.ac.uk/student-life/accommodation

Where do the students come from?

Social inclusion ranking: 16

State schools (non-grammar)	96%	First generation students	51.6%	Black attainment gap	-22%
Grammar schools	1.5%	Deprived areas	7.1%	Disabled	6.7%
Independent schools	2.5%	All ethnic minorities	62.3%	Mature (over 21)	54.7%

University of the West of England

A review of the degree portfolio will bear fruit for the University of the West of England (UWE Bristol) in 2020, when courses in the arts and creative industries will become more practice-oriented. There will also be more cross-disciplinary courses, where faculties work together to address skills gaps and technological advancements in the labour market.

The university is already popular with prospective students – not least because of new academic buildings, teaching facilities, accommodation and equipment, resulting from a £300m investment programme that will run until 2020. The numbers starting courses have risen for three years in succession, adding almost 1,000 to the annual intake. Applications were up again, by 4.5% in 2019.

A new engineering building on the main Frenchay campus is scheduled to open in 2020. It will have specialist workshops, study areas and laboratories for composite manufacturing, machining and metrology, responding to predicted growth in the demand for engineering graduates in the region.

New and enhanced science laboratories for more than 1,000 students opened in May 2019, as did the Foundry Technology Affinity Space, built in partnership with the new Institute of Coding. The Foundry, which also houses UWE's enterprise studios, is intended to equip students with digital skills and enable them to work with industry partners on paid projects that fit around their studies.

The university was also one of the first to launch a holistic mental health strategy, following the deaths of three students in little more than a year. Each student is assigned an academic personal tutor and there is a round-the-clock help centre and crisis text helpline, with out-of-hours online counselling.

UWE Bristol has launched 14 new degree programmes in 2019, more than half of them top-up courses for students with lower-level qualifications. Degrees in environmental management and music and sound design will take their first students in 2020.

By then, UWE Bristol also expects to have added to its 12 degree apprenticeship programmes. It is working with the West of England Combined Authority to develop new programmes to close regional skills gaps in business, engineering and healthcare.

The institution has held its own in our table for the second year in a row, remaining comfortably in the top half and featuring among the top dozen post-1992 universities. But its static position disguises a big improvement in staffing levels and an equally large decline in spending on student facilities.

The university is the biggest in the region, with more than 28,000 undergraduate and postgraduate students. Its three sites in

---

Frenchay Campus
Coldharbour Lane
Bristol BS16 1QY
0117 328 3333
admissions@uwe.ac.uk
www.uwe.ac.uk
www.thestudentsunion.co.uk
Open days 2020:
March 18 (City campus),
March 25 (Frenchay),
April 1 (Glenside)

The Times and The Sunday Times Rankings
Overall Ranking: =58 (last year: 58)

Teaching quality	83.8%	=11
Student experience	83.1%	6
Research quality	8.8%	69
Entry standards	128	=77
Graduate prospects	76.3%	64
Good honours	75.4%	63
Expected completion rate	84.3%	71
Student/staff ratio	15.3	55
Services and facilities	£2,007	95

Bristol are mainly in the north of the city, and those training for the nursing and allied health professions study at regional centres near hospitals in Gloucester and Bath. Since 2008 the main campus, four miles from the city centre, has doubled in size and now has the UK's largest robotics laboratory. The university's exhibition and conference centre is one of the biggest in the southwest.

UWE Bristol's international college, run in partnership with the Kaplan group, prepares those arriving from outside the UK for the rigours of degree study. The university's degrees are also taught in a growing number of institutions overseas.

More than half of the students come from the West Country, however, and the university has broadened its intake considerably in recent years. The proportion of independent school entrants has dropped to about 6% and more than a third of UK undergraduates receive some financial support.

More than 60% of the work submitted for assessment in the 2014 Research Excellence Framework was rated as world-leading or internationally excellent. Health subjects and communication and media studies produced the best results.

The careers and employment service runs an innovative web-based jobs and placement service with the local chamber of commerce. The UWE Bristol Futures Award encourages students to acquire skills that will count in the employment market, and to make sure extracurricular activities are shown to best advantage on their CVs. UWE Bristol has one of the largest internship programmes at any university and graduates can apply to the Centre for Graduate Enterprise for help to set up a business in an incubator hub on the Frenchay campus.

Lively Bristol is a popular student centre – but it isn't cheap. The university owns or endorses more than 4,700 residential places, enough to guarantee accommodation for new entrants who apply by June. Two up-to-date fitness suites are just yards away from Frenchay's student accommodation so there's no excuse to stay on the couch. Hillside Gardens, the £5.5m sports complex opened in 2018, has outdoor facilities a few minutes away and there are teams for American football and ultimate Frisbee as well as more conventional sports leagues.

Tuition fees

» Fees for UK/EU students	£9,250
» Fees for International students 2020–21	£13,500
» For scholarship and bursary information see www1.uwe.ac.uk/students/feesandfunding.aspx	
» Graduate salary	£22,000

Student numbers

Undergraduates	19,231 (2,290)
Postgraduates	2,468 (4,800)
Applications/places	31,765/7,095
Applications per place	4.5
Overall offer rate	81.5%
Unconditional offers	0%
International students	13.2%

Accommodation

University provided places: 4,788
Self-catered: £88–£183 per week
First years guaranteed accommodation
www.uwe.ac.uk/students/accommodation.aspx

Where do the students come from?

State schools (non-grammar)	90.6%	First generation students	43.4%		
Grammar schools	3.4%	Deprived areas	14.8%		
Independent schools	6.1%	All ethnic minorities	17.1%		

Social inclusion ranking: 74

Black attainment gap	-31.9%
Disabled	7.7%
Mature (over 21)	21.2%

University of the West of Scotland

The University of the West of Scotland (UWS), is the most socially inclusive north of the border, topping our first table to rank Scottish universities separately from their counterparts in England and Wales. Almost a third of its intake – easily the largest proportion in Scotland – is recruited from the poorest 20% of areas, according to the Scottish Index of Multiple Deprivation.

Just less than half of the students come from homes where no parent went to university and just over half are aged over 21 when they begin their studies.

In our academic rankings, however, UWS has fallen 16 places and out of the top 100 for the first time since 2016. This is mostly due to a decline in student satisfaction. The university was in the top 30 in the UK for student satisfaction with teaching quality last year but is now outside the top 40 – and there has been an even sharper decline in the university's scores in the National Student Survey for the broader student experience. Once in the top 50, UWS now finds itself outside the top 70 for the student experience.

The student satisfaction scores are a disappointment as UWS is committed to becoming Scotland's most "student-focused" university. Staffing levels are the other main stumbling block in our league table. Although there had been a slight improvement in the latest survey, only one university has more students per member of staff than the 22.4 at UWS.

The university may be a victim of its own success in recruitment. The number of new entrants has risen for the past two years, when others were struggling, and its intake in 2018 was 1,000 higher than in 2014. It took only 7% of undergraduate entrants through clearing. UWS expects to have more than 100 degree apprentices in software development, engineering design, civil engineering and business management in 2020.

The £110m Lanarkshire campus, which opened in 2018 set in 37 acres of woodland, has added significantly to UWS's attractions. Applications were up by 14% at the June 2019 application deadline compared to the previous year. Based in carbon-neutral buildings at the Hamilton International Technology Park, the eco-campus features a street atrium linking its main buildings, which contain ultra-modern teaching and learning spaces and a students' union.

Built for 4,000 students and 250 staff, the campus is the base for courses in health, computing and some business and social science subjects. There are simulated hospital wards, community and primary care settings where students can immerse themselves in authentic healthcare environments using virtual reality technology.

Paisley Campus
Paisley PA1 2BE
0800 027 1000;
+44 141 849 4101 (international)
ask@uws.ac.uk
www.uws.ac.uk
www.sauws.org.uk
Open days 2020:
see website

PAISLEY
Edinburgh
Belfast
London
Cardiff

The Times and The Sunday Times Rankings
Overall Ranking: 108 (last year: 92)

Teaching quality	81.4%	41
Student experience	78%	=72
Research quality	4.3%	=98
Entry standards	135	51
Graduate prospects	80.7%	=42
Good honours	71.3%	=91
Expected completion rate	80.9%	=97
Student/staff ratio	22.4	130
Services and facilities	£2,205	77

UWS headquarters will remain in Paisley, where more than £30m has been spent on better student facilities and more accommodation. The campus has a flexible learning area with interactive technology and a cafe open to staff, students and the public.

In Ayr, £81m has gone into modern facilities for 2,300 students. The campus, which has a prize-winning library, is shared with Scotland's Rural College. The Dumfries campus is the smallest, where 550 UWS students join others from the University of Glasgow and Dumfries and Galloway College on the 85-acre parkland site on the Crichton Estate, half an hour from the town centre.

Founded in 2007 from the merger of Paisley University and Bell College, in Hamilton – serving two areas of low participation in higher education – UWS is one of the largest modern universities in Scotland, with more than 16,000 students. It describes itself as "the local university for a third of Scotland's population" – although there are 1,700 students from outside the UK, a third from other EU countries.

A south London campus opened in Southwark in 2015, where more than 1,000 students are taking courses in business, health, music, quality management, project management, and education.

All UWS students are offered computer training and many take sandwich degrees or have work placements built into their courses. UWS was the first UK university to be approved by Microsoft, Macromedia and Cisco. Sony supported a games development laboratory, part of a £300,000 investment in its multimedia and games facilities.

The School of Health, Nursing and Midwifery, the largest in Scotland, produced easily UWS's best results in the 2014 Research Excellence Framework, when 44% of the submission reached one of the top two categories.

UWS academics are preparing to test their research in space through a collaboration announced in 2018 with the International Space School Education Trust. Their work on the effects of growth hormone on muscle mass and cognitive function will be tested on the International Space Station.

UWS has just 850 residential places, so only international students are guaranteed accommodation. However, the high proportion of home-based students means that, until now, it has been possible to satisfy all new entrants requiring a study bedroom. Until student residences are available at the Lanarkshire campus, students will continue to live in the centre of Hamilton, two miles away.

Tuition fees

» Fees for Scottish/EU students   £0–£1,820
  RUK fees   £9,250 (capped at £27,750 for 4-year courses)
» Fees for International students 2020–21   £13,000–£16,000
» For scholarship and bursary information see
  www.uws.ac.uk/money-fees-funding/
» Graduate salary   £22,000

Student numbers

Undergraduates	11,385	(2,078)
Postgraduates	1,879	(1,093)
Applications/places	20,030/4,770	
Applications per place	4.2	
Overall offer rate	79.8%	
Unconditional offers	0%	
International students	10.4%	

Accommodation

University provided places: 852
Self-catered: £85–£162 per week
www.uws.ac.uk/university-life/accommodation

Where do the students come from?

State schools (non-grammar)	98.8%	First generation students	47.3%	Black attainment gap	-46.2%
Grammar schools	0.3%	Deprived areas	29.4%	Disabled	2.1%
Independent schools	0.9%	All ethnic minorities	9.6%	Mature (over 21)	51.4%

Social inclusion ranking (Scotland): 1

University of Westminster

Applications to study at Westminster rose for the first time in five years during the 2019 admissions cycle – a 4% increase at a time when most of its peer group was seeing the demand for places fall. The university also made a strong pitch in clearing, offering 40 scholarships of £1,500 a year to students who bettered the standard offer, subject to interview.

Westminster said the clearing scholarships acknowledged the costs and benefits of studying in London. More students have actually started courses for the past two years, but almost 90% of applicants were offered places in 2018, compared with 67% four years earlier.

The university will be keeping a close eye on post-Brexit arrangements for European undergraduates. It had nearly 2,300 EU students in 2017–18, one of the 12 largest totals in the UK and close to 20% of the undergraduate population. Westminster attracts even more students from outside the EU and its courses are taught in nine other countries, from Sri Lanka to Uzbekistan.

Until 2018, the university had been moving up our table, but it has dropped five places in the latest edition and is now in the bottom 15. It has fallen significantly in the measures for staffing levels, spending on student facilities and the proportion achieving good honours degrees. It was already well outside the top 100

for student satisfaction, joining a crop of London-based institutions near the bottom of the table on these measures, despite a slight improvement in this year's outcomes.

Westminster has a longstanding commitment to widening participation in higher education, however, and is just outside the top-40 in our social inclusion table for England and Wales. Two-thirds of undergraduates come from ethnic minorities and almost half from working-class families.

The university was given a bronze rating in the Teaching Excellence Framework, which takes account of the backgrounds of students. An unusually brief commentary by the awarding panel praised the consistent support for students at risk of dropping out and acknowledged a strategic approach and commitment to improving employment and entrepreneurship.

All courses were reviewed when the Learning Futures programme came into operation in 2016, with work-related skills woven into degrees and the structure of undergraduate programmes incorporating year-long modules to promote deeper learning. This resulted in new support for employability and international mobility, as well as awards for students' extracurricular activities recognising outstanding contributions of benefit to the public.

New degrees were launched in 2019 in data science and analytics, and business management for digital business, and there are four new joint honours programmes for international business

309 Regent Street
London W1B 2HW
020 7911 5000
ugadmissions@westminster.ac.uk
www.westminster.ac.uk
www.uwsu.com
Open days 2020:
March 14, June 13

The Times and The Sunday Times Rankings
Overall Ranking: 119 (last year: 114)

Teaching quality	75.2%	119
Student experience	75.1%	111
Research quality	9.8%	59
Entry standards	127	=75
Graduate prospects	70.4%	=99
Good honours	70.5%	96
Expected completion rate	81.7%	92
Student/staff ratio	19.3	=118
Services and facilities	£1,857	106

with Arabic, Chinese, French or Spanish. The university teaches one of the widest ranges of languages in the UK and, together with the School of Oriental and African Studies (SOAS) leads the Routes into Languages programme to encourage more people to learn a language.

Westminster aims to be the leading practice-informed university and promises a "dynamic synergy" between the creative arts and design, architecture and the built environment, science and technology, business, law, and the social sciences and humanities. It collaborates with a network of more than 3,000 companies and all students are encouraged to undertake a work placement which can form part of their degree.

The university became the UK's first polytechnic in 1838. There are three sites in central London, including the Marylebone headquarters, near the BBC's Broadcasting House, and a larger campus in Harrow, in the northwest of the capital, which houses the media, arts and design faculty, the university's best-known feature.

Current investment includes new wet laboratory space at the Cavendish campus and more studio space being added to the Harrow campus to support the significant increase in students taking fashion degrees. A technologically advanced space and learning platform is being built at the Marylebone campus to support the business school.

Westminster held its position among the leading institutions for communication and media studies in the 2014 Research Excellence Framework, when almost two-thirds of the work submitted was judged to be world-leading or excellent. There were even better results in art and design, and a good performance in English.

Although less than 30% of the eligible staff entered the exercise, the university is in our top 60 for research, comfortably its best position among the nine measures.

There are 1,500 residential places but only students with medical conditions and those under 18 are guaranteed accommodation. There is a student village for first-years close to Wembley Stadium and a £6m development in Harrow – with 60 rooms already upgraded and up to 150 more in 2020. The Westminster halls in Marylebone were also recently refurbished but there is no way round the expensive private market at some stage.

There is a lively social scene on the Harrow campus but Westminster students tend to be dispersed around the capital. Sports facilities are also decentralised, with playing fields and a boathouse in Chiswick. Student membership for the university gyms in London's Regent Street and on the Harrow campus costs £45 per month.

Tuition fees

» Fees for UK/EU students	£9,250
» Fees for International students 2020–21	£14,000
» For scholarship and bursary information see www.westminster.ac.uk/study/fees-and-funding/	
» Graduate salary	£21,000

Student numbers

Undergraduates	12,337	(2,555)
Postgraduates	2,383	(1,968)
Applications/places		24,680/5,075
Applications per place		4.9
Overall offer rate		88.8%
Unconditional offers		0%
International students		33.2%

Accommodation
University provided places: 1,514
Self-catered: £129–£271 per week
www.westminster.ac.uk/study/accommodation

Where do the students come from?

State schools (non-grammar)	94.5%	First generation students	54.5%	
Grammar schools	2.2%	Deprived areas	5.6%	
Independent schools	3.3%	All ethnic minorities	66.6%	

Social inclusion ranking: 43

Black attainment gap	-22%
Disabled	4.4%
Mature (over 21)	20.5%

University of Winchester

Winchester is only just hanging on in our top 100 after a drop of 19 places this year. Student satisfaction, once the university's greatest strength, has declined significantly and there have been smaller falls in the scores for completion rates and the proportion of students achieving good honours.

The university is more popular than ever in terms of applications, however. Dramatic expansion in the portfolio of degrees, with 50 new programmes launched in two years, helped it to an increase of 12% in applications in 2019 – among the biggest rises.

Much of the increase has come in subject areas taking their first students in 2019. They included seven new law degrees, pairing the subject with cybersecurity, psychology and even sports studies. Other fresh options included three branches of nursing, banking and finance, data science and American studies, with a US study year. Winchester has also launched a new degree in professional policing, part of the new qualifications framework for the force and including new areas such as digital policing.

The pace of development will slow in 2020, but there will still be seven new degrees, including modern English literature, nutrition and dietetics, fashion business and international development. Winchester is also expanding its range of degree apprenticeships in areas such as social care, senior leadership, digital and technology solutions, and a postgraduate apprenticeship which will confer qualified teacher status.

The university is just outside the top 40 in our social inclusion ranking, with almost half the students from homes where parents did not go to university. Winchester was named one of ten UK Universities of Sanctuary in 2018 by the charity, City of Sanctuary. It is the first university in the south of England to be recognised for supportive initiatives to welcome refugees and asylum-seekers who wish to study.

Winchester has a silver rating in the Teaching Excellence Framework. The panel was impressed by the "appropriate" contact hours, tutorials and buddy schemes that produce personalised learning and high levels of commitment from students.

A new digital futures and business management development will include a 250-seat auditorium, art gallery, cafe and food hall, as well as a library and social learning areas. The new building, which is on target to achieve an "excellent" Breeam rating, will help the university in its ambition to be the most sustainable in the UK.

Winchester featured in the top 100 of a global impact ranking published by *Times Higher Education* magazine, based on UN sustainable development goals. The university won an award from the National Union of Students for embedding sustainability and

Sparkford Road
Winchester SO22 4NR
01962 827 234
admissions@winchester.ac.uk
www.winchester.ac.uk
www.winchesterstudents.co.uk
Open days 2020:
see website

The Times and The Sunday Times **Rankings**
Overall Ranking: =98 (last year: 79)

Teaching quality	80.5%	=59
Student experience	78.5%	64
Research quality	5.8%	=83
Entry standards	113	=115
Graduate prospects	63.7%	=122
Good honours	76.4%	=54
Expected completion rate	86.3%	61
Student/staff ratio	16.4	=81
Services and facilities	£1,683	119

social responsibility in all its activities.

Other recent developments include an award-winning extension to the library, which added 450 study spaces and extra computers, and a well-equipped learning and teaching building. Winchester has split its campus into four quarters of which the compact main King Alfred site is on a wooded hillside overlooking the cathedral city, a ten-minute walk away. The West Downs quarter is the site of the £50m digital futures development and Winchester's well-regarded business school, one of six in the UK and 30 in the world selected to champion a United Nations initiative, PRME (the Principles for Responsible Management Education).

Winchester was one the first universities to appoint its own ombudsman to handle complaints. It is still best known for its education courses, which Ofsted rates as outstanding, although they no longer dominate in terms of student numbers. A new faculty of health and wellbeing was established in 2019 to reflect the growth in this area, which is expected to expand further. Media courses are another growth area, with an industry-standard newsroom, and new sound recording studios at the School of Media and Film's multimedia centre.

The university held its own in the 2014 Research Excellence Framework. Almost 45% of its work was considered world-leading or internationally excellent, with communications and history producing the best results. John Denham, the former Labour universities secretary, heads Winchester's Centre for English Identity and Politics.

The opening of the Sport and Exercise Research Centre marked the 175th anniversary in 2015 of the institution's establishment as a Church of England foundation for teacher training (it was known as King Alfred College until 2004). Sports facilities are good, with a gym, fitness suite and sports hall supplemented by the Winchester Sports Stadium.

The gym is at the heart of a £12m student village of more than 700 rooms. Two other complexes bring the number of residential places to more than 2,200. UK entrants are guaranteed accommodation.

The university campus is within walking distance of the city, which *The Sunday Times* named the best place to live in 2016 and which topped the Royal Mail Happiness Index for 2019.

Winchester has a rich cultural and architectural heritage, but it also has a lively contemporary social and entertainment vibe with a well-regarded music scene and bars and venues catering to student tastes and budgets.

Tuition fees

» Fees for UK/EU students	£9,250
» Fees for International students 2020–21	£13,500
» For scholarship and bursary information see www.winchester.ac.uk/accommodation-and-winchester-life/scholarships-bursaries-and-awards/	
» Graduate salary	£20,000

Student numbers

Undergraduates	5,975	(316)
Postgraduates	543	(749)
Applications/places		8,940/2,600
Applications per place		3.4
Overall offer rate		90.2%
Unconditional offers		0%
International students		6.1%

Accommodation

University provided places: 2,215
Catered costs: £167 per week
Self-catered: £86–£159 per week
First years guaranteed accommodation
www.winchester.ac.uk/accommodation-and-winchester-life/accommodation

Where do the students come from?

State schools (non-grammar)	91.8%	First generation students	49.5%	Black attainment gap	-24.3%
Grammar schools	4.1%	Deprived areas	13.4%	Disabled	12.2%
Independent schools	4.1%	All ethnic minorities	9.7%	Mature (over 21)	14.6%

Social inclusion ranking: 42

University of Wolverhampton

The £100m redevelopment of the derelict Springfield Brewery site in Wolverhampton to create a new campus for construction and the built environment is the centrepiece of a wider £250m investment programme currently under way at the university. The site is being transformed into Europe's largest specialist campus in these areas, bringing together businesses and the education sector to maximise impact on the economy.

Wolverhampton's School of Architecture and Built Environment will move to its new home there in 2020. The site will also house the West Midlands University Technical College and the Elite Centre for Manufacturing Skills.

Elsewhere, a £9m cutting-edge centre for cybersecurity will open in 2020 at Skylon Park, Hereford. It is a collaboration between the university and Herefordshire Council, offering high quality research facilities through the university's cyber research institute and providing office space for cyber businesses and advanced training facilities designed specifically to tackle threats in cyberspace.

The development programme has already seen the opening of an £18m building for the business school, and £10m of new engineering facilities are being provided in Telford and Wolverhampton to support the university's courses in automotive and motorsport engineering, electronic and telecommunications engineering, and chemical and aerospace engineering.

Wolverhampton delivers higher education courses in leadership and management, education, travel and tourism, hospitality and computing on a 50-acre campus in Stafford bought by the Chinese-based New Beacon Group from Staffordshire University. Students are recruited directly from China and locally in Staffordshire, and in March 2019 the university extended its international reach in China even further when it signed a five-year partnership agreement with the University of Hong Kong.

Wolverhampton enjoyed a 13% increase in new enrolments in 2018, the year that the university returned to the league tables after an eight-year boycott, although there has been an almost 9% drop in applications since.

The university has gone up three places in our latest table, but remains in the bottom ten. There have been big improvements in staffing levels and in both measures of student satisfaction. Wolverhampton is well inside the top-50 for satisfaction with teaching quality and in the top-60 for the broader student experience.

It is also ranked 7th in England and Wales in our new social inclusion ranking, with almost 60% of undergraduates the first in their family to go to university and more than half from ethnic minorities. The university draws two-thirds of its students from the West Midlands and leads a regional scheme to encourage young

Wulfruna Street
Wolverhampton WV1 1LY
01902 321 000
enquiries@wlv.ac.uk
www.wlv.ac.uk
www.wolvesunion.org/
Open days 2020:
June 13

The Times and The Sunday Times Rankings
Overall Ranking: 124 (last year: 127)

Teaching quality	81.3%	=42
Student experience	78.8%	58
Research quality	5.9%	82
Entry standards	112	=119
Graduate prospects	68.9%	103
Good honours	66.2%	119
Expected completion rate	72.9%	127
Student/staff ratio	18	=104
Services and facilities	£1,913	103

people to consider higher education.

Wolverhampton was placed in the bronze category in the first round of Teaching Excellence Framework grades, but was upgraded to silver in 2018. The university still missed its benchmarks for student satisfaction and progression to highly-skilled employment, but the panel praised the commitment to enhancing students' learning experience and the involvement of employers in the development and review of courses.

The university has three bases in the West Midlands: the original campus in Wolverhampton and the Walsall campus that is dedicated to sport and performance, education, and which houses the Institute of Health, where facilities are undergoing a £4.8m upgrade. The third, purpose-built campus at Telford in Shropshire focuses on business and engineering.

The university has linked with West Midlands Ambulance Service to create the UK's first university-ambulance trust, which will see closer working on collaborative projects, research, sharing clinical expertise, joint curriculum development and staff exchanges. Wolverhampton's paramedic science students are guaranteed a job with the service if they pass their course and all necessary professional tests.

New degrees include a BSc in demolition practice, another in emergency and disaster management and BAs in sports journalism and professional policing. In addition, there are 14 degree apprenticeship programmes with 500 apprentices in areas as diverse as engineering,

healthcare and teaching. The university expects to double the number of apprentices by 2020.

Research mainly serves the needs of business and industry, as well as underpinning teaching. Best results in the Research Excellence Framework were in information science, almost 90% considered world-leading or internationally excellent.

The recent redevelopment of the students' union on the City campus and a new union bar on the Walsall campus upgraded student facilities, and the Performance Hub, in Walsall, has exceptional provision for music, dance and drama. There are 1,200 study bedrooms available, including a 350-bed student village.

Sports facilities include a research centre for sport, exercise and performance. Students and locals can buy gym membership valid on the City and Walsall campuses for £20 a month and have access to facilities that include the swimming pool at Walsall.

The city of Wolverhampton has a growing nightlife, with 25,000 revellers travelling from miles around each weekend to enjoy the bars and clubs of the buzzing Entertainment Quarter.

Tuition fees

» Fees for UK/EU students	£9,250
Foundation courses £8,400	
» Fees for International students 2020–21	£12,250
» For scholarship and bursary information see	
www.wlv.ac.uk/study-here/money-matters/fees-and-costs	
» Graduate salary	£18,000

Student numbers

Undergraduates	12,720	(3,333)
Postgraduates	1,257	(2,320)
Applications/places	17,470/4,630	
Applications per place	3.8	
Overall offer rate	90%	
Unconditional offers	0.4%	
International students	5.2%	

Accommodation

University provided places: 1,208
Self-catered: £88–£106 per week
www.wlv.ac.uk/university-life/accommodation

Where do the students come from?

State schools (non-grammar)	97.1%	First generation students	59.8%	Black attainment gap	-26.3%
Grammar schools	1.2%	Deprived areas	20.7%	Disabled	7.7%
Independent schools	1.7%	All ethnic minorities	52%	Mature (over 21)	45.4%

Social inclusion ranking: =7

University of Worcester

Worcester is in the top eight in both of our measures of student satisfaction – sixth for teaching quality and eighth for the wider student experience – but ranks below 90th place in all but one of the other measures in our table. Consequently, despite its stellar performance in the National Student Survey, Worcester has fallen one place in our overall ranking this year.

The university is only just outside the top-30 in our new social inclusion table, however. More than half of the undergraduates are the first in their family to go to university and 95% went to non-selective state schools or colleges. More than a third of new entrants are mature students, aged 21 or older when they start their courses.

A team of graduate ambassadors works with more than 200 primary schools to try to broaden the intake further. The Reach scheme gives most students access to e-books, stationery, art supplies, digital equipment, or other course-specific equipment at discounted prices. New undergraduates paying full fees will receive £100 bursaries to spend through the scheme. Students also have access to an extensive earn-as-you-learn programme.

Worcester was given a silver rating in the Teaching Excellence Framework. The panel said that the teaching encourages high levels of student engagement and commitment, with "excellent" levels of contact time, and schemes which involve students in the enhancement of their learning experience.

Enrolments dropped by 10% in 2018, but the total was still on a par with the years before recruitment restrictions were lifted. Those starting courses in 2019 had new options to choose from, including a foundation year for degrees in the biological sciences. The university also launched seven new foundation degrees, mainly in sport, education and wellbeing, at a time when many others are phasing out the two-year qualification.

Worcester's portfolio of degree apprenticeships is modest, with only 63 apprentices on five programmes in 2019. The university is expecting more than 100 in 2020, after adding new programmes in departmental management, nursing and teaching.

The university's three teaching campuses are less than a mile from each other and all close to the city centre. The main St John's campus is set in parkland a 15-minute walk from the centre. It houses science facilities, the National Pollen and Aerobiology Research Unit, the digital arts centre and drama studio, and an AstroTurf pitch.

The other star facility is a 2,000-seat indoor sporting arena, which is one of only two sports venues in the UK designed specifically for wheelchair athletes as well as the able-bodied. The Arena is on the Riverside Campus, which is being developed as an International Centre

Henwick Grove
Worcester WR2 6AJ
01905 855 111
admissions@worc.ac.uk
www.worcester.ac.uk
www.worcsu.com
Open days 2020:
March 28, June 28

The Times and The Sunday Times **Rankings**
Overall Ranking: =92 (last year: 91)

Teaching quality	85.1%	6
Student experience	82.8%	8
Research quality	4.3%	=98
Entry standards	120	=94
Graduate prospects	75.0%	70
Good honours	67.1%	117
Expected completion rate	81.8%	91
Student/staff ratio	17.2	=92
Services and facilities	£1,629	122

for Inclusive Sport and Health to include a new facility in partnership with Worcestershire County Cricket Club.

Worcester has also added the Lakeside Campus, a short drive from the main campus, which has sports pitches and a ten-acre lake, which has been adapted for a range of inclusive water sports and other outdoor activities. The university's commitment to disability sports extends to the UK's first disability sport degree.

A new Art House, in the city centre, was officially opened in 2019, providing high-quality facilities for art and illustration courses. The grade II-listed building was built in 1939 as a car showroom, and many of its art deco features, including a distinctive clock tower, have been retained.

The Art House is located opposite the City campus, which houses the business school and occupies the historic buildings of the former Worcester Royal Infirmary. Almost next door is the university's spectacular library and history centre, The Hive, which was the first joint public and university library to open in Britain and has won several awards.

Worcester now has approaching 11,000 students, two-thirds of them female. The university, which was originally a post-war emergency teacher training college, has applied to open a medical school to serve the three counties of Gloucestershire, Herefordshire and Worcestershire. All six NHS trusts in the region have backed the proposal, which rests on the institution's strength in nursing and other health disciplines.

The university has been shortlisted five times for nurse education provider of the year and is the partner institution for the National Childbirth Trust, for example, delivering all of the trust's antenatal training.

Worcester was one of the most improved universities in the 2014 Research Excellence Framework compared with previous assessments: it went up 20 places in our research ranking, partly because it entered five times as many academics as in 2008. A third of the work was considered world leading or internationally excellent, with history and art and design achieving the best scores.

An active students' union acts as a social hub and Worcester has 1,210 residential places on the St John's and City campuses – enough to guarantee accommodation to new entrants who apply before the end of May. The cathedral city is not large but is safer than many university locations and has its share of pubs and clubs that cater for a growing student clientele.

Tuition fees

» Fees for UK/EU students	£9,250
» Fees for International students 2020–21	£12,700
» For scholarship and bursary information see www.worcester.ac.uk/study/fees-and-finance/1	
» Graduate salary	£21,000

Student numbers

Undergraduates	8,084	(861)
Postgraduates	783	(1,070)
Applications/places		11,610/2,825
Applications per place		4.1
Overall offer rate		92%
Unconditional offers		0%
International students		5.8%

Accommodation

University provided places: 1,210
Self-catered: £102–£165 per week
First years guaranteed accommodation
www.worcester.ac.uk/life/accommodation

Where do the students come from?

State schools (non-grammar)	95%	First generation students	51.7%	Black attainment gap	-21.5%
Grammar schools	2.1%	Deprived areas	15.9%	Disabled	10.1%
Independent schools	3.0%	All ethnic minorities	13%	Mature (over 21)	36.6%

Social inclusion ranking: 32

Wrexham Glyndŵr University

Wrexham Glyndŵr remains the most socially inclusive university in England and Wales – but sits only one place off the bottom of our main academic league table. It has dropped one place because of a decline in student satisfaction with the quality of teaching, and lower staffing levels.

The Wrexham-based university is even further ahead of the rest than it was last year in terms of social inclusion, with the highest proportions of disabled students and mature students. Just one other university recruits more students educated in non-selective state schools and well over half its undergraduates are the first in their family to go to university.

More than 50 new programmes were launched in 2019, almost half of them foundation years preparing students for entry to existing degrees. New subject areas include children's books, computer networks and security, sports injury rehabilitation, and comics. A new degree in public services leadership will be launched in 2020.

Wrexham Glyndŵr also offers two-year fast-track degrees and four-year master's degrees in art and design, and computing. The university has developed a model for its degree programmes called "the Glyndŵr Graduate", in consultation with local and national employers, highlighting the core skills and attributes that are most valued in the labour market. A standalone module includes a programme of lectures and workshops with employers and careers advisors to help students to understand, develop and document their skills and achievements.

The university gained silver in the Teaching Excellence Framework (TEF), scoring well for its part-time courses. Part-timers who live in Wales are eligible for a scholarship waiving 40% of the tuition fee. The TEF panel was impressed by the high levels of interaction with industry, business and the public sector and commented favourably on the quality of work-based learning that matches the region's priorities.

The Campus 2025 strategy aims to update and modernise the university's campuses. Two new social study spaces have been developed at the heart of the main campus to support the evolution of collaborative learning. Wrexham Glyndŵr is exploring new teaching methods that promote group work and problem-solving so teaching sessions are freed up for tackling ideas. In a refurbished classroom block, there are new learning spaces with high-end IT improvements.

The main campus is on the outskirts of Wrexham, with a town centre base for the Art School. There are two further sites at Northop, in Flintshire, and St Asaph, in Denbighshire. The university also owns the Racecourse stadium – the oldest in the world. As well as

Mold Road
Wrexham LL11 2AW
01978 293 439
enquiries@glyndwr.ac.uk
www.glyndwr.ac.uk
www.wrexhamglyndwrsu.org.uk
Open days 2020:
February 29, June 6,
August 15

Edinburgh
Belfast
WREXHAM
Cardiff
London

being home to Wrexham FC, the football ground gives media and sound technology students a good place to practise their skills – and has been used to host music events featuring Sterophonics and Olly Murs.

The Centre for the Creative Industries hosts the regional home of BBC Cymru Wales and has high-quality studios used by students on television production degree courses. The university's facilities reflect its diverse subject areas and emphasis on collaboration across disciplines: there is a complementary medicine clinic and laboratories for computer game development and the study of crime scenes – as well as a flight simulator and supersonic wind tunnel.

Northop hosts the university's rural campus, specialising in courses on animal studies and biodiversity, where students have access to a small animal unit and an equine centre.

The St Asaph campus houses Glyndŵr Innovations, a research centre that brings together academia and industry, focusing on the technology to make high-resolution telescopes. At Broughton, the university's Advanced Composite Training and Development Centre works in partnership with Airbus, which has a plant nearby. Research carried out there will help to improve the efficiency of aircraft and feed into the university's engineering courses.

Wrexham Glyndŵr became a university in 2008 after a long campaign, taking the name of the 15th-century Welsh prince Owain Glyndŵr, who championed the establishment of universities throughout Wales. There are now 6,400 students, more than half of them part-timers and including 1,000 from outside the UK.

The university entered only 34 academics for the 2014 Research Excellence Framework, but a third of their work was judged to be internationally excellent, with some world-leading, notably in media subjects.

A high proportion of the students are local so many remain living at home, which eases the pressure on accommodation. There are currently only 351 residential places, although more will be added as part of the Campus 2025 strategy. First-years are guaranteed accommodation if they apply by the deadline.

Wrexham is not without nightlife, and the upgraded students' union runs the popular Centenary bar in the Racecourse stadium. The campus also has a modern sports centre with two floodlit artificial pitches, a human performance laboratory and indoor facilities.

Tuition fees

» Fees for UK/EU students	£9,000
» Fees for International students 2020–21	£11,750
» For scholarship and bursary information see www.glyndwr.ac.uk/en/feesandstudentfinance/	
» Graduate salary	£20,000

Student numbers

Undergraduates	2,665	(2,467)
Postgraduates	142	(470)
Applications/places		1,815/915
Applications per place		2
Overall offer rate		81%
Unconditional offers		0%
International students		17.5%

Accommodation

University provided places: 351
Self-catered: £88–£165 per week
www.glyndwr.ac.uk/en/Accommodation

Where do the students come from?

State schools (non-grammar)	99.2%	First generation students	56.8%	Black attainment gap	-25.5%
Grammar schools	0.4%	Deprived areas	23.6%	Disabled	22.1%
Independent schools	0.4%	All ethnic minorities	5.7%	Mature (over 21)	72%

Social inclusion ranking: 1

University of York

York finishes more than 30 places higher in our rankings for student satisfaction with teaching quality than any other Russell Group university, an achievement that came close to making it our University of the Year for Teaching Quality. High levels of satisfaction in this key area have proved notoriously hard to achieve for the most selective universities, but York rises to 25th on this measure this year.

It achieves a similar rank for the wider student experience, also a considerable improvement on its score and ranking in 2018. However, these twin successes have not been sufficient to move York in our rankings overall, and it remains on the fringes of the UK top-20, where it was formerly a fixture for more than two decades.

The university has launched a £120m fundraising campaign, which blends enhancing on-campus teaching and research facilities with broader global challenges such as improving access to education, mental health services and jobs. York Unlimited also covers expanded scholarship and bursary schemes and new research into mental health and other global challenges, as well as greater support for innovation and entrepreneurship.

York has already invested £800,000 in enhanced mental health services, having carried out a review following five student suicides in a single year. The Open Door team provides professional support to students experiencing mental health or psychological difficulties, and there have been campaigns on the benefits of sleep, studying methods, how to identify signs of distress and where to seek help.

The university also has a prize-winning personal development programme to boost undergraduates' employment prospects. The York Strengths scheme, launched in partnership with employers such as PwC, Clifford Chance, the NHS and IBM, focuses on nine qualities valued by the recruiters of graduates. A three-stage programme gives students the opportunity to engage with employers early in their studies to arrange work experience, placements, internships or volunteering.

York has made a commitment to give all students the opportunity to pursue a work placement of up to a year. Degree modules have been designed to develop the skills that will boost employability. Careers advice is delivered through the 29 academic departments.

The development of employability skills and provision of careers support were among the factors behind the 2018 upgrading of York's rating to gold in the Teaching Excellence Framework. The panel found excellent academic support and a research-strong environment that engages students and provides outstanding levels of stretch.

A new degree in finance, operations research, management and statistics, with the

Heslington
York YO10 5DD
01904 324 000
ug-admissions@york.ac.uk
www.york.ac.uk
www.yusu.org
Open days 2020: see website

The Times and The Sunday Times Rankings
Overall Ranking: 22 (last year: 22)

Teaching quality	82.6%	25
Student experience	81%	24
Research quality	38.3%	17
Entry standards	158	=29
Graduate prospects	82%	29
Good honours	80.5%	36
Expected completion rate	92.8%	=20
Student/staff ratio	14.6	=41
Services and facilities	£1,810	110

option of a year in industry, took its first students in 2019. Six more new programmes are planned for 2020, nearly all of them offering a placement year. They include medical, micro-mechanical or robotic engineering, as well as global development and business of the creative industries.

All students join one of the nine colleges – small communities based on the two linked Heslington campuses. They combine academic and social roles and provide a network of support, events and activities. Some departments have their headquarters in one of the colleges, but the student communities are a mix of disciplines, years and sexes.

York has invested £750m on its estate since deciding that the university was too small to maximise its research capability and satisfy the demand for its places. The student population has grown by 50% since then, although there was a small drop in the number of new entrants in 2018.

The main university campuses are situated within walking distance of York's historic centre, where archaeology and medieval studies are based in suitably medieval buildings. Every student has a supervisor responsible for their academic and personal welfare, as well as support for their studies. Beyond graduation, they can take advantage of the York University for Life initiative, which provides support from a community of 123,000 graduates in 180 countries.

York's undergraduates are studying abroad in growing numbers, at leading universities in Europe, the United States, China, South Africa and Brazil.

The university lost ground on some of its competitors in the 2014 Research Excellence Framework, when it submitted a lower proportion of its academics for assessment than most of the leading universities. Nevertheless, more than 80% of the research was considered world leading or internationally excellent, and York was in the top ten for the impact of its research and top 20 overall.

Sports facilities are good and include four sports halls and a dance studio. The £12m York Sports Village features a 25-metre pool, trainer pool, 120-station gym, 3G pitch and three further five-a-side pitches. The university has the only velodrome in Yorkshire, a 1km cycling track and an athletics track, and its own boathouse.

Cultural events abound on campus and in the city, which is also famous for a high concentration of pubs. The free Festival of Ideas, run by the university, is the largest of its type in the UK and is heading for its 10th anniversary in 2021.

Tuition fees

» Fees for UK/EU students	£9,250
» Fees for International students 2020–21	£17,890–£22,080
Medicine £33,700 (Hull-York Medical School 2019–20)	
» For scholarship and bursary information see	
www.york.ac.uk/study/undergraduate/fees-funding/	
» Graduate salary	£22,000

Student numbers

Undergraduates	13,260	(552)
Postgraduates	3,961	(1,051)
Applications/places		23,685/4,485
Applications per place		5.3
Overall offer rate		86%
Unconditional offers		0%
International students		21.6%

Accommodation

University provided places: 6,048
Catered costs: £148–£190 per week
Self-catered: £96–£169 per week
First years guaranteed accommodation
www.york.ac.uk/study/accommodation/

Where do the students come from?

State schools (non-grammar)	71.2%	First generation students	31.4%
Grammar schools	11.4%	Deprived areas	8.2%
Independent schools	17.4%	All ethnic minorities	13.1%

Social inclusion ranking: 103

Black attainment gap	-16.8%
Disabled	5.2%
Mature (over 21)	8.5%

York St John University

York St John (YSJ) has achieved one of the biggest rises in our latest league table, moving up 21 places to build on last year's rise of 16 places. The university has gone from well outside the top 100 in 2017 to rank 81 now, thanks to improvements in student satisfaction and completion rates, more top-class degrees and increased spending on student facilities. It is now in the top ten for satisfaction with the quality of teaching.

YSJ's aim is to be "the best of England's small universities" and to have 7,300 students by 2020, compared with 6,000 in 2016–17, when the recent increases began working through the system. League tables will be one of the university's measures of success.

Applications dropped by 11% in 2019, but only after a period of sustained growth. The numbers starting degrees rose by 40% in the three years up to 2018.

The university attributes its increased popularity with applicants to dramatic diversification in its portfolio of courses. Korean was added in 2019, as well as biochemistry, data science and nutrition. New offerings for 2020 will include Chinese (Mandarin), digital marketing and data analysis, events and experience management, music theatre and sport business management.

Low rates of graduate employment in highly-skilled jobs contributed to a bronze rating in the Teaching Excellence Framework, but the proportion of leavers going straight into graduate-level work or further study had risen by 18 percentage points in the latest survey. The panel was impressed by a scheme that involves undergraduates in research and by the innovative measures to support vulnerable students, including those with mental health difficulties.

The university is a Church of England foundation that dates back to 1841, when the Diocesan Training School opened with just one pupil on the register, in whose honour the students' union is named. Full university status finally arrived in 2006. YSJ continues to charge the lowest fees in England – only £4,200 in the 2019–20 academic year – for its foundation degrees in education and theology. But the courses are for a limited range of mature students without traditional qualifications; the fees for all honours degrees are £9,250.

Divided between York and Ripon for most of its existence, the university now concentrates all its activities on York. The 11-acre campus faces York Minster across the city walls and is a five-minute walk from the city centre. It has seen more than £100m of development and more is planned. By September 2020, new sports science laboratories and teaching rooms should be open on the Haxby Road site, and a new medical centre, support spaces for the creative arts and laboratories for

Lord Mayor's Walk
York YO31 7EX
01904 876 598
admissions@yorksj.ac.uk
www.yorksj.ac.uk
http://ysjsu.com
Open days 2020:
see website

The Times and The Sunday Times Rankings
Overall Ranking: 81 (last year: 102)

Teaching quality	83.9%	10
Student experience	79.9%	=35
Research quality	4.1%	=101
Entry standards	114	=112
Graduate prospects	73.6%	=77
Good honours	68.6%	108
Expected completion rate	87.7%	54
Student/staff ratio	18	=104
Services and facilities	£2,068	90

biology and physiotherapy are scheduled to open on the main Lord Mayor's Walk campus.

The Fountains Learning Centre at the entrance to the university has 530 computer workstations, multimedia group-work facilities, 24-hour access and an internet cafe and lecture theatre. The prize-winning De Grey Court nearby serves the health and life sciences and links the university quarter with the city centre.

The York Business School is the biggest school and offers a number of degree apprenticeships as well as conventional degrees. The university is adding degree apprenticeships for data scientists and police constables in the next year, and expects to have 460 apprentices by September 2020.

Two-thirds of the students are female and more than one in six comes from an area of low participation in higher education – well above average for YSJ's courses and entry qualifications. A new offer scheme has been introduced in 2019 providing a mixture of unconditional, reduced and standard offers to applicants whose UCAS forms demonstrate that they come from schools, areas or families with low participation in higher education. The Aspire scheme gives all UK undergraduates £100 a year towards course materials, with those whose household income is below £25,000 receiving an extra £400.

Psychology produced the best results in the 2014 research ratings, when the 30% of research regarded as world-leading or internationally excellent represented a big improvement on the 2008 assessments. The research strategy promotes interdisciplinary research, building on current areas of expertise and targeting further improvement in the 2021 exercise.

New entrants are guaranteed one of almost 2,000 residential places if they apply by mid-July with York St John as their firm choice. Another 105 en-suite rooms will be available in 2020 through a private provider.

On campus, there is a sports hall, climbing wall, basketball, netball, indoor football and cricket nets. A sports park, 15 minutes' walk from the campus, has a 3G pitch; outdoor tennis and netball courts; and a sprint track. The indoor centre has a sports hall; strength and conditioning suite; and six changing rooms. All facilities are open to the public as well as students and staff.

An active students' union is the social centre for many students, especially in their first year. But York is popular as a student city with a growing range of clubs as well as, supposedly, a pub for every day of the year.

Tuition fees

»	Fees for UK/EU students	£9,250
	Foundation courses from	£4,200
»	Fees for International students 2019–20	£12,750
	Foundation courses	£10,000
»	For scholarship and bursary information see	
	www.yorksj.ac.uk/study/undergraduate/funding-opportunities	
»	Graduate salary	£20,000

Student numbers

Undergraduates	5,222	(240)
Postgraduates	506	(281)
Applications/places		9,840/2,205
Applications per place		4.5
Overall offer rate		91.6%
Unconditional offers		0%
International students		5.3%

Accommodation

University provided places: 1,951
Self-catered: £100–£181 per week
First years guaranteed accommodation
www.yorksj.ac.uk/study/accommodation

Where do the students come from?

State schools (non-grammar)	93.6%	First generation students	47.8%	Black attainment gap	n/a
Grammar schools	2.8%	Deprived areas	18.4%	Disabled	7.6%
Independent schools	3.6%	All ethnic minorities	5.8%	Mature (over 21)	10.9%

Social inclusion ranking: 67

Specialist and Private Institutions

1 Specialist colleges of the University of London

This listing gives contact details for specialist degree-awarding colleges within the University of London not listed elsewhere within the book. Those marked * are members of GuildHE (**www.guildhe.ac.uk**). Fees are given for UK/EU undergraduates for a single year of study.

Courtauld Institute of Art
Somerset House Strand
London WC2R 0RN
020 3947 7673
www.courtauld.ac.uk
Fees 2020–21: £9,250

London Business School
Regent's Park London NW1 4SA
020 7000 7000
www.london.edu
Postgraduate only

London School of Hygiene and Tropical Medicine
Keppel Street
London WC1E 7HT
020 7299 4646
www.lshtm.ac.uk
Postgraduate medical courses

Royal Academy of Music
Marylebone Road London NW1 5HT
020 7873 7373
www.ram.ac.uk
Fees 2019–20: £9,250

Royal Central School of Speech and Drama*
Eton Avenue
London NW3 3HY
020 7722 8183
www.cssd.ac.uk
Fees 2020–21: £9,250

Royal Veterinary College
Royal College Street London NW1 0TU
020 7468 5147
www. rvc.ac.uk
Fees 2020–21: £9,250

University of London Institute in Paris
9–11 rue de Constantine
75340 Paris Cedex 07, France
(+33) 1 44 11 73 83
https://ulip.london.ac.uk
Degrees offered in conjunction with Queen Mary and Royal Holloway colleges
Fees 2019–20: £9,250

2 Specialist colleges and private institutions

This listing gives contact details for other degree-awarding higher education institutions not mentioned elsewhere within the book. All the institutions listed below offer degree courses, some providing a wide range of courses while others are specialist colleges with a small intake. Those marked * are members of GuildHE (www.guildhe.ac.uk). Fees are given for UK/EU undergraduates for a single year of study.

BPP University
Mainly law, business & health
Aldine Place, 142–144 Uxbridge Road,
London W12 8AW
    Campuses in Abingdon, Birmingham,
    Bristol, Cambridge, Doncaster, Leeds,
    Liverpool, London, Manchester,
    Maidstone, Milton Keynes, Newcastle,
    Nottingham, Reading, Southampton.
03300 603 100
www.bpp.com
Fees 2020–21: £13,500 (two-year course);
£6,000–£9,000 (three-year course)

Conservatoire for Dance and Drama
Comprised of:
    Bristol Old Vic Theatre School Central
    School of Ballet
    London Academy of Music and Dramatic
    Art (LAMDA)
    London Contemporary Dance School,
    National Centre for Circus Arts,
    Northern School of Contemporary
    Dance, Rambert School of Ballet and
    Contemporary Dance, Royal Academy of
    Dramatic Art (RADA)
    The Energy Centre, Units 1–3,
    Bowling Green Walk, London N1 6AL
020 7387 5101
www.cdd.ac.uk
Fees 2020–21: £9,250

Dyson Institute of Engineering and Technology
Tetbury Hill Malmesbury
Wiltshire SN16 0RP
01285 705228
dysoninstitute@dyson.com
www.dysoninstitute.com
Paid degree courses – no fees

Glasgow School of Art
167 Renfrew Street, Glasgow G3 6RQ
0141 353 4500
www.gsa.ac.uk
Fees 2019–20: Scotland / EU, no fee,
RUK £9,250

Guildhall School of Music and Drama
Silk Street, Barbican,
London EC2Y 8DT
020 7628 2571
www.gsmd.ac.uk
Fees 2019–20: £9,250

Hartpury University
Animal, agriculture & sport
Gloucester
GL19 3BE
www.hartpury.ac.uk
Fees 2019–20: £9,250

The University of Law
Birmingham, Bristol, Chester, Exeter,
Guildford, Leeds, London (Bloomsbury and
Moorgate), Manchester, Nottingham
0800 289997
www.law.ac.uk
Fees 2020–21: £11,100 (two-year course)
£9,250 (three-year course)

Liverpool Institute for Performing Arts*
Mount Street,
Liverpool L1 9HF
0151 330 3084
www.lipa.ac.uk
Fees 2019–20: £9,250

**The London Institute of Banking and
Finance**
4–9 Burgate Lane
Canterbury, Kent CT1 2XJ
01227 818609
Student campus:
    25 Lovat Lane, London EC3R 8EB
020 7337 6293
www.libf.ac.uk
ftp@libf.ac.uk
Fees 2019–20: £9,000

New College of the Humanities
19 Bedford Square,
London WC1B 3HH
020 7637 4550
www.nchlondon.ac.uk
Fees 2019–20: £9,250

Pearson College
Business, law & video games
190 High Holborn,
London WC1V 7BH
020 3733 7166
www.pearsoncollegelondon.ac.uk
Fees 2020–21: £9,250

Plymouth College of Art*
Tavistock Place,
Plymouth PL4 8AT
01752 203434
www.plymouthart.ac.uk
Fees 2020–21: £9,250

Regent's University London*
Business, design, media & psychology
Inner Circle,
Regent's Park, London NW1 4NS
020 7487 7700
www.regents.ac.uk
Fees 2019–20: £17,500

**Rose Bruford College of Theatre and
Performance***
Lamorbey Park,
Burnt Oak Lane,
Sidcup, Kent DA15 9DF
020 8308 2600
www.bruford.ac.uk
Fees 2019–20: £9,250

Royal College of Music
Prince Consort Road,
London SW7 2BS
020 7591 4300
www.rcm.ac.uk
Fees 2020–21: £9,250

Royal Conservatoire of Scotland
100 Renfrew Street,
Glasgow G2 3DB
0141 332 4101
www.rcs.ac.uk
Fees 2019–20: Scotland/EU, no fee;
RUK £9,250

Royal Northern College of Music
124 Oxford Road,
Manchester M13 9RD
0161 907 5200
www.rncm.ac.uk
Fees 2019–20: £9,250

Royal Welsh College of Music and Drama
Castle Grounds, Cathays Park,
Cardiff CF10 3ER
029 2034 2854
www.rwcmd.ac.uk
Fees 2020–21: £9,000

St Mary's University College*
Teaching & liberal arts
191 Falls Road, Belfast BT12 6FE
028 9032 7678
www.stmarys-belfast.ac.uk
Fees 2019–20: £4,275; RUK £9,250

Scotland's Rural College
Agriculture, environment & land
management
    Campuses at Aberdeen, Ayr, Cupar,
    Dumfries, Ecclesmachan, near Broxburn,
    Edinburgh
0800 269453
www.sruc.ac.uk
Fees 2019–20: Scotland/EU, no fee;
RUK £6,950

Stranmillis University College
Teaching courses
Stranmillis Road, Belfast BT9 5DY
028 9038 1271
www.stran.ac.uk
Fees 2019–20: £4,160; RUK £9,250

Trinity Laban Conservatoire of Music and Dance
Music Faculty: King Charles Court
Old Royal Naval College,
Greenwich, London SE10 9JF
020 8305 4444
Dance Faculty: Laban Building, Creekside
London SE8 3DZ
020 8305 9400
www.trinitylaban.ac.uk
Fees 2020–21: £9,250

University Academy 92
Business, media & sport
UA92 Campus,
Talbot Road, Trafford,
Manchester M16 0PU
0161 507 1992
www.ua92.ac.uk
Fees 2019–20: £9,000

UCFB (University College of Football Business)
Burnley FC Turf Moor
Harry Potts Way Burnley
Lancashire BB10 4BX
Wembley Stadium
London HA9 0WS
Etihad Campus, Manchester M11 3FF
0333 060 3800
www.ucfb.com
Fees 2019–20: £9,250

Writtle University College*
Land management
Lordship Road,
Chelmsford, Essex CM1 3RR
01245 424200
www.writtle.ac.uk
Fees 2020–21: £9,250

Index